THE ORACLE 11G PERFORMANCE TUNING

THE ORACLE 11G PERFORMANCE TUNING

By

Rajeev A. Parida
MCA, OCP

UNIVERSITY SCIENCE PRESS

(An Imprint of Laxmi Publications (P) Ltd.)

BANGALORE • CHENNAI • COCHIN • GUWAHATI • HYDERABAD
JALANDHAR • KOLKATA • LUCKNOW • MUMBAI • RANCHI • NEW DELHI
INDIA • USA • GHANA • KENYA

THE ORACLE 11G PERFORMANCE TUNING

Printed and bound in India
Typeset at Excellent Graphics
First Edition: 2015
ISBN 978-93-83828-31-9

PUBLISHED IN INDIA BY

UNIVERSITY SCIENCE PRESS
(An Imprint of Laxmi Publications Pvt.Ltd.)
113, GOLDEN HOUSE, DARYAGANJ,
NEW DELHI - 110002, INDIA
Telephone : 91-11-4353 2500, 4353 2501
Fax : 91-11-2325 2572, 4353 2528
www.laxmipublications.com info@laxmipublications.com

Branches

✆	Bangalore	080-26 75 69 30	
✆	Chennai	044-24 34 47 26,	24 35 95 07
✆	Cochin	0484-237 70 04,	405 13 03
✆	Guwahati	0361-254 36 69,	251 38 81
✆	Hyderabad	040-27 55 53 83,	27 55 53 93
✆	Jalandhar	0181-222 12 72	
✆	Kolkata	033-22 27 43 84	
✆	Lucknow	0522-220 99 16	
✆	Mumbai	022-24 91 54 15,	24 92 78 69
✆	Ranchi	0651-220 44 64	

C—
Printed at:

Contents

Chapters Pages

PREFACE

In today's Internet-centric economy, too many organizations respond to Oracle performance problems by throwing money at these problems by buying larger and more expensive computers or by hiring expert consultants. But there's a lot you can do on your own to increase dramatically the performance of your existing system. Whatever version of Oracle you're running from Version 10g to Oracle 11g, proper tuning can save your organization a huge amount of money in additional equipment, extra memory, and hardware upgrades. The first edition of Oracle 11g Performance Tuning became a classic for programmers, managers, database administrators, system administrators, and anyone who cares about improving the performance of an Oracle database system.

Oracle 11g Performance Tuning is a must-have reference guide for all Oracle professionals. It provides much-needed information on best practices, tips, and techniques in debugging and tuning of the Oracle 11g database. It will bring you the insider information that you can't get anywhere else. It is a book for people who administer the operation of an Oracle Database system. Referred to as database administrators (DBAs), they are responsible for creating Oracle Database, ensuring its smooth operation, and monitoring its use.

PURPOSE OF THIS BOOK

My main purpose is to give you a foundation for using, the Oracle database effectively and efficiently. Therefore, I wrote with these principles in mind:

- I have tried to concentrate on the most important Oracle 11g performance tuning issues. Every topic provides a comprehensive but concise discussion of how Oracle 11g handles a tuning issue and the repercussions of that action.
- One of the first decisions I made was to concentrate on principles rather than syntax. There simply isn't room for myriad syntax diagrams and examples in this book.
- I have tried to make this an ideal first oracle 11g tuning book for a wide spectrum of oracle users but not the last you will very likely have to refer to Oracle documentation or other, more specific books for more details about using Oracle 11g tuning. However, I hope this book will act as information from other sources and put it to the best use.

This book is the result of over 14 years of experience with oracle and other databases. I have tried to apply that experience as best I can here.

WHO THIS BOOK IS FOR

This book is an aid for people responsible for the operation, maintenance, and performance of Oracle database. This book describes detailed ways to enhance Oracle performance by writing and tuning SQL properly, using performance tools, and optimizing instance performance. It also explains how to create an initial database for good performance and includes performance-related reference information. This book could be useful for database administrators, application designers, and programmers.

Good Luck, be patient, and I look forward to work with you.

- AUTHOR

ACKNOWLEDGEMENT

"You must be the change you wish to see in the world"

Mahatma Gandhi

There have been many who have helped me become who I currently am, and who have directly or indirectly participated in this project. I must start with my gratitude to God, the source of all wisdom, knowledge, and ever-present help. On earth, I acknowledge the consistent support from my wife Anupama and my son Ayush. They patiently put up with my absences as I sat at the PC, typing away late in the night and on weekends, missing family time together. Without Anu, none of this would have been possible. She is not only a wonderful mother but also my true love and best friend.

I would like to express my special gratitude to my wife Anupama Parida for her eagle eye and gentle correction of my text and her expert technical review of the content and her encyclopedic knowledge of all things oracle.

I would also like to thank the following technical reviewers who have provided very useful and critical comments to improve the presentation and content of the book in its first edition: Mr. Kaushal Sawhney, NIIT Technologies Ltd, India, Mr. Nick Lukin, Oracle Corporation; Ms. Binodini Paital, IBM, India ; Mr. Paul Anderson, Accenture, Australia.

A book such as this would not have seen the light of day without the dedicated efforts of all the Firewall Media Publishing staff who helped me.

Many of my professional colleagues at NIIT Technologies Ltd were a source of both inspiration and guidance, especially Late Amitabh Gupta, Somnath Das Gupta, Biswarup Dey, Sameer Grover, Sanjay Karambelkar, Amiya Maharatha , Shashank Batra, Neeraj Jain, Naveen Kumar and Pravat Roy. Thanks to all of those above who made both big and small differences in my life and in this book.

An acknowledgement to all those whom I have worked with in the past is most in order. I dare not print a list of all those people for fear of leaving someone out. To all of you I owe more thanks than I can say. Thanks to previous employers who gave me wonderful opportunities.

Furthermore, my special thanks to Mr. Abhiram Behera and Mrs. Nirupama Behera for formulating the original concept and made many suggestions for the topic covered in this book via email from Florida, USA.

Last but not least, to my parents, thanks for your enduring level of patience, love, encouragement, support, and sacrifice during the past 24 months. Without them, none of this would have been possible.

- AUTHOR

1 Getting Started with Oracle Architecture

Learning Objectives

This chapter provides an introduction to performance tuning and contains the following sections:

- Oracle Database
- Connecting to a Server
- Oracle Database Server Architecture
- Instance: Database Configurations
- Connecting to the Database Instance
- Oracle Database Memory Structures
- Shared Pool
- Database Buffer Cache
- Program Global Area (PGA)
- Process Architecture
- Database Storage Architecture
- Logical and Physical Database Structures
- SYSTEM and SYSAUX Tablespaces
- Automatic Storage Management
- Introduction to Performance Tuning
- SQL Tuning
- Introduction to Performance Tuning Features and Tools
- Additional Oracle Database Tools

ORACLE DATABASE

A database is a collection of data treated as a unit. The purpose of a database is to store and retrieve related information.

The Oracle Relational Database Management System (RDBMS) reliably manages a large amount of data in a multiuser environment so that many users can concurrently access the same data. This is accomplished while delivering high performance. At the same time, it prevents unauthorized access and provides efficient solutions for failure recovery.

CONNECTING TO A SERVER

A database user can connect to an Oracle server in one of three ways:

The user logs on to the operating system running the Oracle instance and starts an application or tool that accesses the database on that system. The communication pathway is established using the interprocess communication mechanisms available on the host operating system.

The user starts the application or tool on a local computer and connects over a network to the computer running the Oracle database. In this configuration (called *client/server*), network software is used to communicate between the user and the back-end server. The client/server architecture database system has two parts: a front end (client) and a back end (server) connected through a network. Network software is used to communicate between the user and the Oracle server.

The client is a database application that initiates a request for an operation to be performed on the database server. It requests, processes, and presents data managed by the server. The client workstation can be optimized for its job. For example, the client might not need large disk capacity, or it might benefit from graphic capabilities. Often, the client runs on a different computer than the database server. Many clients can simultaneously run against one server.

The server runs Oracle Database software and handles the functions required for concurrent, shared data access. The server receives and processes requests that originate from client applications. The computer that manages the server can be optimized for its duties. For example, the server computer can have large disk capacity and fast processors.

The user accesses an application server through a tool (such as a Web browser) on the local computer (client). The application server then interacts with a back-end database server on behalf of the client.

A traditional multitier architecture has the following components:

- A client or initiator process that starts an operation.
- One or more application servers that perform parts of the operation. An application server contains a large part of the application logic, provides access to the data for the client, and performs some query processing, thus removing some of the load from the database server. The application server can serve as an interface between clients and multiple database servers and can provide an additional level of security.

An end server or database server that stores most of the data used in the operation.

This architecture enables use of an application server to do the following:

- Validate the credentials of a client (such as a Web browser).
- Connect to an Oracle Database server.
- Perform the requested operation on behalf of the client.

ORACLE DATABASE SERVER ARCHITECTURE

There are three major structures in Oracle database server architecture: memory structures, process structures, and storage structures. A basic Oracle database system consists of an Oracle database and a database instance.

The database consists of both physical structures and logical structures. Because the physical and logical structures are separate, the physical storage of data can be managed without affecting access to logical storage structures.

The instance consists of memory structures and background processes associated with that instance. Every time an instance is started, a shared memory area called the System Global Area (SGA) is allocated and the background processes are started. Processes are jobs that work in the memory of computers. A process is defined as a "thread of control" or a mechanism in an operating system that can run a series of steps. After starting a database instance, the Oracle software associates the instance with a specific database. This is called *mounting the database*. The database is then ready to be opened, which makes it accessible to authorized users.

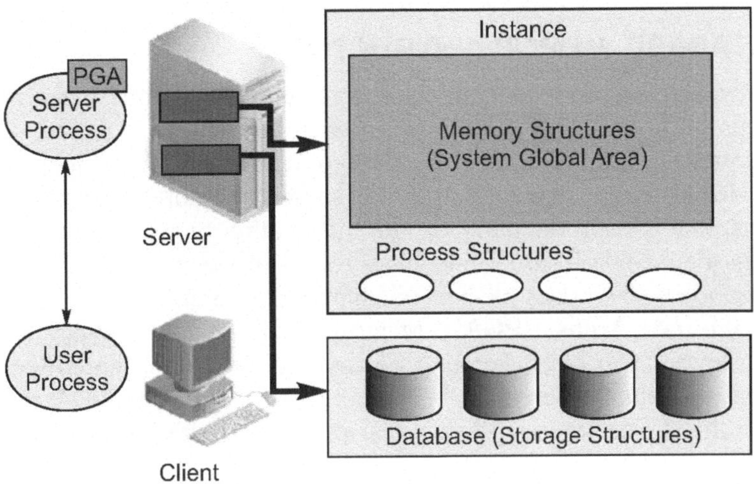

Figure 1.1. Oracle Architecture

The Oracle Automatic Storage Management (ASM) uses the concept of an instance for the memory and process components, but is not associated with a specific database.

INSTANCE: DATABASE CONFIGURATIONS

Each database instance is associated with one and only one database. If there are multiple databases on the same server, then there is a separate and distinct database instance for each database. A database instance cannot be shared. A Real Applications Cluster (RAC) database usually has multiple instances on separate servers for the same shared database. In this model, the same database is associated with each RAC instance, which meets the requirement that at most only one database is associated with an instance.

CONNECTING TO THE DATABASE INSTANCE

Connections and sessions are closely related to user processes but are very different in meaning.

A *connection* is a communication pathway between a user process and an Oracle Database instance. A communication pathway is established using available interprocess communication mechanisms (on a computer that runs both the user process and Oracle Database) or network software (when different computers run the database application and Oracle Database, and communicate through a network).

A *session* represents the state of a current user login to the database instance. For example, when a user starts SQL*Plus, the user must provide a valid username and password, and then a session is established for that user. A session lasts from the time a user connects until the user disconnects or exits the database application.

Multiple sessions can be created and exist concurrently for a single Oracle database user using the same username. For example, a user with the username/password of HR/HR can connect to the same Oracle Database instance several times.

ORACLE DATABASE MEMORY STRUCTURES

Oracle Database creates and uses memory structures for various purposes. For example, memory stores program code being run, data that is shared among users, and private data areas for each connected user. Two basic memory structures are associated with an instance:

- **System Global Area (SGA):** Group of shared memory structures, known as SGA components, that contain data and control information for one Oracle database instance. The SGA is shared by all server and background processes. Examples of data stored in the SGA include cached data blocks and shared SQL areas.
- **Program Global Areas (PGA):** Memory regions that contain data and control information for a server or background process. A PGA is nonshared memory created by Oracle Database when a server or background process is started. Access to the PGA is exclusive to the server process. Each server process and background process has its own PGA.

The SGA is the memory area that contains data and control information for the instance. The SGA includes the following data structures:

- **Shared pool:** Caches various constructs that can be shared among users
- **Database buffer cache:** Caches blocks of data retrieved from the database
- **KEEP buffer pool:** A specialized type of database buffer cache that is tuned to retain blocks of data in memory for long periods of time
- **RECYCLE buffer pool:** A specialized type of database buffer cache that is tuned to recycle or remove block from memory quickly
- **nK buffer cache:** One of several specialized database buffer caches designed to hold block sizes different than the default database block size
- **Redo log buffer:** Caches redo information (used for instance recovery) until it can be written to the physical redo log files stored on the disk
- **Large pool:** Optional area that provides large memory allocations for certain large processes, such as Oracle backup and recovery operations, and I/O server processes
- **Java pool:** Used for all session-specific Java code and data in the Java Virtual Machine (JVM)
- **Streams pool:** Used by Oracle Streams to store information required by capture and apply.

When you start the instance by using Enterprise Manager or SQL*Plus, the amount of memory allocated for the SGA is displayed.

A Program Global Area (PGA) is a memory region that contains data and control information for each server process. An Oracle server process services a client's requests. Each server process has its own private PGA that is allocated when the server process is started. Access to the PGA is exclusive to that server process, and the PGA is read and written only by the Oracle code acting on its behalf. The PGA is divided into two major areas: stack space and the User Global Area (UGA).

With the dynamic SGA infrastructure, the sizes of the database buffer cache, the shared pool, the large pool, the Java pool, and the Streams pool can change without shutting down the instance.

The Oracle database uses initialization parameters to create and manage memory structures. The simplest way to manage memory is to allow the database to automatically manage and tune it for you. To do so (on most platforms), you only have to set a target memory size initialization parameter (MEMORY_TARGET) and a maximum memory size initialization parameter (MEMORY_MAX_TARGET).

SHARED POOL

The shared pool portion of the SGA contains the library cache, the data dictionary cache, the SQL query result cache, the PL/SQL function result cache, buffers for parallel execution messages, and control structures.

The *data dictionary* is a collection of database tables and views containing reference information about the database, its structures, and its users. Oracle Database accesses the data dictionary frequently during SQL statement parsing. This access is essential to the continuing operation of Oracle Database.

The data dictionary is accessed so often by Oracle Database that two special locations in memory are designated to hold dictionary data. One area is called the *data dictionary cache*, also known as the row cache because it holds data as rows instead of buffers (which hold entire blocks of data). The other area in memory to hold dictionary data is the *library cache*. All Oracle Database user processes share these two caches for access to data dictionary information.

Oracle Database represents each SQL statement that it runs with a shared SQL area (as well as a private SQL area kept in the PGA). Oracle Database recognizes when two users are executing the same SQL statement and reuses the shared SQL area for those users.

A shared SQL area contains the parse tree and execution plan for a given SQL statement. Oracle Database saves memory by using one shared SQL area for SQL statements run multiple times, which often happens when many users run the same application.

When a new SQL statement is parsed, Oracle Database allocates memory from the shared pool to store in the shared SQL area. The size of this memory depends on the complexity of the statement.

Oracle Database processes PL/SQL program units (procedures, functions, packages, anonymous blocks, and database triggers) in much the same way it processes individual SQL statements. Oracle Database allocates a shared area to hold the parsed, compiled form of a program unit. Oracle Database allocates a private area to hold values specific to the session that runs the program unit, including local, global, and package variables (also known as package instantiation) and buffers for executing SQL. If more than one user runs the same program unit, then a single, shared area is used by all users, while all users maintain separate copies of their own private SQL areas, holding values specific to their own sessions.

Individual SQL statements contained in a PL/SQL program unit are processed just like other SQL statements. Despite their origins in a PL/SQL program unit, these SQL statements use a shared area to hold their parsed representations and a private area for each session that runs the statement.

The SQL query result cache and PL/SQL function result cache are new to Oracle Database 11*g*. They share the same infrastructure, appear in the same dynamic performance (V$) views, and are administered using the same supplied package.

Results of queries and query fragments can be cached in memory in the SQL query result cache. The database can then use cached results to answer future executions of these queries and query fragments. Because retrieving results from the SQL query result cache is faster than rerunning a query, frequently run queries experience a significant performance improvement when their results are cached.

A PL/SQL function is sometimes used to return the result of a computation whose inputs are one or several parameterized queries issued by the function. In some cases, these queries access data that changes very infrequently compared to the frequency of calling the function. You can include syntax in the source text of a PL/SQL function to request that its results be cached in the PL/SQL function result cache and (to ensure correctness) that the cache be purged when tables in a list of tables experience DML.

The fixed area of the shared pool represents startup overhead for the SGA. It is very small in comparison to a typically sized shared pool or SGA.

DATABASE BUFFER CACHE

The database buffer cache is the portion of the SGA that holds block images read from the data files or constructed dynamically to satisfy the read consistency model. All users who are concurrently connected to the instance share access to the database buffer cache.

The first time an Oracle Database user process requires a particular piece of data, it searches for the data in the database buffer cache. If the process finds the data already in the cache (a cache hit), it can read the data directly from memory. If the process cannot find the data in the cache (a cache miss), it must copy the data block from a data file on disk into a buffer in the cache before accessing the data. Accessing data through a cache hit is faster than data access through a cache miss.

The buffers in the cache are managed by a complex algorithm that uses a combination of Least Recently Used (LRU) lists and touch count. The LRU helps to ensure that the most recently used blocks tend to stay in memory to minimize disk access.

The KEEP buffer pool and the RECYCLE buffer pool are used for specialized buffer pool tuning. The KEEP buffer pool is designed to retain buffers in memory longer than the LRU would normally retain them. The RECYCLE buffer pool is designed to flush buffers from memory faster than the LRU would normally do so.

Additional buffer caches can be configured to hold blocks of a size that is different than the default block size.

Redo Log Buffer

The redo log buffer is a circular buffer in the SGA that holds information about changes made to the database. This information is stored in redo entries. Redo entries contain the information necessary to reconstruct (or redo) changes that are made to the database by DML, DDL, or internal operations. Redo entries are used for database recovery if necessary.

As the server process makes changes to the buffer cache, redo entries are generated and written to the redo log buffer in the SGA. The redo entries take up continuous, sequential space in the buffer. The log writer background process writes the redo log buffer to the active redo log file (or group of files) on disk.

Large Pool

The database administrator can configure an optional memory area called the *large pool* to provide large memory allocations for:

- Session memory for the shared server and the Oracle XA interface (used where transactions interact with multiple databases)

- I/O server processes
- Oracle Database backup and restore operations
- Parallel Query operations
- Advanced Queuing memory table storage.

By allocating session memory from the large pool for shared server, Oracle XA, or parallel query buffers, Oracle Database can use the shared pool primarily for caching shared SQL and avoid the performance overhead that is caused by shrinking the shared SQL cache.

In addition, the memory for Oracle Database backup and restore operations, for I/O server processes, and for parallel buffers is allocated in buffers of a few hundred kilobytes. The large pool is better able to satisfy such large memory requests than the shared pool.

The large pool is not managed by a Least Recently Used (LRU) list.

Java Pool and Streams Pool

Java pool memory is used to store all session-specific Java code and data in the JVM. Java pool memory is used in different ways, depending on the mode in which Oracle Database is running.

The Streams pool is used exclusively by Oracle Streams. The Streams pool stores buffered queue messages, and it provides memory for Oracle Streams capture processes and apply processes.

Unless you specifically configure it, the size of the Streams pool starts at zero. The pool size grows dynamically as needed when Oracle Streams is used.

A detailed discussion of Java programming and Oracle Streams is beyond the scope of this class.

PROGRAM GLOBAL AREA (PGA)

The Program Global Area (PGA) is a private memory region containing data and control information for a server process. Each server process has a distinct PGA. Access to it is exclusive to that the server process is read only by Oracle code acting on behalf of it. It is not available for developer's code.

Every PGA contains stack space. In a dedicated server environment, each user connecting to the database instance has a separate server process. For this type of connection, the PGA contains a subdivision of memory known as the User Global Area (UGA). The UGA is composed of the following:

- Cursor area for storing runtime information on cursors
- User session data storage area for control information about a session
- SQL working areas for processing SQL statements consisting of:
  - A sort area for functions that order data such as ORDER BY and GROUP BY
  - A hash area for performing hash joins of tables
  - A create bitmap area used in bitmap index creation common to data warehouses
  - A bitmap merge area used for resolving bitmap index plan execution

In a shared server environment, multiple client users share the server process. In this model, the UGA is moved into the SGA (shared pool or large pool if configured) leaving the PGA with only stack space.

PROCESS ARCHITECTURE

The processes in an Oracle database system can be divided into three major groups:

- User processes that run the application or Oracle tool code
- Oracle Database processes that run the Oracle database server code (including server processes and background processes)
- Oracle daemons and application processes not specific to a single database.

When a user runs an application program or an Oracle tool such as SQL*Plus, the term *user process* is used to refer to the user's application. The user process may or may not be on the database server machine. Oracle Database also creates a *server process* to execute the commands issued by the user process. In addition, the Oracle server also has a set of *background processes* for an instance that interact with each other and with the operating system to manage the memory structures, asynchronously perform I/O to write data to disk, and perform other required tasks. The process structure varies for different Oracle Database configurations, depending on the operating system and the choice of Oracle Database options. The code for connected users can be configured as a dedicated server or a shared server.

- **Dedicated server:** For each session, the database application is run by a user process that is served by a dedicated server process that executes Oracle database server code.
- **Shared server:** Eliminates the need for a dedicated server process for each connection. A dispatcher directs multiple incoming network session requests to a pool of shared server processes. A shared server process serves any client request.

Server Processes

Oracle Database creates server processes to handle the requests of user processes connected to the instance. The user process represents the application or tool that connects to the Oracle database. It may be on the same machine as the Oracle database or it may exist on a remote client and utilize a network to reach the Oracle database. The user process first communicates with a listener process that creates a server process in a dedicated environment.

Server processes created on behalf of each user's application can perform one or more of the following:

- Parse and run SQL statements issued through the application
- Read necessary data blocks from data files on disk into the shared database buffers of the SGA (if the blocks are not already present in the SGA)
- Return results in such a way that the application can process the information.

Background Processes

To maximize performance and accommodate many users, a multiprocess Oracle Database system uses some additional Oracle Database processes called *background processes*. An Oracle Database instance can have many background processes.

The background processes commonly seen in non-RAC, non-ASM environments can include the following:

1. Database writer process (DBW*n*)
2. Log writer process (LGWR)
3. Checkpoint process (CKPT)
4. System monitor process (SMON)
5. Process monitor process (PMON)
6. Recoverer process (RECO)

7. Job queue coordinator (CJQ0)
8. Job slave processes (J*nnn*)
9. Archiver processes (ARC*n*)
10. Queue monitor processes (QMN*n*).

Other background processes may be found in more advanced configurations such as RAC. See the V$BGPROCESS view for more information on the background processes.

Some background processes are created automatically when an instance is started, whereas others are started as required.

Other process structures are not specific to a single database, but rather can be shared among many databases on the same server. The Grid Infrastructure and networking processes fall into this category.

Oracle Grid Infrastructure processes on Linux and UNIX systems include the following:

1. ohasd: Oracle High Availability Service daemon that is responsible to starting Oracle Clusterware processes
2. ocssd: Cluster Synchronization Service daemon
3. diskmon: Disk Monitor daemon that is responsible for input and output fencing for HP Oracle Exadata Storage Server
4. cssdagent: Starts, stops and check the status of the CSS daemon, ocssd
5. oraagent: Extend clusterware to support Oracle-specific requirements and complex resources
6. orarootagent: A specialized Oracle agent process that helps manage resources owned by root, such as the network.

Database Writer Process (DBW*n*)

The Database Writer process (DBW*n*) writes the contents of buffers to data files. The DBW*n* processes are responsible for writing modified (dirty) buffers in the database buffer cache to disk. Although one Database Writer process (DBW*0*) is adequate for most systems, you can configure additional processes (DBW*1* through DBW*9* and DBW*a* through DBW*z*) to improve write performance if your system modifies data heavily. These additional DBW*n* processes are not useful on uniprocessor systems.

When a buffer in the database buffer cache is modified, it is marked dirty and is added to the head of the checkpoint queue that is kept in SCN order. This order therefore matches the order of redo that is written to the redo logs for these changed buffers. When the number of available buffers in the buffer cache falls below an internal threshold (to the extent that server processes find it difficult to obtain available buffers), DBW*n* writes non frequently used buffers to the data files from the tail of the LRU list so that processes can replace buffers when they need them. DBW*n* also writes from the tail of the checkpoint queue to keep the checkpoint advancing.

The SGA contains a memory structure that has the Redo Byte Address (RBA) of the position in the redo stream where recovery should begin in the case of an instance failure. This structure acts as a pointer into the redo and is written to the control file by the CKPT process once every three seconds. Because the DBW*n* writes dirty buffers in SCN order, and because the redo is in SCN order, every time DBW*n* writes dirty buffers from the LRUW list, it also advances the pointer held in the SGA memory structure so that instance recovery (if required) begins reading the redo from approximately the correct location and avoids unnecessary I/O. This is known as *incremental checkpointing*.

> There are other cases when DBW*n* may write (for example, when tablespaces are made read-only or are placed offline). In such cases, no incremental checkpoint occurs because dirty buffers belonging only to the corresponding data files are written to the database unrelated to the SCN order.

The LRU algorithm keeps more frequently accessed blocks in the buffer cache to minimize disk reads. A CACHE option can be placed on tables to help retain block even longer in memory.

The DB_WRITER_PROCESSES initialization parameter specifies the number of DBW*n* processes. The maximum number of DBW*n* processes is 36. If it is not specified by the user during startup, Oracle Database determines how to set DB_WRITER_PROCESSES based on the number of CPUs and processor groups.

The DBW*n* process writes dirty buffers to disk under the following conditions:

- When a server process cannot find a clean reusable buffer after scanning a threshold number of buffers, it signals DBW*n* to write. DBW*n* writes dirty buffers to disk asynchronously while performing other processing.
- DBW*n* writes buffers to advance the checkpoint, which is the position in the redo thread (log) from which instance recovery begins. This log position is determined by the oldest dirty buffer in the buffer cache.

In all cases, DBW*n* performs batched (multiblock) writes to improve efficiency. The number of blocks written in a multiblock write varies by operating system.

Log Writer Process (LGWR)

The Log Writer process (LGWR) is responsible for redo log buffer management by writing the redo log buffer entries to a redo log file on disk. LGWR writes all redo entries that have been copied into the buffer since the last time it wrote.

The redo log buffer is a circular buffer. When LGWR writes redo entries from the redo log buffer to a redo log file, server processes can then copy new entries over the entries in the redo log buffer that have been written to disk. LGWR normally writes fast enough to ensure that space is always available in the buffer for new entries, even when access to the redo log is heavy. LGWR writes one contiguous portion of the buffer to disk.

LGWR writes:

- When a user process commits a transaction
- When the redo log buffer is one-third full
- Before a DBW*n* process writes modified buffers to disk (if necessary)
- Every three seconds.

Before DBW*n* can write a modified buffer, all redo records that are associated with the changes to the buffer must be written to disk (the write-ahead protocol). If DBW*n* finds that some redo records have not been written, it signals LGWR to write the redo records to disk and waits for LGWR to complete writing the redo log buffer before it can write out the data buffers. LGWR writes to the current log group. If one of the files in the group is damaged or unavailable, LGWR continues writing to other files in the group and logs an error in the LGWR trace file and in the system alert log. If all files in a group are damaged, or if the group is unavailable because it has not been archived, LGWR cannot continue to function.

When a user issues a COMMIT statement, LGWR puts a commit record in the redo log buffer and writes it to disk immediately, along with the transaction's redo entries. The corresponding changes to data blocks are deferred until it is more efficient to write them. This is called a *fast commit mechanism*. The atomic write of the redo entry containing the transaction's commit record is the single event that determines whether the transaction has committed. Oracle Database returns a success code to the committing transaction, although the data buffers have not yet been written to disk.

If more buffer space is needed, LGWR sometimes writes redo log entries before a transaction is committed. These entries become permanent only if the transaction is later committed. When a user commits a transaction, the transaction is assigned a System Change Number (SCN), which Oracle Database records along with the transaction's redo entries in the redo log. SCNs are recorded in the redo log so that recovery operations can be synchronized in Real Application Clusters and distributed databases.

In times of high activity, LGWR can write to the redo log file by using group commits. For example, suppose that a user commits a transaction. LGWR must write the transaction's redo entries to disk. As this happens, other users issue COMMIT statements. However, LGWR cannot write to the redo log file to commit these transactions until it has completed its previous write operation. After the first transaction's entries are written to the redo log file, the entire list of redo entries of waiting transactions (not yet committed) can be written to disk in one operation, requiring less I/O than do transaction entries handled individually. Therefore, Oracle Database minimizes disk I/O and maximizes performance of LGWR. If requests to commit continue at a high rate, every write (by LGWR) from the redo log buffer can contain multiple commit records.

Checkpoint Process (CKPT)

A *checkpoint* is a data structure that defines a System Change Number (SCN) in the redo thread of a database. Checkpoints are recorded in the control file and in each data file header. They are a crucial element of recovery.

When a checkpoint occurs, Oracle Database must update the headers of all data files to record the details of the checkpoint. This is done by the CKPT process. The CKPT process does not write blocks to disk; DBW*n* always performs that work. The SCNs recorded in the file headers guarantee that all changes made to database blocks prior to that SCN have been written to disk.

System Monitor Process (SMON)

The System Monitor Process (SMON) performs recovery at instance startup if necessary. SMON is also responsible for cleaning up temporary segments that are no longer in use. If any terminated transactions were skipped during instance recovery because of file-read or offline errors, SMON recovers them when the tablespace or file is brought back online.

SMON checks regularly to see whether the process is needed. Other processes can call SMON if they detect a need for it.

Process Monitor Process (PMON)

The Process Monitor Process (PMON) performs process recovery when a user process fails. PMON is responsible for cleaning up the database buffer cache and freeing resources that the user process was using. For example, it resets the status of the active transaction table, releases locks, and removes the process ID from the list of active processes.

PMON periodically checks the status of dispatcher and server processes, and restarts any that have stopped running (but not any that Oracle Database has terminated intentionally). PMON also registers information about the instance and dispatcher processes with the network listener.

Like SMON, PMON checks regularly to see whether it is needed; it can be called if another process detects the need for it.

Recoverer Process (RECO)

The recoverer process (RECO) is a background process that is used with the distributed database configuration that automatically resolves failures involving distributed transactions. The RECO process of an instance automatically connects to other databases involved in an in-doubt distributed transaction. When the RECO process reestablishes a connection between involved database servers, it automatically resolves all in-doubt transactions, removing from each database's pending transaction table any rows that correspond to the resolved in-doubt transactions.

If the RECO process fails to connect with a remote server, RECO automatically tries to connect again after a timed interval. However, RECO waits an increasing amount of time (growing exponentially) before it attempts another connection.

Archiver Processes (ARC*n*)

The archiver processes (ARC*n*) copy redo log files to a designated storage device after a log switch has occurred. ARC*n* processes are present only when the database is in ARCHIVELOG mode and automatic archiving is enabled.

If you anticipate a heavy workload for archiving (such as during bulk loading of data), you can increase the maximum number of archiver processes. There can also be multiple archive log destinations. It is recommended that there be at least one archiver process for each destination. The default is to have four archiver processes.

DATABASE STORAGE ARCHITECTURE

The files that constitute an Oracle database are organized into the following:

1. **Control files:** Contain data about the database itself (that is, physical database structure information). These files are critical to the database. Without them, you cannot open data files to access the data in the database. It can also contain metadata related to backups.
2. **Data files:** Contain the user or application data of the database, as well as metadata and the data dictionary
3. **Online redo log files:** Allow for instance recovery of the database. If the database server crashes and does not lose any data files, the instance can recover the database with the information in these files.

The following additional files are important to the successful running of the database:

1. **Parameter file:** Is used to define how the instance is configured when it starts up
2. **Password file:** Allows users using the sysdba, sysoper, and sysasm roles to connect remotely to the instance and perform administrative tasks
3. **Backup files:** Are used for database recovery. You typically restore a backup file when a media failure or user error has damaged or deleted the original file.
4. **Archived redo log files:** Contain an ongoing history of the data changes (redo) that are generated by the instance. Using these files and a backup of the database, you can recover a lost data file. That is, archive logs enable the recovery of restored data files.

5. **Trace files:** Each server and background process can write to an associated trace file. When an internal error is detected by a process, the process dumps information about the error to its trace file. Some of the information written to a trace file is intended for the database administrator, whereas other information is for Oracle Support Services.
6. **Alert log file:** These are special trace entries. The alert log of a database is a chronological log of messages and errors. Oracle recommends that you review the alert log periodically.

LOGICAL AND PHYSICAL DATABASE STRUCTURES

The database has logical structures and physical structures.

Databases, Tablespaces, and Data Files

The relationship among databases, tablespaces, and data files is illustrated in the slide. Each database is logically divided into two or more tablespaces. One or more data files are explicitly created for each tablespace to physically store the data of all segments in a tablespace. If it is a TEMPORARY tablespace, it has a temporary file instead of a data file. A tablespace's datafile can be physically stored on any supported storage technology.

Tablespaces

A database is divided into logical storage units called ***tablespaces***, which group related logical structures or datafiles together. For example, tablespaces commonly group all of an application's segments to simplify some administrative operations.

Data Blocks

At the finest level of granularity, an Oracle database's data is stored in *data blocks*. One data block corresponds to a specific number of bytes of physical space on the disk. A data block size is specified for each tablespace when it is created. A database uses and allocates free database space in Oracle data blocks.

Extents

The next level of logical database space is an *extent*. An extent is a specific number of contiguous Oracle data blocks (obtained in a single allocation) that are used to store a specific type of information. Oracle data blocks in an extent are logically contiguous but can be physically spread out on disk because of RAID striping and file system implementations.

Segments

The level of logical database storage above an extent is called a *segment*. A segment is a set of extents allocated for a certain logical structure. For example:

- **Data segments:** Each nonclustered, non-index-organized table has a data segment, with the exception of external tables, global temporary tables, and partitioned tables in which each table has one or more segments. All of the table's data is stored in the extents of its data segment. For a partitioned table, each partition has a data segment. Each cluster has a data segment. The data of every table in the cluster is stored in the cluster's data segment.
- **Index segments:** Each index has an index segment that stores all of its data. For a partitioned index, each partition has an index segment.

- **Undo segments:** One UNDO tablespace is created for each database instance. This tablespace contains numerous undo segments to temporarily store undo information. The information in an undo segment is used to generate read-consistent database information and, during database recovery, to roll back uncommitted transactions for users.
- **Temporary segments:** Temporary segments are created by the Oracle database when a SQL statement needs a temporary work area to complete execution. When the statement finishes execution, the temporary segment's extents are returned to the instance for future use. Specify either a default temporary tablespace for every user, or a default temporary tablespace that is used database-wide.

There are other types of segments not listed above. There are also schema objects such as views, packages, triggers, etc., that are not considered segments even though they are database objects. A segment owns its respective disk space allocation. The other objects exist as rows stored in a system metadata segment.

The Oracle database server dynamically allocates space. When the existing extents of a segment are full, additional extents are added. Because extents are allocated as needed, the extents of a segment may or may not be contiguous on the disk, and they can come from different datafiles belonging to the same tablespace.

Segments, Extents, and Blocks

A subset of database objects such as tables and indexes are stored as segments in tablespaces. Each segment contains one or more extents. An extent consists of contiguous data blocks, which means that each extent can exist only in one data file. Data blocks are the smallest unit of I/O in the database.

When the database requests a set of data blocks from the Operating System (OS), the OS maps this to an actual file system or disk block on the storage device. Because of this, you do not need to know the physical address of any of the data in your database. This also means that a data file can be striped or mirrored on several disks.

The size of the data block can be set at the time of database creation. The default size of 8 KB is adequate for most databases. If your database supports a data warehouse application that has large tables and indexes, a larger block size may be beneficial.

If your database supports a transactional application in which reads and writes are random, specifying a smaller block size may be beneficial. The maximum block size depends on your OS. The minimum Oracle block size is 2 KB; it should rarely (if ever) be used.

Tablespaces and Data Files

A database is divided into *tablespaces*, which are logical storage units that can be used to group related logical structures. Each database is logically divided into two or more tablespaces: the SYSTEM and SYSAUX tablespaces. One or more data files are explicitly created for each tablespace to physically store the data of all logical structures in a tablespace.

The graphic on the slide illustrates tablespace one composed of two datafiles. A segment of 160 KB size is spanning the two datafiles, composed of two extents. The first extent of size 64 KB is in the first datafile and the second extent of size 96 KB is in the second datafile. Both extents are formed from contiguous 8 Kb Oracle blocks.

You can also create bigfile tablespaces, which have only one file that is often very large. The file may be any size up to the maximum that the row ID architecture permits. The maximum size is the block size for the tablespace multiplied by 236, or 128 TB for a 32 KB block size. Traditional smallfile tablespaces (which are the default) may contain multiple data files, but the files cannot be as large.

SYSTEM AND SYSAUX TABLESPACES

Each Oracle database must contain a SYSTEM tablespace and a SYSAUX tablespace. They are automatically created when the database is created. The system default is to create a smallfile tablespace. You can also create bigfile tablespaces, which enable the Oracle database to manage ultralarge files.

A tablespace can be online (accessible) or offline (not accessible). The SYSTEM tablespace is always online when the database is open. It stores tables that support the core functionality of the database, such as the data dictionary tables.

The SYSAUX tablespace is an auxiliary tablespace to the SYSTEM tablespace. The SYSAUX tablespace stores many database components, and it must be online for the correct functioning of all database components. The SYSTEM and SYSAUX tablespaces are not recommended to be used to store application's data. Additional tablespaces can be created for this purpose.

The SYSAUX tablespace may be offlined to do tablespace recovery, whereas this is not possible for the SYSTEM tablespace. Neither of them may be made read-only.

AUTOMATIC STORAGE MANAGEMENT

Automatic Storage Management (ASM) provides vertical integration of the file system and the volume manager for Oracle database files. ASM can provide management for single symmetric multiprocessing (SMP) machines or across multiple nodes of a cluster for Oracle Real Application Clusters (RAC) support.

Oracle ASM Cluster File System (ACFS) is a multi-platform, scalable file system, and storage management technology that extends ASM functionality to support application files outside of the Oracle Database such as executables, reports, BFILEs, video, audio, text, images, and other general-purpose application file data.

ASM distributes Input/Output (I/O) load across all available resources to optimize performance while removing the need for manual I/O tuning. ASM helps DBAs manage a dynamic database environment by enabling them to increase the database size without having to shut down the database to adjust storage allocation.

ASM can maintain redundant copies of data to provide fault tolerance, or it can be built on top of vendor-supplied storage mechanisms. Data management is done by selecting the desired reliability and performance characteristics for classes of data rather than with human interaction on a per-file basis.

ASM capabilities save the DBA's time by automating manual storage and thereby increasing the administrator's ability to manage more and larger databases with increased efficiency.

ASM Storage Components

ASM does not eliminate any existing database functionality. Existing databases are able to operate as they always have. New files may be created as ASM files, whereas existing ones are administered in the old way or can be migrated to ASM.

The diagram illustrates the relationships between an Oracle database datafile and the ASM storage components. The crow's foot notation represents a one-to-many relationship. An Oracle database datafile has a one-to-one relationship with either a file stored on the operating system in a file system or an ASM file.

An Oracle ASM disk group is a collection of one or more Oracle ASM disks managed as a logical unit. The data structures in a disk group are self-contained using some of the space for metadata needs. Oracle ASM disks are the storage devices provisioned to an Oracle ASM disk group and can be physical disk or partitions, a Logical Unit Number (LUN) from a storage array, a Logical Volume (LV), or a network-attached file. Each ASM disk is divided into many ASM allocation units, the smallest contiguous amount of disk space that ASM allocates. When you create an ASM disk group, you can set the ASM allocation unit size to 1, 2, 4, 8, 16, 32, or 64 MB depending on the disk group compatibility level. One or more ASM allocation units forms an ASM extent. An Oracle ASM extent is the raw storage used to hold the contents of an Oracle ASM file. An Oracle ASM file consists of one or more file extents. Variable extent sizes of 1*AU size, 4*AU size, and 16*AU size are used for supporting very large ASM files.

INTRODUCTION TO PERFORMANCE TUNING

This guide provides information about tuning Oracle Database for performance. Topics discussed in this guide include:

- Performance Planning
- Instance Tuning
- SQL Tuning.

Performance Planning

Based on years of designing and performance experience, Oracle has designed a performance methodology. This part describes activities that can dramatically improve system performance and contains the following topics:

- Understanding Investment Options
- Understanding Scalability
- System Architecture
- Application Design Principles
- Workload Testing, Modeling, and Implementation
- Deploying New Applications.

Instance Tuning

When considering instance tuning, take care in the initial design of the database to avoid bottlenecks that could lead to performance problems. In addition, you must consider:

- Allocating memory to database structures
- Determining I/O requirements of different parts of the database
- Tuning the operating system for optimal performance of the database.

After the database instance has been installed and configured, you must monitor the database as it is running to check for performance-related problems.

Performance Principles

Performance tuning requires a different, although related, method to the initial configuration of a system. Configuring a system involves allocating resources in an ordered manner so that the initial system configuration is functional.

Tuning is driven by identifying the most significant bottleneck and making the appropriate changes to reduce or eliminate the effect of that bottleneck. Usually, tuning is performed reactively, either while the system is in preproduction or after it is live.

Baselines

The most effective way to tune is to have an established performance baseline that you can use for comparison if a performance issue arises. Most database administrators (DBAs) know their system well and can easily identify peak usage periods. For example, the peak periods could be between 10.00 am and 12.00 pm and also between 1.30 pm and 3.00 pm. This could include a batch window of 12.00 am midnight to 6 am.

It is important to identify these peak periods at the site and install a monitoring tool that gathers performance data for those high-load times. Optimally, data gathering should be configured from when the application is in its initial trial phase during the QA cycle. Otherwise, this should be configured when the system is first in production.

Ideally, baseline data gathered should include the following:

- Application statistics (transaction volumes, response time)
- Database statistics
- Operating system statistics
- Disk I/O statistics
- Network statistics.

In the Automatic Workload Repository, baselines are identified by a range of snapshots that are preserved for future comparisons.

The Symptoms and the Problems

A common pitfall in performance tuning is to mistake the symptoms of a problem for the actual problem itself. It is important to recognize that many performance statistics indicate the symptoms, and that identifying the symptom is not sufficient data to implement a remedy. For example:

- Slow physical I/O
  Generally, this is caused by poorly-configured disks. However, it could also be caused by a significant amount of unnecessary physical I/O on those disks issued by poorly-tuned SQL.
- Latch contention
  Rarely is latch contention tunable by reconfiguring the instance. Rather, latch contention usually is resolved through application changes.
- Excessive CPU usage
  Excessive CPU usage usually means that there is little idle CPU on the system. This could be caused by an inadequately-sized system, by untuned SQL statements, or by inefficient application programs.

When to Tune

There are two distinct types of tuning:

- Proactive Monitoring
- Bottleneck Elimination.

Proactive Monitoring

Proactive monitoring usually occurs on a regularly scheduled interval, where several performance statistics are examined to identify whether the system behavior and resource usage has changed. Proactive monitoring can also be considered as proactive tuning.

Usually, monitoring does not result in configuration changes to the system, unless the monitoring exposes a serious problem that is developing. In some situations, experienced performance engineers can identify potential problems through statistics alone, although accompanying performance degradation is usual.

Experimenting with or tweaking a system when there is no apparent performance degradation as a proactive action can be a dangerous activity, resulting in unnecessary performance drops. Tweaking a system should be considered reactive tuning, and the steps for reactive tuning should be followed.

Monitoring is usually part of a larger capacity planning exercise, where resource consumption is examined to see changes in the way the application is being used, and the way the application is using the database and host resources.

Bottleneck Elimination

Tuning usually implies fixing a performance problem. However, tuning should be part of the life cycle of an application—through the analysis, design, coding, production, and maintenance stages. Often, the tuning phase is left until the database is in production. At this time, tuning becomes a reactive process, where the most important bottleneck is identified and fixed.

Usually, the purpose for tuning is to reduce resource consumption or to reduce the elapsed time for an operation to complete. Either way, the goal is to improve the effective use of a particular resource. In general, performance problems are caused by the overuse of a particular resource. The overused resource is the bottleneck in the system. There are several distinct phases in identifying the bottleneck and the potential fixes. These are discussed in the sections that follow.

Remember that the different forms of contention are symptoms that can be fixed by making changes in the following places:

- Changes in the application, or the way the application is used
- Changes in Oracle
- Changes in the host hardware configuration.

Often, the most effective way of resolving a bottleneck is to change the application.

SQL TUNING

Many application programmers consider SQL a messaging language, because queries are issued and data is returned. However, client tools often generate inefficient SQL statements. Therefore, a good understanding of the database SQL processing engine is necessary for writing optimal SQL. This is especially true for high transaction processing systems.

Typically, SQL statements issued by OLTP applications operate on relatively few rows at a time. If an index can point to the exact rows that are required, then Oracle Database can construct an accurate plan to access those rows efficiently through the shortest possible path. In decision support system (DSS) environments, selectivity is less important, because they often access most of a table's rows. In such situations, full table scans are common, and indexes are not even used. This book is primarily focussed on OLTP-type applications.

Query Optimizer and Execution Plans

When a SQL statement is executed on an Oracle database, the query optimizer determines the most efficient execution plan after considering many factors related to the objects referenced and the conditions specified in the query. This determination is an important step in the processing of any SQL statement and can greatly affect execution time.

During the evaluation process, the query optimizer reviews statistics gathered on the system to determine the best data access path and other considerations. You can override the execution plan of the query optimizer with hints inserted in SQL statement.

INTRODUCTION TO PERFORMANCE TUNING FEATURES AND TOOLS

Effective data collection and analysis is essential for identifying and correcting performance problems. Oracle Database provides several tools that allow a performance engineer to gather information regarding database performance. In addition to gathering data, Oracle Database provides tools to monitor performance, diagnose problems, and tune applications.

The Oracle Database gathering and monitoring features are mainly automatic, managed by Oracle background processes. To enable automatic statistics collection and automatic performance features, the STATISTICS_LEVEL initialization parameter must be set to TYPICAL or ALL. You can administer and display the output of the gathering and tuning tools with Oracle Enterprise Manager, or with APIs and views. For ease of use and to take advantage of its numerous automated monitoring and diagnostic tools, Oracle Enterprise Manager Database Control is recommended.

Automatic Performance Tuning Features

The Oracle Database automatic performance tuning features include:

- Automatic Workload Repository (AWR) collects, processes, and maintains performance statistics for problem detection and self-tuning purposes.
- Automatic Database Diagnostic Monitor (ADDM) analyzes the information collected by the AWR for possible performance problems with the Oracle database.
- SQL Tuning Advisor allows a quick and efficient technique for optimizing SQL statements without modifying any statements.
- SQLAccess Advisor provides advice on materialized views, indexes, and materialized view logs.
- End to End Application tracing identifies excessive workloads on the system by specific user, service, or application component.
- Server-generated alerts automatically provide notifications when impending problems are detected.
- Additional advisors that can be launched from Oracle Enterprise Manager, such as memory advisors to optimize memory for an instance. The memory advisors are commonly used when automatic memory management is not set up for the database. Other advisors are used to optimize mean time to recovery (MTTR), shrinking of segments, and undo tablespace settings.

- The Database Performance page in Oracle Enterprise Manager displays host, instance service time, and throughput information for real time monitoring and diagnosis. The page can be set to refresh automatically in selected intervals or manually.

ADDITIONAL ORACLE DATABASE TOOLS

This section describes additional Oracle Database tools that you can use for determining performance problems.

V$ Performance Views

The V$ views are the performance information sources used by all Oracle Database performance tuning tools. The V$ views are based on memory structures initialized at instance startup. The memory structures, and the views that represent them, are automatically maintained by Oracle Database for the life of the instance. See Chapter 10, "Instance Tuning Using Performance Views" for information diagnosing tuning problems using the V$ performance views.

Oracle recommends using the Automatic Workload Repository to gather performance data. These tools have been designed to capture all of the data needed for performance analysis.

2

Designing and Developing for Performance

Learning Objectives

Optimal system performance begins with design and continues throughout the life of your system. Carefully consider performance issues during the initial design phase so that you can tune your system more easily during production.

This chapter contains the following sections:

- Oracle Methodology
- Understanding Investment Options
- Understanding Scalability
- System Architecture
- Application Design Principles
- Workload Testing, Modeling, and Implementation
- Deploying New Applications

ORACLE METHODOLOGY

System performance has become increasingly important as computer systems get larger and more complex as the Internet plays a bigger role in business applications. To accommodate this, Oracle has produced a performance methodology based on years of designing and performance experience. This methodology explains clear and simple activities that can dramatically improve system performance.

Performance strategies vary in their effectiveness, and systems with different purposes—such as operational systems and decision support systems—require different performance skills. This book examines the considerations that any database designer, administrator, or performance expert should focus their efforts on.

System performance is designed and built into a system. It does not just happen. Performance problems are usually the result of contention for, or exhaustion of, some system resource. When a system resource is exhausted, the system cannot scale to higher levels of performance. This new performance methodology is based on careful planning and design of the database, to prevent system resources from becoming exhausted and causing down-time. By eliminating resource conflicts, systems can be made scalable to the levels required by the business.

UNDERSTANDING INVESTMENT OPTIONS

With the availability of relatively inexpensive, high-powered processors, memory, and disk drives, there is a temptation to buy more system resources to improve performance. In many situations, new CPUs, memory, or more disk drives can indeed provide an immediate performance improvement. However, any performance increases achieved by adding hardware should be considered a short-term relief to an immediate problem. If the demand and load rates on the application continue to grow, then the chance of the same problem occurring soon is likely.

In other situations, additional hardware does not improve the system's performance at all. Poorly designed systems perform poorly no matter how much extra hardware is allocated. Before purchasing additional hardware, ensure that serialization or single threading is not occurring within the application. Long-term, it is generally more valuable to increase the efficiency of your application in terms of the number of physical resources used for each business transaction.

UNDERSTANDING SCALABILITY

The word *scalability* is used in many contexts in development environments. The following section provides an explanation of scalability that is aimed at application designers and performance specialists.

This section covers the following topics:

- What is Scalability?
- System Scalability
- Factors Preventing Scalability.

What is Scalability?

Scalability is a system's ability to process more workload, with a proportional increase in system resource usage. In other words, in a scalable system, if you double the workload, then the system uses twice as many system resources. This sounds obvious, but due to conflicts within the system, the resource usage might exceed twice the original workload.

Examples of poor scalability due to resource conflicts include the following:

- Applications requiring significant concurrency management as user populations increase
- Increased locking activities
- Increased data consistency workload
- Increased operating system workload
- Transactions requiring increases in data access as data volumes increase
- Poor SQL and index design resulting in a higher number of logical I/Os for the same number of rows returned
- Reduced availability, because database objects take longer to maintain.

An application is said to be unscalable if it exhausts a system resource to the point where no more throughput is possible when its workload is increased. Such applications result in fixed throughputs and poor response times.

Examples of resource exhaustion include the following:

- Hardware exhaustion
- Table scans in high-volume transactions causing inevitable disk I/O shortages
- Excessive network requests, resulting in network and scheduling bottlenecks

- Memory allocation causing paging and swapping
- Excessive process and thread allocation causing operating system thrashing.

This means that application designers must create a design that uses the same resources, regardless of user populations and data volumes, and does not put loads on the system resources beyond their limits.

System Scalability

Applications that are accessible through the Internet have more complex performance and availability requirements. Some applications are designed and written only for Internet use, but even typical back-office applications—such as a general ledger application—might require some or all data to be available online.

Characteristics of Internet age applications include the following:

- Availability 24 hours a day, 365 days a year
- Unpredictable and imprecise number of concurrent users
- Difficulty in capacity planning
- Availability for any type of query
- Multitier architectures
- Stateless middleware
- Rapid development timescale
- Minimal time for testing.

Figure 2.1 illustrates the classic workload growth curve, with demand growing at an increasing rate. Applications must scale with the increase of workload and also when additional hardware is added to support increasing demand. Design errors can cause the implementation to reach its maximum, regardless of additional hardware resources or re-design efforts.

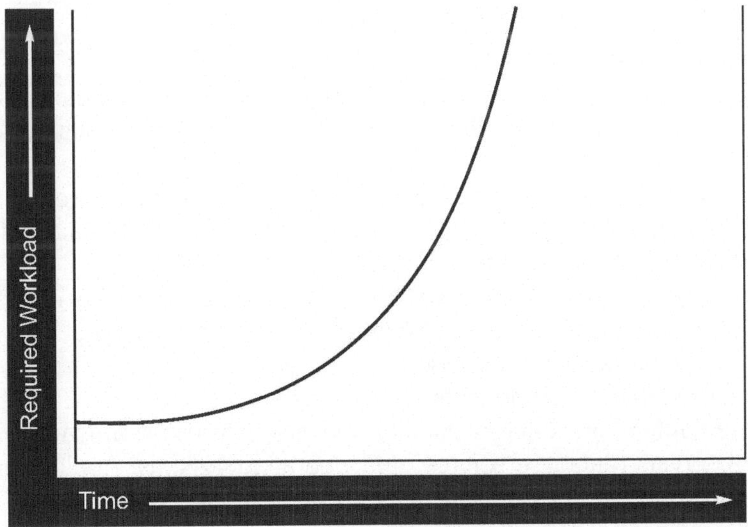

Figure 2.1. Workload Growth Curve

Applications are challenged by very short development timeframes with limited time for testing and evaluation. However, bad design typically means that you must later rearchitect and reimplement the system. If you deploy an application with known architectural and implementation limitations on the Internet, and if the workload exceeds the anticipated demand, then failure is a real possibility. From a business perspective, poor performance can mean a loss of customers. If Web users do not get a response in seven seconds, then the user's attention could be lost forever.

In many cases, the cost of re-designing a system with the associated downtime costs in migrating to new implementations exceeds the costs of properly building the original system. The moral of the story is simple: design and implement with scalability in mind from the start.

Factors Preventing Scalability

When building applications, designers and architects should aim for as close to perfect scalability as possible. This is sometimes called *linear* scalability, where system throughput is directly proportional to the number of CPUs.

In real life, linear scalability is impossible for reasons beyond a designer's control. However, making the application design and implementation as scalable as possible should ensure that current and future performance objectives can be achieved through expansion of hardware components and the evolution of CPU technology.

Factors that may prevent linear scalability include:

- Poor application design, implementation, and configuration.
  The application has the biggest impact on scalability. For example:
  - Poor schema design can cause expensive SQL that do not scale.
  - Poor transaction design can cause locking and serialization problems.
  - Poor connection management can cause poor response times and unreliable systems.

  However, the design is not the only problem. The physical implementation of the application can be the weak link. For example:
  - Systems can move to production environments with bad I/O strategies.
  - The production environment could use different execution plans than those generated in testing.
  - Memory-intensive applications that allocate a large amount of memory without much thought for freeing the memory at run time can cause excessive memory usage.
  - Inefficient memory usage and memory leaks put a high stress on the operating virtual memory subsystem. This impacts performance and availability.
- Incorrect sizing of hardware components.
  Bad capacity planning of all hardware components is becoming less of a problem as relative hardware prices decrease. However, too much capacity can mask scalability problems as the workload is increased on a system.
- Limitations of software components.
  All software components have scalability and resource usage limitations. This applies to application servers, database servers, and operating systems. Application design should not place demands on the software beyond what it can handle.
- Limitations of hardware components.
  Hardware is not perfectly scalable. Most multiprocessor computers can get close to linear scaling with a finite number of CPUs, but after a certain point each additional CPU can increase performance overall, but not proportionately. There might come a time when an additional CPU offers no increase in performance, or even degrades performance. This behavior is very closely linked to the workload and the operating system setup.

These factors are based on Oracle Server Performance group's experience of tuning unscalable systems.

SYSTEM ARCHITECTURE

There are two main parts to a system's architecture:

- Hardware and Software Components.
- Configuring the Right System Architecture for Your Requirements.

Hardware and Software Components

This section discusses:

- Hardware Components
- Software Components.

Hardware Components

Today's designers and architects are responsible for sizing and capacity planning of hardware at each tier in a multitier environment. It is the architect's responsibility to achieve a balanced design. This is analogous to a bridge designer who must consider all the various payload and structural requirements for the bridge. A bridge is only as strong as its weakest component. As a result, a bridge is designed in balance, such that all components reach their design limits simultaneously.

The main hardware components include:

- CPU
- Memory
- I/O Subsystem
- Network.

CPU

There can be one or more CPUs, and they can vary in processing power from simple CPUs found in hand-held devices to high-powered server CPUs. Sizing of other hardware components is usually a multiple of the CPUs on the system. See Chapter 9, "Managing Operating System Resources".

Memory

Database and application servers require considerable amounts of memory to cache data and avoid time-consuming disk access. See Chapter 7, "Configuring and Using Memory".

I/O Subsystem

The I/O subsystem can vary between the hard disk on a client PC and high performance disk arrays. Disk arrays can perform thousands of I/Os each second and provide availability through redundancy in terms of multiple I/O paths and hot pluggable mirrored disks. See Chapter 8, "I/O Configuration and Design".

Network

All computers in a system are connected to a network, from a modem line to a high speed internal LAN. The primary concerns with network specifications are bandwidth (volume) and latency (speed).

Software Components

The same way computers have common hardware components, applications have common functional components. By dividing software development into functional components, it is possible to better comprehend the application design and architecture. Some components of the system are performed by existing software bought to accelerate application implementation, or to avoid re-development of common components.

The difference between software components and hardware components is that while hardware components only perform one task, a piece of software can perform the roles of various software components. For example, a disk drive only stores and retrieves data, but a client program can manage the user interface and perform business logic.

Most applications involve the following components:

- Managing the User Interface
- Implementing Business Logic
- Managing User Requests and Resource Allocation
- Managing Data and Transactions.

Managing the User Interface

This component is the most visible to application users, and includes the following functions:

- Displaying the screen to the user
- Collecting user data and transferring it to business logic
- Validating data entry
- Navigating through levels or states of the application.

Implementing Business Logic

This component implements core business rules that are central to the application function. Errors made in this component can be very costly to repair. This component is implemented by a mixture of declarative and procedural approaches. An example of a declarative activity is defining unique and foreign keys. An example of procedure-based logic is implementing a discounting strategy.

Common functions of this component include:

- Moving a data model to a relational table structure
- Defining constraints in the relational table structure
- Coding procedural logic to implement business rules.

Managing User Requests and Resource Allocation

This component is implemented in all pieces of software. However, there are some requests and resources that can be influenced by the application design and some that cannot.

In a multiuser application, most resource allocation by user requests are handled by the database server or the operating system. However, in a large application where the number of users and their usage pattern is unknown or growing rapidly, the system architect must be proactive to ensure that no single software component becomes overloaded and unstable.

Common functions of this component include:

- Connection management with the database
- Executing SQL efficiently (cursors and SQL sharing)
- Managing client state information

- Balancing the load of user requests across hardware resources
- Setting operational targets for hardware and software components
- Persistent queuing for asynchronous execution of tasks.

Managing Data and Transactions

This component is largely the responsibility of the database server and the operating system. Common functions of this component include:

- Providing concurrent access to data using locks and transactional semantics
- Providing optimized access to the data using indexes and memory cache
- Ensuring that data changes are logged in the event of a hardware failure
- Enforcing any rules defined for the data.

Configuring the Right System Architecture for Your Requirements

Configuring the initial system architecture is a largely iterative process. System architects must satisfy the system requirements within budget and schedule constraints. If the system requires interactive users transacting business-making decisions based on the contents of a database, then user requirements drive the architecture. If there are few interactive users on the system, then the architecture is process-driven.

Examples of interactive user applications:

- Accounting and bookkeeping applications
- Order entry systems
- Email servers
- Web-based retail applications
- Trading systems.

Examples of process-driven applications:

- Utility billing systems
- Fraud detection systems
- Direct mail.

In many ways, process-driven applications are easier to design than multiuser applications because the user interface element is eliminated. However, because the objectives are process-oriented, system architects not accustomed to dealing with large data volumes and different success factors can become confused. Process-driven applications draw from the skills sets used in both user-based applications and data warehousing. Therefore, this book focuses on evolving system architectures for interactive users.

> Generating a system architecture is not a deterministic process. It requires careful consideration of business requirements, technology choices, existing infrastructure and systems, and actual physical resources, such as budget and manpower.

The following questions should stimulate thought on system architecture, though they are not a definitive guide to system architecture. These questions demonstrate how business requirements can influence the architecture, ease of implementation, and overall performance and availability of a system. For example:

- How many users must the system support?
  Most applications fall into one of the following categories:
  - Very few users on a lightly-used or exclusive computer.
    For this type of application, there is usually one user. The focus of the application design is to make the single user as productive as possible by providing good response time, yet make the application require minimal administration. Users of these applications rarely interfere with each other and have minimal resource conflicts.
  - A medium to large number of users in a corporation using shared applications.
    For this type of application, the users are limited by the number of employees in the corporation actually transacting business through the system. Therefore, the number of users is predictable. However, delivering a reliable service is crucial to the business. The users must share a resource, so design efforts must address response time under heavy system load, escalation of resource for each session usage, and room for future growth.
  - An infinite user population distributed on the Internet.
    For this type of application, extra engineering effort is required to ensure that no system component exceeds its design limits. This creates a bottleneck that halts or destabilizes the system. These applications require complex load balancing, stateless application servers, and efficient database connection management. In addition, use statistics and governors to ensure that the user receives feedback if the database cannot satisfy their requests because of system overload.
- What will be the user interaction method?
  The choices of user interface range from a simple Web browser to a custom client program.
- Where are the users located?
  The distance between users influences how the application is engineered to cope with network latencies. The location also affects which times of the day are busy, when it is impossible to perform batch or system maintenance functions.
- What is the network speed?
  Network speed affects the amount of data and the conversational nature of the user interface with the application and database servers. A highly conversational user interface can communicate with back-end servers on every key stroke or field level validation. A less conversational interface works on a screen-sent and a screen-received model. On a slow network, it is impossible to achieve high data entry speeds with a highly conversational user interface.
- How much data will the user access, and how much of that data is largely read only?
  The amount of data queried online influences all aspects of the design, from table and index design to the presentation layers. Design efforts must ensure that user response time is not a function of the size of the database. If the application is largely read only, then replication and data distribution to local caches in the application servers become a viable option. This also reduces workload on the core transactional server.
- What is the user response time requirement?
  Consideration of the user type is important. If the user is an executive who requires accurate information to make split second decisions, then user response time cannot be compromised. Other types of users, such as users performing data entry activities, might not need such a high level of performance.

- Do users expect 24 hour service?
  This is mandatory for today's Internet applications where trade is conducted 24 hours a day. However, corporate systems that run in a single time zone might be able to tolerate after-hours downtime. You can use this after-hours downtime to run batch processes or to perform system administration. In this case, it might be more economic not to run a fully-available system.
- Must all changes be made in real time?
  It is important to determine whether transactions must be executed within the user response time, or if they can be queued for asynchronous execution.

The following are secondary questions, which can also influence the design, but really have more impact on budget and ease of implementation. For example:

- How big will the database be?
  This influences the sizing of the database server. On servers with a very large database, it might be necessary to have a bigger computer than dictated by the workload. This is because the administration overhead with large databases is largely a function of the database size. As tables and indexes grow, it takes proportionately more CPUs to allow table reorganizations and index builds to complete in an acceptable time limit.
- What is the required throughput of business transactions?
- What are the availability requirements?
- Do skills exist to build and administer this application?
- What compromises are forced by budget constraints?

APPLICATION DESIGN PRINCIPLES

This section describes the following design decisions that are involved in building applications:

- Simplicity In Application Design
- Data Modeling
- Table and Index Design
- Using Views
- SQL Execution Efficiency
- Implementing the Application
- Trends in Application Development.

Simplicity in Application Design

Applications are no different than any other designed and engineered product. Well-designed structures, computers, and tools are usually reliable, easy to use and maintain, and simple in concept. In the most general terms, if the design looks correct, then it probably is. This principle should always be kept in mind when building applications.

Consider the following design issues:

- If the table design is so complicated that nobody can fully understand it, then the table is probably poorly designed.
- If SQL statements are so long and involved that it would be impossible for any optimizer to effectively optimize it in real time, then there is probably a bad statement, underlying transaction, or table design.
- If there are indexes on a table and the same columns are repeatedly indexed, then there is probably a poor index design.

- If queries are submitted without suitable qualification for rapid response for online users, then there is probably a poor user interface or transaction design.
- If the calls to the database are abstracted away from the application logic by many layers of software, then there is probably a bad software development method.

Data Modeling

Data modeling is important to successful relational application design. You must perform this modeling in a way that quickly represents the business practices. Heated debates may occur about the correct data model. The important thing is to apply greatest modeling efforts to those entities affected by the most frequent business transactions. In the modeling phase, there is a great temptation to spend too much time modeling the non-core data elements, which results in increased development lead times. Use of modeling tools can then rapidly generate schema definitions and can be useful when a fast prototype is required.

Table and Index Design

Table design is largely a compromise between flexibility and performance of core transactions. To keep the database flexible and able to accommodate unforeseen workloads, the table design should be very similar to the data model, and it should be normalized to at least 3rd normal form. However, certain core transactions required by users can require selective denormalization for performance purposes.

Examples of this technique include storing tables pre-joined, the addition of derived columns, and aggregate values. Oracle Database provides numerous options for storage of aggregates and pre-joined data by clustering and materialized view functions. These features allow a simpler table design to be adopted initially.

Again, focus and resources should be spent on the business critical tables, so that optimal performance can be achieved. For non-critical tables, shortcuts in design can be adopted to enable a more rapid application development. However, if prototyping and testing a non-core table becomes a performance problem, then remedial design effort should be applied immediately.

Index design is also a largely iterative process, based on the SQL generated by application designers. However, it is possible to make a sensible start by building indexes that enforce primary key constraints and indexes on known access patterns, such as a person's name. As the application evolves, and as you perform testing on realistic amounts of data, you may need to improve the performance of specific queries by building a better index. Consider the following list of indexing design ideas when building a new index:

- Appending Columns to an Index or Using Index-Organized Tables
- Using a Different Index Type
- Finding the Cost of an Index
- Serializing within Indexes
- Ordering Columns in an Index.

Appending Columns to an Index or Using Index-Organized Tables

One of the easiest ways to speed up a query is to reduce the number of logical I/Os by eliminating a table access from the execution plan. This can be done by appending to the index all columns referenced by the query. These columns are the select list columns, and any required join or sort columns. This technique is particularly useful in speeding up online applications response times when time-consuming I/Os are reduced. This is best applied when testing the application with properly sized data for the first time.

The most aggressive form of this technique is to build an Index-Organized Table (IOT). However, you must be careful that the increased leaf size of an IOT does not undermine the efforts to reduce I/O.

Using a Different Index Type

There are several index types available, and each index has benefits for certain situations. The following list gives performance ideas associated with each index type.

B-Tree Indexes: These indexes are the standard index type, and they are excellent for primary key and highly-selective indexes. Used as concatenated indexes, the database can use B-tree indexes to retrieve data sorted by the index columns.

Bitmap Indexes: These indexes are suitable for low cardinality data. Through compression techniques, they can generate a large number of rowids with minimal I/O. Combining bitmap indexes on non-selective columns allows efficient AND and OR operations with a great number of rowids with minimal I/O. Bitmap indexes are particularly efficient in queries with COUNT(), because the query can be satisfied within the index.

Function-based Indexes: These indexes allow access through a B-tree on a value derived from a function on the base data. Function-based indexes have some limitations with regards to the use of nulls, and they require that you have the query optimizer enabled.

Function-based indexes are particularly useful when querying on composite columns to produce a derived result or to overcome limitations in the way data is stored in the database. An example is querying for line items in an order exceeding a certain value derived from (sales price-discount) x quantity, where these were columns in the table. Another example is to apply the UPPER function to the data to allow case-insensitive searches.

Partitioned Indexes: Partitioning a global index allows partition pruning to take place within an index access, which results in reduced I/Os. By definition of good range or list partitioning, fast index scans of the correct index partitions can result in very fast query times.

Reverse Key Indexes: These indexes are designed to eliminate index hot spots on insert applications. These indexes are excellent for insert performance, but they are limited because the database cannot use them for index range scans.

Finding the Cost of an Index

Building and maintaining an index structure can be expensive, and it can consume resources such as disk space, CPU, and I/O capacity. Designers must ensure that the benefits of any index outweigh the negatives of index maintenance.

Use this simple estimation guide for the cost of index maintenance: each index maintained by an INSERT, DELETE, or UPDATE of the indexed keys requires about three times as much resource as the actual DML operation on the table. Thus, if you INSERT into a table with three indexes, then the insertion is approximately 10 times slower than an INSERT into a table with no indexes. For DML, and particularly for INSERT-heavy applications, the index design should be seriously reviewed, which might require a compromise between the query and INSERT performance.

Serializing within Indexes

Use of sequences, or timestamps, to generate key values that are indexed themselves can lead to database hotspot problems, which affect response time and throughput. This is usually the result of a monotonically growing key that results in a right-growing index. To avoid this problem, try to generate keys that insert over the full range of the index. This results in a well-balanced index that is more scalable and space efficient. You can achieve this by using a reverse key index or using a cycling sequence to prefix and sequence values.

Ordering Columns in an Index

Designers should be flexible in defining any rules for index building. Depending on your circumstances, use one of the following two ways to order the keys in an index:

- Order columns with most selectivity first. This method is the most commonly used because it provides the fastest access with minimal I/O to the actual rowids required. This technique is used mainly for primary keys and for very selective range scans.
- Order columns to reduce I/O by clustering or sorting data. In large range scans, I/Os can usually be reduced by ordering the columns in the least selective order, or in a manner that sorts the data in the way it should be retrieved. See Chapter 14, "Using Indexes and Clusters".

Using Views

Views can speed up and simplify application design. A simple view definition can mask data model complexity from the programmers whose priorities are to retrieve, display, collect, and store data.

However, while views provide clean programming interfaces, they can cause sub-optimal, resource-intensive queries. The worst type of view use is when a view references other views, and when they are joined in queries. In many cases, developers can satisfy the query directly from the table without using a view. Usually, because of their inherent properties, views make it difficult for the optimizer to generate the optimal execution plan.

SQL Execution Efficiency

In the design and architecture phase of any system development, care should be taken to ensure that the application developers understand SQL execution efficiency. To achieve this goal, the development environment must support the following characteristics:

- Good database connection management:
  Connecting to the database is an expensive operation that is highly unscalable. Therefore, the number of concurrent connections to the database should be minimized as much as possible. A simple system, where a user connects at application initialization, is ideal. However, in a Web-based or multitiered application, where application servers are used to multiplex database connections to users, this can be difficult. With these types of applications, design efforts should ensure that database connections are pooled and are not reestablished for each user request.
- Good cursor usage and management:
  Maintaining user connections is equally important to minimizing the parsing activity on the system. Parsing is the process of interpreting a SQL statement and creating an execution plan for it. This process has many phases, including syntax checking, security checking, execution plan generation, and loading shared structures into the shared pool. There are two types of parse operations:
  - Hard parsing:
    A SQL statement is submitted for the first time, and no match is found in the shared pool. Hard parses are the most resource-intensive and unscalable, because they perform all the operations involved in a parse.

- Soft parsing:
  A SQL statement is submitted for the first time, and a match is found in the shared pool. The match can be the result of previous execution by another user. The SQL statement is shared, which is good for performance. However, soft parses are not ideal, because they still require syntax and security checking, which consume system resources.

Because parsing should be minimized as much as possible, application developers should design their applications to parse SQL statements once and execute them many times. This is done through cursors. Experienced SQL programmers should be familiar with the concept of opening and re-executing cursors.

Application developers must also ensure that SQL statements are shared within the shared pool. To achieve this goal, use bind variables to represent the parts of the query that change from execution to execution. If this is not done, then the SQL statement is likely to be parsed once and never re-used by other users. To ensure that SQL is shared, use bind variables and do not use string literals with SQL statements. For example:

Statement with string literals:

```
SELECT * FROM employees
  WHERE last_name LIKE 'KING';
```

Statement with bind variables:

```
SELECT * FROM employees
  WHERE last_name LIKE :1;
```

The following example shows the results of some tests on a simple OLTP application.

Test	#Users Supported
No Parsing all statements	270
Soft Parsing all statements	150
Hard Parsing all statements	60
Re-Connecting for each Transaction	30

These tests were performed on a four-CPU computer. The differences increase as the number of CPUs on the system increase. See Chapter 16, "SQL Tuning Overview" for information about optimizing SQL statements.

Implementing the Application

The choice of development environment and programming language is largely a function of the skills available in the development team and architectural decisions made when specifying the application. There are, however, some simple performance management rules that can lead to scalable, high-performance applications.

1. Choose a development environment suitable for software components, and do not let it limit your design for performance decisions. If it does, then you probably chose the wrong language or environment.
   - User interface:
     The programming model can vary between HTML generation and calling the windowing system directly. The development method should focus on response time of the user interface code. If HTML or Java is being sent over a network, then try to minimize network volume and interactions.

- Business logic:
  Interpreted languages, such as Java and PL/SQL, are ideal to encode business logic. They are fully portable, which makes upgrading logic relatively easy. Both languages are syntactically rich to allow code that is easy to read and interpret. If business logic requires complex mathematical functions, then a compiled binary language might be needed. The business logic code can be on the client computer, the application server, and the database server. However, the application server is the most common location for business logic.
- User requests and resource allocation:
  Most of this is not affected by the programming language, but tools and fourth generation languages that mask database connection and cursor management might use inefficient mechanisms. When evaluating these tools and environments, check their database connection model and their use of cursors and bind variables.
- Data management and transactions:
  Most of this is not affected by the programming language.

2. When implementing a software component, implement its function and not the functionality associated with other components. Implementing another component's functionality results in sub-optimal designs and implementations. This applies to all components.
3. Do not leave gaps in functionality or have software components under-researched in design, implementation, or testing. In many cases, gaps are not discovered until the application is rolled out or tested at realistic volumes. This is usually a sign of poor architecture or initial system specification. Data archival and purge modules are most frequently neglected during initial system design, build, and implementation.
4. When implementing procedural logic, implement in a procedural language, such as C, Java, or PL/SQL. When implementing data access (queries) or data changes (DML), use SQL. This rule is specific to the business logic modules of code where procedural code is mixed with data access (nonprocedural SQL) code. There is great temptation to put procedural logic into the SQL access. This tends to result in poor SQL that is resource-intensive. SQL statements with DECODE case statements are very often candidates for optimization, as are statements with a large amount of OR predicates or set operators, such as UNION and MINUS.
5. Cache frequently accessed, rarely changing data that is expensive to retrieve on a repeated basis. However, make this cache mechanism easy to use, and ensure that it is indeed cheaper than accessing the data in the original method. This is applicable to all modules where frequently used data values should be cached or stored locally, rather than be repeatedly retrieved from a remote or expensive data store.
   The most common examples of candidates for local caching include the following:
   - Today's date. SELECT SYSDATE FROM DUAL can account for over 60% of the workload on a database.
   - The current user name.
   - Repeated application variables and constants, such as tax rates, discounting rates, or location information.
   - Caching data locally can be further extended into building a local data cache into the application server middle tiers. This helps take load off the central database

servers. However, care should be taken when constructing local caches so that they do not become so complex that they cease to give a performance gain.

- Local sequence generation.

The design implications of using a cache should be considered. For example, if a user is connected at midnight and the date is cached, then the user's date value becomes invalid.

6. Optimize the interfaces between components, and ensure that all components are used in the most scalable configuration. This rule requires minimal explanation and applies to all modules and their interfaces.
7. Use foreign key references. Enforcing referential integrity through an application is expensive. You can maintain a foreign key reference by selecting the column value of the child from the parent and ensuring that it exists. The foreign key constraint enforcement supplied by Oracle—which does not use SQL—is fast, easy to declare, and does not create network traffic.
8. Consider setting up action and module names in the application to use with End to End Application Tracing. This allows greater flexibility in tracing workload problems.

Trends in Application Development

The two biggest challenges in application development today are the increased use of Java to replace compiled C or C++ applications, and increased use of object-oriented techniques, influencing the schema design.

Java provides better portability of code and availability to programmers. However, there are several performance implications associated with Java. Because Java is an interpreted language, it is slower at executing similar logic than compiled languages, such as C. As a result, resource usage of client computers increases. This requires more powerful CPUs to be applied in the client or middle tier computers and greater care from programmers to produce efficient code.

Because Java is an object-oriented language, it encourages insulation of data access into classes not performing the business logic. As a result, programmers might invoke methods without knowledge of the efficiency of the data access method being used. This tends to result in minimal database access and uses the simplest and crudest interfaces to the database.

With this type of software design, queries do not always include all the WHERE predicates to be efficient, and row filtering is performed in the Java program. This is very inefficient. In addition, for DML operations—and especially for INSERTs—single INSERTs are performed, making use of the array interface impossible. In some cases, this is made more inefficient by procedure calls. More resources are used moving the data to and from the database than in the actual database calls.

In general, it is best to place data access calls next to the business logic to achieve the best overall transaction design.

The acceptance of object-orientation at a programming level has led to the creation of object-oriented databases within the Oracle Server. This has manifested itself in many ways, from storing object structures within BLOBs and only using the database effectively as an indexed card file to the use of the Oracle Database object-relational features.

If you adopt an object-oriented approach to schema design, then ensure that you do not lose the flexibility of the relational storage model. In many cases, the object-oriented approach to schema design ends up in a heavily denormalized data structure that requires considerable maintenance and REF pointers associated with objects. Often, these designs represent a step backward to the hierarchical and network database designs that were replaced with the relational storage method.

In summary, if you are storing your data in your database for the long-term, and if you anticipate a degree of ad hoc queries or application development on the same schema, then the relational storage method probably gives the best performance and flexibility.

WORKLOAD TESTING, MODELING, AND IMPLEMENTATION

This section describes workload estimation, modeling, implementation, and testing. This section covers the following topics:

- Sizing Data
- Estimating Workloads
- Application Modeling
- Testing, Debugging, and Validating a Design.

Sizing Data

You could experience errors in your sizing estimates when dealing with variable length data if you work with a poor sample set. As data volumes grow, your key lengths could grow considerably, altering your assumptions for column sizes.

When the system becomes operational, it becomes more difficult to predict database growth, especially for indexes. Tables grow over time, and indexes are subject to the individual behavior of the application in terms of key generation, insertion pattern, and deletion of rows. The worst case is where you insert using an ascending key, and then delete most rows from the left-hand side but not all the rows. This leaves gaps and wasted space. If you have index use like this, then ensure that you know how to use the online index rebuild facility.

DBAs should monitor space allocation for each object and look for objects that may grow out of control. A good understanding of the application can highlight objects that may grow rapidly or unpredictably. This is a crucial part of both performance and availability planning for any system. When implementing the production database, the design should attempt to ensure that minimal space management takes place when interactive users are using the application. This applies for all data, temp, and rollback segments.

Estimating Workloads

Considering the number of variables involved, estimation of workloads for capacity planning and testing purposes is extremely difficult. However, designers must specify computers with CPUs, memory, and disk drives, and eventually roll out an application. There are several techniques used for sizing, and each technique has merit. When sizing, it is best to use the following two methods to validate your decision-making process and provide supporting documentation:

- Extrapolating From a Similar System
- Benchmarking.

Extrapolating from a Similar System

This is an entirely empirical approach where an existing system of similar characteristics and known performance is used as a basis system. The specification of this system is then modified by the sizing specialist according to the known differences. This approach has merit in that it correlates with an existing system, but it provides little assistance when dealing with the differences.

This approach is used in nearly all large engineering disciplines when preparing the cost of an engineering project, such as a large building, a ship, a bridge, or an oil rig. If the reference system is an order of magnitude different in size from the anticipated system, then some components may have exceeded their design limits.

Benchmarking

The benchmarking process is both resource and time consuming, and it might not produce the correct results. By simulating an application in early development or prototype form, there is a danger of measuring something that has no resemblance to the actual production system. This sounds strange, but over the many years of benchmarking customer applications with the database development organization, Oracle has yet to see reliable correlation between the benchmark application and the actual production system. This is mainly due to the number of application inefficiencies introduced in the development process.

However, benchmarks have been used successfully to size systems to an acceptable level of accuracy. In particular, benchmarks are very good at determining the actual I/O requirements and testing recovery processes when a system is fully loaded.

Benchmarks by their nature stress all system components to their limits. As the benchmark stresses all components, be prepared to see all errors in application design and implementation manifest themselves while benchmarking. Benchmarks also test database, operating system, and hardware components. Because most benchmarks are performed in a rush, expect setbacks and problems when a system component fails. Benchmarking is a stressful activity, and it takes considerable experience to get the most out of a benchmarking exercise.

Application Modeling

Modeling the application can range from complex mathematical modeling exercises to the classic simple calculations performed on the back of an envelope. Both methods have merit, with one attempting to be very precise and the other making gross estimates. The downside of both methods is that they do not allow for implementation errors and inefficiencies.

The estimation and sizing process is an imprecise science. However, by investigating the process, some intelligent estimates can be made. The whole estimation process makes no allowances for application inefficiencies introduced by poor SQL, index design, or cursor management. A sizing engineer should build in margin for application inefficiencies. A performance engineer should discover the inefficiencies and make the estimates look realistic. The Oracle performance method describes how to discover the application inefficiencies.

Testing, Debugging, and Validating a Design

The testing process mainly consists of functional and stability testing. At some point in the process, performance testing is performed.

The following list describes some simple rules for performance testing an application. If correctly documented, then this list provides important information for the production application and the capacity planning process after the application has gone live.

- Use the Automatic Database Diagnostic Monitor (ADDM) and SQL Tuning Advisor for design validation.
- Test with realistic data volumes and distributions.
  All testing must be done with fully populated tables. The test database should contain data representative of the production system in terms of data volume and cardinality between tables. All the production indexes should be built and the schema statistics should be populated correctly.
- Use the correct optimizer mode.
  Perform all testing with the optimizer mode that you plan to use in production. All Oracle Database research and development effort is focused on the query optimizer. Therefore, the use of the query optimizer is recommended.
- Test a single user performance.
  Test a single user on an idle or lightly-used database for acceptable performance. If a single user cannot achieve acceptable performance under ideal conditions, then multiple users cannot achieve acceptable performance under real conditions.
- Obtain and document plans for all SQL statements.
  Obtain an execution plan for each SQL statement. Use this process to verify that the optimizer is obtaining an optimal execution plan, and that the relative cost of the SQL statement is understood in terms of CPU time and physical I/Os. This process assists in identifying the heavy use transactions that require the most tuning and performance work in the future.
- Attempt multiuser testing.
  This process is difficult to perform accurately, because user workload and profiles might not be fully quantified. However, transactions performing DML statements should be tested to ensure that there are no locking conflicts or serialization problems.
- Test with the correct hardware configuration.
  Test with a configuration as close to the production system as possible. Using a realistic system is particularly important for network latencies, I/O subsystem bandwidth, and processor type and speed. Failing to use this approach may result in an incorrect analysis of potential performance problems.
- Measure steady state performance.
  When benchmarking, it is important to measure the performance under steady state conditions. Each benchmark run should have a ramp-up phase, where users are connected to the application and gradually start performing work on the application. This process allows for frequently cached data to be initialized into the cache and single execution operations—such as parsing—to be completed before the steady state condition. Likewise, at the end of a benchmark run, there should be a ramp-down period, where resources are freed from the system and users cease work and disconnect.

DEPLOYING NEW APPLICATIONS

This section describes the following design decisions involved in deploying applications:

- Rollout Strategies
- Performance Checklist.

Rollout Strategies

When new applications are rolled out, two strategies are commonly adopted:

- Big Bang approach—all users migrate to the new system at once.
- Trickle approach—users slowly migrate from existing systems to the new one.

Both approaches have merits and disadvantages. The Big Bang approach relies on reliable testing of the application at the required scale, but has the advantage of minimal data conversion and synchronization with the old system, because it is simply switched off. The Trickle approach allows debugging of scalability issues as the workload increases, but might mean that data must be migrated to and from legacy systems as the transition takes place.

It is difficult to recommend one approach over the other, because each method has associated risks that could lead to system outages as the transition takes place. Certainly, the Trickle approach allows profiling of real users as they are introduced to the new application, and allows the system to be reconfigured while only affecting the migrated users. This approach affects the work of the early adopters, but limits the load on support services. This means that unscheduled outages only affect a small percentage of the user population.

The decision on how to roll out a new application is specific to each business. Any adopted approach has its own unique pressures and stresses. The more testing and knowledge that you derive from the testing process, the more you realize what is best for the rollout.

Performance Checklist

To assist in the rollout, build a list of tasks that increase the chance of optimal performance in production and enable rapid debugging of the application. Do the following:

1. When you create the control file for the production database, allow for growth by setting MAXINSTANCES, MAXDATAFILES, MAXLOGFILES, MAXLOGMEMBERS, and MAXLOGHISTORY to values higher than what you anticipate for the rollout. This technique results in more disk space usage and larger control files, but saves time later should these need extension in an emergency.
2. Set block size to the value used to develop the application. Export the schema statistics from the development or test environment to the production database if the testing was done on representative data volumes and the current SQL execution plans are correct.
3. Set the minimal number of initialization parameters. Ideally, most other parameters should be left at default. If there is more tuning to perform, then this appears when the system is under load. See Chapter 4, "Configuring a Database for Performance" for information about parameter settings in an initial instance configuration.
4. Be prepared to manage block contention by setting storage options of database objects. Tables and indexes that experience high INSERT/UPDATE/DELETE rates should be created with automatic segment space management. To avoid contention of rollback segments, use automatic undo management. See Chapter 4, "Configuring a Database for Performance" for information about undo and temporary segments.
5. All SQL statements should be verified to be optimal and their resource usage understood.
6. Validate that middleware and programs that connect to the database are efficient in their connection management and do not logon or logoff repeatedly.
7. Validate that the SQL statements use cursors efficiently. The database should parse each SQL statement once and then execute it multiple times. The most common reason this

does not happen is because bind variables are not used properly and WHERE clause predicates are sent as string literals. If you use precompilers to develop the application, then make sure to reset the parameters MAXOPENCURSORS, HOLD_CURSOR, and RELEASE_CURSOR from the default values before precompiling the application.

8. Validate that all schema objects have been correctly migrated from the development environment to the production database. This includes tables, indexes, sequences, triggers, packages, procedures, functions, Java objects, synonyms, grants, and views. Ensure that any modifications made in testing are made to the production system.
9. As soon as the system is rolled out, establish a baseline set of statistics from the database and operating system. This first set of statistics validates or corrects any assumptions made in the design and rollout process.
10. Start anticipating the first bottleneck (which is inevitable) and follow the Oracle performance method to make performance improvement. For more information, see Chapter 3, "Performance Improvement Methods".

3 Performance Improvement Methods

Learning Objectives

This chapter discusses Oracle Database improvement methods and contains the following sections:

- The Oracle Performance Improvement Method
- Emergency Performance Methods

THE ORACLE PERFORMANCE IMPROVEMENT METHOD

Oracle performance methodology helps you to identify performance problems in an Oracle database. This involves identifying bottlenecks and fixing them. It is recommended that changes be made to a system only after you have confirmed that there is a bottleneck.

Performance improvement, by its nature, is iterative. For this reason, removing the first bottleneck might not lead to performance improvement immediately, because another bottleneck might be revealed. Also, in some cases, if serialization points move to a more inefficient sharing mechanism, then performance could degrade. With experience, and by following a rigorous method of bottleneck elimination, applications can be debugged and made scalable.

Performance problems generally result from either a lack of throughput, unacceptable user/job response time, or both. The problem might be localized between application modules, or it might be for the entire system.

Before looking at any database or operating system statistics, it is crucial to get feedback from the most important components of the system: the users of the system and the people ultimately paying for the application. Typical user feedback includes statements like the following:

- "The online performance is so bad that it prevents my staff from doing their jobs."
- "The billing run takes too long."
- "When I experience high amounts of Web traffic, the response time becomes unacceptable, and I am losing customers."
- "I am currently performing 5000 trades a day, and the system is maxed out. Next month, we roll out to all our users, and the number of trades is expected to quadruple."

From candid feedback, it is easy to set critical success factors for any performance work. Determining the performance targets and the performance engineer's exit criteria make managing the performance process much simpler and more successful at all levels. These critical success factors are better defined in terms of real business goals rather than system statistics.

Some real business goals for these typical user statements might be:

- "The billing run must process 1,000,000 accounts in a three-hour window."
- "At a peak period on a Website, the response time must not exceed five seconds for a page refresh."
- "The system must be able to process 25,000 trades in an eight-hour window."

The ultimate measure of success is the user's perception of system performance. The performance engineer's role is to eliminate any bottlenecks that degrade performance. These bottlenecks could be caused by inefficient use of limited shared resources or by abuse of shared resources, causing serialization. Because all shared resources are limited, the goal of a performance engineer is to maximize the number of business operations with efficient use of shared resources. At a very high level, the entire database server can be seen as a shared resource. Conversely, at a low level, a single CPU or disk can be seen as shared resources.

You can apply the Oracle performance improvement method until performance goals are met or deemed impossible. This process is highly iterative. Inevitably, some investigations may have little or no impact on database performance. Time and experience are necessary to develop the skills to accurately and quickly pinpoint critical bottlenecks. However, prior experience can sometimes work against the experienced engineer who neglects to use the data and statistics available. This type of behavior encourages database tuning by myth and folklore. This is a very risky, expensive, and unlikely to succeed method of database tuning.

The Automatic Database Diagnostic Monitor (ADDM) implements parts of the performance improvement method and analyzes statistics to provide automatic diagnosis of major performance issues. Using ADDM can significantly shorten the time required to improve the performance of a system. See Chapter 6, "Automatic Performance Diagnostics" for a description of ADDM.

Systems are so different and complex that hard and fast rules for performance analysis are impossible. In essence, the Oracle performance improvement method defines a way of working, but not a definitive set of rules. With bottleneck detection, the only rule is that there are no rules! The best performance engineers use the data provided and think laterally to determine performance problems.

Steps in the Oracle Performance Improvement Method

1. Perform the following initial standard checks:
   (*a*) Get candid feedback from users. Determine the performance project's scope and subsequent performance goals, and performance goals for the future. This process is key in future capacity planning.

   (*b*) Get a full set of operating system, database, and application statistics from the system when the performance is both good and bad. If these are not available, then get whatever is available. Missing statistics are analogous to missing evidence at a crime scene: They make detectives work harder and it is more time-consuming.

(c) Sanity-check the operating systems of all computers involved with user performance. By sanity-checking the operating system, you look for hardware or operating system resources that are fully utilized. List any over-used resources as symptoms for analysis later. In addition, check that all hardware shows no errors or diagnostics.

2. Check for the top ten most common mistakes with Oracle Database, and determine if any of these are likely to be the problem. List these as symptoms for later analysis. These are included because they represent the most likely problems. ADDM automatically detects and reports nine of these top ten issues.
3. Build a conceptual model of what is happening on the system using the symptoms as clues to understand what caused the performance problems.
4. Propose a series of remedy actions and the anticipated behavior to the system, then apply them in the order that can benefit the application the most. ADDM produces recommendations each with an expected benefit. A golden rule in performance work is that you only change one thing at a time and then measure the differences. Unfortunately, system downtime requirements might prohibit such a rigorous investigation method. If multiple changes are applied at the same time, then try to ensure that they are isolated so that the effects of each change can be independently validated.
5. Validate that the changes made have had the desired effect, and see if the user's perception of performance has improved. Otherwise, look for more bottlenecks, and continue refining the conceptual model until your understanding of the application becomes more accurate.
6. Repeat the last three steps until performance goals are met or become impossible due to other constraints.

This method identifies the biggest bottleneck and uses an objective approach to performance improvement. The focus is on making large performance improvements by increasing application efficiency and eliminating resource shortages and bottlenecks. In this process, it is anticipated that minimal (less than 10%) performance gains are made from instance tuning, and large gains (100% +) are made from isolating application inefficiencies.

A Sample Decision Process for Performance Conceptual Modeling

Conceptual modeling is almost deterministic. However, as you gain experience in performance tuning, you begin to appreciate that no real rules exist. A flexible heads-up approach is required to interpret statistics and make good decisions.

For a quick and easy approach to performance tuning, use ADDM. ADDM automatically monitors your Oracle system and provides recommendations for solving performance problems should problems occur. For example, suppose a DBA receives a call from a user complaining that the system is slow. The DBA simply examines the latest ADDM report to see which of the recommendations should be implemented to solve the problem.

The following steps illustrate how a performance engineer might look for bottlenecks without using automatic diagnostic features. These steps are only intended as a guideline for the manual process. With experience, performance engineers add to the steps involved. This analysis assumes that statistics for both the operating system and the database have been gathered.

1. Is the response time/batch run-time acceptable for a single user on an empty or lightly loaded computer?
   If it is not acceptable, then the application is probably not coded or designed optimally, and it will never be acceptable in a multiple user situation when system resources are shared. In this case, get application internal statistics, and get SQL Trace and SQL plan information. Work with developers to investigate problems in data, index, transaction SQL design, and potential deferral of work to batch and background processing.
2. Is all the CPU being utilized?
   If the kernel utilization is over 40%, then investigate the operating system for network transfers, paging, swapping, or process thrashing. Continue to check CPU utilization in user space to verify if there are any non-database jobs consuming CPU on the system limiting the amount of shared CPU resources, such as backups, file transforms, print queues, and so on. After determining that the database is using most of the CPU, investigate the top SQL by CPU utilization. These statements form the basis of all future analysis. Check the SQL and the transactions submitting the SQL for optimal execution. Oracle Database provides CPU statistics in `V$SQL` and `V$SQLSTATS`.
   If the application is optimal and no inefficiencies exist in the SQL execution, then consider rescheduling some work to off-peak hours or using a bigger computer.
3. At this point, the system performance is unsatisfactory, yet the CPU resources are not fully utilized.
   In this case, you have serialization and unscalable behavior within the server. Get the `WAIT_EVENTS` statistics from the server, and determine the biggest serialization point. If there are no serialization points, then the problem is most likely outside the database, and this should be the focus of investigation. Elimination of `WAIT_EVENTS` involves modifying application SQL and tuning database parameters. This process is very iterative and requires the ability to drill down on the `WAIT_EVENTS` systematically to eliminate serialization points.

Top Ten Mistakes Found in Oracle Systems

This section lists the most common mistakes found in Oracle databases. By following the Oracle performance improvement methodology, you should be able to avoid these mistakes altogether. If you find these mistakes in your system, then re-engineer the application where the performance effort is worthwhile. See Chapter 10, "Instance Tuning Using Performance Views" for a discussion on how wait event data reveals symptoms of problems that can be impacting performance.

1. Bad connection management.
   The application connects and disconnects for each database interaction. This problem is common with stateless middleware in application servers. It has over two orders of magnitude impact on performance, and is totally unscalable.
2. Bad use of cursors and the shared pool.
   Not using cursors results in repeated parses. If bind variables are not used, then there is hard parsing of all SQL statements. This has an order of magnitude impact in performance, and it is totally unscalable. Use cursors with bind variables that open the cursor and execute it many times. Be suspicious of applications generating dynamic SQL.

3. Bad SQL.
   Bad SQL is SQL that uses more resources than appropriate for the application requirement. This can be a Decision Support Systems (DSS) query that runs for more than 24 hours, or a query from an online application that takes more than a minute. You should investigate SQL that consumes significant system resources for potential improvement. ADDM identifies high load SQL. SQL Tuning Advisor can provide recommendations for improvement. See Chapter 6, "Automatic Performance Diagnostics" and Chapter 17, "Automatic SQL Tuning".
4. Use of nonstandard initialization parameters.
   These might have been implemented based on poor advice or incorrect assumptions. Most databases provide acceptable performance using only the set of basic parameters. In particular, parameters associated with `SPIN_COUNT` on latches and undocumented optimizer features can cause a great deal of problems that can require considerable investigation.
   Likewise, optimizer parameters set in the initialization parameter file can override proven optimal execution plans. For these reasons, schemas, schema statistics, and optimizer settings should be managed as a group to ensure consistency of performance.
5. Getting database I/O wrong.
   Many sites lay out their databases poorly over the available disks. Other sites specify the number of disks incorrectly, because they configure disks by disk space and not I/O bandwidth. See Chapter 8, "I/O Configuration and Design".
6. Online redo log setup problems.
   Many sites run with too few online redo log files and files that are too small. Small redo log files cause system checkpoints to continuously put a high load on the buffer cache and I/O system. If too few redo log files exist, then the archive cannot keep up, and the database must wait for the archiver to catch up. See Chapter 4, "Configuring a Database for Performance" for information about sizing redo log files for performance.
7. Serialization of data blocks in the buffer cache due to lack of free lists, free list groups, transaction slots `(INITRANS)`, or shortage of rollback segments.
   This is particularly common on `INSERT`-heavy applications, in applications that have raised the block size above 8K, or in applications with large numbers of active users and few rollback segments. Use Automatic Segment-Space Management (ASSM) and automatic undo management to solve this problem.
8. Long full table scans.
   Long full table scans for high-volume or interactive online operations could indicate poor transaction design, missing indexes, or poor SQL optimization. Long table scans, by nature, are I/O intensive and unscalable.
9. High amounts of recursive `(SYS)` SQL
   Large amounts of recursive SQL executed by `SYS` could indicate space management activities, such as extent allocations, taking place. This is unscalable and impacts user response time. Use locally managed tablespaces to reduce recursive SQL due to extent allocation. Recursive SQL executed under another user ID is probably SQL and PL/SQL, and this is not a problem.

10. Deployment and migration errors.
    In many cases, an application uses too many resources because the schema owning the tables has not been successfully migrated from the development environment or from an older implementation. Examples of this are missing indexes or incorrect statistics. These errors can lead to sub-optimal execution plans and poor interactive user performance. When migrating applications of known performance, export the schema statistics to maintain plan stability using the `DBMS_STATS` package.
    Although these errors are not directly detected by ADDM, ADDM highlights the resulting high load SQL.

EMERGENCY PERFORMANCE METHODS

This section provides techniques for dealing with performance emergencies. You presumably have a methodology for establishing and improving application performance. However, in an emergency situation, a component of the system has changed to transform it from a reliable, predictable system to one that is unpredictable and not satisfying user requests.

In this case, the performance engineer must rapidly determine what has changed and take appropriate actions to resume normal service as quickly as possible. In many cases, it is necessary to take immediate action, and a rigorous performance improvement project is unrealistic.

After addressing the immediate performance problem, the performance engineer must collect sufficient debugging information either to get better clarity on the performance problem or to at least ensure that it does not happen again.

The method for debugging emergency performance problems is the same as the method described in the performance improvement method earlier in this book. However, shortcuts are taken in various stages because of the timely nature of the problem. Keeping detailed notes and records of facts found as the debugging process progresses is essential for later analysis and justification of any remedial actions. This is analogous to a doctor keeping good patient notes for future reference.

Steps in the Emergency Performance Method

The Emergency Performance Method is as follows:

1. Survey the performance problem and collect the symptoms of the performance problem. This process should include the following:
    - User feedback on how the system is underperforming. Is the problem throughput or response time?
    - Ask the question, "What has changed since we last had good performance?" This answer can give clues to the problem. However, getting unbiased answers in an escalated situation can be difficult. Try to locate some reference points, such as collected statistics or log files, that were taken before and after the problem.
    - Use automatic tuning features to diagnose and monitor the problem. In addition, you can use Oracle Enterprise Manager performance features to identify top SQL and sessions.
2. Sanity-check the hardware utilization of all components of the application system. Check where the highest CPU utilization is, and check the disk, memory usage, and network performance on all the system components. This quick process identifies which tier is causing the problem. If the problem is in the application, then shift analysis to application debugging. Otherwise, move on to database server analysis.

3. Determine if the database server is constrained on CPU or if it is spending time waiting on wait events. If the database server is CPU-constrained, then investigate the following:
   - Sessions that are consuming large amounts of CPU at the operating system level and database; check `V$SESS_TIME_MODEL` for database CPU usage.
   - Sessions or statements that perform many buffer gets at the database level; check `V$SESSTAT` and `V$SQLSTATS`.
   - Execution plan changes causing sub-optimal SQL execution; these can be difficult to locate.
   - Incorrect setting of initialization parameters.
   - Algorithmic issues caused by code changes or upgrades of all components.

   If the database sessions are waiting on events, then follow the wait events listed in `V$SESSION_WAIT` to determine what is causing serialization. The `V$ACTIVE_SESSION_HISTORY` view contains a sampled history of session activity which you can use to perform diagnosis even after an incident has ended and the system has returned to normal operation. In cases of massive contention for the library cache, it might not be possible to logon or submit SQL to the database. In this case, use historical data to determine why there is suddenly contention on this latch. If most waits are for I/O, then examine `V$ACTIVE_SESSION_HISTORY` to determine the SQL being run by the sessions that are performing all of the inputs and outputs. See Chapter 10, "Instance Tuning Using Performance Views" for a discussion on wait events.
4. Apply emergency action to stabilize the system. This could involve actions that take parts of the application offline or restrict the workload that can be applied to the system. It could also involve a system restart or the termination of job in process. These naturally have service level implications.
5. Validate that the system is stable. Having made changes and restrictions to the system, validate that the system is now stable, and collect a reference set of statistics for the database. Now follow the rigorous performance method described earlier in this book to bring back all functionality and users to the system. This process may require significant application re-engineering before it is complete.

4 Configuring a Database for Performance

Learning Objectives

This chapter contains an overview of the Oracle methodology for configuring a database for performance. Although performance modifications can be made to Oracle Database on an ongoing basis, significant benefits can be gained by proper initial configuration of the database.

This chapter contains the following sections:

- Performance Considerations for Initial Instance Configuration
- Creating Subsequent Tablespaces
- Performance Considerations for Shared Servers

PERFORMANCE CONSIDERATIONS FOR INITIAL INSTANCE CONFIGURATION

This section discusses some initial database instance configuration options that have important performance impacts.

If you use the Database Configuration Assistant (DBCA) to create a database, then the supplied seed database includes the necessary basic initialization parameters and meets the performance recommendations that are discussed in this chapter.

Initialization Parameters

A running Oracle database instance is configured using initialization parameters, which are set in the initialization parameter file. These parameters influence the behavior of the running insta nce, including influencing performance. In general, a very simple initialization file with few relevant settings covers most situations, and the initialization file should not be the first place you expect to do performance tuning, except for the few parameters shown in Table 4.2.

Table 4.1 describes the parameters necessary in a minimal initialization file. Although these parameters are necessary, they have no performance impact.

Table 4.1. Necessary Initialization Parameters Without Performance Impact

Parameter	Description
DB_NAME	Name of the database. This should match the ORACLE_SID environment variable.
DB_DOMAIN	Location of the database in Internet dot notation.
OPEN_CURSORS	Limit on the maximum number of cursors (active SQL statements) for each session. The setting is application-dependent; 500 is recommended.
CONTROL_FILES	Set to contain at least two files on different disk drives to prevent failures from control file loss.
DB_FILES	Set to the maximum number of files that can assigned to the database.

Table 4.2 includes the most important parameters to set with performance implications:

Table 4.2. Important Initialization Parameters With Performance Impact

Parameter	Description
COMPATIBLE	Specifies the release with which the Oracle database must maintain compatibility. It lets you take advantage of the maintenance improvements of a new release immediately in your production systems without testing the new functionality in your environment. If your application was designed for a specific release of Oracle Database, and you are actually installing a later release, then you might want to set this parameter to the version of the previous release.
DB_BLOCK_SIZE	Sets the size of the Oracle database blocks stored in the database files and cached in the SGA. The range of values depends on the operating system, but it is typically 8192 for transaction processing systems and higher values for database warehouse systems.
SGA_TARGET	Specifies the total size of all SGA components. If SGA_TARGET is specified, then the buffer cache (DB_CACHE_SIZE), Java pool (JAVA_POOL_SIZE), large pool (LARGE_POOL_SIZE), and shared pool (SHARED_POOL_SIZE) memory pools are automa-tically sized.
PGA_AGGREGATE_TARGET	Specifies the target aggregate PGA memory available to all server processes attached to the instance.
PROCESSES	Sets the maximum number of processes that can be started by that instance. This is the most important primary parameter to set, because many other parameter values are deduced from this.

SESSIONS	This is set by default from the value of processes. However, if you are using the shared server, then the deduced value is likely to be insufficient.
UNDO_MANAGEMENT	Specifies the undo space management mode used by the database. The default is AUTO. If unspecified, the database uses AUTO.
UNDO_TABLESPACE	Specifies the undo tablespace to be used when an instance starts.

Configuring Undo Space

The database uses undo space to store data used for read consistency, recovery, and rollback statements. This data exists in one or more undo tablespaces. If you use the Database Configuration Assistant (DBCA) to create a database, then the undo tablespace is created automatically. To manually create an undo tablespace, add the UNDO TABLESPACE clause to the CREATE DATABASE statement.

To automate the management of undo data, Oracle Database uses **automatic undo management**, which transparently creates and manages undo segments.To enable automatic undo management, set the UNDO_MANAGEMENT initialization parameter to AUTO (thse default setting). If unspecified, then the UNDO_MANAGEMENT initialization parameter uses the AUTO setting. Oracle strongly recommends using automatic undo management because it significantly simplifies database management and eliminates the need for any manual tuning of undo (rollback) segments. Manual undo management using rollback segments is supported for backward compatibility.

The V$UNDOSTAT view contains statistics for monitoring and tuning undo space. Using this view, you can better estimate the amount of undo space required for the current workload. Oracle Database also uses this information to help tune undo usage. The V$ROLLSTAT view contains information about the behavior of the undo segments in the undo tablespace.

Sizing Redo Log Files

The size of the redo log files can influence performance, because the behaviour of the database writer and archiver processes depend on the redo log sizes. Generally, larger redo log files provide better performance. Undersized log files increase checkpoint activity and reduce performance.

Although the size of the redo log files does not affect LGWR performance, it can affect DBWR and checkpoint behavior. Checkpoint frequency is affected by several factors, including log file size and the setting of the FAST_START_MTTR_TARGET initialization parameter. If the FAST_START_MTTR_TARGET parameter is set to limit the instance recovery time, Oracle Database automatically tries to checkpoint as frequently as necessary. Under this condition, the size of the log files should be large enough to avoid additional checkpointing due to under sized log files. The optimal size can be obtained by querying the OPTIMAL_LOGFILE_SIZE column from the V$INSTANCE_RECOVERY view. You can also obtain sizing advice on the **Redo Log Groups** page of Oracle Enterprise Manager.

It may not always be possible to provide a specific size recommendation for redo log files, but redo log files in the range of 100 MB to a few gigabytes are considered reasonable. Size online redo log files according to the amount of redo your system generates. A rough guide is to switch log files at most once every 20 minutes.

CREATING SUBSEQUENT TABLESPACES

If you use the Database Configuration Assistant (DBCA) to create a database, then the seed database automatically includes the necessary tablespaces. If you choose not to use DBCA, then you must create extra tablespaces after creating the database.

All databases should have several tablespaces in addition to the `SYSTEM` and `SYSAUX` tablespaces. These additional tablespaces include:

- A temporary tablespace, which is used for operations such as sorting.
- An undo tablespace to contain information for read consistency, recovery, and undo statements.
- At least one tablespace for application use (in most cases, applications require several tablespaces).

For extremely large tablespaces with many data files, you can run multiple `ALTER TABLESPACE ... ADD DATAFILE` statements in parallel. During tablespace creation, the data files that make up the tablespace are initialized with special empty block images. Temporary files are not initialized.

Oracle Database does this to ensure that it can write all data files in their entirety, but this can obviously be a lengthy process if done serially. Therefore, run multiple `CREATE TABLESPACE` statements concurrently to speed up tablespace creation. For permanent tables, the choice between local and global extent management on tablespace creation can greatly affect performance. For any permanent tablespace that has moderate to large insert, modify, or delete operations compared to reads, choose local extent management.

Creating Permanent Tablespaces-Automatic Segment-Space Management

For permanent tablespaces, Oracle recommends using automatic segment-space management. Such tablespaces, often referred to as bitmap tablespaces, are locally managed tablespaces with bitmap segment space management.

Creating Temporary Tablespaces

Properly configuring the temporary tablespace helps optimize disk sort performance. Temporary tablespaces can be dictionary-managed or locally managed. Oracle recommends the use of locally managed temporary tablespaces with a `UNIFORM` extent size of `1 MB`.

You should monitor temporary tablespace activity to check how many extents the database allocates for the temporary segment. If an application extensively uses temporary tables, as in a situation when many users are concurrently using temporary tables, then the extent size could be set smaller, such as 256 K, because every usage requires at least one extent. The `EXTENT MANAGEMENT LOCAL` clause is optional for temporary tablespaces because all temporary tablespaces are created with locally managed extents of a uniform size. The default for `SIZE` is `1M`.

Creating and Maintaining Tables for Optimal Performance

When installing applications, an initial step is to create all necessary tables and indexes. When you create a segment, such as a table, the database allocates space for the data. If subsequent database operations cause the data volume to increase and exceed the space allocated, then Oracle Database extends the segment.

When creating tables and indexes, note the following:

- Specify automatic segment-space management for tablespaces.
  In this way Oracle Database automatically manages segment space for best performance.
- Set storage options carefully.
  Applications should carefully set storage options for the intended use of the table or index. This includes setting the value for `PCTFREE`. Note that using automatic segment-space management eliminates the necessity of specifying `PCTUSED`.

Use of free lists is not recommended. To use automatic segment-space management, create locally managed tablespaces, with the segment space management clause set to `AUTO`.

Table Compression

You can store heap-organized tables in a compressed format that is transparent for any kind of application. Compressed data in a database block is self-contained, which means that all information needed to re-create the uncompressed data in a block is available within the block. A block is also compressed in the buffer cache. Table compression not only reduces the disk storage but also the memory usage, specifically the buffer cache requirements. Performance improvements are accomplished by reducing the amount of necessary I/O operations for accessing a table and by increasing the probability of buffer cache hits.

Oracle Database has an advanced compression option that enables you to boost the performance of any type of application workload including data warehousing and `OLTP` applications while reducing the disk storage that is required by the database. You can use the advanced compression feature for all types of data, including structured data, unstructured data, backup data, and network data.

Estimating the Compression Factor

Table compression works by eliminating column value repetitions within individual blocks. Duplicate values in all the rows and columns in a block are stored once at the beginning of the block, in what is called a symbol table for that block. All occurrences of such values are replaced with a short reference to the symbol table. The compression is higher in blocks that have more repeated values.

Before compressing large tables you should estimate the expected compression factor. The compression factor is defined as the number of blocks necessary to store the information in an uncompressed form divided by the number of blocks necessary for a compressed storage. The compression factor can be estimated by sampling a small number of representative data blocks of the table to be compressed and comparing the average number of records for each block for the uncompressed and compressed case. Experience shows that approximately 1000 data blocks provides a very accurate estimation of the compression factor. Note that the more blocks you are sampling, the more accurate the result become.

Tuning to Achieve a Better Compression Ratio

Oracle Database achieves a good compression factor in many cases with no special tuning. As a DBA or application developer, you can try to tune the compression factor by reorganizing the records when the compression takes place. Tuning can improve the compression factor slightly in some cases and substantially in other cases.

To improve the compression factor you must increase the likelihood of value repetitions within a data block. The achievable compression factor depends on the cardinality of a specific column or column pairs (representing the likelihood of column value repetitions) and on the average row length of those columns. Table compression not only compresses duplicate values of a single column but tries to use multi-column value pairs whenever possible. Without a detailed understanding of the data distribution it is very difficult to predict the most optimal order.

Reclaiming Unused Space

Over time, it is common for segment space to become fragmented or for a segment to acquire a lot of free space as the result of update and delete operations. The resulting sparsely populated objects can suffer performance degradation during queries and DML operations.

Oracle Database provides a Segment Advisor that provides advice on whether an object has space available for reclamation based on the level of space fragmentation within an object.

If an object does have space available for reclamation, then you can compact and shrink segments or deallocate unused space at the end of a segment.

Indexing Data

The most efficient time to create indexes is after data has been loaded. In this way, space management becomes simpler, and no index maintenance takes place for each row inserted. SQL*Loader automatically uses this technique, but if you are using other methods to do initial data load, then you may need to create indexes manually. Additionally, you can perform index creation in parallel using the `PARALLEL` clause of the `CREATE INDEX` statement. However, SQL*Loader is not able to parallelize index creation, so you must manually create indexes in parallel after loading data.

Specifying Memory for Sorting Data

During index creation on tables that contain data, the data must be sorted. This sorting is done in the fastest possible way, if all available memory is used for sorting. Oracle recommends that you enable automatic sizing of SQL working areas by setting the `PGA_AGGREGATE_TARGET` initialization parameter.

PERFORMANCE CONSIDERATIONS FOR SHARED SERVERS

Using shared servers reduces the number of processes and the amount of memory consumed on the database host. Shared servers are beneficial for databases where there are many OLTP users performing intermittent transactions.

Using shared servers rather than dedicated servers is also generally better for systems that have a high connection rate to the database. With shared servers, when a connect request is received, a dispatcher is available to handle concurrent connection requests. With dedicated servers, however, a connection-specific dedicated server is sequentially initialized for each connection request.

Performance of certain database features can improve when a shared server architecture is used, and performance of certain database features can degrade slightly when a shared server architecture is used. For example, a session can be prevented from migrating to another shared server while parallel execution is active.

A session can remain nonmigratable even after a request from the client has been processed, because not all the user information has been stored in the UGA. If a server were to process the request from the client, then the part of the user state that was not stored in the UGA would be inaccessible. To avoid this situation, individual shared servers often need to remain bound to a user session.

When using some features, you may need to configure more shared servers, because some servers might be bound to sessions for an excessive amount of time.

This section discusses how to reduce contention for processes used by Oracle Database architecture:

- Identifying Contention Using the Dispatcher-Specific Views
- Identifying Contention for Shared Servers.

Identifying Contention Using the Dispatcher-Specific Views

The following views provide dispatcher performance statistics:

- V$DISPATCHER: general information about dispatcher processes
- V$DISPATCHER_RATE: dispatcher processing statistics.

The V$DISPATCHER_RATE view contains current, average, and maximum dispatcher statistics for several categories. Statistics with the prefix CUR_ are statistics for the current sample. Statistics with the prefix AVG_ are the average values for the statistics after the collection period began. Statistics with the prefix MAX_ are the maximum values for these categories after statistics collection began.

To assess dispatcher performance, query the V$DISPATCHER_RATE view and compare the current values with the maximums. If your present system throughput provides adequate response time and current values from this view are near the average and less than the maximum, then you likely have an optimally tuned shared server environment.

If the current and average rates are significantly less than the maximums, then consider reducing the number of dispatchers. Conversely, if current and average rates are close to the maximums, then you might need to add more dispatchers. A general rule is to examine V$DISPATCHER_RATE statistics during both light and heavy system use periods. After identifying your shared server load patterns, adjust your parameters accordingly.

If necessary, you can also mimic processing loads by running system stress tests and periodically polling V$DISPATCHER_RATE statistics. Proper interpretation of these statistics varies from platform to platform. Different types of applications also can cause significant variations on the statistical values recorded in V$DISPATCHER_RATE.

Reducing Contention for Dispatcher Processes

To reduce contention, consider the following:

- Adding dispatcher processes.
  The total number of dispatcher processes is limited by the value of the initialization parameter MAX_DISPATCHERS. You might need to increase this value before adding dispatcher processes.
- Enabling connection pooling.
  When system load increases and dispatcher throughput is maximized, it is not necessarily a good idea to immediately add more dispatchers. Instead, consider configuring the dispatcher to support more users with connection pooling.
- Enabling Session Multiplexing.
  Multiplexing is used by a connection manager process to establish and maintain network sessions from multiple users to individual dispatchers. For example, several user processes can connect to one dispatcher by way of a single connection from a connection manager

process. Session multiplexing is beneficial because it maximizes use of the dispatcher process connections. Multiplexing is also useful for multiplexing database link sessions between dispatchers.

Identifying Contention for Shared Servers

Steadily increasing wait times in the requests queue indicate contention for shared servers. To examine wait time data, use the dynamic performance view V$QUEUE. This view contains statistics showing request queue activity for shared servers. By default, this view is available only to the user SYS and to other users with SELECT ANY TABLE system privilege, such as SYSTEM. Table 4.3 lists the columns showing the wait times for requests and the number of requests in the queue.

Table 4.3. Wait Time and Request Columns in V$QUEUE

Column	Description
WAIT	Displays the total waiting time, in hundredths of a second, for all requests that have ever been in the queue.
TOTALQ	Displays the total number of requests that have ever been in the queue.

Monitor these statistics occasionally while your application is running by issuing the following SQL statement:

```
SELECT DECODE(TOTALQ, 0, 'No Requests',
WAIT/TOTALQ || 'HUNDREDTHS OF SECONDS') "AVERAGE WAIT TIME PER
REsQUESTS" FROM V$QUEUE WHERE TYPE = 'COMMON';
```

This query returns the results of a calculation that show the following:

```
AVERAGE WAIT TIME PER REQUEST
------------------------------
.090909 HUNDREDTHS OF SECONDS
```

From the result, you can tell that a request waits an average of 0.09 hundredths of a second in the queue before processing.

You can also determine how many shared servers are currently running by issuing the following query:

```
SELECT COUNT(*) "Shared Server Processes"
 FROM V$SHARED_SERVER
 WHERE STATUS != 'QUIT';
```

The result of this query could look like the following:

```
Shared Server Processes
------------------------------
10
```

If you detect resource contention with shared servers, then first ensure that this is not a memory contention issue by examining the shared pool and the large pool. If performance remains poor, then you might want to create more resources to reduce shared server process contention. You can do this by modifying the optional server process initialization parameters:

- MAX_DISPATCHERS
- MAX_SHARED_SERVERS
- DISPATCHERS
- SHARED_SERVERS.

5 Automatic Performance Statistics

Learning Objectives

This chapter discusses the gathering of performance statistics. This chapter contains the following topics:

- Overview of Data Gathering
- Overview of the Automatic Workload Repository
- Managing the Automatic Workload Repository

OVERVIEW OF DATA GATHERING

To effectively diagnose performance problems, statistics must be available. Oracle Database generates many types of cumulative statistics for the system, sessions, and individual SQL statements. Oracle Database also tracks cumulative statistics on segments and services. When analyzing a performance problem in any of these scopes, you typically look at the change in statistics (delta value) over the period you are interested in. Specifically, you look at the difference between the cumulative value of a statistic at the start of the period and the cumulative value at the end.

Cumulative values for statistics are generally available through dynamic performance views, such as the V$SESSTAT and V$SYSSTAT views. Note that the cumulative values in dynamic views are reset when the database instance is shutdown. The Automatic Workload Repository (AWR) automatically persists the cumulative and delta values for most of the statistics at all levels except the session level. This process is repeated on a regular time period and the result is called an AWR snapshot. The delta values captured by the snapshot represent the changes for each statistic over the time period.

A metric is another type of statistic collected by Oracle Database. A metric is defined as the rate of change in some cumulative statistic. That rate can be measured against a variety of units, including time, transactions, or database calls. For example, the number database calls per second is a metric. Metric values are exposed in some V$ views, where the values are the average over a fairly small time interval, typically 60 seconds. A history of recent metric values is available through V$ views, and some data is also persisted by AWR snapshots.

A third type of statistical data collected by Oracle is sampled data. The Active Session History (ASH) sampler performs the sampling. ASH samples the current state of all active sessions. The database collects this data into memory, where you can access it with a `V$` view. AWR snapshot processing also writes it to persistent storage.

A powerful tool for diagnosing performance problems is the use of statistical baselines. A statistical baseline is collection of statistic rates usually taken over time period where the system is performing well at peak load. Comparing statistics captured during a period of bad performance to a baseline helps discover specific statistics that have increased significantly and could be the cause of the problem.

AWR supports the capture of baseline data by enabling you to specify and preserve a pair or range of AWR snapshots as a baseline. Carefully consider the time period you choose as a baseline; the baseline should be a good representation of the peak load on the system. In the future, you can compare these baselines with snapshots captured during periods of poor performance.

Oracle Enterprise Manager is the recommended tool for viewing both real time data in the dynamic performance views and historical data from the AWR history tables. Enterprise Manager can also be used to capture operating system and network statistical data that can be correlated with AWR data.

This section covers the following topics:

- Database Statistics
- Operating System Statistics
- Interpreting Statistics.

Database Statistics

Database statistics provide information on the type of load on the database and the internal and external resources used by the database. This section describes some of the more important statistics.

Wait Events

Wait events are statistics that are incremented by a server process or thread to indicate that it had to wait for an event to complete before being able to continue processing. Wait event data reveals various symptoms of problems that might be impacting performance, such as latch contention, buffer contention, and I/O contention.

To enable easier high-level analysis of the wait events, events are grouped into classes. The classes include: Administrative, Application, Cluster, Commit, Concurrency, Configuration, Idle, Network, Other, Scheduler, System I/O, and User I/O.

The wait classes are based on a common solution that usually applies to fixing a problem with the wait event. For example, exclusive TX locks are generally an application level issue and HW locks are generally a configuration issue.

The following list includes common examples of the waits in some of the classes:

- Application: locks waits caused by row level locking or explicit lock commands
- Commit: waits for redo log write confirmation after a commit
- Idle: wait events that signify the session is inactive, such as `SQL*Net message from client`
- Network: waits for data to be sent over the network
- User I/O: wait for blocks to be read off a disk.

Wait event statistics for an instance include statistics for both background and foreground processes. Because you would typically focus your effort in tuning foreground activities, overall instance activity is broken down into foreground and background statistics in the relevant `V$` views to facilitate tuning.

The `V$SYSTEM_EVENT` view shows wait event statistics for the foreground activities of an instance and the wait event statistics for the instance. The `V$SYSTEM_WAIT_CLASS` view shows these foreground and wait event instance statistics after aggregating to wait classes. `V$SESSION_EVENT` and `V$SYSTEM_WAIT_CLASS` show wait event and wait class statistics at the session level.

Time Model Statistics

When tuning an Oracle database, each component has its own set of statistics. To look at the system as a whole, it is necessary to have a common scale for comparisons. For this reason, most Oracle Database advisories and reports describe statistics in terms of time. In addition, the `V$SESS_TIME_MODEL` and `V$SYS_TIME_MODEL` views provide time model statistics. Using the common time instrumentation helps to identify quantitative effects on the database operations.

The most important of the time model statistics is `DB time`. This statistics represents the total time spent in database calls and is an indicator of the total instance workload. It is calculated by aggregating the CPU and wait times of all sessions not waiting on idle wait events (non-idle user sessions).

`DB time` is measured cumulatively from the time of instance startup. Because `DB time` it is calculated by combining the times from all non-idle user sessions, it is possible that the `DB time` can exceed the actual time elapsed after the instance started. For example, an instance that has been running for 30 minutes could have four active user sessions whose cumulative `DB time` is approximately 120 minutes.

The objective for tuning an Oracle system could be stated as reducing the time that users spend in performing some action on the database, or simply reducing `DB time`. Other time model statistics provide quantitative effects (in time) on specific actions, such as logon operations and hard and soft parses.

Active Session History

The `V$ACTIVE_SESSION_HISTORY` view provides sampled session activity in the instance. Active sessions are sampled every second and are stored in a circular buffer in SGA. Any session that is connected to the database and is waiting for an event that does not belong to the Idle wait class is considered as an active session. This includes any session that was on the CPU at the time of sampling.

Each session sample is a set of rows and the `V$ACTIVE_SESSION_HISTORY` view returns one row for each active session per sample, returning the latest session sample rows first. Because the active session samples are stored in a circular buffer in SGA, the greater the system activity, the smaller the number of seconds of session activity that can be stored in the circular buffer. This means that the duration for which a session sample appears in the `V$` view, or the number of seconds of session activity that is displayed in the `V$` view, is completely dependent on the database activity.

As part of the AWR snapshots, the content of `V$ACTIVE_SESSION_HISTORY` is also flushed to disk. Because the content of this `V$` view can get quite large during heavy system activity, only a portion of the session samples is written to disk.

By capturing only active sessions, a manageable set of data is represented with the size being directly related to the work being performed rather than the number of sessions allowed on the system. Using ASH enables you to examine and perform detailed analysis on both current data in the V$ACTIVE_SESSION_HISTORY view and historical data in the DBA_HIST_ACTIVE_SESS_HISTORY view, often avoiding the need to replay the workload to gather additional performance tracing information. ASH also contains execution plan information for each captured SQL statement. You can use this information to identify which part of SQL execution contributed most to the SQL elapsed time. The data present in ASH can be rolled up on various dimensions that it captures, including the following:

- SQL identifier of SQL statement
- SQL plan identifier and hash value of the SQL plan used to execute the SQL statement
- SQL execution plan information
- Object number, file number, and block number
- Wait event identifier and parameters
- Session identifier and session serial number
- Module and action name
- Client identifier of the session
- Service hash identifier
- Consumer group identifier.

You can gather ASH information over a specified duration into a report.

Active session history sampling is also available for Active Data Guard physical standby instances and Oracle Automatic Storage Management (Oracle ASM) instances. On these instances, the current session activity is collected and displayed in the V$ACTIVE_SESSION_HISTORY view, but not written to disk.

System and Session Statistics

A large number of cumulative database statistics are available on a system and session level through the V$SYSSTAT and V$SESSTAT views.

Operating System Statistics

Operating system statistics provide information on the usage and performance of the main hardware components of the system, and the performance of the operating system itself. This information is crucial for detecting potential resource exhaustion, such as CPU cycles and physical memory, and for detecting bad performance of peripherals, such as disk drives.

Operating system statistics are an indication of how the hardware and operating system are working. Many system analysts react to a hardware resource shortage by installing more hardware. This is a reactionary response to a series of symptoms shown in the operating system statistics. It is best to consider operating system statistics as a diagnostic tool, similar to the way doctors use body temperature, pulse rate, and patient pain when making a diagnosis. To help identify bottlenecks, gather operating system statistics for all servers in the system under performance analysis.

Operating system statistics include the following:

- CPU Statistics
- Virtual Memory Statistics
- Disk I/O Statistics
- Network Statistics.

CPU Statistics

CPU utilization is the most important operating system statistic in the tuning process. Get CPU utilization for the entire system and for each individual CPU on multi-processor environments. Utilization for each CPU can detect single-threading and scalability issues.

Most operating systems report CPU usage as time spent in user space or mode and time spent in kernel space or mode. These additional statistics allow better analysis of what is actually being executed on the CPU.

On a system running Oracle Database, where only one application is typically running, the system runs database activity in user space. Activities required to service database requests (such as scheduling, synchronization, I/O, memory management, and process/thread creation and tear down) run in kernel mode. In a system where CPU is fully utilized, a healthy Oracle database runs between 65% and 95% in user space.

The `V$OSSTAT` view captures machine-level information in the database, making it easier for you to determine if hardware-level resource issues exist. The `V$SYSMETRIC_HISTORY` view shows a one-hour history of the Host CPU Utilization metric, a representation of percentage of CPU usage at each one-minute interval. The `V$SYS_TIME_MODEL` view supplies statistics on the CPU usage by the Oracle database. Using both sets of statistics enable you to determine whether the Oracle database or other system activity is the cause of the CPU problems.

Virtual Memory Statistics

Virtual memory statistics should mainly be used as a check to validate that there is very little paging or swapping activity on the system. System performance degrades rapidly and unpredictably when paging or swapping occurs.

Individual process memory statistics can detect memory leaks due to a programming failure to deallocate memory taken from the process heap. These statistics are necessary to validate that memory usage does not increase after the system has reached a steady state after startup. This problem is particularly acute on shared server applications on middle tier computers where session state may persist across user interactions, and on completion state information that is not fully deallocated.

Disk I/O Statistics

Because the database resides on a set of disks, the performance of the I/O subsystem is very important to the performance of the database. Most operating systems provide extensive statistics on disk performance. The most important disk statistics are the current response time and the length of the disk queues. These statistics show if the disk is performing optimally or if the disk is being overworked.

Measure the normal performance of the I/O system; typical values for a single block read range from 5 to 20 milliseconds, depending on the hardware used. If the hardware shows response times much higher than the normal performance value, then it is performing badly or is overworked. This is your bottleneck. If disk queues start to exceed two, then the disk is a potential bottleneck of the system.

Oracle Database also maintains a consistent set of I/O statistics for the I/O calls it issues. These statistics are captured for both single and multi block read and write operations in the following dimensions:

- Consumer group.
  When Oracle Database Resource Manager is enabled, the V$IOSTAT_CONSUMER_GROUP view captures I/O statistics for all consumer groups that are part of the currently enabled resource plan. The database samples cumulative statistics every hour and stores them as historical statistics in the AWR.
- Database file.
  I/O statistics of database files that are or have been accessed are captured in the V$IOSTAT_FILE view.
- Database function.
  I/O statistics for database functions (such as the LGWR and DBWR) are captured in the V$IOSTAT_FUNCTION view.

Network Statistics

You can use network statistics in much the same way as disk statistics to determine if a network or network interface is overloaded or not performing optimally. In today's networked applications, network latency can be a large portion of the actual user response time. For this reason, these statistics are a crucial debugging tool.

Oracle Database maintains a set of network I/O statistics in the V$IOSTAT_NETWORK view.

Operating System Data Gathering Tools

Table 5.1 shows the various tools for gathering operating statistics on UNIX. For Windows, use the Performance Monitor tool.

Table 5.1. UNIX Tools for Operating Statistics

Component	UNIX Tool
CPU	sar, vmstat, mpstat, iostat
Memory	sar, vmstat
Disk	sar, iostat
Network	netstat

Interpreting Statistics

When initially examining performance data, you can formulate potential theories by examining your statistics. One way to ensure that your interpretation of the statistics is correct is to perform cross-checks with other data. This establishes whether a statistic or event is really of interest. Also, because foreground activities are tunable, it is better to first analyze the statistics from foreground activities before analyzing the statistics from background activities.

Some pitfalls are discussed in the following sections:

- Hit ratios.
  When tuning, it is common to compute a ratio that helps determine whether there is a problem. Such ratios include the buffer cache hit ratio, the soft-parse ratio, and the latch hit ratio. Do not use these ratios as definitive identifiers of whether a performance bottleneck exists. Rather, use them as indicators. To identify whether a bottleneck exists, examine other related evidence.
- Wait events with timed statistics.
  Setting TIMED_STATISTICS to true at the instance level directs the database to gather wait time for events, in addition to available wait counts. This data is useful for comparing

the total wait time for an event to the total elapsed time between the data collections. For example, if the wait event accounts for only 30 seconds out of a 2-hour period, then little is to be gained by investigating this event, although it may be the highest ranked wait event when ordered by time waited. However, if the event accounts for 30 minutes of a 45-minute period, then the event is worth investigating.

Timed statistics are automatically collected for the database if the initialization parameter STATISTICS_LEVEL is set to TYPICAL or ALL. If STATISTICS_LEVEL is set to BASIC, then you must set TIMED_STATISTICS to TRUE to enable collection of timed statistics. Note that setting STATISTICS_LEVEL to BASIC disables many automatic features and is not recommended.

If you explicitly set DB_CACHE_ADVICE, TIMED_STATISTICS, or TIMED_OS_STATISTICS, either in the initialization parameter file or by using ALTER_SYSTEM or ALTER SESSION, then the explicitly set value overrides the value derived from STATISTICS_LEVEL.

- Comparing Oracle Database statistics with other factors.

  When looking at statistics, it is important to consider other factors that influence whether the statistic is of value. Such factors include the user load and the hardware capability. Even an event that had a wait of 30 minutes in a 45-minute period might not be indicative of a problem if you discover that there were 2000 users on the system, and the host hardware was a 64-node computer.
- Wait events without timed statistics.

  If TIMED_STATISTICS is false, then the amount of time waited for an event is not available. Therefore, it is only possible to order wait events by the number of times each event was waited for. Although the events with the largest number of waits might indicate the potential bottleneck, they might not be the main bottleneck. This can happen when an event is waited for a large number of times, but the total time waited for that event is small. The converse is also true: an event with fewer waits might be a problem if the wait time is a significant proportion of the total wait time. Without having the wait times to use for comparison, it is difficult to determine whether a wait event is really of interest.
- Idle wait events.

  Oracle Database uses some wait events to indicate if the Oracle server process is idle. Typically, these events are of no value when investigating performance problems, and they should be ignored when examining the wait events.
- Computed statistics.

  When interpreting computed statistics (such as rates, statistics normalized over transactions, or ratios), it is important to cross-verify the computed statistic with the actual statistic counts. This confirms whether the derived rates are really of interest: small statistic counts usually can discount an unusual ratio. For example, on initial examination, a soft-parse ratio of 50% generally indicates a potential tuning area. If, however, there was only one hard parse and one soft parse during the data collection interval, then the soft-parse ratio would be 50%, even though the statistic counts show this is not an area of concern. In this case, the ratio is not of interest due to the low raw statistic counts.

OVERVIEW OF THE AUTOMATIC WORKLOAD REPOSITORY

The Automatic Workload Repository (AWR) collects, processes, and maintains performance statistics for problem detection and self-tuning purposes. This data is both in memory and stored in the database. The gathered data can be displayed in both reports and views.

The statistics collected and processed by AWR include:

- Object statistics that determine both access and usage statistics of database segments
- Time model statistics based on time usage for activities, displayed in the `V$SYS_TIME_MODEL` and `V$SESS_TIME_MODEL` views
- Some of the system and session statistics collected in the `V$SYSSTAT` and `V$SESSTAT` views
- SQL statements that are producing the highest load on the system, based on criteria such as elapsed time and CPU time
- ASH statistics, representing the history of recent sessions activity.

Gathering database statistics using the AWR is enabled by default and is controlled by the `STATISTICS_LEVEL` initialization parameter. The `STATISTICS_LEVEL` parameter should be set to the `TYPICAL` or `ALL` to enable statistics gathering by the AWR. The default setting is `TYPICAL`. Setting `STATISTICS_LEVEL` to `BASIC` disables many Oracle Database features, including the AWR, and is not recommended. If `STATISTICS_LEVEL` is set to `BASIC`, you can still manually capture AWR statistics using the `DBMS_WORKLOAD_REPOSITORY` package. However, because in-memory collection of many system statistics such as segments statistics and memory advisor information will be disabled, the statistics captured in these snapshots may not be complete.

Snapshots

Snapshots are sets of historical data for specific time periods that are used for performance comparisons by ADDM. By default, Oracle Database automatically generates snapshots of the performance data once every hour and retains the statistics in the workload repository for 8 days. You can also manually create snapshots, but this is usually not necessary. The data in the snapshot interval is then analyzed by the Automatic Database Diagnostic Monitor (ADDM.

AWR compares the difference between snapshots to determine which SQL statements to capture based on the effect on the system load. This reduces the number of SQL statements that must be captured over time.

Baselines

A baseline contains performance data from a specific time period that is preserved for comparison with other similar workload periods when performance problems occur. The snapshots contained in a baseline are excluded from the automatic AWR purging process and are retained indefinitely.

There are several types of available baselines in Oracle Database:

- Fixed Baselines
- Moving Window Baseline
- Baseline Templates.

Fixed Baselines

A fixed baseline corresponds to a fixed, contiguous time period in the past that you specify. Before creating a fixed baseline, carefully consider the time period you choose as a baseline, because the baseline should represent the system operating at an optimal level. In the future, you can compare the baseline with other baselines or snapshots captured during periods of poor performance to analyze performance degradation over time.

Moving Window Baseline

A moving window baseline corresponds to all AWR data that exists within the AWR retention period. This is useful when using adaptive thresholds because the database can use AWR data in the entire AWR retention period to compute metric threshold values.

Oracle Database automatically maintains a system-defined moving window baseline. The default window size for the system-defined moving window baseline is the current AWR retention period, which by default is 8 days. If you are planning to use adaptive thresholds, consider using a larger moving window such as 30 days to accurately compute threshold values. You can resize the moving window baseline by changing the number of days in the moving window to a value that is equal to or less than the number of days in the AWR retention period. Therefore, to increase the size of a moving window, you must first increase the AWR retention period accordingly.

Baseline Templates

You can also create baselines for a contiguous time period in the future using baseline templates. There are two types of baseline templates: single and repeating.

You can use a single baseline template to create a baseline for a single contiguous time period in the future. This technique is useful if you know beforehand of a time period that you intend to capture in the future. For example, you may want to capture the AWR data during a system test that is scheduled for the upcoming weekend. In this case, you can create a single baseline template to automatically capture the time period when the test occurs.

You can use a repeating baseline template to create and drop baselines based on a repeating time schedule. This is useful if you want Oracle Database to automatically capture a contiguous time period on an ongoing basis. For example, you may want to capture the AWR data during every Monday morning for a month. In this case, you can create a repeating baseline template to automatically create baselines on a repeating schedule for every Monday, and automatically remove older baselines after a specified expiration interval, such as one month.

Adaptive Thresholds

Adaptive thresholds enable you to monitor and detect performance issues while minimizing administrative overhead. Adaptive thresholds can automatically set warning and critical alert thresholds for some system metrics using statistics derived from metric values captured in the moving window baseline. The statistics for these thresholds are recomputed weekly and might result in new thresholds as system performance evolves over time. In addition to recalculating thresholds weekly, adaptive thresholds might compute different thresholds values for different times of the day or week based on periodic workload patterns.

For example, many databases support an Online Transaction Processing (OLTP) workload during the day and batch processing at night. The performance metric for response time per transaction can be useful for detecting degradation in OLTP performance during the day. However, a useful OLTP threshold value is almost certainly too low for batch workloads, where long-running transactions might be common. As a result, threshold values appropriate to OLTP might trigger frequent false performance alerts during batch processing. Adaptive thresholds can detect such a workload pattern and automatically set different threshold values for the daytime and nighttime.

In Oracle Database 11g Release 2 (11.2), Oracle Database automatically determines the appropriate time groupings for a database. However, before Oracle Database 11g Release 2 (11.2), time groupings were specified manually by the database administrator.

There are two types of adaptive thresholds:

- Percentage of maximum: The threshold value is computed as a percentage multiple of the maximum value observed for the data in the moving window baseline.
- Significance level: The threshold value is set to a statistical percentile that represents how unusual it is to observe values above the threshold value based the data in the moving window baseline. Specify one of the following percentiles:
  - o High (.95): Only 5 in 100 observations are expected to exceed this value.
  - o Very High (.99): Only 1 in 100 observations are expected to exceed this value.
  - o Severe (.999): Only 1 in 1,000 observations are expected to exceed this value.
  - o Extreme (.9999): Only 1 in 10,000 observations are expected to exceed this value.

When you specify Severe (.999) or Extreme (.9999), Oracle Database performs an internal calculation to set the threshold value. In some cases, Oracle Database cannot establish the threshold value at these levels using the data in the baseline, and the significance level threshold is not set.

If you are not receiving alerts as expected, and you specified a Severe (.999) or Extreme (.9999) significance level threshold, then you can try setting the significance level threshold to a lower value, such as Very High (.99) or High (.95). Alternatively, you can set a percentage of maximum threshold instead of a significance level threshold. If you change the threshold and find that you are receiving too many alerts, then you can try increasing the number of occurrences to cause an alert.

Percentage of maximum thresholds are most useful when a system is sized for peak workloads, and you want to be alerted when the current workload volume is approaching or exceeding previous high values. Metrics that have an unknown but definite limiting value are good candidates for these settings. For example, the redo generated per second metric is typically a good candidate for a percentage of maximum threshold.

Significance level thresholds are most useful for metrics that should exhibit statistically stable behavior when the system is operating normally, but might vary over a wide range when the system is performing poorly. For example, the response time per transaction metric should be stable for a well-tuned OLTP system, but may fluctuate widely when performance issues arise. Significance level thresholds are meant to generate alerts when conditions produce both unusual metric values and unusual system performance.

The primary interface for managing baseline metrics is Oracle Enterprise Manager.

Space Consumption

The space consumed by the AWR is determined by several factors:

- Number of active sessions in the system at any given time
- Snapshot interval
  The snapshot interval determines the frequency at which snapshots are captured. A smaller snapshot interval increases the frequency, which increases the volume of data collected by the AWR.
- Historical data retention period.
  The retention period determines how long this data is retained before being purged. A longer retention period increases the space consumed by the AWR.

By default, snapshots are captured once every hour and are retained in the database for 8 days. With these default settings, a typical system with an average of 10 concurrent active sessions can require approximately 200 to 300 MB of space for its AWR data. It is possible to change the default values for both snapshot interval and retention period.

The AWR space consumption can be reduced by the increasing the snapshot interval and reducing the retention period. When reducing the retention period, note that several Oracle Database self-managing features depend on AWR data for proper functioning. Not having enough data can affect the validity and accuracy of these components and features, including:

- Automatic Database Diagnostic Monitor
- SQL Tuning Advisor
- Undo Advisor
- Segment Advisor.

If possible, Oracle recommends that you set the AWR retention period large enough to capture at least one complete workload cycle. If your system experiences weekly workload cycles, such as OLTP workload during weekdays and batch jobs during the weekend, you do not need to change the default AWR retention period of 8 days. However if your system is subjected to a monthly peak load during month end book closing, you may have to set the retention period to one month.

Under exceptional circumstances, you can turn off automatic snapshot collection by setting the snapshot interval to 0. Under this condition, the automatic collection of the workload and statistical data is stopped and much of the Oracle Database self-management functionality is not operational. In addition, you cannot manually create snapshots. For this reason, Oracle strongly recommends that you do not turn off automatic snapshot collection.

MANAGING THE AUTOMATIC WORKLOAD REPOSITORY

This section describes how to manage the AWR and contains the following topics:

- Managing Snapshots
- Managing Baselines
- Managing Baseline Templates
- Transporting Automatic Workload Repository Data
- Using Automatic Workload Repository Views
- Generating Automatic Workload Repository Reports
- Generating Automatic Workload Repository Compare Periods Reports
- Generating Active Session History Reports
- Using Active Session History Reports.

Managing Snapshots

By default, Oracle Database generates snapshots once every hour, and retains the statistics in the workload repository for 8 days. When necessary, you can use DBMS_WORKLOAD_REPOSITORY procedures to manually create, drop, and modify the snapshots. To invoke these procedures, a user must be granted the DBA role.

The primary interface for managing snapshots is Oracle Enterprise Manager. Whenever possible, you should manage snapshots using Oracle Enterprise Manager. If Oracle Enterprise Manager is unavailable, you can manage snapshots using the DBMS_WORKLOAD_REPOSITORY package, as described in the following sections:

- Creating Snapshots
- Dropping Snapshots
- Modifying Snapshot Settings.

Creating Snapshots

You can manually create snapshots with the CREATE_SNAPSHOT procedure to capture statistics at times different than those of the automatically generated snapshots. For example:

```
BEGIN
  DBMS_WORKLOAD_REPOSITORY.CREATE_SNAPSHOT ();
END;
/
```

In this example, a snapshot for the instance is created immediately with the flush level specified to the default flush level of TYPICAL. You can view this snapshot in the DBA_HIST_SNAPSHOT view.

Dropping Snapshots

You can drop a range of snapshots using the DROP_SNAPSHOT_RANGE procedure. To view a list of the snapshot IDs along with database IDs, check the DBA_HIST_SNAPSHOT view. For example, you can drop the following range of snapshots:

```
BEGIN
  DBMS_WORKLOAD_REPOSITORY.DROP_SNAPSHOT_RANGE
(low_snap_id => 22,high_snap_id => 32, dbid =>
3310949047);
END;
/
```

In the example, the range of snapshot IDs to drop is specified from 22 to 32. The optional database identifier is 3310949047. If you do not specify a value for dbid, the local database identifier is used as the default value.

Active Session History data (ASH) that belongs to the time period specified by the snapshot range is also purged when the DROP_SNAPSHOT_RANGE procedure is called.

Modifying Snapshot Settings

You can adjust the interval, retention, and captured Top SQL of snapshot generation for a specified database ID, but note that this can affect the precision of the Oracle Database diagnostic tools.

The INTERVAL setting affects how often the database automatically generates snapshots. The RETENTION setting affects how long the database stores snapshots in the workload repository. The TOPNSQL setting affects the number of Top SQL to flush for each SQL criteria (Elapsed

Time, CPU Time, Parse Calls, sharable Memory, and Version Count). The value for this setting is not affected by the statistics/flush level and will override the system default behavior for the AWR SQL collection. It is possible to set the value for this setting to `MAXIMUM` to capture the complete set of SQL in the shared SQL area, though by doing so (or by setting the value to a very high number) may lead to possible space and performance issues because there will more data to collect and store. To adjust the settings, use the `MODIFY_SNAPSHOT_SETTINGS` procedure. For example:

```
BEGIN
 DBMS_WORKLOAD_REPOSITORY.MODIFY_SNAPSHOT_SETTINGS(retention
=> 43200,interval => 30, topnsql => 100, dbid => 3310949047);
END;
/
```

In this example, the retention period is specified as 43200 minutes (30 days), the interval between each snapshot is specified as 30 minutes, and the number of Top SQL to flush for each SQL criteria as 100. If NULL is specified, the existing value is preserved. The optional database identifier is `3310949047`. If you do not specify a value for `dbid`, the local database identifier is used as the default value. You can check the current settings for your database instance with the `DBA_HIST_WR_CONTROL` view.

Managing Baselines

This section describes how to manage baselines. The primary interface for managing baselines is Oracle Enterprise Manager. Whenever possible, you should manage baselines using Oracle Enterprise Manager. If Oracle Enterprise Manager is unavailable, you can manage baselines using the `DBMS_WORKLOAD_REPOSITORY` package, as described in the following sections:

- Creating a Baseline
- Dropping a Baseline
- Renaming a Baseline
- Displaying Baseline Metrics
- Modifying the Window Size of the Default Moving Window Baseline.

Creating a Baseline

This section describes how to create a baseline using an existing range of snapshots.

To create a baseline:

1. Review the existing snapshots in the `DBA_HIST_SNAPSHOT` view to determine the range of snapshots to use.
2. Use the `CREATE_BASELINE` procedure to create a baseline using the desired range of snapshots:

```
BEGIN
DBMS_WORKLOAD_REPOSITORY.CREATE_BASELINE (start_snap_id =>
270,end_snap_id => 280, baseline_name => 'peak baseline',
                   dbid => 3310949047, expiration => 30);
END;
/
```

In this example, `270` is the start snapshot sequence number and `280` is the end snapshot sequence. The name of baseline is `peak baseline`. The optional database identifier is `3310949047`. If you do not specify a value for `dbid`, then the local database identifier is used as the default value. The optional expiration parameter is set to 30, so the baseline will expire and be dropped automatically after 30 days. If you do not specify a value for expiration, the baseline will never expire.

The system automatically assign a unique baseline ID to the new baseline when the baseline is created. The baseline ID and database identifier are displayed in the DBA_HIST_BASELINE view.

Dropping a Baseline

This section describes how to drop an existing baseline. Periodically, you may want to drop a baseline that is no longer used to conserve disk space. The snapshots associated with a baseline are retained indefinitely until you explicitly drop the baseline or the baseline has expired.

To drop a baseline:

1. Review the existing baselines in the DBA_HIST_BASELINE view to determine the baseline to drop.
2. Use the DROP_BASELINE procedure to drop the desired baseline:

```
BEGIN
DBMS_WORKLOAD_REPOSITORY.DROP_BASELINE        (baseline_name  =>  'peak
baseline',cascade => FALSE, dbid => 3310949047);
END;
/
```

In the example, the name of baseline is peak baseline. The cascade parameter is set to FALSE, which specifies that only the baseline is dropped. Setting this parameter to TRUE specifies that the drop operation will also remove the snapshots associated with the baseline. The optional dbid parameter specifies the database identifier, which in this example is 3310949047. If you do not specify a value for dbid, then the local database identifier is used as the default value.

Renaming a Baseline

This section describes how to rename a baseline.

To rename a baseline:

1. Review the existing baselines in the DBA_HIST_BASELINE view to determine the baseline to rename.
2. Use the RENAME_BASELINE procedure to rename the desired baseline:

```
BEGIN
    DBMS_WORKLOAD_REPOSITORY.RENAME_BASELINE
                    (old_baseline_name => 'peak baseline',
                    new_baseline_name => 'peak mondays',
                    dbid => 3310949047);
END;
/
```

In this example, the name of the baseline is renamed from peak baseline, as specified by the old_baseline_name parameter, to peak mondays, as specified by the new_baseline_name parameter. The optional dbid parameter specifies the database identifier, which in this example is 3310949047. If you do not specify a value for dbid, then the local DBID is the default value.

Displaying Baseline Metrics

This section describes how to display metric threshold settings during the time period captured in a baseline. When used with adaptive thresholds, a baseline contains AWR data that the database can use to compute metric threshold values. The `SELECT_BASELINE_METRICS` function enables you to display the summary statistics for metric values in a baseline period.

To display metric information in a baseline:

1. Review the existing baselines in the `DBA_HIST_BASELINE` view to determine the baseline for which you want to display metric information.
2. Use the `SELECT_BASELINE_METRICS` function to display the metric information for the desired baseline:

```
BEGIN
    DBMS_WORKLOAD_REPOSITORY.SELECT_BASELINE_METRICS
                   (baseline_name => 'peak baseline',
                   dbid => 3310949047,
                   instance_num => '1');
END;
/
```

In this example, the name of baseline is `peak baseline`. The optional `dbid` parameter specifies the database identifier, which in this example is `3310949047`. If you do not specify a value for `dbid`, then the local database identifier is used as the default value. The optional `instance_num` parameter specifies the instance number, which in this example is `1`. If you do not specify a value for `instance_num`, then the local instance is used as the default value.

Modifying the Window Size of the Default Moving Window Baseline

This section describes how to modify the window size of the default moving window baseline. For information about the default moving window baseline.

To resize the default moving window baseline, use the `MODIFY_BASELINE_WINDOW_SIZE` procedure:

```
BEGIN
    DBMS_WORKLOAD_REPOSITORY.MODIFY_BASELINE_WINDOW_SIZE
           (window_size => 30, dbid => 3310949047);
END;
/
```

The `window_size` parameter is used to specify the new window size, in number of days, for the default moving window size. In this example, the `window_size` parameter is set to 30. The window size must be set to a value that is equal to or less than the value of the AWR retention setting. To set a window size that is greater than the current AWR retention period, you must first increase the value of the `retention` parameter.

In this example, the optional `dbid` parameter specifies the database identifier is `3310949047`. If you do not specify a value for `dbid`, then the local database identifier is used as the default value.

Managing Baseline Templates

This section describes how to manage baseline templates. You can automatically create baselines to capture specified time periods in the future using baseline templates.

The primary interface for managing baseline templates is Oracle Enterprise Manager. Whenever possible, you should manage baseline templates using Oracle Enterprise Manager. If Oracle Enterprise Manager is unavailable, you can manage baseline templates using the `DBMS_WORKLOAD_REPOSITORY` package, as described in the following sections:

- Creating a Single Baseline Template
- Creating a Repeating Baseline Template
- Dropping a Baseline Template.

Creating a Single Baseline Template

This section describes how to create a single baseline template. You can use a single baseline template to create a baseline during a single, fixed time interval in the future. For example, you can create a single baseline template to generate a baseline that is captured on April 2, 2009 from 5:00 p.m. to 8:00 p.m.

To create a single baseline template, use the `CREATE_BASELINE_TEMPLATE` procedure:

```
BEGIN
    DBMS_WORKLOAD_REPOSITORY.CREATE_BASELINE_TEMPLATE
     (start_time => '2009-04-02 17:00:00 PST',
      end_time => '2009-04-02 20:00:00 PST',
      baseline_name => 'baseline_090402',
      template_name => 'template_090402',expiration => 30,
                      dbid => 3310949047);
END;
/
```

The `start_time` parameter specifies the start time for the baseline to be created. The `end_time` parameter specifies the end time for the baseline to be created. The `baseline_name` parameter specifies the name of the baseline to be created. The `template_name` parameter specifies the name of the baseline template. The optional `expiration` parameter specifies the expiration, in number of days, for the baseline. If unspecified, then the baseline never expires. The optional `dbid` parameter specifies the database identifier. If unspecified, then the local database identifier is used as the default value.

In this example, a baseline template named `template_090402` is created that will generate a baseline named `baseline_090402` for the time period from 5:00 p.m. to 8:00 p.m. on April 2, 2009 on the database with a database ID of `3310949047`. The baseline will expire after 30 days.

Creating a Repeating Baseline Template

This section describes how to create a repeating baseline template. A repeating baseline template can be used to automatically create baselines that repeat during a particular time interval over a specific period in the future. For example, you can create a repeating baseline template to generate a baseline that repeats every Monday from 5:00 p.m. to 8:00 p.m. for the year 2009.

To create a repeating baseline template, use the `CREATE_BASELINE_TEMPLATE` procedure:

```
BEGIN
    DBMS_WORKLOAD_REPOSITORY.CREATE_BASELINE_TEMPLATE
      (day_of_week => 'monday', hour_in_day => 17,
      duration => 3, expiration => 30,
      start time => '2009-04-02 17:00:00 PST',
```

```
        end_time => '2009-12-31 20:00:00 PST',
        baseline_name_prefix => 'baseline_2009_mondays_',
        template_name => 'template_2009_mondays',
                        dbid => 3310949047);
END;
/
```

The `day_of_week` parameter specifies the day of the week on which the baseline will repeat. The `hour_in_day` parameter specifies the hour in the day when the baseline will start. The `duration` parameter specifies the duration, in number of hours, that the baseline will last. The `expiration` parameter specifies the number of days to retain each created baseline. If set to `NULL`, then the baselines never expires. The `start_time` parameter specifies the start time for the baseline to be created. The `end_time` parameter specifies the end time for the baseline to be created. The `baseline_name_prefix` parameter specifies the name of the baseline prefix that will be appended to the data information when the baseline is created. The `template_name` parameter specifies the name of the baseline template. The optional `dbid` parameter specifies the database identifier. If unspecified, then the local database identifier is used as the default value.

In this example, a baseline template named `template_2009_mondays` is created that will generate a baseline on every Monday from 5:00 p.m. to 8:00 p.m. beginning on April 2, 2009 at 5:00 p.m. and ending on December 31, 2009 at 8:00 p.m. on the database with a database ID of `3310949047`. Each of the baselines will be created with a baseline name with the prefix `baseline_2009_mondays_` and will expire after 30 days.

Dropping a Baseline Template

This section describes how to drop an existing baseline template. Periodically, you may want to remove baselines templates that are no longer used to conserve disk space.

To drop a baseline template:

1. Review the existing baselines in the `DBA_HIST_BASELINE_TEMPLATE` view to determine the baseline template you want to drop.
2. Use the `DROP_BASELINE_TEMPLATE` procedure to drop the desired baseline template:

```
BEGIN
  DBMS_WORKLOAD_REPOSITORY.DROP_BASELINE_TEMPLATE
                    (template_name => 'template_2009_mondays',
                    dbid => 3310949047);
END;
/
```

The `template_name` parameter specifies the name of the baseline template that will be dropped. In the example, the name of baseline template that will be dropped is `template_2009_mondays`. The optional `dbid` parameter specifies the database identifier, which in this example is `3310949047`. If you do not specify a value for `dbid`, then the local database identifier is used as the default value.

Transporting Automatic Workload Repository Data

Oracle Database enables you to transport AWR data between systems. This is useful in cases where you want to use a separate system to perform analysis of the AWR data. To transport

AWR data, you must first extract the AWR snapshot data from the database on the source system, then load the data into the database on the target system, as described in the following sections:

- Extracting AWR Data
- Loading AWR Data.

Extracting AWR Data

The `awrextr.sql` script extracts the AWR data for a range of snapshots from the database into a Data Pump export file. After it is created, you can transport this dump file to another database where you can load the extracted data. To run the `awrextr.sql` script, you must be connected to the database as the `SYS` user.

To extract AWR data:

1. At the SQL prompt, enter:
   @$ORACLE_HOME/rdbms/admin/awrextr.sql
   A list of the databases in the AWR schema is displayed.
2. Specify the database from which the AWR data will be extracted:
   ```
   Enter value for db_id: 1377863381
   ```
   In this example, the database with the database identifier of `1377863381` is selected.
3. Specify the number of days for which you want to list snapshot IDs.
   ```
   Enter value for num_days: 2
   ```
   A list of existing snapshots for the specified time range is displayed. In this example, snapshots captured in the last 2 days are displayed.
4. Define the range of snapshots for which AWR data will be extracted by specifying a beginning and ending snapshot ID:
   ```
   Enter value for begin_snap: 30
   Enter value for end_snap: 40
   ```
   In this example, the snapshot with a snapshot ID of 30 is selected as the beginning snapshot, and the snapshot with a snapshot ID of 40 is selected as the ending snapshot.
5. A list of directory objects is displayed.
   Specify the directory object pointing to the directory where the export dump file will be stored:
   ```
   Enter value for directory_name: DATA_PUMP_DIR
   ```
   In this example, the directory object `DATA_PUMP_DIR` is selected.
6. Specify the prefix for name of the export dump file (the `.dmp` suffix will be automatically appended):
   Enter value for file_name: awrdata_30_40
   In this example, an export dump file named `awrdata_30_40` will be created in the directory corresponding to the directory object you specified:
   ```
   Dump file set for SYS.SYS_EXPORT_TABLE_01 is:
   C:\ORACLE\PRODUCT\11g\DB_1\RDBMS\LOG\AWRDATA_30_40.DMP
   Job "SYS"."SYS_EXPORT_TABLE_01" successfully completed at 08:58:20
   ```
   Depending on the amount of AWR data that must be extracted, the AWR extract operation may take a while to complete. After the dump file is created, you can use Data Pump to transport the file to another system.

Loading AWR Data

After the export dump file is transported to the target system, you can load the extracted AWR data using the `awrload.sql` script. The `awrload.sql` script will first create a staging schema where the snapshot data is transferred from the Data Pump file into the database. The data is then transferred from the staging schema into the appropriate AWR tables. To run the `awrload.sql` script, you must be connected to the database as the `SYS` user.

To load AWR data:

1. At the SQL prompt, enter:
   `@$ORACLE_HOME/rdbms/admin/awrload.sql`
   A list of directory objects is displayed.
2. Specify the directory object pointing to the directory where the export dump file is located:
   `Enter value for directory_name: DATA_PUMP_DIR`
   In this example, the directory object `DATA_PUMP_DIR` is selected.
3. Specify the prefix for name of the export dump file (the `.dmp` suffix will be automatically appended):
   `Enter value for file_name: awrdata_30_40`
   In this example, the export dump file named `awrdata_30_40` is selected.
4. Specify the name of the staging schema where the AWR data will be loaded:
   `Enter value for schema_name: AWR_STAGE`
   In this example, a staging schema named `AWR_STAGE` will be created where the AWR data will be loaded.
5. Specify the default tablespace for the staging schema:
   `Enter value for default_tablespace: SYSAUX`
   In this example, the `SYSAUX` tablespace is selected.
6. Specify the temporary tablespace for the staging schema:
   `Enter value for temporary_tablespace: TEMP`
   In this example, the `TEMP` tablespace is selected.
7. A staging schema named `AWR_STAGE` will be created where the AWR data will be loaded. After the AWR data is loaded into the `AWR_STAGE` schema, the data will be transferred into the AWR tables in the `SYS` schema.

Depending on the amount of AWR data that must be loaded, the AWR load operation may take a while to complete. After the AWR data is loaded, the staging schema will be dropped automatically.

Using Automatic Workload Repository Views

Typically, you would view the AWR data through Oracle Enterprise Manager or AWR reports. However, you can also view the statistics using the following views:

- `V$ACTIVE_SESSION_HISTORY`.
  This view displays active database session activity, sampled once every second.
- `V$` metric views provide metric data to track the performance of the system.
  The metric views are organized into various groups, such as event, event class, system, session, service, file, and tablespace metrics. These groups are identified in the `V$METRICGROUP` view.
- `DBA_HIST` views.
  The `DBA_HIST` views displays historical data stored in the database. This group of views includes:

- o `DBA_HIST_ACTIVE_SESS_HISTORY` displays the history of the contents of the in-memory active session history for recent system activity
- o `DBA_HIST_BASELINE` displays information about the baselines captured on the system, such as the time range of each baseline and the baseline type
- o `DBA_HIST_BASELINE_DETAILS` displays details about a specific baseline
- o `DBA_HIST_BASELINE_TEMPLATE` displays information about the baseline templates used by the system to generate baselines
- o `DBA_HIST_DATABASE_INSTANCE` displays information about the database environment
- o `DBA_HIST_DB_CACHE_ADVICE` displays historical predictions of the number of physical reads for the cache size corresponding to each row
- o `DBA_HIST_DISPATCHER` displays historical information for each dispatcher process at the time of the snapshot
- o `DBA_HIST_DYN_REMASTER_STATS` displays statistical information about the dynamic remastering process
- o `DBA_HIST_IOSTAT_DETAIL` displays historical I/O statistics aggregated by file type and function
- o `DBA_HIST_SHARED_SERVER_SUMMARY` displays historical information for shared servers, such as shared server activity, common queues and dispatcher queues
- o `DBA_HIST_SNAPSHOT` displays information on snapshots in the system
- o `DBA_HIST_SQL_PLAN` displays the SQL execution plans
- o `DBA_HIST_WR_CONTROL` displays the settings for controlling AWR.

Generating Automatic Workload Repository Reports

An AWR report shows data captured between two snapshots (or two points in time). The AWR reports are divided into multiple sections. The HTML report includes links that can be used to navigate quickly between sections. The content of the report contains the workload profile of the system for the selected range of snapshots.

The primary interface for generating AWR reports is Oracle Enterprise Manager. Whenever possible, you should generate AWR reports using Oracle Enterprise Manager. If Oracle Enterprise Manager is unavailable, you can generate AWR reports by running SQL scripts, as described in the following sections:

- Generating an AWR Report
- Generating an Oracle RAC AWR Report
- Generating an AWR Report on a Specific Database Instance
- Generating an Oracle RAC AWR Report on Specific Database Instances
- Generating an AWR Report for a SQL Statement
- Generating an AWR Report for a SQL Statement on a Specific Database Instance.

To run these scripts, you must be granted the DBA role.

> If you run a report on a database that does not have any workload activity during the specified range of snapshots, calculated percentages for some report statistics can be less than 0 or greater than 100. This result simply means that there is no meaningful value for the statistic.

Generating an AWR Report

The `awrrpt.sql` SQL script generates an HTML or text report that displays statistics for a range of snapshot IDs.

To generate an AWR report:

1. At the SQL prompt, enter:
   `@$ORACLE_HOME/rdbms/admin/awrrpt.sql`
2. Specify whether you want an HTML or a text report:
   `Enter value for report_type: text`
   In this example, a text report is chosen.
3. Specify the number of days for which you want to list snapshot IDs:
   `Enter value for num_days: 2`
   A list of existing snapshots for the specified time range is displayed. In this example, snapshots captured in the last 2 days are displayed.
4. Specify a beginning and ending snapshot ID for the workload repository report:
   ```
   Enter value for begin_snap: 150
   Enter value for end_snap: 160
   ```
   In this example, the snapshot with a snapshot ID of 150 is selected as the beginning snapshot, and the snapshot with a snapshot ID of 160 is selected as the ending snapshot.
5. Enter a report name, or accept the default report name:
   ```
   Enter value for report_name:
   Using the report name awrrpt_1_150_160
   ```
   In this example, the default name is accepted and an AWR report named `awrrpt_1_150_160` is generated.

Generating an Oracle RAC AWR Report

The `awrgrpt.sql` SQL script generates an HTML or text report that displays statistics for a range of snapshot IDs using the current database identifier and all available database instances in an Oracle Real Application Clusters (Oracle RAC) environment.

In an Oracle RAC environment, you should always try to generate an HTML report (instead of a text report) because they are much easier to read.

To generate an AWR report in an Oracle RAC environment:

1. At the SQL prompt, enter:
   `@$ORACLE_HOME/rdbms/admin/awrgrpt.sql`
2. Specify whether you want an HTML or a text report:
   `Enter value for report_type: html`
   In this example, an HTML report is chosen.
3. Specify the number of days for which you want to list snapshot IDs.
   `Enter value for num_days: 2`
   A list of existing snapshots for the specified time range is displayed. In this example, snapshots captured in the last day are displayed.
4. Specify a beginning and ending snapshot ID for the workload repository report:
   ```
   Enter value for begin_snap: 150
   Enter value for end_snap: 160
   ```

In this example, the snapshot with a snapshot ID of 150 is selected as the beginning snapshot, and the snapshot with a snapshot ID of 160 is selected as the ending snapshot.

5. Enter a report name, or accept the default report name:

   Enter value for report_name:

   Using the report name awrrpt_rac_150_160.html

   In this example, the default name is accepted and an AWR report named `awrrpt_rac_150_160.html` is generated.

Generating an AWR Report on a Specific Database Instance

The `awrrpti.sql` SQL script generates an HTML or text report that displays statistics for a range of snapshot IDs using a specific database and instance. This script enables you to specify a database identifier and instance for which the AWR report will be generated.

To generate an AWR report on a specific database instance:

1. At the SQL prompt, enter:

   ```
   @$ORACLE_HOME/rdbms/admin/awrrpti.sql
   ```

2. Specify whether you want an HTML or a text report:

   ```
   Enter value for report_type: text
   ```

   In this example, a text report is chosen.

   A list of available database identifiers and instance numbers are displayed:

   ```
   Instances in this Workload Repository schema
   ~~~~~~~~~~~~~~~~~~~~~~~~~~~~~~~~~~~~~~~~~ ~~~~~~~~~~~~
   DB Id          Inst Num      DB Name     Instance     Host
   -------        ---------     --------    -------      -----
   3309173529     1 MAIN        main        examp1690
   3309173529     1 TINT251     tint251     samp251
   ```

3. Enter the values for the database identifier (`dbid`) and instance number (`inst_num`):

   ```
   Enter value for dbid: 3309173529
   Using 3309173529 for database Id
   Enter value for inst_num: 1
   ```

4. Specify the number of days for which you want to list snapshot IDs:

   ```
   Enter value for num_days: 2
   ```

   A list of existing snapshots for the specified time range is displayed. In this example, snapshots captured in the last 2 days are displayed.

5. Specify a beginning and ending snapshot ID for the workload repository report:

   ```
   Enter value for begin_snap: 150
   Enter value for end_snap: 160
   ```

   In this example, the snapshot with a snapshot ID of 150 is selected as the beginning snapshot, and the snapshot with a snapshot ID of 160 is selected as the ending snapshot.

6. Enter a report name, or accept the default report name:

   ```
   Enter value for report_name:
   Using the report name awrrpt_1_150_160
   ```

   In this example, the default name is accepted and an AWR report named `awrrpt_1_150_160` is generated on the database instance with a database ID value of `3309173529`.

Generating an Oracle RAC AWR Report on Specific Database Instances

The `awrgrpti.sql` SQL script generates an HTML or text report that displays statistics for a range of snapshot IDs using specific databases and instances running in an Oracle RAC environment. This script enables you to specify database identifiers and a comma-delimited list of database instances for which the AWR report will be generated.

In an Oracle RAC environment, you should always try to generate an HTML report (instead of a text report) because they are much easier to read.

To generate an AWR report on a specific database instance in an Oracle RAC environment:

1. At the SQL prompt, enter:
   ```
   @$ORACLE_HOME/rdbms/admin/awrgrpti.sql
   ```
2. Specify whether you want an HTML or a text report:
   ```
   Enter value for report_type: html
   ```
   In this example, an HTML report is chosen.
   A list of available database identifiers and instance numbers are displayed:
   ```
   Instances in this Workload Repository schema
   ~~~~~~~~~~~~~~~~~~~~~~~~~~~~~~~~~~~~~~~~~~~~
   DB Id        Inst Num    DB Name     Instance    Host
   -------      -------     -------     -------     -------
   3309173529         1     MAIN        main        examp1690
   3309173529         1     TINT251     tint251     samp251
   3309173529         2     TINT251     tint252     samp252
   ```
3. Enter the value for the database identifier (`dbid`):
   ```
   Enter value for dbid: 3309173529
   Using 3309173529 for database Id
   ```
4. Enter the value for the instance numbers (`instance_numbers_or_all`) of the Oracle RAC instances you want to include in the report:
   ```
   Enter value for instance_numbers_or_all: 1,2
   ```
5. Specify the number of days for which you want to list snapshot IDs:
   ```
   Enter value for num_days: 2
   ```
   A list of existing snapshots for the specified time range is displayed. In this example, snapshots captured in the last 2 days are displayed.
6. Specify a beginning and ending snapshot ID for the workload repository report:
   ```
   Enter value for begin_snap: 150
   Enter value for end_snap: 160
   ```
   In this example, the snapshot with a snapshot ID of 150 is selected as the beginning snapshot, and the snapshot with a snapshot ID of 160 is selected as the ending snapshot.
7. Enter a report name, or accept the default report name:
   Enter value for report_name:
   Using the report name awrrpt_rac_150_160.html
   In this example, the default name is accepted and an AWR report named `awrrpt_rac_150_160.html` is generated on the database instance with a database ID value of `3309173529`.

Generating an AWR Report for a SQL Statement

The `awrsqrpt.sql` SQL script generates an HTML or text report that displays statistics of a particular SQL statement for a range of snapshot IDs. Run this report to inspect or debug the performance of a SQL statement.

To generate an AWR report for a particular SQL statement:

1. At the SQL prompt, enter:
   `@$ORACLE_HOME/rdbms/admin/awrsqrpt.sql`
2. Specify whether you want an HTML or a text report:
   `Enter value for report_type: html`
   In this example, an HTML report is chosen.
3. Specify the number of days for which you want to list snapshot IDs:
   `Enter value for num_days: 1`
   A list of existing snapshots for the specified time range is displayed. In this example, snapshots captured in the previous day are displayed.
4. Specify a beginning and ending snapshot ID for the workload repository report:
   ```
   Enter value for begin_snap: 146
   Enter value for end_snap: 147
   ```
   In this example, the snapshot with a snapshot ID of 146 is selected as the beginning snapshot, and the snapshot with a snapshot ID of 147 is selected as the ending snapshot.
5. Specify the SQL ID of a particular SQL statement to display statistics:
   `Enter value for sql_id: 2b064ybzkwf1y`
   In this example, the SQL statement with a SQL ID of `2b064ybzkwf1y` is selected.
6. Enter a report name, or accept the default report name:
   ```
   Enter value for report_name:
   Using the report name awrrpt_1_146_147.html
   ```
   In this example, the default name is accepted and an AWR report named `awrrpt_1_146_147` is generated.

Generating an AWR Report for a SQL Statement on a Specific Database Instance

The `awrsqrpi.sql` SQL script generates an HTML or text report that displays statistics of a particular SQL statement for a range of snapshot IDs using a specific database and instance.This script enables you to specify a database identifier and instance for which the AWR report will be generated. Run this report to inspect or debug the performance of a SQL statement on a specific database and instance.

To generate an AWR report for a particular SQL statement on a specified database instance:

1. At the SQL prompt, enter:
   `@$ORACLE_HOME/rdbms/admin/awrsqrpi.sql`
2. Specify whether you want an HTML or a text report:
   Enter value for report_type: html
   In this example, an HTML report is chosen.
   A list of available database identifiers and instance numbers are displayed:

```
Instances in this Workload Repository schema
~~~~~~~~~~~~~~~~~~~~~~~~~~~~~~~~~~~~~~~~~~~~
DB Id        Inst Num   DB Name     Instance    Host
-------      -------    -------     -------     -------
3309173529        1     MAIN        main        examp1690
3309173529        1     TINT251     tint251     samp251
```

3. Enter the values for the database identifier (`dbid`) and instance number (`inst_num`):
```
Enter value for dbid: 3309173529
Using 3309173529 for database Id
Enter value for inst_num: 1
Using 1 for instance number
```
4. Specify the number of days for which you want to list snapshot IDs:
```
Enter value for num_days: 1
```
A list of existing snapshots for the specified time range is displayed. In this example, snapshots captured in the previous day are displayed.
5. Specify a beginning and ending snapshot ID for the workload repository report:
```
Enter value for begin_snap: 146
Enter value for end_snap: 147
```
In this example, the snapshot with a snapshot ID of 146 is selected as the beginning snapshot, and the snapshot with a snapshot ID of 147 is selected as the ending snapshot.
6. Specify the SQL ID of a particular SQL statement to display statistics:
```
Enter value for sql_id: 2b064ybzkwf1y
```
In this example, the SQL statement with a SQL ID of `2b064ybzkwf1y` is selected.
7. Enter a report name, or accept the default report name:
```
Enter value for report_name:
Using the report name awrrpt_1_146_147.html
```
In this example, the default name is accepted and an AWR report named `awrrpt_1_146_147` is generated on the database instance with a database ID value of `3309173529`.

Generating Automatic Workload Repository Compare Periods Reports

While an AWR report shows AWR data between two snapshots (or two points in time), the AWR Compare Periods report shows the difference between two periods (or two AWR reports, which equates to four snapshots). Using the AWR Compare Periods report helps you to identify detailed performance attributes and configuration settings that differ between two time periods.

For example, if the application workload is known to be stable between 10:00 p.m. and midnight every night, but the performance on a particular Thursday was poor between 10:00 p.m. and 11:00 p.m., generating an AWR Compare Periods report for Thursday from 10:00 p.m. to 11:00 p.m. and Wednesday from 10:00 p.m. to 11:00 p.m. should identify configuration settings, workload profile, and statistics that were different in these time periods. Based on the differences, you can more easily diagnose the cause of the performance degradation. The two time periods selected for the AWR Compare Periods Report can be of different durations because the report normalizes the statistics by the amount of time spent on the database for each time period, and presents statistical data ordered by the largest difference between the periods.

The AWR Compare Periods reports are divided into multiple sections. The HTML report includes links that can be used to navigate quickly between sections. The content of the report contains the workload profile of the system for the selected range of snapshots.

The primary interface for generating AWR Compare Periods reports is Oracle Enterprise Manager. Whenever possible, you should generate AWR Compare Periods reports using Oracle Enterprise Manager. If Oracle Enterprise Manager is unavailable, you can generate AWR Compare Periods reports by running SQL scripts, as described in the following sections:

- Generating an AWR Compare Periods Report
- Generating an Oracle RAC AWR Compare Periods Report
- Generating an AWR Compare Periods Report on a Specific Database Instance
- Generating an Oracle RAC AWR Compare Periods Report on Specific Database Instances.

To run these scripts, you must be granted the DBA role.

Generating an AWR Compare Periods Report

The `awrddrpt.sql` SQL script generates an HTML or text report that compares detailed performance attributes and configuration settings between two selected time periods.

To generate an AWR Compare Periods report:

1. At the SQL prompt, enter:
   ```
   @$ORACLE_HOME/rdbms/admin/awrddrpt.sql
   ```
2. Specify whether you want an HTML or a text report:
   ```
   Enter value for report_type: html
   ```
   In this example, an HTML report is chosen.
3. Specify the number of days for which you want to list snapshot IDs in the first time period:
   ```
   Enter value for num_days: 2
   ```
   A list of existing snapshots for the specified time range is displayed. In this example, snapshots captured in the last 2 days are displayed.
4. Specify a beginning and ending snapshot ID for the first time period:
   ```
   Enter value for begin_snap: 102
   Enter value for end_snap: 103
   ```
   In this example, the snapshot with a snapshot ID of 102 is selected as the beginning snapshot, and the snapshot with a snapshot ID of 103 is selected as the ending snapshot for the first time period.
5. Specify the number of days for which you want to list snapshot IDs in the second time period:
   ```
   Enter value for num_days2: 1
   ```
   A list of existing snapshots for the specified time range is displayed. In this example, snapshots captured in the previous day are displayed.
6. Specify a beginning and ending snapshot ID for the second time period:
   ```
   Enter value for begin_snap2: 126
   Enter value for end_snap2: 127
   ```
   In this example, the snapshot with a snapshot ID of 126 is selected as the beginning snapshot, and the snapshot with a snapshot ID of 127 is selected as the ending snapshot for the second time period.

7. Enter a report name, or accept the default report name:
   `Enter value for report_name:`
   `Using the report name awrdiff_1_102_1_126.txt`
   In this example, the default name is accepted and an AWR report named `awrdiff_1_102_126` is generated.

Generating an Oracle RAC AWR Compare Periods Report

The `awrgdrpt.sql` SQL script generates an HTML or text report that compares detailed performance attributes and configuration settings between two selected time periods using the current database identifier and all available database instances in an Oracle RAC environment.

In an Oracle RAC environment, you should always try to generate an HTML report (instead of a text report) because they are much easier to read.

To generate an AWR Compare Periods report in an Oracle RAC environment:

1. At the SQL prompt, enter:
   `@$ORACLE_HOME/rdbms/admin/awrgdrpt.sql`
2. Specify whether you want an HTML or a text report:
   `Enter value for report_type: html`
   In this example, an HTML report is chosen.
3. Specify the number of days for which you want to list snapshot IDs in the first time period:
   `Enter value for num_days: 2`
   A list of existing snapshots for the specified time range is displayed. In this example, snapshots captured in the last 2 days are displayed.
4. Specify a beginning and ending snapshot ID for the first time period:
   `Enter value for begin_snap: 102`
   `Enter value for end_snap: 103`
   In this example, the snapshot with a snapshot ID of 102 is selected as the beginning snapshot, and the snapshot with a snapshot ID of 103 is selected as the ending snapshot for the first time period.
5. Specify the number of days for which you want to list snapshot IDs in the second time period:
   `Enter value for num_days2: 1`
   A list of existing snapshots for the specified time range is displayed. In this example, snapshots captured in the previous day are displayed.
6. Specify a beginning and ending snapshot ID for the second time period:
   `Enter value for begin_snap2: 126`
   `Enter value for end_snap2: 127`
   In this example, the snapshot with a snapshot ID of 126 is selected as the beginning snapshot, and the snapshot with a snapshot ID of 127 is selected as the ending snapshot for the second time period.
7. Enter a report name, or accept the default report name:
   `Enter value for report_name:`
   `Using the report name awrracdiff_1st_1_2nd_1.html`
   In this example, the default name is accepted and an AWR report named `awrrac_1st_1_2nd_1.html` is generated.

Generating an AWR Compare Periods Report on a Specific Database Instance

The `awrddrpi.sql` SQL script generates an HTML or text report that compares detailed performance attributes and configuration settings between two selected time periods on a specific database and instance. This script enables you to specify a database identifier and instance for which the AWR Compare Periods report will be generated.

To generate an AWR Compare Periods report on a specified database instance:

1. At the SQL prompt, enter:
   ```
   @$ORACLE_HOME/rdbms/admin/awrddrpi.sql
   ```
2. Specify whether you want an HTML or a text report:
   ```
   Enter value for report_type: text
   ```
   In this example, a text report is chosen.
3. A list of available database identifiers and instance numbers are displayed:
   ```
   Instances in this Workload Repository schema
   ~~~~~~~~~~~~~~~~~~~~~~~~~~~~~~~~~~~~~~~~~~~~~
   DB Id        Inst Num    DB Name     Instance    Host
   -------      --------    -------     -------     -------
   3309173529          1    MAIN        main        examp1690
   3309173529          1    TINT251     tint251     samp251
   ```
   Enter the values for the database identifier (`dbid`) and instance number `inst_num`) for the first time period:
   ```
   Enter value for dbid: 3309173529
   Using 3309173529 for Database Id for the first pair of snapshots
   Enter value for inst_num: 1
   Using 1 for Instance Number for the first pair of snapshots
   ```
4. Specify the number of days for which you want to list snapshot IDs in the first time period:
   ```
   Enter value for num_days: 2
   ```
   A list of existing snapshots for the specified time range is displayed. In this example, snapshots captured in the last 2 days are displayed.
5. Specify a beginning and ending snapshot ID for the first time period:
   ```
   Enter value for begin_snap: 102
   Enter value for end_snap: 103
   ```
   In this example, the snapshot with a snapshot ID of 102 is selected as the beginning snapshot, and the snapshot with a snapshot ID of 103 is selected as the ending snapshot for the first time period.
6. Enter the values for the database identifier (`dbid`) and instance number (`inst_num`) for the second time period:
   ```
   Enter value for dbid2: 3309173529
   Using 3309173529 for Database Id for the second pair of snapshots
   Enter value for inst_num2: 1
   Using 1 for Instance Number for the second pair of snapshots
   ```
7. Specify the number of days for which you want to list snapshot IDs in the second time period:
   ```
   Enter value for num_days2: 1
   ```
   A list of existing snapshots for the specified time range is displayed. In this example, snapshots captured in the previous day are displayed.

8. Specify a beginning and ending snapshot ID for the second time period:
   ```
   Enter value for begin_snap2: 126
   Enter value for end_snap2: 127
   ```
   In this example, the snapshot with a snapshot ID of 126 is selected as the beginning snapshot, and the snapshot with a snapshot ID of 127 is selected as the ending snapshot for the second time period.
9. Enter a report name, or accept the default report name:
   ```
   Enter value for report_name:
   Using the report name awrdiff_1_102_1_126.txt
   ```
   In this example, the default name is accepted and an AWR report named `awrdiff_1_102_126` is generated on the database instance with a database ID value of `3309173529`.

Generating an Oracle RAC AWR Compare Periods Report on Specific Database Instances

The `awrgdrpi.sql` SQL script generates an HTML or text report that compares detailed performance attributes and configuration settings between two selected time periods using specific databases and instances in an Oracle RAC environment. This script enables you to specify database identifiers and a comma-delimited list of database instances for which the AWR Compare Periods report will be generated.

In an Oracle RAC environment, you should always try to generate an HTML report (instead of a text report) because they are much easier to read.

To generate an AWR Compare Periods report on a specified database instance in an Oracle RAC environment:

1. At the SQL prompt, enter:
   ```
   @$ORACLE_HOME/rdbms/admin/awrgdrpi.sql
   ```
2. Specify whether you want an HTML or a text report:
   ```
   Enter value for report_type: html
   ```
   In this example, an HTML report is chosen.
3. A list of available database identifiers and instance numbers are displayed:
   ```
   Instances in this Workload Repository schema
   ~~~~~~~~~~~~~~~~~~~~~~~~~~~~~~~~~~~~~~~~~~~~~~
   DB Id        Inst Num    DB Name    Instance    Host
   -------      --------    -------    -------     -------
   3309173529         1     MAIN       main        examp1690
   3309173529         1     TINT251    tint251     samp251
   3309173529         2     TINT251    tint252     samp252
   3309173529         3     TINT251    tint253     samp253
   3309173529         4     TINT251    tint254     samp254
   ```
   Enter the values for the database identifier (`dbid`) and instance number (`instance_numbers_or_all`) for the first time period:
   ```
   Enter value for dbid: 3309173529
   Using 3309173529 for Database Id for the first pair of snapshots
   Enter value for inst_num: 1,2
   Using instances 1 for the first pair of snapshots
   ```

4. Specify the number of days for which you want to list snapshot IDs in the first time period:

   `Enter value for num_days: 2`

   A list of existing snapshots for the specified time range is displayed. In this example, snapshots captured in the last 2 days are displayed.

5. Specify a beginning and ending snapshot ID for the first time period:

   ```
   Enter value for begin_snap: 102
   Enter value for end_snap: 103
   ```

   In this example, the snapshot with a snapshot ID of 102 is selected as the beginning snapshot, and the snapshot with a snapshot ID of 103 is selected as the ending snapshot for the first time period.

6. A list of available database identifiers and instance numbers are displayed:

   ```
   Instances in this Workload Repository schema
   ~~~~~~~~~~~~~~~~~~~~~~~~~~~~~~~~~~~~~~~~~~~~
   DB Id          Inst Num    DB Name     Instance    Host
   -------        -------     -------     -------     -------
   3309173529           1     MAIN        main        examp1690
   3309173529           1     TINT251     tint251     samp251
   3309173529           2     TINT251     tint252     samp252
   3309173529           3     TINT251     tint253     samp253
   3309173529           4     TINT251     tint254     samp254
   ```

   Enter the values for the database identifier (`dbid2`) and instance numbers (`instance_numbers_or_all2`) for the second time period:

   ```
   Enter value for dbid2: 3309173529
   Using 3309173529 for Database Id for the second pair of snapshots
   Enter value for instance_numbers_or_all2: 3,4
   ```

7. Specify the number of days for which you want to list snapshot IDs in the second time period:

   `Enter value for num_days2: 1`

   A list of existing snapshots for the specified time range is displayed. In this example, snapshots captured in the previous day are displayed.

8. Specify a beginning and ending snapshot ID for the second time period:

   ```
   Enter value for begin_snap2: 126
   Enter value for end_snap2: 127
   ```

   In this example, the snapshot with a snapshot ID of 126 is selected as the beginning snapshot, and the snapshot with a snapshot ID of 127 is selected as the ending snapshot for the second time period.

9. Enter a report name, or accept the default report name:

   ```
   Enter value for report_name:
   Using the report name awrracdiff_1st_1_2nd_1.html
   ```

   In this example, the default name is accepted and an AWR report named `awrrac_1st_1_2nd_1.html` is generated.

Generating Active Session History Reports

Use Active Session History (ASH) reports to perform analysis of:

- Transient performance problems that typically last for a few minutes
- Scoped or targeted performance analysis by various dimensions or their combinations, such as time, session, module, action, or `SQL_ID`.

Transient performance problems are short-lived and do not appear in the Automatic Database Diagnostics Monitor (ADDM) analysis. ADDM tries to report the most significant performance problems during an analysis period in terms of their impact on DB time. If a particular problem lasts for a very short duration, then its severity might be averaged out or minimized by other performance problems in the analysis period. Therefore, the problem may not appear in the ADDM findings. Whether a performance problem is captured by ADDM depends on its duration compared to the interval between the AWR snapshots.

If a performance problem lasts for a significant portion of the time between snapshots, it will be captured by ADDM. For example, if the snapshot interval is set to one hour, a performance problem that lasts for 30 minutes should not be considered as a transient performance problem because its duration represents a significant portion of the snapshot interval and will likely be captured by ADDM.

However, a performance problem that lasts for only 2 minutes could be a transient performance problem because its duration represents a small portion of the snapshot interval and will likely not show up in the ADDM findings. For example, if the user notifies you that the system was slow between 10:00 p.m. and 10:10 p.m., but the ADDM analysis for the time period between 10:00 p.m. and 11:00 p.m. does not show a performance problem, a transient performance problem probably occurred that lasted for only a few minutes of the 10-minute interval reported by the user.

The ASH reports are divided into multiple sections. The HTML report includes links that can be used to navigate quickly between sections. The content of the report contains ASH information used to identify blocker and waiter identities and their associated transaction identifiers and SQL for a specified duration.

The primary interface for generating ASH reports is Oracle Enterprise Manager. Whenever possible, you should generate ASH reports using Oracle Enterprise Manager. If Oracle Enterprise Manager is unavailable, you can generate ASH reports by running SQL scripts, as described in the following sections:

- Generating an ASH Report
- Generating an ASH Report on a Specific Database Instance
- Generating an Oracle RAC ASH Report.

Generating an ASH Report

The `ashrpt.sql` SQL script generates an HTML or text report that displays ASH information for a specified duration.

To generate an ASH report:

1. At the SQL prompt, enter:
   ```
   @$ORACLE_HOME/rdbms/admin/ashrpt.sql
   ```
2. Specify whether you want an HTML or a text report:
   ```
   Enter value for report_type: text
   ```
   In this example, a text report is chosen.

3. Specify the begin time in minutes before the system date:
   ```
   Enter value for begin_time: -10
   ```
   In this example, 10 minutes before the current time is selected.
4. Enter the duration in minutes that the report for which you want to capture ASH information from the begin time:
   ```
   Enter value for duration:
   ```
   In this example, the default duration of system date minus begin time is accepted.
5. Enter a report name, or accept the default report name:
   ```
   Enter value for report_name:
   Using the report name ashrpt_1_0310_0131.txt
   ```
   In this example, the default name is accepted and an ASH report named `ashrpt_1_0310_0131` is generated. The report will gather ASH information beginning from 10 minutes before the current time and ending at the current time.

Generating an ASH Report on a Specific Database Instance

The `ashrpti.sql` SQL script generates an HTML or text report that displays ASH information for a specified duration for a specified database and instance. This script enables you to specify a database and instance before setting the time frame to collect ASH information.

To generate an ASH report on a specified database instance:

1. At the SQL prompt, enter:
   ```
   @$ORACLE_HOME/rdbms/admin/ashrpti.sql
   ```
2. Specify whether you want an HTML or a text report:
   ```
   Enter value for report_type: html
   ```
   In this example, an HTML report is chosen.
3. A list of available database IDs and instance numbers are displayed:
   ```
   Instances in this Workload Repository schema
   ~~~~~~~~~~~~~~~~~~~~~~~~~~~~~~~~~~~~~~~~~~~~~~
   DB Id        Inst Num    DB Name     Instance    Host
   -------      --------    --------    --------    -------
   3309173529          1    MAIN        main        examp1690
   3309173529          1    TINT251     tint251     samp251
   ```
   Enter the values for the database identifier (`dbid`) and instance number (`inst_num`):
   ```
   Enter value for dbid: 3309173529
   Using 3309173529 for database id
   Enter value for inst_num: 1
   ```
4. This step is applicable only if you are generating an ASH report on an Active Data Guard physical standby instance. If this is not the case, you may skip this step.
   To generate an ASH report on a physical standby instance, the standby database must be opened read-only. The ASH data on disk represents activity on the primary database and the ASH data in memory represents activity on the standby database.
   Specify whether to generate the report using data sampled from the primary or standby database:
   ```
   You are running ASH report on a Standby database.
   To generate the report over data sampled on the Primary database,
   enter 'P'.
   ```

```
Defaults to 'S' data sampled in the Standby database.
Enter value for stdbyflag:
Using Primary (P) or Standby (S): S
```

In this example, the default value of Standby (S) is selected.

5. Specify the begin time in minutes before the system date:

   ```
   Enter value for begin_time: -10
   ```

   In this example, 10 minutes before the current time is selected.
6. Enter the duration in minutes that the report for which you want to capture ASH information from the begin time.

   ```
   Enter value for duration:
   ```

   In this example, the default duration of system date minus begin time is accepted.
7. Specify the slot width in seconds that will be used in the Activity Over Time section of the report:

   ```
   Enter value for slot_width:
   ```

   In this example, the default value is accepted.
8. Follow the instructions as explained in the subsequent prompts and enter values for the following report targets:
   - `target_session_id`
   - `target_sql_id`
   - `target_wait_class`
   - `target_service_hash`
   - `target_module_name`
   - `target_action_name`
   - `target_client_id`
   - `target_plsql_entry`.
9. Enter a report name, or accept the default report name:

   ```
   Enter value for report_name:
   Using the report name ashrpt_1_0310_0131.txt
   ```

   In this example, the default name is accepted and an ASH report named `ashrpt_1_0310_0131` is generated. The report will gather ASH information on the database instance with a database ID value of `3309173529` beginning from 10 minutes before the current time and ending at the current time.

Generating an Oracle RAC ASH Report

The `ashrpti.sql` SQL script generates an HTML or text report that displays ASH information for a specified duration for specified databases and instances in an Oracle RAC environment. Only ASH data that is written to disk will be used to generate the report. This report will only use ASH samples from the last 10 minutes that are found in the `DBA_HIST_ACTIVE_SESS_HISTORY` table.

To generate an ASH report in an Oracle RAC environment:

1. At the SQL prompt, enter:

   ```
   @$ORACLE_HOME/rdbms/admin/ashrpti.sql
   ```
2. Specify whether you want an HTML or a text report:

   ```
   Enter value for report_type: html
   ```

   In this example, an HTML report is chosen.

3. A list of available database IDs and instance numbers are displayed:

```
Instances in this Workload Repository schema
~~~~~~~~~~~~~~~~~~~~~~~~~~~~~~~~~~~~~~~~~~~~
DB Id        Inst Num    DB Name     Instance    Host
-------      --------    -------     -------     -------
3309173529          1    MAIN        main        examp1690
3309173529          1    TINT251     tint251     samp251
3309173529          2    TINT251     tint252     samp252
3309173529   3 TINT251   tint253     samp253
3309173529   4 TINT251   tint254     samp254
```

Enter the values for the database identifier (`dbid`) and instance number (`inst_num`):

```
Enter value for dbid: 3309173529
Using database id: 3309173529
Enter instance numbers. Enter 'ALL' for all instances in an Oracle
RAC cluster or explicitly specify list of instances (e.g., 1,2,3).
Defaults to current instance.
Enter value for inst_num: ALL
Using instance number(s): ALL
```

4. Specify the begin time in minutes before the system date:

```
Enter value for begin_time: -1:10
```

In this example, 1 hour and 10 minutes before the current time is selected.

5. Enter the duration in minutes that the report for which you want to capture ASH information from the begin time:

```
Enter value for duration: 10
```

In this example, the duration is set to 10 minutes.

6. Specify the slot width in seconds that will be used in the Activity Over Time section of the report:

```
Enter value for slot_width:
```

In this example, the default value is accepted.

7. Follow the instructions as explained in the subsequent prompts and enter values for the following report targets:
   - `target_session_id`
   - `target_sql_id`
   - `target_wait_class`
   - `target_service_hash`
   - `target_module_name`
   - `target_action_name`
   - `target_client_id`
   - `target_plsql_entry`.

8. Enter a report name, or accept the default report name:

```
Enter value for report_name:
Using the report name ashrpt_rac_0310_0131.txt
```

In this example, the default name is accepted and an ASH report named `ashrpt_rac_0310_0131` is generated. The report will gather ASH information on all instances belonging to the database with a database ID value of `3309173529` beginning from 10 minutes before the current time and ending at the current time.

Using Active Session History Reports

After generating an ASH report, you can review the contents to identify transient performance problems.

The contents of the ASH report are divided into the following sections:

- Top Events
- Load Profile
- Top SQL
- Top PL/SQL
- Top Java
- Top Sessions
- Top Objects/Files/Latches
- Activity Over Time.

Top Events

The Top Events section describes the top wait events of the sampled session activity categorized by user, background, and priority. Use the information in this section to identify the wait events that may be the cause of the transient performance problem.

The Top Events section contains the following subsections:

- Top User Events.
  This subsection lists the top wait events from user processes that accounted for the highest percentages of sampled session activity.
- Top Background Events.
  This subsection lists the top wait events from backgrounds that accounted for the highest percentages of sampled session activity.
- Top Event P1/P2/P3.
  This subsection lists the wait event parameter values of the top wait events that accounted for the highest percentages of sampled session activity, ordered by the percentage of total wait time (% Event). For each wait event, values in the P1 Value, P2 Value, P3 Value column correspond to wait event parameters displayed in the Parameter 1, Parameter 2, and Parameter 3 columns.

Load Profile

The Load Profile section describes the load analyzed in the sampled session activity. Use the information in this section to identify the service, client, or SQL command type that may be the cause of the transient performance problem.

The Load Profile section contains the following subsections:

- Top Service/Module.
  This subsection lists the services and modules that accounted for the highest percentages of sampled session activity.
- Top Client IDs.
  This subsection lists the clients that accounted for the highest percentages of sampled session activity based on their client ID, which is the application-specific identifier of the database session.
- Top SQL Command Types.
  This subsection lists the SQL command types, such as `SELECT` or `UPDATE`, that accounted for the highest percentages of sampled session activity.

- Top Phases of Execution.
  This subsection lists the phases of execution, such as SQL, PL/SQL, and Java compilation and execution, that accounted for the highest percentages of sampled session activity.

Top SQL

The Top SQL section describes the top SQL statements of the sampled session activity. Use this information to identify high-load SQL statements that may be the cause of the transient performance problem.

The Top SQL section contains the following subsections:

- Top SQL with Top Events
- Top SQL with Top Row Sources
- Top SQL Using Literals
- Top Parsing Module/Action
- Complete List of SQL Text.

Top SQL with Top Events: The Top SQL with Top Events subsection lists the SQL statements that accounted for the highest percentages of sampled session activity and the top wait events that were encountered by these SQL statements. The Sampled # of Executions column shows how many distinct executions of a particular SQL statement were sampled.

Top SQL with Top Row Sources: The Top SQL with Top Row Sources subsection lists the SQL statements that accounted for the highest percentages of sampled session activity and their detailed execution plan information. You can use this information to identify which part of the SQL execution contributed significantly to the SQL elapsed time.

Top SQL Using Literals: The Top SQL Using Literals subsection lists the SQL statements using literals that accounted for the highest percentages of sampled session activity. You should review the statements listed in this report to determine whether the literals can be replaced with bind variables.

Top Parsing Module/Action: The Top Parsing Module/Action subsection lists the module and action that accounted for the highest percentages of sampled session activity while parsing the SQL statement.

Complete List of SQL Text: The Complete List of SQL Text subsection displays the entire text of the Top SQL statements shown in this section.

Top PL/SQL

The Top PL/SQL section lists the PL/SQL procedures that accounted for the highest percentages of sampled session activity. The PL/SQL Entry Subprogram column lists the application's top-level entry point into PL/SQL. The PL/SQL Current Subprogram column lists the PL/SQL subprogram being executed at the point of sampling. If the value of this column is `SQL`, then the % Current column shows the percentage of time spent executing SQL for this subprogram.

Top Java

The Top Java section describes the top Java programs in the sampled session activity.

Top Sessions

The Top Sessions section describes the sessions that were waiting for a particular wait event. Use this information to identify the sessions that accounted for the highest percentages of sampled session activity, which may be the cause of the transient performance problem.

The Top Sessions section contains the following subsections:

- Top Sessions
- Top Blocking Sessions
- Top Sessions Running PQs.

Top Sessions: The Top Session subsection lists the sessions that were waiting for a particular wait event that accounted for the highest percentages of sampled session activity.

Top Blocking Sessions: The Top Blocking Sessions subsection lists the blocking sessions that accounted for the highest percentages of sampled session activity.

Top Sessions Running PQs: The Top Sessions Running PQs subsection lists the sessions running Parallel Queries (PQs) that were waiting for a particular wait event, which accounted for the highest percentages of sampled session activity.

Top Objects/Files/Latches

The Top Objects/Files/Latches section provides additional information about the most commonly-used database resources and contains the following subsections:

- Top DB Objects
- Top DB Files
- Top Latches.

Top DB Objects: The Top DB Objects subsection lists the database objects (such as tables and indexes) that accounted for the highest percentages of sampled session activity.

Top DB Files: The Top DB Files subsection lists the database files that accounted for the highest percentages of sampled session activity.

Top Latches: The Top Latches subsection lists the latches that accounted for the highest percentages of sampled session activity.

Latches are simple, low-level serialization mechanisms to protect shared data structures in the System Global Area (SGA). For example, latches protect the list of users currently accessing the database and the data structures describing the blocks in the buffer cache. A server or background process acquires a latch for a very short time while manipulating or looking at one of these structures. The implementation of latches is operating system-dependent, particularly regarding whether and how long a process waits for a latch.

Activity Over Time

The Activity Over Time section is one of the most informative sections of the ASH report. This section is particularly useful for longer time periods because it provides in-depth details about activities and workload profiles during the analysis period. The Activity Over Time section is divided into 10 time slots. The size of each time slot varies based on the duration of the analysis period. The first and last slots are usually odd-sized. All inner slots are equally sized and can be compared to each other. For example, if the analysis period lasts for 10 minutes, then all time slots will 1 minute each. However, if the analysis period lasts for 9 minutes and 30 seconds, then the outer slots may be 15 seconds each and the inner slots will be 1 minute each.

Each of the time slots contains information regarding that particular time slot, as described in Table 5.2.

Table 5. . ctivity Over Time

Column	escription
Slot Time (Duration)	Duration of the slot
Slot Count	Number of sampled sessions in the slot
Event	Top three wait events in the slot
Event Count	Number of ASH samples waiting for the wait event
% Event	Percentage of ASH samples waiting for wait events in the entire analysis period

When comparing the inner slots, perform a skew analysis by identifying spikes in the Event Count and Slot Count columns. A spike in the Event Count column indicates an increase in the number of sampled sessions waiting for a particular event. A spike in the Slot Count column indicates an increase in active sessions, because ASH data is sampled from active sessions only and a relative increase in database workload. Typically, when the number of active session samples and the number of sessions associated with a wait event increases, the slot may be the cause of the transient performance problem.

6

Automatic Performance Diagnostics

Learning Objectives

This chapter describes Oracle Database automatic features for performance diagnosing and tuning.

This chapter contains the following topics:

- Overview of the Automatic Database Diagnostic Monitor
- Setting Up ADDM
- Diagnosing Database Performance Problems with ADDM
- Views with ADDM Information

OVERVIEW OF THE AUTOMATIC DATABASE DIAGNOSTIC MONITOR

When problems occur with a system, it is important to perform accurate and timely diagnosis of the problem before making any changes to a system. Oftentimes, a Database Administrator (DBA) simply looks at the symptoms and immediately starts changing the system to fix those symptoms. However, an accurate diagnosis of the actual problem in the initial stage significantly increases the probability of success in resolving the problem.

With Oracle Database, the statistical data needed for accurate diagnosis of a problem is stored in the Automatic Workload Repository (AWR). The Automatic Database Diagnostic Monitor (ADDM):

- Analyzes the AWR data on a regular basis
- Diagnoses the root causes of performance problems
- Provides recommendations for correcting any problems
- Identifies non-problem areas of the system.

Because AWR is a repository of historical performance data, ADDM can analyze performance issues after the event, often saving time and resources in reproducing a problem.

In most cases, ADDM output should be the first place that a DBA looks when notified of a performance problem. ADDM provides the following benefits:

- Automatic performance diagnostic report every hour by default
- Problem diagnosis based on decades of tuning expertise
- Time-based quantification of problem impacts and recommendation benefits

- Identification of root cause, not symptoms
- Recommendations for treating the root causes of problems
- Identification of non-problem areas of the system
- Minimal overhead to the system during the diagnostic process.

It is important to realize that tuning is an iterative process, and fixing one problem can cause the bottleneck to shift to another part of the system. Even with the benefit of ADDM analysis, it can take multiple tuning cycles to reach acceptable system performance. ADDM benefits apply beyond production systems; on development and test systems, ADDM can provide an early warning of performance issues.

This section contains the following topics:

- ADDM Analysis
- Using ADDM with Oracle Real Application Clusters
- ADDM Analysis Results
- Reviewing ADDM Analysis Results: Example.

ADDM Analysis

An ADDM analysis can be performed on a pair of AWR snapshots and a set of instances from the same database. The pair of AWR snapshots define the time period for analysis, and the set of instances define the target for analysis.

If you are using Oracle Real Application Clusters (Oracle RAC), ADDM has three analysis modes:

- **Database**

  In Database mode, ADDM analyzes all instances of the database.
- **Instance**

  In Instance mode, ADDM analyzes a particular instance of the database.
- **Partial**

  In Partial mode, ADDM analyzes a subset of all database instances.

If you are not using Oracle RAC, ADDM can only function in Instance mode because there is only one instance of the database.

An ADDM analysis is performed each time an AWR snapshot is taken and the results are saved in the database. The time period analyzed by ADDM is defined by the last two snapshots (the last hour by default). ADDM will always analyze the specified instance in Instance mode. For non-Oracle RAC or single instance environments, the analysis performed in the Instance mode is the same as a database-wide analysis. If you are using Oracle RAC, ADDM will also analyze the entire database in Database mode. After an ADDM completes its analysis, you can view the results using Oracle Enterprise Manager, or by viewing a report in a SQL*Plus session.

ADDM analysis is performed top down, first identifying symptoms, and then refining them to reach the root causes of performance problems. The goal of the analysis is to reduce a single throughput metric called `DB time`. `DB time` is the cumulative time spent by the database in processing user requests. It includes wait time and CPU time of all non-idle user sessions. `DB time` is displayed in the `V$SESS_TIME_MODEL` and `V$SYS_TIME_MODEL` views.

By reducing `DB time`, the database is able to support more user requests using the same resources, which increases throughput. The problems reported by ADDM are sorted by the amount of `DB time` they are responsible for. System areas that are not responsible for a significant portion of `DB time` are reported as non-problem areas.

The types of problems that ADDM considers include the following:

- CPU bottlenecks—Is the system CPU bound by Oracle Database or some other application?
- Undersized Memory Structures—Are the Oracle Database memory structures, such as the SGA, PGA, and buffer cache, adequately sized?
- I/O capacity issues—Is the I/O subsystem performing as expected?
- High load SQL statements—Are there any SQL statements which are consuming excessive system resources?
- High load PL/SQL execution and compilation, and high-load Java usage
- Oracle RAC specific issues—What are the global cache hot blocks and objects; are there any interconnect latency issues?
- Sub-optimal use of Oracle Database by the application—Are there problems with poor connection management, excessive parsing, or application level lock contention?
- Database configuration issues—Is there evidence of incorrect sizing of log files, archiving issues, excessive checkpoints, or sub-optimal parameter settings?
- Concurrency issues—Are there buffer busy problems?
- Hot objects and top SQL for various problem areas.

This is not a comprehensive list of all problem types that ADDM considers in its analysis.

ADDM also documents the non-problem areas of the system. For example, wait event classes that are not significantly impacting the performance of the system are identified and removed from the tuning consideration at an early stage, saving time and effort that would be spent on items that do not impact overall system performance.

Using ADDM with Oracle Real Application Clusters

If you are using Oracle RAC, you can run ADDM in Database analysis mode to analyze the throughput performance of all instances of the database. In Database mode, ADDM considers DB time as the sum of the database time for all database instances. Using the Database analysis mode enables you to view all findings that are significant to the entire database in a single report, instead of reviewing a separate report for each instance.

The Database mode report includes findings about database resources (such as I/O and interconnect). The report also aggregates findings from the various instances if they are significant to the entire database. For example, if the CPU load on a single instance is high enough to affect the entire database, the finding will appear in the Database mode analysis, which will point to the particular instance responsible for the problem.

ADDM Analysis Results

In addition to problem diagnostics, ADDM recommends possible solutions. ADDM analysis results are represented as a set of findings. See for an example of ADDM analysis result. Each ADDM finding can belong to one of the following types:

- Problem findings describe the root cause of a database performance problem.
- Symptom findings contain information that often lead to one or more problem findings.
- Information findings are used for reporting information that are relevant to understanding the performance of the database, but do not constitute a performance problem (such as non-problem areas of the database and the activity of automatic database maintenance).

- Warning findings contain information about problems that may affect the completeness or accuracy of the ADDM analysis (such as missing data in the AWR).

Each problem finding is quantified by an impact that is an estimate of the portion of `DB time` caused by the finding's performance issue. A problem finding can be associated with a list of recommendations for reducing the impact of the performance problem. The types of recommendations include:

- Hardware changes: adding CPUs or changing the I/O subsystem configuration
- Database configuration: changing initialization parameter settings
- Schema changes: hash partitioning a table or index, or using Automatic Segment-Space Management (ASSM)
- Application changes: using the cache option for sequences or using bind variables
- Using other advisors: running SQL Tuning Advisor on high-load SQL or running the Segment Advisor on hot objects.

A list of recommendations can contain various alternatives for solving the same problem; you do not have to apply all the recommendations to solve a specific problem. Each recommendation has a benefit which is an estimate of the portion of `DB time` that can be saved if the recommendation is implemented. Recommendations are composed of actions and rationales. You must apply all the actions of a recommendation to gain the estimated benefit. The rationales are used for explaining why the set of actions were recommended and to provide additional information to implement the suggested recommendation.

Reviewing ADDM Analysis Results: Example

Consider the following section of an ADDM report in.

Example 6.1: Example ADDM Report

```
FINDING 1: 31% impact (7798 seconds)
--------------------------------------
SQL statements were not shared due to the usage of literals. This
resulted in additional hard parses which were consuming significant
database time.
RECOMMENDATION 1: Application Analysis, 31% benefit (7798 seconds)
ACTION: Investigate application logic for possible use of bind
variables instead of literals. Alternatively, you may set the
parameter "cursor_sharing" to "force".
RATIONALE: SQL statements with PLAN_HASH_VALUE 3106087033 were found
to be using literals. Look in V$SQL for examples of such SQL
statements.
```

In , the finding points to a particular root cause, the usage of literals in SQL statements, which is estimated to have an impact of about 31% of total `DB time` in the analysis period.

The finding has a recommendation associated with it, composed of one action and one rationale. The action specifies a solution to the problem found and is estimated to have a maximum benefit of up to 31% `DB time` in the analysis period. Note that the benefit is given as a portion of the total `DB time` and not as a portion of the finding's impact. The rationale provides additional information on tracking potential SQL statements that were using literals and causing this performance issue. Using the specified plan hash value of SQL statements that could be a problem, a DBA could quickly examine a few sample statements.

When a specific problem has multiple causes, the ADDM may report multiple problem and symptom findings. In this case, the impacts of these multiple findings can contain the same portion of DB time. Because the performance issues of findings can overlap, the sum of the impacts of the findings can exceed 100% of DB time. For example, if a system performs many reads, then ADDM might report a SQL statement responsible for 50% of DB time due to I/O activity as one finding, and an undersized buffer cache responsible for 75% of DB time as another finding.

When multiple recommendations are associated with a problem finding, the recommendations may contain alternatives for solving the problem. In this case, the sum of the recommendations' benefits may be higher than the finding's impact.

When appropriate, an ADDM action may have multiple solutions for you to choose from. In the example, the most effective solution is to use bind variables. However, it is often difficult to modify the application. Changing the value of the CURSOR_SHARING initialization parameter is much easier to implement and can provide significant improvement.

SETTING UP ADDM

Automatic database diagnostic monitoring is enabled by default and is controlled by the CONTROL_MANAGEMENT_PACK_ACCESS and the STATISTICS_LEVEL initialization parameters.

The CONTROL_MANAGEMENT_PACK_ACCESS parameter should be set to DIAGNOSTIC or DIAGNOSTIC+TUNING to enable automatic database diagnostic monitoring. The default setting is DIAGNOSTIC+TUNING. Setting CONTROL_MANAGEMENT_PACK_ACCESS to NONE disables ADDM.

The STATISTICS_LEVEL parameter should be set to the TYPICAL or ALL to enable automatic database diagnostic monitoring. The default setting is TYPICAL. Setting STATISTICS_LEVEL to BASIC disables many Oracle Database features, including ADDM, and is strongly discouraged.

ADDM analysis of I/O performance partially depends on a single argument, DBIO_EXPECTED, that describes the expected performance of the I/O subsystem. The value of DBIO_EXPECTED is the average time it takes to read a single database block in microseconds. Oracle Database uses the default value of 10 milliseconds, which is an appropriate value for most modern hard drives. If your hardware is significantly different, such as very old hardware or very fast RAM disks, consider using a different value.

To determine the correct setting for DBIO_EXPECTED parameter:

1. Measure the average read time of a single database block read for your hardware. Note that this measurement is for random I/O, which includes seek time if you use standard hard drives. Typical values for hard drives are between 5000 and 20000 microseconds.
2. Set the value one time for all subsequent ADDM executions. For example, if the measured value if 8000 microseconds, you should execute the following command as SYS user:

```
EXECUTE DBMS_ADVISOR.SET_DEFAULT_TASK_PARAMETER
                              ('ADDM', 'DBIO_EXPECTED', 8000);
```

DIAGNOSING DATABASE PERFORMANCE PROBLEMS WITH ADDM

To diagnose database performance problems, first review the ADDM analysis results that are automatically created each time an AWR snapshot is taken. If a different analysis is required (such as a longer analysis period, using a different DBIO_EXPECTED setting, or changing the analysis mode), you can run ADDM manually as described in this section.

ADDM can analyze any two AWR snapshots (on the same database), as long as both snapshots are still stored in the AWR (have not been purged). ADDM can only analyze instances that are started before the beginning snapshot and remain running until the ending snapshot. Additionally, ADDM will not analyze instances that experience significant errors when generating the AWR snapshots. In such cases, ADDM will analyze the largest subset of instances that did not experience these problems.

The primary interface for diagnostic monitoring is Oracle Enterprise Manager. Whenever possible, you should run ADDM using Oracle Enterprise Manager. If Oracle Enterprise Manager is unavailable, you can run ADDM using the `DBMS_ADDM` package. In order to run the `DBMS_ADDM` APIs, the user must be granted the `ADVISOR` privilege.

This section contains the following topics:

- Running ADDM in Database Mode
- Running ADDM in Instance Mode
- Running ADDM in Partial Mode
- Displaying an ADDM Report.

Running ADDM in Database Mode

For Oracle RAC configurations, you can run ADDM in Database mode to analyze all instances of the databases. For single-instance configurations, you can still run ADDM in Database mode; ADDM will simply behave as if running in Instance mode.

To run ADDM in Database mode, use the `DBMS_ADDM.ANALYZE_DB` procedure:

```
BEGIN
DBMS_ADDM.ANALYZE_DB
    (task_name          IN     OUT VARCHAR2,
    begin_snapshot      IN     NUMBER,
    end_snapshot        IN     NUMBER,
    db_id               IN     NUMBER := NULL);
END;
/
```

The `task_name` parameter specifies the name of the analysis task that will be created. The `begin_snapshot` parameter specifies the snapshot number of the beginning snapshot in the analysis period. The `end_snapshot` parameter specifies the snapshot number of the ending snapshot in the analysis period. The `db_id` parameter specifies the database identifier of the database that will be analyzed. If unspecified, this parameter defaults to the database identifier of the database to which you are currently connected.

The following example creates an ADDM task in database analysis mode, and executes it to diagnose the performance of the entire database during the time period defined by snapshots 137 and 145:

```
VAR tname VARCHAR2(30);
BEGIN
    :tname := 'ADDM for 7PM to 9PM';
    DBMS_ADDM.ANALYZE_DB(:tname, 137, 145);
END;
/
```

Running ADDM in Instance Mode

To analyze a particular instance of the database, you can run ADDM in Instance mode. To run ADDM in Instance mode, use the DBMS_ADDM.ANALYZE_INST procedure:

```
BEGIN
DBMS_ADDM.ANALYZE_INST
    (task_name          IN    OUT VARCHAR2,
    begin_snapshot      IN    NUMBER,
    end_snapshot        IN    NUMBER,
    instance_number     IN    NUMBER := NULL,
    db_id               IN    NUMBER := NULL);
END;
/
```

The task_name parameter specifies the name of the analysis task that will be created. The begin_snapshot parameter specifies the snapshot number of the beginning snapshot in the analysis period. The end_snapshot parameter specifies the snapshot number of the ending snapshot in the analysis period. The instance_number parameter specifies the instance number of the instance that will be analyzed. If unspecified, this parameter defaults to the instance number of the instance to which you are currently connected. The db_id parameter specifies the database identifier of the database that will be analyzed. If unspecified, this parameter defaults to the database identifier of the database to which you are currently connected.

The following example creates an ADDM task in instance analysis mode, and executes it to diagnose the performance of instance number 1 during the time period defined by snapshots 137 and 145:

```
VAR tname VARCHAR2(30);
BEGIN
    :tname := 'my ADDM for 7PM to 9PM';
    DBMS_ADDM.ANALYZE_INST(:tname, 137, 145, 1);
END;
/
```

Running ADDM in Partial Mode

To analyze a subset of all database instances, you can run ADDM in Partial mode. To run ADDM in Partial mode, use the DBMS_ADDM.ANALYZE_PARTIAL procedure:

```
BEGIN
DBMS_ADDM.ANALYZE_PARTIAL
    (task_name          IN    OUT VARCHAR2,
    instance_numbers    IN    VARCHAR2,
    begin_snapshot      IN    NUMBER,
    end_snapshot        IN    NUMBER,
    db_id               IN    NUMBER := NULL);
END;
/
```

The task_name parameter specifies the name of the analysis task that will be created. The instance_numbers parameter specifies a comma-delimited list of instance numbers of instances that will be analyzed. The begin_snapshot parameter specifies the snapshot number of the beginning snapshot in the analysis period. The end_snapshot parameter specifies the snapshot number of the ending snapshot in the analysis period. The db_id parameter specifies the database identifier of the database that will be analyzed. If unspecified, this parameter defaults to the database identifier of the database to which you are currently connected.

The following example creates an ADDM task in partial analysis mode, and executes it to diagnose the performance of instance numbers 1, 2, and 4, during the time period defined by snapshots 137 and 145:

```
VAR tname VARCHAR2(30);
BEGIN
    :tname := 'my ADDM for 7PM to 9PM';
    DBMS_ADDM.ANALYZE_PARTIAL(:tname, '1,2,4', 137, 145);
END;
/
```

Displaying an ADDM Report

To display a text report of an executed ADDM task, use the DBMS_ADDM.GET_REPORT function:

```
DBMS_ADDM.GET_REPORT
    (task_name  IN     VARCHAR2
    RETURN CLOB);
```

The following example displays a text report of the ADDM task specified by its task name using the tname variable:

```
SET LONG 1000000 PAGESIZE 0;
SELECT DBMS_ADDM.GET_REPORT(:tname) FROM DUAL;
```

Note that the return type of a report is a CLOB, formatted to fit line size of 80.

VIEWS WITH ADDM INFORMATION

Typically, you should view output and information from ADDM using Oracle Enterprise Manager or ADDM reports.

However, you can display ADDM information through the DBA_ADVISOR views. This group of views includes:

- DBA_ADVISOR_FINDINGS
  This view displays all the findings discovered by all advisors. Each finding is displayed with an associated finding ID, name, and type. For tasks with multiple executions, the name of each task execution associated with each finding is also listed.
- DBA_ADDM_FINDINGS
  This view contains a subset of the findings displayed in the related DBA_ADVISOR_FINDINGS view. This view only displays the ADDM findings discovered by all advisors. Each ADDM finding is displayed with an associated finding ID, name, and type.

- `DBA_ADVISOR_FINDING_NAMES`
  List of all finding names registered with the advisor framework.
- `DBA_ADVISOR_RECOMMENDATIONS`
  This view displays the results of completed diagnostic tasks with recommendations for the problems identified in each execution. The recommendations should be reviewed in the order of the **RANK** column, as this relays the magnitude of the problem for the recommendation. The **BENEFIT** column displays the benefit to the system you can expect after the recommendation is performed. For tasks with multiple executions, the name of each task execution associated with each advisor task is also listed.
- `DBA_ADVISOR_TASKS`
  This view provides basic information about existing tasks, such as the task ID, task name, and when the task was created. For tasks with multiple executions, the name and type of the last or current execution associated with each advisor task is also listed.

7 Configuring and Using Memory

Learning Objectives

This chapter explains how to allocate memory to Oracle Database memory caches, and how to use those caches. Proper sizing and effective use of the Oracle Database memory caches greatly improves database performance. Oracle recommends using automatic memory management to manage the memory on your system. However, you can choose to manually adjust the memory pools on your system, as described in this chapter.

This chapter contains the following sections:

- Understanding Memory Allocation Issues
- Configuring and Using the Buffer Cache
- Configuring and Using the Shared Pool and Large Pool
- Configuring and Using the Redo Log Buffer
- PGA Memory Management
- Managing the Server and Client Result Caches

UNDERSTANDING MEMORY ALLOCATION ISSUES

Oracle Database stores information in memory caches and on disk. Memory access is much faster than disk access. Disk access (physical I/O) take a significant amount of time, compared with memory access, typically in the order of 10 milliseconds. Physical I/O also increases the CPU resources required, because of the path length in device drivers and operating system event schedulers. For this reason, it is more efficient for data requests of frequently accessed objects to be perform by memory, rather than also requiring disk access.

A performance goal is to reduce the physical I/O overhead as much as possible, either by making it more likely that the required data is in memory, or by making the process of retrieving the required data more efficient.

This section contains the following topics:

- Oracle Memory Caches
- Automatic Memory Management
- Automatic Shared Memory Management
- Dynamically Changing Cache Sizes

- Application Considerations
- Operating System Memory Use
- Iteration During Configuration.

Oracle Memory Caches

The main Oracle Database memory caches that affect performance are:

- Shared pool
- Large pool
- Java pool
- Buffer cache
- Streams pool size
- Log buffer
- Process-private memory, such as memory used for sorting and hash joins.

Automatic Memory Management

Oracle strongly recommends the use of automatic memory management to manage the memory on your system. Automatic memory management enables Oracle Database to automatically manage and tune the instance memory. Automatic memory management can be configured using a target memory size initialization parameter (`MEMORY_TARGET`) and a maximum memory size initialization parameter (`MEMORY_MAX_TARGET`). The database tunes to the target memory size, redistributing memory as needed between the system global area (SGA) and the instance program global area (instance PGA). Before setting any memory pool sizes, consider using the automatic memory management feature of Oracle Database. If you must configure memory allocations, consider using the Memory Advisor for managing memory.

Automatic Shared Memory Management

Automatic Shared Memory Management simplifies the configuration of the SGA. To use Automatic Shared Memory Management, set the `SGA_TARGET` initialization parameter to a nonzero value and set the `STATISTICS_LEVEL` initialization parameter to `TYPICAL` or `ALL`. Set the value of the `SGA_TARGET` parameter to the amount of memory that you intend to dedicate for the SGA. In response to the workload on the system, the automatic SGA management distributes the memory appropriately for the following memory pools:

- Database buffer cache (default pool)
- Shared pool
- Large pool
- Java pool
- Streams pool.

If these automatically tuned memory pools had been set to nonzero values, those values are used as minimum levels by Automatic Shared Memory Management. You would set minimum values if an application component needs a minimum amount of memory to function properly.

`SGA_TARGET` is a dynamic parameter that can be changed by accessing the SGA Size Advisor from the Memory Parameters SGA page in Oracle Enterprise Manager, or by querying the `V$SGA_TARGET_ADVICE` view and using the `ALTER SYSTEM` command. `SGA_TARGET` can be set less than or equal to the value of `SGA_MAX_SIZE` initialization parameter. Changes in the value of `SGA_TARGET` automatically resize the automatically tuned memory pools.

If you dynamically disable `SGA_TARGET` by setting its value to 0 at instance startup, Automatic Shared Memory Management will be disabled and the current auto-tuned sizes will be used for each memory pool. If necessary, you can manually resize each memory pool using the `DB_CACHE_SIZE`, `SHARED_POOL_SIZE`, `LARGE_POOL_SIZE`, `JAVA_POOL_SIZE`, and `STREAMS_POOL_SIZE` initialization parameters.

The following pools are manually sized components and are not affected by Automatic Shared Memory Management:

- Log buffer
- Other buffer caches (such as KEEP, RECYCLE, and other nondefault block size)
- Fixed SGA and other internal allocations.

To manually size these memory pools, you must set the `DB_KEEP_CACHE_SIZE`, `DB_RECYCLE_CACHE_SIZE`, `DB_nK_CACHE_SIZE`, and `LOG_BUFFER` initialization parameters. The memory allocated to these pools is deducted from the total available for `SGA_TARGET` when Automatic Shared Memory Management computes the values of the automatically tuned memory pools.

Dynamically Changing Cache Sizes

If the system is not using Automatic Memory Management or Automatic Shared Memory Management, you can choose to dynamically reconfigure the sizes of the shared pool, the large pool, the buffer cache, and the process-private memory. The following sections contain details on sizing of caches:

- Configuring and Using the Buffer Cache
- Configuring and Using the Shared Pool and Large Pool
- Configuring and Using the Redo Log Buffer.

The size of these memory caches is configurable using initialization configuration parameters, such as `DB_CACHE_SIZE`, `JAVA_POOL_SIZE`, `LARGE_POOL_SIZE`, `LOG_BUFFER`, and `SHARED_POOL_SIZE`. The values for these parameters are also dynamically configurable using the `ALTER SYSTEM` statement except for the log buffer pool and process-private memory, which are static after startup.

Memory for the shared pool, large pool, java pool, and buffer cache is allocated in units of **granules**. The granule size is 4 MB if the SGA size is less than 1 GB. If the SGA size is greater than 1 GB, the granule size changes to 16 MB. The granule size is calculated and fixed when the instance starts up. The size does not change during the lifetime of the instance.

The granule size that is currently being used for SGA can be viewed in the view `V$SGA_DYNAMIC_COMPONENTS`. The same granule size is used for all dynamic components in the SGA.

You can expand the total SGA size to a value equal to the `SGA_MAX_SIZE` parameter. If the `SGA_MAX_SIZE` is not set, you can decrease the size of one cache and reallocate that memory to another cache if necessary. `SGA_MAX_SIZE` defaults to the aggregate setting of all the components.

`SGA_MAX_SIZE` cannot be dynamically resized.

The maximum amount of memory usable by the instance is determined at instance startup by the initialization parameter `SGA_MAX_SIZE`. You can specify `SGA_MAX_SIZE` to be larger than the sum of all of the memory components, such as buffer cache and shared pool.

Otherwise, SGA_MAX_SIZE defaults to the actual size used by those components. Setting SGA_MAX_SIZE larger than the sum of memory used by all of the components lets you dynamically increase a cache size without needing to decrease the size of another cache.

Viewing Information About Dynamic Resize Operations

The following views provide information about dynamic resize operations:

- V$MEMORY_CURRENT_RESIZE_OPS displays information about memory resize operations (both automatic and manual) which are currently in progress.
- V$MEMORY_DYNAMIC_COMPONENTS displays information about the current sizes of all dynamically tuned memory components, including the total sizes of the SGA and instance PGA.
- V$MEMORY_RESIZE_OPS displays information about the last 800 completed memory resize operations (both automatic and manual). This does not include in-progress operations.
- V$MEMORY_TARGET_ADVICE displays tuning advice for the MEMORY_TARGET initialization parameter.
- V$SGA_CURRENT_RESIZE_OPS displays information about SGA resize operations that are currently in progress. An operation can be a grow or a shrink of a dynamic SGA component.
- V$SGA_RESIZE_OPS displays information about the last 800 completed SGA resize operations. This does not include any operations currently in progress.
- V$SGA_DYNAMIC_COMPONENTS displays information about the dynamic components in SGA. This view summarizes information based on all completed SGA resize operations that occurred after startup.
- V$SGA_DYNAMIC_FREE_MEMORY displays information about the amount of SGA memory available for future dynamic SGA resize operations.

Application Considerations

When configuring memory, size the cache appropriately for the application's needs. Conversely, tuning the application's use of the caches can greatly reduce resource requirements. Efficient use of Oracle Database memory caches also reduces the load on related resources such as the latches, the CPU, and the I/O system.

For best performance, you should consider the following:

- The cache should be optimally designed to use the operating system and database resources most efficiently.
- Memory allocations to Oracle Database memory structures should best reflect the needs of the application.

Making changes or additions to an existing application might require resizing Oracle Database memory structures to meet the needs of your modified application.

If your application uses Java, you should investigate whether you need to modify the default configuration for the Java pool.

Operating System Memory Use

For most operating systems, it is important to consider the following:

- Reduce Paging
- Fit the SGA into Main Memory
- Allow Adequate Memory to Individual Users.

Reduce Paging: Paging occurs when an operating system transfers memory-resident pages to disk solely to allow new pages to be loaded into memory. Many operating systems page to accommodate large amounts of information that do not fit into real memory. On most operating systems, paging reduces performance.

Use operating system utilities to examine the operating system, to identify whether there is a lot of paging on your system. If so, then the total system memory may not be large enough to hold everything for which you have allocated memory. Either increase the total memory on your system, or decrease the amount of memory allocated.

Fit the SGA into Main Memory: Because the purpose of the SGA is to store data in memory for fast access, the SGA should be within main memory. If pages of the SGA are swapped to disk, then the data is no longer quickly accessible. On most operating systems, the disadvantage of paging significantly outweighs the advantage of a large SGA.

> You can use the `LOCK_SGA` parameter to lock the SGA into physical memory and prevent it from being paged out. The database does not use the `MEMORY_TARGET` and `MEMORY_MAX_TARGET` parameters when the `LOCK_SGA` parameter is enabled.

To see how much memory is allocated to the SGA and each of its internal structures, enter the following SQL*Plus statement:

```
SHOW SGA
```

The output of this statement will look similar to the following:

```
Total System Global Area     840205000   bytes
Fixed Size                      279240   bytes
Variable Size                520093696   bytes
Database Buffers             318767104   bytes
Redo Buffers                   1064960   bytes
```

Allow Adequate Memory to Individual Users: When sizing the SGA, ensure that you allow enough memory for the individual server processes and any other programs running on the system.

Iteration During Configuration

Configuring memory allocation involves distributing available memory to Oracle Database memory structures, depending on the needs of the application. The distribution of memory to Oracle Database structures can affect the amount of physical I/O necessary for Oracle Database t operate. Having a good first initial memory configuration also provides an indication of whether the I/O system is effectively configured.

It might be necessary to repeat the steps of memory allocation after the initial pass through the process. Subsequent passes let you make adjustments in earlier steps, based on changes in later steps. For example, decreasing the size of the buffer cache lets you increase the size of another memory structure, such as the shared pool.

CONFIGURING AND USING THE BUFFER CACHE

For many types of operations, Oracle Database uses the buffer cache to store blocks read from disk. Oracle Database bypasses the buffer cache for particular operations, such as sorting and parallel reads. For operations that use the buffer cache, this section explains the following:

- Using the Buffer Cache Effectively
- Sizing the Buffer Cache
- Interpreting and Using the Buffer Cache Advisory Statistics
- Considering Multiple Buffer Pools.

Using the Buffer Cache Effectively

To use the buffer cache effectively, tune SQL statements for the application to avoid unnecessary resource consumption. To meet this goal, verify that frequently executed SQL statements and SQL statements that perform many buffer gets have been tuned.

When using parallel query, you can configure the database to use the database buffer cache instead of performing direct reads into the PGA. This configuration may be appropriate when the database servers have a large amount of memory.

Sizing the Buffer Cache

When configuring a new instance, it is impossible to know the correct size for the buffer cache. Typically, a database administrator makes a first estimate for the cache size, then runs a representative workload on the instance and examines the relevant statistics to see whether the cache is under or over configured.

Buffer Cache Advisory Statistics

You can use several statistics to examine buffer cache activity, including the following:

- V$DB_CACHE_ADVICE
- Buffer cache hit ratio.

Using V$DB_CACHE_ADVICE

This view is populated when the DB_CACHE_ADVICE initialization parameter is set to ON. This view shows the simulated miss rates for a range of potential buffer cache sizes.

Each cache size simulated has its own row in this view, with the predicted physical I/O activity that would take place for that size. The DB_CACHE_ADVICE parameter is dynamic, so the advisory can be enabled and disabled dynamically to allow you to collect advisory data for a specific workload.

There is some overhead associated with this advisory. When the advisory is enabled, there is a small increase in CPU usage, because additional bookkeeping is required.

Oracle Database uses DBA-based sampling to gather cache advisory statistics. Sampling substantially reduces both CPU and memory overhead associated with bookkeeping. Sampling is not used for a buffer pool if the number of buffers in that buffer pool is small to begin with.

To use V$DB_CACHE_ADVICE, the parameter DB_CACHE_ADVICE should be set to ON, and a representative workload should be running on the instance. Allow the workload to stabilize before querying the V$DB_CACHE_ADVICE view.

The following SQL statement returns the predicted I/O requirement for the default buffer pool for various cache sizes:

```
COLUMN size_for_estimate FORMAT 999,999,999,999 heading 'Cache Size
(MB)'
COLUMN buffers_for_estimate FORMAT 999,999,999 heading 'Buffers'
COLUMN estd_physical_read_factor FORMAT 999.90 heading 'Estd Phys|Read
Factor'
```

```
COLUMN estd_physical_reads FORMAT 999,999,999 heading 'Estd Phys|
Reads'

SELECT size_for_estimate, buffers_for_estimate,
       estd_physical_read_factor, estd_physical_reads
       FROM V$DB_CACHE_ADVICE WHERE name = 'DEFAULT'
       AND block_size = (SELECT value FROM V$PARAMETER WHERE
        name = 'db_block_size') AND advice_status = 'ON';
```

The following output shows that if the cache was 212 MB, rather than the current size of 304 MB, the estimated number of physical reads would increase by a factor of 1.74 or 74%. This means it would not be advisable to decrease the cache size to 212 MB.

However, increasing the cache size to 334 MB would potentially decrease reads by a factor of .93 or 7%. If an additional 30 MB memory is available on the host computer and the `SGA_MAX_SIZE` setting allows the increment, it would be advisable to increase the default buffer cache pool size to 334 MB.

This view assists in cache sizing by providing information that predicts the number of physical reads for each potential cache size. The data also includes a physical read factor, which is a factor by which the current number of physical reads is estimated to change if the buffer cache is resized to a given value.

With Oracle Database, physical reads do not necessarily indicate disk reads; physical reads may well be satisfied from the file system cache.

The relationship between successfully finding a block in the cache and the size of the cache is not always a smooth distribution. When sizing the buffer pool, avoid the use of additional buffers that contribute little or nothing to the cache hit ratio. In the example illustrated in Figure 7.1, only narrow bands of increments to the cache size may be worthy of consideration.

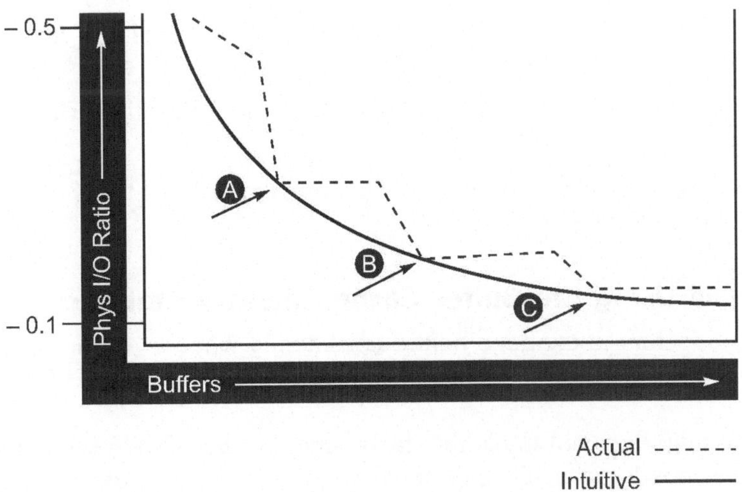

Figure 7.1. Physical I/O and Buffer Cache Size

Examining Figure 7.1 leads to the following observations:

- The benefit from increasing buffers from point A to point B is considerably higher than from point B to point C.
- The decrease in the physical I/O between points A and B and points B and C is not smooth, as indicated by the dotted line in the graph.

Calculating the Buffer Cache Hit Ratio

The buffer cache hit ratio calculates how often a requested block has been found in the buffer cache without requiring disk access. This ratio is computed using data selected from the dynamic performance view `V$SYSSTAT`. You can use the buffer cache hit ratio to verify the physical I/O as predicted by `V$DB_CACHE_ADVICE`.

Table 7.1. Statistics for Calculating the Hit Ratio

Statistic	Description
`consistent gets from cache`	Number of times a consistent read was requested for a block from the buffer cache.
`db block gets from`	Number of times a CURRENT block was requested from the `cache` buffer cache.
`physical reads cache`	Total number of data blocks read from disk into buffer cache.

The statistics in Table 7.1 are used to calculate the hit ratio has been simplified by using values selected directly from the `V$SYSSTAT` table, rather than over an interval. It is best to calculate the delta of these statistics over an interval while your application is running, then use them to determine the hit ratio.

Example 7.1: Calculating the Buffer Cache Hit Ratio

```
SELECT NAME, VALUE
       FROM V$SYSSTAT
WHERE NAME IN ('db block gets from cache', 'consistent gets from cache',
'physical reads cache');
```

Using the values in the output of the query, calculate the hit ratio for the buffer cache with the following formula:

```
1 - (('physical reads cache') / ('consistent gets from cache' + 'db
block gets from cache')
```

Interpreting and Using the Buffer Cache Advisory Statistics

There are many factors to examine before considering whether to increase or decrease the buffer cache size. For example, you should examine `V$DB_CACHE_ADVICE` data and the buffer cache hit ratio.

A low cache hit ratio does not imply that increasing the size of the cache would be beneficial for performance. A good cache hit ratio could wrongly indicate that the cache is adequately sized for the workload.

To interpret the buffer cache hit ratio, you should consider the following:

- Repeated scanning of the same large table or index can artificially inflate a poor cache hit ratio. Examine frequently executed SQL statements with a large number of buffer gets, to ensure that the execution plan for such SQL statements is optimal. If possible, avoid repeated scanning of frequently accessed data by performing all of the processing in a single pass or by optimizing the SQL statement.

- If possible, avoid requerying the same data, by caching frequently accessed data in the client program or middle tier.
- Database blocks accessed during a long full table scan are put on the tail end of the least recently used LRU list and not on the head of the list. Therefore, the blocks are aged out faster than blocks read when performing indexed lookups or small table scans. When interpreting the buffer cache data, poor hit ratios when valid large full table scans are occurring should also be considered.

Short table scans are scans performed on tables under a certain size threshold. The definition of a small table is the maximum of 2% of the buffer cache and 20, whichever is bigger.

- In any large database running OLTP applications in any given unit of time, most rows are accessed either one or zero times. On this basis, there might be little purpose in keeping the block in memory for very long following its use.
- A common mistake is to continue increasing the buffer cache size. Such increases have no effect if you are doing full table scans or operations that do not use the buffer cache.

Increasing Memory Allocated to the Buffer Cache

As a general rule, investigate increasing the size of the cache if the cache hit ratio is low and your application has been tuned to avoid performing full table scans.

To increase cache size, first set the `DB_CACHE_ADVICE` initialization parameter to ON, and let the cache statistics stabilize. Examine the advisory data in the `V$DB_CACHE_ADVICE` view to determine the next increment required to significantly decrease the amount of physical I/O performed. If it is possible to allocate the required extra memory to the buffer cache without causing the host operating system to page, then allocate this memory. To increase the amount of memory allocated to the buffer cache, increase the value of the `DB_CACHE_SIZE` initialization parameter.

If required, resize the buffer pools dynamically, rather than shutting down the instance to perform this change.

When the cache is resized significantly (greater than 20%), the old cache advisory value is discarded and the cache advisory is set to the new size. Otherwise, the old cache advisory value is adjusted to the new size by the interpolation of existing values.

The `DB_CACHE_SIZE` parameter specifies the size of the default cache for the database's standard block size. To create and use tablespaces with block sizes different than the database's standard block sizes (such as to support transportable tablespaces), you must configure a separate cache for each block size used. You can use the `DB_nK_CACHE_SIZE` parameter to configure the nonstandard block size needed (where *n* is 2, 4, 8, 16 or 32 and *n* is not the standard block size).

The process of choosing a cache size is the same, regardless of whether the cache is the default standard block size cache, the KEEP or RECYCLE cache, or a nonstandard block size cache.

Reducing Memory Allocated to the Buffer Cache

If the cache hit ratio is high, then the cache is probably large enough to hold the most frequently accessed data. Check V$DB_CACHE_ADVICE data to see whether decreasing the cache size significantly causes the number of physical I/Os to increase. If not, and if you require memory for another memory structure, then you might be able to reduce the cache size and still maintain good performance. To make the buffer cache smaller, reduce the size of the cache by changing the value for the parameter DB_CACHE_SIZE.

Considering Multiple Buffer Pools

A single default buffer pool is generally adequate for most systems. However, users with detailed knowledge of an application's buffer pool might benefit from configuring multiple buffer pools.

With segments that have atypical access patterns, store blocks from those segments in two different buffer pools: the KEEP pool and the RECYCLE pool. A segment's access pattern may be atypical if it is constantly accessed (that is, hot) or infrequently accessed (for example, a large segment accessed by a batch job only once a day).

Multiple buffer pools let you address these differences. You can use a KEEP buffer pool to maintain frequently accessed segments in the buffer cache, and a RECYCLE buffer pool to prevent objects from consuming unnecessary space in the cache. When an object is associated with a cache, all blocks from that object are placed in that cache. Oracle Database maintains a DEFAULT buffer pool for objects that have not been assigned to a specific buffer pool. The default buffer pool is of size DB_CACHE_SIZE. Each buffer pool uses the same Least Recently Used (LRU) replacement policy (for example, if the KEEP pool is not large enough to store all of the segments allocated to it, then the oldest blocks age out of the cache).

By allocating objects to appropriate buffer pools, you can:

- Reduce or eliminate I/Os
- Isolate or limit an object to a separate cache.

Random Access to Large Segments

A problem can occur with an LRU aging method when a very large segment is accessed with a large or unbounded index range scan. Here, very large means large compared to the size of the cache. Any single segment that accounts for a substantial portion (more than 10%) of nonsequential physical reads can be considered very large. Random reads to a large segment can cause buffers that contain data for other segments to be aged out of the cache. The large segment ends up consuming a large percentage of the cache, but it does not benefit from the cache.

Very frequently accessed segments are not affected by large segment reads because their buffers are warmed frequently enough that they do not age out of the cache. However, the problem affects warm segments that are not accessed frequently enough to survive the buffer aging caused by the large segment reads. There are three options for solving this problem:

1. If the object accessed is an index, find out whether the index is selective. If not, tune the SQL statement to use a more selective index.

2. If the SQL statement is tuned, you can move the large segment into a separate RECYCLE cache so that it does not affect the other segments. The RECYCLE cache should be smaller than the DEFAULT buffer pool, and it should reuse buffers more quickly than the DEFAULT buffer pool.
3. Alternatively, you can move the small warm segments into a separate KEEP cache that is not used at all for large segments. The KEEP cache can be sized to minimize misses in the cache. You can make the response times for specific queries more predictable by putting the segments accessed by the queries in the KEEP cache to ensure that they do not age out.

Oracle Real Application Clusters Instances

You can create multiple buffer pools for each database instance. The same set of buffer pools need not be defined for each instance of the database. Among instances, the buffer pools can be different sizes or not defined at all. Tune each instance according to the application requirements for that instance.

Using Multiple Buffer Pools

To define a default buffer pool for an object, use the BUFFER_POOL keyword of the STORAGE clause. This clause is valid for CREATE and ALTER TABLE, CLUSTER, and INDEX SQL statements. After a buffer pool has been specified, all subsequent blocks read for the object are placed in that pool.

If a buffer pool is defined for a partitioned table or index, then each partition of the object inherits the buffer pool from the table or index definition, unless you override it with a specific buffer pool.

When the buffer pool of an object is changed using the ALTER statement, all buffers currently containing blocks of the altered segment remain in the buffer pool they were in before the ALTER statement. Newly loaded blocks and any blocks that have aged out and are reloaded go into the new buffer pool.

Buffer Pool Data in V$DB_CACHE_ADVICE

You can use V$DB_CACHE_ADVICE to size all pools configured on a database instance. Make the initial cache size estimate, run the representative workload, then simply query the V$DB_CACHE_ADVICE view for the pool you want to use.

For example, to query data from the KEEP pool:

```
SELECT SIZE_FOR_ESTIMATE, BUFFERS_FOR_ESTIMATE,
ESTD_PHYSICAL_READ_FACTOR, ESTD_PHYSICAL_READS FROM V$DB_CACHE_ADVICE
WHERE NAME = 'KEEP' AND BLOCK_SIZE = (SELECT VALUE FROM V$PARAMETER
WHERE NAME = 'db_block_size')AND ADVICE_STATUS = 'ON';
```

Buffer Pool Hit Ratios

The data in V$SYSSTAT reflects the logical and physical reads for all buffer pools within one set of statistics. To determine the hit ratio for the buffer pools individually, query the V$BUFFER_POOL_STATISTICS view. This view maintains statistics for each pool on the number of logical reads and writes.

The buffer pool hit ratio can be determined using the following formula:

```
1 - (physical_reads/(db_block_gets + consistent_gets))
```

The ratio can be calculated with the following query:

```
SELECT NAME, PHYSICAL_READS, DB_BLOCK_GETS, CONSISTENT_GETS,1 -
(PHYSICAL_READS / (DB_BLOCK_GETS + CONSISTENT_GETS)) "Hit Ratio" FROM
V$BUFFER_POOL_STATISTICS;
```

Determining which Segments have Many Buffers in the Pool

The V$BH view shows the data object ID of all blocks that currently reside in the SGA. To determine which segments have many buffers in the pool, you can use one of the two methods described in this section. You can either look at the buffer cache usage pattern for all segments (Method 1) or examine the usage pattern of a specific segment, (Method 2).

Method 1: The following query counts the number of blocks for all segments that reside in the buffer cache at that point in time. Depending on buffer cache size, this might require a lot of sort space.

```
COLUMN OBJECT_NAME FORMAT A40
COLUMN NUMBER_OF_BLOCKS FORMAT 999,999,999,999

SELECT o.OBJECT_NAME, COUNT(*) NUMBER_OF_BLOCKS
 FROM DBA_OBJECTS o, V$BH bh
 WHERE o.DATA_OBJECT_ID = bh.OBJD
 AND o.OWNER != 'SYS'
 GROUP BY o.OBJECT_NAME
 ORDER BY COUNT(*);
     OBJECT_NAME                                        NUMBER_OF_BLOCKS
--------------------------------------------------------------------------
     OA_PREF_UNIQ_KEY                                                  1
     SYS_C002651                                                       1
     ..
     DS_PERSON                                                        78
     OM_EXT_HEADER                                                   701
     OM_SHELL                                                      1,765
     OM_HEADER                                                     5,826
     OM_INSTANCE                                                  12,644
```

Method 2: Use the following steps to determine the percentage of the cache used by an individual object at a given point in time:

1. Find the Oracle Database internal object number of the segment by entering the following query:

   ```
   SELECT DATA_OBJECT_ID, OBJECT_TYPE
         FROM DBA_OBJECTS
         WHERE OBJECT_NAME = UPPER('segment_name');
   ```

   Because two objects can have the same name (if they are different types of objects), use the `OBJECT_TYPE` column to identify the object of interest.

2. Find the number of buffers in the buffer cache for `SEGMENT_NAME`:

   ```
   SELECT COUNT(*) BUFFERS
         FROM V$BH WHERE OBJD = data_object_id_value;
   ```

   where *`data_object_id_value`* is from step 1.

3. Find the number of buffers in the instance:

```
SELECT NAME, BLOCK_SIZE, SUM(BUFFERS)
      FROM V$BUFFER_POOL GROUP BY NAME, BLOCK_SIZE
      HAVING SUM(BUFFERS) 0;
```

4. Calculate the ratio of buffers to total buffers to obtain the percentage of the cache currently used by SEGMENT_NAME:

```
% cache used by segment_name = [buffers(Step2)/total
buffers(Step3)]
```

This technique works only for a single segment. You must run the query for each partition for a partitioned object.

KEEP Pool

If there are certain segments in your application that are referenced frequently, then store the blocks from those segments in a separate cache called the KEEP buffer pool. Memory is allocated to the KEEP buffer pool by setting the parameter DB_KEEP_CACHE_SIZE to the required size. The memory for the KEEP pool is not a subset of the default pool. Typical segments that can be kept are small reference tables that are used frequently. Application developers and DBAs can determine which tables are candidates.You can check the number of blocks from candidate tables by querying V$BH.

The NOCACHE clause has no effect on a table in the KEEP cache.

The goal of the KEEP buffer pool is to retain objects in memory, thus avoiding I/O operations. The size of the KEEP buffer pool, therefore, depends on the objects to be kept in the buffer cache. You can compute an approximate size for the KEEP buffer pool by adding the blocks used by all objects assigned to this pool. If you gather statistics on the segments, you can query DBA_TABLES.BLOCKS and DBA_TABLES.EMPTY_BLOCKS to determine the number of blocks used.

Calculate the hit ratio by taking two snapshots of system performance at different times, using the previous query. Subtract the more recent values for physical reads, block gets, and consistent gets from the older values, and use the results to compute the hit ratio.

A buffer pool hit ratio of 100% might not be optimal. Often, you can decrease the size of your KEEP buffer pool and still maintain a sufficiently high hit ratio. Allocate blocks removed from the KEEP buffer pool to other buffer pools.

If an object grows in size, then it might no longer fit in the KEEP buffer pool. You will begin to lose blocks out of the cache.

Each object kept in memory results in a trade-off. It is beneficial to keep frequently-accessed blocks in the cache, but retaining infrequently-used blocks results in less space for other, more active blocks.

RECYCLE Pool

It is possible to configure a RECYCLE buffer pool for blocks belonging to those segments that you do not want to remain in memory. The RECYCLE pool is good for segments that are scanned rarely or are not referenced frequently. If an application accesses the blocks of a very large object in a random fashion, then there is little chance of reusing a block stored in the buffer pool before it is aged out. This is true regardless of the size of the buffer pool (given the constraint of the amount of available physical memory). Consequently, the object's blocks need not be cached; those cache buffers can be allocated to other objects.

Memory is allocated to the RECYCLE buffer pool by setting the parameter DB_RECYCLE_CACHE_SIZE to the required size. This memory for the RECYCLE buffer pool is not a subset of the default pool.

Do not discard blocks from memory too quickly. If the buffer pool is too small, then blocks can age out of the cache before the transaction or SQL statement has completed execution. For example, an application might select a value from a table, use the value to process some data, and then update the record. If the block is removed from the cache after the SELECT statement, then it must be read from disk again to perform the update. The block should be retained for the duration of the user transaction.

CONFIGURING AND USING THE SHARED POOL AND LARGE POOL

Oracle Database uses the shared pool to cache many different types of data. Cached data includes the textual and executable forms of PL/SQL blocks and SQL statements, dictionary cache data, result cache data, and other data.

Proper use and sizing of the shared pool can reduce resource consumption in at least four ways:

- Parse overhead is avoided if the SQL statement is in the shared pool. This saves CPU resources on the host and elapsed time for the end user.
- Latching resource usage is significantly reduced, which results in greater scalability.
- Shared pool memory requirements are reduced, because all applications use the same pool of SQL statements and dictionary resources.
- I/O resources are saved, because dictionary elements that are in the shared pool do not require disk access.

This section covers the following:

- Shared Pool Concepts
- Using the Shared Pool Effectively
- Sizing the Shared Pool
- Interpreting Shared Pool Statistics
- Using the Large Pool
- Using CURSOR_SPACE_FOR_TIME
- Caching Session Cursors
- Configuring the Reserved Pool
- Keeping Large Objects to Prevent Aging
- Sharing Cursors for Existing Applications
- Maintaining Connections.

The **server result cache** is an optional cache of query and function results within the shared pool.

Shared Pool Concepts

The main components of the shared pool are the library cache, the dictionary cache, and, depending on your configuration, the server result cache. The library cache stores the executable (parsed or compiled) form of recently referenced SQL and PL/SQL code. The dictionary cache stores data referenced from the data dictionary. The server result cache stores the results of queries and PL/SQL function results.

Many of the caches in the shared pool automatically increase or decrease in size, as needed, including the library cache and the dictionary cache. Old entries are aged out to accommodate new entries when the shared pool does not have free space.

A cache miss on the data dictionary cache or library cache is more expensive than a miss on the buffer cache. For this reason, the shared pool should be sized to ensure that frequently used data is cached.

Several features make large memory allocations in the shared pool: for example, the shared server, parallel query, or Recovery Manager. Oracle recommends segregating the SGA memory used by these features by configuring a distinct memory area, called the large pool.

Allocation of memory from the shared pool is performed in chunks. This chunking enables large objects (over 5 KB) to be loaded into the cache without requiring a single contiguous area. In this way, the database reduces the possibility of running out of enough contiguous memory due to fragmentation.

Infrequently, Java, PL/SQL, or SQL cursors may make allocations out of the shared pool that are larger than 5 KB. To allow these allocations to occur most efficiently, Oracle Database segregates a small amount of the shared pool. This memory is used if the shared pool does not have enough space. The segregated area of the shared pool is called the reserved pool.

Dictionary Cache Concepts

Information stored in the data dictionary cache includes usernames, segment information, profile data, tablespace information, and sequence numbers. The dictionary cache also stores descriptive information, or metadata, about schema objects. Oracle Database uses this metadata when parsing SQL cursors or during the compilation of PL/SQL programs.

Library Cache Concepts

The library cache holds executable forms of SQL cursors, PL/SQL programs, and Java classes. This section focuses on tuning as it relates to cursors, PL/SQL programs, and Java classes. These are collectively referred to as application code.

When application code is run, Oracle Database attempts to reuse existing code if it has been executed previously and can be shared. If the parsed representation of the statement does exist in the library cache and it can be shared, then the database reuses the existing code. This is known as a **soft parse**, or a **library cache hit.** If Oracle Database cannot use existing code, then the database must build a new executable version of the application code. This is known as a **hard parse**, or a **library cache miss.**

Library cache misses can occur on either the parse step or the execute step when processing a SQL statement. When an application makes a parse call for a SQL statement, if the parsed representation of the statement does not exist in the library cache, then Oracle Database parses the statement and stores the parsed form in the shared pool. This is a hard parse. You might be able to reduce library cache misses on parse calls by ensuring that all sharable SQL statements are in the shared pool whenever possible.

If an application makes an execute call for a SQL statement, and if the executable portion of the previously built SQL statement has been aged out (that is, deallocated) from the library cache to make room for another statement, then Oracle Database implicitly reparses the statement, creating a new shared SQL area for it, and executes it. This also results in a hard parse. Usually, you can reduce library cache misses on execution calls by allocating more memory to the library cache.

In order to perform a hard parse, Oracle Database uses more resources than during a soft parse. Resources used for a soft parse include CPU and library cache latch gets. Resources required for a hard parse include additional CPU, library cache latch gets, and shared pool latch gets.

SQL Sharing Criteria

Oracle Database automatically determines whether a SQL statement or PL/SQL block being issued is identical to another statement currently in the shared pool.

Oracle Database performs the following steps to compare the text of the SQL statement to existing SQL statements in the shared pool:

1. The text of the statement is hashed. If there is no matching hash value, then the SQL statement does not currently exist in the shared pool, and a hard parse is performed.
2. If there is a matching hash value for an existing SQL statement in the shared pool, then Oracle Database compares the text of the matched statement to the text of the statement hashed to see if they are identical. The text of the SQL statements or PL/SQL blocks must be identical, character for character, including spaces, case, and comments. For example, the following statements cannot use the same shared SQL area:

   ```
   SELECT * FROM employees;
   SELECT * FROM Employees;
   SELECT * FROM  employees;
   ```

   Usually, SQL statements that differ only in literals cannot use the same shared SQL area. For example, the following statements do not resolve to the same SQL area:

   ```
   SELECT count(1) FROM employees WHERE manager_id = 121;
   SELECT count(1) FROM employees WHERE manager_id = 247;
   ```

   The only exception to this rule is when the parameter CURSOR_SHARING has been set to `SIMILAR` or `FORCE`. Similar statements can share SQL areas when the `CURSOR_SHARING` is set to `SIMILAR` or `FORCE`.
3. The objects referenced in the issued statement are compared to the referenced objects of all existing statements in the shared pool to ensure that they are identical.

   References to schema objects in the SQL statements or PL/SQL blocks must resolve to the same object in the same schema. For example, if two users each issue the following SQL statement and they each have their own `employees` table, then this statement is not considered identical, because the statement references different tables for each user:

   ```
   SELECT * FROM employees;
   ```

4. Bind variables in the SQL statements must match in name, data type, and length. For example, the following statements cannot use the same shared SQL area, because the bind variable names differ:

```
SELECT * FROM employees WHERE department_id = :department_id;
SELECT * FROM employees WHERE department_id = :dept_id;
```

   Many Oracle products, such as Oracle Forms and the precompilers, convert the SQL before passing statements to the database. Characters are uniformly changed to uppercase, white space is compressed, and bind variables are renamed so that a consistent set of SQL statements is produced.
5. The session's environment must be identical. For example, SQL statements must be optimized using the same optimization goal.

Using the Shared Pool Effectively

An important purpose of the shared pool is to cache the executable versions of SQL and PL/SQL statements. This allows multiple executions of the same SQL or PL/SQL code to be performed without the resources required for a hard parse, which results in significant reductions in CPU, memory, and latch usage.

The shared pool is also able to support unshared SQL in data warehousing applications, which execute low-concurrency, high-resource SQL statements. In this situation, using unshared SQL with literal values is recommended. Using literal values rather than bind variables allows the optimizer to make good column selectivity estimates, thus providing an optimal data access plan.

In an OLTP system, there are several ways to ensure efficient use of the shared pool and related resources. Discuss the following items with application developers and agree on strategies to ensure that the shared pool is used effectively:

- Shared Cursors
- Single-User Logon and Qualified Table Reference
- Use of PL/SQL
- Avoid Performing DDL
- Cache Sequence Numbers
- Cursor Access and Management.

Efficient use of the shared pool in high-concurrency OLTP systems significantly reduces the probability of parse-related application scalability issues.

Shared Cursors

Reuse of shared SQL for multiple users running the same application, avoids hard parsing. Soft parses provide a significant reduction in the use of resources such as the shared pool and library cache latches. To share cursors, do the following:

- Use bind variables rather than literals in SQL statements whenever possible. For example, the following two statements cannot use the same shared area because they do not match character for character:
- `SELECT employee_id FROM employees WHERE department_id = 10;`
- `SELECT employee_id FROM employees WHERE department_id = 20;`

  By replacing the literals with a bind variable, only one SQL statement would result, which could be executed twice:

```
SELECT employee_id FROM employees WHERE department_id = :dept_id;
```

For existing applications where rewriting the code to use bind variables is impractical, you can use the `CURSOR_SHARING` initialization parameter to avoid some of the hard parse overhead.

- Avoid application designs that result in large numbers of users issuing dynamic, unshared SQL statements. Typically, the majority of data required by most users can be satisfied using preset queries. Use dynamic SQL where such functionality is required.
- Ensure that users of the application do not change the optimization approach and goal for their individual sessions.
- Establish the following policies for application developers:
    - Standardize naming conventions for bind variables and spacing conventions for SQL statements and PL/SQL blocks.
    - Consider using stored procedures whenever possible. Multiple users issuing the same stored procedure use the same shared PL/SQL area automatically. Because stored procedures are stored in a parsed form, their use reduces run-time parsing.
- For SQL statements which are identical but are not being shared, you can query `V$SQL_SHARED_CURSOR` to determine why the cursors are not shared. This would include optimizer settings and bind variable mismatches.

Single-User Logon and Qualified Table Reference

Large OLTP systems where users log in to the database as their own user ID can benefit from explicitly qualifying the segment owner, rather than using public synonyms. This significantly reduces the number of entries in the dictionary cache. For example:

```
SELECT employee_id FROM hr.employees WHERE department_id = :dept_id;
```

An alternative to qualifying table names is to connect to the database through a single user ID, rather than individual user IDs. User-level validation can take place locally on the middle tier. Reducing the number of distinct userIDs also reduces the load on the dictionary cache.

Use of PL/SQL

Using stored PL/SQL packages can overcome many of the scalability issues for systems with thousands of users, each with individual user sign-on and public synonyms. This is because a package is executed as the owner, rather than the caller, which reduces the dictionary cache load considerably.

Oracle encourages the use of definer's rights packages to overcome scalability issues. The benefits of reduced dictionary cache load are not as obvious with invoker's rights packages.

Avoid Performing DDL

Avoid performing DDL operations on high-usage segments during peak hours. Performing DDL on such segments often results in the dependent SQL being invalidated and hence reparsed on a later execution.

Cache Sequence Numbers

Allocating sufficient cache space for frequently updated sequence numbers significantly reduces the frequency of dictionary cache locks, which improves scalability. The `CACHE` keyword on the `CREATE SEQUENCE` or `ALTER SEQUENCE` statement lets you configure the number of cached entries for each sequence.

Cursor Access and Management

Depending on the application tool that you are using, you can control how frequently your application performs parse calls.

The frequency with which your application either closes cursors or reuses existing cursors for new SQL statements affects the amount of memory used by a session and often the amount of parsing performed by that session.

An application that closes cursors or reuses cursors (for a different SQL statement), does not need as much session memory as an application that keeps cursors open. Conversely, that same application may need to perform more parse calls, using extra CPU and Oracle Database resources.

Cursors associated with SQL statements that are not executed frequently can be closed or reused for other statements, because the likelihood of reexecuting (and reparsing) that statement is low.

Extra parse calls are required when a cursor containing a SQL statement that will be reexecuted is closed or reused for another statement. Had the cursor remained open, it could have been reused without the overhead of issuing a parse call.

The ways in which you control cursor management depends on your application development tool. The following sections introduce the methods used for some Oracle Database t.

Reducing Parse Calls with OCI: When using Oracle Call Interface (OCI), do not close and reopen cursors that you will be reexecuting. Instead, leave the cursors open, and change the literal values in the bind variables before execution.

Avoid reusing statement handles for new SQL statements when the existing SQL statement will be reexecuted in the future.

Reducing Parse Calls with the Oracle Precompilers: When using the Oracle precompilers, you can control when cursors are closed by setting precompiler clauses. In Oracle mode, the clauses are as follows:

- `HOLD_CURSOR = YES`
- `RELEASE_CURSOR = NO`
- `MAXOPENCURSORS =` *`desired_value`*

Oracle Database recommends that you not use ANSI mode, in which the values of `HOLD_CURSOR` and `RELEASE_CURSOR` are switched.

The precompiler clauses can be specified on the precompiler command line or within the precompiler program. With these clauses, you can employ different strategies for managing cursors during execution of the program.

Reducing Parse Calls with SQLJ: Prepare the statement, then reexecute the statement with the new values for the bind variables. The cursor stays open for the duration of the session.

Reducing Parse Calls with JDBC: Avoid closing cursors if they will be reexecuted, because the new literal values can be bound to the cursor for reexecution. Alternatively, JDBC provides a SQL statement cache within the JDBC client using the `setStmtCacheSize()` method. Using this method, JDBC creates a SQL statement cache that is local to the JDBC program.

Reducing Parse Calls with Oracle Forms: With Oracle Forms, it is possible to control some aspects of cursor management. You can exercise this control either at the trigger level, at the form level, or at run-time.

Sizing the Shared Pool

When configuring a brand new instance, it is impossible to know the correct size to make the shared pool cache. Typically, a DBA makes a first estimate for the cache size, then runs a representative workload on the instance, and examines the relevant statistics to see whether the cache is under-configured or over-configured.

For most OLTP applications, shared pool size is an important factor in application performance. Shared pool size is less important for applications that issue a very limited number of discrete SQL statements, such as Decision Support Systems (DSS).

If the shared pool is too small, then extra resources are used to manage the limited amount of available space. This consumes CPU and latching resources, and causes contention. Optimally, the shared pool should be just large enough to cache frequently accessed objects. Having a significant amount of free memory in the shared pool is a waste of memory. When examining the statistics after the database has been running, a DBA should check that none of these mistakes are in the workload.

Shared Pool: Library Cache Statistics

When sizing the shared pool, the goal is to ensure that SQL statements that will be executed multiple times are cached in the library cache, without allocating too much memory.

The statistic that shows the amount of reloading (that is, reparsing) of a previously cached SQL statement that was aged out of the cache is the `RELOADS` column in the `V$LIBRARYCACHE` view. In an application that reuses SQL effectively, on a system with an optimal shared pool size, the `RELOADS` statistic will have a value near zero.

The `INVALIDATIONS` column in `V$LIBRARYCACHE` view shows the number of times library cache data was invalidated and had to be reparsed. `INVALIDATIONS` should be near zero. This means SQL statements that could have been shared were invalidated by some operation (for example, a DDL). This statistic should be near zero on OLTP systems during peak loads.

Another key statistic is the amount of free memory in the shared pool at peak times. The amount of free memory can be queried from V$SGASTAT, looking at the free memory for the shared pool. Optimally, free memory should be as low as possible, without causing any reloads on the system.

Lastly, a broad indicator of library cache health is the library cache hit ratio. This value should be considered along with the other statistics discussed in this section and other data, such as the rate of hard parsing and whether there is any shared pool or library cache latch contention.

These statistics are discussed in more detail in the following section.

V$LIBRARYCACHE

You can monitor statistics reflecting library cache activity by examining the dynamic performance view `V$LIBRARYCACHE`. These statistics reflect all library cache activity after the most recent instance startup.

Each row in this view contains statistics for one type of item kept in the library cache. The item described by each row is identified by the value of the `NAMESPACE` column. Rows with the following `NAMESPACE` values reflect library cache activity for SQL statements and PL/SQL blocks:

- `SQL AREA`
- `TABLE/PROCEDURE`
- `BODY`
- `TRIGGER`

Rows with other NAMESPACE values reflect library cache activity for object definitions that Oracle Database uses for dependency maintenance.

To examine each namespace individually, use the following query:

```
SELECT NAMESPACE, PINS, PINHITS, RELOADS, INVALIDATIONS
 FROM V$LIBRARYCACHE
 ORDER BY NAMESPACE;
```

The output of this query could look like the following:

NAMESPACE	PINS	PINHITS	RELOADS	INVALIDATIONS
BODY	8870	8819	0	0
CLUSTER	393	380	0	0
INDEX	29	0	0	0
OBJECT	0	0	0	0
PIPE	55265	55263	0	0
SQL AREA	21536413	21520516	11204	2
TABLE/PROCEDURE	10775684	10774401	0	0
TRIGGER	1852	1844	0	0

To calculate the library cache hit ratio, use the following formula:

```
Library Cache Hit Ratio = sum(pinhits) / sum(pins)
```

Using the library cache hit ratio formula, the cache hit ratio is the following:

```
SUM(PINHITS)/SUM(PINS)
----------------------
     .999466248
```

These queries return data from instance startup, rather than statistics gathered during an interval; interval statistics can better identify the problem.

Examining the returned data leads to the following observations:

- For the SQL AREA namespace, there were 21,536,413 executions.
- 11,204 of the executions resulted in a library cache miss, requiring Oracle Database t implicitly reparse a statement or block or reload an object definition because it aged out of the library cache (that is, a RELOAD).
- SQL statements were invalidated two times, again causing library cache misses.
- The hit percentage is about 99.94%. This means that only .06% of executions resulted in reparsing.

The amount of free memory in the shared pool is reported in V$SGASTAT. Report the current value from this view using the following query:

```
SELECT * FROM V$SGASTAT
 WHERE NAME = 'free memory'
   AND POOL = 'shared pool';
```

The output will be similar to the following:

POOL	NAME	BYTES
shared pool	free memory	4928280

If free memory is always available in the shared pool, then increasing the size of the pool offers little or no benefit. However, just because the shared pool is full does not necessarily mean there is a problem. It may be indicative of a well-configured system.

Shared Pool Advisory Statistics

The amount of memory available for the library cache can drastically affect the parse rate of an Oracle database instance. The shared pool advisory statistics provide a database administrator with information about library cache memory, allowing a DBA to predict how changes in the size of the shared pool can affect aging out of objects in the shared pool.

The shared pool advisory statistics track the library cache's use of shared pool memory and predict how the library cache will behave in shared pools of different sizes. Two fixed views provide the information to determine how much memory the library cache is using, how much is currently pinned, how much is on the shared pool's LRU list, and how much time might be lost or gained by changing the size of the shared pool.

The following views of the shared pool advisory statistics are available. These views display any data when shared pool advisory is on. These statistics reset when the advisory is turned off.

V$SHARED_POOL_ADVICE

This view displays information about estimated parse time in the shared pool for different pool sizes. The sizes range from 10% of the current shared pool size or the amount of pinned library cache memory, whichever is higher, to 200% of the current shared pool size, in equal intervals. The value of the interval depends on the current size of the shared pool.

V$LIBRARY_CACHE_MEMORY

This view displays information about memory allocated to library cache memory objects in different namespaces. A memory object is an internal grouping of memory for efficient management. A library cache object may consist of one or more memory objects.

V$JAVA_POOL_ADVICE and V$JAVA_LIBRARY_CACHE_MEMORY

These views contain Java pool advisory statistics that track information about library cache memory used for Java and predict how changes in the size of the Java pool can affect the parse rate.

`V$JAVA_POOL_ADVICE` displays information about estimated parse time in the Java pool for different pool sizes. The sizes range from 10% of the current Java pool size or the amount of pinned Java library cache memory, whichever is higher, to 200% of the current Java pool size, in equal intervals. The value of the interval depends on the current size of the Java pool.

Shared Pool: Dictionary Cache Statistics

Typically, if the shared pool is adequately sized for the library cache, it will also be adequate for the dictionary cache data.

Misses on the data dictionary cache are to be expected in some cases. On instance startup, the data dictionary cache contains no data. Therefore, any SQL statement issued is likely to result in cache misses. As more data is read into the cache, the likelihood of cache misses decreases. Eventually, the database reaches a steady state, in which the most frequently used dictionary data is in the cache. At this point, very few cache misses occur.

Each row in the `V$ROWCACHE` view contains statistics for a single type of data dictionary item. These statistics reflect all data dictionary activity since the most recent instance startup. The columns in the `V$ROWCACHE` view that reflect the use and effectiveness of the data dictionary cache are listed in Table 7.2.

Table 7.2. V$ROWCACHE Columns

Column	Description
PARAMETER	Identifies a particular data dictionary item. For each row, the value in this column is the item prefixed by dc_. For example, in the row that contains statistics for file descriptions, this column has the value dc_files.
GETS	Shows the total number of requests for information about the corresponding item. For example, in the row that contains statistics for file descriptions, this column has the total number of requests for file description data.
GETMISSES	Shows the number of data requests which were not satisfied by the cache, requiring an I/O.
MODIFICATIONS	Shows the number of times data in the dictionary cache was updated.

Use the following query to monitor the statistics in the V$ROWCACHE view over a period while your application is running. The derived column PCT_SUCC_GETS can be considered the item-specific hit ratio:

```
column parameter format a21
column pct_succ_gets format 999.9
column updates format 999,999,999

SELECT parameter, sum(gets) , sum(getmisses)
 , 100*sum(gets - getmisses) / sum(gets) pct_succ_gets
 , sum(modifications)updates FROM V$ROWCACHE
 WHERE gets 0
 GROUP BY parameter;
```

The output of this query will be similar to the following:

```
PARAMETER UPDATES           SUM(GETS)   SUM(GETMISSES)   PCT_SUCC_GETS
-----------------------   ----------    --------------   -------------
dc_database_links                  81                1            98.8
0
dc_free_extents                 44876            20301            54.8
40,453
dc_global_oids                     42                9            78.6
0
dc_histogram_defs                9419              651            93.1
0
dc_object_ids                   29854              239            99.2
52
dc_objects                      33600              590            98.2
53
```

```
dc_profiles                   19001          1       100.0
0
dc_rollback_segments          47244         16       100.0
19
dc_segments                  100467      19042        81.0
40,272
dc_sequence_grants              119         16        86.6
0
dc_sequences                  26973         16        99.9
26,811
dc_synonyms                    6617        168        97.5
0
dc_tablespace_quotas            120          7        94.2
51
dc_tablespaces               581248         10       100.0
0
dc_used_extents               51418      20249        60.6
42,811
dc_user_grants                76082         18       100.0
0
dc_usernames                 216860         12       100.0
0
dc_users                     376895         22       100.0
0
```

Examining the data returned by the sample query leads to these observations:

- There are large numbers of misses and updates for used extents, free extents, and segments. This implies that the instance had a significant amount of dynamic space extension.
- Based on the percentage of successful gets, and comparing that statistic with the actual number of gets, the shared pool is large enough to store dictionary cache data adequately.

It is also possible to calculate an overall dictionary cache hit ratio using the following formula; however, summing up the data over all the caches will lose the finer granularity of data:

```
SELECT (SUM(GETS - GETMISSES - FIXED)) / SUM(GETS) "ROW CACHE" FROM
V$ROWCACHE;
```

Interpreting Shared Pool Statistics

Shared pool statistics indicate adjustments that can be made. The following sections describe some of your choices.

Increasing Memory Allocation

Increasing the amount of memory for the shared pool increases the amount of memory available to the library cache, the dictionary cache, and the result.

Allocating Additional Memory for the Library Cache

To ensure that shared SQL areas remain in the cache after their SQL statements are parsed, increase the amount of memory available to the library cache until the `V$LIBRARYCACHE.RELOADS` value is near zero. To increase the amount of memory available to the library cache, increase the value of the initialization parameter `SHARED_POOL_SIZE`. The maximum value for this parameter depends on your operating system. This measure reduces implicit reparsing of SQL statements and PL/SQL blocks on execution.

Allocating Additional Memory to the Data Dictionary Cache

Examine cache activity by monitoring the `GETS` and `GETMISSES` columns. For frequently accessed dictionary caches, the ratio of total `GETMISSES` to total `GETS` should be less than 10% or 15%, depending on the application.

Consider increasing the amount of memory available to the cache if all of the following are true:

- Your application is using the shared pool effectively.
- Your system has reached a steady state, any of the item-specific hit ratios are low, and there are a large numbers of gets for the caches with low hit ratios.

Increase the amount of memory available to the data dictionary cache by increasing the value of the initialization parameter `SHARED_POOL_SIZE`.

Reducing Memory Allocation

If your `RELOADS` are near zero, and if you have a small amount of free memory in the shared pool, then the shared pool is probably large enough to hold the most frequently accessed data.

If you always have significant amounts of memory free in the shared pool, and if you would like to allocate this memory elsewhere, then you might be able to reduce the shared pool size and still maintain good performance.

To make the shared pool smaller, reduce the size of the cache by changing the value for the parameter `SHARED_POOL_SIZE`.

Using the Large Pool

Unlike the shared pool, the large pool does not have an LRU list. Oracle Database does not attempt to age objects out of the large pool.

You should consider configuring a large pool if your instance uses any of the following:

- Parallel query Parallel query uses shared pool memory to cache parallel execution message buffers.
- Recovery Manager Recovery Manager uses the shared pool to cache I/O buffers during backup and restore operations. For I/O server processes and backup and restore operations, Oracle Database allocates buffers that are a few hundred kilobytes in size.
- Shared server

In a shared server architecture, the session memory for each client process is included in the shared pool.

Tuning the Large Pool and Shared Pool for the Shared Server Architecture

As Oracle Database allocates shared pool memory for shared server session memory, the amount of shared pool memory available for the library cache and dictionary cache decreases.

If you allocate this session memory from a different pool, then Oracle Database can use the shared pool primarily for caching shared SQL and not incur the performance overhead from shrinking the shared SQL cache.

Oracle Database recommends using the large pool to allocate the shared server-related User Global Area (UGA), rather that using the shared pool. This is because Oracle Database uses the shared pool to allocate System Global Area (SGA) memory for other purposes, such as shared SQL and PL/SQL procedures. Using the large pool instead of the shared pool decreases fragmentation of the shared pool.

To store shared server-related UGA in the large pool, specify a value for the initialization parameter `LARGE_POOL_SIZE`. To see which pool (shared pool or large pool) the memory for an object resides in, check the column `POOL` in `V$SGASTAT`. The large pool is not configured by default; its minimum value is 300K. If you do not configure the large pool, then Oracle Database uses the shared pool for shared server user session memory.

Configure the size of the large pool based on the number of simultaneously active sessions. Each application requires a different amount of memory for session information, and your configuration of the large pool or SGA should reflect the memory requirement. For example, assuming that the shared server requires 200K to 300K to store session information for each active session. If you anticipate 100 active sessions simultaneously, then configure the large pool to be 30 M, or increase the shared pool accordingly if the large pool is not configured.

If a shared server architecture is used, then Oracle Database allocates some fixed amount of memory (about 10K) for each configured session from the shared pool, even if you have configured the large pool. The `CIRCUITS` initialization parameter specifies the maximum number of concurrent shared server connections that the database allows.

Determining an Effective Setting for Shared Server UGA Storage

The exact amount of UGA that Oracle Database uses depends on each application. To determine an effective setting for the large or shared pools, observe UGA use for a typical user and multiply this amount by the estimated number of user sessions.

Even though use of shared memory increases with shared servers, the total amount of memory use decreases. This is because there are fewer processes; therefore, Oracle Database uses less PGA memory with shared servers when compared to dedicated server environments.

For best performance with sorts using shared servers, set `SORT_AREA_SIZE` and `SORT_AREA_RETAINED_SIZE` to the same value. This keeps the sort result in the large pool instead of having it written to disk.

Checking System Statistics in the V$SESSTAT View

Oracle Database collects statistics on total memory used by a session and stores them in the dynamic performance view `V$SESSTAT`. Table 7.3 lists these statistics.

Table 7.3. V$SESSTAT Statistics Reflecting Memory

Statistic	Description
`session UGA memory`	The value of this statistic is the amount of memory in bytes allocated to the session.
`Session UGA memory max`	The value of this statistic is the maximum amount of memory in bytes ever allocated to the session.

To find the value, query `V$STATNAME`. If you are using a shared server, you can use the following query to decide how much larger to make the shared pool. Issue the following queries while your application is running:

```
SELECT SUM(VALUE) || 'BYTES' "TOTAL MEMORY FOR ALL SESSIONS"
 FROM V$SESSTAT, V$STATNAME
 WHERE NAME = 'session uga memory'
 AND V$SESSTAT.STATISTIC# = V$STATNAME.STATISTIC#;
SELECT SUM(VALUE) || 'BYTES' "TOTAL MAX MEM FOR ALL SESSIONS"
 FROM V$SESSTAT, V$STATNAME
 WHERE NAME = 'session uga memory max'
 AND V$SESSTAT.STATISTIC# = V$STATNAME.STATISTIC#;
```

These queries also select from the dynamic performance view V$STATNAME to obtain internal identifiers for session memory and max session memory. The results of these queries could look like the following:

```
TOTAL MEMORY FOR ALL SESSIONS
----------------------------------------------
157125 BYTES

TOTAL MAX MEM FOR ALL SESSIONS
------------------------------
417381 BYTES
```

The result of the first query indicates that the memory currently allocated to all sessions is 157,125 bytes. This value is the total memory with a location that depends on how the sessions are connected to Oracle. If the sessions are connected to dedicated server processes, then this memory is part of the memories of the user processes. If the sessions are connected to shared server processes, then this memory is part of the shared pool.

The result of the second query indicates that the sum of the maximum size of the memory for all sessions is 417,381 bytes. The second result is greater than the first because some sessions have deallocated memory since allocating their maximum amounts.

If you use a shared server architecture, you can use the result of either of these queries to determine how much larger to make the shared pool. The first value is likely to be a better estimate than the second unless nearly all sessions are likely to reach their maximum allocations at the same time.

Limiting Memory Use for Each User Session by Setting PRIVATE_SGA

You can set the `PRIVATE_SGA` resource limit to restrict the memory used by each client session from the `SGA.` `PRIVATE_SGA` defines the number of bytes of memory used from the SGA by a session. However, this parameter is used rarely, because most DBAs do not limit SGA consumption on a user-by-user basis.

Reducing Memory Use with Three-Tier Connections

If you have a high number of connected users, then you can reduce memory usage by implementing three-tier connections. This by-product of using a Transaction Process (TP) monitor is feasible only with pure transactional models because locks and uncommitted DMLs cannot be held between calls. A shared server environment offers the following advantages:

- It is much less restrictive of the application design than a TP monitor.
- It dramatically reduces operating system process count and context switches by enabling users to share a pool of servers.
- It substantially reduces overall memory usage, even though more SGA is used in shared server mode.

Using CURSOR_SPACE_FOR_TIME

If you have no library cache misses, then you might be able to accelerate execution calls by setting the value of the initialization parameter `CURSOR_SPACE_FOR_TIME` to true. This parameter specifies whether a cursor can be deallocated from the library cache to make room for a new SQL statement. `CURSOR_SPACE_FOR_TIME` has the following values meanings:

- If `CURSOR_SPACE_FOR_TIME` is set to `false` (the default), then a cursor can be deallocated from the library cache regardless of whether application cursors associated with its SQL statement are open. In this case, Oracle Database must verify that the cursor containing the SQL statement is in the library cache.
- If `CURSOR_SPACE_FOR_TIME` is set to `true`, then a cursor can be deallocated only when all application cursors associated with its statement are closed. In this case, Oracle Database need not verify that a cursor is in the cache because it cannot be deallocated while an application cursor associated with it is open.

Setting the value of the parameter to `true` saves Oracle Database a small amount of time and can slightly improve the performance of execution calls. This value also prevents the deallocation of cursors until associated application cursors are closed.

Do not set the value of `CURSOR_SPACE_FOR_TIME` to `true` if you have found library cache misses on execution calls. Such library cache misses indicate that the shared pool is not large enough to hold the shared SQL areas of all concurrently open cursors. If the value is `true`, and if the shared pool has no space for a new SQL statement, then the statement cannot be parsed, and Oracle Database returns an error saying that there is no more shared memory. If the value is `false`, and if there is no space for a new statement, then Oracle Database deallocates an existing cursor. Although deallocating a cursor could result in a library cache miss later (only if the cursor is reexecuted), it is preferable to an error halting your application because a SQL statement cannot be parsed.

Do not set the value of `CURSOR_SPACE_FOR_TIME` to `true` if the amount of memory available to each user for private SQL areas is scarce. This value also prevents the deallocation of private SQL areas associated with open cursors. If the private SQL areas for all concurrently open cursors fills your available memory so that there is no space for a new SQL statement, then the statement cannot be parsed. Oracle Database returns an error indicating that there is not enough memory.

Caching Session Cursors

The **session cursor cache** contains closed session cursors for SQL and PL/SQL, including recursive SQL.

This cache can be useful for applications that use Oracle Forms because switching from one form to another closes all session cursors associated with the first form. If an application repeatedly issues parse calls on the same set of SQL statements, then reopening session cursors can degrade performance. By reusing cursors, the database can reduce parse times, leading to faster overall execution times.

How the Session Cursor Cache Works

A **session cursor** represents an instantiation of a **shared child cursor**, which is stored in the shared pool, for a specific session. Each session cursor stores a reference to a child cursor that it has instantiated.

Oracle Database checks the library cache to determine whether more than three parse requests have been issued on a given statement. If a cursor has been closed three times, then Oracle Database assumes that the session cursor associated with the statement should be cached and moves the cursor into the session cursor cache.

Subsequent requests to parse a SQL statement by the same session search an array for pointers to the shared cursor. If the pointer is found, then the database dereferences the pointer to determine whether the shared cursor exists. To reuse a cursor from the cache, the cache manager checks whether the cached states of the cursor match the current session and system environment.

Reuse of a cached cursor still registers as a parse, even though it is not a hard parse.

An LRU algorithm removes entries in the session cursor cache to make room for new entries when needed. The cache also uses an internal time-based algorithm to evict cursors that have been idle for an certain amount of time.

Enabling the Session Cursor Cache

The following initialization parameters are relevant to the cursor cache:

- `SESSION_CACHED_CURSORS`
  This parameter sets the maximum number of cached closed cursors for each session. The default setting is 50. You can use this parameter to prevent a session from opening an excessive number of cursors, thereby filling the library cache or forcing excessive hard parses.
- `OPEN_CURSORS`
  This parameter specifies the maximum number of cursors a session can have open simultaneously. For example, if OPEN_CURSORS is set to 1000, then each session can have up to 1000 cursors open at one time.

`SESSION_CACHED_CURSORS` and `OPEN_CURSORS` parameters are independent. For example, you can set `SESSION_CACHED_CURSORS` higher than `OPEN_CURSORS` because session cursors are not cached in an open state.

To enable caching of session cursors:

1. Determine the maximum number of session cursors to keep in the cache.
2. Do one of the following:
   - To enable caching statically, set the initialization parameter `SESSION_CACHED_CURSORS` to the number determined in the previous step.
   - To enable caching dynamically, execute the following statement:
     `ALTER SESSION SET SESSION_CACHED_CURSORS = *value*;`

Tuning the Session Cursor Cache

You can query V$SYSSTAT to determine whether the session cursor cache is sufficiently large for the database instance.

To tune the session cursor cache:

1. Determine how many cursors are currently cached in a particular session.

For example, enter the following query for session 35:

```
SELECT a.value curr_cached, p.value max_cached,
s.username, s.sid, s.serial# FROM v$sesstat a, v$statname b,
v$session s, v$parameter2 p
WHERE a.statistic# = b.statistic# and s.sid=a.sid and a.sid=&sid AND
p.name='session_cached_cursors'
AND b.name = 'session cursor cache count';

Enter value for sid: 35
old 4: WHERE a.statistic# = b.statistic# and s.sid=a.sid and
a.sid=&sid
new 4: WHERE a.statistic# = b.statistic# and s.sid=a.sid and a.sid=35

CURR_CACHED        MAX_CACHED    USERNAME       SID        SERIAL#
------------------ ------------- -------------  -----      -----------
   49                 50           APP          35           263
```

The preceding result shows that the number of cursors currently cached for session 35 is close to the maximum.

2. Find the percentage of parse calls that found a cursor in the session cursor cache.

For example, enter the following query for session 35:

```
SELECT cach.value cache_hits, prs.value all_parses,
round((cach.value/prs.value)*100,2) as "% found in cache"
 FROM v$sesstat cach, v$sesstat prs, v$statname nm1,
 v$statname nm2 WHERE cach.statistic# = nm1.statistic#
 AND nm1.name = 'session cursor cache hits'
 AND prs.statistic#=nm2.statistic#
 AND nm2.name= 'parse count (total)'
 AND cach.sid= &sid and prs.sid= cach.sid;

Enter value for sid: 35
old 8: AND cach.sid= &sid and prs.sid= cach.sid
new 8: AND cach.sid= 35 and prs.sid= cach.sid

CACHE_HITS          ALL_PARSES         % found in cache
----------------    ----------------   --------------------------
        34            700                   4.57
```

The preceding result shows that the number of hits in the session cursor cache for session 35 is low compared to the total number of parses.

3. Consider increasing SESSION_CURSOR_CACHE when the following statements are true:
    - The session cursor cache count is close to the maximum.
    - The percentage of session cursor cache hits is low relative to the total parses.

- The application repeatedly makes parse calls for the same queries.

In this example, setting SESSION_CURSOR_CACHE to 100 may help boost performance.

Configuring the Reserved Pool

Although Oracle Database breaks down very large requests for memory into smaller chunks, on some systems there might still be a requirement to find a contiguous chunk (for example, over 5 KB) of memory. (The default minimum reserved pool allocation is 4,400 bytes.)

If there is not enough free space in the shared pool, then Oracle Database must search for and free enough memory to satisfy this request. This operation could conceivably hold the latch resource for detectable periods of time, causing minor disruption to other concurrent attempts at memory allocation.

Thus, Oracle Database internally reserves a small memory area in the shared pool that the database can use if the shared pool does not have enough space. This reserved pool makes allocation of large chunks more efficient.

By default, Oracle Database configures a small reserved pool. The database can use this memory for operations such as PL/SQL and trigger compilation or for temporary space while loading Java objects. After the memory allocated from the reserved pool is freed, it returns to the reserved pool.

You probably will not need to change the default amount of space Oracle Database reserves. However, if necessary, the reserved pool size can be changed by setting the SHARED_POOL_RESERVED_SIZE initialization parameter. This parameter sets aside space in the shared pool for unusually large allocations.

For large allocations, Oracle Database attempts to allocate space in the shared pool in the following order:

1. From the unreserved part of the shared pool.
2. From the reserved pool. If there is not enough space in the unreserved part of the shared pool, then Oracle Database checks whether the reserved pool has enough space.
3. From memory. If there is not enough space in the unreserved and reserved parts of the shared pool, then Oracle Database attempts to free enough memory for the allocation. It then retries the unreserved and reserved parts of the shared pool.

Using SHARED_POOL_RESERVED_SIZE

The default value for SHARED_POOL_RESERVED_SIZE is 5% of the SHARED_POOL_SIZE. This means that, by default, the reserved list is configured.

If you set SHARED_POOL_RESERVED_SIZE to more than half of SHARED_POOL_SIZE, then Oracle Database signals an error. Oracle Database does not let you reserve too much memory for the reserved pool. The amount of operating system memory, however, might constrain the size of the shared pool. In general, set SHARED_POOL_RESERVED_SIZE to 10% of SHARED_POOL_SIZE. For most systems, this value is sufficient if you have tuned the shared pool. If you increase this value, then the database takes memory from the shared pool. (This reduces the amount of unreserved shared pool memory available for smaller allocations.)

Statistics from the V$SHARED_POOL_RESERVED view help you tune these parameters. On a system with ample free memory to increase the size of the SGA, the goal is to have the value of REQUEST_MISSES equal zero. If the system is constrained for operating system memory, then the goal is to not have REQUEST_FAILURES or at least prevent this value from increasing.

If you cannot achieve these target values, then increase the value for SHARED_POOL_RESERVED_SIZE. Also, increase the value for SHARED_POOL_SIZE by the same amount, because the reserved list is taken from the shared pool.

When SHARED_POOL_RESERVED_SIZE is Too Small

The reserved pool is too small when the value for REQUEST_FAILURES is more than zero and increasing. To resolve this, increase the value for the SHARED_POOL_RESERVED_SIZE and SHARED_POOL_SIZE accordingly. The settings you select for these parameters depend on your system's SGA size constraints.

Increasing the value of SHARED_POOL_RESERVED_SIZE increases the amount of memory available on the reserved list without having an effect on users who do not allocate memory from the reserved list.

When SHARED_POOL_RESERVED_SIZE is Too Large

Too much memory might have been allocated to the reserved list if:

- REQUEST_MISSES is zero or not increasing
- FREE_SPACE is greater than or equal to 50% of SHARED_POOL_RESERVED_SIZE minimum.

If either of these conditions is true, then decrease the value for SHARED_POOL_RESERVED_SIZE.

When SHARED_POOL_SIZE is Too Small

The V$SHARED_POOL_RESERVED fixed view can also indicate when the value for SHARED_POOL_SIZE is too small. This can be the case if REQUEST_FAILURES is greater than zero and increasing.

If you have enabled the reserved list, then decrease the value for SHARED_POOL_RESERVED_SIZE. If you have not enabled the reserved list, then you could increase SHARED_POOL_SIZE.

Keeping Large Objects to Prevent Aging

After an entry has been loaded into the shared pool, it cannot be moved. Sometimes, as entries are loaded and aged, the free memory can become fragmented.

Use the PL/SQL package DBMS_SHARED_POOL to manage the shared pool. Shared SQL and PL/SQL areas age out of the shared pool according to a least recently used LRU algorithm, similar to database buffers. To improve performance and prevent reparsing, you might want to prevent large SQL or PL/SQL areas from aging out of the shared pool.

The DBMS_SHARED_POOL package lets you keep objects in shared memory, so that they do not age out with the normal LRU mechanism. By using the DBMS_SHARED_POOL package and by loading the SQL and PL/SQL areas before memory fragmentation occurs, the objects can be kept in memory. This ensures that memory is available, and it prevents the sudden, inexplicable slowdowns in user response time that occur when SQL and PL/SQL areas are accessed after aging out.

The DBMS_SHARED_POOL package is useful for the following:

- When loading large PL/SQL objects, such as the STANDARD and DIUTIL packages. When large PL/SQL objects are loaded, user response time may be affected if smaller objects that must age out of the shared pool to make room. In some cases, there might be insufficient memory to load the large objects.
- Frequently executed triggers. You might want to keep compiled triggers on frequently used tables in the shared pool.

- `DBMS_SHARED_POOL` supports sequences. Sequence numbers are lost when a sequence ages out of the shared pool. `DBMS_SHARED_POOL` keeps sequences in the shared pool, thus preventing the loss of sequence numbers.

To use the `DBMS_SHARED_POOL` package to pin a SQL or PL/SQL area, complete the following steps:

1. Decide which packages or cursors to pin in memory.
2. Start up the database.
3. Make the call to `DBMS_SHARED_POOL.KEEP` to pin your objects.

   This procedure ensures that your system does not run out of shared memory before the kept objects are loaded. By pinning the objects early in the life of the instance, you prevent memory fragmentation that could result from pinning a large portion of memory in the middle of the shared pool.

Sharing Cursors for Existing Applications

In the context of SQL parsing, an **identical statement** is a statement whose text is identical to another, character for character, including spaces, case, and comments. A **similar statement** is identical except for the values of some literals.

The parse phase compares the statement text with statements in the shared pool to determine whether the statement can be shared. If the initialization parameter `CURSOR_SHARING=EXACT` (default), and if a statement in the pool is not identical, then the database does not share the SQL area. Each statement has its own parent cursor and its own execution plan based on the literal in the statement.

How Similar Statements Can Share SQL Areas

When SQL statements use literals rather than bind variables, a nondefault setting for `CURSOR_SHARING` enables the database to replace literals with system-generated bind variables. Using this technique, the database can sometimes reduce the number of parent cursors in the shared SQL area.

When `CURSOR_SHARING` is set to a nondefault value, the database performs the following steps during the parse:

1. Searches for an identical statement in the shared pool:

   If an identical statement is found, then the database skips to Step 3. Otherwise, the database proceeds to the next step.
2. Searches for a similar statement in the shared pool:

   If a similar statement is *not* found, then the database performs a hard parse. If a similar statement *is* found, then the database proceeds to the next step.
3. Proceeds through the remaining steps of the parse phase to ensure that the execution plan of the existing statement is applicable to the new statement:

   If the plan is not applicable, then the database performs a hard parse. If the plan is applicable, then the database proceeds to the next step.
4. Shares the SQL area of the statement.

When to Set CURSOR_SHARING to a Nondefault Value

The best practice is to write sharable SQL and use the default of EXACT for `CURSOR_SHARING`. However, for applications with many similar statements, setting `CURSOR_SHARING` can significantly improve cursor sharing, resulting in reduced memory usage, faster parses, and reduced latch contention. Consider this approach when statements in the shared pool differ only in the values of literals, and when response time is poor because of a very high number of library cache misses.

If stored outlines were generated with CURSOR_SHARING set to EXACT, then the database does not use stored outlines generated with literals. To avoid this problem, generate outlines with CURSOR_SHARING set to FORCE or SIMILAR and use the CREATE_STORED_OUTLINES parameter.

Setting CURSOR_SHARING to FORCE or SIMILAR has the following drawbacks:

- The database must perform extra work during the soft parse to find a similar statement in the shared pool.
- There is an increase in the maximum lengths (as returned by DESCRIBE) of any selected expressions that contain literals in a SELECT statement. However, the actual length of the data returned does not change.
- Star transformation is not supported.
- Excessive child cursors may be generated if CURSOR_SHARING is set to SIMILAR.

When deciding whether to set CURSOR_SHARING to FORCE or SIMILAR, consider the performance implications of each setting. When CURSOR_SHARING is set to FORCE, the database uses one parent cursor and one child cursor for each distinct SQL statement. The database uses the same plan for each execution of the same statement. When set to SIMILAR, database behavior depends on the presence of histograms:

- Histogram absent for column with system-generated bind value:
  Only one parent cursor and one child cursor exists for each distinct SQL statement. In this case, all executions of a SQL statement use the same plan.
- Histogram present for column with system-generated bind value:
  If the same SQL statement is executed multiple times, each execution has its own child cursor. In this case, the database peeks at bind variable values and create a new child cursor for each distinct value. Thus, each statement execution uses a plan based on the specific literals in the statement.

For example, consider the following statement:

```
SELECT * FROM hr.employees WHERE employee_id = 101
```

If FORCE is used, or if SIMILAR is used when no histogram exists, then the database optimizes this statement as if it contained a bind variable and uses bind peeking to estimate cardinality. Statements that differ only in the bind variable share the same execution plan. If SIMILAR is used, and if a histogram *does* exist, then the database does not treat the statement as if a bind variable were used. The same query for a different employee may not use the same plan.

If you set CURSOR_SHARING, then Oracle recommends the FORCE setting unless you are in a DSS environment. FORCE limits the growth of child cursors that can occur when the setting is SIMILAR. Also, function-based indexes may not work when using SIMILAR because the database converts index parameters to bind variables. For example, if the index is SUBSTR(id,1,3), then the database converts it to SUBSTR("ID",:SYS_B_0,:SYS_B_1) =:id, rendering the index invalid.

In Oracle Database 11*g* Release 2, the number of child cursors in the shared pool associated with a single parent is no longer limited by the database. Setting CURSOR_SHARING to SIMILAR is not recommended. Consider using adaptive cursor sharing instead.

Maintaining Connections

Large OLTP applications with middle tiers should maintain connections, rather than connecting and disconnecting for each database request. Maintaining persistent connections saves CPU resources and database resources, such as latches.

CONFIGURING AND USING THE REDO LOG BUFFER

Server processes making changes to data blocks in the buffer cache generate redo data into the log buffer. LGWR begins writing to copy entries from the redo log buffer to the online redo log if any of the following are true:

- The log buffer becomes one third full
- LGWR is posted by a server process performing a `COMMIT` or `ROLLBACK`
- DBWR posts LGWR to do so.

When LGWR writes redo entries from the redo log buffer to a redo log file or disk, user processes can then copy new entries over the entries in memory that have been written to disk. LGWR usually writes fast enough to ensure that space is available in the buffer for new entries, even when access to the redo log is heavy.

A larger buffer makes it more likely that there is space for new entries, and also gives LGWR the opportunity to efficiently write out redo records (too small a log buffer on a system with large updates means that LGWR is continuously flushing redo to disk so that the log buffer remains 2/3 empty).

On computers with fast processors and relatively slow disks, the processors might be filling the rest of the buffer in the time it takes the redo log writer to move a portion of the buffer to disk. A larger log buffer can temporarily mask the effect of slower disks in this situation. Alternatively, you can do one of the following:

- Improve the checkpointing or archiving process
- Improve the performance of log writer (perhaps by moving all online logs to fast raw devices).

Good usage of the redo log buffer is a simple matter of:

- Batching commit operations for batch jobs, so that log writer is able to write redo log entries efficiently.
- Using `NOLOGGING` operations when you are loading large quantities of data.

The size of the redo log buffer is determined by the initialization parameter `LOG_BUFFER`. You cannot modify the log buffer size after instance startup.

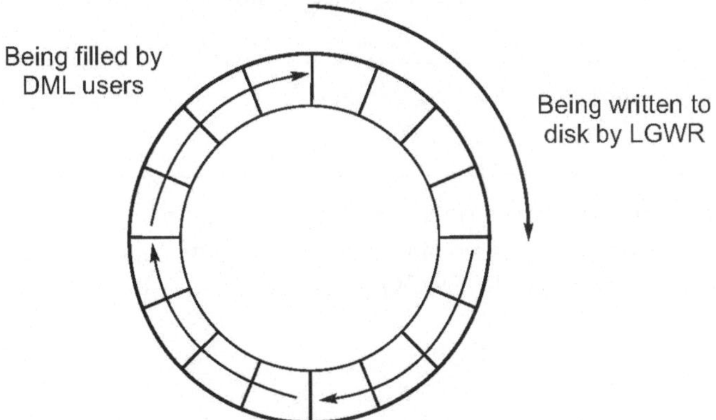

Figure 7.2. Redo Log Buffer

Sizing the Log Buffer

Applications that insert, modify, or delete large volumes of data usually need to change the default log buffer size. The log buffer is small compared with the total SGA size, and a modestly sized log buffer can significantly enhance throughput on systems that perform many updates.

A reasonable first estimate for such systems is to the default value, which is:

```
MAX(0.5M, (128K * number of cpus))
```

On most systems, sizing the log buffer larger than 1M does not provide any performance benefit. Increasing the log buffer size does not have any negative implications on performance or recoverability. It merely uses extra memory.

Log Buffer Statistics

The statistic `REDO BUFFER ALLOCATION RETRIES` reflects the number of times a user process waits for space in the redo log buffer. This statistic can be queried through the dynamic performance view `V$SYSSTAT`.

Use the following query to monitor these statistics over a period while your application is running:

```
SELECT NAME, VALUE FROM V$SYSSTAT
 WHERE NAME = 'redo buffer allocation retries';
```

The value of `redo buffer allocation retries` should be near zero over an interval. If this value increments consistently, then processes have had to wait for space in the redo log buffer. The wait can be caused by the log buffer being too small or by checkpointing. Increase the size of the redo log buffer, if necessary, by changing the value of the initialization parameter `LOG_BUFFER`. The value of this parameter is expressed in bytes. Alternatively, improve the checkpointing or archiving process.

Another data source is to check whether the `log buffer space` wait event is not a significant factor in the wait time for the instance; if not, the log buffer size is most likely adequate.

PGA MEMORY MANAGEMENT

The Program Global Area (PGA) is a private memory region containing data and control information for a server process. Access to it is exclusive to the server process and is read and written only by the Oracle Database code acting on behalf of it. An example of such information is the run-time area of a cursor. Each time a cursor is executed, a new run-time area is created for that cursor in the PGA memory region of the server process executing that cursor.

Part of the run-time area can be located in the SGA when using shared servers.

For complex queries (for example, decision support queries), a big portion of the run-time area is dedicated to work areas allocated by memory intensive operators, such as the following:

- Sort-based operators, such as `ORDER BY, GROUP BY, ROLLUP,` and window functions
- Hash-join
- Bitmap merge
- Bitmap create
- Write buffers used by bulk load operations.

A sort operator uses a work area (the sort area) to perform the in-memory sort of a set of rows. Similarly, a hash-join operator uses a work area (the hash area) to build a hash table from its left input.

The size of a work area can be controlled and tuned. Generally, bigger work areas can significantly improve the performance of a particular operator at the cost of higher memory consumption. Ideally, the size of a work area is big enough that it can accommodate the input data and auxiliary memory structures allocated by its associated SQL operator. This is known as the optimal size of a work area. When the size of the work area is smaller than optimal, the response time increases, because an extra pass is performed over part of the input data. This is known as the one-pass size of the work area. Under the one-pass threshold, when the size of a work area is far too small compared to the input data size, multiple passes over the input data are needed. This could dramatically increase the response time of the operator. This is known as the multi-pass size of the work area. For example, a serial sort operation that must sort 10 GB of data needs a little more than 10 GB to run optimal and at least 40 MB to run one-pass. If this sort gets less that 40 MB, then it must perform several passes over the input data.

The goal is to have most work areas running with an optimal size (for example, more than 90% or even 100% for pure OLTP systems), while a smaller fraction of them run with a one-pass size (for example, less than 10%). Multi-pass execution should be avoided. Even for DSS systems running large sorts and hash-joins, the memory requirement for the one-pass executions is relatively small. A system configured with a reasonable amount of PGA memory should not need to perform multiple passes over the input data.

Automatic PGA memory management simplifies and improves the way PGA memory is allocated. By default, PGA memory management is enabled. In this mode, Oracle Database dynamically adjusts the size of the portion of the PGA memory dedicated to work areas, based on 20% of the SGA memory size. The minimum value is 10 MB.

For backward compatibility, automatic PGA memory management can be disabled by setting the value of the PGA_AGGREGATE_TARGET initialization parameter to 0. When automatic PGA memory management is disabled, the maximum size of a work area can be sized with the associated _AREA_SIZE parameter, such as the SORT_AREA_SIZE initialization parameter.

Configuring Automatic PGA Memory

When running under the automatic PGA memory management mode, sizing of work areas for all sessions becomes automatic and the *_AREA_SIZE parameters are ignored by all sessions running in that mode. At any given time, the total amount of PGA memory available to active work areas in the instance is automatically derived from the PGA_AGGREGATE_TARGET initialization parameter. This amount is set to the value of PGA_AGGREGATE_TARGET minus the amount of PGA memory allocated by other components of the system (for example, PGA memory allocated by sessions). The resulting PGA memory is then assigned to individual active work areas, based on their specific memory requirements.

Under automatic PGA memory management mode, the main goal of Oracle Database is to honor the PGA_AGGREGATE_TARGET limit set by the DBA, by controlling dynamically the amount of PGA memory allotted to SQL work areas. At the same time, Oracle Database t to maximize the performance of all the memory-intensive SQL operations, by maximizing the number of work areas that are using an optimal amount of PGA memory (cache memory).

The rest of the work areas are executed in one-pass mode, unless the PGA memory limit set by the DBA with the parameter **PGA_AGGREGATE_TARGET** is so low that multi-pass execution is required to reduce even more the consumption of PGA memory and honor the PGA target limit.

When configuring a brand new instance, it is hard to know precisely the appropriate setting for **PGA_AGGREGATE_TARGET**. You can determine this setting in three stages:

1. Make a first estimate for PGA_AGGREGATE_TARGET. By default, Oracle Database uses 20% of the SGA size. However, this initial setting may be too low for a large DSS system.
2. Run a representative workload on the instance and monitor performance, using PGA statistics collected by Oracle Database, to see whether the maximum PGA size is under-configured or over-configured.
3. Tune PGA_AGGREGATE_TARGET, using Oracle PGA advice statistics.

The following sections explain this in detail:

- Setting PGA_AGGREGATE_TARGET Initially
- Monitoring the Performance of the Automatic PGA Memory Management
- Tuning PGA_AGGREGATE_TARGET.

Setting PGA_AGGREGATE_TARGET Initially

The value of the PGA_AGGREGATE_TARGET initialization parameter (for example, 100000 KB, 2500 MB, or 50 GB) should be set based on the total amount of memory available for the Oracle database instance. This value can then be tuned and dynamically modified at the instance level. illustrates a typical situation.

Example 7.2: Initial Setting of PGA_AGGREGATE_TARGET

Assume that an Oracle database instance is configured to run on a system with 4 GB of physical memory. Part of that memory should be left for the operat ing system and other non-Oracle applications running on the same hardware system. You might decide to dedicate only 80% (3.2 GB) of the available memory to the Oracle database instance.

You must then divide the resulting memory between the SGA and the PGA:

- For OLTP systems, the PGA memory typically accounts for a small fraction of the total memory available (for example, 20%), leaving 80% for the SGA.
- For DSS systems running large, memory-intensive queries, PGA memory can typically use up to 70% of that total (up to 2.2 GB in this example).

Good initial values for the parameter PGA_AGGREGATE_TARGET might be:

- For OLTP: PGA_AGGREGATE_TARGET = (*total_mem* * 80%) * 20%
- For DSS: PGA_AGGREGATE_TARGET = (*total_mem* * 80%) * 50%.

Where *total_mem* is the total amount of physical memory available on the system.

In this example, with a value of *total_mem* equal to 4 GB, you can initially set PGA_AGGREGATE_TARGET to 1600 MB for a DSS system and to 655 MB for an OLTP system.

Monitoring the Performance of the Automatic PGA Memory Management

Before starting the tuning process, you need to know how to monitor and interpret the key statistics collected by Oracle Database to help in assessing the performance of the automatic PGA memory management component. Several dynamic performance views are available for this purpose:

- V$PGASTAT
- V$PROCESS

- V$PROCESS_MEMORY
- V$SQL_WORKAREA_HISTOGRAM
- V$SQL_WORKAREA_ACTIVE
- V$SQL_WORKAREA.

V$PGASTAT

This view gives instance-level statistics on the PGA memory usage and the automatic PGA memory manager. For example:

```
SELECT * FROM V$PGASTAT;
```

The main statistics displayed in `V$PGASTAT` are as follows:

- `aggregate PGA target parameter`: This is the current value of the initialization parameter `PGA_AGGREGATE_TARGET`. The default value is 20% of the SGA size. If you set this parameter to 0, automatic management of the PGA memory is disabled.
- `aggregate PGA auto target`: This gives the amount of PGA memory Oracle Database can use for work areas running in automatic mode. This amount is dynamically derived from the value of the parameter `PGA_AGGREGATE_TARGET` and the current work area workload. Hence, it is continuously adjusted by Oracle. If this value is small compared to the value of `PGA_AGGREGATE_TARGET`, then a lot of PGA memory is used by other components of the system (for example, PL/SQL or Java memory) and little is left for sort work areas. You must ensure that enough PGA memory is left for work areas running in automatic mode.
- `global memory bound`. This gives the maximum size of a work area executed in `AUTO` mode. This value is continuously adjusted by Oracle Database to reflect the current state of the work area workload. The global memory bound generally decreases when the number of active work areas is increasing in the system. As a rule of thumb, the value of the global bound should not decrease to less than one megabyte. If it does, then the value of `PGA_AGGREGATE_TARGET` should probably be increased.
- `total PGA allocated`: This gives the current amount of PGA memory allocated by the instance. Oracle Database tries to keep this number less than the value of `PGA_AGGREGATE_TARGET`. However, it is possible for the PGA allocated to exceed that value by a small percentage and for a short period, when the work area workload is increasing very rapidly or when the initialization parameter `PGA_AGGREGATE_TARGET` is set to a too small value.
- `total freeable PGA memory`: This indicates how much allocated PGA memory which can be freed.
- `total PGA used for auto workareas`: This indicates how much PGA memory is currently consumed by work areas running under automatic memory management mode. This number can be used to determine how much memory is consumed by other consumers of the PGA memory (for example, PL/SQL or Java):
- `PGA other = total PGA allocated - total PGA used for auto workareas.`
- `over allocation count`: This statistic is cumulative from instance startup. Over-allocating PGA memory can happen if the value of `PGA_AGGREGATE_TARGET` is too small to accommodate the PGA other component in the previous equation plus the minimum memory required to execute the work area workload. When this happens, Oracle Database cannot honor the initialization parameter `PGA_AGGREGATE_TARGET`, and extra PGA memory must be allocated. If over-allocation occurs, you should increase the

value of PGA_AGGREGATE_TARGET using the information provided by the advice view V$PGA_TARGET_ADVICE.

- total bytes processed: This is the number of bytes processed by memory-intensive SQL operators since instance startup. For example, the number of byte processed is the input size for a sort operation. This number is used to compute the cache hit percentage metric.
- extra bytes read/written: When a work area cannot run optimally, one or more extra passes is performed over the input data. extra bytes read/written represents the number of bytes processed during these extra passes since instance startup. This number is also used to compute the cache hit percentage. Ideally, it should be small compared to total bytes processed.
- cache hit percentage: This metric is computed by Oracle Database to reflect the performance of the PGA memory component. It is cumulative from instance startup. A value of 100% means that all work areas executed by the system since instance startup have used an optimal amount of PGA memory. This is, of course, ideal but rarely happens except maybe for pure OLTP systems. In reality, some work areas run one-pass or even multi-pass, depending on the overall size of the PGA memory. When a work area cannot run optimally, one or more extra passes is performed over the input data. This reduces the cache hit percentage in proportion to the size of the input data and the number of extra passes performed. shows how cache hit percentage is affected by extra passes.

Example 7.3: Calculating Cache Hit Percentage

Consider a simple example: Four sort operations have been executed, three were small (1 MB of input data) and one was bigger (100 MB of input data). The total number of bytes processed (BP) by the four operations is 103 MB. If one of the small sorts runs one-pass, an extra pass over 1 MB of input data is performed. This 1 MB value is the number of extra bytes read/written, or EBP. The cache hit percentage is calculated by the following formula:

```
BP × 100 / (BP + EBP)
```

The cache hit percentage in this case is 99.03%, almost 100%. This value reflects the fact that only one of the small sorts had to perform an extra pass while all other sorts were able to run optimally. Hence, the cache hit percentage is almost 100%, because this extra pass over 1 MB represents a tiny overhead. However, if the big sort is the one to run one-pass, then EBP is 100 MB instead of 1 MB, and the cache hit percentage falls to 50.73%, because the extra pass has a much bigger impact.

V$PROCESS

This view has one row for each Oracle process connected to the instance. The columns PGA_USED_MEM, PGA_ALLOC_MEM, PGA_FREEABLE_MEM and PGA_MAX_MEM can be used to monitor the PGA memory usage of these processes. For example:

```
SELECT PROGRAM, PGA_USED_MEM, PGA_ALLOC_MEM, PGA_FREEABLE_MEM,
PGA_MAX_MEM
 FROM V$PROCESS;
```

V$PROCESS_MEMORY

This view displays dynamic PGA memory usage by named component categories for each Oracle process. This view will contain up to six rows for each Oracle process, one row for:

- Each named component category: Java, PL/SQL, OLAP, and SQL.
- Freeable: memory that has been allocated to the process by the operating system, but not to a specific category.
- Other: memory that has been allocated to a category, but not to one of the named categories.

You can use the columns CATEGORY, ALLOCATED, USED, and MAX_ALLOCATED to dynamically monitor the PGA memory usage of Oracle processes for each of the six categories.

V$SQL_WORKAREA_HISTOGRAM

This view shows the number of work areas executed with optimal memory size, one-pass memory size, and multi-pass memory size since instance startup. Statistics in this view are subdivided into buckets that are defined by the optimal memory requirement of the work area. Each bucket is identified by a range of optimal memory requirements specified by the values of the columns LOW_OPTIMAL_SIZE and HIGH_OPTIMAL_SIZE.

and show two ways of using V$SQL_WORKAREA_HISTOGRAM.

Example 7.4: Querying V$SQL_WORKAREA_HISTOGRAM: Non-empty Buckets

Consider a sort operation that requires 3 MB of memory to run optimally (cached). Statistics about the work area used by this sort are placed in the bucket defined by LOW_OPTIMAL_SIZE = 2097152 (2 MB) and HIGH_OPTIMAL_SIZE = 4194303 (4 MB minus 1 byte), because 3 MB falls within that range of optimal sizes. Statistics are segmented by work area size, because the performance impact of running a work area in optimal, one-pass or multi-pass mode depends mainly on the size of that work area.

The following query shows statistics for all non-empty buckets. Empty buckets are removed with the predicate WHERE TOTAL_EXECUTION!= 0.

```
SELECT LOW_OPTIMAL_SIZE/1024 low_kb,HIGH_OPTIMAL_SIZE+1)/1024 high_kb,OPTIMAL_EXECUTIONS, ONEPASS_EXECUTIONS, MULTIPASSES_EXECUTIONSFROM V$SQL_WORKAREA_HISTOGRAM WHERE TOTAL_EXECUTIONS != 0;
```

The query result shows that, in the 1024 KB to 2048 KB bucket, 551 work areas used an optimal amount of memory, while 16 ran in one-pass mode and none ran in multi-pass mode. It also shows that all work areas under 1 MB were able to run in optimal mode.

Example 7.5: Querying V$SQL_WORKAREA_HISTOGRAM: Percent Optimal

You can also use V$SQL_WORKAREA_HISTOGRAM to find the percentage of times work areas were executed in optimal, one-pass, or multi-pass mode since startup. This query only considers work areas of a certain size, with an optimal memory requirement of at least 64 KB.

```
SELECT optimal_count, round(optimal_count*100/total, 2) optimal_perc, onepass_count, round(onepass_count*100/total, 2) onepass_perc, multipass_count, round(multipass_count*100/total, 2) multipass_perc FROM(SELECT decode(sum(total_executions), 0, 1, sum(total_executions)) total,sum(OPTIMAL_EXECUTIONS) optimal_count,sum(ONEPASS_EXECUTIONS) onepass_count, sum(MULTIPASSES_EXECUTIONS) multipass_count FROM v$sql_workarea_histogram WHERE low_optimal_size >= 64*1024);
```

This result shows that 81.63% of these work areas have been able to run using an optimal amount of memory. The rest (18.37%) ran one-pass. None of them ran multi-pass. Such behavior is preferable, for the following reasons:

- Multi-pass mode can severely degrade performance. A high number of multi-pass work areas has an exponentially adverse effect on the response time of its associated SQL operator.
- Running one-pass does not require a large amount of memory; only 22 MB is required to sort 1 GB of data in one-pass mode.

V$SQL_WORKAREA_ACTIVE

You can use this view to display the work areas that are active (or executing) in the instance. Small active sorts (under 64 KB) are excluded from the view. Use this view to precisely monitor the size of all active work areas and to determine if these active work areas spill to a temporary segment. shows a typical query of this view:

Example 7.6: Querying V$SQL_WORKAREA_ACTIVE

```
SELECT          to_number(decode(SID, 65535, NULL, SID)) sid,
                operation_type OPERATION,
                trunc(EXPECTED_SIZE/1024) ESIZE,
                trunc(ACTUAL_MEM_USED/1024) MEM,
                trunc(MAX_MEM_USED/1024) “MAX MEM”,
                NUMBER_PASSES PASS,
                trunc(TEMPSEG_SIZE/1024) TSIZE
 FROM V$SQL_WORKAREA_ACTIVE ORDER BY 1,2;
```

The output of this query might look like the following:

SID	OPERATION	ESIZE	MEM	MAX MEM	PASS	TSIZE
8	GROUP BY (SORT)	315	280	904	0	
8	HASH-JOIN	2995	2377	2430	1	20000
9	GROUP BY (SORT)	34300	22688	22688	0	
11	HASH-JOIN	18044	54482	54482	0	
12	HASH-JOIN	18044	11406	21406	1	120000

This output shows that session 12 (column SID) is running a hash-join having its work area running in one-pass mode (PASS column). This work area is currently using 11406 KB of memory (MEM column) and has used, in the past, up to 21406 KB of PGA memory (MAX MEM column). It has also spilled to a temporary segment of size 120000 KB. Finally, the column ESIZE indicates the maximum amount of memory that the PGA memory manager expects this hash-join to use. This maximum is dynamically computed by the PGA memory manager according to workload.

When a work area is deallocated—that is, when the execution of its associated SQL operator is complete—the work area is automatically removed from the V$SQL_WORKAREA_ACTIVE view.

V$SQL_WORKAREA

Oracle Database maintains cumulative work area statistics for each loaded cursor whose execution plan uses one or more work areas. Every time a work area is deallocated, the V$SQL_WORKAREA table is updated with execution statistics for that work area.

V$SQL_WORKAREA can be joined with V$SQL to relate a work area to a cursor. It can even be joined to V$SQL_PLAN to precisely determine which operator in the plan uses a work area.

Shows three typical queries on the V$SQL_WORKAREA dynamic view:

Example 7.7: Querying V$SQL_WORKAREA

The following query finds the top 10 work areas requiring most cache memory:

```
SELECT * FROM (SELECT workarea_address, operation_type, policy,
estimated_optimal_size FROM V$SQL_WORKAREA
 ORDER BY estimated_optimal_size DESC) WHERE ROWNUM <= 10;
```

The following query finds the cursors with one or more work areas that have been executed in one or even multiple passes:

```
col sql_text format A80 wrap
SELECT sql_text, sum(ONEPASS_EXECUTIONS) onepass_cnt,
sum(MULTIPASSES_EXECUTIONS) mpass_cnt FROM V$SQL s, V$SQL_WORKAREA wa
WHERE s.address = wa.address
GROUP BY sql_text HAVING sum(ONEPASS_EXECUTIONS+MULTIPASSES_EXECUTIONS)>0;
```

Using the hash value and address of a particular cursor, the following query displays the cursor execution plan, including information about the associated work areas.

```
col "O/1/M" format a10
col name format a20
SELECT operation, options, object_name name, trunc(bytes/1024/1024)
"input(MB)",
trunc(last_memory_used/1024) last_mem, trunc(estimated_optimal_size/
1024) optimal_mem,
trunc(estimated_onepass_size/1024) onepass_mem,
decode(optimal_executions, null, null, optimal_executions||'/'
 ||onepass_executions||'/'||
 multipasses_executions) "O/1/M"
 FROM V$SQL_PLAN p, V$SQL_WORKAREA w
 WHERE p.address=w.address(+)
 AND p.hash_value=w.hash_value(+)
 AND p.id=w.operation_id(+)
 AND p.address='88BB460C'
 AND p.hash_value=3738161960;
```

You can get the address and hash value from the V$SQL view by specifying a pattern in the query. For example:

```
SELECT address, hash_value
 FROM V$SQL WHERE sql_text LIKE '%my_pattern%';
```

Tuning PGA_AGGREGATE_TARGET

To help you tune the initialization parameter `PGA_AGGREGATE_TARGET`, Oracle Database provides the `V$PGA_TARGET_ADVICE` and `V$PGA_TARGET_ADVICE_HISTOGRAM` views. By examining these views, you no longer need to use an empirical approach to tune the value of `PGA_AGGREGATE_TARGET`. Instead, you can use these views to determine how key PGA statistics will be impacted if you change the value of `PGA_AGGREGATE_TARGET`.

In both views, values of `PGA_AGGREGATE_TARGET` used for the prediction are derived from fractions and multiples of the current value of that parameter, to assess possible higher and lower values. Values used for the prediction range from 10 MB to a maximum of 256 GB.

Oracle Database generates PGA advice performance views by recording the workload history and then simulating this history for different values of PGA_AGGREGATE_TARGET. The simulation process happens in the background and continuously updates the workload history to produce the simulation result. You can view the result at any time by querying V$PGA_TARGET_ADVICE or V$PGA_TARGET_ADVICE_HISTOGRAM.

To enable automatic generation of PGA advice performance views, make sure the following parameters are set:

- PGA_AGGREGATE_TARGET, to enable automatic PGA memory.
- STATISTICS_LEVEL. Set this to TYPICAL (the default) or ALL; setting this parameter to BASIC turns off generation of PGA performance advice views.

The content of these PGA advice performance views is reset at instance startup or when PGA_AGGREGATE_TARGET is altered.

Simulation cannot include all factors of real execution, so derived statistics may not exactly match up with real performance statistics. Always monitor the system after changing PGA_AGGREGATE_TARGET to verify that the new performance is what you expect.

V$PGA_TARGET_ADVICE

This view predicts how the statistics cache hit percentage and over allocation count in V$PGASTAT will be impacted if you change the value of the initialization parameter PGA_AGGREGATE_TARGET. shows a typical query of this view.

Example 7.8: Querying V$PGA_TARGENT_ADVICE

```
SELECT round(PGA_TARGET_FOR_ESTIMATE/1024/1024) target_mb,
 ESTD_PGA_CACHE_HIT_PERCENTAGE cache_hit_perc,
 ESTD_OVERALLOC_COUNT
 FROM V$PGA_TARGET_ADVICE;
```

The output of this query might look like the following:

```
TARGET_MB          CACHE_HIT_PERC        ESTD_OVERALLOC_COUNT
----------         ----------------      ---------------------
      63                   23                    367
     125                   24                     30
     250                   30                      3
     375                   39                      0
     500                   58                      0
     600                   59                      0
     700                   59                      0
     800                   60                      0
     900                   60                      0
    1000                   61                      0
    1500                   67                      0
    2000                   76                      0
    3000                   83                      0
    4000                   85                      0
```

The result of the this query can be plotted as shown in Figure 7.3:

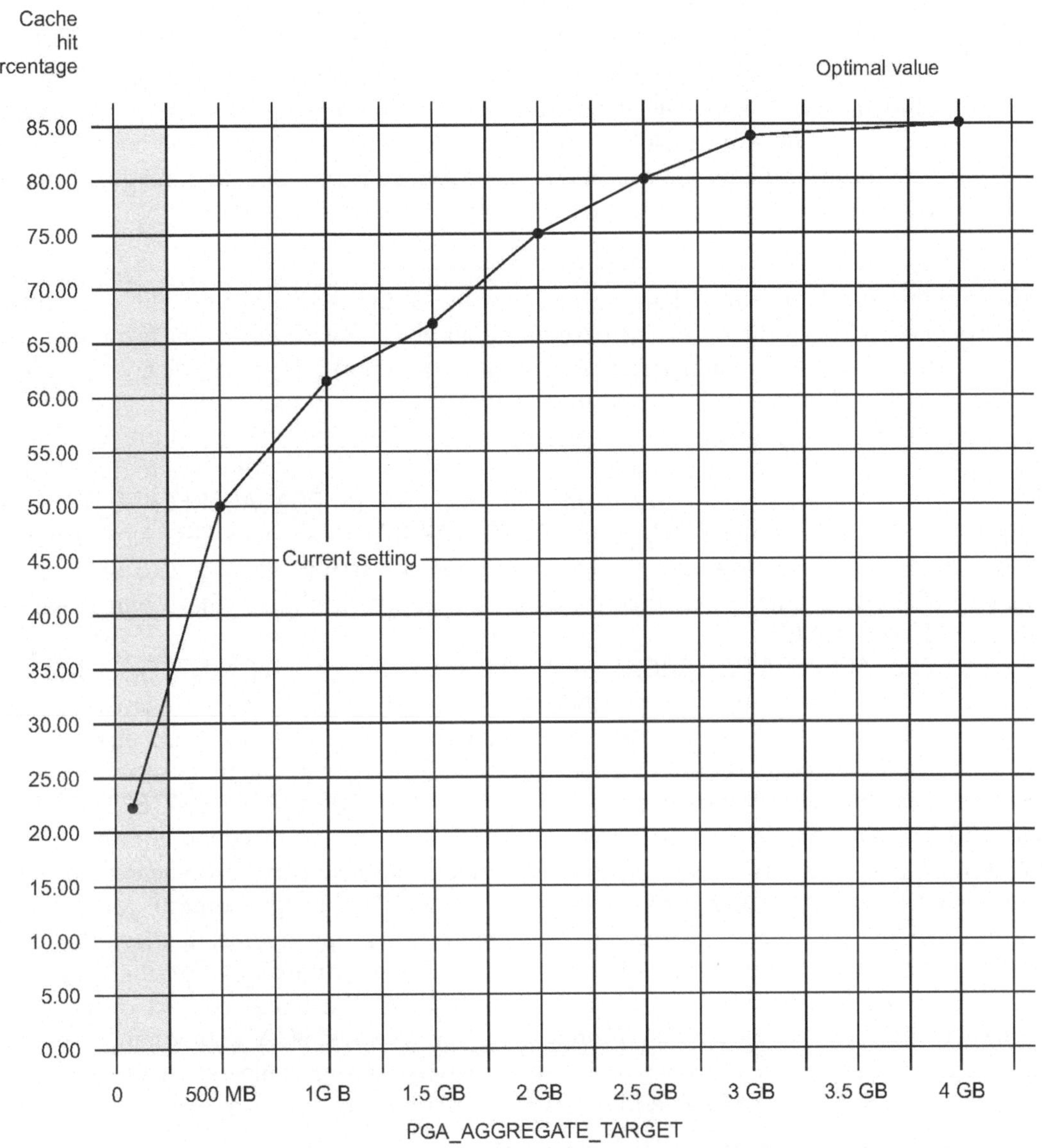

Figure 7.3. Graphical Representation of V$PGA_TARGET_ADVICE

The curve shows how the PGA `cache hit percentage` improves as the value of `PGA_AGGREGATE_TARGET` increases. The shaded zone in the graph is the `over allocation` zone, where the value of the column `ESTD_OVERALLOCATION_COUNT` is nonzero. It indicates that `PGA_AGGREGATE_TARGET` is too small to even meet the minimum PGA memory needs. If `PGA_AGGREGATE_TARGET` is set within the `over allocation` zone, the memory manager will over-allocate memory and actual PGA memory consumed will be more than the limit you set. It is therefore meaningless to set a value of `PGA_AGGREGATE_TARGET` in that zone. In this particular example `PGA_AGGREGATE_TARGET` should be set to at least 375 MB.

Although the theoretical maximum for the PGA `cache hit percentage` is 100%, there is a practical limit on the maximum size of a work area, which may prevent this theoretical maximum from being reached, even if you further increase PGA_AGGREGATE_TARGET. This should happen only in large DSS systems where the optimal memory requirement is large and might cause the value of the `cache hit percentage` to taper off at a lower percentage, like 90%.

Beyond the `over allocation` zone, the value of the PGA `cache hit percentage` increases rapidly. This is due to an increase in the number of work areas which run optimally or one-pass and a decrease in the number of multi-pass executions. At some point, around 500 MB in this example, an inflection in the curve corresponds to the point where most (probably all) work areas can run optimally or at least one-pass. After this inflection, the `cache hit percentage` keeps increasing, though at a lower pace, up to the point where it starts to taper off and shows only slight improvement with increase in PGA_AGGREGATE_TARGET. In Figure 7.3, this happens when GA_AGGREGATE_TARGET reaches 3 GB. At that point, the `cache hit percentage` is 83% and only improves marginally (by 2%) with one extra gigabyte of PGA memory. In this example, 3 GB is probably the optimal value for PGA_AGGREGATE_TARGET.

Ideally, PGA_AGGREGATE_TARGET should be set at the optimal value, or at least to the maximum value possible in the region beyond the `over allocation` zone. As a rule of thumb, the PGA `cache hit percentage` should be higher than 60%, because at 60% the system is almost processing double the number of bytes it actually needs to process in an ideal situation. Using this particular example, it makes sense to set PGA_AGGREGATE_TARGET to at least 500 MB and as close as possible to 3 GB. But the right setting for the parameter PGA_AGGREGATE_TARGET depends on how much memory can be dedicated to the PGA component. Generally, adding PGA memory requires reducing memory for some SGA components, like the shared pool or buffer cache, because the overall memory dedicated to the instance is often bound by the amount of physical memory available on the system. Thus, any decisions to increase PGA memory must be taken in the larger context of the available memory in the system and the performance of the various SGA components (which you monitor with shared pool advisory and buffer cache advisory statistics). If you cannot take memory from the SGA, consider adding physical memory to the computer.

How to Tune PGA_AGGREGATE_TARGET

You can use the following steps as a tuning guideline in tuning PGA_AGGREGATE_TARGET:

1. Set PGA_AGGREGATE_TARGET so there is no memory over-allocation; avoid setting it in the over-allocation zone. In , PGA_AGGREGATE_TARGET should be set to at least 375 MB.
2. After eliminating over-allocations, aim at maximizing the PGA `cache hit percentage,` based on your response-time requirement and memory constraints. In , assume you have a limit *X* on memory you can allocate to PGA.
   - If this limit *X* is beyond the optimal value, then you would set PGA_AGGREGATE_TARGET to the optimal value. After this point, the incremental benefit with higher memory allocation to PGA_AGGREGATE_TARGET is very small. In, if you have 10 GB to dedicate to PGA, set PGA_AGGREGATE_TARGET to 3 GB, the optimal value. The remaining 7 GB is dedicated to the SGA.

- If the limit is less than the optimal value, then you would set PGA_AGGREGATE_TARGET to . In , if you have only 2 GB to dedicate to PGA, set PGA_AGGREGATE_TARGET to 2 GB and accept a cache hit percentage of 75%.

Finally, like most statistics collected by Oracle Database that are cumulative since instance startup, you can take a snapshot of the view at the beginning and at the end of a time interval. You can then derive the predicted statistics for that time interval as follows:

```
estd_overalloc_count = (difference in estd_overalloc_count between
the two snapshots)(difference in bytes_processed between the two
snapshots)estd_pga_cache_hit_percentage = (difference in bytes_
processed + extra_bytes_rw between the two snapshots)
```

V$PGA_TARGET_ADVICE_HISTOGRAM

This view predicts how the statistics displayed by the performance view V$SQL_WORKAREA_HISTOGRAM will be impacted if you change the value of the initialization parameter PGA_AGGREGATE_TARGET. You can use the dynamic view V$PGA_TARGET_ADVICE_HISTOGRAM to view detailed information on the predicted number of optimal, one-pass and multi-pass work area executions for the set of PGA_AGGREGATE_TARGET values you use for the prediction.

The V$PGA_TARGET_ADVICE_HISTOGRAM view is identical to the V$SQL_WORKAREA_HISTOGRAM view, with two additional columns to represent the PGA_AGGREGATE_TARGET values used for the prediction. Therefore, any query executed against the V$SQL_WORKAREA_HISTOGRAM view can be used on this view, with an additional predicate to select the desired value of PGA_AGGREGATE_TARGET.

Example 7.9: Querying V$PGA_TARGET_ADVICE_HISTOGRAM

The following query displays the predicted content of V$SQL_WORKAREA_HISTOGRAM for a value of the initialization parameter PGA_AGGREGATE_TARGET set to twice its current value.

```
SELECT LOW_OPTIMAL_SIZE/1024 low_kb, (HIGH_OPTIMAL_SIZE+1)/1024 high_kb,
estd_optimal_executions estd_opt_cnt, estd_onepass_executions
estd_onepass_cnt, estd_multipasses_executions estd_mpass_cnt FROM
v$pga_target_advice_histogram WHERE pga_target_factor = 2
 AND estd_total_executions != 0 ORDER BY 1;
```

V$SYSSTAT and V$SESSTAT

Statistics in the V$SYSSTAT and V$SESSTAT views show the total number of work areas executed with optimal memory size, one-pass memory size, and multi-pass memory size. These statistics are cumulative since the instance or the session was started.

The following query gives the total number and the percentage of times work areas were executed in these three modes since the instance was started:

```
SELECT name profile, cnt, decode(total, 0, 0, round(cnt*100/total))
percentage
 FROM (SELECT name, value cnt, (sum(value) over ()) total
 FROM V$SYSSTAT
 WHERE name like 'workarea exec%');
```

The output of this query might look like the following:

```
PROFILE                                   CNT       PERCENTAGE
--------------------------------------    --------  ----------
workarea executions - optimal             5395      95
workarea executions - onepass             284       5
workarea executions - multipass           0         0
```

Configuring OLAP_PAGE_POOL_SIZE

The `OLAP_PAGE_POOL_SIZE` initialization parameter specifies (in bytes) the maximum size of the paging cache to be allocated to an OLAP session.

For performance reasons, it is usually preferable to configure a small OLAP paging cache and set a larger default buffer pool with `DB_CACHE_SIZE`. An OLAP paging cache of 4 MB is fairly typical, with 2 MB used for systems with limited memory.

MANAGING THE SERVER AND CLIENT RESULT CACHES

A **result cache** is an area of memory, either in the SGA or client application memory, that stores the result of a database query or query block for reuse. The cached rows are shared across statements and sessions unless they become stale.

This section contains the following topics:

- Managing the Server Result Cache
- Managing the Client Result Cache
- Managing Memory for the Server Result Cache
- Specifying Queries for Result Caching
- Requirements for the Result Cache
- Accessing Result Cache Information.

Managing the Server Result Cache

The **server result cache** is a memory pool within the shared pool. This pool contains a **SQL query result cache**, which stores results of SQL queries, and a **PL/SQL function result cache**, which stores values returned by PL/SQL functions.

OLAP applications can benefit significantly from the use of the server result cache. The benefits highly depend on the application. Good candidates for caching are queries that access a high number of rows but return a small number, as in a data warehouse. For example, you can use advanced query rewrite with equivalences to create materialized views that materialize queries in the result cache instead of using tables.

How the Server Result Cache Works

When a query executes, the database looks in the cache memory to determine whether the result exists in the cache. If the result exists, then the database retrieves the result from memory instead of executing the query. If the result is not cached, then the database executes the query, returns the result as output, and stores the result in the result cache.

When users execute queries and functions repeatedly, the database retrieves rows from the cache, decreasing response time. Cached results become invalid when data in dependent database objects is modified.

queries `hr.employees` and uses the `RESULT_CACHE` hint to retrieve rows from the server result cache. includes a portion of the execution plan, which shows that in step 1 the results are retrieved directly from the cache. The value in the Name column is the cache ID of the result.

Example 7.10: Using the RESULT_CACHE Hint in a Query

```
SELECT /*+ RESULT_CACHE */ department_id, AVG(salary)
FROM hr.employees
GROUP BY department_id;
----------------------------------------------------------------
| Id | Operation         | Name                        | Rows
----------------------------------------------------------------
| 0  | SELECT STATEMENT  |                             | 11
| 1  | RESULT CACHE      | 8fpza04gtwsfr6n595au15yj4y  |
| 2  | HASH GROUP BY     |                             | 11
| 3  | TABLE ACCESS FULL| EMPLOYEES                    | 107
----------------------------------------------------------------
```

As shown in , after the query is executed you can obtain detailed statistics about the cached result by querying V$RESULT_CACHE_OBJECTS, where the cache ID obtained from the explain plan is equal to the CACHE_ID value.

Example 7.11: Querying Statistics for Cached Results

```
SELECT ID, TYPE, CREATION_TIMESTAMP, BLOCK_COUNT, COLUMN_COUNT,
 PIN_COUNT, ROW_COUNT
FROM V$RESULT_CACHE_OBJECTS
WHERE CACHE_ID = '8fpza04gtwsfr6n595au15yj4y';
```

Uses the RESULT_CACHE hint within a WITH clause view. The example shows a portion of the execution plan. In step 3, the RESULT CACHE Operation indicates that the summary view results are retrieved directly from the cache.

Example 7.12: Using the RESULT_CACHE Hint in a WITH Clause View

```
WITH summary AS
( SELECT /*+ RESULT_CACHE */ department_id, avg(salary) avg_sal
 FROM hr.employees
 GROUP BY department_id )
SELECT d.*, avg_sal
FROM hr.departments d, summary s
WHERE d.department_id = s.department_id;
```

Server Result Cache Initialization Parameters

The following database initialization parameters control the server result cache:

- RESULT_CACHE_MAX_SIZE.
  This parameter sets the memory allocated to the server result cache. The server result cache is enabled unless you set this parameter to 0, in which case the cache is disabled.
- RESULT_CACHE_MAX_RESULT.
  This parameter sets the maximum amount of server result cache memory that can be used for a single result. The default is 5%, but you can specify any percentage value between 1 and 100. You can set this parameter at the system or session level.
- RESULT_CACHE_REMOTE_EXPIRATION.
  This parameter specifies the expiration time for a result in the server result cache that depends on remote database objects. The default value is 0 minutes, which implies that results using remote objects should not be cached.

When you use a non zero value for this parameter, DML on the remote database does not invalidate the server result cache.

Managing Memory for the Server Result Cache

You can manage memory for the server result cache by setting database initialization parameters and by using the DBMS_RESULT_CACHE package.

Managing Server Result Cache Memory with Initialization Parameters

By default, on database startup, Oracle Database allocates memory to the server result cache in the shared pool. The memory size allocated depends on the memory size of the shared pool and the memory management system. The database uses the following algorithm:

- When using the `MEMORY_TARGET` initialization parameter to specify the memory allocation, Oracle Database allocates 0.25% of `MEMORY_TARGET` to the result cache.
- When you set the size of the shared pool using the `SGA_TARGET` initialization parameter, Oracle Database allocates 0.50% of `SGA_TARGET` to the result cache.
- If you specify the size of the shared pool using the `SHARED_POOL_SIZE` initialization parameter, then Oracle Database allocates 1% of the shared pool size to the result cache.

The size of the server result cache grows until reaching the maximum size. Query results larger than the available space in the cache are not cached. The database employs an LRU algorithm to age out cached results, but does not otherwise automatically release memory from the server result cache. You can use the `DBMS_RESULT_CACHE.FLUSH` procedure to purge memory.

You can change the memory allocated to the result cache by setting the `RESULT_CACHE_MAX_SIZE` initialization parameter. In an Oracle RAC environment, the result cache itself is specific to each instance and can be sized differently on each instance. However, invalidations work across instances. To disable the server result cache in a cluster, you must explicitly set this parameter to `0` for each instance startup.

Oracle Database will not allocate more than 75% of the shared pool to the server result cache.

Managing Server Result Cache Memory with DBMS_RESULT_CACHE

The `DBMS_RESULT_CACHE` package provides statistics, information, and operators that enable you to manage memory allocation for the server result cache. You can use the `DBMS_RESULT_CACHE` package to perform operations such as bypassing the cache, retrieving statistics on the cache memory usage, flushing the cache, and so on.

For example, use the following SQL procedure to view the memory allocation statistics for the result cache:

```
SQLSET SERVEROUTPUT ON
EXECUTE DBMS_RESULT_CACHE.MEMORY_REPORT
```

The output of this command will be similar to the following:

```
Result Cache Memory Report
[Parameters]
Block Size = 1024 bytes
Maximum Cache Size = 950272 bytes (928 blocks)
```

```
Maximum Result Size = 47104 bytes (46 blocks)
[Memory]
Total Memory = 46340 bytes [0.048% of the Shared Pool]
... Fixed Memory = 10696 bytes [0.011% of the Shared Pool]
... State Object Pool = 2852 bytes [0.003% of the Shared Pool]
... Cache Memory = 32792 bytes (32 blocks) [0.034% of the Shared
Pool]
....... Unused Memory = 30 blocks
....... Used Memory = 2 blocks
........... Dependencies = 1 blocks
........... Results = 1 blocks
............... SQL = 1 blocks

PL/SQL procedure successfully completed.
```

To remove all existing results and clear the result cache memory, use the command:

```
EXECUTE DBMS_RESULT_CACHE.FLUSH
```

Managing the Client Result Cache

The **Oracle Call Interface (OCI) client result cache** is a memory area inside a client process that caches SQL query result sets for OCI applications. This client cache exists for each client process and is shared by all sessions inside the process. Oracle Database recommends client result caching for queries of read-only or read-mostly tables.

> The client result cache is distinct from the server result cache, which resides in the SGA. When client result caching is enabled, the query result set can be cached on the client, server, or both. Client caching can be enabled even if the server result cache is disabled.

OCI drivers such as OCCI, the JDBC OCI driver, and ODP.NET support client result caching. Performance benefits of the client result cache include:

- Reduced query response time:
  When queries are executed repeatedly, the application retrieves results directly from the client cache memory, resulting in faster query response time.
- More efficient use of database resources:
  The reduction in server round trips can result in huge performance savings for server resources, for example, server CPU and I/O. These resources are freed for other tasks, thereby making the server more scalable.
- Reduced memory cost:
  The cache uses client memory that may be cheaper than server memory.

How the Client Result Cache Works

The client result cache stores the results of the outermost query, which are the columns defined by the OCI application. Subqueries and query blocks are not cached.

Figure 7.4 shows a client process with a database login session. This client process has one client result cache shared among multiple application sessions running in the client process. If the first application session runs a query, then it retrieves rows from the database and caches them in the client result cache. If other application sessions run the same query, then they also retrieve rows from the client result cache.

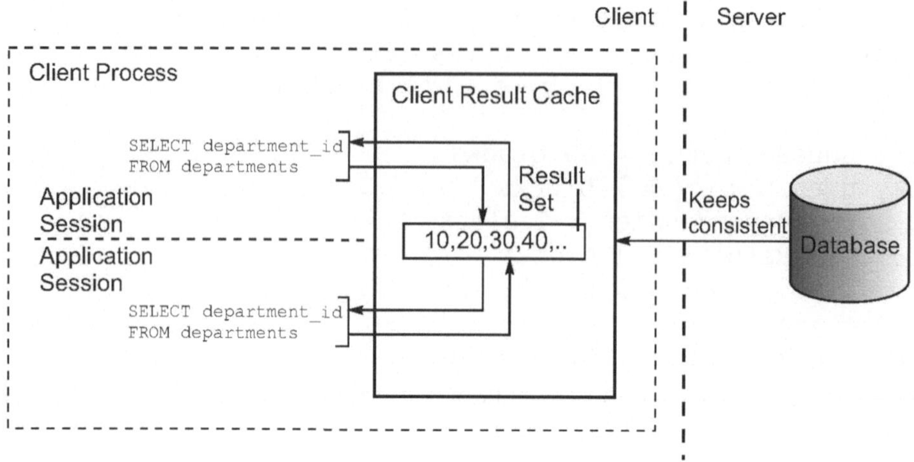

Figure 7.4. Client Result Cache

The client result cache transparently keeps the result set consistent with session state or database changes that affect it. When a transaction changes the data or metadata of database objects used to build the cached result, the database sends an invalidation to the OCI client on its next round trip to the server.

Client Result Cache Initialization Parameters

Table 7.4 lists the database initialization parameters that enable or influence the behavior of the client result cache.

Table 7.4. Client Result Cache Initialization Parameters

Initialization Parameter	Description
`CLIENT_RESULT_CACHE_SIZE`	Sets the maximum size of the client result cache for each client process. To enable the client result cache, set the size to `32768` bytes or greater. A lesser value, including the default of `0`, disables the client result cache. **Note:** If the `CLIENT_RESULT_CACHE_SIZE` setting disables the client cache, then a client node cannot enable it. If the `CLIENT_RESULT_CACHE_SIZE` setting enables the client cache, however, then a client node can override the setting. For example, a client node can disable client result caching or increase the size of its cache.
`CLIENT_RESULT_CACHE_LAG`	Specifies the amount of lag time for the client result cache. If the OCI application performs no database calls for a period, then the **client cache lag** setting forces the next statement execution call to

	check for validations. If the OCI application accesses the database infrequently, then setting this parameter to a low value results in more round trips from the OCI client to the database to keep the client result cache synchronized with the database. The client cache lag is specified in milliseconds, with a default value of `3000` (3 seconds).
`COMPATIBLE`	Specifies the release with which Oracle Database must maintain compatibility. For the client result cache to be enabled, this parameter must be set to `11.0.0.0` or higher. For client caching on views, this parameter must be set to `11.2.0.0.0` or higher.

For the client result cache, an optional client configuration file overrides cache parameters set in the server parameter file. Note that you can only set the client result cache lag with a database initialization parameter.

Specifying Queries for Result Caching

If the server or client result cache is enabled, then Oracle Database gives you control over which queries are eligible to be cached.

About the Result Cache Mode

The **result cache mode** is a database setting that determines which queries are eligible to store result sets in the client and server result caches. Oracle Database recommends that applications cache results for queries of read-only or read-mostly database objects.

The `RESULT_CACHE_MODE` initialization parameter determines the result cache behavior. Table 7.5 describes the possible values for this initialization parameter.

Table 7.5. Values for the RESULT_CACHE_MODE Initialization Parameter

Value	Default	Description
`MANUAL`	Yes	Query results can only be stored in the result cache by using a query hint or table annotation. This is the recommended value.
`FORCE`	No	All results are stored in the result cache. If a query result is not in the cache, then the database executes the query and stores the result in the cache. Subsequent executions of the same statement, including the result cache hint, retrieve data from the cache. Sessions uses these results if possible. To exclude query results from the cache, you must use the `/*+ NO_RESULT_CACHE */` query hint. ***Note:*** FORCE mode is not recommended because the database and clients attempt to cache all queries, which can create significant performance and latching overhead.

You can set the RESULT_CACHE_MODE initialization parameter for the instance (ALTER SYSTEM), session (ALTER SESSION), or in the server parameter file.

If a query is eligible for caching, then the application checks the result cache to determine whether the query result set exists in the cache. If it exists, then the result is retrieved directly from the result cache. Otherwise, the database executes the query and returns the result as output and stores it in the result cache.

Using SQL Result Cache Hints

You can use **result cache hints** at the application level to control caching behavior. The SQL result cache hints take precedence over the result cache mode and result cache table annotations.

When the result cache mode is MANUAL, the /*+ RESULT_CACHE */ hint instructs the database to cache the results of a query block and to use the cached results in future executions. instructs the database to cache rows for a query of the sales table.

Example 7.13: RESULT_CACHE Hint

```
SELECT /*+ RESULT_CACHE */ prod_id, SUM(amount_sold)
FROM sales
GROUP BY prod_id
ORDER BY prod_id;
```

The /*+ NO_RESULT_CACHE */ hint instructs the database *not* to cache the results in either the server or client result caches. instructs the database not to cache rows for a query of the sales table.

Example 7.14: NO_RESULT_CACHE Hint

```
SELECT /*+ NO_RESULT_CACHE */ prod_id, SUM(amount_sold)
FROM sales
GROUP BY prod_id
ORDER BY prod_id;
```

RESULT_CACHE Hint in Query Blocks: Example

The RESULT_CACHE hint applies only to the query block in which the hint is specified. If the hint is specified only in a view, then only these results are cached. Note the following characteristics of view caching:

- The view must be a standard view (a view created with the CREATE ... VIEW statement), an inline view specified in the FROM clause of a SELECT statement, or an inline view created with the WITH clause.
- The result of a view query with a **correlated column**, which is a reference to an outer query block, cannot be cached.
- Query results are stored in the server result cache, not the client result cache.
- A caching view is not merged into its outer (or referring) query block. Adding the RESULT_CACHE hint to inline views disables optimizations between the outer query and inline view to maximize reusability of the cached result.

Queries the inline view view1. The SELECT from view1 is the outer block, whereas the SELECT from employees is the inner block. Because the RESULT_CACHE hint is specified only in the inner block, the results of the outer query are not cached. The results of the inner query are stored in the server result cache.

Example 7.15: RESULT_CACHE Hint Specified in Inline View

```
SELECT *
FROM (SELECT /*+ RESULT_CACHE */ department_id, manager_id, count(*)
count
  FROM hr.employees
  GROUP BY department_id, manager_id) view1
WHERE department_id = 30;
```

Assume that the same session runs the statement in . This statement queries view2. Because the RESULT_CACHE hint is specified only in the query block in the WITH clause, the results of the employees query are eligible to be cached. Because cached these results, the SELECT statement in the WITH clause in can retrieve the cached rows.

Example 7.16: RESULT_CACHE Hint Specified in WITH View

```
WITH view2 AS
( SELECT /*+ RESULT_CACHE */ department_id, manager_id, count(*)
count FROM hr.employees
  GROUP BY department_id, manager_id)
SELECT * FROM view2
WHERE count BETWEEN 1 and 5;
```

Using Result Cache Table Annotations

You can use **table annotations** to control result caching. Table annotations are in effect only for the whole query, not for query segments. The primary benefit of these annotations is avoiding the necessity of adding result cache hints to queries at the application level.

A table annotation has a lower precedence than a SQL hint. Thus, you can override table and session settings by using hints at the query level. Permitted values for the RESULT_CACHE table annotation are as follows:

- DEFAULT
  If at least one table in a query is set to DEFAULT, then result caching is *not* enabled at the table level for this query, unless the RESULT_CACHE_MODE initialization parameter is set to FORCE or the RESULT_CACHE hint is specified. This is the default value.
- FORCE
  If all the tables of a query are marked as FORCE, then the query result is considered for caching. The table annotation FORCE takes precedence over the RESULT_CACHE_MODE parameter value of MANUAL set at the session level.

Shows the creation of the sales table with a table annotation that disables result caching. The example also shows a query of sales, whose results are not considered for caching because of the table annotation.

Example 7.17: DEFAULT Table Annotation

```
CREATE TABLE sales (...) RESULT_CACHE (MODE DEFAULT);

SELECT prod_id, SUM(amount_sold) FROM sales
GROUP BY prod_id ORDER BY prod_id;
```

Assume that later you decide to force result caching for the sales table as shown in. This example includes two queries of sales. The first query, which is frequently used and returns few rows, is eligible for caching because of the table annotation. The second query, which is a one-time query that returns many rows, uses a hint to prevent result caching.

Example 7.18: FORCE Table Annotation

```
ALTER TABLE sales RESULT_CACHE (MODE FORCE);

SELECT prod_id, SUM(amount_sold)
FROM sales GROUP BY prod_id
HAVING prod_id=136;

SELECT /*+ NO_RESULT_CACHE */ * FROM sales
ORDER BY time_id DESC;
```

Requirements for the Result Cache

If you enable the result cache, then this setting does not *guarantee* that a specific result set will be included in the client or server cache.

Read Consistency Requirements for the Result Cache

For a snapshot to be reusable, it must have read consistency. One of the following statements must be true for a result set to be eligible to be cached:

- The read-consistent snapshot used to build the result must retrieve the most current committed state of the data.
- The query points to an explicit point in time using flashback query.

If the current session has an active transaction referencing objects in a query, then the results from this query are not eligible for caching.

Additional Requirements for the Result Cache

You cannot cache results when the following objects or functions are in a query:

- Temporary tables and tables in the `SYS` or `SYSTEM` schemas
- Sequence `CURRVAL` and `NEXTVAL` pseudo columns
- SQL functions `CURRENT_DATE`, `CURRENT_TIMESTAMP`, `LOCAL_TIMESTAMP`, `USERENV/SYS_CONTEXT` (with non-constant variables), `SYS_GUID`, `SYSDATE`, and `SYS_TIMESTAMP`

The client result cache has additional limitations for result caching.

Query Parameter Requirements for the Result Cache

Cache results can be reused when they are **parameterized** with variable values when queries are equivalent and the parameter values are the same. Different values or bind variable names may cause cache misses. Results are parameterized if any of the following constructs are used in the query:

- Bind variables
- The SQL functions `DBTIMEZONE`, `SESSIONTIMEZONE`, `USERENV/SYS_CONTEXT` (with constant variables), `UID`, and `USER`
- NLS parameters.

Accessing Result Cache Information

You can query database views and tables to obtain information about the server and client result caches. Table 7-6 describes the most useful views and tables. The description column specifies the result cache to which they are applicable.

Table 7.6. Views and Tables Related to the Server and Client Result Caches

View/Table	Description
V$RESULT_CACHE_STATISTICS	Lists various server result cache settings and memory usage statistics.
V$RESULT_CACHE_MEMORY	Lists all the memory blocks in the server result cache and their corresponding statistics.
V$RESULT_CACHE_OBJECTS	Lists all the objects whose results are in the server result cache along with their attributes.
V$RESULT_CACHE_DEPENDENCY	Lists the dependency details between the results in the server cache and dependencies among these results.
CLIENT_RESULT_CACHE_STATS$	Stores cache settings and memory usage statistics for the client result caches obtained from the OCI client processes. This statistics table has entries for each client process that is using result caching. After the client processes terminate, the database removes their entries from this table. The client table lists information similar to V$RESULT_CACHE_ STATISTICS.
DBA_TABLES, USER_TABLES, ALL_TABLES	Includes a RESULT_CACHE column that shows the result cache mode annotation for the table. If the table has not been annotated, then this column shows DEFAULT. This column applies to both server and client result caching.

The following sample query monitors the server result cache statistics (sample output included):

```
COLUMN NAME FORMAT A20
SELECT NAME, VALUE FROM V$RESULT_CACHE_STATISTICS;

NAME                                VALUE
---------------------------------   -------------------------
Block Size (Bytes)                  1024
Block Count Maximum                 3136
Block Count Current                   32
Result Size Maximum (Blocks)         156
Create Count Success                   2
Create Count Failure                   0
```

Find Count	0
Invalidation Count	0
Delete Count Invalid	0
Delete Count Valid	0

The following sample query monitors the client result cache statistics (sample output included):

```
SELECT STAT_ID, SUBSTR(NAME,1,20), VALUE, CACHE_ID
FROM CLIENT_RESULT_CACHE_STATS$
ORDER BY CACHE_ID, STAT_ID;
```

STAT_ID	NAME OF STATISTICS	VALUE	CACHE_ID
1	Block Size	256	124
2	Block Count Max	256	124
3	Block Count Current	128	124
4	Hash Bucket Count	1024	124
5	Create Count Success	10	124
6	Create Count Failure	0	124
7	Find Count	12	124
8	Invalidation Count	8	124
9	Delete Count Invalid	0	124
10	Delete Count Valid	0	124

The `CLIENT_RESULT_CACHE_STATS$` table has statistics entries for each active client process performing client result caching. Every client process has a unique cache ID. To find the client connection information (for example, process IDs) for the sessions performing client caching, do the following:

- Obtain the session IDs from `GV$SESSION_CONNECT_INFO` for the `CLIENT_REGID` that exists in `CLIENT_RESULT_CACHE_STATS$` (the column name is `CACHE_ID`).
- Query the relevant columns from `GV$SESSION_CONNECT_INFO` and `GV$SESSION`.

For both client and server result cache statistics, a database that makes good use of result caching should show relatively low values for `Create Count Failure` and `Delete` Count `Valid`, while showing relatively high values for `Find Count`.

8 I/O Configuration and Design

Learning Objectives

The I/O subsystem is a vital component of an Oracle database. This chapter introduces fundamental I/O concepts, discusses the I/O requirements of different parts of the database, and provides sample configurations for I/O subsystem design.

This chapter includes the following topics:

- About I/O
- I/O Configuration
- I/O Calibration Inside the Database
- I/O Calibration with the Oracle Orion Calibration Tool

ABOUT I/O

Every Oracle Database reads or write data on disk, the database generates **disk I/O**. The performance of many software applications is inherently limited by disk I/O. Applications that spend the majority of CPU time waiting for I/O activity to complete are said to be **I/O-bound**.

Oracle Database is designed so that if an application is well written, its performance should not be limited by I/O. Tuning I/O can enhance the performance of the application if the I/O system is operating at or near capacity and is not able to service the I/O requests within an acceptable time. However, tuning I/O cannot help performance if the application is not I/O-bound (for example, when CPU is the limiting factor).

Consider the following database requirements when designing an I/O system:

- Storage, such as minimum disk capacity.
- Availability, such as continuous (24 x 7) or business hours only.
- Performance, such as I/O throughput and application response times.

Many I/O designs plan for storage and availability requirements with the assumption that performance will not be an issue. This is not always the case. Optimally, the number of disks and controllers to be configured should be determined by I/O throughput and redundancy requirements. The size of disks can then be determined by the storage requirements.

When developing an I/O design plan, consider using **Oracle Automatic Storage Management (Oracle ASM)**. Oracle ASM is an integrated, high-performance database file system and disk manager that is based on the principle that the database should manage storage instead of requiring an administrator to do it.

Oracle recommends that you use Oracle ASM for your database file storage, instead of raw devices or the operating system file system. Oracle ASM provides the following key benefits:

- Striping
- Mirroring
- Online storage reconfiguration and dynamic rebalancing
- Managed file creation and deletion.

I/O CONFIGURATION

This section describes the basic information to be gathered and decisions to be made when defining a system's I/O configuration. You want to keep the configuration as simple as possible, while maintaining the required availability, recoverability, and performance. The more complex a configuration becomes, the more difficult it is to administer, maintain, and tune.

This section contains the following topics:

- Lay Out the Files Using Operating System or Hardware Striping
- Manually Distributing I/O
- When to Separate Files
- Three Sample Configurations
- Oracle Managed Files
- Choosing Data Block Size.

Lay Out the Files Using Operating System or Hardware Striping

If your operating system has LVM software or hardware-based striping, then it is possible to distribute I/O using these tools. Decisions to be made when using an LVM or hardware striping include **stripe depth** and **stripe width**.

- Stripe depth is the size of the stripe, sometimes called stripe unit.
- Stripe width is the product of the stripe depth and the number of drives in the striped set.

Choose these values wisely so that the system is capable of sustaining the required throughput. For an Oracle database, reasonable stripe depths range from 256 KB to 1 MB. Different types of applications benefit from different stripe depths. The optimal stripe depth and stripe width depend on the following:

- Requested I/O Size
- Concurrency of I/O Requests
- Alignment of Physical Stripe Boundaries with Block Size Boundaries
- Manageability of the Proposed System.

Requested I/O Size

Table 8.1 lists the Oracle Database and operating system parameters that you can use to set I/O size:

Table 8.1. Oracle Database and Operating System Operational Parameters

Parameter	Description
DB_BLOCK_SIZE	The size of single-block I/O requests. This parameter is also used in combination with multiblock parameters to determine multiblock I/O request size.
OS block size	Determines I/O size for redo log and archive log operations.
Maximum OS I/O size	Places an upper bound on the size of a single I/O request.
DB_FILE_MULTIBLOCK_READ_COUNT	The maximum I/O size for full table scans is computed by multiplying this parameter with DB_BLOCK_SIZE. (the upper value is subject to operating system limits). If this value is not set explicitly (or is set to 0), the default value corresponds to the maximum I/O size that can be efficiently performed and is platform-dependent.
SORT_AREA_SIZE	Determines I/O sizes and concurrency for sort operations.
HASH_AREA_SIZE	Determines the I/O size for hash operations.

In addition to I/O size, the degree of concurrency also helps in determining the ideal stripe depth. Consider the following when choosing stripe width and stripe depth:

- On low-concurrency (sequential) systems, ensure that no single I/O visits the same disk twice. For example, assume that the stripe width is four disks, and the stripe depth is 32 K. If a single 1 MB I/O request (for example, for a full table scan) is issued by an Oracle server process, then each disk in the stripe must perform eight I/Os to return the requested data. To avoid this situation, the size of the average I/O should be smaller than the stripe width multiplied by the stripe depth. If this is not the case, then a single I/O request made by Oracle Database to the operating system results in multiple physical I/O requests to the same disk.
- On high-concurrency (random) systems, ensure that no single I/O request is broken up into multiple physical I/O calls. Failing to do this multiplies the number of physical I/O requests performed in your system, which in turn can severely degrade the I/O response times.

Concurrency of I/O Requests

In a system with a high degree of concurrent small I/O requests, such as in a traditional OLTP environment, it is beneficial to keep the stripe depth large. Using stripe depths larger than the I/O size is called **coarse grain striping**. In high-concurrency systems, the stripe depth can be as follows, where n > 1:

```
n * DB_BLOCK_SIZE
```

Coarse grain striping allows a disk in the array to service several I/O requests. In this way, a large number of concurrent I/O requests can be serviced by a set of striped disks with minimal I/O setup costs. Coarse grain striping strives to maximize overall I/O throughput. Multiblock reads, as in full table scans, will benefit when stripe depths are large and can be serviced from one drive. Parallel query in a data warehouse environment is also a candidate for coarse grain striping because many individual processes each issue separate I/Os. If coarse grain striping is used in systems that do not have high concurrent requests, then hot spots could result.

In a system with a few large I/O requests, such as in a traditional DSS environment or a low-concurrency OLTP system, then it is beneficial to keep the stripe depth small. This is called **fine grain striping**. In such systems, the stripe depth is as follows, where n is smaller than the multiblock read parameters, such as DB_FILE_MULTIBLOCK_READ_COUNT:

```
n * DB_BLOCK_SIZE
```

Fine grain striping allows a single I/O request to be serviced by multiple disks. Fine grain striping strives to maximize performance for individual I/O requests or response time.

Alignment of Physical Stripe Boundaries with Block Size Boundaries

On some Oracle Database ports, a database block boundary may not align with the stripe. If your stripe depth is the same size as the database block, then a single I/O issued by Oracle Database may result in two physical I/O operations.

This is not optimal in an OLTP environment. To ensure a higher probability of one logical I/O resulting in no more than one physical I/O, the minimum stripe depth should be at least twice the Oracle block size. Table 8-2 shows recommended minimum stripe depth for random access and for sequential reads.

Table 8.2. Minimum Stripe Depth

Disk Access	Minimum Stripe Depth
Random reads and writes	The minimum stripe depth is twice the Oracle block size.
Sequential reads	The minimum stripe depth is twice the value of DB_FILE_MULTIBLOCK_READ_COUNT, multiplied by the Oracle block size.

Manageability of the Proposed System

With an LVM, the simplest configuration to manage is one with a single striped volume over all available disks. In this case, the stripe width encompasses all available disks. All database files reside within that volume, effectively distributing the load evenly. This single-volume layout provides adequate performance in most situations.

A single-volume configuration is viable only when used in conjunction with RAID technology that allows easy recoverability, such as RAID 1. Otherwise, losing a single disk means losing all files concurrently and, hence, performing a full database restore and recovery.

In addition to performance, there is a manageability concern: the design of the system must allow disks to be added simply, to allow for database growth. The challenge is to do so while keeping the load balanced evenly.

For example, an initial configuration can involve the creation of a single striped volume over 64 disks, each disk being 16 GB. This is total disk space of 1 terabyte (TB) for the primary data. Sometime after the system is operational, an additional 80 GB (that is, five disks) must be added to account for future database growth.

The options for making this space available to the database include creating a second volume that includes the five new disks. However, an I/O bottleneck might develop, if these new disks are unable to sustain the I/O throughput required for the files placed on them.

Another option is to increase the size of the original volume. LVMs are becoming sophisticated enough to allow dynamic reconfiguration of the stripe width, which allows disks to be added while the system is online. This begins to make the placement of all files on a single striped volume feasible in a production environment.

If your LVM cannot support dynamically adding disks to the stripe, then it is likely that you need to choose a smaller, more manageable stripe width. Then, when new disks are added, the system can grow by a stripe width.

In the preceding example, eight disks might be a more manageable stripe width. This is only feasible if eight disks are capable of sustaining the required number of I/Os each second. Thus, when extra disk space is required, another eight-disk stripe can be added, keeping the I/O balanced across the volumes.

The smaller the stripe width becomes, the more likely it is that you will need to spend time distributing the files on the volumes, and the closer the procedure becomes to manually distributing I/O.

Manually Distributing I/O

If your system does not have an LVM or hardware striping, then I/O must be manually balanced across the available disks by distributing the files according to each file's I/O requirements. In order to make decisions on file placement, you should be familiar with the I/O requirements of the database files and the capabilities of the I/O system. If you are not familiar with this data and do not have a representative workload to analyze, you can make a first guess and then tune the layout as the usage becomes known.

To stripe disks manually, you need to relate a file's storage requirements to its I/O requirements:

1. Evaluate database disk-storage requirements by checking the size of the files and the disks.
2. Identify the expected I/O throughput for each file. Determine which files have the highest I/O rate and which do not have many I/Os. Lay out the files on all the available disks so as to even out the I/O rate.

One popular approach to manual I/O distribution suggests separating a frequently used table from its index. This is not correct. During the course of a transaction, the index is read first, and then the table is read. Because these I/Os occur sequentially, the table and index can be stored on the same disk without contention. It is not sufficient to separate a data file simply because the data file contains indexes or table data. The decision to segregate a file should be made only when the I/O rate for that file affects database performance.

When to Separate Files

Regardless of whether you use operating system striping or manual I/O distribution, if the I/O system or I/O layout is not able to support the I/O rate required, then you need to separate files with high I/O rates from the remaining files. You can identify such files either at the planning stage or after the system is live.

The decision to segregate files should only be driven by I/O rates, recoverability concerns, or manageability issues. (For example, if your LVM does not support dynamic reconfiguration of stripe width, then you might need to create smaller stripe widths to be able to add *n* disks at a time to create a new stripe of identical configuration.)

Before segregating files, verify that the bottleneck is truly an I/O issue. The data produced from investigating the bottleneck identifies which files have the highest I/O rates.

The following sections describe how to segregate the following file types:

- Tables, Indexes, and TEMP Tablespaces
- Redo Log Files
- Archived Redo Logs.

Tables, Indexes, and TEMP Tablespaces: If the files with high I/O are data files belonging to tablespaces that contain tables and indexes, then identify whether the I/O for those files can be reduced by tuning SQL or application code.

If the files with high-I/O are data files that belong to the **TEMP** tablespace, then investigate whether to tune the SQL statements performing disk sorts to avoid this activity, or to tune the sorting.

After the application has been tuned to avoid unnecessary I/O, if the I/O layout is still not able to sustain the required throughput, then consider segregating the high-I/O files.

Redo Log Files: If the high-I/O files are redo log files, then consider splitting the redo log files from the other files. Possible configurations can include the following:

- Placing all redo logs on one disk without any other files. Also consider availability; members of the same group should be on different physical disks and controllers for recoverability purposes.
- Placing each redo log group on a separate disk that does not store any other files.
- Striping the redo log files across several disks, using an operating system striping tool. (Manual striping is not possible in this situation.)
- Avoiding the use of RAID 5 for redo logs.

Redo log files are written sequentially by the Log Writer (LGWR) process. This operation can be made faster if there is no concurrent activity on the same disk. Dedicating a separate disk to redo log files usually ensures that LGWR runs smoothly with no further tuning necessary. If your system supports asynchronous I/O but this feature is not currently configured, then test to see if using this feature is beneficial. Performance bottlenecks related to LGWR are rare.

Archived Redo Logs: If the archiver is slow, then it might be prudent to prevent I/O contention between the archiver process and LGWR by ensuring that archiver reads and LGWR writes are separated. This is achieved by placing logs on alternating drives.

For example, suppose a system has four redo log groups, each group with two members. To create separate-disk access, the eight log files should be labeled 1a, 1b, 2a, 2b, 3a, 3b, 4a, and 4b. This requires at least four disks, plus one disk for archived files.

Figure 8.1 illustrates how redo members should be distributed across disks to minimize contention.

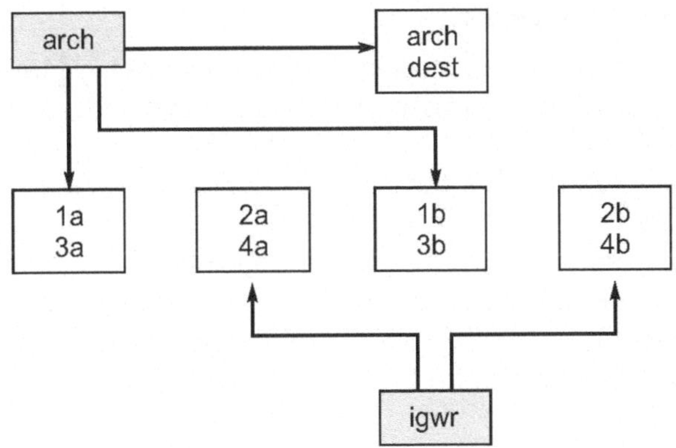

Figure 8.1. Distributing Redo Members Across Disks

In this example, LGWR switches out of log group 1 (member 1a and 1b) and writes to log group 2 (2a and 2b). Concurrently, the archiver process reads from group 1 and writes to its archive destination. Note how the redo log files are isolated from contention.

Mirroring redo log files, or maintaining multiple copies of each redo log file on separate disks, does not slow LGWR considerably. LGWR writes to each disk in parallel and waits until each part of the parallel write is complete. Thus, a parallel write does not take longer than the longest possible single-disk write.

Because redo logs are written serially, drives dedicated to redo log activity generally require limited head movement. This significantly accelerates log writing.

Three Sample Configurations

This section contains three high-level examples of configuring I/O systems. These examples include sample calculations that define the disk topology, stripe depths, and so on:

- Stripe Everything Across Every Disk
- Move Archive Logs to Different Disks
- Move Redo Logs to Separate Disks.

Stripe Everything Across Every Disk

The simplest approach to I/O configuration is to build one giant volume, striped across all available disks. To account for recoverability, the volume is mirrored (RAID 1). The striping unit for each disk should be larger than the maximum I/O size for the frequent I/O operations. This provides adequate performance for most cases.

Move Archive Logs to Different Disks

If archived redo log files are striped on the same set of disks as other files, then any I/O requests on those disks could suffer when the database is archiving the redo logs. Moving archived redo log files to separate disks provides the following benefits:

- The archive can be performed at very high rate (using sequential I/O).
- Nothing else is affected by the degraded response time on the archive destination disks.

The number of disks for archive logs is determined by the rate of archive log generation and the amount of archive storage required.

Move Redo Logs to Separate Disks

In high-update OLTP systems, the redo logs are write-intensive. Moving the redo log files to disks that are separate from other disks and from archived redo log files has the following benefits:

- Writing redo logs is performed at the highest possible rate. Hence, transaction processing performance is at its best.
- Writing of the redo logs is not impaired with any other I/O.

The number of disks for redo logs is mostly determined by the redo log size, which is generally small compared to current technology disk sizes. Typically, a configuration with two disks (possibly mirrored to four disks for fault tolerance) is adequate. In particular, by having the redo log files alternating on two disks, writing redo log information to one file does not interfere with reading a completed redo log for archiving.

Oracle Managed Files

When file systems can contain all Oracle Database data, database administration is simplified by using **Oracle Managed Files**. Oracle Database internally uses standard file system interfaces to create and delete files as needed for tablespaces, temp files, online logs, and control files. Administrators only specify the file system directory to be used for a particular type of file. You can specify one default location for data files and up to five multiplexed locations for the control and online redo log files.

Oracle Database ensures that a unique file is created and then deleted when it is no longer needed. This reduces corruption caused by administrators specifying the wrong file, reduces wasted disk space consumed by obsolete files, and simplifies creation of test and development databases. It also makes development of portable third-party tools easier, because it eliminates the need to put operating system-specific file names in SQL scripts.

New files can be created as Oracle Managed Files, while old ones are administered in the old way. Thus, a database can have a mixture of Oracle Managed Files and user-managed files.

Oracle Managed Files cannot be used with raw devices.

Several points should be considered when tuning Oracle Managed Files:

- Because Oracle Managed Files require the use of a file system, DBAs give up control over how the data is laid out. Therefore, it is important to correctly configure the file system.
- Build the file system for Oracle Managed Files on top of an LVM that supports striping. For load balancing and improved throughput, stripe the disks in the file system.
- Oracle Managed Files work best if used on an LVM that supports dynamically extensible logical volumes. Otherwise, configure the logical volumes as large as possible.
- Oracle Managed Files work best if the file system provides large extensible files.

Choosing Data Block Size

A block size of 8 KB is optimal for most systems. However, OLTP systems occasionally use smaller block sizes and DSS systems occasionally use larger block sizes. This section discusses considerations when choosing database block size for optimal performance and contains the following topics:

- Reads
- Writes
- Block Size Advantages and Disadvantages.

The use of multiple block sizes in a single database instance is not encouraged because of manageability issues.

Reads

Regardless of the size of the data, the goal is to minimize the number of reads required to retrieve the desired data.

- If the rows are small and access is predominantly random, then choose a smaller block size.
- If the rows are small and access is predominantly sequential, then choose a larger block size.
- If the rows are small and access is both random and sequential, then it might be effective to choose a larger block size.
- If the rows are large, such as rows containing large object (LOB) data, then choose a larger block size.

Writes

For high-concurrency OLTP systems, consider appropriate values for `INITRANS`, `MAXTRANS`, and `FREELISTS` when using a larger block size. These parameters affect the degree of update concurrency allowed within a block. However, you do not need to specify the value for `FREELISTS` when using automatic segment-space management.

If you are uncertain about which block size to choose, then try a database block size of 8 KB for most systems that process a large number of transactions. This represents a good compromise and is usually effective. Only systems processing LOB data need more than 8 KB.

Block Size Advantages and Disadvantages

Table 8.3 lists the advantages and disadvantages of different block sizes.

Table 8.3. Block Size Advantages and Disadvantages

Block Size	Advantages	Disadvantages
Smaller	Good for small rows with lots of random access. Reduces block contention.	Has relatively large space overhead due to metadata (that is, block header). Not recommended for large rows. There might only be a few rows stored for each block, or worse, row chaining if a single row does not fit into a block.
Larger	Has lower overhead, so there is more room to store data. Permits reading several rows into the buffer cache with a single I/O (depending on row size and block size). Good for sequential access or very large rows (such as LOB data).	Wastes space in the buffer cache, if you are doing random access to small rows and have a large block size. For example, with 8 KB block size and an 50 byte row size, you waste 7,950 bytes in the buffer cache when doing random access. Not good for index blocks used in an OLTP environment, because they increase block contention on the index leaf blocks.

I/O CALIBRATION INSIDE THE DATABASE

The I/O calibration feature of Oracle Database enables you to assess the performance of the storage subsystem, and determine whether I/O performance problems are caused by the database or the storage subsystem. Unlike other external I/O calibration tools that issue I/Os sequentially, the I/O calibration feature of Oracle Database issues I/Os randomly using Oracle data files to access the storage media, producing results that more closely match the actual performance of the database.

The section describes how to use the I/O calibration feature of Oracle Database and contains the following topics:

- Prerequisites for I/O Calibration
- Running I/O Calibration.

Oracle Database also provides Orion, an I/O calibration tool. Orion is a tool for predicting the performance of an Oracle database without having to install Oracle or create a database. Unlike other I/O calibration tools, Oracle Orion is expressly designed for simulating Oracle database I/O workloads using the same I/O software stack as Oracle. Orion can also simulate the effect of striping performed by Oracle Automatic Storage Management.

Prerequisites for I/O Calibration

Before running I/O calibration, ensure that the following requirements are met:

- The user must be granted the SYSDBA privilege timed_statistics must be set to TRUE Asynchronous I/O must be enabled.
  When using file systems, asynchronous I/O can be enabled by setting the FILESYSTEMIO _OPTIONS initialization parameter to SETALL.
- Ensure that asynchronous I/O is enabled for data files by running the following query:

```
COL NAME FORMAT A50
SELECT  NAME,ASYNCH_IO FROM V$DATAFILE F,V$IOSTAT_FILE I
WHERE   F.FILE#=I.FILE_NO
AND     FILETYPE_NAME= 'Data File';
```

Additionally, only one calibration can be performed on a database instance at a time.

Running I/O Calibration

The I/O calibration feature of Oracle Database is accessed using the DBMS_ RESOURCE_MANAGER.CALIBRATE_IO procedure. This procedure issues an I/O intensive read-only workload, made up of one megabyte of random of I/Os, to the database files to determine the maximum IOPS (I/O requests per second) and MBPS (megabytes of I/O per second) that can be sustained by the storage subsystem.

The I/O calibration occurs in two steps:

- In the first step of I/O calibration with the DBMS_RESOURCE_MANAGER.CALIBRATE_IO procedure, the procedure issues random database-block-sized reads, by default, 8 KB, to all data files from all database instances. This step provides the maximum IOPS, in the output parameter max_iops, that the database can sustain. The value max_iops is an important metric for OLTP databases. The output parameter actual_latency provides the average latency for this workload. When you need a specific target latency, you can specify the target latency with the input parameter max_latency (specifies the maximum tolerable latency in milliseconds for database-block-sized IO requests).

- The second step of calibration using the DBMS_RESOURCE_MANAGER.CALIBRATE_IO procedure issues random, 1 MB reads to all data files from all database instances. The second step yields the output parameter max_mbps, which specifies the maximum MBPS of I/O that the database can sustain. This step provides an important metric for data warehouses.

The calibration runs more efficiently if the user provides the num_physical_disks input parameter, which specifies the approximate number of physical disks in the database storage system.

Due to the overhead from running the I/O workload, I/O calibration should only be performed when the database is idle, or during off-peak hours, to minimize the impact of the I/O workload on the normal database workload.

To run I/O calibration and assess the I/O capability of the storage subsystem used by Oracle Database, use the DBMS_RESOURCE_MANAGER.CALIBRATE_IO procedure:

```
SET SERVEROUTPUT ON
DECLARE
    lat   INTEGER;
    iops  INTEGER;
    mbps  INTEGER;
BEGIN
-- DBMS_RESOURCE_MANAGER.CALIBRATE_IO (<DISKS>, <MAX_LATENCY>, iops, mbps, lat);
    DBMS_RESOURCE_MANAGER.CALIBRATE_IO (2, 10, iops, mbps, lat);
    DBMS_OUTPUT.PUT_LINE ('max_iops = ' || iops);
    DBMS_OUTPUT.PUT_LINE ('latency  = ' || lat);
    dbms_output.put_line('max_mbps = ' || mbps);
end;
/
```

When running the DBMS_RESOURCE_MANAGER.CALIBRATE_IO procedure, consider the following:

- Only run one calibration at a time on databases that use the same storage subsystem. If you simultaneously run the calibration across separate databases that use the same storage subsystem, the calibration will fail.
- Quiesce the database to minimize I/O on the instance.
- For Oracle Real Application Clusters (Oracle RAC) configurations, ensure that all instances are opened to calibrate the storage subsystem across nodes.
- For an Oracle Real Application Clusters (Oracle RAC) database, the workload is simultaneously generated from all instances.
- The num_physical_disks input parameter is optional. By setting the num_physical_disks parameter to the approximate number of physical disks in the database's storage system, the calibration can be faster and more accurate.
- In some cases, asynchronous I/O is permitted for data files, but the I/O subsystem for submitting asynchronous I/O may be maximized, and I/O calibration cannot continue. In such cases, refer to the port-specific documentation for information about checking the maximum limit for asynchronous I/O on the system.

At any time during the I/O calibration process, you can query the calibration status in the V$IO_CALIBRATION_STATUS view. After I/O calibration is successfully completed, you can view the results in the DBA_RSRC_IO_CALIBRATE table.

I/O CALIBRATION WITH THE ORACLE ORION CALIBRATION TOOL

This section describes the Oracle Orion Calibration Tool and includes the following sections:

- Introduction to the Oracle Orion Calibration Tool
- Getting Started with Orion
- Orion Input Files
- Orion Parameters
- Orion Output Files
- Orion Troubleshooting.

Introduction to the Oracle Orion Calibration Tool

Oracle Orion is a tool for predicting the performance of an Oracle database without having to install Oracle or create a database. Unlike other I/O calibration tools, Oracle Orion is expressly designed for simulating Oracle database I/O workloads using the same I/O software stack as Oracle. Orion can also simulate the effect of striping performed by Oracle Automatic Storage Management.

Table 8.4 lists the types of I/O workloads that Orion supports.

For each type of workload shown in Table 8.4, Orion can run tests using different I/O loads to measure performance metrics such as MBPS, IOPS, and I/O latency. Load is expressed in terms of the number of outstanding asynchronous I/Os. Internally, for each such load level, the Orion software keeps issuing I/O requests as fast as they complete to maintain the I/O load at that level. For random workloads, using either large or small sized I/Os, the load level is the number of outstanding I/Os. For large sequential workloads, the load level is a combination of the number of sequential streams and the number of outstanding I/Os per stream. Testing a given workload at a range of load levels can help you understand how performance is affected by load.

Note the following when you use Orion:

- Run Orion when the storage is idle (or pretty close to idle). Orion calibrates the performance of the storage based on the I/O load it generates; Orion is not able to properly assess the performance if non-Orion I/O workloads run simultaneously.
- If a database has been created on the storage, the storage can alternatively be calibrated using the PL/SQL routine `dbms_resource_manager.calibrate_io()`.

Table 8.4. Orion I/O Workload Support

Workload	Description
Small Random I/O	OLTP applications typically generate random reads and writes whose size is equivalent to the database block size, typically 8 KB. Such applications typically care about the throughput in I/Os Per Second (IOPS) and about the average latency (I/O turn-around time) per request. These parameters translate to the transaction rate and transaction turn-around time at the application layer. Orion simulates a random I/O workload with a given percentage of reads compared to writes, a given I/O size, and a given number of outstanding I/Os. In this Orion workload simulation, the I/Os are distributed across all disks.

Large Sequential I/O	Data warehousing applications, data loads, backups, and restores generate sequential read and write streams composed of multiple outstanding 1 MB I/Os. Such applications are processing large amounts of data, such as a whole table or a whole database and they typically care about the overall data throughput in MegaBytes Per Second (MBPS). Orion can simulate a given number of sequential read or write streams of a given I/O size with a given number of outstanding I/Os. Orion can optionally simulate Oracle Automatic Storage Management striping when testing sequential streams.
Large Random I/O	A sequential stream typically accesses the disks concurrently with other database traffic. With striping, a sequential stream is spread across many disks. Consequently, at the disk level, multiple sequential streams are seen as random 1 MB I/Os.
Mixed Workloads	Orion can simulate two simultaneous workloads: Small Random I/O and either Large Sequential I/O or Large Random I/O. This workload type enables you to simulate, for example, an OLTP workload of 8 KB random reads and writes with a backup workload of four sequential read streams of 1 MB I/Os.

Each Orion data point is a test for a specific mix of small and large I/O loads sustained for a duration. An Orion test consists of multiple data point tests. These data point tests can be represented as a two-dimensional matrix. Each column in the matrix represents data point tests with the same small I/O load, but varying large I/O loads. Each row represents data point tests with the same large I/O load, but varying small I/O loads. An Orion test can be for a single point, a single row, a single column, or for the whole matrix.

Orion Test Targets

You can use Orion to test any disk-based character device that supports asynchronous I/O. Orion has been tested on the following types of targets:

- *DAS (direct-attached) storage:* You can use Orion to test the performance of one or more local disks, volumes, or files on the local host.
- *SAN (storage-area network) storage:* Orion can be run on any host that has all or parts of the SAN storage mapped as character devices. The devices can correspond to striped or un-striped volumes exported by the storage array(s), or individual disks, or one or more whole arrays.
- *NAS (network-attached storage):* You can use Orion to test the performance on data files on NAS storage. In general, the performance results on NAS storage are dependent on the I/O patterns with which the data files have been created and updated. Therefore, you should initialize the data files appropriately before running Orion.

Orion for Oracle Administrators

Oracle administrators can use Orion to evaluate and compare different storage arrays, based on the expected workloads. Oracle administrators can also use Orion to determine the optimal number of network connections, storage arrays, storage array controllers, and disks for the expected peak workloads.

Getting Started with Orion

To get started using Orion, do the following:

1. Select a test name to use with the Orion `-testname` parameter. This parameter specifies a unique identifier for your Orion run. For example, use the test name "mytest".
2. Create an Orion input file, based on the test name. For example, create a file named `mytest.lun`. In the input file list the raw volumes or files to test. Add one volume name per line. Do not put comments or anything else in the `.lun` file.
   For example, an Orion input file could contain the following:
   ```
   /dev/raw/raw1
   /dev/raw/raw2
   /dev/raw/raw3
   /dev/raw/raw4
   /dev/raw/raw5
   /dev/raw/raw6
   /dev/raw/raw7
   /dev/raw/raw8
   ```
3. Verify that the all volumes specified in the input file, for example mytest.lun, are accessible using the command `dd` or another equivalent file viewing utility. For example, for a typical sanity-check try the following on a Linux system:
   ```
   $ dd if=/dev/raw/raw1 of=/dev/null bs=32k count=1024
   ```
   Depending on your platform, the file viewing utility you use and its interface may be different.
4. Verify that your platform has the necessary libraries installed to do asynchronous I/Os. The Orion test is completely dependent on asynchronous I/O. On Linux and Solaris, the library `libaio` must be in the standard `lib` directories or accessible through the shell environment's library path variable (usually `LD_LIBRARY_PATH` or `LIBPATH`, depending on your shell). Windows has built-in asynchronous I/O libraries, so this issue does not apply.
5. As a first test with Orion, use `-run` with either the `oltp` or `dss` option. If the database is primarily OLTP, then use `-run oltp`. If the database is primarily for data warehousing or analytics, then use `-run dss`.
   For example, use the following command to run an OLTP-like workload using the default input file name, `orion.lun`:
   ```
   $ ./orion -run oltp
   ```
   The I/O load levels generated by Orion take into account the number of disk spindles being tested (or specified with the `-num_disks` parameter). Keep in mind that the number of spindles *may or may not be* related to the number of volumes specified in the input file, depending on how these volumes are mapped.

6. The section, "Orion Output Files" provides sample results showing the Orion output files. Using the sample file mytest_summary.txt is a good starting point for verifying the input parameters and analyzing the output. The sample files mytest_*.csv contain comma-delimited values for several I/O performance measures.

Orion Input Files

When you specify the Orion `-testname` *<testname>* parameter, this sets the test name prefix for the Orion input and output filenames. The default value for the `-testname` option is "orion".

The Orion input file, *<testname>*`.lun` should contain a carriage-return-separated list of LUNs.

Orion Parameters

Use the Orion command parameters to specify the I/O workload type and to specify other Orion options.

Orion Required Parameter

The`-run` parameter is required with the Orion command. Table 8.5 describes the `-run` parameter.

Table 8.5. Required Orion Parameter

Optimal	Description	Default

`-run` *level*	Specifies the test run level to be *level*. This option provides the run level and allows complex commands to be specified at the advanced level. If not set as `-run advanced`, then setting any other parameter, besides `-cache_size` or `-verbose`, results in an error.
	Except **advanced**, all of the `-run` *level* settings use a pre-specified set of parameters
	The *level* must be one of:
	• **oltp**
	Tests with random small (8K) I/Os at increasing loads to determine the maximum IOPS.
	This parameter corresponds to the following Orion invocation:
	`%> ./orion -run advanced \`
	`-num_large 0 -size_small 8 -type rand \`
	`-simulate concat -write 0 -duration 60 \`
	`-matrix row`
	• **dss**
	Tests with random large (1M) I/Os at increasing loads to determine the maximum throughput.
	This parameter corresponds to the following Orion invocation:
	`%> ./orion -run advanced \`
	`-num_small 0 -size_large 1024 -type`
	`rand \`
	`-simulate concat -write 0 -duration 60 \`
	`-matrix column`
		`normal`

<table>
<tr>
<td></td>
<td>

• **simple**
Generates the Small Random I/O and the Large Random I/O workloads for a range of load levels. In this option, small and large I/Os are tested in isolation. The only optional parameters that can be specified at this run level are `–cache_size` and `–verbose`.
This parameter corresponds to the following Orion invocation:
<code>%> ./orion -run advanced \</code>
<code>size_small 8 -size_large 1024 -type rand \</code>
<code>-simulate concat -write 0 -duration 60 \</code>
<code>-matrix basic</code>
• **normal**
Same as `simple`, but also generates combinations of the small random I/O and large random I/O workloads for a range of loads. The only optional parameters that can be specified at this run level are `–cache_size` and `–verbose`.
This parameter corresponds to the following Orion invocation:
<code>%> ./orion -run advanced \</code>
<code>-size_small 8 -size_large 1024 -type rand \</code>
<code>-simulate concat -write 0 -duration 60 \</code>
<code>-matrix detailed</code>
• **advanced**
Tests the workload you specify with optional parameters.
Any of the optional parameters can be specified at this run level.

</td>
<td></td>
</tr>
</table>

Orion Optional Parameters

Table 8.6. Optional Orion Parameters

Optimal	Description	Default
`–cache_size` *num*	Size of the storage array's read or write cache *num* (in MB). For Large Sequential I/O workloads, Orion warms the cache by doing random large I/Os before each data point. Orion uses the cache size to determine the duration for this cache warming operation. If set to 0, do not perform cache warming. Unless this option is set to 0, Orion issues several unmeasured, random I/Os before each large sequential data point. These I/Os fill up the storage array's cache, if any, with random data so that I/Os from one data point do not result in cache hits for the next data point. Read tests are preceded with junk reads and write tests are preceded with junk writes. If specified, this 'cache warming' is performed until *num* MBs of I/O have been read or written.	Default Value: If not specified, warming occurs for a default amount of time (two minutes). That is, issue two minutes of unmeasured random I/Os before each data point.

-duration num_seconds	Set the duration to test each data point in seconds to the value num_seconds.	Default value: 60
-help	Prints Orion help information. All other options are ignored with help set.	
-matrix type	Type of mixed workloads to test over a range of loads. An Orion test consists of multiple data point tests. The data point tests can be represented as a two-dimensional matrix. Each column in the matrix represents data point tests with the same small I/O load, but varying large I/O loads. Each row represents data point tests with the same large I/O load, but varying small I/O loads. An Orion test can be for a single point, a single row, a single column, or the whole matrix, depending on the matrix type: • basic: No mixed workload. The Small Random and Large Random/ Sequential workloads are tested separately. Test small I/Os only, then large I/Os only. • etaile : Small Random and Large Random/Sequential workloads are tested in combination. Test entire matrix. • point: A single data point with S outstanding Small Random I/Os and L outstanding Large Random I/Os or sequential streams. S is set by the -num_small parameter. L is set by the -num_large parameter. Test with -num_small small I/Os, -num_large large I/Os. • col: Large Random/Sequential workloads only. Test a varying large I/O load with -num_small small I/Os. • ro : Small Random workloads only. Test a varying small I/O load with -num_large large I/Os. • max: Same as detailed, but only tests the workload at the maximum load, specified by the -num_small and -num_large parameters. Test varying loads up to the -num_small and -num_large limits.	Default value: basic

num_disks value	Specify the number of physical disks used by the test. Used to generate a range for the load. Specifies the number of disks (physical spindles). This number value is used to gauge the range of loads that Orion should test at. Increasing this parameter results in Orion using heavier I/O loads.	Default value: the number of LUNs in <testname>.lun. -num_large value
num_Large value	Controls the large I/O load. Note: this option only applies when -matrix is specified as: row, point, or max. When the -type option is set to rand, the parameter argument value specifies the number of outstanding large I/Os. When the -type option is set to seq, the parameter argument value specifies the number of sequential I/O streams.	Default value: no default
num_Small	Specify the maximum number of outstanding I/Os for the Small Random I/O workload. Note: This only applies when -matrix is specified as col, point, or max.	Default value: no default
num_stream IO num	Specify the number of concurrent I/Os per stream as num. Note: this parameter is only used if -type is seq.	Default value: 4
-simulate type	Data layout to simulate for Large Sequential I/O workload. Orion tests on a virtual LUN formed by combining specified LUNs in one of these ways. The type is one: • concat: A virtual volume is simulated by serially chaining the specified LUNs. A sequential test over this virtual volume will go from some point to the end of each one LUN, followed by the beginning to end of the next LUN, and so on. • rai : A virtual volume is simulated by striping across the specified LUNs. Each sequential stream issues I/Os across all LUNs using raid0 striping. The stripe depth is 1M by default, to match the Oracle Automatic Storage Management stripe depth, and can be changed with the -stripe parameter.	Default value: concat

	The offsets for I/Os are determined as follows: For Small Random and Large Random workloads: • The LUNs are concatenated into a single virtual LUN (VLUN) and random offsets are chosen within the VLUN. For Large Sequential workloads: • With striping (`-simulate raid0`). The LUNs are used to create a single striped VLUN. With no concurrent Small Random workload, the sequential streams start at fixed offsets within the striped VLUN. For n streams, stream i start at offset VLUNsize * (i + 1) / (n + 1), unless n is 1, in which case the single stream start at offset 0. With a concurrent Small Random workload, streams start at random offsets within the striped VLUN. • Without striping (`-simulate CONCAT`). The LUNs are concatenated into a single VLUN. The streams start at random offsets within the single VLUN. This parameter is typically only used if `-type` is `seq`.	
`-size_large` num	Specify the num, size of the I/Os (in KB) for the Large Random or Sequential I/O workload.	Default value: `1024`
`-size_small` num	Specify the num, size of the I/Os (in KB) for the Small Random I/O workload.	Default value: `8`
`-testname` tname	Specify the tname identifier for the test run. When specified, the input file containing the LUN disk or file names must be named <tname>.lun. The output files are named with the prefix <tname>_.	Default value: `orion`
`-type [rand | seq]`	Type of the Large I/O workload: • ran : Randomly distributed large I/Os. • se : Sequential streams of large I/Os.	Default value: `rand`
`-verbose`	Prints status and tracing information to standard output.	Default value: option not set

`-write` *num_write*	Specify the percentage of I/Os that are writes to *num_write*; the rest being reads. This parameter applies to both the Large and Small I/O workloads. For Large Sequential I/Os, each stream is either read-only or write-only; the parameter specifies the percentage of steams that are write-only. The data written to disk is garbage and unrelated to any existing data on the disk. **Caution:** write tests obliterate all data on the specified LUNS.	Default Value: `0`

Caution: Write tests obliterate all data on the specified LUNS.

Orion Command Line Samples

The following provides sample Orion commands for different types of I/O workloads:

1. To evaluate storage for an OLTP database:
   ```
   -run oltp
   ```
2. To evaluate storage for a data warehouse:
   ```
   -run dss
   ```
3. For a basic set of data:
   ```
   -run normal
   ```
4. To understand your storage performance with read-only, small and large random I/O workload:
   ```
   $ orion -run simple
   ```
5. To understand your storage performance with a mixed small and large random I/O workload:
   ```
   $ orion -run normal
   ```
6. To generate combinations of 32KB and 1MB reads to random locations:
   ```
   $ orion -run advanced -size_small 32 \
   -size_large 1024 -type rand -matrix detaileds
   ```
7. To generate multiple sequential 1 MB write streams, simulating 1 MB RAID-0 stripes:
   ```
   $ orion -run advanced -simulate raid0 \
   -stripe 1024 -write 100 -type seq -matrix col -num_small 0
   ```
8. To generate combinations of 32 KB and 1 MB reads to random locations:
   ```
   -run advanced -size_small 32 -size_large 1024 -type rand -matrix
   detailed
   ```
9. To generate multiple sequential 1 MB write streams, simulating RAID0 striping:
   ```
   -run advanced -simulate raid0 -write 100 -type seq -matrix col -
   num_small 0
   ```

Orion Output Files

The output files for a test run are prefixed by *<testname>_<date>* where *date* is *yyyymmdd_hhmm*.

Table 8.7 lists the Orion output files.

Table 8.7. Orion Generated Output Files

Output File	Description
*<testname>_<date>*_hist.csv	Histogram of I/O latencies.
*<testname>_<date>*_iops.csv	Performance results of small I/Os in IOPS.
*<testname>_<date>*_lat.csv	Latency of small I/Os in microseconds.
*<testname>_<date>*_mbps.csv	Performance results of large I/Os in MBPS.
*<testname>_<date>*_summary.txt	Summary of the input parameters, along with the minimum small I/O latency (in secs), the maximum MBPS, and the maximum IOPS observed.
*<testname>_<date>*_trace.txt	Extended, unprocessed output.

Caution: If you are performing write tests, be prepared to lose any data stored on the LUNs.

Orion Sample Output Files

Orion creates several output files as specified in Table 8.7. For the sample "mytest" shown in the section, "Getting Started with Orion", the output files are:

- **mytest_summary.txt:** This file contains:
  - Input parameters
  - Maximum throughput observed for the Large Random/Sequential workload
  - Maximum I/O rate observed for the Small Random workload
  - Minimum latency observed for the Small Random workload.
- **mytest_mbps.csv:** comma-delimited value file containing the data transfer rate (MBPS) results for the Large Random/Sequential workload. In the general case, this and all other CSV files contains a two-dimensional table. Each row in the table corresponds to a large I/O load level and each column corresponds to a specific small I/O load level. Thus, the column headings are the number of outstanding small I/Os and the row headings are the number of outstanding large I/Os (for random large I/O tests) or the number of sequential streams (for sequential large I/O tests).

  Shows the first few data points of the Orion MBPS output CSV file for "mytest". The simple mytest command-line does not test combinations of large and small I/Os. Hence, the MBPS file has just one column corresponding to 0 outstanding small I/Os. In, at a load level of 8 outstanding large reads and no small I/Os, the report data indicates a throughput of 103.06 MBPS.

Example 8.1: Mytest Sample Data Points

```
Large/Small,    0
1,      9.18
2,      37.59
4,      65.53
```

```
6,     87.03
8,     103.06
10,    109.67
```

Figure 8.2 shows a sample data transfer rate measured at different large I/O load levels. This chart can be generated by loading mytest_mbps.csv into a spreadsheet and graphing the data points. Orion does not directly generate such graphs. The x-axis corresponds to the number of outstanding large reads and the y-axis corresponds to the throughput observed.

The graph shown in Figure 8.2 shows typical storage system behavior. As the number of outstanding I/O requests is increased, the throughput increases. However, at a certain point the throughput level stabilizes, indicating the storage system's maximum throughput value.

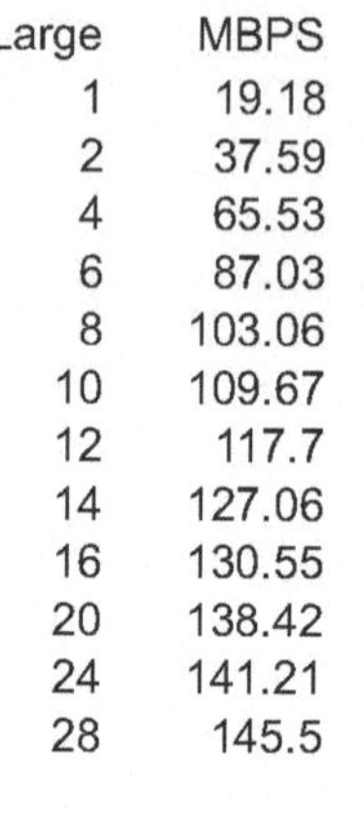

Large	MBPS
1	19.18
2	37.59
4	65.53
6	87.03
8	103.06
10	109.67
12	117.7
14	127.06
16	130.55
20	138.42
24	141.21
28	145.5

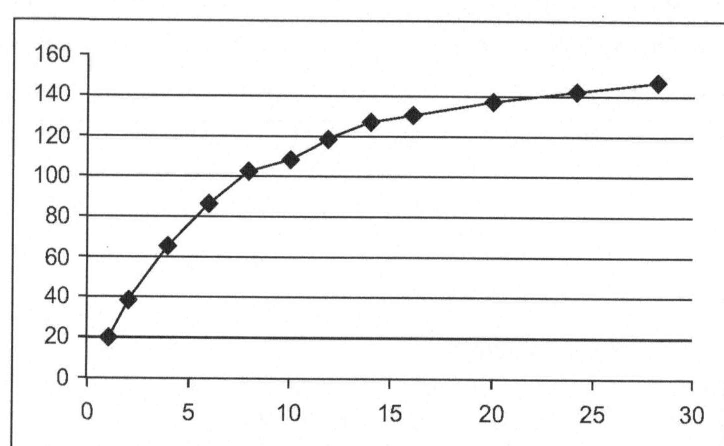

Figure 8.2. Sample I/O Load Levels

- **mytest_iops.csv:** Comma-delimited value file containing the I/O throughput (in IOPS) results for the Small Random workload. Like in the MBPS file, the column headings are the number of outstanding small I/Os and the row headings are the number of outstanding large I/Os, when testing large random, or the number of sequential streams (for large sequential).

  In the general case, a CSV file contains a two-dimensional table. However, for a simple test where you are not testing combinations of large and small I/Os the results file has just one row. Hence, the IOPS results file just has one row with 0 large I/Os. As shown in , an example data point with 12 outstanding small reads and no large I/Os provides a sample throughput of 951 IOPS.

Example 8.2: Sample Data Points with 12 Small Reads and No Large Reads

```
Large/Small,     1,     2,     3,     6,     9,     12   .
0,             105,   208,   309,   569,   782,    951   .
```

The graph shown in Figure 8.3, generated by loading mytest_iops.csv into Excel and charting the data, illustrates the IOPS throughput seen at different small I/O load levels. Figure 8.3 shows typical storage system behavior. As the number of outstanding I/O requests is increased, the throughput increases. However, at a certain point, the throughput level stabilizes, indicating the storage system reaches a maximum throughput value. At higher throughput levels, the latency for the I/O requests also increase significantly. Therefore, it is important to view this data with the latency data provided in the generated latency results in mytest_lat.csv.

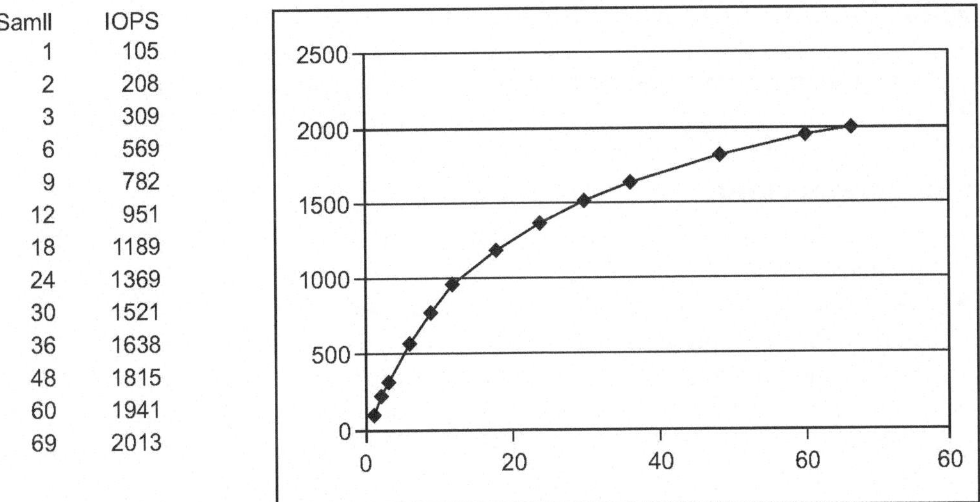

Samll	IOPS
1	105
2	208
3	309
6	569
9	782
12	951
18	1189
24	1369
30	1521
36	1638
48	1815
60	1941
69	2013

Figure 8.3. I/O Throughput at Different Small I/O Load Levels

mytest_lat.csv: Comma-delimited value file containing the latency results for the Small Random workload. As with the MBPS and IOPS files, the column headings are the number of outstanding small I/Os and the row headings are the number of outstanding large I/Os (when testing large random I/Os) or the number of sequential streams.

In the general case, a CSV file contains a two-dimensional table. However, for a simple test where you are not testing combinations of large and small I/Os the results file has just one row. Hence, the IOPS results file just has one row with 0 large I/Os. In the example shown in , at a sustained load level of 12 outstanding small reads and no large I/Os, the generated results show an I/O turn-around latency of 22.25 milliseconds.

Example 8.3: Sample CSV file with 12 Small Reads and No Large Reads

```
Large/Small, 1, 2, 3, 6, 9, 12 . . . .
0, 14.22, 14.69, 15.09, 16.98, 18.91, 21.25 . . . .
```

The graph in Figure 8.4, generated by loading mytest_lat.csv into Excel and charting the data, illustrates the small I/O latency at different small I/O load levels for mytest.

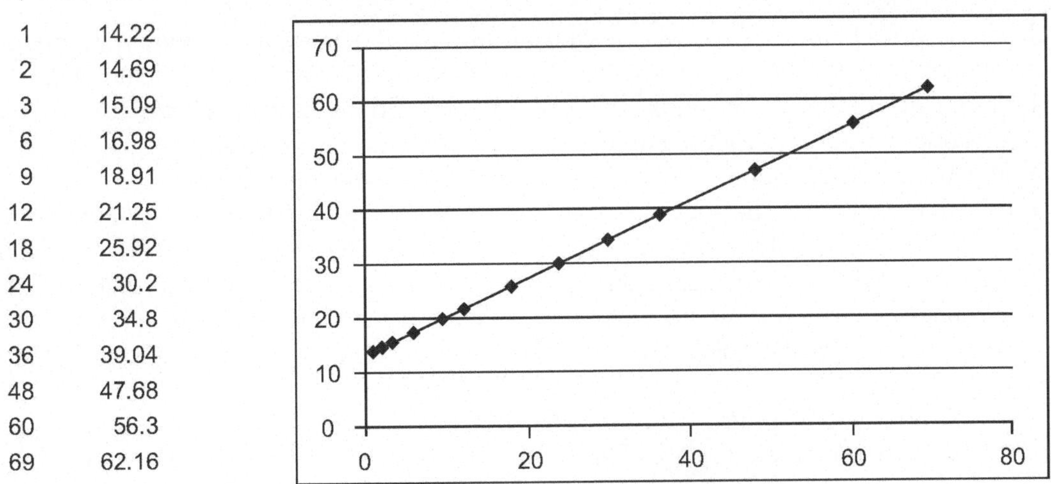

1	14.22
2	14.69
3	15.09
6	16.98
9	18.91
12	21.25
18	25.92
24	30.2
30	34.8
36	39.04
48	47.68
60	56.3
69	62.16

Figure 8.4. I/O Latency at Small I/O Load Levels

- **mytest_trace.txt:** Contains the extended, unprocessed test output.

Orion reports errors that occur during a test on standard output.

Orion Troubleshooting

1. If you are getting an I/O error on one or more of the volumes specified in the <*testname*>.lun file:
    - Verify that you can access the volume in the same mode as the test, read or write, using a file copy program such as `dd`.
    - Verify that your host operating system version can do asynchronous I/O.
    - On Linux and Solaris, the library `libaio` must be in the standard lib directories or accessible through the shell environment's library path variable (usually LD_LIBRARY_PATH or LIBPATH, depending on your shell).
2. If you run on NAS storage:
    - The file system must be properly mounted for Orion to run. Please consult your Oracle Installation Guide for directions (for example, the section, Appendix B "Using NAS Devices" in the Database Installation Guide for Linux x86).
    - The mytest.lun file should contain one or more paths of existing files. Orion does not work on directories or mount points. The file has to be large enough for a meaningful test. The size of this file should represent the eventual expected size of your datafiles (say, after a few years of use).
    - You may see poor performance doing asynchronous I/O over NFS on Linux (including 2.6 kernels).
    - If you are doing read tests and the reads are hitting untouched blocks of the file that were not initialized or previously written, some smart NAS systems may "fake" the read by returning zeroed-out blocks. When this occurs, you see unexpectedly good performance.

      The workaround is to write all blocks, using a tool such as `dd`, before performing the read test.
3. If you run Orion on Windows: Testing on raw partitions requires temporarily mapping the partitions to drive letters and specifying these drive letters in the test.lun file.
4. If you run Orion 32-bit Linux/x86 binary on an x86_64 system: Please copy a 32-bit libaio.so file from a 32-bit computer running the same Linux version.
5. If you are testing with a lot of disks (`num_disks` greater than around 30):
    - You should use the -duration option (see the optional parameters section for more details) to specify a long duration (like 120 seconds or more) for each data point. Since Orion tries to keep all the spindles running at a particular load level, each data point requires a ramp-up time, which implies a longer duration for the test.
    - You may get the following error message, instructing you to increase the duration value:

      `Specify a longer -duration value.`

      A duration of 2x the number of spindles seems to be a good rule of thumb. Depending on your disk technology, your platform may need more or less time.

6. If you get an error about libraries being used by Orion:
   - Linux/Solaris: See I/O error troubleshooting.
   - **NT-Only:** Do not move/remove the Oracle libraries included in the distribution. These must be in the same directory as orion.exe.
7. If you are seeing performance numbers that are "unbelievably good":
   - You may have a large read or write cache, or read and write cache somewhere between the Orion program and the disk spindles. Typically, the storage array controller has the biggest effect. Find out the size of this cache and use the-cache_size advanced option to specify it to Orion (see the optional parameters section for more details).
   - The total size of your volumes may be really small compared to one or more caches along the way. Try to turn off the cache. This is needed if the other volumes sharing your storage show significant I/O activity in a production environment (and end up using large parts of the shared cache).
8. If Orion is reporting a long estimated run time:
   - The run time increases when `-num_disks` is high. Orion internally uses a linear formula to determine how long it takes to saturate the given number of disks.
   - The `-cache_size` parameter affects the run time, even when it is not specified. Orion does cache warming for two minutes per data point by default. If you have turned off the cache, specify `-cache_size 0`.
   - The run time increases when a long-duration value is specified, as expected.

9 Managing Operating System Resources

Learning Objectives

This chapter explains how to tune the operating system for optimal performance of Oracle Database.
This chapter contains the following sections:

- Understanding Operating System Performance Issues
- Resolving Operating System Issues
- Understanding CPU
- Resolving CPU Issues

UNDERSTANDING OPERATING SYSTEM PERFORMANCE ISSUES

Operating system performance issues commonly involve process management, memory management, and scheduling. If you have tuned the Oracle database instance and still need to improve performance, verify your work or try to reduce system time. Ensure that there is enough I/O bandwidth, CPU power, and swap space. Do not expect, however, that further tuning of the operating system will have a significant effect on application performance. Changes in the Oracle Database configuration or in the application are likely to result in a more significant difference in operating system efficiency than simply tuning the operating system.

For example, if an application experiences excessive buffer busy waits, then the number of system calls increases. If you reduce the buffer busy waits by tuning the application, then the number of system calls decreases.

This section covers the following topics related to operating system performance issues:

- Using Operating System Caches
- Memory Usage
- Using Operating System Resource Managers.

Using Operating System Caches

Operating systems and device controllers provide data caches that do not directly conflict with Oracle Database cache management. Nonetheless, these structures can consume resources while offering little or no performance benefit. This situation is most noticeable when database files are stored in a Linux or UNIX file system. By default, all database I/O goes through the file system cache.

On some Linux and UNIX systems, direct I/O is available to the filestore. This arrangement allows the database files to be accessed within the file system, bypassing the file system cache. Direct I/O saves CPU resources and allows the file system cache to be dedicated to non-database activity, such as program texts and spool files.

This problem does not occur on Windows. All file requests by the database bypass the caches in the file system.

Although the operating system cache is often redundant because the Oracle Database buffer cache buffers blocks, in some cases the database does not use the database buffer cache. In these cases, using direct I/O or raw devices may yield worse performance than using operating system buffering. Examples include:

- Reads or writes to the `TEMP` tablespace
- Data stored in `NOCACHE` LOBs
- Parallel Query slaves reading data.

In some cases the database can cache parallel query data in the database buffer cache instead of performing direct reads from disk into the PGA. This configuration may be appropriate when the database servers have a large.

You may want to cache but not all files at the operating system level.

Asynchronous I/O

With synchronous I/O, when an I/O request is submitted to the operating system, the writing process blocks until the write is confirmed as complete. It can then continue processing. With asynchronous I/O, processing continues while the I/O request is submitted and processed. Use asynchronous I/O when possible to avoid bottlenecks.

Some platforms support asynchronous I/O by default, others need special configuration, and some only support asynchronous I/O for certain underlying file system types.

FILESYSTEMIO_OPTIONS Initialization Parameter

You can use the FILESYSTEMIO_OPTIONS initialization parameter to enable or disable asynchronous I/O or direct I/O on file system files. This parameter is platform-specific and has a default value that is best for a particular platform.

`FILESYTEMIO_OPTIONS` can be set to one of the following values:

- `ASYNCH`: enable asynchronous I/O on file system files, which has no timing requirement for transmission.
- `DIRECTIO`: enable direct I/O on file system files, which bypasses the buffer cache.
- `SETALL`: enable both asynchronous and direct I/O on file system files.
- `NONE`: disable both asynchronous and direct I/O on file system files.

Memory Usage

Memory usage is affected by both buffer cache limits and initialization parameters.

Buffer Cache Limits

The UNIX buffer cache consumes operating system memory resources. Although in some versions of UNIX, the UNIX buffer cache may be allocated a set amount of memory, it is common today for more sophisticated memory management mechanisms to be used. Typically, these will allow free memory pages to be used to cache I/O. In such systems, it is common for operating system reporting tools to show that there is no free memory, which is not generally a problem. If processes require more memory, the memory caching I/O data is usually released to allow the process memory to be allocated.

Parameters Affecting Memory Usage

The memory required by anyone Oracle Database session depends on many factors. Typically the major contributing factors are:

- Number of open cursors
- Memory used by PL/SQL, such as PL/SQL tables
- `SORT_AREA_SIZE` initialization parameter

In Oracle Database, the `PGA_AGGREGATE_TARGET` initialization parameter gives greater control over a session's memory usage.

Using Operating System Resource Managers

Some platforms provide operating system resource managers. These are designed to reduce the impact of peak load use patterns by prioritizing access to system resources. They usually implement administrative policies that govern which resources users can access and how much of those resources each user is permitted to consume.

Operating system resource managers are different from domains or other similar facilities. Domains provide one or more completely separated environments within one system. Disk, CPU, memory, and all other resources are dedicated to each domain and cannot be accessed from any other domain. Other similar facilities completely separate just a portion of system resources into different areas, usually separate CPU or memory areas. Like domains, the separate resource areas are dedicated only to the processing assigned to that area; processes cannot migrate across boundaries. Unlike domains, all other resources (usually disk) are accessed by all partitions on a system.

Oracle Database runs within domains, and within these other less complete partitioning constructs, as long as the allocation of partitioned memory (RAM) resources is fixed, not dynamic.

Operating system resource managers prioritize resource allocation within a global pool of resources, usually a domain or an entire system. Processes are assigned to groups, which are in turn assigned resources anywhere within the resource pool.

Oracle Database is not supported for use with any UNIX operating system resource manager's memory management and allocation facility. Oracle Database Resource Manager, which provides resource allocation capabilities within an Oracle database instance, cannot be used with any operating system resource manager.

If you have multiple instances on a node, and you want to distribute resources among them, then each instance should be assigned to a dedicated operating-system resource manager group or managed entity. To run multiple instances in the managed entity, use instance caging to manage how the CPU resources within the managed entity should be distributed among the instances. When Oracle Database Resource Manager is managing CPU resources, it expects a fixed amount of CPU resources for the instance. Without instance caging, it expects the available CPU resources to be equal to the number of CPUs in the managed entity. With instance caging, it expects the available CPU resources to be equal to the value of the `CPU_COUNT` initialization parameter. If there are less CPU resources than expected, then Oracle Database Resource Manager is not as effective at enforcing the resource allocations in the resource plan.

RESOLVING OPERATING SYSTEM ISSUES

This section provides hints for tuning various systems by explaining the following topics:

- Performance Hints on UNIX-Based Systems
- Performance Hints on Windows Systems
- Performance Hints on HP OpenVMS Systems.

Familiarize yourself with platform-specific issues so that you know what performance options the operating system provides.

Performance Hints on UNIX-Based Systems

On UNIX systems, try to establish a good ratio between the amount of time the operating system spends fulfilling system calls and doing process scheduling and the amount of time the application runs. The goal should be to run most of the time in application mode, also called user mode, rather than system mode.

The ratio of time spent in each mode is only a symptom of the underlying problem, which might involve the following:

- Paging or swapping
- Executing too many operating system calls
- Running too many processes.

If such conditions exist, then there is less time available for the application to run. The more time you can release from the operating system side, the more transactions an application can perform.

Performance Hints on Windows Systems

On Windows systems, as with UNIX-based systems, establish an appropriate ratio between time in application mode and time in system mode. You can easily monitor many factors with the Windows administrative performance tool: CPU, network, I/O, and memory are all displayed on the same graph to assist you in avoiding bottlenecks in any of these areas.

Performance Hints on HP OpenVMS Systems

Consider the paging parameters on a mainframe, and remember that Oracle Database can exploit a very large working set.

Free memory in HP OpenVMS environments is actually memory that is not mapped to any operating system process. On a busy system, free memory likely contains a page belonging to one or more currently active process. When that access occurs, a `soft page fault` takes place, and the page is included in the working set for the process. If the process cannot expand its working set, then one of the pages currently mapped by the process must be moved to the free set.

Any number of processes might have pages of shared memory within their working sets. The sum of the sizes of the working sets can thus markedly exceed the available memory. When the

Oracle server is running, the SGA, the Oracle Database kernel code, and the Oracle Forms run-time executable are normally all sharable and account for perhaps 80% or 90% of the pages accessed.

UNDERSTANDING CPU

To address CPU problems, first establish appropriate expectations for the amount of CPU resources your system should be using. Then, determine whether sufficient CPU resources are available and recognize when your system is consuming too many resources. Begin by determining the amount of CPU resources the Oracle database instance utilizes with your system in the following three cases:

- System is idle, when little Oracle Database and non-Oracle activity exists
- System at average workloads
- System at peak workloads.

You can capture various workload snapshots using the Automatic Workload Repository, Statspack, or the `UTLBSTAT/UTLESTAT` utility. Operating system utilities—such as `vmstat`, `sar`, and `iostat` on UNIX and the administrative performance monitoring tool on Windows—can be used along with the `V$OSSTAT` or `V$SYSMETRIC_HISTORY` view during the same time interval as Automatic Workload Repository, Statspack, or `UTLBSTAT/UTLESTAT` to provide a complimentary view of the overall statistics.

Workload is an important factor when evaluating your system's level of CPU utilization. During peak workload hours, 90% CPU utilization with 10% idle and waiting time can be acceptable. Even 30% utilization at a time of low workload can be understandable. However, if your system shows high utilization at normal workload, then there is no room for a peak workload. For example, Figure 9.1 illustrates workload over time for an application having peak periods at 10:00 AM and 2:00 PM.

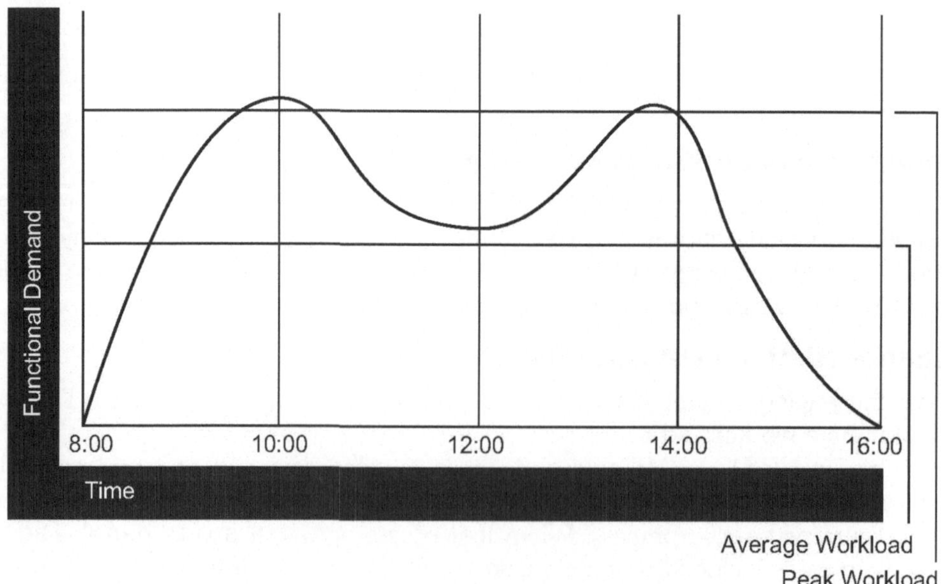

Figure 9.1. Average Workload and Peak Workload

This example application has 100 users working 8 hours a day. Each user entering one transaction every 5 minutes translates into 9,600 transactions daily. Over an 8-hour period, the system must support 1,200 transactions an hour, which is an average of 20 transactions a minute. If the demand rate were constant, then you could build a system to meet this average workload.

However, usage patterns are not constant and in this context, 20 transactions a minute can be understood as merely a minimum requirement. If the peak rate you need to achieve is 120 transactions a minute, then you must configure a system that can support this peak workload.

For this example, assume that at peak workload, Oracle Database uses 90% of the CPU resource. For a period of average workload, then, Oracle Database uses no more than about 15% of the available CPU resource, as illustrated in the following equation:

```
20 tpm / 120 tpm * 90% = 15% of available CPU resource
```

where `tpm` is transactions a minute.

If the system requires 50% of the CPU resource to achieve 20 tpm, then a problem exists: the system cannot achieve 120 transactions a minute using 90% of the CPU. However, if you tuned this system so that it achieves 20 tpm using only 15% of the CPU, then, assuming linear scalability, the system might achieve 120 transactions a minute using 90% of the CPU resources.

As users are added to an application, the workload can rise to what had previously been peak levels. No further CPU capacity is then available for the new peak rate, which is actually higher than the previous.

RESOLVING CPU ISSUES

You can resolve CPU capacity issues by:

- Detecting and solving CPU problems from excessive consumption.
- Reducing the impact of peak load use patterns by prioritizing CPU resource allocation using Oracle Database Resource Manager.
- Using instance caging to limit the number of CPUs that a database instance can use simultaneously when running multiple database instances on a multi-CPU system.
- Increasing hardware capacity and improving the system architecture.

Finding and Tuning CPU Utilization

Every process running on your system affects the available CPU resources. Therefore, tuning non-database factors can also improve database performance.

Use the `V$OSSTAT` or `V$SYSMETRIC_HISTORY` view to monitor system utilization statistics from the operating system.Useful statistics contained in`V$OSSTAT` and `V$SYSMETRIC_HISTORY` include:

- Number of CPUs
- CPU utilization
- Load
- Paging
- Physical memory.

You can use operating system monitoring tools to determine which processes run on the system as a whole. If the system is too heavily loaded, check the memory, I/O, and process management areas described later in this section.

You can use tools such as `sar -u` on many UNIX-based systems to examine the level of CPU utilization on the system. In UNIX, statistics show user time, system time, idle time, and time waiting for I/O. A CPU problem exists if idle time and time waiting for I/O are both close to zero (less than 5%) at a normal or low workload.

On Windows, you can use the administrative performance tool to monitor CPU utilization. This utility provides statistics on processor time, user time, privileged time, interrupt time, and DPC time.

This section contains the following topics related to checking system CPU utilization:

- Checking Memory Management
- Checking I/O Management
- Checking Network Management
- Checking Process Management.

This section describes how to check system CPU utilization on most UNIX-based and Windows systems. For other platforms, see your operating system documentation.

Checking Memory Management

Check the following memory management areas:

- Paging and Swapping
- Oversize Page Tables.

Paging and Swapping: Use the `V$OSSTAT` view, utilities such as `sar` or `vmstat` on UNIX, or the administrative performance tool on Windows, to investigate the cause of paging and swapping.

Oversize Page Tables: On UNIX, if the processing space becomes too large, then it can result in the page tables becoming too large. This is not an issue on Windows systems.

Checking I/O Management

Thrashing is an I/O management issue. Ensure that your workload fits into memory, so the computer is not thrashing (swapping and paging processes in and out of memory). The operating system allocates fixed portions of time during which CPU resources are available to your process. If the process wastes a large portion of each time period checking to ensure that it can run and ensuring that all necessary components are in the computer, then the process might be using only 50% of the time allotted to actually perform work.

Checking Network Management

Check client/server round trips. There is an overhead in processing messages. When an application generates many messages that need to be sent through the network, the latency of sending a message can result in CPU overload. To alleviate this problem, bundle multiple messages rather than perform lots of round trips. For example, you can use array inserts, array fetches, and so on.

Checking Process Management

Several process management issues discussed in this section should be checked.

Scheduling and Switching: The operating system can spend excessive time scheduling and switching processes. Examine the way in which you are using the operating system, because it is possible that too many processes are in use. On Windows systems, do not overload the server with too many non-database processes.

Context Switching: Due to operating system specific characteristics, your system could be spending a lot of time in context switches. Context switching can be expensive, especially with a large SGA. Context switching is not an issue on Windows, which has only one process for each instance. All threads share the same page table.

Oracle Database has several features for context switching:

- Post-wait driver:

  An Oracle process must be able to post another Oracle process (give it a message) and also must be able to wait to be posted. For example, a foreground process may need to post LGWR to tell it to write out all blocks up to a given point so that it can acknowledge a commit.

  Often this post-wait mechanism is implemented through UNIX Semaphores, but these can be resource intensive. Therefore, some platforms supply a post-wait driver, typically a kernel device driver that is a lightweight method of implementing a post-wait interface.
- Memory-mapped system timer:

  Oracle Database often needs to query the system time for timing information. This can involve an operating system call that incurs a relatively costly context switch. Some platforms implement a memory-mapped timer that uses an address within the processes virtual address space to contain the current time information. Reading the time from this memory-mapped timer is less expensive than the overhead of a context switch for a system call.
- List I/O interfaces to submit multiple asynchronous I/Os in One Call:

  List I/O is an application programming interface that allows several asynchronous I/O requests to be submitted in a single system call, rather than submitting several I/O requests through separate system calls. The main benefit of this feature is to reduce the number of context switches required.

Starting New Operating System Processes: There is a high cost in starting new operating system processes. Developers often create a single-purpose process, exit the process, and then create a new one. This technique re-creates and destroys the process each time, consuming excessive amounts of CPU, especially in applications that have large SGAs. The CPU is needed to build the page tables each time. The problem is aggravated when you pin or lock shared memory because you must access every page.

For example, if you have a 1 gigabyte SGA, then you might have page table entries for every 4 KB, and a page table entry might be 8 bytes. You could end up with (1 GB / 4 KB) * 8 byte entries. This becomes expensive, because you need to continually ensure that the page table is loaded.

Managing CPU Resources Using Oracle Database Resource Manager

Oracle Database Resource Manager allocates and manages CPU resources among database users and applications in the following ways:

- Preventing CPU saturation:

  If the CPUs run at 100%, then you can use Oracle Database Resource Manager to allocate a maximum amount of CPU to sessions in each consumer group. This feature can ensure that high-priority sessions can run immediately and lower the CPU consumption of low-priority sessions.
- Limiting CPU usage for a consumer group:

  You can use the Resource Manager directive `max_utilization_limit` to place a hard limit on the percentage of CPU that a consumer group can use. This feature restricts the

CPU consumption of low-priority sessions and can help provide more consistent performance for the workload in a consumer group.

- Limiting damage from runaway queries:
  Starting with Oracle Database 11g Release 2 (11.2.0.2), Oracle Database Resource Manager can limit the damage from runaway queries by limiting the maximum execution time for a call, or by moving a long-running query to a lower-priority consumer group.
- Limiting the parallel statement activity for a consumer group:
  Starting with Oracle Database 11g Release 2 (11.2.0.2), you can use the Resource Manager directive `parallel_target_percentage` to prevent one consumer group from monopolizing all parallel servers. The database queues parallel statements if they would cause this limit to be exceeded.
  For example, assume that the target number of parallel servers is 64, and the consumer group `ETL` has this directive set to 50%. If consumer group `ETL` is using 30 parallel servers, and if a new parallel statement needs 4 parallel servers, then the database would queue this statement.

Managing CPU Resources Using Instance Caging

When running multiple database instances on a single system, the instances compete for CPU resources. One resource-intensive database instance may significantly degrade the performance of the other instances. To avoid this problem, you can use instance caging to limit the number of CPUs that can used by each instance. Oracle Database Resource Manager then allocates CPU among the various database sessions according to the resource plan that you set for the instance, thereby minimizing the likelihood of the instance becoming CPU-bound.

10

Instance Tuning Using Performance Views

Learning Objectives

After the initial configuration of a database, monitoring and tuning an instance regularly is important to eliminate any potential performance bottlenecks. This chapter discusses the tuning process using Oracle V$ performance views.

This chapter contains the following sections:

- Instance Tuning Steps
- Interpreting Oracle Database Statistics
- Wait Events Statistics
- Real-Time SQL Monitoring
- Tuning Instance Recovery Performance: Fast-Start Fault Recovery

INSTANCE TUNING STEPS

These are the main steps in the Oracle performance method for instance tuning:

1. Define the Problem.
   Get candid feedback from users about the scope of the performance problem.
2. Examine the Host System and Examine the Oracle Database Statistics.
   - After obtaining a full set of operating system, database, and application statistics, examine the data for any evidence of performance problems.
   - Consider the list of common performance errors to see whether the data gathered suggests that they are contributing to the problem.
   - Build a conceptual model of what is happening on the system using the performance data gathered.
3. Implement and Measure Change.
   Propose changes to be made and the expected result of implementing the changes. Then, implement the changes and measure application performance.
4. Determine whether the performance objective defined in step 1 has been met. If not, then repeat steps 2 and 3 until the performance goals are met.

The remainder of this chapter discusses instance tuning using the Oracle Database dynamic performance views. However, Oracle recommends using the Automatic Workload Repository (AWR) and Automatic Database Diagnostic Monitor (ADDM) for statistics gathering, monitoring, and tuning due to the extended feature list.

If your site does not have the AWR and ADDM features, then you can use Statspack to gather Oracle database instance statistics.

Define the Problem

It is vital to develop a good understanding of the purpose of the tuning exercise and the nature of the problem before attempting to implement a solution. Without this understanding, it is virtually impossible to implement effective changes. The data gathered during this stage helps determine the next step to take and what evidence to examine.

Gather the following data:

1. Identify the performance objective.
   What is the measure of acceptable performance? How many transactions an hour, or seconds, response time will meet the required performance level?
2. Identify the scope of the problem.
   What is affected by the slowdown? For example, is the whole instance slow? Is it a particular application, program, specific operation, or a single user?
3. Identify the time frame when the problem occurs.
   Is the problem only evident during peak hours? Does performance deteriorate over the course of the day? Was the slowdown gradual (over the space of months or weeks) or sudden?
4. Quantify the slowdown.
   This helps identify the extent of the problem and also acts as a measure for comparison when deciding whether changes implemented to fix the problem have actually made an improvement. Find a consistently reproducible measure of the response time or job run time. How much worse are the timings than when the program was running well?
5. Identify any changes.
   Identify what has changed since performance was acceptable. This may narrow the potential cause quickly. For example, has the operating system software, hardware, application software, or Oracle Database release been upgraded? Has more data been loaded into the system, or has the data volume or user population grown?

At the end of this phase, you should have a good understanding of the symptoms. If the symptoms can be identified as local to a program or set of programs, then the problem is handled in a different manner than instance-wide performance issues.

Examine the Host System

Look at the load on the database server and the database instance. Consider the operating system, the I/O subsystem, and network statistics, because examining these areas helps determine what might be worth further investigation. In multitier systems, also examine the application server middle-tier hosts.

Examining the host hardware often gives a strong indication of the bottleneck in the system. This determines which Oracle Database performance data could be useful for cross-reference and further diagnosis.

Data to examine includes the following:

- CPU Usage
- Identifying I/O Problems
- Identifying Network Issues.

CPU Usage

If there is a significant amount of idle CPU, then there could be an I/O, application, or database bottleneck. Note that wait I/O should be considered as idle CPU.

If there is high CPU usage, then determine whether the CPU is being used effectively. Is the majority of CPU usage attributable to a small number of high-CPU using programs, or is the CPU consumed by an evenly distributed workload?

If a small number of high-usage programs use the CPU, then look at the programs to determine the cause. Check whether some processes alone consume the full power of one CPU. Depending on the process, this could indicate a CPU or process-bound workload that can be tackled by dividing or parallelizing process activity.

Non-Oracle Processes: If the programs are not Oracle programs, then identify whether they are legitimately requiring that amount of CPU. If so, determine whether their execution be delayed to off-peak hours. Identifying these CPU intensive processes can also help narrowing what specific activity, such as I/O, network, and paging, is consuming resources and how can it be related to the database workload.

Oracle Processes: If a small number of Oracle processes consumes most of the CPU resources, then use `SQL_TRACE` and `TKPROF` to identify the SQL or PL/SQL statements to see if a particular query or PL/SQL program unit can be tuned. For example, a SELECT statement could be CPU-intensive if its execution involves many reads of data in cache (logical reads) that could be avoided with better SQL optimization.

Oracle Database CPU Statistics: Oracle Database CPU statistics are available in several `V$` views:

- `V$SYSSTAT` shows Oracle Database CPU usage for all sessions. The `CPU used by this session` statistic shows the aggregate CPU used by all sessions. The `parse time cpu` statistic shows the total CPU time used for parsing.
- `V$SESSTAT` shows Oracle Database CPU usage for each session. Use this view to determine which particular session is using the most CPU.
- `V$RSRC_CONSUMER_GROUP` shows CPU utilization statistics for each consumer group when the Oracle Database Resource Manager is running.

Interpreting CPU Statistics

It is important to recognize that CPU time and real time are distinct. With eight CPUs, for any given minute in real time, there are eight minutes of CPU time available. On Windows and UNIX, this can be either user time or system time (privileged mode on Windows). Thus, average CPU time utilized by all processes (threads) on the system could be greater than one minute for everyone minute real time interval.

At any given moment, you know how much time Oracle Database has used on the system. So, if eight minutes are available and Oracle Database uses four minutes of that time, then you know that 50% of all CPU time is used by Oracle. If your process is not consuming that time, then some other process is. Identify the processes that are using CPU time, figure out why, and then attempt to tune them. See Chapter 21, "Using Application Tracing Tools".

If the CPU usage is evenly distributed over many Oracle server processes, examine the `V$SYS_TIME_MODEL` view to help get a precise understanding of where most time is spent. See Table 10-1, "Wait Events and Potential Causes".

Identifying I/O Problems

An overly active I/O system can be evidenced by disk queue lengths greater than two, or disk service times that are over 20-30ms. If the I/O system is overly active, then check for potential hot spots that could benefit from distributing the I/O across more disks. Also identify whether the load can be reduced by lowering the resource requirements of the programs using those resources. If the I/O problems are caused by Oracle Database, then I/O tuning can begin. If Oracle Database is not consuming the available I/O resources, then identify the process that is using up the I/O. Determine why the process is using up the I/O, and then tune this process.

I/O problems can be identified using `V$` views in Oracle Database and monitoring tools in the operating system, as described in the following sections:

- Identifying I/O Problems Using `V$` Views
- Identifying I/O Problems Using Operating System Monitoring Tools.

Identifying I/O Problems Using V$ Views: Check the Oracle wait event data in `V$SYSTEM_EVENT` to see whether the top wait events are I/O related. I/O related events include db file sequential read, `db file scattered read, db file single write, db file parallel write, and log file parallel write.` These are all events corresponding to I/Os performed against data files and log files. If any of these wait events correspond to high average time, then investigate the I/O contention.

Cross reference the host I/O system data with the I/O sections in the Automatic Repository report to identify hot data files and tablespaces. Also compare the I/O times reported by the operating system with the times reported by Oracle Database to see if they are consistent.

An I/O problem can also manifest itself with non-I/O related wait events. For example, the difficulty in finding a free buffer in the buffer cache or high wait times for logs to be flushed to disk can also be symptoms of an I/O problem. Before investigating whether the I/O system should be reconfigured, determine if the load on the I/O system can be reduced.

To reduce I/O load caused by Oracle Database, examine the I/O statistics collected for all I/O calls made by the database using the following views:

- `V$IOSTAT_CONSUMER_GROUP`.

  The `V$IOSTAT_CONSUMER_GROUP` view captures I/O statistics for consumer groups. If Oracle Database Resource Manager is enabled, I/O statistics for all consumer groups that are part of the currently enabled resource plan are captured.

- `V$IOSTAT_FILE`.

  The `V$IOSTAT_FILE` view captures I/O statistics of database files that are or have been accessed. The `SMALL_SYNC_READ_LATENCY` column displays the latency for single block synchronous reads (in milliseconds), which translates directly to the amount of time that clients need to wait before moving onto the next operation. This defines the responsiveness of the storage subsystem based on the current load. If there is a high latency for critical data files, you may want to consider relocating these files to improve their service time. To calculate latency statistics, `timed_statistics` must be set to `TRUE`.

- `V$IOSTAT_FUNCTION`.

  The `V$IOSTAT_FUNCTION` view captures I/O statistics for database functions (such as the LGWR and DBWR).

An I/O can be issued by various Oracle processes with different functionalities. The top database functions are classified in the **V$IOSTAT_FUNCTION** view. In cases when there is a conflict of I/O functions, the I/O is placed in the bucket with the lower **FUNCTION_ID**. For example, if XDB issues an I/O from the buffer cache, the I/O would be classified as an XDB I/O because it has a lower **FUNCTION_ID** value. Any unclassified function is placed in the Others bucket. You can display the **FUNCTION_ID** hierarchy by querying the **V$IOSTAT_FUNCTION** view:

```
select FUNCTION_ID, FUNCTION_NAME
from v$iostat_function
order by FUNCTION_ID;
```

```
         FUNCTION_ID    FUNCTION_NAME
        ------------    ----------------
                   0    RMAN
                   1    DBWR
                   2    LGWR
                   3    ARCH
                   4    XDB
                   5    Streams AQ
                   6    Data Pump
                   7    Recovery
                   8    Buffer Cache Reads
                   9    Direct Reads
                  10    Direct Writes
                  11    Others
```

These **V$IOSTAT** views contains I/O statistics for both single and multi block read and write operations. Single block operations are small I/Os that are less than or equal to 128 kilobytes. Multi block operations are large I/Os that are greater than 128 kilobytes. For each of these operations, the following statistics are collected:

- Identifier
- Total wait time (in milliseconds)
- Number of waits executed (for consumer groups and functions)
- Number of requests for each operation
- Number of single and multi block bytes read
- Number of single and multi block bytes written.

You should also look at SQL statements that perform many physical reads by querying the **V$SQLAREA** view, or by reviewing the "SQL ordered by Reads" section of the Automatic Workload Repository report. Examine these statements to see how they can be tuned to reduce the number of I/Os.

Identifying I/O Problems Using Operating System Monitoring Tools: Use operating system monitoring tools to determine what processes are running on the system as a whole and to monitor disk access to all files. Remember that disks holding data files and redo log files can also hold files that are not related to Oracle Database. Reduce any heavy access to disks that contain database files. You can monitor access to non-database files only through operating system facilities, rather than through the **V$** views.

Utilities, such as `sar -d` (or `iostat`) on many UNIX systems and the administrative performance monitoring tool on Windows systems, examine I/O statistics for the entire system.

Identifying Network Issues

Using operating system utilities, look at the network round-trip ping time and the number of collisions. If the network is causing large delays in response time, then investigate possible causes.

To identify network I/O caused by remote access of database files, examine the V$IOSTAT_NETWORK view. This view contains network I/O statistics caused by accessing files on a remote database instance, including:

- Database client initiating the network I/O (such as RMAN and PLSQL)
- Number of read and write operations issued
- Number of kilobytes read and written
- Total wait time in milliseconds for read operations
- Total wait in milliseconds for write operations.

After the cause of the network issue is identified, network load can be reduced by scheduling large data transfers to off-peak times, or by coding applications to batch requests to remote hosts, rather than accessing remote hosts once (or more) for one request.

Examine the Oracle Database Statistics

You should examine Oracle Database statistics and cross-reference them with operating system statistics to ensure a consistent diagnosis of the problem. Operating system statistics can indicate a good place to begin tuning. However, if the goal is to tune the Oracle database instance, then look at the Oracle Database statistics to identify the resource bottleneck from a database perspective before implementing corrective action.

The following sections discuss the common Oracle data sources used while tuning.

Setting the Level of Statistics Collection

Oracle Database provides the initialization parameter STATISTICS_LEVEL, which controls all major statistics collections or advisories in the database. This parameter sets the statistics collection level for the database.

Depending on the setting of STATISTICS_LEVEL, certain advisories or statistics are collected, as follows:

- BASIC: No advisories or statistics are collected. Monitoring and many automatic features are disabled. Oracle does not recommend this setting because it disables important Oracle Database features.
- TYPICAL: This is the default value and ensures collection for all major statistics while providing best overall database performance. This setting should be adequate for most environments.
- ALL: All of the advisories or statistics that are collected with the TYPICAL setting are included, plus timed operating system statistics and row source execution statistics.

V$STATISTICS_LEVEL

This view lists the status of the statistics or advisories controlled by STATISTICS_LEVEL.

Wait Event

Wait events are statistics that are incremented by a server process or thread to indicate that it had to wait for an event to complete before being able to continue processing. Wait event data reveals various symptoms of problems that might be impacting performance, such as latch contention, buffer contention, and I/O contention. Remember that these are only symptoms of problems, not the actual causes.

Wait events are grouped into classes. The wait event classes include: Administrative, Application, Cluster, Commit, Concurrency, Configuration, Idle, Network, Other, Scheduler, System I/O, and User I/O.

A server process can wait for the following:

- A resource to become available, such as a buffer or a latch.
- An action to complete, such as an I/O.
- More work to do, such as waiting for the client to provide the next SQL statement to execute. Events that identify that a server process is waiting for more work are known as idle events.

Wait event statistics include the number of times an event was waited for and the time waited for the event to complete. If the initialization parameter `TIMED_STATISTICS` is set to `true`, then you can also see how long each resource was waited for.

To minimize user response time, reduce the time spent by server processes waiting for event completion. Not all wait events have the same wait time. Therefore, it is more important to examine events with the most total time waited rather than wait events with a high number of occurrences. Usually, it is best to set the dynamic parameter `TIMED_STATISTICS` to true at least while monitoring performance.

Dynamic Performance Views Containing Wait Event Statistics

These dynamic performance views can be queried for wait event statistics:

- `V$ACTIVE_SESSION_HISTORY`.
  The `V$ACTIVE_SESSION_HISTORY` view displays active database session activity, sampled once every second.
- `V$SESS_TIME_MODEL and V$SYS_TIME_MODEL`.
  The `V$SESS_TIME_MODEL` and `V$SYS_TIME_MODEL` views contain time model statistics, including `DB time` which is the total time spent in database calls.
- `V$SESSION_WAIT`.
  The `V$SESSION_WAIT` view displays information about the current or last wait for each session (such as wait ID, class, and time).
- `V$SESSION`.
  The `V$SESSION` view displays information about each current session and contains the same wait statistics as those found in the `V$SESSION_WAIT` view. If applicable, this view also contains detailed information about the object that the session is currently waiting for (such as object number, block number, file number, and row number), the blocking session responsible for the current wait (such as the blocking session ID, status, and type), and the amount of time waited.
- `V$SESSION_EVENT`.
  The `V$SESSION_EVENT` view provides summary of all the events the session has waited for since it started.
- `V$SESSION_WAIT_CLASS`.
  The `V$SESSION_WAIT_CLASS` view provides the number of waits and the time spent in each class of wait events for each session.
- `V$SESSION_WAIT_HISTORY`.
  The `V$SESSION_WAIT_HISTORY` view displays information about the last ten wait events for each active session (such as event type and wait time).
- `V$SYSTEM_EVENT`.
  The `V$SYSTEM_EVENT` view provides a summary of all the event waits on the instance since it started.

- V$EVENT_HISTOGRAM.
  The V$EVENT_HISTOGRAM view displays a histogram of the number of waits, the maximum wait, and total wait time on an event basis.
- V$FILE_HISTOGRAM.
  The V$FILE_HISTOGRAM view displays a histogram of times waited during single block reads for each file.
- V$SYSTEM_WAIT_CLASS.
  The V$SYSTEM_WAIT_CLASS view provides the instance wide time totals for the number of waits and the time spent in each class of wait events.
- V$TEMP_HISTOGRAM.
  The V$TEMP_HISTOGRAM view displays a histogram of times waited during single block reads for each temporary file.

Investigate wait events and related timing data when performing reactive performance tuning. The events with the most time listed against them are often strong indications of the performance bottleneck. For example, by looking at V$SYSTEM_EVENT, you might notice lots of buffer busy waits. It might be that many processes are inserting into the same block and must wait for each other before they can insert. The solution could be to use automatic segment space management or partitioning for the object in question.

System Statistics

System statistics are typically used in conjunction with wait event data to find further evidence of the cause of a performance problem.

For example, if V$SYSTEM_EVENT indicates that the largest wait event (in terms of wait time) is the event buffer busy waits, then look at the specific buffer wait statistics available in the view V$WAITSTAT to see which block type has the highest wait count and the highest wait time.

After the block type has been identified, also look at V$SESSION real-time while the problem is occurring or V$ACTIVE_SESSION_HISTORY and DBA_HIST_ACTIVE_SESS_HISTORY views after the problem has been experienced to identify the contended-for objects using the object number indicated. The combination of this data indicates the appropriate corrective action.

Statistics are available in many V$ views. Some common views include the following:

- V$ACTIVE_SESSION_HISTORY
- V$SYSSTAT
- V$FILESTAT
- V$ROLLSTAT
- V$ENQUEUE_STAT
- V$LATCH

V$ACTIVE_SESSION_HISTORY

This view displays active database session activity, sampled once every second.

V$SYSSTAT

This contains overall statistics for many different parts of Oracle Database, including rollback, logical and physical I/O, and parse data. Data from V$SYSSTAT is used to compute ratios, such as the buffer cache hit ratio.

V$FILESTAT

This contains detailed file I/O statistics for each file, including the number of I/Os for each file and the average read time.

V$ROLLSTAT

This contains detailed rollback and undo segment statistics for each segment.

V$ENQUEUE_STAT

This contains detailed enqueue statistics for each enqueue, including the number of times an enqueue was requested and the number of times an enqueue was waited for, and the wait time.

V$LATCH

This contains detailed latch usage statistics for each latch, including the number of times each latch was requested and the number of times the latch was waited for.

Segment-Level Statistics

You can gather segment-level statistics to help you spot performance problems associated with individual segments. Collecting and viewing segment-level statistics is a good way to effectively identify hot tables or indexes in an instance.

After viewing wait events and system statistics to identify the performance problem, you can use segment-level statistics to find specific tables or indexes that are causing the problem. Consider, for example, that `V$SYSTEM_EVENT` indicates that buffer busy waits cause a fair amount of wait time. You can select from `V$SEGMENT_STATISTICS` the top segments that cause the buffer busy waits. Then you can focus your effort on eliminating the problem in those segments.

You can query segment-level statistics through the following dynamic performance views:

- `V$SEGSTAT_NAME` This view lists the segment statistics being collected and the properties of each statistic (for instance, if it is a sampled statistic).
- `V$SEGSTAT` This is a highly efficient, real-time monitoring view that shows the statistic value, statistic name, and other basic information.
- `V$SEGMENT_STATISTICS` This is a user-friendly view of statistic values. In addition to all the columns of `V$SEGSTAT`, it has information about such things as the segment owner and table space name. It makes the statistics easy to understand, but it is more costly.

Implement and Measure Change

Often at the end of a tuning exercise, it is possible to identify two or three changes that could potentially alleviate the problem. To identify which change provides the most benefit, it is recommended that only one change be implemented at a time. The effect of the change should be measured against the baseline data measurements found in the problem definition phase.

Typically, most sites with dire performance problems implement several overlapping changes at once, and thus cannot identify which changes provided any benefit. Although this is not immediately an issue, this becomes a significant hindrance if similar problems subsequently appear, because it is not possible to know which of the changes provided the most benefit and which efforts to prioritize.

If it is not possible to implement changes separately, then try to measure the effects of dissimilar changes. For example, measure the effect of making an initialization change to optimize redo generation separately from the effect of creating a new index to improve the performance of a modified query. It is impossible to measure the benefit of performing an operating system upgrade if SQL is tuned, the operating system disk layout is changed, and the initialization parameters are also changed at the same time.

Performance tuning is an iterative process. It is unlikely to find a 'silver bullet' that solves an instance-wide performance problem. In most cases, excellent performance requires iteration through the performance tuning phases, because solving one bottleneck often uncovers another (sometimes worse) problem.

Knowing when to stop tuning is also important. The best measure of performance is user perception, rather than how close the statistic is to an ideal value.

INTERPRETING ORACLE DATABASE STATISTICS

Gather statistics that cover the time when the instance had the performance problem. If you previously captured baseline data for comparison, then you can compare the current data to the data from the baseline that most represents the problem workload.

When comparing two reports, ensure that the two reports are from times where the system was running comparable workloads.

Examine Load

Usually, wait events are the first data examined. However, if you have a baseline report, then check to see if the load has changed. Regardless of whether you have a baseline, it is useful to see whether the resource usage rates are high.

Load-related statistics to examine include `redo size`, `session logical reads`, `db block changes`, `physical reads`, `physical read total bytes`, `physical writes`, `physical write total bytes`, `parse count (total)`, `parse count (hard)`, and `user calls`. This data is queried from `V$SYSSTAT`. It is best to normalize this data over seconds and over transactions. It is also useful to examine the total I/O load in MB per second by using the sum of physical read total bytes and physical write total bytes. The combined value includes the I/O's used to buffer cache, redo logs, archive logs, by Recovery Manager (RMAN) backup and recovery and any Oracle Database background process.

In the AWR report, look at the Load Profile section. The data has been normalized over transactions and over seconds.

Changing Load

The load profile statistics over seconds show the changes in throughput (that is, whether the instance is performing more work each second). The statistics over transactions identify changes in the application characteristics by comparing these to the corresponding statistics from the baseline report.

High Rates of Activity

Examine the statistics normalized over seconds to identify whether the rates of activity are very high. It is difficult to make blanket recommendations on high values, because the thresholds are different on each site and are contingent on the application characteristics, the number and speed of CPUs, the operating system, the I/O system, and the Oracle Database release.

The following are some generalized examples (acceptable values vary at each site):

- A hard parse rate of more than 100 a second indicates that there is a very high amount of hard parsing on the system. High hard parse rates cause serious performance issues and must be investigated. Usually, a high hard parse rate is accompanied by latch contention on the shared pool and library cache latches.

- Check whether the sum of the wait times for library cache and shared pool latch events (latch: library cache, latch: library cache pin, latch: library cache lock and latch: shared pool) is significant compared to statistic `DB time` found in `V$SYSSTAT`. If so, examine the `SQL ordered by Parse Calls` section of the AWR report.
- A high soft parse rate could be in the rate of 300 a second or more. Unnecessary soft parses also limit application scalability. Optimally, a SQL statement should be soft parsed once in each session and executed many times.

Using Wait Event Statistics to Drill Down to Bottlenecks

Whenever an Oracle process waits for something, it records the wait using one of a set of predefined wait events. These wait events are grouped in wait classes. The Idle wait class groups all events that a process waits for when it does not have work to do and is waiting for more work to perform. Non-idle events indicate nonproductive time spent waiting for a resource or action to complete.

Not all symptoms can be evidenced by wait events.

The most effective way to use wait event data is to order the events by the wait time. This is only possible if `TIMED_STATISTICS` is set to true. Otherwise, the wait events can only be ranked by the number of times waited, which is often not the ordering that best represents the problem.

To get an indication of where time is spent, follow these steps:

1. Examine the data collection for `V$SYSTEM_EVENT`. The events of interest should be ranked by wait time.

   Identify the wait events that have the most significant percentage of wait time. To determine the percentage of wait time, add the total wait time for all wait events, excluding idle events, such as `Null event`, `SQL*Net message from client`, `SQL*Net message to client`, and `SQL*Net more data to client`. Calculate the relative percentage of the five most prominent events by dividing each event's wait time by the total time waited for all events.

   Alternatively, look at the Top 5 Timed Events section at the beginning of the Automatic Workload Repository report. This section automatically orders the wait events (omitting idle events), and calculates the relative percentage:

```
Top 5 Timed Events
~~~~~~~~~~~~~~~~~~~~
% Total Event Waits Time (s) Call Time
-------------------------------------- ----------- ---
CPU time 88.80
log file parallel write 2,181  28    4.42
SQL*Net data from client 516,611     27    4.24
db file parallel write    13,383     13    2.04
db file sequential read   563   2     .27
```

   In some situations, there might be a few events with similar percentages. This can provide extra evidence if all the events are related to the same type of resource request (for example, all I/O related events).

   Look at the number of waits for these events, and the average wait time. For example, for I/O related events, the average time might help identify whether the I/O system is slow.

2. The top wait events identify the next places to investigate. A table of common wait events is listed in Table 10.1. It is usually a good idea to also have quick look at high-load SQL.
3. Examine the related data indicated by the wait events to see what other information this data provides. Determine whether this information is consistent with the wait event data. In most situations, there is enough data to begin developing a theory about the potential causes of the performance bottleneck.
4. To determine whether this theory is valid, cross-check data you have examined with other statistics available for consistency. The appropriate statistics vary depending on the problem, but usually include load profile-related data in V$SYSSTAT, operating system statistics, and so on. Perform cross-checks with other data to confirm or refute the developing theory.

Table of Wait Events and Potential Causes

Table 10.1 links wait events to possible causes and gives an overview of the Oracle data that could be most useful to review next.

Table 10.1. Wait Events and Potential Causes

Wait Event	General Area	Possible Causes	Look for/Examine
`buffer busy waits`	Buffer cache, DBWR	Depends on buffer type. For example, waits for an index block may be caused by a primary key that is based on an ascending sequence.	Examine `V$SESSION` while the problem is occurring to determine the type of block in contention.
`free buffer waits`	Buffer cache, DBWR, I/O	Slow DBWR (possibly due to I/O?) Cache too small	Examine write time using operating system statistics. Check buffer cache statistics for evidence of too small cache.
`db file scattered read`	I/O, SQL statement tuning	Poorly tuned SQL Slow I/O system	Investigate `V$SQLAREA` to see whether there are SQL statements performing many disk reads. Cross-check I/O system and `V$FILESTAT` for poor read time.
`db file sequential read`	I/O, SQL statement tuning	Poorly tuned SQL Slow I/O system	Investigate `V$SQLAREA` to see whether there are SQL statements performing many disk reads. Cross-check I/O system and `V$FILESTAT` for poor read time.

enqueue waits (waits starting with enq:)	Locks	Depends on type of enqueue	Look at V$ENQUEUE_STAT.
library cache latch waits: library cache, library cache pin, and library cache lock	Latch contention	SQL parsing or sharing	Check V$SQLAREA to see whether there are SQL statements with a relatively high number of parse calls or a high number of child cursors (column VERSION_COUNT). Check parse statistics in V$SYSSTAT and their corresponding rate for each second.
log buffer space	Log buffer, I/O	Log buffer small Slow I/O system	Check the statistic redo buffer allocation retries in V$SYSSTAT. Check configuring log buffer section in configuring memory chapter. Check the disks that house the online redo logs for resource contention.
log file sync	I/O, overcommitting	Slow disks that store the online logs Unbatched commits	Check the disks that house the online redo logs for resource contention. Check the number of transactions (commits + rollbacks) each second, from V$SYSSTAT.

You may also want to review the My Oracle Support notices on buffer busy waits (34405.1) and free buffer waits (62172.1). You can also access these notices and related notices by searching for busy buffer waits and free buffer waits at:

Additional Statistics

There are several statistics that can indicate performance problems that do not have corresponding wait events.

Redo Log Space Requests Statistic

The V$SYSSTAT statistic redo log space requests indicates how many times a server process had to wait for space in the online redo log, not for space in the redo log buffer. Use this statistic and the wait events as an indication that you must tune checkpoints, DBWR, or archiver activity, not LGWR. Increasing the size of the log buffer does not help.

Read Consistency

Your system might spend excessive time rolling back changes to blocks in order to maintain a consistent view. Consider the following scenarios:

- If there are many small transactions and an active long-running query is running in the background on the same table where the changes are happening, then the query might need to roll back those changes often, in order to obtain a read-consistent image of the table. Compare the following `V$SYSSTAT` statistics to determine whether this is happening:
  - o `consistent: changes` statistic indicates the number of times a database block has rollback entries applied to perform a consistent read on the block. Workloads that produce a great deal of `consistent changes` can consume a great deal of resources.
  - o `consistent gets`: statistic counts the number of logical reads in consistent mode.
- If there are few very, large rollback segments, then your system could be spending a lot of time rolling back the transaction table during delayed block cleanout in order to find out exactly which System Change Number (SCN) a transaction was committed. When Oracle Database commits a transaction, all modified blocks are not necessarily updated with the commit SCN immediately. In this case, it is done later on demand when the block is read or updated. This is called delayed block cleanout.

The ratio of the following `V$SYSSTAT` statistics should be close to one:

```
ratio = transaction tables consistent reads - undo records applied
/transaction tables consistent read rollbacks
```

The recommended solution is to use automatic undo management.

- If there are insufficient rollback segments, then there is rollback segment (header or block) contention. Evidence of this problem is available by the following:
  - o Comparing the number of `WAITS` to the number of `GETS` in `V$ROLLSTAT;` the proportion of `WAITS` to `GETS` should be small.
  - o Examining `V$WAITSTAT` to see whether there are many `WAITS` for buffers of `CLASS 'undo header'`.

The recommended solution is to use automatic undo management.

Table Fetch by Continued Row

You can detect migrated or chained rows by checking the number of `table fetch continued row` statistic in `V$SYSSTAT`. A small number of chained rows (less than 1%) is unlikely to impact system performance. However, a large percentage of chained rows can affect performance.

Chaining on rows larger than the block size is inevitable. Consider using a tablespace with a larger block size for such data.

However, for smaller rows, you can avoid chaining by using sensible space parameters and good application design. For example, do *not* insert a row with key values filled in and nulls in most other columns, then update that row with the real data, causing the row to grow in size. Rather, insert rows filled with data from the start.

If an `UPDATE` statement increases the amount of data in a row so that the row no longer fits in its data block, then Oracle Database tries to find another block with enough free space to hold the entire row. If such a block is available, then Oracle Database moves the entire row to the new block. This operation is called **row migratio.** If the row is too large to fit into any available block, then the database splits the row into multiple pieces and stores each piece in a separate block. This operation is called **row chaining**. The database can also chain rows when they are inserted.

Migration and chaining are especially detrimental to performance with the following:

- UPDATE statements that cause migration and chaining to perform poorly.
- Queries that select migrated or chained rows because these must perform additional input and output.

The definition of a sample output table named CHAINED_ROWS appears in a SQL script available on your distribution medium. The common name of this script is UTLCHN1.SQL, although its exact name and location varies depending on your platform. Your output table must have the same column names, data types, and sizes as the CHAINED_ROWS table.

Increasing PCTFREE can help to avoid migrated rows. If you leave more free space available in the block, then the row has room to grow. You can also reorganize or re-create tables and indexes that have high deletion rates. If tables frequently have rows deleted, then data blocks can have partially free space in them. If rows are inserted and later expanded, then the inserted rows might land in blocks with deleted rows but still not have enough room to expand. Reorganizing the table ensures that the main free space is totally empty blocks.

PCTUSED is not the opposite of PCTFREE.

Parse-Related Statistics

The more your application parses, the more potential for contention exists, and the more time your system spends waiting. If parse time CPU represents a large percentage of the CPU time, then time is being spent parsing instead of executing statements. If this is the case, then it is likely that the application is using literal SQL and so SQL cannot be shared, or the shared pool is poorly configured.

There are several statistics available to identify the extent of time spent parsing by Oracle. Query the parse related statistics from V$SYSSTAT. For example:

```
SELECT NAME, VALUE
    FROM V$SYSSTAT
WHERE NAME IN ('parse time cpu', 'parse time elapsed',
    'parse count (hard)', 'CPU used by this session');
```

There are various ratios that can be computed to assist in determining whether parsing may be a problem:

- Parse time CPU / parse time elapsed.
  This ratio indicates how much of the time spent parsing was due to the parse operation itself, rather than waiting for resources, such as latches. A ratio of one is good, indicating that the elapsed time was not spent waiting for highly contended resources.
- Parse time CPU / CPU used by this session.
  This ratio indicates how much of the total CPU used by Oracle server processes was spent on parse-related operations. A ratio closer to zero is good, indicating that the majority of CPU is not spent on parsing.

WAIT EVENTS STATISTICS

The V$SESSION, V$SESSION WAIT, V$SESSION_HISTORY, V$SESSION_EVENT, and V$SYSTEM_EVENT views provide information on what resources were waited for, and, if the configuration parameter TIMED_STATISTICS is set to true, how long each resource was waited for.

Investigate wait events and related timing data when performing reactive performance tuning. The events with the most time listed against them are often strong indications of the performance bottleneck.

The following views contain related, but different, views of the same data:

- V$SESSION lists session information for each current session. It lists either the event currently being waited for, or the event last waited for on each session. This view also contains information about blocking sessions, the wait state, and the wait time.
- V$SESSION_WAIT is a current state view. It lists either the event currently being waited for, or the event last waited for on each session, the wait state, and the wait time.
- V$SESSION_WAIT_HISTORY lists the last 10 wait events for each current session and the associated wait time.
- V$SESSION_EVENT lists the cumulative history of events waited for on each session. After a session exits, the wait event statistics for that session are removed from this view.
- V$SYSTEM_EVENT lists the events and times waited for by the whole instance (that is, all session wait events data rolled up) since instance startup.

Because V$SESSION_WAIT is a current state view, it also contains a finer-granularity of information than V$SESSION_EVENT or V$SYSTEM_EVENT. It includes additional identifying data for the current event in three parameter columns: P1, P2, and P3.

For example, V$SESSION_EVENT can show that session 124 (SID=124) had many waits on the db file scattered read, but it does not show which file and block number. However, V$SESSION_WAIT shows the file number in P1, the block number read in P2, and the number of blocks read in P3 (P1 and P2 let you determine for which segments the wait event is occurring).

This section concentrates on examples using V$SESSION_WAIT. However, Oracle recommends capturing performance data over an interval and keeping this data for performance and capacity analysis. This form of rollup data is queried from the V$SYSTEM_EVENT view by AWR.

Most commonly encountered events are described in this chapter, listed in case-sensitive alphabetical order. Other event-related data to examine is also included. The case used for each event name is that which appears in the V$SYSTEM_EVENT view.

Oracle Database 11g accumulates wait counts and time outs for wait events (such as in the V$SYSTEM_EVENT view) differently than in past releases. Continuous waits for certain types of resources (such as enqueues) are internally divided into a set of shorter wait calls. In prior releases, each individual internal wait call was counted as a separate wait. Starting with release 11.1, a single resource wait is recorded as a single wait, irrespective of the number of internal time outs experienced by the session during the wait.

This change allows Oracle Database to display a more representative wait count, and an accurate total time spent waiting for the resource. Time outs now refer to the resource wait, instead of the individual internal wait calls. This change also affects the average wait time and the maximum wait time. For example, if a user session must wait for an enqueue in order for a transaction row lock to update a single row in a table, and it takes 10 seconds to acquire the enqueue, Oracle Database breaks down the enqueue wait into 3-second wait calls. In this example, there will be three 3-second wait calls, followed by a 1-second wait call. From the session's perspective, however, there is only one wait on an enqueue.

In prior releases, the V$SYSTEM_EVENT view would represent this wait scenario as follows:

- TOTAL_WAITS: 4 waits (three 3-second waits, one 1-second wait)
- TOTAL_TIMEOUTS: 3 time outs (the first three waits time out and the enqueue is acquired during the final wait)
- TIME_WAITED: 10 seconds (sum of the times from the 4 waits)
- AVERAGE_WAIT: 2.5 seconds
- MAX_WAIT: 3 seconds.

In Oracle Database 11*g*, this wait scenario is represented as:

- TOTAL_WAITS: 1 wait (one 10-second wait)
- TOTAL_TIMEOUTS: 0 time outs (the enqueue is acquired during the resource wait)
- TIME_WAITED: 10 seconds (time for the resource wait)
- AVERAGE_WAIT: 10 seconds
- MAX_WAIT: 10 seconds.

The following common wait events are affected by this change:

- Enqueue waits (such as enq: name - reason waits)
- Library cache lock waits
- Library cache pin waits
- Row cache lock waits

The following statistics are affected by this change:

- Wait counts
- Wait time outs
- Average wait time
- Maximum wait time.

The following views are affected by this change:

- V$EVENT_HISTOGRAM
- V$EVENTMETRIC
- V$SERVICE_EVENT
- V$SERVICE_WAIT_CLASS
- V$SESSION_EVENT
- V$SESSION_WAIT
- V$SESSION_WAIT_CLASS
- V$SESSION_WAIT_HISTORY
- V$SYSTEM_EVENT
- V$SYSTEM_WAIT_CLASS
- V$WAITCLASSMETRIC
- V$WAITCLASSMETRIC_HISTORY.

Buffer Busy Waits

This wait indicates that there are some buffers in the buffer cache that multiple processes are attempting to access concurrently. Query V$WAITSTAT for the wait statistics for each class of buffer. Common buffer classes that have buffer busy waits include data block, segment header, undo header, and undo block.

Check the following V$SESSION_WAIT parameter columns:

- P1: File ID
- P2: Block ID
- P3: Class ID.

Causes

To determine the possible causes, first query V$SESSION to identify the value of ROW_WAIT_OBJ# when the session waits for buffer busy waits. For example:

```
SELECT row_wait_obj#
  FROM V$SESSION
WHERE EVENT = 'buffer busy waits';
```

To identify the object and object type contended for, query DBA_OBJECTS using the value for ROW_WAIT_OBJ# that is returned from V$SESSION. For example:

```
SELECT owner, object_name, subobject_name, object_type
    FROM DBA_OBJECTS
WHERE data_object_id = &row_wait_obj;
```

Actions

The action required depends on the class of block contended for and the actual segment.

Segment Header

If the contention is on the segment header, then this is most likely free list contention.

Automatic segment-space management in locally managed tablespaces eliminates the need to specify the PCTUSED, FREELISTS, and FREELIST GROUPS parameters. If possible, switch from manual space management to Automatic Segment-Space Management (ASSM).

The following information is relevant if you are unable to use ASSM (for example, because the tablespace uses dictionary space management).

A free list is a list of free data blocks that usually includes blocks existing in several different extents within the segment. Free lists are composed of blocks in which free space has not yet reached PCTFREE or used space has shrunk below PCTUSED. Specify the number of process free lists with the FREELISTS parameter. The default value of FREELISTS is one. The maximum value depends on the data block size.

To find the current setting for free lists for that segment, run the following:

```
SELECT    SEGMENT_NAME,     FREELISTS
    FROM  DBA_SEGMENTS
WHERE     SEGMENT_NAME      =      segment name
    AND   SEGMENT_TYPE      =      segment type;
```

Set free lists, or increase the number of free lists. If adding more free lists does not alleviate the problem, then use free list groups (even in single instance this can make a difference). If using Oracle RAC, then ensure that each instance has its own free list group(s).

Data Block

If the contention is on tables or indexes (not the segment header):

- Check for right-hand indexes. These are indexes that are inserted into at the same point by many processes. For example, those that use sequence number generators for the key values.
- Consider using ASSM, global hash partitioned indexes, or increasing free lists to avoid multiple processes attempting to insert into the same block.

Undo Header

For contention on rollback segment header:

- If you are not using automatic undo management, then add more rollback segments.

Undo Block

For contention on rollback segment block:

- If you are not using automatic undo management, then consider making rollback segment sizes larger.

DB File Scattered Read

This event signifies that the user process is reading buffers into the SGA buffer cache and is waiting for a physical I/O call to return. A `db file scattered read` issues a scattered read to read the data into multiple discontinuous memory locations. A scattered read is usually a multiblock read. It can occur for a fast full scan (of an index) in addition to a full table scan.

The `db file scattered read` wait event identifies that a full scan is occurring. When performing a full scan into the buffer cache, the blocks read are read into memory locations that are not physically adjacent to each other. Such reads are called scattered read calls, because the blocks are scattered throughout memory. This is why the corresponding wait event is called 'db file scattered read'. multiblock (up to `DB_FILE_MULTIBLOCK_READ_COUNT` blocks) reads due to full scans into the buffer cache show up as waits for 'db file scattered read'.

Check the following `V$SESSION_WAIT` parameter columns:

- `P1`: The absolute file number
- `P2`: The block being read
- `P3`: The number of blocks (should be greater than 1).

Actions

On a healthy system, physical read waits should be the biggest waits after the idle waits. However, also consider whether there are direct read waits (signifying full table scans with parallel query) or `db file scattered read` waits on an operational (OLTP) system that should be doing small indexed accesses.

Other things that could indicate excessive I/O load on the system include the following:

- Poor buffer cache hit ratio
- These wait events accruing most of the wait time for a user experiencing poor response time

Managing Excessive I/O

There are several ways to handle excessive I/O waits. In the order of effectiveness, these are as follows:

- Reduce the I/O activity by SQL tuning.
- Reduce the need to do I/O by managing the workload.
- Gather system statistics with `DBMS_STATS` package, allowing the query optimizer to accurately cost possible access paths that use full scans.
- Use Automatic Storage Management.
- Add more disks to reduce the number of I/Os for each disk.
- Alleviate I/O hot spots by redistributing I/O across existing disks.

The first course of action should be to find opportunities to reduce I/O. Examine the SQL statements being run by sessions waiting for these events and statements causing high physical I/Os from `V$SQLAREA`. Factors that can adversely affect the execution plans causing excessive I/O include the following:

- Improperly optimized SQL
- Missing indexes

- High degree of parallelism for the table (skewing the optimizer toward scans)
- Lack of accurate statistics for the optimizer
- Setting the value for DB_FILE_MULTIBLOCK_READ_COUNT initialization parameter too high which favors full scans.

Inadequate I/O Distribution

Besides reducing I/O, also examine the I/O distribution of files across the disks. Is I/O distributed uniformly across the disks, or are there hot spots on some disks? Are the number of disks sufficient to meet the I/O needs of the database?

See the total I/O operations (reads and writes) by the database, and compare those with the number of disks used. Remember to include the I/O activity of LGWR and ARCH processes.

Finding the SQL Statement Executed by Sessions Waiting for I/O

Use the following query to determine, at a point in time, which sessions are waiting for I/O:

```
SELECT SQL_ADDRESS, SQL_HASH_VALUE FROM V$SESSION
WHERE EVENT LIKE 'db file%read';
```

Finding the Object Requiring I/O

To determine the possible causes, first query V$SESSION to identify the value of ROW_WAIT_OBJ# when the session waits for db file scattered read. For example:

```
SELECT row_wait_obj# FROM V$SESSION
 WHERE EVENT = 'db file scattered read';
```

To identify the object and object type contended for, query DBA_OBJECTS using the value for ROW_WAIT_OBJ# that is returned from V$SESSION. For example:

```
SELECT owner, object_name, subobject_name, object_type
FROM DBA_OBJECTS WHERE data_object_id = &row_wait_obj;
```

DB File Sequential Read

This event signifies that the user process is reading a buffer into the SGA buffer cache and is waiting for a physical I/O call to return. A sequential read is a single-block read.

Single block I/Os are usually the result of using indexes. Rarely, full table scan calls could get truncated to a single block call because of extent boundaries, or buffers present in the buffer cache. These waits would also show up as db file sequential read.

Check the following V$SESSION_WAIT parameter columns:

- P1: The absolute file number
- P2: The block being read
- P3: The number of blocks (should be 1).

Actions

On a healthy system, physical read waits should be the biggest waits after the idle waits. However, also consider whether there are db file sequential reads on a large data warehouse that should be seeing mostly full table scans with parallel query.

Figure 10.1 depicts the differences between the following wait events:

- db file sequential read (single block read into one SGA buffer)
- db file scattered read (multiblock read into many discontinuous SGA buffers)
- direct read (single or multiblock read into the PGA, bypassing the SGA).

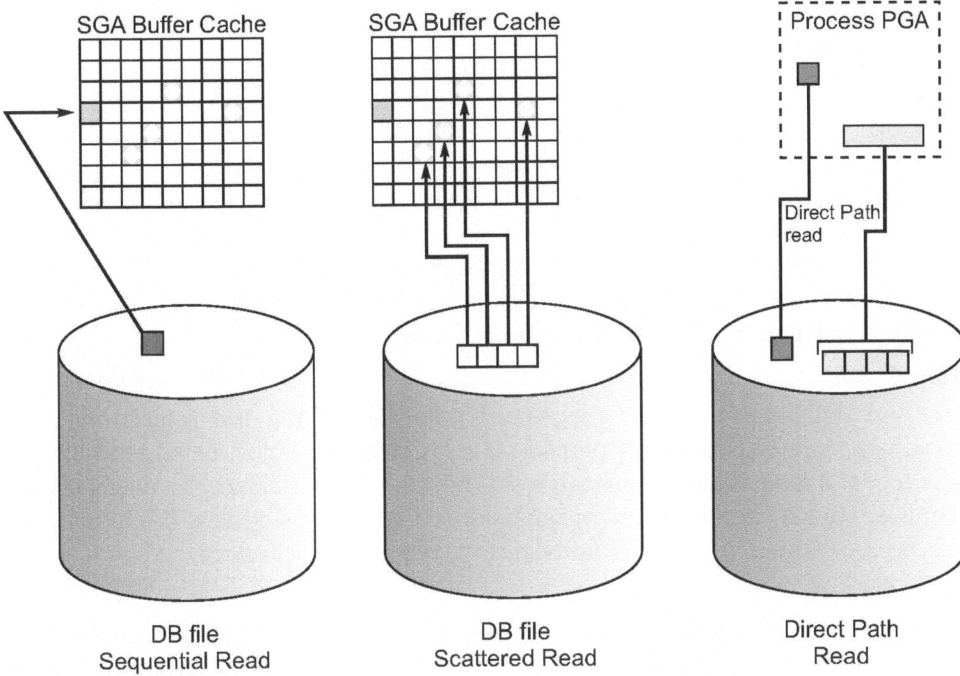

Figure 10.1. Scattered Read, Sequential Read, and Direct Path Read

Direct Path Read and Direct Path Read Temp

When a session is reading buffers from disk directly into the PGA (opposed to the buffer cache in SGA), it waits on this event. If the I/O subsystem does not support asynchronous I/Os, then each wait corresponds to a physical read request.

If the I/O subsystem supports asynchronous I/O, then the process is able to overlap issuing read requests with processing the blocks existing in the PGA. When the process attempts to access a block in the PGA that has not yet been read from disk, it then issues a wait call and updates the statistics for this event. Hence, the number of waits is not necessarily the same as the number of read requests (unlike `db file scattered read` and `db file sequential read`).

Check the following `V$SESSION_WAIT` parameter columns:

- `P1`: File_id for the read call
- `P2`: Start block_id for the read call
- `P3`: Number of blocks in the read call.

Causes

This situation occurs in the following situations:

- The sorts are too large to fit in memory and some of the sort data is written out directly to disk. This data is later read back in, using direct reads.
- Parallel slaves are used for scanning data.
- The server process is processing buffers faster than the I/O system can return the buffers. This can indicate an overloaded I/O system.

Actions

The `file_id` shows if the reads are for an object in `TEMP` tablespace (sorts to disk) or full table scans by parallel slaves. This wait is the largest wait for large data warehouse sites.

However, if the workload is not a Decision Support Systems (DSS) workload, then examine why this situation is happening.

Sorts to Disk

Examine the SQL statement currently being run by the session experiencing waits to see what is causing the sorts. Query V$TEMPSEG_USAGE to find the SQL statement that is generating the sort. Also query the statistics from V$SESSTAT for the session to determine the size of the sort. See if it is possible to reduce the sorting by tuning the SQL statement. If WORKAREA_SIZE_POLICY is MANUAL, then consider increasing the SORT_AREA_SIZE for the system (if the sorts are not too big) or for individual processes. If WORKAREA_SIZE_POLICY is AUTO, then investigate whether to increase PGA_AGGREGATE_TARGET.

Full Table Scans

If tables are defined with a high degree of parallelism, then this setting could skew the optimizer to use full table scans with parallel slaves. Check the object being read into using the direct path reads. If the full table scans are a valid part of the workload, then ensure that the I/O subsystem is adequate for the degree of parallelism. Consider using disk striping if you are not already using it or Oracle Automatic Storage Management (Oracle ASM).

Hash Area Size

For query plans that call for a hash join, excessive I/O could result from having HASH_AREA_SIZE too small. If WORKAREA_SIZE_POLICY is MANUAL, then consider increasing the HASH_AREA_SIZE for the system or for individual processes. If WORKAREA_SIZE_POLICY is AUTO, then investigate whether to increase PGA_AGGREGATE_TARGET.

Direct Path Write and Direct Path Write Temp

When a process is writing buffers directly from PGA (as opposed to the DBWR writing them from the buffer cache), the process waits on this event for the write call to complete. Operations that could perform direct path writes include sorts on disk, parallel DML operations, direct-path INSERTs, parallel create table as select, and some LOB operations.

Like direct path reads, the number of waits is not the same as number of write calls issued if the I/O subsystem supports asynchronous writes. The session waits if it has processed all buffers in the PGA and cannot continue work until an I/O request completes.

Check the following V$SESSION_WAIT parameter columns:

- P1: File_id for the write call
- P2: Start block_id for the write call
- P3: Number of blocks in the write call.

Causes

This happens in the following situations:

- Sorts are too large to fit in memory and are written to disk
- Parallel DML are issued to create/populate objects
- Direct path loads

Actions

For parallel DML, check the I/O distribution across disks and ensure that the I/O subsystem is adequately configured for the degree of parallelism.

Enqueue (enq:) Waits

Enqueues are locks that coordinate access to database resources. This event indicates that the session is waiting for a lock that is held by another session.

The name of the enqueue is included as part of the wait event name, in the form `enq: enqueue_type - related_details`. In some cases, the same enqueue type can be held for different purposes, such as the following related TX types:

- `enq: TX - allocate ITL entry`
- `enq: TX - contention`
- `enq: TX - index contention`
- `enq: TX - row lock contention.`

The `V$EVENT_NAME` view provides a complete list of all the `enq`: wait events.

You can check the following `V$SESSION_WAIT` parameter columns for additional information:

- `P1`: Lock `TYPE` (or name) and `MODE`
- `P2`: Resource identifier ID1 for the lock
- `P3`: Resource identifier ID2 for the lock.

Finding Locks and Lock Holders

Query `V$LOCK` to find the sessions holding the lock. For every session waiting for the event enqueue, there is a row in `V$LOCK` with `REQUEST` <> `0`. Use one of the following two queries to find the sessions holding the locks and waiting for the locks.

If there are enqueue waits, you can see these using the following statement:

```
SELECT * FROM V$LOCK WHERE request > 0;
```

To show only holders and waiters for locks being waited on, use the following:

```
SELECT DECODE(request,0,'Holder: ','Waiter: ') ||
sid sess, id1, id2, lmode, request, type
FROM V$LOCK WHERE (id1, id2, type) IN (SELECT id1, id2,
type FROM V$LOCK WHERE request > 0)
ORDER BY id1, request;
```

Actions

The appropriate action depends on the type of enqueue.

Enqueue

If the contended-for enqueue is the ST enqueue, then the problem is most likely to be dynamic space allocation. Oracle Database dynamically allocates an extent to a segment when there is no more free space available in the segment. This enqueue is only used for dictionary managed tablespaces.

To solve contention on this resource:

- Check to see whether the temporary (that is, sort) tablespace uses `TEMPFILES`. If not, then switch to using `TEMPFILES`.
- Switch to using locally managed tablespaces if the tablespace that contains segments that are growing dynamically is dictionary managed.
- If it is not possible to switch to locally managed tablespaces, then ST enqueue resource usage can be decreased by changing the next extent sizes of the growing objects to be large enough to avoid constant space allocation. To determine which segments are growing constantly, monitor the `EXTENTS` column of the `DBA_SEGMENTS` view for all `SEGMENT_NAMEs`.
- Preallocate space in the segment, for example, by allocating extents using the `ALTER TABLE ALLOCATE EXTENT` SQL statement.

HW Enqueue

The HW enqueue is used to serialize the allocation of space beyond the high water mark of a segment.

- V$SESSION_WAIT.P2 / V$LOCK.ID1 is the tablespace number.
- V$SESSION_WAIT.P3 / V$LOCK.ID2 is the relative data block address (dba) of segment header of the object for which space is being allocated.

If this is a point of contention for an object, then manual allocation of extents solves the problem.

TM Enqueue

The most common reason for waits on TM locks tend to involve foreign key constraints where the constrained columns are not indexed. Index the foreign key columns to avoid this problem.

TX Enqueue

These are acquired exclusive when a transaction initiates its first change and held until the transaction does a COMMIT or ROLLBACK.

- Waits for TX in mode 6: occurs when a session is waiting for a row level lock that is held by another session. This occurs when one user is updating or deleting a row, which another session wants to update or delete. This type of TX enqueue wait corresponds to the wait event enq: TX - row lock contention.
  The solution is to have the first session holding the lock perform a COMMIT or ROLLBACK.
- Waits for TX in mode 4 can occur if the session is waiting for an ITL (interested transaction list) slot in a block. This happens when the session wants to lock a row in the block but one or more other sessions have rows locked in the same block, and there is no free ITL slot in the block. Usually, Oracle Database dynamically adds another ITL slot. This may not be possible if there is insufficient free space in the block to add an ITL. If so, the session waits for a slot with a TX enqueue in mode 4. This type of TX enqueue wait corresponds to the wait event enq: TX - allocate ITL entry.
  The solution is to increase the number of ITLs available, either by changing the INITRANS or MAXTRANS for the table (either by using an ALTER statement, or by re-creating the table with the higher values).
- Waits for TX in mode 4 can also occur if a session is waiting due to potential duplicates in UNIQUE index. If two sessions try to insert the same key value the second session has to wait to see if an ORA-0001 should be raised or not. This type of TX enqueue wait corresponds to the wait event enq: TX - row lock contention.
  The solution is to have the first session holding the lock perform a COMMIT or ROLLBACK.
- Waits for TX in mode 4 is also possible if the session is waiting due to shared bitmap index fragment. Bitmap indexes index key values and a range of rowids. Each entry in a bitmap index can cover many rows in the actual table. If two sessions want to update rows covered by the same bitmap index fragment, then the second session waits for the first transaction to either COMMIT or ROLLBACK by waiting for the TX lock in mode 4. This type of TX enqueue wait corresponds to the wait event enq: TX - row lock contention.
- Waits for TX in Mode 4 can also occur waiting for a PREPARED transaction.
- Waits for TX in mode 4 also occur when a transaction inserting a row in an index has to wait for the end of an index block split being done by another transaction. This type of TX enqueue wait corresponds to the wait event enq: TX - index contention.

Events in Wait Class Other

This event belong to Other wait class and typically should not occur on a system. This event is an aggregate of all other events in the Other wait class, such as `latch free`, and is used in the `V$SESSION_EVENT` and `V$SERVICE_EVENT` views only. In these views, the events in the Other wait class will not be maintained individually in every session. Instead, these events will be rolled up into this single event to reduce the memory used for maintaining statistics on events in the Other wait class.

Free Buffer Waits

This wait event indicates that a server process was unable to find a free buffer and has posted the database writer to make free buffers by writing out dirty buffers. A dirty buffer is a buffer whose contents have been modified. Dirty buffers are freed for reuse when DBWR has written the blocks to disk.

Causes

DBWR may not be keeping up with writing dirty buffers in the following situations:

- The I/O system is slow.
- There are resources it is waiting for, such as latches.
- The buffer cache is so small that DBWR spends most of its time cleaning out buffers for server processes.
- The buffer cache is so big that one DBWR process is not enough to free enough buffers in the cache to satisfy requests.

Actions

If this event occurs frequently, then examine the session waits for DBWR to see whether there is anything delaying DBWR.

Writes

If it is waiting for writes, then determine what is delaying the writes and fix it. Check the following:

- Examine `V$FILESTAT` to see where most of the writes are happening.
- Examine the host operating system statistics for the I/O system. Are the write times acceptable?

If I/O is slow:

- Consider using faster I/O alternatives to speed up write times.
- Spread the I/O activity across large number of spindles (disks) and controllers.

Cache is Too Small

It is possible DBWR is very active because the cache is too small. Investigate whether this is a probable cause by looking to see if the buffer cache hit ratio is low. Also use the `V$DB_CACHE_ADVICE` view to determine whether a larger cache size would be advantageous.

Cache is Too Big for One DBWR

If the cache size is adequate and the I/O is evenly spread, then you can potentially modify the behavior of DBWR by using asynchronous I/O or by using multiple database writers.

Consider Multiple Database Writer (DBWR) Processes or I/O Slaves

Configuring multiple database writer processes, or using I/O slaves, is useful when the transaction rates are high or when the buffer cache size is so large that a single DBW*n* process cannot keep up with the load.

DB_WRITER_PROCESSES

The `DB_WRITER_PROCESSES` initialization parameter lets you configure multiple database writer processes (from DBW0 to DBW9 and from DBWa to DBWj). Configuring multiple DBWR processes distributes the work required to identify buffers to be written, and it also distributes the I/O load over these processes. Multiple db writer processes are highly recommended for systems with multiple CPUs (at least one db writer for every 8 CPUs) or multiple processor groups (at least as many db writers as processor groups).

Based upon the number of CPUs and the number of processor groups, Oracle Database either selects an appropriate default setting for `DB_WRITER_PROCESSES` or adjusts a user-specified setting.

DBWR_IO_SLAVES

If it is not practical to use multiple DBWR processes, then Oracle Database provides a facility whereby the I/O load can be distributed over multiple slave processes. The DBWR process is the only process that scans the buffer cache LRU list for blocks to be written out. However, the I/O for those blocks is performed by the I/O slaves. The number of I/O slaves is determined by the parameter `DBWR_IO_SLAVES`.

`DBWR_IO_SLAVES` is intended for scenarios where you cannot use multiple `DB_WRITER_PROCESSES` (for example, where you have a single CPU). I/O slaves are also useful when asynchronous I/O is not available, because the multiple I/O slaves simulate nonblocking, asynchronous requests by freeing DBWR to continue identifying blocks in the cache to be written. Asynchronous I/O at the operating system level, if you have it, is generally preferred.

DBWR I/O slaves are allocated immediately following database open when the first I/O request is made. The DBWR continues to perform all of the DBWR-related work, apart from performing I/O. I/O slaves simply perform the I/O on behalf of DBWR. The writing of the batch is parallelized between the I/O slaves.

Implementing `DBWR_IO_SLAVES` requires that extra shared memory be allocated for I/O buffers and request queues. Multiple DBWR processes cannot be used with I/O slaves. Configuring I/O slaves forces only one DBWR process to start.

Choosing between Multiple DBWR Processes and I/O Slaves

Configuring multiple DBWR processes benefits performance when a single DBWR process cannot keep up with the required workload. However, before configuring multiple DBWR processes, check whether asynchronous I/O is available and configured on the system. If the system supports asynchronous I/O but it is not currently used, then enable asynchronous I/O to see if this alleviates the problem. If the system does not support asynchronous I/O, or if asynchronous I/O is configured and there is still a DBWR bottleneck, then configure multiple DBWR processes.

If asynchronous I/O is not available on your platform, then asynchronous I/O can be disabled by setting the `DISK_ASYNCH_IO` initialization parameter to `FALSE`.

Using multiple DBWRs parallelizes the gathering and writing of buffers. Therefore, multiple DBW*n* processes should deliver more throughput than one DBWR process with the same number of I/O slaves. For this reason, the use of I/O slaves has been deprecated in favor of multiple DBWR processes. I/O slaves should only be used if multiple DBWR processes cannot be configured.

Idle Wait Events

These events belong to Idle wait class and indicate that the server process is waiting because it has no work. This usually implies that if there is a bottleneck, then the bottleneck is not for database resources. The majority of the idle events should be ignored when tuning, because they do not indicate the nature of the performance bottleneck. Some idle events can be useful in indicating what the bottleneck is not. An example of this type of event is the most commonly encountered idle wait-event `SQL Net message from client`. This and other idle events (and their categories) are listed in Table 10.2.

Table 10.2 Idle Wait Events

Wait Name	Background Process Idle Event	User Process Idle Event	Parallel Query Idle Event	Shared Server Idle Event	Oracle Real Application Clusters Idle Event
`dispatcher timer`	.	.	.	X	.
`pipe get`	.	X	.	.	.
`pmon timer`	X	.	.	.	.
`PX Idle Wait`	.	.	X	.	.
`PX Deq Credit: need buffer`	.	.	X	.	.
`rdbms ipc message`	X .	. .	. .	. X	. .
`Shared server idle wait`					
`smon timer`	X	.	.	.	.
`SQL*Net message from client`	.	X	.	.	.

Latch Events

A latch is a low-level internal lock used by Oracle Database to protect memory structures. The latch free event is updated when a server process attempts to get a latch, and the latch is unavailable on the first attempt.

There is a dedicated latch-related wait event for the more popular latches that often generate significant contention. For those events, the name of the latch appears in the name of the wait event, such as `latch: library cache` or `latch: cache buffers chains`. This enables you to quickly figure out if a particular type of latch is responsible for most of the latch-related contention. Waits for all other latches are grouped in the generic `latch free` wait event.

Actions

This event should only be a concern if latch waits are a significant portion of the wait time on the system as a whole, or for individual users experiencing problems.

- Examine the resource usage for related resources. For example, if the library cache latch is heavily contended for, then examine the hard and soft parse rates.
- Examine the SQL statements for the sessions experiencing latch contention to see if there is any commonality.

Check the following `V$SESSION_WAIT` parameter columns:

- `P1`: Address of the latch
- `P2`: Latch number
- `P3`: Number of times process has slept, waiting for the latch

Example 10.1: Find Latches Currently Waited For

```
SELECT EVENT, SUM(P3) SLEEPS, SUM(SECONDS_IN_WAIT)
SECONDS_IN_WAITFROM V$SESSION_WAIT
WHERE EVENT LIKE 'latch%' GROUP BY EVENT;
```

A problem with the previous query is that it tells more about session tuning or instant instance tuning than instance or long-duration instance tuning.

The following query provides more information about long duration instance tuning, showing whether the latch waits are significant in the overall database time.

```
SELECT EVENT, TIME_WAITED_MICRO,
ROUND(TIME_WAITED_MICRO*100/S.DBTIME,1) PCT_DB_TIME
FROM V$SYSTEM_EVENT, (SELECT VALUE DBTIME FROM
V$SYS_TIME_MODEL WHERE STAT_NAME = 'DB time') s
WHERE EVENT LIKE 'latch%'
ORDER BY PCT_DB_TIME ASC;
```

A more general query that is not specific to latch waits is the following:

```
SELECT EVENT, WAIT_CLASS,TIME_WAITED_MICRO,
ROUND     (TIME_WAITED_MICRO*100/S.DBTIME,1) PCT_DB_TIME
          FROM V$SYSTEM_EVENT E, V$EVENT_NAME N,
          (SELECT VALUE DBTIME FROM V$SYS_TIME_MODEL WHERE
STAT_NAME = 'DB time') S WHERE E.EVENT_ID =
N.EVENT_ID AND N.WAIT_CLASS NOT IN ('Idle', 'System
I/O')     ORDER BY PCT_DB_TIME ASC;
```

Table 10.3. Latch Wait Event

Latch	SGA Area	Possible Causes	Look For:
Shared pool, library cache	Shared pool	Lack of statement reuse. Statements not using bind variables. Insufficient size of application cursor cache Cursors closed explicitly after each execution.	Sessions (in `V$SESSTAT`) with high: • `parse time CPU` • `parse time elapsed` • Ratio of `parse count (hard) / execute count` • Ratio of `parse count (total) / execute count.`

		Frequent logins and logoffs. Underlying object structure being modified (for example truncate). Shared pool too small.	Cursors (in `V$SQLAREA/V$SQLSTATS`) with: • High ratio of `PARSE_CALLS / EXECUTIONS` • `EXECUTIONS` = 1 differing only in literals in the `WHERE` clause (that is, no bind variables used) • High `RELOADS` • High `INVALIDATIONS` • Large (> 1mb) `SHARABLE_MEM`
`cache buffers lru chain`	Buffer cache LRU lists	Excessive buffer cache throughput. For example, inefficient SQL that accesses incorrect indexes iteratively (large index range scans) or many full table scans DBWR not keeping up with the dirty workload; hence, foreground process spends longer holding the latch looking for a free buffer. Cache may be too small.	Statements with very high logical I/O or physical I/O, using unselective indexes.
`cache buffers chains`	Buffer cache buffers.	Repeated access to a block (or small number of blocks), known as a hot block.	Sequence number generation code that updates a row in a table to generate the number, rather than using a sequence number generator. Index leaf chasing from very many processes scanning the same unselective index with very similar predicate. Identify the segment the hot block belongs to.
`row cache objects`			

Shared Pool and Library Cache Latch Contention

A main cause of shared pool or library cache latch contention is parsing. There are several techniques that you can use to identify unnecessary parsing and several types of unnecessary parsing:

- Unshared SQL
- Reparsed Sharable SQL
- By Session
- cache buffers lru chain
- cache buffers chains
- row cache objects.

Unshared SQL

This method identifies similar SQL statements that could be shared if literals were replaced with bind variables. The idea is to either:

- Manually inspect SQL statements that have only one execution to see whether they are dsimilar:

```
SELECT SQL_TEXT   FROM V$SQLSTATS
WHERE EXECUTIONS  < 4 ORDER BY SQL_TEXT;
```

- Or, automate this process by grouping what may be similar statements. Estimate the number of bytes of a SQL statement that are likely the same, and group the SQL statements by this number of bytes. For example, the following example groups statements that differ only after the first 60 bytes.

```
SELECT SUBSTR(SQL_TEXT, 1, 60), COUNT(*)
FROM V$SQLSTATS WHERE EXECUTIONS < 4
GROUP BY SUBSTR(SQL_TEXT, 1, 60)
HAVING COUNT(*) > 1;
```

- Or report distinct SQL statements that have the same execution plan. The following query selects distinct SQL statements that share the same execution plan at least four times. These SQL statements are likely to be using literals instead of bind variables.

```
SELECT SQL_TEXT FROM V$SQLSTATS WHERE PLAN_HASH_VALUE
IN (SELECT PLAN_HASH_VALUE FROM V$SQLSTATS GROUP BY
PLAN_HASH_VALUE HAVING COUNT(*) > 4)
      ORDER BY PLAN_HASH_VALUE;
```

Reparsed Sharable SQL

Check the V$SQLSTATS view. Enter the following query:

```
SELECT SQL_TEXT, PARSE_CALLS, EXECUTIONS
      FROM V$SQLSTATS
ORDER BY PARSE_CALLS;
```

When the PARSE_CALLS value is close to the EXECUTIONS value for a given statement, you might be continually reparsing that statement. Tune the statements with the higher numbers of parse calls.

By Session

Identify unnecessary parse calls by identifying the session in which they occur. It might be that particular batch programs or certain types of applications do most of the reparsing. To achieve this goal, run the following query:

```
SELECT pa.SID, pa.VALUE "Hard Parses", ex.VALUE "Execute
Count" FROM V$SESSTAT pa, V$SESSTAT ex
        WHERE pa.SID = ex.SID AND pa.STATISTIC#=(SELECT STATISTIC#
        FROM V$STATNAME WHERE NAME = 'parse count (hard)')
        AND ex.STATISTIC#=(SELECT STATISTIC# FROM V$STATNAME WHERE
        NAME = 'execute count') AND pa.VALUE > 0;
```

The result is a list of all sessions and the amount of reparsing they do. For each session identifier (SID), go to V$SESSION to find the name of the program that causes the reparsing.

Because this query counts all parse calls since instance startup, it is best to look for sessions with high *rates* of parse. For example, a connection which has been up for 50 days might show a high parse figure, but a second connection might have been up for 10 minutes and be parsing at a much faster rate.

The output is similar to the following:

```
SID   Hard ParsesExecute    Count
------ ---------- ------------
  7       1              20
  8       3              12690
  6       26             325
  11      84             1619
```

Cache Buffers Lru Chain

The `cache buffers lru chain` latches protect the lists of buffers in the cache. When adding, moving, or removing a buffer from a list, a latch must be obtained.

For symmetric multiprocessor (SMP) systems, Oracle Database automatically sets the number of LRU latches to a value equal to one half the number of CPUs on the system. For non-SMP systems, one LRU latch is sufficient.

Contention for the LRU latch can impede performance on SMP computers with a large number of CPUs. LRU latch contention is detected by querying `V$LATCH`,`V$SESSION_EVENT`, and `V$SYSTEM_EVENT`. To avoid contention, consider tuning the application, bypassing the buffer cache for DSS jobs, or redesigning the application.

Cache Buffers Chains

The `cache buffers chains` latches are used to protect a buffer list in the buffer cache. These latches are used when searching for, adding, or removing a buffer from the buffer cache. Contention on this latch usually means that there is a block that is greatly contended for (known as a hot block).

To identify the heavily accessed buffer chain, and hence the contended for block, look at latch statistics for the `cache buffers chains` latches using the view `V$LATCH_CHILDREN`. If there is a specific `cache buffers chains` child latch that has many more `GETS`, `MISSES`, and `SLEEPS` when compared with the other child latches, then this is the contended for child latch.

This latch has a memory address, identified by the `ADDR` column. Use the value in the `ADDR` column joined with the `X$BH` table to identify the blocks protected by this latch. For example, given the address (`V$LATCH CHILDREN.ADDR`) of a heavily contended latch, this queries the file and block numbers:

```
SELECT OBJ data_object_id, FILE#, DBABLK CLASS, STATE, TCH
        FROM X$BH   WHERE HLADDR = 'address of latch'
        ORDER BY TCH;
```

X$BH.TCH is a touch count for the buffer. A high value for X$BH.TCH indicates a hot block.

Many blocks are protected by each latch. One of these buffers will probably be the hot block. Any block with a high TCH value is a potential hot block. Perform this query several times, and identify the block that consistently appears in the output. After you have identified the hot block, query DBA_EXTENTS using the file number and block number, to identify the segment.

After you have identified the hot block, you can identify the segment it belongs to with the following query:

```
SELECT OBJECT_NAME, SUBOBJECT_NAME FROM DBA_OBJECTS
        WHERE DATA_OBJECT_ID = &obj;
```

In the query, &obj is the value of the OBJ column in the previous query on X$BH.

Row Cache Objects

The row cache objects latches protect the data dictionary.

Log file Parallel Write

This event involves writing redo records to the redo log files from the log buffer.

library Cache Pin

This event manages library cache concurrency. Pinning an object causes the heaps to be loaded into memory. If a client wants to modify or examine the object, the client must acquire a pin after the lock.

Library Cache Lock

This event controls the concurrency between clients of the library cache. It acquires a lock on the object handle so that either:

- One client can prevent other clients from accessing the same object
- The client can maintain a dependency for a long time which does not allow another client to change the object

This lock is also obtained to locate an object in the library cache.

Log Buffer Space

This event occurs when server processes are waiting for free space in the log buffer, because all the redo is generated faster than LGWR can write it out.

Actions

Modify the redo log buffer size. If the size of the log buffer is reasonable, then ensure that the disks on which the online redo logs reside do not suffer from I/O contention. The log buffer space wait event could be indicative of either disk I/O contention on the disks where the redo logs reside, or of a too-small log buffer. Check the I/O profile of the disks containing the redo logs to investigate whether the I/O system is the bottleneck. If the I/O system is not a problem, then the redo log buffer could be too small. Increase the size of the redo log buffer until this event is no longer significant.

Log File Switch

There are two wait events commonly encountered:

- log file switch (archiving needed)
- log file switch (checkpoint incomplete).

In both of the events, the LGWR cannot switch into the next online redo log file. All the commit requests wait for this event.

Actions

For the `log file switch (archiving needed)` event, examine why the archiver cannot archive the logs in a timely fashion. It could be due to the following:

- Archive destination is running out of free space.
- Archiver is not able to read redo logs fast enough (contention with the LGWR).
- Archiver is not able to write fast enough (contention on the archive destination, or not enough ARCH processes). If you have ruled out other possibilities (such as slow disks or a full archive destination) consider increasing the number of ARCn processes. The default is 2.
- If you have mandatory remote shipped archive logs, check whether this process is slowing down because of network delays or the write is not completing because of errors.

Depending on the nature of bottleneck, you might need to redistribute I/O or add more space to the archive destination to alleviate the problem. For the `log file switch (checkpoint incomplete)` event:

- Check if DBWR is slow, possibly due to an overloaded or slow I/O system. Check the DBWR write times, check the I/O system, and distribute I/O if necessary.
- Check if there are too few, or too small redo logs. If you have a few redo logs or small redo logs (for example, 2 x 100k logs), and your system produces enough redo to cycle through all of the logs before DBWR has been able to complete the checkpoint, then increase the size or number of redo logs.

Log File Sync

When a user session commits (or rolls back), the session's redo information must be flushed to the redo logfile by LGWR. The server process performing the `COMMIT` or `ROLLBACK` waits under this event for the write to the redo log to complete.

Actions

If this event's waits constitute a significant wait on the system or a significant amount of time waited by a user experiencing response time issues or on a system, then examine the average time waited.

If the average time waited is low, but the number of waits are high, then the application might be committing after every `INSERT`, rather than batching `COMMIT`s. Applications can reduce the wait by committing after 50 rows, rather than every row.

If the average time waited is high, then examine the session waits for the log writer and see what it is spending most of its time doing and waiting for. If the waits are because of slow I/O, then try the following:

- Reduce other I/O activity on the disks containing the redo logs, or use dedicated disks.
- Alternate redo logs on different disks to minimize the effect of the archiver on the log writer.
- Move the redo logs to faster disks or a faster I/O subsystem (for example, switch from RAID 5 to RAID 1).

- Consider using raw devices (or simulated raw devices provided by disk vendors) to speed up the writes.
- Depending on the type of application, it might be possible to batch COMMITs by committing every *N* rows, rather than every row, so that fewer log file syncs are needed.

RDBMS Ipc Reply

This event is used to wait for a reply from one of the background processes.

SQL*Net Events

The following events signify that the database process is waiting for acknowledgment from a database link or a client process:

- `SQL*Net break/reset to client`
- `SQL*Net break/reset to dblink`
- `SQL*Net message from client`
- `SQL*Net message from dblink`
- `SQL*Net message to client`
- `SQL*Net message to dblink`
- `SQL*Net more data from client`
- `SQL*Net more data from dblink`
- `SQL*Net more data to client`
- `SQL*Net more data to dblink`

If these waits constitute a significant portion of the wait time on the system or for a user experiencing response time issues, then the network or the middle-tier could be a bottleneck.

Events that are client-related should be diagnosed as described for the event `SQL*Net message from client`. Events that are dblink-related should be diagnosed as described for the event `SQL*Net message from dblink.`

*SQL*Net Message From Client*

Although this is an idle event, it is important to explain when this event can be used to diagnose what is not the problem. This event indicates that a server process is waiting for work from the client process. However, there are several situations where this event could accrue most of the wait time for a user experiencing poor response time. The cause could be either a network bottleneck or a resource bottleneck on the client process.

Network Bottleneck

A network bottleneck can occur if the application causes a lot of traffic between server and client and the network latency (time for a round-trip) is high. Symptoms include the following:

- Large number of waits for this event
- Both the database and client process are idle (waiting for network traffic) most of the time

To alleviate network bottlenecks, try the following:

- Tune the application to reduce round trips.
- Explore options to reduce latency (for example, terrestrial lines opposed to VSAT links).
- Change system configuration to move higher traffic components to lower latency links.

Resource Bottleneck on the Client Process

If the client process is using most of the resources, then there is nothing that can be done in the database. Symptoms include the following:

- Number of waits might not be large, but the time waited might be significant
- Client process has a high resource usage.

In some cases, you can see the wait time for a waiting user tracking closely with the amount of CPU used by the client process. The term client here refers to any process other than the database process (middle-tier, desktop client) in the *n*-tier architecture.

*SQL*Net Message From Dblink*

This event signifies that the session has sent a message to the remote node and is waiting for a response from the database link. This time could go up because of the following:

- Network bottleneck
- Time taken to execute the SQL on the remote node
  It is useful to see the SQL being run on the remote node. Login to the remote database, find the session created by the database link, and examine the SQL statement being run by it.
- Number of round trip messages
  Each message between the session and the remote node adds latency time and processing overhead. To reduce the number of messages exchanged, use array fetches and array inserts.

*SQL*Net More Data to Client*

The server process is sending more data or messages to the client. The previous operation to the client was also a send.

REAL-TIME SQL MONITORING

The real-time SQL monitoring feature of Oracle Database enables you to monitor the performance of SQL statements while they are executing. By default, SQL monitoring automatically starts when a SQL statement runs parallel, or when it has consumed at least 5 seconds of CPU or I/O time in a single execution.

You can monitor the statistics for SQL statement execution using the `V$SQL_MONITOR` and `V$SQL_PLAN_MONITOR` views. You can use these views in conjunction with the following views to get additional information about the execution being monitored:

- `V$ACTIVE_SESSION_HISTORY`
- `V$SESSION`
- `V$SESSION_LONGOPS`
- `V$SQL`
- `V$SQL_PLAN`.

After monitoring is initiated, the database adds an entry to the dynamic performance view `V$SQL_MONITOR`. This entry tracks key performance metrics collected for the execution, including the elapsed time, CPU time, number of reads and writes, I/O wait time and various other wait times. These statistics are refreshed in near real-time as the statement executes, generally once every second. After the execution ends, monitoring information is not deleted immediately, but is kept in the `V$SQL_MONITOR` view for at least one minute. The entry will eventually be deleted so its space can be reclaimed as new statements are monitored.

The `V$SQL_MONITOR` view contains a subset of the statistics available in `V$SQL`. However, unlike `V$SQL`, monitoring statistics are not cumulative over several executions. Instead, one entry in `V$SQL_MONITOR` is dedicated to a single execution of a SQL statement. If the database monitors two executions of the same SQL statement, then each execution has a separate entry in `V$SQL_MONITOR`.

To uniquely identify two executions of the same SQL statement, a composite key called an execution key is generated. This execution key is composed of three attributes, each corresponding to a column in V$SQL_MONITOR:

- SQL identifier to identify the SQL statement (SQL_ID)
- Start execution timestamp (SQL_EXEC_START)
- An internally generated identifier to ensure that this primary key is truly unique (SQL_EXEC_ID)

This section contains the following topics:

- SQL Plan Monitoring
- Parallel Execution Monitoring
- Generating the SQL Monitor Report
- Enabling and Disabling SQL Monitoring.

SQL Plan Monitoring

Real-time SQL monitoring also includes monitoring statistics for each operation in the execution plan of the SQL statement being monitored. This data is visible in the V$SQL_PLAN_MONITOR view. Similar to the V$SQL_MONITOR view, statistics in V$SQL_PLAN_MONITOR are updated every second as the SQL statement is being executed. These statistics persist after the execution ends, with the same duration as V$SQL_MONITOR. There will be multiple entries in V$SQL_PLAN_MONITOR for every SQL statement being monitored; each entry will correspond to an operation in the execution plan of the statement.

Parallel Execution Monitoring

The database automatically monitors parallel queries, DML, and DDL statements as soon as execution begins. The V$SQL_MONITOR and V$SQL_PLAN_MONITOR views records monitoring information for each process participating in the parallel execution is recorded as separate entries.

V$SQL_MONITOR has one entry for the parallel execution coordinator process, and one entry for each parallel execution server process. Each entry has corresponding entries in V$SQL_PLAN_MONITOR. Because the processes allocated for the parallel execution of a SQL statement are cooperating for the same execution, these entries share the same execution key (the composite SQL_ID, SQL_EXEC_START and SQL_EXEC_ID). You can therefore aggregate the execution key to determine the overall statistics for a parallel execution.

Generating the SQL Monitor Report

You can use the SQL monitor report to view SQL monitoring data. The SQL monitor report uses data from several views, including:

- GV$SQL_MONITOR
- GV$SQL_PLAN_MONITOR
- GV$SQL
- GV$SQL_PLAN
- GV$ACTIVE_SESSION_HISTORY
- GV$SESSION_LONGOPS

To generate the SQL monitor report, run the REPORT_SQL_MONITOR function in the DBMS_SQLTUNE package:

```
variable my_rept CLOB;
BEGIN
        :my_rept :=DBMS_SQLTUNE.REPORT_SQL_MONITOR();
END;
/
print :my_rept
```

The DBMS_SQLTUNE.REPORT_SQL_MONITOR function accepts several input parameters to specify the execution, the level of detail in the report, and the report type ('TEXT', 'HTML', or 'XML'). By default, a text report is generated for the last execution that was monitored if no parameters are specified as shown in the example.

Shows the output of the SQL Monitor Report for the last execution of a SQL statement that was monitored.

Example 10.1: Sample SQL Monitor Report

```
set long 10000000
set longchunksize 10000000
set linesize 200
select dbms_sqltune.report_sql_monitor from dual;
SQL Text
-----------------------------------------------------------------
select * from (select O_ORDERDATE, sum(O_TOTALPRICE)
        from orders o, lineitem l
        where l.l_orderkey = o.o_orderkey
        group by o_orderdate
        order by o_orderdate) where rownum < 100
-----------------------------------------------------------------
Global Information
Status                :     EXECUTING
Instance ID           :     1
Session ID            :     980
SQL ID                :     br4m75c20p97h
SQL Execution ID      :     16777219
Plan Hash Value       :     2992965678
Execution Started     :     06/07/2007 08:36:42
First Refresh Time    :     06/07/2007 08:36:46
Last Refresh Time     :     06/07/2007 08:40:02
```

In the Global Information section of this report, the Status field shows that this statement is still executing. The Time Active(s) column shows how long the operation has been active (the delta in seconds between the first and the last active time). The Start Active column shows, in seconds, when the operation in the execution plan started relative to the SQL statement execution start time. In this report, the fast full scan operation at ID 5 was the first to start (+1s Start Active) and ran for the first 82 seconds.The Starts column shows the number of times the operation in the execution plan was executed. The Rows (Actual) column indicates the number of rows produced, and the Rows (Estim) column shows the estimated cardinality from the optimizer. The Memory and Temp columns indicate the amount of memory and temporary space consumed by each operation of the execution plan.The Activity (percent) and Activity Detail (sample #) columns are derived by joining the V$SQL_PLAN_MONITOR and V$ACTIVE_SESSION_HISTORY views. Activity (percent) shows the percentage of database time consumed by each operation of the execution plan. Activity Detail (sample#) shows the nature of that activity (such as CPU or wait event). In this report, this column shows that most of the database time, 36.68%, is consumed by operation ID 8 (TABLE ACCESS FULL of ORDERS). This activity consists of 73 samples (28+3+42), of which more than half of the activity is attributed to direct path read (42 samples), and a third to CPU (28 samples).The last column, Progress, shows progress monitoring information for the operation from the V$SESSION_LONGOPS view. In this report, it shows that the hash-join operation is 87% complete.

Enabling and Disabling SQL Monitoring

The SQL monitoring feature is enabled by default when the STATISTICS_LEVEL initialization parameter is either set to ALL or TYPICAL (the default value).

Additionally, the CONTROL_MANAGEMENT_PACK_ACCESS parameter must be set to DIAGNOSTIC+TUNING (the default value) because SQL monitoring is a feature of the Oracle Database Tuning Pack. SQL monitoring starts automatically for all long running queries.

Two statement-level hints are available to force or prevent a SQL statement from being monitored. To force SQL monitoring, use the MONITOR hint:

```
select /*+MONITOR*/ from dual;
```

This hint is effective only when the CONTROL_MANAGEMENT_PACK_ACCESS parameter is set to DIAGNOSTIC+TUNING. To prevent the hinted SQL statement from being monitored, use the NO_MONITOR reverse hint.

TUNING INSTANCE RECOVERY PERFORMANCE: FAST-START FAULT RECOVERY

This section describes instance recovery, and how Oracle's Fast-Start Fault Recovery improves availability in the event of a crash or instance failure. It also offers guidelines for tuning the time required to perform crash and instance recovery.

This section contains the following topics:

- About Instance Recovery
- Configuring the Duration of Cache Recovery: FAST_START_MTTR_TARGET
- Tuning FAST_START_MTTR_TARGET and Using MTTR Advisor.

About Instance Recovery

Instance and crash recovery are the automatic application of redo log records to Oracle data blocks after a crash or system failure. During normal operation, if an instance is shut down cleanly (as when using a SHUTDOWN IMMEDIATE statement), rather than terminated abnormally, then the in-memory changes that have not been written to the data files on disk are written to disk as part of the checkpoint performed during shutdown.

However, if a single instance database crashes or if all instances of an Oracle RAC configuration crash, then Oracle Database performs crash recovery at the next startup. If one or more instances of an Oracle RAC configuration crash, then a surviving instance performs instance recovery automatically. Instance and crash recovery occur in two steps: cache recovery followed by transaction recovery.

The database can be opened as soon as cache recovery completes, so improving the performance of cache recovery is important for increasing availability.

Cache Recovery (Rolling Forward)

During the cache recovery step, Oracle Database applies all committed and uncommitted changes in the redo log files to the affected data blocks. The work required for cache recovery processing is proportional to the rate of change to the database (update transactions each second) and the time between checkpoints.

Transaction Recovery (Rolling Back)

To make the database consistent, the changes that were not committed at the time of the crash must be undone (in other words, rolled back). During the transaction recovery step, Oracle Database applies the rollback segments to undo the uncommitted changes.

Checkpoints and Cache Recovery

Periodically, Oracle Database records a checkpoint. A **checkpoint** is the highest system change number (SCN) such that all data blocks less than or equal to that SCN are known to be written out to the data files. If a failure occurs, then only the redo records containing changes at SCNs higher than the checkpoint need to be applied during recovery. The duration of cache recovery processing is determined by two factors: the number of data blocks that have changes at SCNs higher than the SCN of the checkpoint, and the number of log blocks that need to be read to find those changes.

How Checkpoints Affect Performance

Frequent checkpointing writes dirty buffers to the data files more often than otherwise, and so reduces cache recovery time in the event of an instance failure. If checkpointing is frequent, then applying the redo records in the redo log between the current checkpoint position and the end of the log involves processing relatively few data blocks. This means that the cache recovery phase of recovery is fairly short.

However, in a high-update system, frequent checkpointing can reduce run-time performance, because checkpointing causes DBW*n* processes to perform writes.

Fast Cache Recovery Tradeoffs

To minimize the duration of cache recovery, you must force Oracle Database to checkpoint often, thus keeping the number of redo log records to be applied during recovery to a minimum. However, in a high-update system, frequent checkpointing increases the overhead for normal database operations.

If daily operational efficiency is more important than minimizing recovery time, then decrease the frequency of writes to data files due to checkpoints. This should improve operational efficiency, but also increase cache recovery time.

Configuring the Duration of Cache Recovery: FAST_START_MTTR_TARGET

The Fast-Start Fault Recovery feature reduces the time required for cache recovery, and makes the recovery bounded and predictable by limiting the number of dirty buffers and the number of redo records generated between the most recent redo record and the last checkpoint.

The foundation of Fast-Start Fault Recovery is the Fast-Start checkpointing architecture. Instead of conventional event-driven (that is, log switching) checkpointing, which does bulk writes, fast-start checkpointing occurs incrementally. Each DBW*n* process periodically writes buffers to disk to advance the checkpoint position. The oldest modified blocks are written first to ensure that every write lets the checkpoint advance. Fast-Start checkpointing eliminates bulk writes and the resultant I/O spikes that occur with conventional checkpointing.

With the Fast-Start Fault Recovery feature, the FAST_START_MTTR_TARGET initialization parameter simplifies the configuration of recovery time from instance or system failure. FAST_START_MTTR_TARGET specifies a target for the expected Mean Time to Recover (MTTR), that is, the time (in seconds) that it should take to start up the instance and perform cache recovery. After FAST_START_MTTR_TARGET is set, the database manages incremental checkpoint writes in an attempt to meet that target. If you have chosen a practical value for FAST_START_MTTR_TARGET, you can expect your database to recover, on average, in approximately the number of seconds you have chosen.

You must disable or remove the FAST_START_IO_TARGET, LOG_CHECKPOINT_INTERVAL, and LOG_CHECKPOINT_TIMEOUT initialization parameters when using FAST_START_MTTR_TARGET. Setting these parameters interferes with the mechanisms used to manage cache recovery time to meet FAST_START_MTTR_TARGET.

Practical Values for FAST_START_MTTR_TARGET

The maximum value for FAST_START_MTTR_TARGET is 3600 seconds (one hour). If you set the value to more than 3600, then Oracle Database rounds it to 3600.

The following example shows how to set the value of FAST_START_MTTR_TARGET:

```
SQL> ALTER SYSTEM SET FAST_START_MTTR_TARGET=30;
```

In principle, the minimum value for FAST_START_MTTR_TARGET is one second. However, the fact that you can set FAST_START_MTTR_TARGET this low does not mean that this target can be achieved. There are practical limits to the minimum achievable MTTR target, due to such factors as database startup time.

The MTTR target that your database can achieve given the current value of, FAST_START_MTTR_TARGET is called the **effective MTTR target**. You can view your current effective MTTR by viewing the TARGET_MTTR column of the V$INSTANCE_RECOVERY view.

The practical range of MTTR target values for your database is defined to be the range between the lowest achievable effective MTTR target for your database and the longest that startup and cache recovery will take in the worst-case scenario (that is, when the whole buffer cache is dirty).

It is usually not useful to set your FAST_START_MTTR_TARGET to a value outside the practical range. If your FAST_START_MTTR_TARGET value is shorter than the lower limit of the practical range, the effect is as if you set it to the lower limit of the practical range. In such a case, the effective MTTR target will be the best MTTR target the system can achieve, but checkpointing will be at a maximum, which can affect normal database performance. If you set FAST_START_MTTR_TARGET to a time longer than the practical range, the MTTR target will be no better than the worst-case situation.

Reducing Checkpoint Frequency to Optimize Run-Time Performance

To reduce the checkpoint frequency and optimize run-time performance, you can do the following:

- Set the value of FAST_START_MTTR_TARGET to 3600. This enables Fast-Start checkpointing and the Fast-Start Fault Recovery feature, but minimizes its effect on run-time performance while avoiding the need for performance tuning of FAST_START_MTTR_TARGET.
- Size your online redo log files according to the amount of redo your system generates. Try to switch logs at most every twenty minutes. Having your log files too small can increase checkpoint activity and reduce performance. Also note that all redo log files should be the same size.

Monitoring Cache Recovery with V$INSTANCE_RECOVERY

The V$INSTANCE_RECOVERY view displays the current recovery parameter settings. You can also use statistics from this view to determine which factor has the greatest influence on checkpointing.

The following table lists those columns most useful in monitoring predicted cache recovery performance:

Table 10.4. V$INSTANCE_RECOVERY Columns

Column	Description
TARGET_MTTR	Effective MTTR target in seconds. This field is 0 if FAST_START_MTTR_TARGET is not specified.
ESTIMATED_MTTR	The current estimated MTTR in seconds, based on the current number of dirty buffers and log blocks. This field is always calculated, whether FAST_START_MTTR_TARGET is specified.

As part of the ongoing monitoring of your database, you can periodically compare V$INSTANCE_RECOVERY.TARGET_MTTR to your FAST_START_MTTR_TARGET. The two values should generally be the same if the FAST_START_MTTR_TARGET value is in the practical range. If TARGET_MTTR is consistently longer than FAST_START_MTTR_TARGET, then set FAST_START_MTTR_TARGET to a value no less than TARGET_MTTR. If TARGET_MTTR is consistently shorter, then set FAST_START_MTTR_TARGET to a value no greater than TARGET_MTTR.

Tuning FAST_START_MTTR_TARGET and Using MTTR Advisor

To determine the appropriate value for FAST_START_MTTR_TARGET for your database, use the following four step process:

- Calibrate the FAST_START_MTTR_TARGET
- Determine the Practical Range for FAST_START_MTTR_TARGET
- Evaluate Different Target Values with MTTR Advisor
- Determine Optimal Size for Redo Logs.

Calibrate the FAST_START_MTTR_TARGET

The FAST_START_MTTR_TARGET initialization parameter causes the database to calculate internal system trigger values, in order to limit the length of the redo log and the number of dirty data buffers in the data cache. This calculation uses estimated time to read a redo block, estimates of the time to read and write a data block and characteristics of typical workload of the system, such as how many dirty buffers corresponds to how many change vectors, and so on.

Initially, internal defaults are used in the calculation. These defaults are replaced over time by data gathered on I/O performance during system operation and actual cache recoveries.

You will have to perform several instance recoveries in order to calibrate your FAST_START_MTTR_TARGET value properly. Before starting calibration, you must decide whether FAST_START_MTTR_TARGET is being calibrated for a database crash or a hardware crash. This is a consideration if your database files are stored in a file system or if your I/O subsystem has a memory cache, because there is a considerable difference in the read and write time to disk depending on whether the files are cached. The appropriate value for FAST_START_MTTR_TARGET will depend upon which type of crash is more important to recover from quickly.

To effectively calibrate FAST_START_MTTR_TARGET, ensure that you run the typical workload of the system for long enough, and perform several instance recoveries to ensure that the time to read a redo block and the time to read or write a data block during recovery are recorded accurately.

Determine the Practical Range for FAST_START_MTTR_TARGET

After calibration, you can perform tests to determine the practical range for FAST_START_MTTR_TARGET for your database.

Determining Lower Bound for FAST_START_MTTR_TARGET: Scenario

To determine the lower bound of the practical range, set FAST_START_MTTR_TARGET to 1, and start up your database. Then check the value of V$INSTANCE_RECOVERY.TARGET_MTTR, and use this value as a good lower bound for FAST_START_MTTR_TARGET. Database startup time, rather than cache recovery time, is usually the dominant factor in determining this limit.

For example, set the FAST_START_MTTR_TARGET to 1:

```
SQL> ALTER SYSTEM SET FAST_START_MTTR_TARGET=1;
```

Then, execute the following query immediately after opening the database:

```
SQL> SELECT TARGET_MTTR, ESTIMATED_MTTR
 FROM V$INSTANCE_RECOVERY;
```

Oracle Database responds with the following:

```
TARGET_MTTR ESTIMATED_MTTR
18          15
```

The TARGET_MTTR value of 18 seconds is the minimum MTTR target that the system can achieve, that is, the lowest practical value for FAST_START_MTTR_TARGET. This minimum is calculated based on the average database startup time.

The ESTIMATED_MTTR field contains the estimated mean time to recovery based on the current state of the running database. Because the database has just opened, the system contains few dirty buffers, so not much cache recovery would be required if the instance failed at this moment. That is why ESTIMATED_MTTR can, for the moment, be lower than the minimum possible TARGET_MTTR.

ESTIMATED_MTTR can be affected in the short term by recent database activity. Assume that you query V$INSTANCE_RECOVERY immediately after a period of heavy update activity in the database. Oracle Database responds with the following:

```
TARGET_MTTR ESTIMATED_MTTR
18          30
```

Now the effective MTTR target is still 18 seconds, and the estimated MTTR (if a crash happened at that moment) is 30 seconds. This is an acceptable result. This means that some checkpoints writes might not have finished yet, so the buffer cache contains more dirty buffers than targeted.

Now wait for sixty seconds and reissue the query to V$INSTANCE_RECOVERY. Oracle Database responds with the following:

```
TARGET_MTTR ESTIMATED_MTTR
18          25
```

The estimated MTTR at this time has dropped to 25 seconds, because some of the dirty buffers have been written out during this period

Determining Upper Bound for FAST_START_MTTR_TARGET

To determine the upper bound of the practical range, set FAST_START_MTTR_TARGET to 3600, and operate your database under a typical workload for a while. Then check the value of V$INSTANCE_RECOVERY.TARGET_MTTR. This value is a good upper bound for FAST_START_MTTR_TARGET.

Selecting Preliminary Value for FAST_START_MTTR_TARGET

After you have determined the practical bounds for the FAST_START_MTTR_TARGET parameter, select a preliminary value for the parameter. Choose a higher value within the practical range if your concern is with database performance, and a lower value within the practical range if your priority is shorter recovery times. The narrower the practical range, of course, the easier the choice becomes.

For example, if you discovered that the practical range was between 17 and 19 seconds, it would be quite simple to choose 19, because it makes relatively little difference in recovery time and at the same time minimizes the effect of checkpointing on system performance. However, if you found that the practical range was between 18 and 40 seconds, you might choose a compromise value of 30, and set the parameter accordingly:

```
SQL> ALTER SYSTEM SET FAST_START_MTTR_TARGET=30;
```

You might then go on to use the MTTR Advisor to determine an optimal value.

Evaluate Different Target Values with MTTR Advisor

After you have selected a preliminary value for FAST_START_MTTR_TARGET, you can use MTTR Advisor to evaluate the effect of different FAST_START_MTTR_TARGET settings on system performance, compared to your chosen setting.

Enabling MTTR Advisor: To enable MTTR Advisor, set the two initialization parameters STATISTICS_LEVEL and FAST_START_MTTR_TARGET.

STATISTICS_LEVEL governs whether all advisors are enabled and is not specific to MTTR Advisor. Ensure that it is set to TYPICAL or ALL. Then, when FAST_START_MTTR_TARGET is set to a nonzero value, the MTTR Advisor is enabled.

Using MTTR Advisor: After enabling MTTR Advisor, run a typical database workload for a while. When MTTR Advisor is ON, the database simulates checkpoint queue behavior under the current value of FAST_START_MTTR_TARGET, and up to four other different MTTR settings within the range of valid FAST_START_MTTR_TARGET values. (The database will in this case determine the valid range for FAST_START_MTTR_TARGET itself before testing different values in the range.)

Viewing MTTR Advisor Results: V$MTTR_TARGET_ADVICE

The dynamic performance view V$MTTR_TARGET_ADVICE lets you view statistics or advisories collected by MTTR Advisor.

The database populates V$MTTR_TARGET_ADVICE with advice about the effects of each of the FAST_START_MTTR_TARGET settings for your database. For each possible value of FAST_START_MTTR_TARGET, the row contains details about how many cache writes would be performed under the workload tested for that value of FAST_START_MTTR_TARGET.

Specifically, each row contains information about cache writes, total physical writes (including direct writes), and total I/O (including reads) for that value of FAST_START_MTTR_TARGET, expressed both as a total number of operations and a ratio compared to the operations under your chosen FAST_START_MTTR_TARGET value. For instance, a ratio of 1.2 indicates 20% more cache writes.

Knowing the effect of different FAST_START_MTTR_TARGET settings on cache write activity and other I/O enables you to decide better which FAST_START_MTTR_TARGET value best fits your recovery and performance needs.

If MTTR Advisor is currently on, then V$MTTR_TARGET_ADVICE shows the Advisor information collected. If MTTR Advisor is currently OFF, then the view shows information collected the last time MTTR Advisor was ON since database startup, if any. If the database has been restarted since the last time the MTTR Advisor was used, or if it has never been used, the view will not show any rows.

Determine Optimal Size for Redo Logs

You can use the V$INSTANCE_RECOVERY view column OPTIMAL_LOGFILE_SIZE to determine the size of your online redo logs. This field shows the redo log file size in megabytes that is considered optimal based on the current setting of FAST_START_MTTR_TARGET. If this field consistently shows a value greater than the size of your smallest online log, then you should configure all your online logs to be at least this size.

Note, however, that the redo log file size affects the MTTR. In some cases, you may be able to refine your choice of the optimal FAST_START_MTTR_TARGET value by re-running the MTTR Advisor with your suggested optimal log file size.

11 The Query Optimizer

Learning Objectives

*This chapter discusses SQL processing, optimization methods, and how the **query optimizer** (usually called the **optimizer**) chooses a specific plan to execute SQL.*

The chapter contains the following sections:

- Overview of the Query Optimizer
- Overview of Optimizer Access Paths
- Overview of Joins
- Reading and Understanding Execution Plans
- Controlling Optimizer Behaviour

OVERVIEW OF THE QUERY OPTIMIZER

The **optimizer** is built-in software that determines the most efficient way to execute a SQL statement.

This section contains the following topics:

- Optimizer Operations
- Components of the Query Optimizer
- Bind Variable Peeking.

Optimizer Operations

The database can execute a SQL statement in multiple ways, such as **full table scans**, index scans, nested loops, and **hash joins**. The optimizer considers many factors related to the objects and the conditions in the query when determining an execution plan. This determination is an important step in SQL processing and can greatly affect execution time.

The optimizer might not make the same decisions from one version of Oracle Database to the next. In recent versions, the optimizer might make different decisions because better information is available.

When the user submits a SQL statement for execution, the optimizer performs the following steps:

1. The optimizer generates a set of potential plans for the SQL statement based on available access paths and hints.
2. The optimizer estimates the cost of each plan based on statistics in the data dictionary. Statistics include information on the data distribution and storage characteristics of the tables, indexes, and partitions accessed by the statement.
   The **cost** is an estimated value proportional to the expected resource use needed to execute the statement with a particular plan. The optimizer calculates the cost of access paths and join orders based on the estimated computer resources, which includes I/O, CPU, and memory.
   Serial plans with higher costs take longer to execute than those with smaller costs. When using a parallel plan, resource use is not directly related to elapsed time.
3. The optimizer compares the plans and chooses the plan with the lowest cost.
   The output from the optimizer is an **execution plan** that describes the optimum method of execution. The plans shows the combination of the steps Oracle Database uses to execute a SQL statement. Each step either retrieves rows physically from the database or prepares them for the user issuing the statement.

For any SQL statement processed by Oracle Database, the optimizer performs the operations listed in Table 11.1.

Table 11.1. Optimizer Operations

Operation	Description
Evaluation of expressions and conditions	The optimizer first evaluates expressions and containing constants as fully as possible.
Statement transformation	For complex statements involving, for example, correlated subqueries or views, the optimizer might transform the original statement into an equivalent join statement.
Choice of optimizer goals	The optimizer determines the goal of optimization.
Choice of access paths	For each table accessed by the statement, the optimizer chooses one or more of the available access paths to obtain table data.
Choice of join orders	For a join statement that joins more than two tables, the optimizer chooses which pair of tables is joined first, and then which table is joined to the result, and so on.

Sometimes, you may have more information about a particular application's data than is available to the optimizer. In such cases you can use **hints** in SQL statements to instruct the optimizer about how a statement should be executed.

Components of the Query Optimizer

The query optimizer operations include:

- Query Transformation
- Estimation
- Plan Generation.

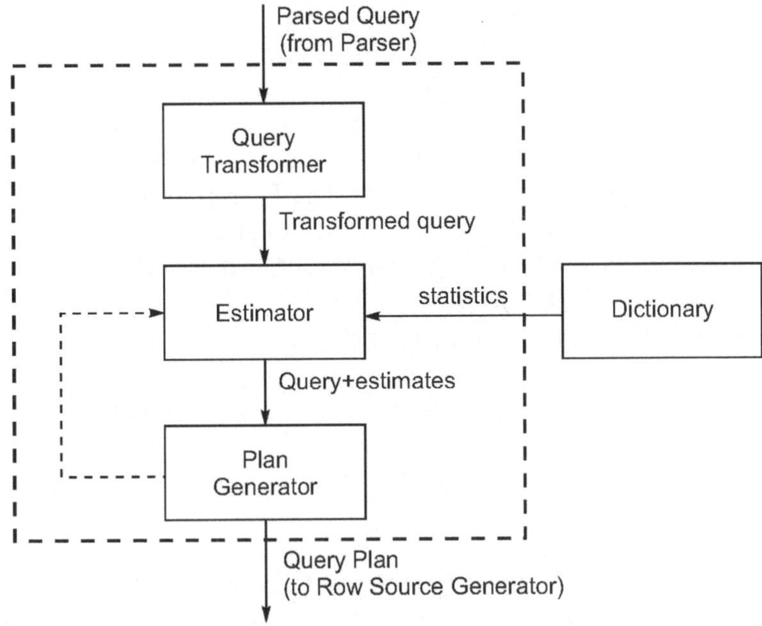

Figure 11.1. Illustrates Optimizer Components

Query Transformation

Each query portion of a statement is called a **query block**. The input to the query transformer is a parsed query, which is represented by a set of query blocks.

In the following example, the SQL statement consists of two query blocks. The subquery in parentheses is the **inner query block**. The **outer query block**, which is the rest of the SQL statement, retrieves names of employees in the departments whose IDs were supplied by the subquery.

```
SELECT first_name, last_name
FROM   employees WHERE  department_id
IN     (SELECT department_id FROM departments WHERE
location_id = 1800);
```

The query form determines how query blocks are interrelated. The transformer determines whether it is advantageous to rewrite the original SQL statement into a semantically equivalent SQL statement that can be processed more efficiently.

The query transformer employs several query transformation techniques, including the following:

- View Merging
- Predicate Pushing
- Subquery Unnesting
- Query Rewrite with Materialized Views.

Any combination of these transformations can apply to a given query.

View Merging: Each view referenced in a query is expanded by the parser into a separate query block. The block essentially represents the view definition, and thus the result of a view. One option for the optimizer is to analyze the view query block separately and generate a view subplan. The optimizer then processes the rest of the query by using the view subplan to generate an overall query plan. This technique usually leads to a suboptimal query plan because the view is optimized separately.

In **view merging**, the transformer merges the query block representing the view into the containing query block. For example, suppose you create a view as follows:

```
CREATE VIEW employees_50_vw AS  SELECT employee_id, last_name,
job_id, salary, commission_pct, department_id
  FROM   employees  WHERE  department_id = 50;
```

You then query the view as follows:

```
SELECT employee_id FROM   employees_50_vw
WHERE  employee_id > 150;
```

The optimizer can use view merging to transform the query of `employees_50_vw` into the following equivalent query:

```
SELECT employee_id FROM   employees
WHERE  department_id = 50
AND    employee_id > 150;
```

The view merging optimization applies to views that contain only selections, projections, and joins. That is, mergeable views do not contain set operators, aggregate functions, `DISTINCT`, `GROUP BY`, `CONNECT BY`, and so on.

To enable the optimizer to use view merging for any query issued by the user, you must grant the `MERGE ANY VIEW` privilege to the user. Grant the `MERGE VIEW` privilege to a user on specific views to enable the optimizer to use view merging for queries on these views. These privileges are required only under specific conditions, such as when a view is not merged because the security checks fail.

Predicate Pushing: In **predicate pushing**, the optimizer "pushes" the relevant predicates from the containing query block into the view query block. For views that are not merged, this technique improves the subplan of the unmerged view because the database can use the pushed-in predicates to access indexes or to use as filters.

For example, suppose you create a view that references two employee tables. The view is defined with a compound query that uses the `UNION` set operator, as follows:

```
CREATE VIEW all_employees_vw AS
  ( SELECT employee_id, last_name, job_id, commission_pct,
  department_id   FROM   employees )
  UNION ( SELECT employee_id, last_name, job_id,
  commission_pct, department_id
    FROM   contract_workers );
```

You then query the view as follows:

```
SELECT last_name FROM   all_employees_vw
WHERE  department_id = 50;
```

Because the view is a compound query, the optimizer cannot merge the view's query into the accessing query block. Instead, the optimizer can transform the accessing statement by pushing its predicate, the `WHERE` clause condition `department_id=50`, into the view's compound query. The equivalent transformed query is as follows:

```
SELECT  last_name  FROM    ( SELECT  employee_id,  last_name,  job_id,
commission_pct, department_id
```

```
  FROM   employees WHERE  department_id=50
  UNION
 SELECT employee_id, last_name, job_id, commission_pct, department_id
FROM contract_workers WHERE department_id=50 );
```

Subquery Unnesting: In **subquery unnesting**, the optimizer transforms a nested query into an equivalent join statement, and then optimizes the join. This transformation enables the optimizer to take advantage of the join optimizer technique. The optimizer can perform this transformation only if the resulting join statement is guaranteed to return exactly the same rows as the original statement, and if subqueries do not contain aggregate functions such as AVG.

For example, suppose you connect as user sh and execute the following query:

```
SELECT * FROM   sales
WHERE  cust_id IN ( SELECT cust_id FROM customers );
```

Because the customers.cust_id column is a primary key, the optimizer can transform the complex query into the following join statement that is guaranteed to return the same data:

```
SELECT sales.* FROM   sales, customers
WHERE  sales.cust_id = customers.cust_id;
```

If the optimizer cannot transform a complex statement into a join statement, it selects execution plans for the parent statement and the subquery as though they were separate statements. The optimizer then executes the subquery and uses the rows returned to execute the parent query. To improve execution speed of the overall query plan, the optimizer orders the subplans efficiently.

Query Rewrite with Materialized Views: A **materialized view** is like a query with a result that the database materializes and stores in a table. When the database finds a user query compatible with the query associated with a materialized view, then the database can rewrite the query in terms of the materialized view. This technique improves query execution because most of the query result has been precomputed.

The query transformer looks for any materialized views that are compatible with the user query and selects one or more materialized views to rewrite the user query. The use of materialized views to rewrite a query is cost-based. That is, the optimizer does not rewrite the query if the plan generated without the materialized views has a lower cost than the plan generated with the materialized views.

Consider the following materialized view, cal_month_sales_mv, which aggregates the dollar amount sold each month:

```
CREATE MATERIALIZED VIEW cal_month_sales_mv
  ENABLE QUERY REWRITE AS
  SELECT t.calendar_month_desc, SUM(s.amount_sold) AS dollars
  FROM   sales s, times t
  WHERE  s.time_id = t.time_id
  GROUP BY t.calendar_month_desc;
```

Assume that sales number is around one million in a typical month. The view has the precomputed aggregates for the dollar amount sold for each month. Consider the following query, which asks for the sum of the amount sold for each month:

```
SELECT t.calendar_month_desc, SUM(s.amount_sold)
FROM   sales s, times t
WHERE  s.time_id = t.time_id
GROUP BY t.calendar_month_desc;
```

Without query rewrite, the database must access `sales` directly and compute the sum of the amount sold. This method involves reading many million rows from `sales`, which invariably increases query response time. The join also further slows query response because the database must compute the join on several million rows. With query rewrite, the optimizer transparently rewrites the query as follows:

```
SELECT calendar_month, dollars FROM   cal_month_sales_mv;
```

Estimation

The **estimator** determines the overall cost of a given execution plan. The estimator generates three different types of measures to achieve this goal:

- Selectivity.

  This measure represents a fraction of rows from a row set. The selectivity is tied to a query predicate, such as `last_name='Smith'`, or a combination of predicates.

- Cardinality.

  This measure represents the number of rows in a row set.

- Cost.

  This measure represents units of work or resource used. The query optimizer uses disk I/O, CPU usage, and memory usage as units of work.

  If statistics are available, then the estimator uses them to compute the measures. The statistics improve the degree of accuracy of the measures.

Selectivity: The **selectivity** represents a fraction of rows from a row set. The row set can be a base table, a view, or the result of a join or a `GROUP BY` operator. The selectivity is tied to a query predicate, such as `last_name = 'Smith'`, or a combination of predicates, such as `last_name = 'Smith' AND job_type = 'Clerk'`.

A predicate filters a specific number of rows from a row set. Thus, the selectivity of a predicate indicates how many rows pass the predicate test. Selectivity ranges from 0.0 to 1.0. A selectivity of 0.0 means that no rows are selected from a row set, whereas a selectivity of 1.0 means that all rows are selected. A predicate becomes more selective as the value approaches 0.0 and less selective (or more unselective) as the value approaches 1.0.

The optimizer estimates selectivity depending on whether statistics are available:

- Statistics not available.

  Depending on the value of the `OPTIMIZER_DYNAMIC_SAMPLING` initialization parameter, the optimizer either uses **dynamic sampling** or an internal default value. The database uses different internal defaults depending on the predicate type. For example, the internal default for an equality predicate (`last_name = 'Smith'`) is lower than for a range predicate (`last_name > 'Smith'`) because an equality predicate is expected to return a smaller fraction of rows.

- Statistics available.

  When statistics are available, the estimator uses them to estimate selectivity. Assume there are 150 distinct employee last names. For an equality predicate `last_name = 'Smith'`, selectivity is the reciprocal of the number `n` of distinct values of `last_name`, which in this example is .006 because the query selects rows that contain 1 out of 150 distinct values.

  If a histogram is available on the `last_name` column, then the estimator uses the histogram instead of the number of distinct values. The histogram captures the distribution of different values in a column, so it yields better selectivity estimates, especially for columns that contain **skewed data.**

Cardinality: Cardinality represents the number of rows in a row set. In this context, the row set can be a base table, a view, or the result of a join or `GROUP BY` operator.

Cost: The **cost** represents units of work or resource used in an operation. The optimizer uses disk I/O, CPU usage, and memory usage as units of work. The operation can be scanning a table, accessing rows from a table by using an index, joining two tables together, or sorting a row set. The cost is the number of work units expected to be incurred when the database executes the query and produces its result.

The **access path** determines the number of units of work required to get data from a base table. The access path can be a table scan, a fast full index scan, or an index scan.

- Table scan or fast full index scan.
  During a table scan or **fast full index scan**, the database reads multiple blocks from disk in a single I/O. Therefore, the cost of the scan depends on the number of blocks to be scanned and the multiblock read count value.
- Index scan.
  The cost of an index scan depends on the levels in the B-tree, the number of index leaf blocks to be scanned, and the number of rows to be fetched using the rowid in the index keys. The cost of fetching rows using rowids depends on the **index clustering factor.**

The **join cost** represents the combination of the individual access costs of the two row sets being joined, plus the cost of the join operation.

Plan Generation

The **plan generator** explores various plans for a query block by trying out different access paths, join methods, and join orders. Many plans are possible because of the various combinations of different access paths, join methods, and join orders that the database can use to produce the same result. The purpose of the generator is to pick the plan with the lowest cost.

Join Order

A **join order** is the order in which different join items, such as tables, are accessed and joined together. Assume that the database joins `table1`, `table2`, and `table3`. The join order might be as follows:

1. The database accesses `table1`.
2. The database accesses `table2` and joins its rows to `table1`.
3. The database accesses `table3` and joins its data to the result of the join between `table1` and `table2`.

Query Subplans

The optimizer represents each nested subquery or unmerged view by a separate query block and generates a **subplan**. The database optimizes query blocks separately from the bottom up. Thus, the database optimizes the innermost query block first and generates a subplan for it, and then lastly generates the outer query block representing the entire query.

The number of possible plans for a query block is proportional to the number of join items in the `FROM` clause. This number rises exponentially with the number of join items. For example, the possible plans for a join of five tables will be significantly higher than the possible plans for a join of two tables.

Cutoff for Plan Selection

The plan generator uses an internal cutoff to reduce the number of plans it tries when finding the lowest-cost plan. The cutoff is based on the cost of the current best plan. If the current best cost is large, then the plan generator explores alternative plans to find a lower cost plan. If the current best cost is small, then the generator ends the search swiftly because further cost improvement will not be significant.

The cutoff works well if the plan generator starts with an initial join order that produces a plan with cost close to optimal. Finding a good initial join order is a difficult problem.

Bind Variable Peeking

In **bind variable peeking** (also known as **bind peeking**), the optimizer looks at the value in a bind variable when the database performs a hard parse of a statement.

When a query uses literals, the optimizer can use the literal values to find the best plan. However, when a query uses bind variables, the optimizer must select the best plan without the presence of literals in the SQL text. This task can be extremely difficult. By peeking at bind values the optimizer can determine the selectivity of a `WHERE` clause condition as if literals *had* been used, thereby improving the plan.

Example 11.1: Bind Peeking

Assume that the following 100,000 row `emp` table exists in the database. The table has the following definition:

```
SQL> DESCRIBE emp
Name                          Null?             Type
---------------------------------------------------------------
ENAME                                           VARCHAR2(20)
EMPNO                                           NUMBER
PHONE                                           VARCHAR2(20)
DEPTNO                                          NUMBER
```

The data is significantly skewed in the `deptno` column. The value 10 is found in 99.9% of the rows. Each of the other `deptno` values (`0` through `9`) is found in 1% of the rows. You have gathered statistics for the table, resulting in a histogram on the `deptno` column. You define a bind variable and query `emp` using the bind value `9` as follows:

```
VARIABLE deptno NUMBER
EXEC :deptno := 9

SELECT /*ACS_1*/ count(*), max(empno)
FROM   emp
WHERE  deptno = :deptno;
```

The query returns 10 rows:

```
COUNT(*)      MAX(EMPNO)
---------     ---------
   10            99
```

To generate the execution plan for the query, the database peeked at the value `9` during the hard parse. The optimizer generated selectivity estimates as if the user had executed the following query:

```
select /*ACS_1*/ count(*), max(empno)
from emp
where deptno = 9;
```

When choosing a plan, the optimizer only peeks at the bind value during the hard parse. This plan may not be optimal for all possible values.

Adaptive Cursor Sharing

The **adaptive cursor sharing** feature enables a single statement that contains bind variables to use multiple execution plans. Cursor sharing is "adaptive" because the cursor adapts its behavior so that the database does not always use the same plan for each execution or bind variable value.

For appropriate queries, the database monitors data accessed over time for different bind values, ensuring the optimal choice of cursor for a specific bind value. For example, the optimizer might choose one plan for bind value 9 and a different plan for bind value `10`. Cursor sharing is "adaptive" because the cursor adapts its behavior so that the same plan is not always used for each execution or bind variable value.

Adaptive cursor sharing is enabled for the database by default and cannot be disabled. Note that adaptive cursor sharing does not apply to SQL statements containing more than 14 bind variables.

Adaptive cursor sharing is independent of the `CURSOR_SHARING` initialization parameter. Adaptive cursor sharing is equally applicable to statements that contain user-defined and system-generated bind variables.

Bind-Sensitive Cursors

A **bind-sensitive cursor** is a cursor whose optimal plan may depend on the value of a bind variable. The database monitors the behavior of a bind-sensitive cursor that uses different bind values to determine whether a different plan is beneficial.

The criteria used by the optimizer to decide whether a cursor is bind-sensitive include the following:

- The optimizer has peeked at the bind values to generate selectivity estimates.
- A histogram exists on the column containing the bind value.

Example 11.2: Bind-Sensitive Cursors

In you queried the `emp` table using the bind value 9 for `deptno`. Now you run the `DBMS_XPLAN.DISPLAY_CURSOR` function to show the query plan:

```
SELECT * FROM TABLE(DBMS_XPLAN.DISPLAY_CURSOR);
```

The plan indicates that the optimizer chose an index range scan, which is expected because of the selectivity (only 1%) of the value 9. You can query `V$SQL` to view statistics about the cursor.

```
COL BIND_SENSI FORMAT a10
COL BIND_AWARE FORMAT a10
COL BIND_SHARE FORMAT a10
SELECT CHILD_NUMBER, EXECUTIONS, BUFFER_GETS, IS_BIND_SENSITIVE AS
"BIND_SENSI", IS_BIND_AWARE AS "BIND_AWARE", IS_SHAREABLE AS
"BIND_SHARE"
FROM   V$SQL
WHERE  SQL_TEXT LIKE 'select /*ACS_1%';
```

As shown in the following output, one child cursor exists for this statement and has been executed once. A small number of buffer gets are associated with the child cursor. Because the `deptno` data is skewed, the database created a histogram. This histogram led the database to mark the cursor as bind-sensitive (`IS_BIND_SENSITIVE` is Y).

```
CHILD_NUMBER EXECUTIONS BUFFER_GETS BIND_SENSI BIND_AWARE BIND_SHARE
------------ ---------- ----------- ---------- ---------- ----------
           0          1          56          Y          N          Y
```

For each execution of the query with a new bind value, the database records the execution statistics for the new value and compares them to the execution statistics for the previous value. If execution statistics vary greatly, then the database marks the cursor bind-aware.

Bind-Aware Cursors

A **bind-aware cursor** is a bind-sensitive cursor eligible to use different plans for different bind values. After a cursor has been made bind-aware, the optimizer chooses plans for future executions based on the bind value and its selectivity estimate.

When a statement with a bind-sensitive cursor executes, the database decides whether to mark the cursor bind-aware. The decision depends on whether the cursor produces significantly different data access patterns for different bind values. If the database marks the cursor bind-aware, then the next time that the cursor executes the database does the following:

- Generates a new plan based on the new bind value.
- Marks the original cursor generated for the statement as not shareable (`V$SQL.IS_SHAREABLE` is `N`). This cursor is no longer usable and will be among the first to be aged out of the shared SQL area.

Example 11.3: Bind-Aware Cursors

In you queried emp using the bind value `9`. Now you query `emp` using the bind value `10`. The query returns 99,900 rows that contain the value `10`:

```
COUNT(*)        MAX(EMPNO)
-------         ---------
 99900           100000
```

Because the cursor for this statement is bind-sensitive, the optimizer assumes that the cursor can be shared. Consequently, the optimizer uses the same index range scan for the value `10` as for the value `9`.

The `V$SQL` output shows that the same bind-sensitive cursor was executed a second time (the query using `10`) and required many more buffer gets than the first execution:

```
SELECT CHILD_NUMBER, EXECUTIONS, BUFFER_GETS,
IS_BIND_SENSITIVE AS "BIND_SENSI",
IS_BIND_AWARE AS "BIND_AWARE", IS_SHAREABLE AS "BIND_SHARE"
FROM   V$SQL WHERE  SQL_TEXT LIKE 'select /*ACS_1%';
CHILD_NUMBER EXECUTIONS BUFFER_GETS BIND_SENSI BIND_AWARE BIND_SHARE
------------ ---------- ----------- ---------- ---------- ----------
           0          2          10 10       Y          N          Y
```

Now you execute the query using the value `10` a second time. The database compares statistics for previous executions and marks the cursor as bind-aware. In this case, the optimizer decides that a new plan is warranted, so it performs a hard parse of the statement and generates a new plan. The new plan uses a full table scan instead of an index range scan:

```
-------------------------------------------------------------------------
| Id   | Operation              | Name     | Rows     | Bytes    | Cost
(% CPU)| Time          |        |
-------------------------------------------------------------------------
|    0 | SELECT STATEMENT       |          |          |          |    208
(100) |                |
|    1 | SORT AGGREGATE         |          |        1 |       16 |
|          |
```

```
|*   2 | TABLE ACCESS FULL|  EMP         |  95000 |   1484K|    208
(1) | 00:00:03 |
---------------------------------------------------------------------
```

A query of V$SQL shows that the database created an additional child cursor (child number 1) that represents the plan containing the full table scan. This new cursor shows a lower number of buffer gets and is marked bind-aware:

```
SELECT CHILD_NUMBER, EXECUTIONS, BUFFER_GETS,
IS_BIND_SENSITIVE AS "BIND_SENSI",IS_BIND_AWARE AS
"BIND_AWARE", IS_SHAREABLE AS "BIND_SHARE"
FROM   V$SQL  WHERE  SQL_TEXT LIKE 'select /*ACS_1%';
CHILD_NUMBER EXECUTIONS BUFFER_GETS BIND_SENSI BIND_AWARE BIND_SHARE
------------ ---------- ----------- ---------- ---------- ----------
       0          2         1010        Y          N          Y
       1          2         1522        Y          Y          Y
```

After you execute the query twice with value 10, you execute it again using the more selective value 9. Because of adaptive cursor sharing, the optimizer "adapts" the cursor and chooses an index range scan rather than a full table scan for this value.

A query of V$SQL indicates that the database created a new child cursor (child number 2) for the execution of the query:

```
CHILD_NUMBER EXECUTIONS BUFFER_GETS BIND_SENSI BIND_AWARE BIND_SHARE
------------ ---------- ----------- ---------- ---------- ----------
       0          2         1010        Y          N          N
       1          1         1522        Y          Y          Y
       2          1            7        Y          Y          Y
```

Because the database is now using adaptive cursor sharing, the database no longer uses the original cursor (child 0), which is not bind-aware. The shared SQL area will age out the defunct cursor.

Cursor Merging

If the optimizer creates a plan for a bind-aware cursor, and if this plan is the same as an existing cursor, then the optimizer can perform **cursor merging**. In this case, the database merges cursors to save space in the shared SQL area. The database increases the selectivity range for the cursor to include the selectivity of the new bind.

Suppose you execute a query with a bind value that does not fall within the selectivity ranges of the existing cursors. The database performs a hard parse and generates a new plan and new cursor. If this new plan is the same plan used by an existing cursor, then the database merges these two cursors and deletes one of the old cursors.

Viewing Bind-Related Performance Data

You can use the V$ views for adaptive cursor sharing to see selectivity ranges, cursor information (such as whether a cursor is bind-aware or bind-sensitive), and execution statistics:

- V$SQL shows whether a cursor is bind-sensitive or bind-aware.
- V$SQL_CS_HISTOGRAM shows the distribution of the execution count across a three-bucket execution history histogram.
- V$SQL_CS_SELECTIVITY shows the selectivity ranges stored for every predicate containing a bind variable if the selectivity was used to check cursor sharing.
- V$SQL_CS_STATISTICS summarizes the information that the optimizer uses to determine whether to mark a cursor bind-aware.

OVERVIEW OF OPTIMIZER ACCESS PATHS

Access paths are ways in which data is retrieved from the database. In general, index access paths are useful for statements that retrieve a small subset of table rows, whereas full scans are more efficient when accessing a large portion of the table. Online transaction processing (OLTP) applications, which consist of short-running SQL statements with high selectivity, often are characterized by the use of index access paths. Decision support systems, however, tend to use partitioned tables and perform full scans of the relevant partitions.

This section describes the data access paths that the database can use to locate and retrieve any row in any table:

- Full Table Scans
- Rowid Scans
- Index Scans
- Cluster Access
- Hash Access
- Sample Table Scans
- How the Query Optimizer Chooses an Access Path.

Full Table Scans

This type of scan reads all rows from a table and filters out those that do not meet the selection criteria. During a full table scan, all blocks in the table that are under the high water mark are scanned. The high water mark indicates the amount of used space, or space that had been formatted to receive data. Each row is examined to determine whether it satisfies the statement's `WHERE` clause.

When Oracle Database performs a full table scan, the blocks are read sequentially. Because the blocks are adjacent, the database can make I/O calls larger than a single block to speed up the process. The size of the read calls range from one block to the number of blocks indicated by the initialization parameter `DB_FILE_MULTIBLOCK_READ_COUNT`. Using multiblock reads, the database can perform a full table scan very efficiently. The database reads each block only once. Contains an example of a full table scan on the `employees` table.

Why a Full Table Scan is Faster for Accessing Large Amounts of Data

Full table scans are cheaper than index range scans when accessing a large fraction of the blocks in a table. Full table scans can use larger I/O calls, and making fewer large I/O calls is cheaper than making many smaller calls.

When the Optimizer Uses Full Table Scans

The optimizer uses a full table scan in any of the following cases:

Lack of Index: If the query cannot use existing indexes, then it uses a full table scan. For example, if there is a function used on the indexed column in the query, then the optimizer cannot use the index and instead uses a full table scan.

If you need to use the index for case-independent searches, then either do not permit mixed-case data in the search columns or create a function-based index, such as `UPPER(last_name)`, on the search column.

Large Amount of Data: If the optimizer thinks that the query requires most of the blocks in the table, then it uses a full table scan, even though indexes are available.

Small Table: If a table contains less than DB_FILE_MULTIBLOCK_READ_COUNT blocks under the high water mark, which the database can read in a single I/O call, then a full table scan might be cheaper than an index range scan, regardless of the fraction of tables being accessed or indexes present.

High Degree of Parallelism: A high degree of parallelism for a table skews the optimizer toward full table scans over range scans. Examine the DEGREE column in ALL_TABLES for the table to determine the degree of parallelism.

Full Table Scan Hints: Use the hint FULL(table alias) to instruct the optimizer to use a full table scan.

You can use the CACHE and NOCACHE hints to indicate where the retrieved blocks are placed in the buffer cache. The CACHE hint instructs the optimizer to place the retrieved blocks at the most recently used end of the LRU list in the buffer cache when the database performs a full table scan.

Small tables are automatically cached according to the criteria in Table 11.2.

Table 11.2. Table Caching Criteria

Table Size	Size Criteria	Caching
Small	Number of blocks < 20 or 2% of total cached blocks, whichever is larger	If STATISTICS_LEVEL is se to TYPICAL or higher, then Oracle Database decides whether to cache a table depending on the table scan history. The database caches the table only if a future table scan is likely to find the cached blocks.If STATISTICS_LEVEL is set to BASIC, then the table is not cached.
Medium	Larger than a small table, but < 10% of total cached blocks	Oracle Database decides whether to cache a table based on its table scan and workload history. It caches the table only if a future table scan is likely to find the cached blocks.
Large	> 10% of total cached blocks	Not cached

Automatic caching of small tables is disabled for tables that are created or altered with the CACHE attribute.

Parallel Query Execution: When a full table scan is required, the database can improve response time by using multiple parallel execution servers. In some cases, as when the database has a large amount of memory, the database can cache parallel query data in the SGA instead of using direct reads into the PGA. Typically, parallel queries occur in low-concurrency data warehouses because of the potential resource usage.

Rowid Scans

The rowid of a row specifies the data file and data block containing the row and the location of the row in that block. Locating a row by specifying its rowid is the fastest way to retrieve a single row, because the exact location of the row in the database is specified.

To access a table by rowid, Oracle Database first obtains the rowids of the selected rows, either from the statement's WHERE clause or through an index scan of one or more of the table's indexes. Oracle Database then locates each selected row in the table based on its rowid.

In, the plan includes an index scan on the jobs and departments tables. The database uses the rowids retrieved to return the rows.

When the Optimizer Uses Rowids

This is generally the second step after retrieving the rowid from an index. The table access might be required for any columns in the statement not present in the index.

Access by rowid does not need to follow every index scan. If the index contains all the columns needed for the statement, then table access by rowid might not occur.

Rowids are an internal representation of where the database stores data. Rowids can change between versions. Accessing data based on position is not recommended because rows can move around due to row migration and chaining, export and import, and some other operations. Foreign keys should be based on primary keys.

Index Scans

In this method, a row is retrieved by traversing the index, using the indexed column values specified by the statement. An index scan retrieves data from an index based on the value of one or more columns in the index. To perform an index scan, Oracle Database searches the index for the indexed column values accessed by the statement. If the statement accesses only columns of the index, then Oracle Database reads the indexed column values directly from the index, rather than from the table.

The index contains not only the indexed value, but also the rowids of rows in the table having that value. Therefore, if the statement accesses other columns in addition to the indexed columns, then Oracle Database can find the rows in the table by using either a table access by rowid or a cluster scan.

An index scan can be one of the following types:

- Assessing I/O for Blocks, not Rows
- Index Unique Scans
- Index Range Scans
- Index Range Scans Descending
- Index Skip Scans
- Full Scans
- Fast Full Index Scans
- Index Joins
- Bitmap Indexes.

Assessing I/O for Blocks, not Rows

Oracle Database performs I/O by blocks. Therefore, the optimizer's decision to use full table scans is influenced by the percentage of blocks accessed, not rows. This is called the **index clustering factor**. If blocks contain single rows, then rows accessed and blocks accessed are the same.

However, most tables have multiple rows in each block. Consequently, the desired number of rows may be clustered in a few blocks or spread out over a larger number of blocks.

Although the clustering factor is a property of the index, the clustering factor actually relates to the spread of similar indexed column values within data blocks in the table. A lower clustering factor indicates that the individual rows are concentrated within fewer blocks in the table. Conversely, a high clustering factor indicates that the individual rows are scattered more randomly across blocks in the table. Therefore, a high clustering factor means that it costs more to use a range scan to fetch rows by rowid, because more blocks in the table need to be visited to return the data. shows how the clustering factor can affect cost.

Example 11.4: Effects of Clustering Factor on Cost

Assume the following situation:

- There is a table with 9 rows.
- There is a non-unique index on `col1` for table.
- The `c1` column currently stores the values A, B, and C.
- The table only has three data blocks.

Case 1: The index clustering factor is low for the rows as they are arranged in the following diagram.

```
Block 1        Block 2          Block 3
-------        -------          -------
A  A  A        B  B  B          C  C  C
```

This is because the rows that have the same indexed column values for `c1` are located within the same physical blocks in the table. The cost of using a range scan to return all rows that have the value A is low because only one block in the table must be read.

Case 2: If the same rows in the table are rearranged so that the index values are scattered across the table blocks (rather than collocated), then the index clustering factor is higher.

```
Block 1        Block 2          Block 3
-------        -------          -------
A  B  C        A  B  C          A  B  C
```

This is because all three blocks in the table must be read in order to retrieve all rows with the value A in `col1`.

Index Unique Scans

This scan returns, at most, a single rowid. Oracle Database performs a unique scan if a statement contains a `UNIQUE` or a `PRIMARY KEY` constraint that guarantees that only a single row is accessed.

In, the database performs an index scan on the `jobs` and `departments` tables, using the `job_id_pk` and `dept_id_pk` indexes respectively.

When the Optimizer Uses Index Unique Scans: The database uses this access path when the user specifies all columns of a unique (B-tree) index or an index created as a result of a primary key constraint with equality conditions.

Index Unique Scan Hints: In general, you should not need to use a hint to do a unique scan. There might be cases where the table is across a database link and being accessed from a local table, or where the table is small enough for the optimizer to prefer a full table scan.

The hint `INDEX(alias index_name)` specifies the index to use, but not an access path (range scan or unique scan.

Index Range Scans

An index range scan is a common operation for accessing selective data. It can be bounded (bounded on both sides) or unbounded (on one or both sides). Data is returned in the ascending order of index columns. Multiple rows with identical values are sorted in ascending order by rowid.

If you require the data to be sorted by order, then use the **ORDER BY** clause, and do not rely on an index. If an index can satisfy an **ORDER BY** clause, then the optimizer uses this option and avoids a sort.

In, the order has been imported from a legacy system, and you are querying the order by the reference used in the legacy system. Assume this reference is the `order_date`.

Example 11.5. Index Range Scan

```
SELECT order_status, order_id
  FROM orders
 WHERE order_date = :b1;
---------------------------------------------------------------------
| Id   | Operation                    |  Name               |
Rows   | Bytes    | Cost (%CPU)|
---------------------------------------------------------------------
|    0 | SELECT STATEMENT             |                     |
1 |      20 |      3  (34)|
|    1 | TABLE ACCESS BY INDEX ROWID  | ORDERS              |
1 |       20 |     3  (34)|
|*  2 | INDEX RANGE SCAN             | ORD_ORDER_DATE_IX   |
1 |          |     2  (50)|
---------------------------------------------------------------------
Predicate Information (identified by operation id):
---------------------------------------------------------------------
   2 - access("ORDERS"."ORDER_DATE"=:Z)
```

This should be a highly selective query, and you should see the query using the index on the column to retrieve the desired rows. The data returned is sorted in ascending order by the rowids for the `order_date`. Because the index column `order_date` is identical for the selected rows here, the data is sorted by rowid.

When the Optimizer Uses Index Range Scans: The optimizer uses a range scan when it finds one or more leading columns of an index specified in conditions, such as the following:

- `col1 = :b1`
- `col1 < :b1`
- `col1 > :b1`
- **AND** combination of the preceding conditions for leading columns in the index
- `col1 like 'ASD%'` wild-card searches should not be in a leading position otherwise the condition `col1 like '%ASD'` does not result in a range scan.

Range scans can use unique or non-unique indexes. Range scans avoid sorting when index columns constitute the **ORDER BY/GROUP BY** clause.

Index Range Scan Hints: A hint might be required if the optimizer chooses some other index or uses a full table scan. The hint `INDEX(table_alias index_name)` instructs the optimizer to use a specific index.

Index Range Scans Descending

An index range scan descending is identical to an index range scan, except that the data is returned in descending order. Indexes, by default, are stored in ascending order. Usually, the database uses this scan when ordering data in a descending order to return the most recent data first, or when seeking a value less than a specified value.

When the Optimizer Uses Index Range Scans Descending: The optimizer uses index range scan descending when an index can satisfy an order by descending clause.

Index Range Scan Descending Hints: Use the hint `INDEX_DESC(table_alias index_name)` for this access path.

Index Skip Scans

Index skip scans improve index scans by nonprefix columns. Often, scanning index blocks is faster than scanning table data blocks.

Skip scanning lets a composite index be split logically into smaller subindexes. In skip scanning, the initial column of the composite index is not specified in the query. In other words, it is skipped.

The database determines the number of logical subindexes by the number of distinct values in the initial column. Skip scanning is advantageous when there are few distinct values in the leading column of the composite index and many distinct values in the nonleading key of the index.

The database may choose an index skip scan when the leading column of the composite index is not specified in a query predicate. For example, assume that you run the following query for a customer in the `sh.customers` table:

```
SELECT * FROM sh.customers WHERE cust email =
'Abbey@company.com';
```

The `customers` table has a column `cust_gender` whose values are either `M` or `F`. Assume that a composite index exists on the columns (`cust_gender`, `cust_email`) that was created as follows:

```
CREATE INDEX customers_gender_email ON sh.customers
(cust_gender, cust_email);
```

shows a portion of the index entries.

Example 11.6: Composite Index Entries

```
F, Wolf@company.com,rowid
F, Wolsey@company.com,rowid
F, Wood@company.com,rowid
F, Woodman@company.com,rowid
F, Yang@company.com,rowid
F, Zimmerman@company.com,rowid
M, Abbassi@company.com,rowid
M, Abbey@company.com,rowid
```

The database can use a skip scan of this index even though `cust_gender` is not specified in the `WHERE` clause.

In a skip scan, the number of logical subindexes is determined by the number of distinct values in the leading column. In, the leading column has two possible values. The database logically splits the index into one subindex with the key F and a second subindex with the key M.

When searching for the record for the customer whose email is Abbey@company.com, the database searches the subindex with the value F first and then searches the subindex with the value M. Conceptually, the database processes the query as follows:

```
SELECT * FROM sh.customers WHERE cust_gender = 'F'
  AND cust_email = 'Abbey@company.com'
UNION ALL
SELECT * FROM sh.customers WHERE cust_gender = 'M'
  AND cust_email = 'Abbey@company.com';
```

Full Scans

A full index scan eliminates a sort operation, because the data is ordered by the index key. It reads the blocks singly. Oracle Database may use a full scan in any of the following situations:

- An ORDER BY clause that meets the following requirements is present in the query:
  - All of the columns in the ORDER BY clause must be in the index.
  - The order of the columns in the ORDER BY clause must match the order of the leading index columns.

  The ORDER BY clause can contain all of the columns in the index or a subset of the columns in the index.
- The query requires a sort merge join. The database can perform a full index scan instead of doing a full table scan followed by a sort when the query meets the following requirements:
  - All of the columns referenced in the query must be in the index.
  - The order of the columns referenced in the query must match the order of the leading index columns.

  The query can contain all of the columns in the index or a subset of the columns in the index.
- A GROUP BY clause is present in the query, and the columns in the GROUP BY clause are present in the index. The columns do not need to be in the same order in the index and the GROUP BY clause. The GROUP BY clause can contain all of the columns in the index or a subset of the columns in the index.

Fast Full Index Scans

Fast full index scans are an alternative to a full table scan when the index contains all the columns that are needed for the query, and at least one column in the index key has the NOT NULL constraint. A fast full scan accesses the data in the index itself, without accessing the table. The database cannot use this scan to eliminate a sort operation because the data is not ordered by the index key. The database reads the entire index using multiblock reads, unlike a full index scan, and can scan in parallel.

You can specify fast full index scans with the initialization parameter OPTIMIZER_FEATURES_ENABLE or the INDEX_FFS hint. A fast full scan is faster than a normal full index scan because it can use multiblock I/O and can run in parallel just like a table scan.

Setting PARALLEL for indexes does not impact the cost calculation.

Fast Full Index Scan Hints: The fast full scan has a special index hint, INDEX_FFS, which has the same format and arguments as the regular INDEX hint.

Index Joins

An **index join** is a hash join of several indexes that together contain all the table columns referenced in the query. If the database uses an index join, then table access is not needed because the database can retrieve all the relevant column values from the indexes. The database cannot use an index join cannot to eliminate a sort operation.

Index Join Hints: You can specify an index join with the INDEX_JOIN hint.

Bitmap Indexes

A bitmap join uses a bitmap for key values and a mapping function that converts each bit position to a rowid. Bitmaps can efficiently merge indexes that correspond to several conditions in a WHERE clause, using Boolean operations to resolve AND and OR conditions.

Bitmap indexes and bitmap join indexes are available only in the Oracle Enterprise Edition.

Cluster Access

The database uses a cluster scan to retrieve all rows that have the same cluster key value from a table stored in an indexed cluster. In an indexed cluster, the database stores all rows with the same cluster key value in the same data block. To perform a cluster scan, Oracle Database first obtains the rowid of one of the selected rows by scanning the cluster index.

Hash Access

The database uses a hash scan to locate rows in a hash cluster based on a hash value. In a hash cluster, all rows with the same hash value are stored in the same data block. To perform a hash scan, Oracle Database first obtains the hash value by applying a hash function to a cluster key value specified by the statement. Oracle Database then scans the data blocks containing rows with that hash value.

Sample Table Scans

A sample table scan retrieves a random sample of data from a simple table or a complex SELECT statement, such as a statement involving joins and views. The database uses this access path when a statement's FROM clause includes the SAMPLE clause or the SAMPLE BLOCK clause. To perform a sample table scan when sampling by rows with the SAMPLE clause, the database reads a specified percentage of rows in the table. To perform a sample table scan when sampling by blocks with the SAMPLE BLOCK clause, the database reads a specified percentage of table blocks.

Uses a sample table scan to access 1% of the employees table, sampling by blocks.

Example 11.7: Sample Table Scan

```
SELECT *
    FROM employees SAMPLE BLOCK (1);
```

The `EXPLAIN PLAN` output for this statement might look like this:

```
-------------------------------------------------------------------------
| Id  | Operation              | Name        | Rows   | Bytes |
 Cost   (%CPU)
-------------------------------------------------------------------------
|   0 | SELECT STATEMENT       |             |      1 |    68 |
3 (34)|
|   1 | TABLE ACCESS SAMPLE    | EMPLOYEES   |      1 |    68 |
3 (34)|
-------------------------------------------------------------------------
```

How the Query Optimizer Chooses an Access Path

The query optimizer chooses an access path based on the following factors:

- The available access paths for the statement.
- The estimated cost of executing the statement, using each access path or combination of paths.

To choose an access path, the optimizer first determines which access paths are available by examining the conditions in the statement's WHERE clause and its FROM clause. The optimizer then generates a set of possible execution plans using available access paths and estimates the cost of each plan, using the statistics for the index, columns, and tables accessible to the statement. Finally, the optimizer chooses the execution plan with the lowest estimated cost.

When choosing an access path, the query optimizer is influenced by the following:

- Optimizer Hints.
  You can instruct the optimizer to use a specific access path using a hint, except when the statement's FROM clause contains SAMPLE or SAMPLE BLOCK.
- Old Statistics.
  For example, if a table has not been analyzed since it was created, and if it has less than DB_FILE_MULTIBLOCK_READ_COUNT blocks under the high water mark, then the optimizer thinks that the table is small and uses a full table scan. Review the LAST_ANALYZED and BLOCKS columns in the ALL_TABLES table to examine the statistics.

OVERVIEW OF JOINS

Joins are statements that retrieve data from multiple tables. A join is characterized by multiple tables in the FROM clause. The existence of a join condition in the WHERE clause defines the relationship between the tables. In a join, one row set is called inner, and the other is called outer.

This section discusses:

- How the Query Optimizer Executes Join Statements
- How the Query Optimizer Chooses Execution Plans for Joins
- Nested Loop Joins
- Hash Joins
- Sort Merge Joins
- Cartesian Joins
- Outer Joins.

How the Query Optimizer Executes Join Statements

To choose an execution plan for a join statement, the optimizer must make these interrelated decisions:

- Access Paths.
  As for simple statements, the optimizer must choose an access path to retrieve data from each table in the join statement.
- Join Method.
  To join each pair of row sources, Oracle Database must perform a join operation. Join methods include nested loop, sort merge, cartesian, and hash joins.
- Join Order.
  To execute a statement that joins more than two tables, Oracle Database joins two of the tables and then joins the resulting row source to the next table. This process continues until all tables are joined into the result.

How the Query Optimizer Chooses Execution Plans for Joins

The query optimizer considers the following when choosing an execution plan:

- The optimizer first determines whether joining two or more tables definitely results in a row source containing at most one row. The optimizer recognizes such situations based on `UNIQUE` and `PRIMARY KEY` constraints on the tables. If such a situation exists, then the optimizer places these tables first in the join order. The optimizer then optimizes the join of the remaining set of tables.
- For join statements with outer join conditions, the table with the outer join operator must come after the other table in the condition in the join order. The optimizer does not consider join orders that violate this rule. Similarly, when a subquery has been converted into an antijoin or semijoin, the tables from the subquery must come after those tables in the outer query block to which they were connected or correlated. However, hash antijoins and semijoins are able to override this ordering condition in certain circumstances.

With the query optimizer, the optimizer generates a set of execution plans, according to possible join orders, join methods, and available access paths. The optimizer then estimates the cost of each plan and chooses the one with the lowest cost. The optimizer estimates costs in the following ways:

- The cost of a nested loops operation is based on the cost of reading each selected row of the outer table and each of its matching rows of the inner table into memory. The optimizer estimates these costs using the statistics in the data dictionary.
- The cost of a sort merge join is based largely on the cost of reading all the sources into memory and sorting them.
- The cost of a hash join is based largely on the cost of building a hash table on one of the input sides to the join and using the rows from the other of the join to probe it.

The optimizer also considers other factors when determining the cost of each operation. For example:

- A smaller sort area size is likely to increase the cost for a sort merge join because sorting takes more CPU time and I/O in a smaller sort area.
- A larger multiblock read count is likely to decrease the cost for a sort merge join in relation to a nested loop join. If the database can read a large number of sequential blocks from disk in a single I/O, then an index on the inner table for the nested loop join is less likely to improve performance over a full table scan. The multiblock read count is specified by the initialization parameter `DB_FILE_MULTIBLOCK_READ_COUNT`.

You can use the **ORDERED** hint to override the optimizer's choice of join orders. If the **ORDERED** hint specifies a join order that violates the rule for an outer join, then the optimizer ignores the hint and chooses the order. Also, you can override the optimizer's choice of join method with hints.

Nested Loop Joins

Nested loop joins are useful when the following conditions are true:

- The database joins small subsets of data.
- The join condition is an efficient method of accessing the second table.

It is important to ensure that the inner table is driven from (dependent on) the outer table. If the inner table's access path is independent of the outer table, then the same rows are retrieved for every iteration of the outer loop, degrading performance considerably. In such cases, hash joins joining the two independent row sources perform better.

A nested loop join involves the following steps:

1. The optimizer determines the driving table and designates it as the outer table.
2. The other table is designated as the inner table.
3. For every row in the outer table, Oracle Database accesses all the rows in the inner table. The outer loop is for every row in the outer table and the inner loop is for every row in the inner table. The outer loop appears before the inner loop in the execution plan, as follows:

```
NESTED LOOPS
  outer_loop
  inner_loop
```

Original and New Implementation for Nested Loop Joins

Oracle Database 11*g* introduces a new implementation for nested loop joins. As a result, execution plans that include nested loops might appear different than they did in previous releases of Oracle Database. Both the new implementation and the original implementation for nested loop joins are possible in Oracle Database 11*g*. So, when analyzing execution plans, it is important to understand that the number of **NESTED LOOPS** join row sources might be different.

Original Implementation for Nested Loop Joins

Consider the following query:

```
SELECT e.first_name, e.last_name, e.salary, d.department_name
    FROM hr.employees e, hr.departments d
    WHERE d.department_name IN ('Marketing', 'Sales')
      AND e.department_id = d.department_id;
```

Before Oracle Database 11*g*, the execution plan for this query might appear similar to the following execution plan:

```
-----------------------------------------------------------------------
| Id  | Operation                       | Name                 | Rows
| Bytes | Cost (%CPU)| Time    |
-----------------------------------------------------------------------
|  0  | SELECT STATEMENT                |                      |
19 |    722 |      3  (0)| 00:00:01 |
| 1   | TABLE ACCESS BY INDEX ROWID     | EMPLOYEES            |
10 |    220 |      1  (0)| 00:00:01 |
```

```
| 2   | NESTED LOOPS                       |                    |
19 |    722 |      3   (0)| 00:00:01 |
|*3   | TABLE ACCESS FULL                  | DEPARTMENTS        |
2  |    32 |      2   (0)| 00:00:01 |
|*4   | INDEX RANGE SCAN                   | EMP_DEPARTMENT_IX |
10 |       |          0   (0)| 00:00:01 |
---------------------------------------------------------------------

Predicate Information (identified by operation id):
---------------------------------------------------------------------
   3 - filter("D"."DEPARTMENT_NAME"='Marketing' OR
"D"."DEPARTMENT_NAME"='Sales')
   4 - access("E"."DEPARTMENT_ID"="D"."DEPARTMENT_ID")
```

In this example, the outer side of the join consists of a scan of the `hr.departments` table that returns the rows that match the condition `department_name IN ('Marketing', 'Sales')`. The inner loop retrieves the employees in the `hr.employees` table that are associated with those departments.

New Implementation for Nested Loop Joins

Oracle Database 11 introduces a new implementation for nested loop joins to reduce overall latency for physical I/O. When an index or a table block is not in the buffer cache and is needed to process the join, a physical I/O is required. Oracle Database 11 can batch multiple physical I/O requests and process them using a vector I/O instead of processing them one at a time.

As part of the new implementation for nested loop joins, two `NESTED LOOPS` join row sources might appear in the execution plan where only one would have appeared in prior releases. In such cases, Oracle Database allocates one `NESTED LOOPS` join row source to join the values from the table on the outer side of the join with the index on the inner side. A second row source is allocated to join the result of the first join, which includes the rowids stored in the index, with the table on the inner side of the join.

In Oracle Database 11 , with the new implementation for nested loop joins, the execution plan for this query might appear similar to the following execution plan:

```
---------------------------------------------------------------------
| Id | Operation                          | Name              |
Rows | Bytes   |  Cost(%CPU)| Time      |
---------------------------------------------------------------------
|  0 | SELECT STATEMENT                   |                   |
19   | 722     |    3    (0)| 00:00:01 |
|  1 | NESTED LOOPS
|      |       |          |
|  2 | NESTED LOOPS                       |                   |
19   | 722     |    3    (0)| 00:00:01 |
|* 3 | TABLE ACCESS FULL                  | DEPARTMENTS |
2    | 32      |    2    (0)| 00:00:01 |
|* 4 | INDEX RANGE SCAN              | EMP_DEPARTMENT_IX |
10   |         |    0    (0)| 00:00:01 |
|    5 |   TABLE ACCESS BY INDEX ROWID| EMPLOYEES
10   | 220 |      1    (0)| 00:00:01 |
---------------------------------------------------------------------
```

```
Predicate Information (identified by operation id):
---------------------------------------------------
 3 - filter("D"."DEPARTMENT_NAME"='Marketing' OR
"D"."DEPARTMENT_NAME"='Sales')
 4 - access("E"."DEPARTMENT_ID"="D"."DEPARTMENT_ID")
```

In this case, the rows from the `hr.departments` table constitute the outer side of the first join. The inner side of the first join is the index `emp_department_ix`. The results of the first join constitute the outer side of the second join, which has the `hr.employees` table as its inner side.

There are cases where a second join row source is not allocated, and the execution plan looks the same as it did in prior releases. The following list describes such cases:

- All of the columns needed from the inner side of the join are present in the index, and there is no table access required. In this case, Oracle Database allocates only one join row source.
- The order of the rows returned might be different than it was in previous releases. Hence, when Oracle Database tries to preserve a specific ordering of the rows, for example to eliminate the need for an `ORDER BY` sort, Oracle Database might use the original implementation for nested loop joins.
- The `OPTIMIZER_FEATURES_ENABLE` initialization parameter is set to a release before Oracle Database 11*g*. In this case, Oracle Database uses the original implementation for nested loop joins.

When the Optimizer Uses Nested Loop Joins

The optimizer uses nested loop joins when joining small number of rows, with a good driving condition between the two tables. You drive from the outer loop to the inner loop, so the order of tables in the execution plan is important.

The outer loop is the driving row source. It produces a set of rows for driving the join condition. The row source can be a table accessed using an index scan or a full table scan. Also, the rows can be produced from any other operation. For example, the output from a nested loop join can serve as a row source for another nested loop join.

The inner loop is iterated for every row returned from the outer loop, ideally by an index scan. If the access path for the inner loop is not dependent on the outer loop, then you can end up with a Cartesian product; for every iteration of the outer loop, the inner loop produces the same set of rows. Therefore, you should use other join methods when two independent row sources are joined together.

Nested Loop Join Hints

If the optimizer chooses to use some other join method, then you can use the `USE_NL(table1 table2)` hint, where `table1` and `table2` are the aliases of the tables being joined.

For some SQL examples, the data is small enough for the optimizer to prefer full table scans and use hash joins. This is the case for the SQL example shown in . However, you can add a `USE_NL` to instruct the optimizer to change the join method to nested loop.

Nesting Nested Loops

The outer loop of a nested loop can be a nested loop itself. You can nest two or more outer loops to join as many tables as needed. Each loop is a data access method, as follows:

```
SELECT STATEMENT
 NESTED LOOP 3
  NESTED LOOP 2          (OUTER LOOP 3.1)
   NESTED LOOP 1         (OUTER LOOP 2.1)
    OUTER LOOP 1.1     - #1
    INNER LOOP 1.2     - #2
   INNER LOOP 2.2      - #3
  INNER LOOP 3.2       - #4
```

Hash Joins

The database uses hash oins to join large data sets. The optimizer uses the smaller of two tables or data sources to build a hash table on the join key in memory. It then scans the larger table, probing the hash table to find the joined rows.

This method is best when the smaller table fits in available memory. The cost is then limited to a single read pass over the data for the two tables.

When the Optimizer Uses Hash Joins

The optimizer uses a hash join to join two tables if they are joined using an equijoin and if either of the following conditions are true:

- A large amount of data must be joined.
- A large fraction of a small table must be joined.

In, the database uses the table `orders` to build the hash table. The database scans the larger `order_items` later.

Example 11.8: Hash Joins

```
SELECT o.customer_id, l.unit_price * l.quantity
  FROM orders o ,order_items l
 WHERE l.order_id = o.order_id;
--------------------------------------------------------------------
| Id  | Operation                 | Name        | Rows     | Bytes    |
  Cost  (%CPU)|
--------------------------------------------------------------------
|   0 | SELECT STATEMENT          |             |      665 | 13300    |
8 (25)|
|*  1 | HASH JOIN                 |             |      665 | 13300    |
8 (25)|
  |   2 | TABLE ACCESS FULL    | ORDERS        |      105 |    840 |
4 (25)|
|   3 | TABLE ACCESS FULL    | ORDER_ITEMS |    665 |    7980 |
4  25)|
--------------------------------------------------------------------

Predicate Information (identified by operation id):
--------------------------------------------------------------------
   1 - access("L"."ORDER_ID"="O"."ORDER_ID")
```

Hash Join Hints

Apply the `USE_HASH` hint to instruct the optimizer to use a hash join when joining two tables together.

Sort Merge Joins

Sort merge joins can join rows from two independent sources. Hash joins generally perform better than sort merge joins. However, sort merge joins can perform better than hash joins if both of the following conditions exist:

- The row sources are sorted already.
- A sort operation does not have to be done.

However, if a sort merge join involves choosing a slower access method (an index scan as opposed to a full table scan), then the benefit of using a sort merge might be lost.

Sort merge joins are useful when the join condition between two tables is an inequality condition such as <, <=, >, or >=. Sort merge joins perform better than nested loop joins for large data sets. You cannot use hash joins unless there is an equality condition.

In a merge join, there is no concept of a driving table. The join consists of two steps:

1. Sort join operation: Both the inputs are sorted on the join key.
2. Merge join operation: The sorted lists are merged together.

If the input is sorted by the join column, then a sort join operation is not performed for that row source. However, a sort merge join always creates a positionable sort buffer for the right side of the join so that it can seek back to the last match in the case where duplicate join key values come out of the left side of the join.

When the Optimizer Uses Sort Merge Joins

The optimizer can choose a sort merge join over a hash join for joining large amounts of data if any of the following conditions are true:

- The join condition between two tables is not an equijoin.
- Because of sorts required by other operations, the optimizer finds it is cheaper to use a sort merge than a hash join.

Sort Merge Join Hints

To instruct the optimizer to use a sort merge join, apply the `USE_MERGE` hint. You might also need to give hints to force an access path.

There are situations where it makes sense to override the optimizer with the `USE_MERGE` hint. For example, the optimizer can choose a full scan on a table and avoid a sort operation in a query. However, there is an increased cost because a large table is accessed through an index and single block reads, as opposed to faster access through a full table scan.

Cartesian Joins

The database uses a **Cartesian join** when one or more of the tables does not have any join conditions to any other tables in the statement. The optimizer joins every row from one data source with every row from the other data source, creating the Cartesian product of the two sets.

When the Optimizer Uses Cartesian Joins

The optimizer uses Cartesian joins when it is asked to join two tables with no join conditions. In some cases, a common filter condition between the two tables could be picked up by the optimizer as a possible join condition. In other cases, the optimizer may decide to generate a Cartesian product of two very small tables that are both joined to the same large table.

Cartesian Join Hints

Applying the `ORDERED` hint, instructs the optimizer to use a Cartesian join. By specifying a table before its join table is specified, the optimizer does a Cartesian join.

Outer Joins

An outer join extends the result of a simple join. An outer join returns all rows that satisfy the join condition and also returns some or all of those rows from one table for which no rows from the other satisfy the join condition.

Nested Loop Outer Joins

The database uses this operation to loop through an outer join between two tables. The outer join returns the outer (preserved) table rows, even when no corresponding rows are in the inner (optional) table.

In a regular outer join, the optimizer chooses the order of tables (driving and driven) based on the cost. However, in a nested loop outer join, the join condition determines the order of tables. The database uses the outer table, with rows that are being preserved, to drive to the inner table.

The optimizer uses nested loop joins to process an outer join in the following circumstances:

- It is possible to drive from the outer table to inner table.
- Data volume is low enough to make the nested loop method efficient.

For an example of a nested loop outer join, you can add the `USE_NL` hint to to instruct the optimizer to use a nested loop. For example:

```
SELECT /*+ USE_NL(c o) */ cust_last_name,
sum(nvl2(o.customer_id,0,1)) "Count"
```

Hash Join Outer Joins

The optimizer uses hash joins for processing an outer join if the data volume is high enough to make the hash join method efficient or if it is not possible to drive from the outer table to inner table.

The order of tables is determined by the cost. The outer table, including preserved rows, may be used to build the hash table, or it may be used to probe one.

Shows a typical hash join outer join query. In this example, all the customers with credit limits greater than 1000 are queried. An outer join is needed so that you do not miss the customers who do not have any orders.

Example 11.9: Hash Join Outer Joins

```
SELECT cust_last_name, sum(nvl2(o.customer_id,0,1)) "Count"
  FROM customers c, orders o
 WHERE c.credit_limit > 1000
   AND c.customer_id = o.customer_id(+)
 GROUP BY cust_last_name;

-------------------------------------------------------------------

| Id  | Operation                 | Name              | Rows  | Bytes |
| Cost (%CPU)|

-------------------------------------------------------------------

|   0 | SELECT STATEMENT          |                   |   168 |  3192 |
|     6 (17)  |
|   1 | HASH GROUP BY             |                   |   168 |  3192 |
|     6 (17)|
```

```
|* 2 | NESTED LOOPS OUTER    |                 |  260 | 4940 |
     5 (0) |
|* 3 | TABLE ACCESS FULL     | CUSTOMERS       |  260 | 3900 |
     5 (0) |
|* 4 |  INDEX RANGE SCAN     | ORD_CUSTOMER_IX |  105 |  420 |
    0  (0) |
--------------------------------------------------------------
Predicate Information (identified by operation id):
--------------------------------------------------------------

   3 - filter("C"."CREDIT_LIMIT">1000)
   4 - access("C"."CUSTOMER_ID"="O"."CUSTOMER_ID"(+))
       filter("O"."CUSTOMER_ID"(+)>0)
```

The query looks for customers which satisfy various conditions. An outer join returns `NULL` for the inner table columns along with the outer (preserved) table rows when it does not find any corresponding rows in the inner table. This operation finds all the `customers` rows that do not have any `orders` rows.

In this case, the outer join condition is the following:

`customers.customer_id = orders.customer_id(+)`

The components of this condition represent the following:

- The outer table is `customers`.
- The inner table is `orders`.
- The join preserves the `customers` rows, including those rows without a corresponding row in `orders`.

You could use a `NOT EXISTS` subquery to return the rows. However, because you are querying all the rows in the table, the hash join performs better (unless the `NOT EXISTS` subquery is not nested).

In, the outer join is to a multitable view. The optimizer cannot drive into the view like in a normal join or push the predicates, so it builds the entire row set of the view.

Example 11.10: Outer Join to a Multitable View

```
SELECT c.cust_last_name, sum(revenue)
  FROM customers c, v_orders o
 WHERE c.credit_limit > 2000
   AND o.customer_id(+) = c.customer_id
 GROUP BY c.cust_last_name;

--------------------------------------------------------------
| Id  | Operation                 | Name          | Rows     | Bytes
|Cost  (%CPU)|
--------------------------------------------------------------
|   0 | SELECT STATEMENT          |               |  144 | 4608 |
    16  (32)|
|   1 |  HASH GROUP BY            |               |  144 | 4608 |
    16  (32)|
|*  2 |   HASH JOIN OUTER         |               |  663 | 21216 |
    15  (27)|
```

```
|* 3 |    TABLE ACCESS FULL    | CUSTOMERS     |  195 |  2925 |
      6  (17)|
|  4 |    VIEW                 | V_ORDERS      |  665 | 11305 |
                |
|  5 |     HASH GROUP BY       |               |  665 | 15960 |
      9  (34)|
|* 6 |      HASH JOIN          |               |  665 | 15960 |
|    8  (25)|
|* 7 |       TABLE ACCESS FULL| ORDERS         |  105 |   840 |
|     4  (25)|
|  8 |       TABLE ACCESS FULL| ORDER_ITEMS    |  665 | 10640 |
|     4  (25)|
--------------------------------------------------------------------

Predicate Information (identified by operation id):
---------------------------------------------------
   2 - access("O"."CUSTOMER_ID"(+)="C"."CUSTOMER_ID")
   3 - filter("C"."CREDIT_LIMIT">2000)
   6 - access("O"."ORDER_ID"="L"."ORDER_ID")
   7 - filter("O"."CUSTOMER_ID">0)
```

The view definition is as follows:

```
CREATE OR REPLACE view v_orders AS
SELECT l.product_id, SUM(l.quantity*unit_price) revenue,
       o.order_id, o.customer_id
  FROM orders o, order_items l
 WHERE o.order_id = l.order_id
 GROUP BY l.product_id, o.order id, o.customer_id;
```

Sort Merge Outer Joins

When an outer join cannot drive from the outer (preserved) table to the inner (optional) table, it cannot use a hash join or nested loop joins. Then it uses the sort merge outer join for performing the join operation.

The optimizer uses sort merge for an outer join:

- If a nested loop join is inefficient. A nested loop join can be inefficient because of data volumes.
- The optimizer finds it is cheaper to use a sort merge over a hash join because of sorts required by other operations.

Full Outer Joins

A full outer join acts like a combination of the left and right outer joins. In addition to the inner join, rows from both tables that have not been returned in the result of the inner join are preserved and extended with nulls. In other words, full outer joins let you join tables together, yet still show rows that do not have corresponding rows in the joined tables.

The query in retrieves all departments and all employees in each department, but also includes:

- Any employees without departments
- Any departments without employees.

Example 11.11: Full Outer Join

```
SELECT d.department_id, e.employee_id
  FROM employees e
  FULL OUTER JOIN departments d
    ON e.department_id = d.department_id
 ORDER BY d.department_id;
```

The statement produces the following output:

```
DEPARTMENT_ID EMPLOYEE_ID
------------- -----------
       10          200
       20          201
       20          202
       30          114
       30          115
       30          116
6 rows selected.
```

Starting with Oracle Database 11 , Oracle Database automatically uses a native execution method based on a hash join for executing full outer joins whenever possible. When the database uses the new method to execute a full outer join, the execution plan for the query contains HASH JOIN FULL OUTER. shows the execution plan for the query in .

Example 11.12: Execution Plan for a Full Outer Join

```
-------------------------------------------------------------------------
| Id  | Operation                  | Name         | Rows   | Bytes |
Cost (%CPU)| Time        |
-------------------------------------------------------------------------
|   0 | SELECT STATEMENT           |              |   122  |  4758 |
6 (34)| 00:0 0:01 |
|   1 |  SORT ORDER BY             |              |   122  |  4758 |
6 (34)| 00:0 0:01 |
|   2 |   VIEW                     | VW_FOJ_0     |   122  |  4758 |
5 (20)| 00:0 0:01 |
|*  3 |    HASH JOIN FULL OUTER    |              |   122  |  1342 |
5 (20)| 00:0 0:01 |
|   4 |     INDEX FAST FULL SCAN| DEPT_ID_PK |    27  |   108 |
2  (0)| 00:0 0:01 |
|   5 |     TABLE ACCESS FULL   | EMPLOYEES    |   107  |   749 |
2  (0)| 00:0 0:01 |
-------------------------------------------------------------------------
Predicate Information (identified by operation id):
-------------------------------------------------------------------------
   3 - access("E"."DEPARTMENT_ID"="D"."DEPARTMENT_ID")
```

Notice that HASH JOIN FULL OUTER is included in the plan. Therefore, the query uses the hash full outer join execution method. Typically, when the full outer join condition between two tables is an equi-join, the hash full outer join execution method is possible, and Oracle Database uses it automatically.

To instruct the optimizer to consider using the hash full outer join execution method, apply the NATIVE_FULL_OUTER_JOIN hint. To instruct the optimizer not to consider using the hash full outer join execution method, apply the NO_NATIVE_FULL_OUTER_JOIN hint. The

NO_NATIVE_FULL_OUTER_JOIN hint instructs the optimizer to exclude the native execution method when joining each specified table. Instead, the full outer join is executed as a union of left outer join and an anti-join.

READING AND UNDERSTANDING EXECUTION PLANS

To execute a SQL statement, Oracle Database may need to perform many steps. Each step either retrieves rows of data physically from the database or prepares them in some way for the user issuing the statement. The combination of the steps that Oracle Database uses to execute a statement is an **execution plan.** An execution plan includes an **access path** for each table that the statement accesses and an ordering of the tables (the **join order**) with the appropriate **join method.**

Overview of EXPLAIN PLAN

You can examine the execution plan chosen by the optimizer for a SQL statement by using the EXPLAIN PLAN statement. When the statement is issued, the optimizer chooses an execution plan and then inserts data describing the plan into a database table. Simply issue the EXPLAIN PLAN statement and then query the output table.

These are the basics of using the EXPLAIN PLAN statement:

- Use the SQL script CATPLAN.SQL to create a sample output table called PLAN_TABLE in your schema.
- Include the EXPLAIN PLAN FOR clause before the SQL statement.
- After issuing the EXPLAIN PLAN statement, use one of the scripts or package provided by Oracle Database to display the most recent plan table output.
- The execution order in EXPLAIN PLAN output begins with the line that is the furthest indented to the right. The next step is the parent of that line. If two lines are indented equally, then the top line is normally executed first.

- The EXPLAIN PLAN output tables in this chapter were displayed with the utlxpls.sql script.
- The steps in the EXPLAIN PLAN output in this chapter may be different on your system. The optimizer may choose different execution plans, depending on database configurations.

Uses EXPLAIN PLAN to examine a SQL statement that selects the employee_id, job_title, salary, and department_name for the employees whose IDs are less than 103.

Example 11.13: Using EXPLAIN PLAN

```
EXPLAIN PLAN FOR
SELECT e.employee_id, j.job_title, e.salary, d.department_name
    FROM employees e, jobs j, departments d
    WHERE  e.employee_id < 103
       AND e.job_id = j.job_id
       AND e.department_id = d.department_id;
```

The resulting output table in shows the execution plan chosen by the optimizer to execute the SQL statement in the example:

Example 11.14: EXPLAIN PLAN Output

```
---------------------------------------------------------------------
| Id  | Operation                         | Name           | Rows  |
Bytes | Cost (%CPU)|
---------------------------------------------------------------------
|   0 | SELECT STATEMENT                  |                |     3 |
189 |    10 (10)|
|   1 |  NESTED LOOPS                     |                |     3 |
189 |   10  (10)|
|   2 |   NESTED LOOPS                    |                |     3 |
141 |    7  (15)|
|*  3 |    TABLE ACCESS FULL              | EMPLOYEES      |     3 |
60  |     4 (25)|
|   4 |    TABLE ACCESS BY INDEX ROWID| JOBS           |    19 |
513 |     2 (50)|
|*  5 |     INDEX UNIQUE SCAN             | JOB_ID_PK      |     1 |
|            |
|   6 |   TABLE ACCESS BY INDEX ROWID | DEPARTMENTS    |    27 |
432 |    2  (50)|
|*  7 |    INDEX UNIQUE SCAN              | DEPT_ID_PK     |     1 |
|            |
---------------------------------------------------------------------

Predicate Information (identified by operation id):
---------------------------------------------------------------------
   3 - filter("E"."EMPLOYEE_ID"<103)
   5 - access("E"."JOB_ID"="J"."JOB_ID")
   7 - access("E"."DEPARTMENT_ID"="D"."DEPARTMENT_ID"

---------------------------------------------------------------------
| Id  | Operation                              | Name            |
| Bytes | Cost (%CPU)| Time     |
---------------------------------------------------------------------
|   0 | SELECT STATEMENT                       |                 |
3 |   189 |     8  (13)| 00:00:01 |
|   1 |  NESTED LOOPS                          |                 |       |
|           |          |
|   2 |   NESTED LOOPS                         |                 |
3 |   189 |     8  (13)| 00:00:01 |
|   3 |    MERGE JOIN                          |                 |
3 |   141 |     5  (20)| 00:00:01 |
|   4 |     TABLE ACCESS BY INDEX ROWID | JOBS            |
19 |  513 |     2   (0)| 00:00:01 |
|   5 |      INDEX FULL SCAN                   | JOB_ID_PK       |
19 |      |     1   (0)| 00:00:01 |
v*  6 |     SORT JOIN                          |                 |
3 |    60 |     3  (34)| 00:00:01 |
|   7 |      TABLE ACCESS BY INDEX ROWID| EMPLOYEES       |
3 |    60 |     2   (0)| 00:00:01 |
```

```
|* 8 |        INDEX RANGE SCAN              | EMP_EMP_ID_PK |
3 |        |    1   (0)| 00:00:01 |
|* 9 |     INDEX UNIQUE SCAN                | DEPT_ID_PK    |
1 |        |    0   (0)| 00:00:01 |
| 10 |    TABLE ACCESS BY INDEX ROWID       | DEPARTMENTS   |
1 |    16 |    1   (0)| 00:00:01 |
----------------------------------------------------------------------

Predicate Information (identified by operation id):
----------------------------------------------------------------------

   6 - access("E"."JOB_ID"="J"."JOB_ID")
       filter("E"."JOB_ID"="J"."JOB_ID")
   8 - access("E"."EMPLOYEE_ID"<103)
   9 - access("E"."DEPARTMENT_ID"="D"."DEPARTMENT_ID")
```

Steps in the Execution Plan

Each row in the output table corresponds to a single step in the execution plan. Note that the step IDs with asterisks are listed in the Predicate Information section.

Each step of the execution plan returns a set of rows. The next step either uses these rows or, in the last step, returns the rows to the user or application issuing the SQL statement. A **row set** is a set of rows returned by a step.

The numbering of the step IDs reflects the order in which they are displayed in response to the `EXPLAIN PLAN` statement. Each step of the execution plan either retrieves rows from the database or accepts rows from one or more row sources as input.

- The following steps in physically retrieve data from an object in the database:
  - o Step 3 reads all rows of the `employees` table.
  - o Step 5 looks up each `job_id` in `JOB_ID_PK` index and finds the rowids of the associated rows in the `jobs` table.
  - o Step 4 retrieves the rows with rowids that were returned by Step 5 from the `jobs` table.
  - o Step 7 looks up each `department_id` in `DEPT_ID_PK` index and finds the rowids of the associated rows in the `departments` table.
  - o Step 6 retrieves the rows with rowids that were returned by Step 7 from the `departments` table.
- The following steps in operate on rows returned by the previous row source:
  - o Step 2 performs the nested loop operation on `job_id` in the `jobs` and `employees` tables, accepting row sources from Steps 3 and 4, joining each row from Step 3 source to its corresponding row in Step 4, and returning the resulting rows to Step 2.
  - o Step 1 performs the nested loop operation, accepting row sources from Step 2 and Step 6, joining each row from Step 2 source to its corresponding row in Step 6, and returning the resulting rows to Step 1.

CONTROLLING OPTIMIZER BEHAVIOUR

Table 11.3 lists initialization parameters that you can use to control the behavior of the query optimizer. You can use these parameters to enable various optimizer features to improve the performance of SQL execution.

Table 11.3. Initialization Parameters that Control Optimizer Behaviour

Initialization Parameter	Description
CURSOR_SHARING	Converts literal values in SQL statements to bind variables. Converting the values improves cursor sharing and can affect the execution plans of SQL statements. The optimizer generates the execution plan based on the presence of the bind variables and not the actual literal values.
DB_FILE_MULTIBLOCK_READ_COUNT	Specifies the number of blocks that are read in a single I/O during a full table scan or index fast full scan. The optimizer uses the value of DB_FILE _MULTIBLOCK_READ_COUNT to cost full table scans and index fast full scans. Larger values result in a cheaper cost for full table scans and can result in the optimizer choosing a full table scan over an index scan. If this parameter is not set explicitly (or is set is 0), then the default value corresponds to the maximum I/O size that can be efficiently performed and is platform-dependent.
OPTIMIZER_INDEX_CACHING	Controls the costing of an index probe in conjunction with a nested loop. The range of values 0 to 100 indicates percentage of index blocks in the buffer cache, which modifies the optimizer's assumptions about index caching for nested loops and IN-list iterators. A value of 100 infers that 100% of the index blocks are likely to be found in the buffer cache and the optimizer adjusts the cost of an index probe or nested loop accordingly. Use caution when using this parameter because execution plans can change in favor of index caching.
OPTIMIZER_INDEX_COST_ADJ	Adjusts the cost of index probes. The range of values is 1 to 10000. The default value is 100, which means that indexes are evaluated as an access path based on the normal costing model. A value of 10 means that the cost of an index access path is one-tenth the normal cost of an index access path.
OPTIMIZER_MODE	Sets the mode of the optimizer at instance startup. The possible values are ALL_ROWS, FIRST_ROWS_n, and FIRST_ROWS.
PGA_AGGREGATE_TARGET	Controls the amount of memory allocated for sorts and hash joins. Larger amounts of memory allocated for sorts or hash joins reduce the optimizer cost of these operations.
STAR_TRANSFORMATION_ENABLED	Enables the optimizer to cost a star transformation for star queries (if true). The star transformation combines the bitmap indexes on the various fact table columns.

Enabling Query Optimizer Features

The OPTIMIZER_FEATURES_ENABLE initialization parameter enables a series of optimizer-related features, depending on the release. It accepts one of a list of valid string values corresponding to the release numbers, such as 10.2.0.1 or 11.2.0.1.

You can use this parameter to preserve the old behavior of the optimizer after a database upgrade. For example, if you upgrade the Oracle Database 11g from Release 1 (11.1.0.7) to Release 2 (11.2.0.2), then the default value of the OPTIMIZER_FEATURES_ENABLE parameter changes from 11.1.0.7 to 11.2.0.2. This upgrade results in the optimizer enabling optimization features based on 11.2.0.2.

For backward compatibility, you might not want the query plans to change because of new optimizer features in a new release. In such a case, you can set the OPTIMIZER_FEATURES_ENABLE parameter to an earlier version.

Oracle does not recommend explicitly setting the OPTIMIZER_FEATURES_ENABLE parameter to an earlier release. To avoid possible SQL performance regression that may result from execution plan changes, consider using SQL plan management instead.

To set OPTIMIZER_FEATURES_ENABLE:

1. Query the current optimizer features settings.
   For example, run the following SQL*Plus command:
   ```
   SQL> SHOW PARAMETER optimizer_features_enable
   NAME                          TYPE        VALUE
   ----------------------------  -------     --------
   optimizer_features_enable     string      11.2.0.2
   ```
2. Set the optimizer features setting at the instance or session level.
   For example, run the following SQL statement to set the optimizer version to 10.2.0.5:
   ```
   SQL> ALTER SYSTEM SET
   optimizer_features_enable='10.2.0.5';
   ```
   The preceding statement disables all new optimizer features that were added in releases following release 10.2.0.5. If you upgrade to a new release and you want to enable the features available with that release, then you do not need to explicitly set the OPTIMIZER_FEATURES_ENABLE initialization parameter.

Choosing an Optimizer Goal

You can influence the optimizer's choices by setting the optimizer goal and by gathering representative statistics for the query optimizer. You can set the following optimizer goals:

- Best throughput (default)
  The database uses the least amount of resources necessary to process all rows accessed by the statement.
  For applications performed in batch, such as Oracle Reports applications, optimize for best throughput. Usually, throughput is more important in batch applications, because the user initiating the application is only concerned with the time necessary for the application to complete. Response time is less important because the user does not examine the results of individual statements while the application is running.

- Best response time
  The database uses the least amount of resources necessary to process the first row accessed by a SQL statement.
  For interactive applications such as Oracle Forms applications or SQL *Plus queries, optimize for best response time. Usually, response time is important in interactive applications because the interactive user is waiting to see the first row or first few rows accessed by the statement.

The optimizer behavior when choosing an optimization approach and goal for a SQL statement is affected by the following factors:

- Setting the OPTIMIZER_MODE Initialization Parameter
- Using Hints to Change the Optimizer Goal
- Optimizer Statistics in the Data Dictionary.

Setting the OPTIMIZER_MODE Initialization Parameter

The `OPTIMIZER_MODE` initialization parameter establishes the default behavior for choosing an optimization approach for the instance. Table 11.4 lists the possible values and description.

Table 11.4. OPTIMIZER_MODE Initialization Parameter Values

Value	December
ALL_ROWS	The optimizer uses a cost-based approach for all SQL statements in the session regardless of the presence of statistics and optimizes with a goal of best throughput (minimum resource use to complete the entire statement). This is the default value.
FIRST_ROWS_n	The optimizer uses a cost-based approach, regardless of the presence of statistics, and optimizes with a goal of best response time to return the first *n* number of rows, where *n* equals 1, 10, 100, or 1000.
FIRST_ROWS	The optimizer uses a mix of cost and heuristics to find a best plan for fast delivery of the first few rows. Note that using heuristics sometimes leads the optimizer to generate a plan with a cost that is significantly larger than the cost of a plan without applying the heuristic. FIRST_ROWS is available for backward compatibility and plan stability; use FIRST_ROWS_n instead.

You can change the goal of the query optimizer for all SQL statements in a session by changing the parameter value in initialization file or by the `ALTER SESSION SET OPTIMIZER_MODE` statement. For example:

- The following statement in an initialization parameter file establishes the goal of the query optimizer for all sessions of the instance to best response time:
- `OPTIMIZER_MODE = FIRST_ROWS_1`
- The following SQL statement changes the goal of the query optimizer for the current session to best response time:
- `ALTER SESSION SET OPTIMIZER_MODE = FIRST_ROWS_1;`

If the optimizer uses the cost-based approach for a SQL statement, and if some tables accessed by the statement have no statistics, then the optimizer uses internal information, such as the number of data blocks allocated to these tables, to estimate other statistics for these tables.

Using Hints to Change the Optimizer Goal

To specify the goal of the optimizer for an individual SQL statement, use a hint from Table 11.5. Any of these hints in an individual SQL statement can override the OPTIMIZER_MODE initialization parameter for that SQL statement.

Table 11.5 Hints for Changing the Query Optimizer Goal

Hint	Description
FIRST_ROWS(n)	This hint instructs Oracle Database to optimize an individual SQL statement with a goal of best response time to return the first n number of rows, where *n* equals any positive integer. The hint uses a cost-based approach for the SQL statement, regardless of the presence of statistic.
ALL_ROWS	This hint explicitly chooses the cost-based approach to optimize a SQL statement with a goal of best throughput.

Optimizer Statistics in the Data Dictionary

The statistics used by the query optimizer are stored in the data dictionary. You can use the DBMS_STATS package to collect exact or estimated statistics about physical storage characteristics and data distribution in these schema objects.

To maintain the effectiveness of the query optimizer, you must have statistics that are representative of the data. For table columns that contain values with large variations in number of duplicates, called **skewed data**, you should collect histograms.

The resulting statistics provide the query optimizer with information about data uniqueness and distribution. Using this information, the query optimizer is able to compute plan costs with a high degree of accuracy and choose the best execution plan based on the least cost.

If no statistics are available when using query optimization, then the optimizer performs dynamic sampling depending on the setting of the OPTMIZER_DYNAMIC_SAMPLING initialization parameter. This sampling may cause slower parse times so for best performance, the optimizer should have representative optimizer statistics.

12 Using Explain Plan

Learning Objectives

This chapter introduces execution plans, describes the SQL statement EXPLAIN PLAN, and explains how to interpret its output. This chapter also provides procedures for managing outlines to control application performance characteristics.
This chapter contains the following sections:

- Understanding EXPLAIN PLAN
- Viewing Parallel Execution with EXPLAIN PLAN
- Viewing Bitmap Indexes with EXPLAIN PLAN
- Viewing Result Cache with EXPLAIN PLAN
- Viewing Partitioned Objects with EXPLAIN PLAN
- PLAN_TABLE Columns

UNDERSTANDING EXPLAIN PLAN

The `EXPLAIN PLAN` statement displays execution plans chosen by the optimizer for `SELECT`, `UPDATE`, `INSERT`, and `DELETE` statements. A statement execution plan is the sequence of operations that the database performs to run the statement.

The **row source tree** is the core of the execution plan. The tree shows the following information:

- An ordering of the tables referenced by the statement
- An access method for each table mentioned in the statement
- A join method for tables affected by join operations in the statement
- Data operations like filter, sort, or aggregation.

In addition to the row source tree, the plan table contains information about the following:

- Optimization, such as the cost and cardinality of each operation
- Partitioning, such as the set of accessed partitions
- Parallel execution, such as the distribution method of join inputs.

The `EXPLAIN PLAN` results let you determine whether the optimizer selects a particular execution plan, such as, nested loops join. The results also help you to understand the optimizer decisions, such as why the optimizer chose a nested loops join instead of a hash join, and lets you understand the performance of a query.

How Execution Plans Can Change

With the query optimizer, execution plans can and do change as the underlying optimizer inputs change. `EXPLAIN PLAN` output shows how Oracle Database would run the SQL statement when the statement was explained. This plan can differ from the actual execution plan a SQL statement because of differences in the execution environment and explain plan environment.

To avoid possible SQL performance regression that may result from execution plan changes, consider using SQL plan management.

Execution plans can differ due to the following:

- Different Schemas
- Different Costs.

Different Schemas

- The execution and explain plan occur on different databases.
- The user explaining the statement is different from the user running the statement. Two users might be pointing to different objects in the same database, resulting in different execution plans.
- Schema changes (usually changes in indexes) between the two operations.

Different Costs

Even if the schemas are the same, the optimizer can choose different execution plans when the costs are different. Some factors that affect the costs include the following:

- Data volume and statistics
- Bind variable types and values
- Initialization parameters set globally or at session level.

Minimizing Throw-Away

Examining an explain plan lets you look for throw-away in cases such as the following:

- Full scans
- Unselective range scans
- Late predicate filters
- Wrong join order
- Late filter operations.

For example, in the following explain plan, the last step is a very unselective range scan that is executed 76563 times, accesses 11432983 rows, throws away 99% of them, and retains 76563 rows. Why access 11432983 rows to realize that only 76563 rows are needed?

Example 12.1: Looking for Throw-Away in an Explain Plan

```
Rows     Execution Plan
--------------------------------------------------------------------
12       SORT AGGREGATE
2        SORT GROUP BY
```

```
76563    NESTED LOOPS
76575    NESTED LOOPS
19       TABLE ACCESS FULL CN_PAYRUNS_ALL
76570    TABLE ACCESS BY INDEX ROWID CN_POSTING_DETAILS_ALL
76570    INDEX RANGE SCAN (object id 178321)
76563    TABLE ACCESS BY INDEX ROWID CN_PAYMENT_WORKSHEETS_ALL
11432983       INDEX RANGE SCAN (object id 186024)
```

Looking Beyond Execution Plans

The execution plan operation alone cannot differentiate between well-tuned statements and those that perform poorly. For example, an EXPLAIN PLAN output that shows that a statement uses an index does not necessarily mean that the statement runs efficiently. Sometimes indexes are extremely inefficient. In this case, you should examine the following:

- The columns of the index being used
- Their selectivity (fraction of table being accessed).

It is best to use EXPLAIN PLAN to determine an access plan, and then later prove that it is the optimal plan through testing. When evaluating a plan, examine the statement's actual resource consumption.

Using V$SQL_PLAN Views

In addition to running the EXPLAIN PLAN command and displaying the plan, you can use the V$SQL_PLAN views to display the execution plan of a SQL statement:

After the statement has executed, you can display the plan by querying the V$SQL_PLAN view. V$SQL_PLAN contains the execution plan for every statement stored in the shared SQL area. Its definition is similar to the PLAN_TABLE.

The advantage of V$SQL_PLAN over EXPLAIN PLAN is that you do not need to know the compilation environment that was used to execute a particular statement. For EXPLAIN PLAN, you would need to set up an identical environment to get the same plan when executing the statement.

The V$SQL_PLAN_STATISTICS view provides the actual execution statistics for every operation in the plan, such as the number of output rows and elapsed time. All statistics, except the number of output rows, are cumulative. For example, the statistics for a join operation also includes the statistics for its two inputs. The statistics in V$SQL_PLAN_STATISTICS are available for cursors that have been compiled with the STATISTICS_LEVEL initialization parameter set to ALL.

The V$SQL_PLAN_STATISTICS_ALL view enables side by side comparisons of the estimates that the optimizer provides for the number of rows and elapsed time. This view combines both V$SQL_PLAN and V$SQL_PLAN_STATISTICS information for every cursor.

EXPLAIN PLAN Restrictions

Oracle Database does not support EXPLAIN PLAN for statements performing implicit type conversion of date bind variables. With bind variables in general, the EXPLAIN PLAN output might not represent the real execution plan.

From the text of a SQL statement, TKPROF cannot determine the types of the bind variables. It assumes that the type is CHARACTER, and gives an error message if this is not the case. You can avoid this limitation by putting appropriate type conversions in the SQL statement.

The PLAN_TABLE Output Table

The PLAN_TABLE is automatically created as a public synonym to a global temporary table. This temporary table holds the output of EXPLAIN PLAN statements for all users. PLAN_TABLE is the default sample output table into which the EXPLAIN PLAN statement inserts rows describing execution plans.

While a PLAN_TABLE table is automatically set up for each user, you can use the SQL script catplan.sql to manually create the global temporary table and the PLAN_TABLE synonym. The name and location of this script depends on your operating system. On UNIX and Linux, the script is located in the $ORACLE_HOME/rdbms/admin directory.

For example, start a SQL*Plus session, connect with SYSDBA privileges, and run the script as follows:

```
@$ORACLE_HOME/rdbms/admin/catplan.sql
```

Oracle recommends that you drop and rebuild your local PLAN_TABLE table after upgrading the version of the database because the columns might change. This can cause scripts to fail or cause TKPROF to fail, if you are specifying the table.

If you do not want to use the name PLAN_TABLE, create a new synonym after running the catplan.sql script. For example:

```
CREATE OR REPLACE PUBLIC SYNONYM my_plan_table for plan_table$
```

Running Explain Plan

To explain a SQL statement, use the EXPLAIN PLAN FOR clause immediately before the statement. For example:

```
EXPLAIN PLAN FOR
        SELECT last_name FROM employees;
```

This explains the plan into the PLAN_TABLE table. You can then select the execution plan from PLAN_TABLE.

Identifying Statements for EXPLAIN PLAN

With multiple statements, you can specify a statement identifier and use that to identify your specific execution plan. Before using SET STATEMENT ID, remove any existing rows for that statement ID.

In, st1 is specified as the statement identifier:

Example 12.2: Using EXPLAIN PLAN with the STATEMENT ID Clause

```
EXPLAIN PLAN
        SET STATEMENT_ID = 'st1' FOR
SELECT last_name FROM employees;
```

Specifying Different Tables for EXPLAIN PLAN

You can specify the INTO clause to specify a different table.

Example 12.3: Using EXPLAIN PLAN with the INTO Clause

```
EXPLAIN PLAN
        INTO my_plan_table
        FOR
SELECT last_name FROM employees;
```

You can specify a statement ID when using the INTO clause.

```
EXPLAIN PLAN
        SET STATEMENT_ID =       'st1'
        INTO my_plan_table       FOR SELECT last_name FROM employees;
```

Displaying PLAN_TABLE Output

After you have explained the plan, use the following SQL scripts or PL/SQL package provided by Oracle Database to display the most recent plan table output:

- `UTLXPLS.SQL`.
  This script displays the plan table output for serial processing. is an example of the plan table output when using the `UTLXPLS.SQL` script.
- `UTLXPLP.SQL`.
  This script displays the plan table output including parallel execution columns.
- `DBMS_XPLAN.DISPLAY` table function.
  This function accepts options for displaying the plan table output. You can specify:
  - A plan table name if you are using a table different than `PLAN_TABLE`
  - A statement ID if you have set a statement ID with the `EXPLAIN PLAN`
  - A format option that determines the level of detail: `BASIC`, `SERIAL`, and `TYPICAL`, `ALL`,

Some examples of the use of `DBMS_XPLAN` to display `PLAN_TABLE` output are:

```
SELECT PLAN_TABLE_OUTPUT FROM
TABLE(DBMS_XPLAN.DISPLAY());
SELECT PLAN_TABLE_OUTPUT
        FROM TABLE(DBMS_XPLAN.DISPLAY('MY_PLAN_TABLE',
'st1','TYPICAL'));
```

Customizing PLAN_TABLE Output

If you have specified a statement identifier, then you can write your own script to query the `PLAN_TABLE`. For example:

- Start with ID = 0 and given `STATEMENT_ID.`
- Use the `CONNECT BY` clause to walk the tree from parent to child, the join keys being `STATEMENT_ID = PRIOR STATEMENT_ID` and `PARENT_ID = PRIOR ID.`
- Use the pseudo-column `LEVEL` (associated with `CONNECT BY`) to indent the children.

```
SELECT cardinality "Rows",lpad(' ',level-
1)||operation||' '||options||' '||object_name "Plan"
        FROM PLAN_TABLE CONNECT BY prior id = parent_id
        AND prior statement_id = statement_id
        START WITH id = 0 AND statement_id = 'st1'
        ORDER BY id;

Rows Plan
------- ----------------------------------------
SELECT STATEMENT TABLE ACCESS FULL EMPLOYEES
```

The `NULL` in the `Rows` column indicates that the optimizer does not have any statistics on the table. Analyzing the table shows the following:

```
Rows Plan
----- ------------------------------------------
        16957 SELECT STATEMENT
        16957 TABLE ACCESS FULL EMPLOYEES
```

You can also select the COST. This is useful for comparing execution plans or for understanding why the optimizer chooses one execution plan over another.

These simplified examples are not valid for recursive SQL.

Reading EXPLAIN PLAN Output

This section uses EXPLAIN PLAN examples to illustrate execution plans. The statement in displays the execution plans.

Example 12.4: Statement to display the EXPLAIN PLAN

```
SELECT PLAN_TABLE_OUTPUT
        FROM TABLE(DBMS_XPLAN.DISPLAY(NULL,
'statement_id','BASIC'));
```

Examples of the output from this statement are shown in and.

Example 12.5: EXPLAIN PLAN for Statement ID ex_plan1

```
EXPLAIN PLAN
        SET statement_id = 'ex_plan1' FOR
SELECT phone_number FROM employees
        WHERE phone_number LIKE '650%';
-----------------------------------
| Id | Operation     | Name        |
-----------------------------------
|        0 | SELECT STATEMENT |  |
|        1 | TABLE ACCESS FULL| EMPLOYEES |
----------------------------------------
```

This plan shows execution of a SELECT statement. The table employees is accessed using a full table scan.

- Every row in the table employees is accessed, and the WHERE clause criteria is evaluated for every row.
- The SELECT statement returns the rows meeting the WHERE clause criteria.

Example 12.6: EXPLAIN PLAN for Statement ID ex_plan2

```
EXPLAIN PLAN
        SET statement_id = 'ex_plan2' FOR
SELECT last_name FROM employees
        WHERE last_name LIKE 'Pe%';
SELECT PLAN_TABLE_OUTPUT
        FROM TABLE(DBMS_XPLAN.DISPLAY(NULL, 'ex_plan2','BASIC'));
-----------------------------------
| Id | Operation     | Name        |
-----------------------------------
|  0 | SELECT STATEMENT | |
|  1 | INDEX RANGE SCAN| EMP_NAME_IX |
-----------------------------------
```

This plan shows execution of a SELECT statement:

- The database range scans EMP_NAME_IX to evaluate the WHERE clause criteria.
- The SELECT statement returns rows satisfying the WHERE clause conditions.

VIEWING PARALLEL EXECUTION WITH EXPLAIN PLAN

Tuning a parallel query begins much like a non-parallel query tuning exercise by choosing the driving table. However, the rules governing the choice are different. In the non-parallel case, the best driving table is typically the one that produces fewest number of rows after limiting conditions are applied. The small number of rows are joined to larger tables using non-unique indexes. For example, consider a table hierarchy consisting of CUSTOMER, ACCOUNT, and TRANSACTION.

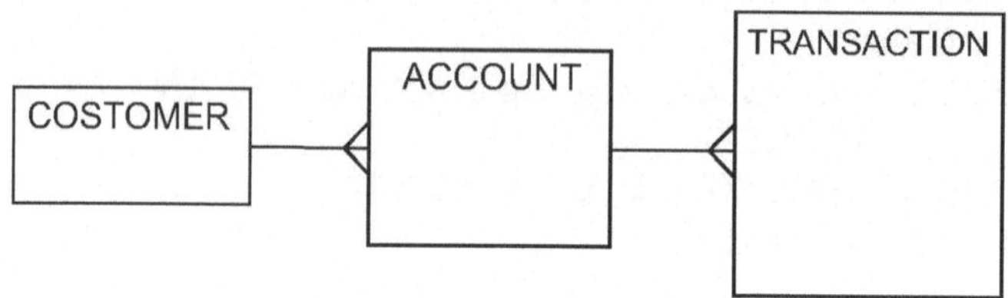

Figure 12.1. A Table Hierarchy

CUSTOMER is the smallest table while TRANSACTION is the largest. A typical OLTP query might retrieve transaction information about a specific customer's account. The query would drive from the CUSTOMER table. The goal in this case is to minimize logical I/O, which typically minimizes other critical resources including physical I/O and CPU time.

For parallel queries, the choice of the driving table is usually the largest table because the database can use parallel query. It would not be efficient to use parallel query in this case because only a few rows from each table are ultimately accessed. However, what if it were necessary to identify all customers that had transactions of a certain type last month? It would be more efficient to drive from the TRANSACTION table because there are no limiting conditions on the customer table. The database would join rows from the TRANSACTION table to the ACCOUNT table, and finally to the CUSTOMER table. In this case, the indexes used on the ACCOUNT and CUSTOMER table are probably highly selective primary key or unique indexes, rather than non-unique indexes used in the first query. Because the TRANSACTION table is large and the column is un-selective, it would be beneficial to utilize parallel query driving from the TRANSACTION table.

Parallel operations include:

- PARALLEL_TO_PARALLEL
- PARALLEL_TO_SERIAL

A PARALLEL_TO_SERIAL operation which is always the step that occurs when rows from a parallel operation are consumed by the query coordinator. Another type of operation that does not occur in this query is a SERIAL operation. If these types of operations occur, then consider making them parallel operations to improve performance because they too are potential bottlenecks.

- PARALLEL_FROM_SERIAL
- PARALLEL_TO_PARALLEL

PARALLEL_TO_PARALLEL operations generally produce the best performance as long as the workloads in each step are relatively equivalent.

- PARALLEL_COMBINED_WITH_CHILD
- PARALLEL_COMBINED_WITH_PARENT

A PARALLEL_COMBINED_WITH_PARENT operation occurs when the database performs the step simultaneously with the parent step.

If a parallel step produces many rows, then the QC may not be able to consume the rows as fast as they are produced. Little can be done to improve this situation.

Viewing Parallel Queries with EXPLAIN PLAN

When using EXPLAIN PLAN with parallel queries, the database compiles and executes one parallel plan. This plan is derived from the serial plan by allocating row sources specific to the parallel support in the QC plan. The table queue row sources (PX Send and PX Receive), the granule iterator, and buffer sorts, required by the two slave set PQ model, are directly inserted into the parallel plan. This plan is the exact same plan for all the slaves if executed in parallel or for the QC if executed in serial.

is a simple query for illustrating an EXPLAIN PLAN for a parallel query.

Example 12.7: Parallel Query Explain Plan

```
CREATE TABLE emp2 AS SELECT * FROM employees;
ALTER TABLE emp2 PARALLEL 2;
EXPLAIN PLAN FOR
        SELECT SUM(salary) FROM emp2 GROUP BY department_id;
SELECT PLAN_TABLE_OUTPUT FROM TABLE(DBMS_XPLAN.DISPLAY());
```

The table EMP2 is scanned in parallel by one set of slaves while the aggregation for the GROUP BY is done by the second set. The PX BLOCK ITERATOR row source represents the splitting up of the table EMP2 into pieces so as to divide the scan workload between the parallel scan slaves. The PX SEND and PX RECEIVE row sources represent the pipe that connects the two slave sets as rows flow up from the parallel scan, get repartitioned through the HASH table queue, and then read by and aggregated on the top slave set. The PX SEND QC row source represents the aggregated values being sent to the QC in random (RAND) order. The PX COORDINATOR row source represents the QC or Query Coordinator which controls and schedules the parallel plan appearing below it in the plan tree.

VIEWING BITMAP INDEXES WITH EXPLAIN PLAN

Index row sources using bitmap indexes appear in the EXPLAIN PLAN output with the word BITMAP indicating the type of the index. Consider the sample query and plan in.

Example 12.8: EXPLAIN PLAN with Bitmap Indexes

```
EXPLAIN PLAN FOR
SELECT * FROM t
WHERE c1 = 2
AND c2 <> 6
OR c3 BETWEEN 10 AND 20;
SELECT STATEMENT
        TABLE ACCESS T BY INDEX ROWID
              BITMAP CONVERSION TO ROWID
                    BITMAP OR
                          BITMAP MINUS
                                BITMAP MINUS
                          BITMAP INDEX C1_IND SINGLE VALUE
                          BITMAP INDEX C2_IND SINGLE VALUE
                    BITMAP INDEX C2_IND SINGLE VALUE
              BITMAP MERGE
                    BITMAP INDEX C3_IND RANGE SCAN
```

In this example, the predicate c1=2 yields a bitmap from which a subtraction can take place. From this bitmap, the bits in the bitmap for c2 = 6 are subtracted. Also, the bits in the bitmap for c2 IS NULL are subtracted, explaining why there are two MINUS row sources in the plan. The NULL subtraction is necessary for semantic correctness unless the column has a NOT NULL constraint. The TO ROWIDS option generates the rowids necessary for the table access.

Queries using bitmap join index indicate the bitmap join index access path. The operation for bitmap join index is the same as bitmap index.

VIEWING RESULT CACHE WITH EXPLAIN PLAN

When your query contains the result_cache hint, the ResultCache operator is inserted into the execution plan.

For example, consider the query:

```
select /*+ result_cache */ deptno, avg(sal)
from emp
group by deptno;
```

To view the EXPLAIN PLAN for this query, use the command:

```
EXPLAIN PLAN FOR
select /*+ result_cache */ deptno, avg(sal)
from emp
group by deptno;
select PLAN_TABLE_OUTPUT from TABLE (DBMS_XPLAN.DISPLAY());
```

The EXPLAIN PLAN output for this query should look similar to the following:

```
--------------------------------------------------------------------
| Id          | Operation        | Name
|Rows         | Bytes |Cost(%CPU)|Time      |
--------------------------------------------------------------------
|      0      | SELECT STATEMENT      |                              |
11      | 77          | 4 (25) | 00:00:01|
|      1 | RESULT CACHE  |b06ppfz9pxzstbttpbqyqnfbmy                 |
|      |     |     |
|      2 |   HASH GROUP BY      |                                    |
11      | 77  | 4 (25) | 00:00:01|
|      3 |   TABLE ACCESS FULL| EMP
|107    | 749 | 3 (0)  | 00:00:01|
--------------------------------------------------------------------
```

In this EXPLAIN PLAN, the ResultCache operator is identified by its CacheId, which is b06ppfz9pxzstbttpbqyqnfbmy. You can now run a query on the V$RESULT_CACHE_OBJECTS view by using this CacheId.

VIEWING PARTITIONED OBJECTS WITH EXPLAIN PLAN

Use EXPLAIN PLAN to see how Oracle Database accesses partitioned objects for specific queries.

Partitions accessed after pruning are shown in the PARTITION START and PARTITION STOP columns. The row source name for the range partition is PARTITION RANGE. For hash partitions, the row source name is PARTITION HASH.

A join is implemented using partial partition-wise join if the DISTRIBUTION column of the plan table of one of the joined tables contains PARTITION(KEY). Partial partition-wise join is possible if one of the joined tables is partitioned on its join column and the table is parallelized.

A join is implemented using full partition-wise join if the partition row source appears before the join row source in the EXPLAIN PLAN output. Full partition-wise joins are possible only if both joined tables are equi-partitioned on their respective join columns. Examples of execution plans for several types of partitioning follow.

Examples of Displaying Range and Hash Partitioning with EXPLAIN PLAN

Consider the following table, emp_range, partitioned by range on hire_date to illustrate how pruning is displayed. Assume that the tables employees and departments from the Oracle Database sample schema exist.

```
CREATE TABLE emp_range
PARTITION BY RANGE(hire_date)
(
PARTITION emp_p1 VALUES LESS THAN (TO_DATE('1-JAN-1992','DD-MON-
YYYY')),
PARTITION emp_p2 VALUES LESS THAN (TO_DATE('1-JAN-1994','DD-MON-
YYYY')),
PARTITION emp_p3 VALUES LESS THAN (TO_DATE('1-JAN-1996','DD-MON-
YYYY')),
PARTITION emp_p4 VALUES LESS THAN (TO_DATE('1-JAN-1998','DD-MON-
YYYY')),
PARTITION emp_p5 VALUES LESS THAN (TO_DATE('1-JAN-2001','DD-MON-
YYYY'))
)
AS SELECT * FROM employees;
```

For the first example, consider the following statement:

```
EXPLAIN PLAN FOR
        SELECT * FROM emp_range;
```

Oracle Database displays something similar to the following:

```
---------------------------------------------------------------------
| Id | Operation      | Name       | Rows | Bytes |
Cost | Pstart| Pstop |
---------------------------------------------------------------------
|       0 | SELECT STATEMENT    |      |      105 | 13965 |
2 |       |      |
|       1 | PARTITION RANGE ALL|       |      105 | 13965 |
2 |       1 |    5 |
|       2 |   TABLE ACCESS FULL | EMP_RANGE |      105 | 13965 |
2 |       1 |    5 |
---------------------------------------------------------------------
```

The database creates a partition row source on top of the table access row source. It iterates over the set of partitions to be accessed. In this example, the partition iterator covers all partitions (option ALL), because a predicate was not used for pruning. The PARTITION_START and PARTITION_STOP columns of the PLAN_TABLE show access to all partitions from 1 to 5.

For the next example, consider the following statement:

```
EXPLAIN PLAN FOR
        SELECT * FROM emp_range
        WHERE hire_date >= TO_DATE('1-JAN-1996','DD-MON-YYYY');
----------------------------------------------------------------------
| Id  | Operation                    | Name        | Rows     | Bytes  |
| Cost | Pstart | Pstop   |
----------------------------------------------------------------------
|  0  | SELECT STATEMENT             |             |     3    |    399
|     2 |        |          |
|  1  |  PARTITION RANGE ITERATOR    |             |     3    |    399
|     2 |    4   |     5    |
|* 2  |   TABLE ACCESS FULL          | EMP_RANGE   |     3    |    399
|     2 |    4   |     5    |
----------------------------------------------------------------------
```

In the previous example, the partition row source iterates from partition 4 to 5 because the database prunes the other partitions using a predicate on `hire_date`.

Finally, consider the following statement:

```
EXPLAIN PLAN FOR
        SELECT * FROM emp_range
        WHERE hire_date < TO_DATE('1-JAN-1992','DD-MON-YYYY');
----------------------------------------------------------------------
| Id | Operation     |     Name |     Rows |     Bytes       |
Cost | Pstart | Pstop     |
----------------------------------------------------------------------
|    0      | SELECT STATEMENT    |     |     1     |           133    |
2    |      |     |
|    1      |     PARTITION RANGE SINGLE|     |     1     |      133    |
2    |     1     |     1      |
|*   2      | TABLE ACCESS FULL    |     EMP_RANGE    |     1     |133    |
2    |     1     |     1      |
----------------------------------------------------------------------
```

In the previous example, only partition 1 is accessed and known at compile time; thus, there is no need for a partition row source.

Plans for Hash Partitioning

Oracle Database displays the same information for hash partitioned objects, except the partition row source name is `PARTITION HASH` instead of `PARTITION RANGE`. Also, with hash partitioning, pruning is only possible using equality or `IN`-list predicates.

Examples of Pruning Information with Composite Partitioned Objects

To illustrate how Oracle Database displays pruning information for composite partitioned objects, consider the table `emp_comp` that is range partitioned on `hiredate` and subpartitioned by hash on `deptno`.

```
CREATE TABLE emp_comp PARTITION BY RANGE(hire_date)
        SUBPARTITION BY HASH(department_id) SUBPARTITIONS 3
```

```
(
PARTITION emp_p1 VALUES LESS THAN (TO_DATE('1-JAN-1992','DD-MON-
YYYY')),
PARTITION emp_p2 VALUES LESS THAN (TO_DATE('1-JAN-1994','DD-MON-
YYYY')),
PARTITION emp_p3 VALUES LESS THAN (TO_DATE('1-JAN-1996','DD-MON-
YYYY')),
PARTITION emp_p4 VALUES LESS THAN (TO_DATE('1-JAN-1998','DD-MON-
YYYY')),
PARTITION emp_p5 VALUES LESS THAN (TO_DATE('1-JAN-2001','DD-MON-
YYYY'))
)
AS SELECT * FROM employees;
```

For the first example, consider the following statement:

```
EXPLAIN PLAN FOR
        SELECT * FROM emp_comp;
--------------------------------------------------------------------
|   Id  | Operation  |    Name   | Rows             |     Bytes      | Cost
|   Pstart| Pstop |
--------------------------------------------------------------------
|   0   | SELECT STATEMENT     | |          10120     |     1314K  |
78   |    |    |
|   1   | PARTITION RANGE ALL  | |          10120     |     1314K  |
78   |  1   |         5   |
|   2   | PARTITION HASH ALL   | |          10120     |     1314K  |
78   |  1   |         3   |
|   3   | TABLE ACCESS FULL    | EMP_COMP |10120     |     1314K  |
78   |  1   |        15   |
--------------------------------------------------------------------
```

This example shows the plan when Oracle Database accesses all subpartitions of all partitions of a composite object. The database uses two partition row sources for this purpose: a range partition row source to iterate over the partitions and a hash partition row source to iterate over the subpartitions of each accessed partition.

In the following example, the range partition row source iterates from partition 1 to 5, because the database performs no pruning. Within each partition, the hash partition row source iterates over subpartitions 1 to 3 of the current partition. As a result, the table access row source accesses subpartitions 1 to 15. In other words, it accesses all subpartitions of the composite object.

```
EXPLAIN PLAN FOR
    SELECT * FROM emp_comp
    WHERE hire_date = TO_DATE('15-FEB-1998', 'DD-MON-YYYY');
--------------------------------------------------------------------
|   Id    | Operation     |    Name |    Rows |    Bytes     |
Cost      | Pstart | Pstop  |
--------------------------------------------------------------------
|   0     | SELECT STATEMENT      |     |    20    |    2660 |
17  |     |     |
|   1     | PARTITION RANGE SINGLE    |     |    20    |    2660 |
```

```
17  |    5   |  5   |
|   2    | PARTITION HASH ALL   |      |   20   |    2660 |
17  |    1   |  3   |
|*  3    | TABLE ACCESS FULL    |   EMP_COMP |   20   |    2660 |
17  |   13   |  15  |
------------------------------------------------------------------
```

In the previous example, only the last partition, partition 5, is accessed. This partition is known at compile time, so the database does not need to show it in the plan. The hash partition row source shows accessing of all subpartitions within that partition; that is, subpartitions 1 to 3, which translates into subpartitions 13 to 15 of the `emp_comp` table.

Now consider the following statement:

```
EXPLAIN PLAN FOR SELECT * FROM emp_comp WHERE department_id = 20;
------------------------------------------------------------------
| Id  | Operation                | Name       | Rows     | Bytes    |
Cost    | Pstart | Pstop |
------------------------------------------------------------------
| 0   | SELECT STATEMENT         |            |      101 |  13433   |
78 |   |    |    |
| 1   | PARTITION RANGE ALL      |            |      101 |  13433   |
78 |  1    |  5 |
| 2   | PARTITION HASH SINGLE    |            |      101 |  13433   |
78 |  3    |  3 |
|* 3  | TABLE ACCESS FULL        | EMP_COMP   |      101 |  13433   |
78 |    |       |
------------------------------------------------------------------
```

In the previous example, the predicate `deptno` = 20 enables pruning on the hash dimension within each partition, so Oracle Database only needs to access a single subpartition. The number of that subpartition is known at compile time, so the hash partition row source is not needed.

Finally, consider the following statement:

```
VARIABLE dno NUMBER;
EXPLAIN PLAN FOR SELECT * FROM emp_comp WHERE department_id = :dno;
------------------------------------------------------------------
| Id | Operation                | Name       | Rows    | Bytes    |
Cost | Pstart | Pstop |
------------------------------------------------------------------
| 0 | SELECT STATEMENT          |            |     101 |  13433   |
78 |       |      |
| 1 |  PARTITION RANGE ALL      |            |     101 |  13433   |
78 |     1 |    5 |
| 2 |   PARTITION HASH SINGLE   |            |     101 |  13433   |
78 |  KEY |   KEY |
|* 3 |    TABLE ACCESS FULL     | EMP_COMP   |     101 |  13433   |
78 |     |    |
------------------------------------------------------------------
```

The last two examples are the same, except that deptno = 20 has been replaced by department_id = :dno. In this last case, the subpartition number is unknown at compile time, and a hash partition row source is allocated. The option is SINGLE for that row source, because Oracle Database accesses only one subpartition within each partition. The PARTITION_START and PARTITION_STOP is set to KEY, which means that Oracle Database determines the number of subpartitions at run time.

Examples of Partial Partition-Wise Joins

In the following example, emp_range_did is joined on the partitioning column department_id and is parallelized. This enables use of partial partition-wise join, because the dept2 table is not partitioned. Oracle Database dynamically partitions the dept2 table before the join.

Example 12.9: Partial Partition-Wise Join with Range Partition

```
CREATE TABLE dept2 AS SELECT * FROM departments;
ALTER TABLE dept2 PARALLEL 2;
CREATE TABLE emp_range_did PARTITION BY RANGE(department_id)
        (PARTITION emp_p1 VALUES LESS THAN (150),
        PARTITION emp_p5 VALUES LESS THAN (MAXVALUE) )
        AS SELECT * FROM employees;
ALTER TABLE emp_range_did PARALLEL 2;
EXPLAIN PLAN FOR SELECT /*+ PQ_DISTRIBUTE(d NONE PARTITION) ORDERED */
e.last_name, d.department_name
        FROM emp_range_did e , dept2 d
        WHERE e.department_id = d.department_id ;
```

```
---------------------------------------------------------------------
| Id | Operation      | Name   | Rows   | Bytes  | Cost   | Pstart | Pstop |
| IN-OUT | PQ Distrib   |
---------------------------------------------------------------------
| 0 | SELECT STATEMENT                |                  | 284    |
16188  | 6 |      |        |        |
| 1 |  PX COORDINATOR                 |                  |        |
|     |      |      |        |        |             |
| 2 |   PX SEND QC (RANDOM)           |:TQ10001          | 284    |
16188 |  6 |      |          | Q1,01 |  P->S | QC (RAND) |
|* 3 |    HASH JOIN                   |                  | 284    |
16188 |  6 |      |          | Q1,01 |  PCWP |           |
| 4 |     PX PARTITION RANGE ALL      |                  | 284    |
7668  | 2 |    1 |   2      | Q1,01 |  PCWC |           |
| 5 |      TABLE ACCESS FULL          |EMP_RANGE_DID |    284    |
7668  |  2 |    1 |   2      |  Q1,01 |  PCWP |          |
| 6 |     BUFFER SORT                 |                  |        |
|     |      |      | Q1,01 | PCWC |              |
| 7|       PX RECEIVE                 |                  | 21     |
630 |   2 |      |      | Q1,01 | PCWP          |         |
| 8|        PX SEND PARTITION (KEY)|:TQ10000             | 21     |
630 |   2 |      |      |        | S->P | PART (KEY) |
| 9|         TABLE ACCESS FULL      | DEPT2               | 21     |
630 |   2 |      |      |        |         |           |
---------------------------------------------------------------------
```

The execution plan shows that the table dept2 is scanned serially and all rows with the same partitioning column value of emp_range_did (department_id) are sent through a PART (KEY), or partition key, table queue to the same slave doing the partial partition-wise join.

In the following example, emp_comp is joined on the partitioning column and is parallelized. This enables use of partial partition-wise join, because the dept2 table is not partitioned. The database dynamically partitions the dept2 table before the join.

Example 12.10: Partial Partition ise Join with omposite Partition

```
ALTER TABLE emp_comp PARALLEL 2;
EXPLAIN PLAN FOR
SELECT /*+ PQ_DISTRIBUTE(d NONE PARTITION) ORDERED */ e.last_name,
d.department_name FROM emp_comp e, dept2 d
        WHERE e.department_id = d.department_id;
SELECT PLAN_TABLE_OUTPUT FROM TABLE(DBMS_XPLAN.DISPLAY());
--------------------------------------------------------------------------
| Id | Operation                     | Name      | Rows    | Bytes   |
Cost | Pstart|Pstop|  TQ   | IN-OUT | PQ Distrib |
--------------------------------------------------------------------------
|  0 | SELECT STATEMENT              |           |  445    |  17800  |
5 |     |     |       |       |              |
|  1 |  PX COORDINATOR               |           |         |         |
|     |     |       |       |              |
|  2 |   PX SEND QC (RANDOM)         |:TQ10001   |  445    |  17800  |
5 |     |     | Q1,01  | P->S  | QC (RAND) |
|* 3 |    HASH JOIN                  |           |  445    |  17800  |
5 |     |     | Q1,01  | PCWP |           |
|  4 |      PX PARTITION RANGE ALL   |           |  107    |  1070   |
3 |  1  |   5 | Q1,01  | PCWC |           |
|  5 |       PX PARTITION HASH ALL   |           |  107    |  1070   |
3 |  1  |   3 | Q1,01 | PCWC |            |
|  6 |       TABLE ACCESS FULL       |EMP_COMP   |  107    |  1070   |
3 |  1  |  15 | Q1,01 | PCWP |            |
|  7 |     PX RECEIVE                |           |  21     |  630    |
1 |     |     | Q1,01 | PCWP |            |
|  8 |     PX SEND PARTITION (KEY)   | :TQ10000  |  21     |  630    |
1 |     |     | Q1,00 | P->P | PART (KEY) |
|  9 |      PX BLOCK ITERATOR        |           |  21     |  630    |
1 |     |     | Q1,00 | PCWC |            |
| 10 |       TABLE ACCESS FULL       |DEPT2      |  21     |  630    |
1 |     |     | Q1,00 | PCWP |            |
--------------------------------------------------------------------------
```

The plan shows that the optimizer selects partial partition-wise join from one of two columns. The PX SEND node type is PARTITION(KEY) and the PQ Distrib column contains the text PART (KEY), or partition key. This implies that the table dept2 is re-partitioned based on the join column department_id to be sent to the parallel slaves executing the scan of EMP_COMP and the join.

Note that in both and the PQ_DISTRIBUTE hint explicitly forces a partial partition-wise join because the query optimizer could have chosen a different plan based on cost in this query.

Examples of Full Partition-wise Joins

In the following example, emp_comp and dept_hash are joined on their hash partitioning columns. This enables use of full partition-wise join. The PARTITION HASH row source appears on top of the join row source in the plan table output.

The PX PARTITION HASH row source appears on top of the join row source in the plan table output while the PX PARTITION RANGE row source appears over the scan of emp_comp. Each parallel slave performs the join of an entire hash partition of emp_comp with an entire partition of dept_hash.

Example 12.11: Full Partition-Wise Join

```
CREATE TABLE dept_hash
        PARTITION BY HASH(department_id)
        PARTITIONS 3
        PARALLEL 2
        AS SELECT * FROM departments;
EXPLAIN PLAN FOR SELECT /*+ PQ_DISTRIBUTE(e NONE NONE) ORDERED */
e.last_name, d.department_name
        FROM emp_comp e, dept_hash d WHERE e.department_id =
d.department_id;
--------------------------------------------------------------------
| Id | Operation                        | Name      | Rows    | Bytes
Cost    | Pstart|Pstop |   TQ   | IN-OUT | PQ Distrib  |
--------------------------------------------------------------------
| 0  | SELECT STATEMENT                 |           |  106    | 2544 |
8        |       |          |        |          |
| 1  |   PX COORDINATOR                 |           |         |      |
|        |       |          |        |          |
| 2  |     PX SEND QC (RANDOM)          | :TQ10000  |  106    | 2544 |
8  |           |     | Q1,00 | P->S | QC (RAND)  |
| 3  |     PX PARTITION HASH ALL        |           |  106    | 2544 |
8  |     1 |     3 | Q1,00 |  PCWC |            |
|* 4 |       HASH JOIN                  |           |  106    | 2544 |
8  |       |       | Q1,00 |  PCWP |            |
| 5  |        PX PARTITION RANGE ALL    |           |  107    | 1070 |
3  |     1 |    5 | Q1,00 |  PCWC |             |
| 6  |          TABLE ACCESS FULL       | EMP_COMP  |  107    | 1070 |
3  |     1 |   15 | Q1,00 |  PCWP |             |
| 7  |        TABLE ACCESS FULL         | DEPT_HASH |  27     | 378  |
4  |     1 |    3 | Q1,00 |  PCWP |             |
--------------------------------------------------------------------
```

Examples of Inlist Iterator and Explain Plan

An INLIST ITERATOR operation appears in the EXPLAIN PLAN output if an index implements an IN-list predicate. For example:

```
SELECT * FROM emp WHERE empno IN (7876, 7900, 7902);
```

The EXPLAIN PLAN output appears as follows:

```
OPERATION               OPTIONS            OBJECT_NAME
---------------         ---------------    ---------------
SELECT STATEMENT
INLIST ITERATOR
TABLE ACCESS            BY ROWID           EMP
INDEX                   RANGE SCAN         EMP_EMPNO
```

The INLIST ITERATOR operation iterates over the next operation in the plan for each value in the IN-list predicate. For partitioned tables and indexes, the three possible types of IN-list columns are described in the following sections.

When the IN-List Column is an Index Column

If the IN-list column empno is an index column but not a partition column, then the plan is as follows (the IN-list operator appears before the table operation but after the partition operation):

```
OPERATION    OPTIONS   OBJECT_NAME   PARTITION_START  PARTITION_STOP
-----------  --------- -----------   ---------------  ---------------
SELECT STATEMENT PARTITION RANGE ALL
KEY(INLIST) KEY(INLIST)INLIST ITERATOR
TABLE ACCESS BY LOCAL INDEX ROWID EMP KEY(INLIST)
KEY(INLIST)INDEX RANGE SCAN EMP_EMPNO KEY(INLIST)
KEY(INLIST)
```

The KEY(INLIST) designation for the partition start and stop keys specifies that an IN-list predicate appears on the index start and stop keys.

When the IN-List Column is an Index and a Partition Column

If empno is an indexed and a partition column, then the plan contains an INLIST ITERATOR operation before the partition operation:

```
OPERATION    OPTIONS   OBJECT_NAME   PARTITION_START  PARTITION_STOP
----------   --------  -----------   ---------------  --------------
SELECT STATEMENT
INLIST ITERATOR
PARTITION RANGE ITERATOR KEY(INLIST) KEY(INLIST)
TABLE ACCESS BY LOCAL INDEX ROWID EMP KEY(INLIST)
KEY(INLIST)INDEX RANGE SCAN EMP_EMPNO KEY(INLIST)
KEY(INLIST)
```

When the IN-List Column is a Partition Column

If empno is a partition column and no indexes exist, then no INLIST ITERATOR operation is allocated:

```
OPERATION OPTIONS      OBJECT_NAME   PARTITION_START  PARTITION_STOP
-----------------      ------------  ---------------  ---------------
SELECT STATEMENT PARTITION RANGE INLIST KEY(INLIST)
KEY(INLIST) TABLE ACCESS FULL EMP KEY(INLIST)
KEY(INLIST)
```

If emp_empno is a bitmap index, then the plan is as follows:

```
OPERATION          OPTIONS                    OBJECT_NAME
---------------    --------------             --------------
SELECT STATEMENT
```

```
INLIST ITERATOR
TABLE ACCESS BY INDEX ROWID          EMP
BITMAP CONVERSION      TO ROWIDS
BITMAP INDEX SINGLE VALUE            EMP_EMPNO
```

Example of Domain Indexes and EXPLAIN PLAN

You can also use EXPLAIN PLAN to derive user-defined CPU and I/O costs for domain indexes. EXPLAIN PLAN displays these statistics in the OTHER column of PLAN_TABLE.

For example, assume table emp has user-defined operator CONTAINS with a domain index emp_resume on the resume column, and the index type of emp_resume supports the operator CONTAINS. You explain the plan for the following query:

```
SELECT * FROM emp WHERE CONTAINS(resume, 'Oracle') = 1
```

The database could display the following plan:

```
OPERATION              OPTIONS        OBJECT_NAME      OTHER
-------------------    ------------   -----------      ----------
SELECT STATEMENT TABLE ACCESS BY ROWID EMP DOMAIN INDEX
EMP_RESUME    CPU: 300, I/O: 4
```

PLAN_TABLE COLUMNS

The PLAN_TABLE used by the EXPLAIN PLAN statement contains the columns listed in Table 12.1.

Table 12.1. PLAN_TABLE Columns

Column	Type	Description
STATEMENT_ID	VARCHAR2(30)	Value of the optional STATEMENT_ID parameter specified in the EXPLAIN PLAN statement.
PLAN_ID	NUMBER	Unique identifier of a plan in the database.
TIMESTAMP	DATE	Date and time when the EXPLAIN PLAN statement was generated.
REMARKS	VARCHAR2(80)	Any comment (of up to 80 bytes) you want to associate with each step of the explained plan. This column indicates whether the database used an outline or SQL profile for the query. If you need to add or change a remark on any row of the PLAN_TABLE, then use the UPDATE statement to modify the rows of the PLAN_TABLE.
OPERATION	VARCHAR2(30)	Name of the internal operation performed in this step. In the first row generated for a statement, the column contains one of the following values: • DELETE STATEMENT • INSERT STATEMENT

		• SELECT STATEMENT • UPDATE STATEMENT See Table 12.3 for more information on values for this column.
OPTIONS	VARCHAR2(225)	A variation on the operation described in the OPERATION column. See Table 12.3 for more information on values for this column.
OBJECT_NODE	VARCHAR2(128)	Name of the database link used to reference the object (a table name or view name). For local queries using parallel execution, this column describes the order in which the database consumes output from operations.
OBJECT_OWNER	VARCHAR2(30)	Name of the user who owns the schema containing the table or index.
OBJECT_NAME	VARCHAR2(30)	Name of the table or index.
OBJECT_ALIAS	VARCHAR2(65)	Unique alias of a table or view in a SQL statement. For indexes, it is the object alias of the underlying table.
OBJECT_INSTANCE	NUMERIC	Number corresponding to the ordinal position of the object as it appears in the original statement. The numbering proceeds from left to right, outer to inner for the original statement text. View expansion results in unpredictable numbers.
OBJECT_TYPE	VARCHAR2(30)	Modifier that provides descriptive information about the object; for example, NON-UNIQUE for indexes.
OPTIMIZER	VARCHAR2(255)	Current mode of the optimizer.
SEARCH_COLUMNS	NUMBERIC	Not currently used.
ID	NUMERIC	A number assigned to each step in the execution plan.
PARENT_ID	NUMERIC	The ID of the next execution step that operates on the output of the ID step.
DEPTH	NUMERIC	Depth of the operation in the row source tree that the plan represents. The value can be used for indenting the rows in a plan table report.

POSITION	NUMERIC	For the first row of output, this indicates the optimizer's estimated cost of executing the statement. For the other rows, it indicates the position relative to the other children of the same parent.
COST	NUMERIC	Cost of the operation as estimated by the optimizer's query approach. Cost is not determined for table access operations. The value of this column does not have any particular unit of measurement; it is merely a weighted value used to compare costs of execution plans. The value of this column is a function of the CPU_COST and IO_COST columns.
CARDINALITY	NUMERIC	Estimate by the query optimization approach of the number of rows accessed by the operation.
BYTES	NUMERIC	Estimate by the query optimization approach of the number of bytes accessed by the operation.
OTHER_TAG	VARCHAR2(255)	Describes the contents of the OTHER column. Values are: • SERIAL (blank): Serial execution. Currently, SQL is not loaded in the OTHER column for this case. • SERIAL_FROM_REMOTE (S -> R): Serial execution at a remote site. • PARALLEL_FROM_SERIAL (S -> P): Serial execution. Output of step is partitioned or broadcast to parallel execution servers. • PARALLEL_TO_SERIAL (P -> S): Parallel execution. Output of step is returned to serial QC process. • PARALLEL_TO_PARALLEL (P -> P): Parallel execution. Output of step is repartitioned to second set of parallel execution servers. • PARALLEL_COMBINED_WITH_PARENT (PWP): Parallel execution; Output of step goes to next step in same parallel process. No interprocess communication to parent. • PARALLEL_COMBINED_WITH_CHIL D (PWC): Parallel execution. Input of step comes from prior step in same parallel

		process. No interprocess communication from child.
PARTITION_START	VARCHAR2(255)	Start partition of a range of accessed partitions. It can take one of the following values: *n* indicates that the start partition has been identified by the SQL compiler, and its partition number is given by *n*. KEY indicates that the start partition is identified at run time from partitioning key values. ROW REMOVE_LOCATION indicates that the database computes the start partition (same as the stop partition) at run time from the location of each retrieved record. The record location is obtained by a user or from a global index. INVALID indicates that the range of accessed partitions is empty.
PARTITION_STOP	VARCHAR2(255)	Stop partition of a range of accessed partitions. It can take one of the following values: *n* indicates that the stop partition has been identified by the SQL compiler, and its partition number is given by *n*. KEY indicates that the stop partition is identified at run time from partitioning key values. ROW REMOVE_LOCATION indicates that the database computes the stop partition (same as the start partition) at run time from the location of each retrieved record. The record location is obtained by a user or from a global index. INVALID indicates that the range of accessed partitions is empty.
PARTITION_ID	NUMERIC	Step that has computed the pair of values of the PARTITION_START and PARTITION_STOP columns.
OTHER	LONG	Other information that is specific to the execution step that a user might find useful. See the OTHER_TAG column.
DISTRIBUTION	VARCHAR2(30)	Method used to distribute rows from producer query servers to consumer query servers.

		See Table 12.2 for more information on the possible values for this column. For more information about consumer and producer query servers.
CPU_COST	NUMERIC	CPU cost of the operation as estimated by the query optimizer's approach. The value of this column is proportional to the number of machine cycles required for the operation. For statements that use the rule-based approach, this column is null.
IO_COST	NUMERIC	I/O cost of the operation as estimated by the query optimizer's approach. The value of this column is proportional to the number of data blocks read by the operation. For statements that use the rule-based approach, this column is null.
TEMP_SPACE	NUMERIC	Temporary space, in bytes, used by the operation as estimated by the query optimizer's approach. For statements that use the rule-based approach, or for operations that do not use any temporary space, this column is null.
ACCESS_PREDICATES	VARCHAR2(4000)	Predicates used to locate rows in an access structure. For example, start or stop predicates for an index range scan.
FILTER_PREDICATES	VARCHAR2(4000)	Predicates used to filter rows before producing them.
PROJECTION	VARCHAR2(4000)	Expressions produced by the operation.
TIME	NUMBER(20,2)	Elapsed time in seconds of the operation as estimated by query optimization. For statements that use the rule-based approach, this column is null.
QBLOCK_NAME	VARCHAR2(30)	Name of the query block, either system-generated or defined by the user with the QB_NAME hint.

Table 12.2 describes the values that can appear in the DISTRIBUTION column:

Table 12.2. Values of DISTRIBUTION Column of the PLAN_TABLE

DISTRIBUTION Text	Interpretation
PARTITION (ROWID)	Maps rows to query servers based on the partitioning of a table or index using the rowid of the row to UPDATE/DELETE.
PARTITION (KEY)	Maps rows to query servers based on the partitioning of a table or index using a set of columns. Used for partial partition-wise join, PARALLEL INSERT, CREATE TABLE AS SELECT of a partitioned table, and CREATE PARTITIONED GLOBAL INDEX.
HASH	Maps rows to query servers using a hash function on the join key. Used for PARALLEL JOIN or PARALLEL GROUP BY.
RANGE	Maps rows to query servers using ranges of the sort key. Used when the statement contains an ORDER BY clause.
ROUND-ROBIN	Randomly maps rows to query servers.
BROADCAST	Broadcasts the rows of the entire table to each query server. Used for a parallel join when one table is very small compared to the other.
QC (ORDER)	The QC consumes the input in order, from the first to the last query server. Used when the statement contains an ORDER BY clause.
QC (RANDOM)	The QC consumes the input randomly. Used when the statement does not have an ORDER BY clause.

Table 12.3 lists each combination of OPERATION and OPTIONS produced by the EXPLAIN PLAN statement and its meaning within an execution plan.

Table 12.3. OPERATION and OPTIONS Values Produced by EXPLAIN PLAN

Operation	Option	Description
AND-EQUAL		Operation accepting multiple sets of rowids, returning the intersection of the sets, eliminating duplicates. Used for the single-column indexes access path.
BITMAP	CONVERSION	TO ROWIDS converts bitmap representations to actual rowids that can be used to access the table. FROM ROWIDS converts the rowids to a bitmap representation. COUNT returns the number of rowids if the actual values are not needed.
BITMAP	INDEX	SINGLE VALUE looks up the bitmap for a single key value in the index.

		RANGE SCAN retrieves bitmaps for a key value range. FULL SCAN performs a full scan of a bitmap index if there is no start or stop key.
BITMAP	MERGE	Merges several bitmaps resulting from a range scan into one bitmap.
BITMAP	MINUS	Subtracts bits of one bitmap from another. Row source is used for negated predicates. Can be used only if there are nonnegated predicates yielding a bitmap from which the subtraction can take place.
BITMAP	OR	Computes the bitwise OR of two bitmaps.
BITMAP	AND	Computes the bitwise AND of two bitmaps.
BITMAP	KEY ITERATION	Takes each row from a table row source and finds the corresponding bitmap from a bitmap index. This set of bitmaps are then merged into one bitmap in a following BITMAP MERGE operation.
CONNECT BY		Retrieves rows in hierarchical order for a query containing a CONNECT BY clause.
CONCATENATION		Operation accepting multiple sets of rows returning the union-all of the sets.
COUNT		Operation counting the number of rows selected from a table.
COUNT	STOPKEY	Count operation where the number of rows returned is limited by the ROWNUM expression in the WHERE clause.
CUBE SCAN		Uses inner joins for all cube access.
CUBE SCAN	PARTIAL OUTER	Uses an outer join for at least one dimension, and inner joins for the other dimensions.
CUBE SCAN	OUTER	Uses outer joins for all cube access.
DOMAIN INDEX		Retrieval of one or more rowids from a domain index. The options column contain information supplied by a user-defined domain index cost function, if any.
FILTER		Operation accepting a set of rows, eliminates some of them, and returns the rest.
FIRST ROW		Retrieval of only the first row selected by a query.

FOR UPDATE		Operation retrieving and locking the rows selected by a query containing a FOR UPDATE clause.
HASH	GROUP BY	Operation hashing a set of rows into groups for a query with a GROUP BY clause.
HASH	GROUP BY PIVOT	Operation hashing a set of rows into groups for a query with a GROUP BY clause. The PIVOT option indicates a pivot-specific optimization for the HASH GROUP BY operator.
HASH JOIN (These are join operations.)		Operation joining two sets of rows and returning the result. This join method is useful for joining large data sets of data (DSS, Batch). The join condition is an efficient way of accessing the second table. Query optimizer uses the smaller of the two tables/ data sources to build a hash table on the join key in memory. Then it scans the larger table, probing the hash table to find the joined rows.
HASH JOIN	ANTI	Hash (left) antijoin
HASH JOIN	SEMI	Hash (left) semijoin
HASH JOIN	RIGHT ANTI	Hash right antijoin
HASH JOIN	RIGHT SEMI	Hash right semijoin
HASH JOIN	OUTER	Hash (left) outer join
HASH JOIN	RIGHT OUTER	Hash right outer join
INDEX (These are access methods.)	UNIQUE SCAN	Retrieval of a single rowid from an index.
INDEX	RANGE SCAN	Retrieval of one or more rowids from an index. Indexed values are scanned in ascending order.
INDEX	RANGE SCAN DESCENDING	Retrieval of one or more rowids from an index. Indexed values are scanned in descending order.
INDEX	FULL SCAN	Retrieval of all rowids from an index when there is no start or stop key. Indexed values are scanned in ascending order.
INDEX	FULL SCAN DESCENDING	Retrieval of all rowids from an index when there is no start or stop key. Indexed values are scanned in descending order.

INDEX	FAST FULL SCAN	Retrieval of all rowids (and column values) using multiblock reads. No sorting order can be defined. Compares to a full table scan on only the indexed columns. Only available with the cost based optimizer.
INDEX	SKIP SCAN	Retrieval of rowids from a concatenated index without using the leading column(s) in the index. Only available with the cost based optimizer.
INLIST ITERATOR		Iterates over the next operation in the plan for each value in the IN-list predicate.
INTERSECTION		Operation accepting two sets of rows and returning the intersection of the sets, eliminating duplicates.
MERGE JOIN (These are join operations.)		Operation accepting two sets of rows, each sorted by a specific value, combining each row from one set with the matching rows from the other, and returning the result.
MERGE JOIN	OUTER	Merge join operation to perform an outer join statement.
MERGE JOIN	ANTI	Merge antijoin.
MERGE JOIN	SEMI	Merge semijoin.
MERGE JOIN	CARTESIAN	Can result from 1 or more of the tables not having any join conditions to any other tables in the statement. Can occur even with a join and it may not be flagged as CARTESIAN in the plan.
CONNECT BY		Retrieval of rows in hierarchical order for a query containing a CONNECT BY clause.
MAT_VIEW REWITE ACCESS (These are access methods.)	FULL	Retrieval of all rows from a materialized view.
MAT_VIEW REWITE ACCESS	SAMPLE	Retrieval of sampled rows from a materialized view.
MAT_VIEW REWITE ACCESS	CLUSTER	Retrieval of rows from a materialized view based on a value of an indexed cluster key.
MAT_VIEW REWITE ACCESS	HASH	Retrieval of rows from materialized view based on hash cluster key value.

MAT_VIEW REWITE ACCESS	BY ROWID RANGE	Retrieval of rows from a materialized view based on a rowid range.
MAT_VIEW REWITE ACCESS	SAMPLE BY ROWID RANGE	Retrieval of sampled rows from a materialized view based on a rowid range.
MAT_VIEW REWITE ACCESS	BY USER ROWID	If the materialized view rows are located using user supplied rowids.
MAT_VIEW REWITE ACCESS	BY INDEX ROWID	If the materialized view is nonpartitioned and rows are located using index(es).
MAT_VIEW REWITE ACCESS	BY GLOBAL INDEX ROWID	If the materialized view is partitioned and rows are located using only global indexes.
MAT_VIEW REWITE ACCESS	BY LOCAL INDEX ROWID	If the materialized view is partitioned and rows are located using one or more local indexes and possibly some global indexes. Partition Boundaries: The partition boundaries might have been computed by: A previous PARTITION step, in which case the PARTITION_START and PARTITION_STOP column values replicate the values present in the PARTITION step, and the PARTITION_ID contains the ID of the PARTITION step. Possible values for PARTITION_START and PARTITION_STOP are NUMBER(*n*), KEY, INVALID. The MAT_VIEW REWRITE ACCESS or INDEX step itself, in which case the PARTITION_ID contains the ID of the step. Possible values for PARTITION_START and PARTITION_STOP are NUMBER(*n*), KEY, ROW REMOVE_LOCATION (MAT_VIEW REWRITE ACCESS only), and INVALID.
MINUS		Operation accepting two sets of rows and returning rows appearing in the first set but not in the second, eliminating duplicates.
NESTED LOOPS (These are join operations.)		Operation accepting two sets of rows, an outer set and an inner set. Oracle Database compares each row of the outer set with each row of the inner set, returning rows that satisfy a condition. This join method is useful for joining small subsets of data (OLTP). The join condition is an efficient way of accessing the second table.

NESTED LOOPS	OUTER	Nested loops operation to perform an outer join statement.
PARTITION		Iterates over the next operation in the plan for each partition in the range given by the PARTITION_START and PARTITION_STOP columns. PARTITION describes partition boundaries applicable to a single partitioned object (table or index) or to a set of equi-partitioned objects (a partitioned table and its local indexes). The partition boundaries are provided by the values of PARTITION_START and PARTITION_STOP of the PARTITION. Refer to Table 12.1 for valid values of partition start and stop.
PARTITION	SINGLE	Access one partition.
PARTITION	ITERATOR	Access many partitions (a subset).
PARTITION	ALL	Access all partitions.
PARTITION	INLIST	Similar to iterator, but based on an IN-list predicate.
PARTITION	INVALID	Indicates that the partition set to be accessed is empty.
PX ITERATOR	BLOCK, CHUNK	Implements the division of an object into block or chunk ranges among a set of parallel slaves.
PX COORDINATOR		Implements the Query Coordinator which controls, schedules, and executes the parallel plan below it using parallel query slaves. It also represents a serialization point, as the end of the part of the plan executed in parallel and always has a PX SEND QC operation below it.
PX PARTITION		Same semantics as the regular PARTITION operation except that it appears in a parallel plan.
PX RECEIVE		Shows the consumer/receiver slave node reading repartitioned data from a send/producer (QC or slave) executing on a PX SEND node. This information was formerly displayed into the DISTRIBUTION column. See Table 12.2.
PX SEND	QC (RANDOM), HASH, RANGE	Implements the distribution method taking place between two parallel set of slaves. Shows the boundary between two slave sets and how data is repartitioned on the send/producer side (QC or side. This information was formerly displayed into the DISTRIBUTION column. See Table 12.2.

REMOTE		Retrieval of data from a remote database.
SEQUENCE		Operation involving accessing values of a sequence.
SORT	AGGREGATE	Retrieval of a single row that is the result of applying a group function to a group of selected rows.
SORT	UNIQUE	Operation sorting a set of rows to eliminate duplicates.
SORT	GROUP BY	Operation sorting a set of rows into groups for a query with a GROUP BY clause.
SORT	GROUP BY PIVOT	Operation sorting a set of rows into groups for a query with a GROUP BY clause. The PIVOT option indicates a pivot-specific optimization for the SORT GROUP BY operator.
SORT	JOIN	Operation sorting a set of rows before a merge-join.
SORT	ORDER BY	Operation sorting a set of rows for a query with an ORDER BY clause.
TABLE ACCESS (These are access methods.)	FULL	Retrieval of all rows from a table.
TABLE ACCESS	SAMPLE	Retrieval of sampled rows from a table.
TABLE ACCESS	CLUSTER	Retrieval of rows from a table based on a value of an indexed cluster key.
TABLE ACCESS	HASH	Retrieval of rows from table based on hash cluster key value.
TABLE ACCESS	BY ROWID RANGE	Retrieval of rows from a table based on a rowid range.
TABLE ACCESS	SAMPLE BY ROWID RANGE	Retrieval of sampled rows from a table based on a rowid range.
TABLE ACCESS	BY USER ROWID	If the table rows are located using user-supplied rowids.
TABLE ACCESS	BY INDEX ROWID	If the table is nonpartitioned and rows are located using index(es).
TABLE ACCESS	BY GLOBAL INDEX ROWID	If the table is partitioned and rows are located using only global indexes.

TABLE ACCESS	BY LOCAL INDEX ROWID	If the table is partitioned and rows are located using one or more local indexes and possibly some global indexes. Partition Boundaries: The partition boundaries might have been computed by: A previous PARTITION step, in which case the PARTITION_START and PARTITION_STOP column values replicate the values present in the PARTITION step, and the PARTITION_ID contains the ID of the PARTITION step. Possible values for PARTITION_START and PARTITION_STOP are NUMBER(*n*), KEY, INVALID. The TABLE ACCESS or INDEX step itself, in which case the PARTITION_ID contains the ID of the step. Possible values for PARTITION_START and PARTITION_STOP are NUMBER(*n*), KEY, ROW REMOVE_LOCATION (TABLE ACCESS only), and INVALID.
TRANSPOSE		Operation evaluating a PIVOT operation by transposing the results of GROUP BY to produce the final pivoted data.
UNION		Operation accepting two sets of rows and returns the union of the sets, eliminating duplicates.
UNPIVOT		Operation that rotates data from columns into rows.
VIEW		Operation performing a view's query and then returning the resulting rows to another operation.

13 Managing Optimizer Statistics

Learning Objectives

This chapter explains why statistics are important for the query optimizer and how to gather and use optimizer statistics with the DBMS_STATS package.

This chapter contains the following sections:

- Overview of Optimizer Statistics
- Managing Automatic Optimizer Statistics Collection
- Gathering Statistics Manually
- System Statistics
- Managing Statistics
- Estimating Statistics with Dynamic Sampling
- Viewing Statistics

OVERVIEW OF OPTIMIZER STATISTICS

Optimizer statistics describe details about the database and the objects in the database. The query optimizer uses these statistics to choose the best execution plan for each SQL statement.

Optimizer statistics include the following:

- Table statistics.
  - o Number of rows
  - o Number of blocks
  - o Average row length.
- Column statistics.
  - o Number of distinct values (NDV) in column
  - o Number of nulls in column
  - o Data distribution (histogram)
  - o Extended statistics.

- Index statistics.
  - o Number of leaf blocks
  - o Levels
  - o Clustering factor.
- System statistics.
  - o I/O performance and utilization
  - o CPU performance and utilization.

Do not confuse optimizer statistics with performance statistics visible through V$ views.

The database stores optimizer statistics in the data dictionary. You can access these statistics using data dictionary views.

Because objects in a database can change constantly, you must update statistics regularly so that they accurately describe these objects. Oracle Database automatically maintains optimizer statistics.

You can maintain optimizer statistics manually using the DBMS_STATS package. For example, you can save and restore copies of statistics. You can export statistics from one database and import those statistics into another database. For example, you can export statistics from a production system to a test system. You can also lock statistics to prevent them from changing.

MANAGING AUTOMATIC OPTIMIZER STATISTICS COLLECTION

Oracle recommends that you enable **automatic optimizer statistics collection.** In this case, the database automatically collects optimizer statistics for tables with absent or stale statistics. If fresh statistics are required for a table, then the database collects them both for the table and associated indexes.

Automatic collection eliminates many manual tasks associated with managing the optimizer. It also significantly reduces the risks of generating poor execution plans because of missing or stale statistics.

Automatic optimizer statistics collection calls the DBMS_STATS.GATHER_DATABASE_STATS_JOB_PROC procedure. This internal procedure operates similarly to the DBMS_STATS.GATHER_DATABASE_STATS procedure using the GATHER AUTO option. The main difference is that GATHER_DATABASE_STATS_JOB_PROC prioritizes database objects that require statistics, so that objects that most need updated statistics are processed first, before the maintenance window closes.

This section contains the following topics:

- Enabling and Disabling Automatic Optimizer Statistics Collection
- Considerations When Gathering Statistics.

Enabling and Disabling Automatic Optimizer Statistics Collection

The automated maintenance tasks infrastructure (known as **AutoTask**) schedules tasks to run automatically in Oracle Scheduler windows known as **maintenance windows**. By default, one window is scheduled for each day of the week. Automatic optimizer statistics collection runs as part of AutoTask and is enabled by default to run in all predefined maintenance windows.

If for some reason automatic optimizer statistics collection is disabled, then you can enable it using the ENABLE procedure in the DBMS_AUTO_TASK_ADMIN package:

```
BEGIN
  DBMS_AUTO_TASK_ADMIN.ENABLE(
    client_name => 'auto optimizer stats collection',
    operation => NULL,
    window_name => NULL);
END;
/
```

When you want to disable automatic optimizer statistics collection, you can disable it using the DISABLE procedure in the DBMS_AUTO_TASK_ADMIN package:

```
BEGIN
  DBMS_AUTO_TASK_ADMIN.DISABLE(
    client_name => 'auto optimizer stats collection',
    operation => NULL,
    window_name => NULL);
END;
/
```

Automatic optimizer statistics collection relies on the modification monitoring feature. If this feature is disabled, then the automatic optimizer statistics collection job cannot detect stale statistics. This feature is enabled when the STATISTICS_LEVEL parameter is set to TYPICAL or ALL. TYPICAL is the default value.

Considerations When Gathering Statistics

This section discusses:

- When to Use Manual Statistics
- Restoring Previous Versions of Statistics
- Locking Statistics.

When to Use Manual Statistics

Automatic optimizer statistics collection should be sufficient for most database objects being modified at a moderate speed. However, in some cases the collection may not be adequate. Because the collection runs during maintenance windows, the statistics on tables that are significantly modified throughout the day may become stale. There are typically two types of such objects:

- Volatile tables that are deleted or truncated and rebuilt during the course of the day.
- Objects that are the target of large bulk loads which add 10% or more to the object's total size.

For highly volatile tables, there are two approaches:

- The statistics on these tables can be null. When Oracle Database encounters a table with no statistics, the database dynamically gathers the necessary statistics as part of query optimization. The OPTIMIZER_DYNAMIC_SAMPLING parameter controls this dynamic sampling feature. Set this parameter to a value of 2 (default) or higher. You can set the statistics to null by deleting and then locking the statistics:

```
BEGIN
  DBMS_STATS.DELETE_TABLE_STATS('OE','ORDERS');
  DBMS_STATS.LOCK_TABLE_STATS('OE','ORDERS');
END;
/
```

- The statistics on these tables can be set to values that represent the typical state of the table. You should gather statistics on the table when the tables has a representative number of rows, and then lock the statistics.
  This may be more effective than automatic optimizer statistic collection, because any statistics generated on the table during the overnight batch window may not be the most appropriate statistics for the daytime workload.

For tables that are bulk-loaded, run the statistics-gathering procedures on the tables immediately following the load process. Preferably, run the procedures as part of the same script or job that is running the bulk load.

The database can collect statistics for external tables in the following ways:

- GATHER_TABLE_STATS procedure
- GATHER_SCHEMA_STATS procedure
- GATHER_DATABASE_STATS procedure
- Automatic optimizer statistics collection processing.

If you are using GATHER_TABLE_STATS, then explicitly set the ESTIMATE_PERCENT option to NULL, 100, or AUTO_SAMPLE because sampling on external tables is not supported. Because the database does not permit data manipulation against external tables, the database never marks statistics on external tables as stale. If new statistics are required for an external table, for example, because the underlying data files change, then drop the existing statistics and regather them.

If the monitoring feature is disabled by setting STATISTICS_LEVEL to BASIC, then automatic optimizer statistics collection cannot detect stale statistics. In this case, you must manually gather statistics.

System statistics are another type of statistic that you must gather manually. The database does not gather these statistics automatically.

You must manually collect statistics on fixed objects, such as the dynamic performance tables, using GATHER_FIXED_OBJECTS_STATS procedure. Fixed objects record current database activity. You should gather statistics when the database has representative activity.

Restoring Previous Versions of Statistics

Whenever statistics in dictionary are modified, old versions of statistics are saved automatically for future restoring. You can restore statistics using RESTORE procedures of DBMS_STATS package.

Locking Statistics

In some cases, you may want to prevent any new statistics from being gathered on a table or schema by the DBMS_STATS_JOB process, such as highly volatile tables. In those cases, the DBMS_STATS package provides procedures for locking the statistics for a table or schema.

GATHERING STATISTICS MANUALLY

If you do not use automatic optimizer statistics collection, then you must run DBMS_STATS to manually collect statistics in all schemas, including system schemas. If the database content changes regularly, then you must also gather statistics regularly to ensure that the statistics accurately represent characteristics of database objects.

This section contains the following topics:

- Gathering Statistics with DBMS_STATS Procedures
- Setting Preferences for Manual Statistics Gathering

- When to Gather Statistics
- Comparing Statistics with DBMS_STATS Functions.

Gathering Statistics with DBMS_STATS Procedures

You can gather statistics with the DBMS_STATS package. This PL/SQL package is also used to modify, view, export, import, and delete statistics.

Do not use the COMPUTE and ESTIMATE clauses of ANALYZE statement to collect optimizer statistics. These clauses are supported solely for backward compatibility and may be removed in a future release. The DBMS_STATS package collects a broader, more accurate set of statistics, and gathers statistics more efficiently.

You may continue to use ANALYZE statement for other purposes not related to optimizer statistics collection:

- To use the VALIDATE or LIST CHAINED ROWS clauses
- To collect information on free list blocks.

The DBMS_STATS package can gather statistics on table and indexes and individual columns and partitions of tables. It does not gather cluster statistics. However, you can use DBMS_STATS to gather statistics on individual tables instead of the whole cluster.

If you generate statistics for a table, column, or index, and if the data dictionary contains statistics for the object, then Oracle Database updates the existing statistics. The older statistics are saved. You can restore them later if necessary.

When gathering statistics on system schemas, you can use the procedure DBMS_STATS. GATHER_DICTIONARY_STATS. This procedure gathers statistics for all system schemas, including SYS and SYSTEM, and other optional schemas, such as CTXSYS and DRSYS.

When statistics are updated for a database object, Oracle Database invalidates any currently parsed SQL statements that access the object. The next time such a statement executes, the statement is re-parsed and the optimizer automatically chooses a new execution plan based on the new statistics. Distributed statements accessing objects with new statistics on remote databases are not invalidated. The new statistics take effect the next time the SQL statement is parsed.

Table 13.1 lists the procedures in the DBMS_STATS package for gathering statistics on database objects.

Table 13.1. Statistics Gathering Procedures in the DBMS_STATS Package

Procedure	Collects
GATHER_INDEX_STATS	Index statistics
GATHER_TABLE_STATS	Table, column, and index statistics
GATHER_SCHEMA_STATS	Statistics for all objects in a schema
GATHER_DICTIONARY_STATS	Statistics for all dictionary objects
GATHER_DATABASE_STATS	Statistics for all objects in a database

When using any of these procedures, there are several important considerations for statistics gathering:

- Statistics Gathering Using Sampling
- Parallel Statistics Gathering
- Statistics on Partitioned Objects
- Column Statistics and Histograms
- Extended Statistics
- Determining Stale Statistics
- User-Defined Statistics.

Statistics Gathering Using Sampling

The statistics-gathering operations can utilize sampling to estimate statistics. Sampling is an important technique for gathering statistics. Gathering statistics without sampling requires full table scans and sorts of entire tables. Sampling minimizes the resources necessary to gather statistics.

Sampling is specified using the `ESTIMATE_PERCENT` argument to the `DBMS_STATS` procedures. While you can set the sampling percentage to any value, Oracle recommends setting the `ESTIMATE_PERCENT` parameter of the `DBMS_STATS` gathering procedures to `DBMS_STATS.AUTO_SAMPLE_SIZE` to maximize performance gains while achieving necessary statistical accuracy. `AUTO_SAMPLE_SIZE` lets Oracle Database determine the best sample size necessary for good statistics, based on the statistical property of the object. Because each type of statistics has different requirements, the size of the actual sample taken may not be the same across the table, columns, or indexes. For example, to collect table and column statistics for all tables in the `OE` schema with auto-sampling, you could use:

```
EXECUTE
DBMS_STATS.GATHER_SCHEMA_STATS('OE',DBMS_STATS.AUTO_SAMPLE_SIZE);
```

When the `ESTIMATE_PERCENT` parameter is manually specified, the `DBMS_STATS` gathering procedures may automatically increase the sampling percentage if the specified percentage did not produce a large enough sample. This ensures the stability of the estimated values by reducing fluctuations.

Parallel Statistics Gathering

The statistics-gathering operations can run either serially or in parallel. You can specify the degree of parallelism with the `DEGREE` argument to the `DBMS_STATS` gathering procedures. The database can use parallel statistics gathering in conjunction with sampling. Oracle recommends setting the `DEGREE` parameter to `DBMS_STATS.AUTO_DEGREE`. This setting allows Oracle Database to choose an appropriate degree of parallelism based on the size of the object and the settings for the parallel-related `init.ora` parameters.

Note that certain types of index statistics are not gathered in parallel, including cluster indexes, domain indexes, and bitmap join indexes.

Statistics on Partitioned Objects

For partitioned tables and indexes, `DBMS_STATS` can gather separate statistics for each partition and global statistics for the entire table or index. Similarly, for composite partitioning,

DBMS_STATS can gather separate statistics for subpartitions, partitions, and the entire table or index.

Granularity of Statistics Gathering: Depending on the SQL statement undergoing optimization, the optimizer can choose to use partition, subpartition, or global statistics. Both global and partition statistics are important for most applications.

You determine the type of partitioning statistics to be gathered using the GRANULARITY argument to the DBMS_STATS procedures. Oracle recommends setting GRANULARITY to AUTO to gather subpartition, partition, or global statistics depending on the partition type. The ALL setting always gathers all types of satistics.

Incremental Statistics Gathering: With partitioned tables, you typically add new data into a new partition. As you add new partitions and load data, you must gather statistics on the new partition and keep global statistics up to date.

You can use INCREMENTAL to decide whether the database performs a full table scan to maintain the global statistics of a partitioned table. You can use the DBMS_STATS. SET_TABLE_PREF procedure to change the INCREMENTAL value.

When INCREMENTAL=false (default), the database always uses a full table scan to maintain global statistics. This is a highly resource-intensive and time-consuming operation for large tables. An alternative to mandatory full table scans is gathering **incremental statistics**. When the following criteria are met, the database updates global statistics incrementally by scanning *only* the partitions that have changed:

- The INCREMENTAL value for the partitioned table is true.
- The PUBLISH value for the partitioned table is true.
- The user specifies AUTO_SAMPLE_SIZE for ESTIMATE_PERCENT and AUTO for GRANULARITY when gathering statistics on the table.

Gathering table statistics incrementally has the following consequences:

- The SYSAUX tablespace consumes additional space to maintain global statistics for partitioned tables.
- If a table uses composite partitioning, then the database only gathers statistics for modified subpartitions. The database does not gather statistics at the subpartition level for unmodified subpartitions. In this way, the database reduces work by skipping unmodified partitions.
- If a table uses incremental statistics, and if this table has a locally partitioned index, then the database gathers index statistics at the global level and for modified (not unmodified) index partitions. The database does not generate global index statistics from the partition-level index statistics. Rather, the database gathers global index statistics by performing a full index scan.

Column Statistics and Histograms

When gathering statistics on a table, DBMS_STATS gathers information about the data distribution of the columns within the table. The most basic information about the data distribution is the maximum value and minimum value of the column. However, this level of statistics may be insufficient for the optimizer's needs if the data within the column is skewed. For skewed data distributions, histograms can also be created as part of the column statistics to describe the data distribution of a given column.

Histograms are specified using the METHOD_OPT argument of the DBMS_STATS gathering procedures. Oracle recommends setting the METHOD_OPT to FOR ALL COLUMNS SIZE AUTO.

With this setting, Oracle Database automatically determines which columns require histograms and the number of buckets (size) of each histogram. You can also manually specify which columns should have histograms and the size of each histogram.

If you need to remove all rows from a table when using DBMS_STATS, use TRUNCATE instead of dropping and re-creating the same table. When you drop a table, workload information used by the auto-histogram gathering feature and saved statistics history used by the RESTORE_*_STATS procedures is lost. Without this data, these features do not function properly.

Extended Statistics

Oracle Database can also gather statistics on a group of columns within a table or an expression on a column. For more details on these, refer to:

- MultiColumn Statistics
- Expression Statistics.

MultiColumn Statistics: When the WHERE clause of a query specifies multiple columns from a single table (multiple single column predicates), the relationship between the columns can strongly affect the combined selectivity for the column group.

For example, consider the customers table in the SH schema. The columns cust_state_province and country_id are related, with cust_state_province determining the country_id for each customer. Suppose you query the customers table where the cust_state_province is California:

```
SELECT COUNT(*)FROM  sh.customers WHERE  cust_state_province = 'CA';
```

The preceding query returns the following value:

```
COUNT(*)
-----------
    3341
```

Adding an extra predicate on the country_id column does not change the result when the country_id is 52790 (United States of America). Assume that you run the following query:

```
SELECT COUNT(*) FROM  customers WHERE  cust_state_province = 'CA'
AND   country_id=52790;
```

The preceding query returns the same value as the previous query:

```
COUNT(*)
-----------
    3341
```

Assume that the country_id has a different value, such as 52775 (Brazil), as in the following query:

```
SELECT COUNT(*) FROM  customers WHERE
cust_state_province = 'CA'
AND   country_id=52775;
```

In this case the returned value is as follows:

```
COUNT(*)
-----------
       0
```

With individual column statistics, the optimizer has no way of knowing that the `cust_state_province` and the `country_id` columns are related. By gathering statistics on these columns as a group (column group), the optimizer has a more accurate selectivity value for the group, instead of having to generate the value based on the individual column statistics.

You can create column groups manually by using the `DBMS_STATS` package. You can use this package to create a column group, get the name of a column group, or delete a column group from a table.

Creating a Column Group: Use the `create_extended_statistics` function to create a column group. The `create_ extended_statistics` function returns the system-generated name of the newly created column group. Table 13.2 lists the input parameters for this function.

Table 13.2. Parameters for the Create_extended_statistics Function

Parameter	Description
owner	Schema owner. NULL indicates current schema.
tab_name	Name of the table to which the column group is added.
extension	Columns in the column group.

For example, to add a column group consisting of the `cust_state_province` and `country_id` columns to the `customers` table in SH schema, run the following PL/SQL block:

```
DECLARE
  cg_name varchar2(30);
BEGIN
  cg_name := dbms_stats.create_extended_stats(null,'customers',
           '(cust_state_province,country_id)');
END;
/
```

Getting a Column Group: Use the `show_extended_stats_name` function to obtain the name of the column group for a given set of columns. Table 13.3 lists the input parameters for this function.

Table 13.3. Parameters for the Show_extended_stats_name Function

Parameter	Description
owner	Schema owner. NULL indicates current schema.
tab_name	Name of the table to which the column group belongs.
extension	Name of the column group.

For example, use the following query to obtain the column group name for a set of columns on the `customers` table:

```
select sys.dbms_stats.show_extended_stats_name
('sh','customers','(cust_state_province,country_id)')
col_group_name from dual;
```

The output is similar to the following:

```
COL_GROUP_NAME
----------------
SYS_STU#S#WF25Z#QAHIHE#MOFFMM
```

Dropping a column group: Use the `drop_extended_stats` function to delete a column group from a table. Table 13.4 lists the input parameters for this function:

Table 13.4. Parameters for the drop_extended_stats Function

Parameter	Description
owner	Schema owner. `NULL` indicates current schema.
tab_name	Name of the table to which the column group belongs.
extension	Name of the column group to be deleted.

For example, the following statement deletes a column group from the `customers` table:

```
exec
dbms_stats.drop_extended_stats('sh','customers','(cust_state_province,
country_id)');
```

Monitoring Column Groups: Use the dictionary table `user_stat_extensions` to obtain information about MultiColumn statistics:

```
Select extension_name, extension from user_stat_extensions
where table_name='CUSTOMERS';
EXTENSION_NAME                    EXTENSION
---------------------------------------------------------------------
SYS_STU#S#WF25Z#QAHIHE#MOFFMM("CUST_STATE_
PROVINCE","COUNTRY_ID")
```

Use the following query to find the number of distinct values and find whether a histogram has been created for a column group:

```
select e.extension col_group, t.num_distinct, t.histogram
  from user_stat_extensions e, user_tab_col_statistics t
  where e.extension_name=t.column_name
  and e.table_name=t.table_name
  and t.table_name='CUSTOMERS';

COL_GROUP              NUM_DISTINCT        HISTOGRAM
---------------------------------------------------------------------
("COUNTRY_ID","CUST_STATE_PROVINCE") 145
FREQUENCY
```

Gathering Statistics on Column Groups: The `METHOD_OPT` argument of the `DBMS_STATS` package enables you to gather statistics on column groups. If you set the value of this argument to `FOR ALL COLUMNS SIZE AUTO`, then the optimizer gathers statistics on all existing column groups. To collect statistics on a new column group, specify the group using `FOR COLUMNS`. The column group is automatically created as part of statistic gathering.

For example, the following statement creates a new column group for the `customers` table on the columns `cust_state_province`, `country_id` and gathers statistics (including histograms) on the entire table and the new column group:

```
EXEC DBMS_STATS.GATHER_TABLE_STATS
('SH','CUSTOMERS',METHOD_OPT =>'FOR ALL COLUMNS SIZE
SKEWONLY FOR COLUMNS (CUST_STATE_PROVINCE,COUNTRY_ID) SIZE
SKEWONLY');
```

The optimizer only uses MultiColumn statistics with equality predicates.

Expression Statistics: When a function is applied to a column in the `where` clause of a query (`function(col1)=constant`), the optimizer has no way of knowing how that function affects the selectivity of the column. By gathering expression statistics on the expression `function(col1)`, the optimizer obtains a more accurate selectivity value.

An example of such a function is:

```
SELECT COUNT(*)FROM  CUSTOMERS
WHERE  LOWER(CUST_STATE_PROVINCE)='CA';
```

Creating Expression Statistics: You can create statistics on an expression as part of the `gather_table_stats` procedure:

```
exec dbms_stats.gather_table_stats('sh','customers', method_opt =>'for
all columns size skewonly
 for columns (lower(cust_state_province)) size skewonly');
```

You can also use the `create_extended_statistics` function to accomplish this:

```
Select dbms_stats.create_extended_stats
(null,'customers','(lower(cust_state_province))')
from dual;
```

Monitoring Expression Statistics: Use the dictionary table `user_stat_extensions` to obtain information about expression statistics:

```
Select extension_name, extension
from user_stat_extensions
where table_name='CUSTOMERS';

EXTENSION_NAME                    EXTENSION
-----------------------------------------------------------------
SYS_STUBPHJSBRKOIK902YV3W8HOUE
(LOWER("CUST_STATE_PROVINCE"))
```

Use the following query to find the number of distinct values and find whether a histogram has been created:

```
select e.extension col_group, t.num_distinct, t.histogram
  from user_stat_extensions e, user_tab_col_statistics t
  where e.extension_name=t.column_name
  and t.table_name='CUSTOMERS';

COL_GROUP    [                NUM_DISTINCT      HISTOGRAM
-----------------------------------------------------------
(LOWER("CUST_STATE_PROVINCE")) 145       FREQUENCY
```

Dropping Expression Statistics: Use the drop_extended_stats function to delete expression statistics from a table:

```
exec dbms_stats. drop_extended_stats
(null,'customers','(lower(country_id))');
```

Determining Stale Statistics

You must regularly gather statistics on database objects as these database objects are modified over time. To determine whether a given database object needs new database statistics, Oracle Database provides a table monitoring facility. This monitoring is enabled by default when STATISTICS_LEVEL is set to TYPICAL or ALL.

Monitoring tracks the approximate number of INSERTs, UPDATEs, and DELETEs for that table and whether the table has been truncated since the last time statistics were gathered. You can access information about changes of tables in the USER_TAB_MODIFICATIONS view. Following a data-modification, there may be a few minutes delay while Oracle Database propagates the information to this view. Use the DBMS_STATS.FLUSH_DATABASE_MONITORING_INFO procedure to immediately reflect the outstanding monitored information kept in the memory.

The GATHER_DATABASE_STATS or GATHER_SCHEMA_STATS procedures gather new statistics for tables with stale statistics when the OPTIONS parameter is set to GATHER STALE or GATHER AUTO. If a monitored table has been modified more than 10%, then these statistics are considered stale and gathered again.

User-Defined Statistics

You can create user-defined optimizer statistics to support user-defined indexes and functions. When you associate a statistics type with a column or domain index, Oracle Database calls the statistics collection method in the statistics type whenever statistics are gathered for database objects.

You should gather new column statistics on a table after creating a function-based index to allow Oracle Database to collect column statistics equivalent information for the expression. You can perform this task by calling the statistics-gathering procedure with the METHOD_OPT argument set to FOR ALL HIDDEN COLUMNS.

Setting Preferences for Manual Statistics Gathering

You can use the DBMS_STATS.SET_*_PREFS procedures to set the default values for parameters used by the DBMS_STATS procedures that gather statistics. You can set a preference for each parameter at a table, schema, database, and global level, thus providing a fine granularity of control.

In previous releases, you used the DBMS_STATS.SET_PARM procedure to set the default parameter values. The scope of these changes was all operations that occurred after running SET_PARM. In Oracle Database 11*g*, SET_PARM is deprecated.

You can use the DBMS_STATS.SET_*_PREFS procedures to change the following parameters:

- AUTOSTATS_TARGET (SET_GLOBAL_PREFS only)
- CASCADE
- DEGREE
- ESTIMATE_PERCENT
- GRANULARITY
- INCREMENTAL
- METHOD_OPT
- NO_INVALIDATE
- PUBLISH
- STALE_PERCENT

Table 13.5 lists the DBMS_STATS procedures for setting preferences. Parameter values set in the DBMS_STAT.GATHER_*_STATS procedures overrule other settings. If a parameter has not been set, then the database checks for a table-level preference. If no table preference exists, then the database uses the GLOBAL preference.

Table 13.5. Setting Preferences for Gathering Statistics

Procedure	Purpose
SET_TABLE_PREFS	Enables you to change the default values of the parameters used by the DBMS_STATS.GATHER_*_STATS procedures for the specified table only.
SET_SCHEMA_PREFS	Enables you to change the default values of the parameters used by the DBMS_STATS.GATHER_*_STATS procedures for all existing objects in the specified schema. This procedure calls SET_TABLE_PREFS for each of the tables in the specified schema. Because it uses SET_TABLE_PREFS, calling SET_SCHEMA_PREFS does not affect any new objects created after it has been run. New objects use the GLOBAL_PREF values for all parameters.
SET_DATABASE_PREFS	Enables you to change the default values of the parameters used by the DBMS_STATS.GATHER_*_STATS procedures for all user-defined schemas in the database. You can include system-owned schemas such as SYS and SYSTEM by setting the ADD_SYS parameter to TRUE. This procedure calls SET_TABLE_PREFS for each table in the specified schema. Because it uses SET_TABLE_PREFS, calling SET_SCHEMA_PREFS does not affect any new objects created after it has been run. New objects use the GLOBAL_PREF values for all parameters.

SET_GLOBAL_PREFS	Enables you to change the default values of the parameters used by the DBMS_STATS.GATHER_*_STATS procedures for any object in the database that does not have an existing table preference. All parameters default to the global setting unless a table preference is set or the parameter is explicitly set in the DBMS_STATS.GATHER_*_STATS command. Changes made by this procedure *will* affect any new objects created after it has been run. New objects use the GLOBAL_PREF values for all parameters. With GLOBAL_PREFS, you can set a default value for the parameter AUTOSTAT_TARGET. This additional parameter controls which objects the automatic statistic gathering job running in the nightly maintenance window looks after. Possible values for this parameter are ALL, ORACLE, and AUTO (default).

When to Gather Statistics

When gathering statistics manually, you not only need to determine how to gather statistics, but also when and how often to gather new statistics.

For an application in which tables are incrementally modified, you may only need to gather new statistics every week or every month. The simplest way to gather statistics in these environments is to use a script or job scheduling tool to regularly run the GATHER_SCHEMA_STATS and GATHER_DATABASE_STATS procedures. The frequency of collection intervals should balance the task of providing accurate statistics for the optimizer against the processing overhead incurred by the statistics collection process.

For tables that are substantially modified in batch operations, such as with bulk loads, gather statistics on these tables as part of the batch operation. Call the DBMS_STATS procedure as soon as the load operation completes.

Sometimes only a single partition is modified. In such cases, you can gather statistics only on the modified partitions rather than on the entire table. However, gathering global statistics for the partitioned table may still be necessary.

Comparing Statistics with DBMS_STATS Functions

DBMS_STATS enables you to compare statistics for a table from two different sources. Table 13.6 lists the functions in the DBMS_STATS package for comparing statistics.

Table 13.6. Functions That Compare Statistics in the DBMS_STATS Package

Procedure	Compares
DIFF_TABLE_STATS_IN_PENDING	Pending statistics and statistics as of a timestamp or statistics from dictionary
DIFF_TABLE_STATS_IN_STATTAB	Statistics for a table from two different sources
DIFF_TABLE_STATS_IN_HISTORY	Statistics for a table from two timestamps in past and statistics as of that timestamp

The functions in Table 13.6 also compare the statistics of dependent objects such as indexes, columns, and partitions. They display statistics of the objects from both sources if the difference between those statistics exceeds a certain threshold. You can specify the threshold as an argument to the function, with a default of 10%. Oracle Database uses the statistics corresponding to the first source as basis for computing the differential percentage.

SYSTEM STATISTICS

System statistics describe the system's hardware characteristics, such as I/O and CPU performance and utilization, to the query optimizer. When choosing an execution plan, the optimizer estimates the I/O and CPU resources required for each query. System statistics enable the query optimizer to more accurately estimate I/O and CPU costs, enabling the query optimizer to choose a better execution plan.

When Oracle Database gathers system statistics, it analyzes system activity in a specified time period (workload statistics) or simulates a workload (noworkload statistics). The statistics are collected using the `DBMS_STATS.GATHER_SYSTEM_STATS` procedure. Oracle highly recommends that you gather system statistics.

You must have DBA privileges or `GATHER_SYSTEM_STATISTICS` role to update dictionary system statistics.

Table 13.7 lists the optimizer system statistics gathered by the `DBMS_STATS` package and the options for gathering or manually setting specific system statistics.

Table 13.7. Optimizer System Statistics in the DBMS_STAT Package

Parameter Name	Description	Initialization	Options for Gathering or Setting Statistics	Unit
`cpuspeedNW`	Represents noworkload CPU speed. CPU speed is the average number of CPU cycles in each second.	At system startup	Set `gathering_mode` = `NOWORKLOAD` or set statistics manually.	Millions/sec.
`ioseektim`	I/O seek time equals seek time + latency time + operating system overhead time.	At system startup 10 (default)	Set `gathering_mode` = `NOWORKLOAD` or set statistics manually.	ms
`iotfrspeed`	I/O transfer speed is the rate at which an Oracle database can read data in the single read request.	At system startup 4096 (default)	Set `gathering_mode` = `NOWORKLOAD` or set statistics manually.	Bytes/ms

`cpuspeed`	Represents workload CPU speed. CPU speed is the average number of CPU cycles in each second.	None	Set `gathering_mode = NOWORKLOAD, INTERVAL,` or `START|STOP`, or set statistics manually.	Millions/sec.
`maxthr`	Maximum I/O throughput is the maximum throughput that the I/O subsystem can deliver.	None	Set `gathering_mode = NOWORKLOAD, INTERVAL,` or `START|STOP`, or set statistics manually.	Bytes/sec.
`slavethr`	Slave I/O throughput is the average parallel slave I/O throughput.	None	Set `gathering_mode = INTERVAL` or `START|STOP`, or set statistics manually.	Bytes/sec.
`sreadtim`	Single block read time is the average time to read a single block randomly.	None	Set `gathering_mode = INTERVAL` or `START|STOP`, or set statistics manually.	ms
`mreadtim`	Multiblock read is the average time to read a multiblock sequentially.	None	Set `gathering_mode = INTERVAL` or `START|STOP`, or set statistics manually.	ms
`mbrc`	Multiblock count is the average multiblock read count sequentially.	None	Set `gathering_mode = INTERVAL` or `START|STOP`, or set statistics manually.	blocks

Unlike table, index, or column statistics, Oracle Database does not invalidate parsed SQL statements when system statistics are updated. All new SQL statements are parsed using new statistics.

Oracle Database offers two options for gathering system statistics:

- Workload Statistics
- Noworkload Statistics.

These options better facilitate the gathering process to the physical database and workload: when workload system statistics are gathered, noworkload system statistics are ignored. Noworkload system statistics are initialized to default values at the first database startup.

Workload Statistics

Workload statistics include the following:

- Single and multiblock read times
- `mbrc`
- CPU speed (`cpuspeed`)
- Maximum system throughput
- Average slave throughput.

single and multiblock read times, `mbrc`, CPU speed (`cpuspeed`), maximum system throughput, and average slave throughput. The database computes `sreadtim`, `mreadtim`, and `mbrc` by comparing the number of physical sequential and random reads between two points in time from the beginning to the end of a workload. The database implements these values through counters that change when the buffer cache completes synchronous read requests.

Because the counters are in the buffer cache, they include not only I/O delays, but also waits related to latch contention and task switching. Workload statistics thus depend on the activity the system had during the workload window. If system is I/O bound (both latch contention and I/O throughput), then the statistics reflect this situation and therefore promotes a less I/O-intensive plan after the database uses the statistics. Furthermore, workload statistics gathering does not generate additional overhead.

Gathering Workload Statistics

To gather workload statistics, perform either of the following tasks:

- Run the `DBMS_STATS.GATHER_SYSTEM_STATS('start')` procedure at the beginning of the workload window, then the `DBMS_STATS.GATHER_SYSTEM_STATS('stop')` procedure at the end of the workload window.
- Run `DBMS_STATS.GATHER_SYSTEM_STATS('interval', interval=>N)` where `N` is the number of minutes when statistics gathering is stopped automatically.

To delete system statistics, run `dbms_stats.delete_system_stats()`. Workload statistics are deleted and reset to the default noworkload statistics.

Multiblock Read Count

If you gather workload statistics, then the `mbrc` value gathered as part of the workload statistics is used to estimate the cost of a full table scan. However, during the gathering process of workload statistics, Oracle Database may not gather the `mbrc` and `mreadtim` values if no table scans are performed during serial workloads, as is often the case with OLTP systems. However, full table scans occur frequently on DSS systems but may run parallel and bypass the buffer cache. In such cases, Oracle Database still gathers the `sreadtim` value because the database performs index lookup using the buffer cache.

If Oracle Database cannot gather or validate gathered `mbrc` or `mreadtim` values, but has gathered `sreadtim` and `cpuspeed` values, then the database uses only the `sreadtim` and `cpuspeed` values for costing. In this case, the optimizer uses the value of the initialization parameter `DB_FILE_MULTIBLOCK_READ_COUNT` to cost a full table scan. However, if `DB_FILE_MULTIBLOCK_READ_COUNT` is not set or is set to 0 (zero), then the optimizer uses a value of 8 for costing.

Noworkload Statistics

Noworkload statistics consist of I/O transfer speed, I/O seek time, and CPU speed (`cpuspeednw`). The major difference between workload statistics and noworkload statistics lies in the gathering method.

Noworkload statistics gather data by submitting random reads against all data files, while workload statistics uses counters updated when database activity occurs. `ioseektim` represents the time it takes to position the disk head to read data. Its value usually varies from 5 ms to 15 ms, depending on disk rotation speed and the disk or RAID specification. The I/O transfer speed represents the speed at which one operating system process can read data from the I/O subsystem. Its value varies greatly, from a few MBs per second to hundreds of MBs per second. Oracle Database uses relatively conservative default settings for I/O transfer speed.

In Oracle Database 10*g*, Oracle Database uses noworkload statistics and the CPU cost model by default. The values of noworkload statistics are initialized to defaults at the first instance startup:

```
ioseektim = 10ms
iotrfspeed = 4096 bytes/ms
cpuspeednw = gathered value, varies based on system
```

If workload statistics are gathered, then Oracle Database ignores noworkload statistics and uses workload statistics instead.

Gathering Noworkload Statistics

To gather noworkload statistics, run `DBMS_STATS.GATHER_SYSTEM_STATS()` with no arguments. There is an overhead on the I/O system during the gathering process of noworkload statistics. The gathering process may take from a few seconds to several minutes, depending on I/O performance and database size.

The information is analyzed and verified for consistency. In some cases, the value of noworkload statistics may remain its default value. In such cases, repeat the statistics gathering process or set the value manually to values that the I/O system has according to its specifications by using the `DBMS_STATS.SET_SYSTEM_STATS` procedure.

MANAGING STATISTICS

This section includes the following topics:

- Pending Statistics
- Restoring Previous Versions of Statistics
- Exporting and Importing Statistics
- Restoring Statistics Versus Importing or Exporting Statistics
- Locking Statistics for a Table or Schema
- Setting Statistics
- Handling Missing Statistics.

Pending Statistics

Starting with Oracle Database 11*g* Release 2 (11.2), you have the following options when gathering statistics:

- Publish the statistics automatically at the end of the gather operation (default behavior)
- Save the new statistics saved as pending.

Saving the new statistics as pending allows you to validate the new statistics and publish them only if they are satisfactory.

To check whether the statistics will be automatically published as soon as they are gathered, use the DBMS_STATS package as follows:

```
SELECT DBMS_STATS.GET_PREFS('PUBLISH') PUBLISH FROM DUAL;
```

The preceding query returns either TRUE or FALSE. TRUE indicates that the statistics will be published as and when they are gathered, while FALSE indicates that the statistics will be kept pending.

The database stores published statistics in data dictionary views such as USER_TAB_STATISTICS and USER_IND_STATISTICS. The database stores pending statistics in views such as USER_TAB_PENDING_STATS and USER_IND_PENDING_STATS.

You can change the PUBLISH setting at either the schema or the table level. For example, to change the PUBLISH setting for the customers table in the SH schema, execute the statement:

```
Exec dbms_stats.set_table_prefs('SH', 'CUSTOMERS',
'PUBLISH', 'false');
```

Subsequently, when you gather statistics on the customers table, the statistics will not be automatically published when the gather job completes. Instead, the database stores the newly gathered statistics in the USER_TAB_PENDING_STATS table.

By default, the optimizer uses the published statistics stored in the data dictionary views. If you want the optimizer to use the newly collected pending statistics, then set the initialization parameter OPTIMIZER_USE_PENDING_STATISTICS to TRUE (the default value is FALSE), and run a workload against the table or schema:

```
alter session set optimizer_use_pending_statistics = TRUE;
```

The optimizer will use the pending statistics instead of the published statistics when compiling SQL statements. If the pending statistics are valid, then you can make them public by executing the following statement:

```
Exec dbms_stats.publish_pending_stats(null, null);
```

You can also publish the pending statistics for a specific database object. For example, by using the following statement:

```
Exec dbms_stats.publish_pending_stats('SH','CUSTOMERS');
```

If you do not want to publish the pending statistics, delete them by executing the following statement:

```
Exec dbms_stats.delete_pending_stats('SH','CUSTOMERS');
```

You can export pending statistics using dbms_stats.export_pending_stats function. Exporting pending statistics to a test system enables you to run a full workload against the new statistics.

Restoring Previous Versions of Statistics

Whenever statistics in dictionary are modified, old versions of statistics are saved automatically for future restoration. You can restore statistics using RESTORE procedures of DBMS_STATS package. These procedures use a time stamp as an argument and restore statistics as of that time stamp. This is useful in case newly collected statistics leads to some sub-optimal execution plans and the administrator wants to revert to the previous set of statistics.

There are dictionary views that display the time of statistics modifications. These views are useful in determining the time stamp to be used for statistics restoration.

- Catalog view DBA_OPTSTAT_OPERATIONS contain history of statistics operations performed at schema and database level using DBMS_STATS.
- The views *_TAB_STATS_HISTORY views (ALL, DBA, or USER) contain a history of table statistics modifications.

The database purges old statistics automatically at regular intervals based on the statistics history retention setting and the time of the recent analysis of the system. You can configure retention using the ALTER_STATS_HISTORY_RETENTION procedure of DBMS_STATS. The default value is 31 days, which means that you would be able to restore the optimizer statistics to any time in last 31 days.

Automatic purging is enabled when STATISTICS_LEVEL parameter is set to TYPICAL or ALL. If automatic purging is disabled, then you must purge the old versions of statistics manually using the PURGE_STATS procedure.

The other DBMS_STATS procedures related to restoring and purging statistics include:

- PURGE_STATS: This procedure can manually purge old versions beyond a time stamp.
- GET_STATS_HISTORY_RETENTION: This function can get the current statistics history retention value.
- GET_STATS_HISTORY_AVAILABILITY: This function gets the oldest time stamp where statistics history is available. Users cannot restore statistics to a time stamp older than the oldest time stamp.

When restoring previous versions of statistics, the following limitations apply:

- RESTORE procedures cannot restore user-defined statistics.
- Old versions of statistics are not stored when the ANALYZE command has been used for collecting statistics.

To remove all rows from a table when using DBMS_STATS, use TRUNCATE instead of dropping and re-creating the same table. When you drop a table, workload information used by the auto-histogram gathering feature and saved statistics history used by the RESTORE_*_STATS procedures is lost. Without this data, these features do not function properly.

Exporting and Importing Statistics

You can export and import statistics from the data dictionary to user-owned tables, enabling you to create multiple versions of statistics for the same schema. You can also copy statistics from one database to another database. You may want to do this to copy the statistics from a production database to a scaled-down test database.

Exporting and importing statistics is a distinct concept from the Data Pump Export and Import utilities.

Before exporting statistics, you first need to create a table for holding the statistics. The procedure DBMS_STATS.CREATE_STAT_TABLE creates the statistics table. After table creation, you can export statistics from the data dictionary into the statistics table using the DBMS_STATS.EXPORT_*_STATS procedures. You can then import statistics using the DBMS_STATS.IMPORT_*_STATS procedures.

Note that the optimizer does not use statistics stored in a user-owned table. The only statistics used by the optimizer are the statistics stored in the data dictionary. To have the optimizer use the statistics in a user-owned tables, you must import those statistics into the data dictionary using the statistics import procedures.

To move statistics from one database to another, you must first export the statistics on the first database, then copy the statistics table to the second database, using the Data Pump Export and Import utilities or other mechanisms, and finally import the statistics into the second database.

> The Data Pump Export and Import utilities export and import optimizer statistics from the database along with the table. When a column has system-generated names, Original Export does not export statistics with the data, but this restriction does not apply to Data Pump Export.

Restoring Statistics Versus Importing or Exporting Statistics

The functionality for restoring statistics is similar in some respects to the functionality of importing and exporting statistics. In general, use the restore capability when:

- You want to recover older versions of the statistics. For example, to restore the optimizer behavior to an earlier date.
- You want the database to manage the retention and purging of statistics histories.

You should use EXPORT/IMPORT_*_STATS procedures when:

- You want to experiment with multiple sets of statistics and change the values back and forth.
- You want to move the statistics from one database to another database. For example, moving statistics from a production system to a test system.
- You want to preserve a known set of statistics for a longer period than the desired retention date for restoring statistics.

Locking Statistics for a Table or Schema

Statistics for a table or schema can be locked. After statistics are locked, you can make no modifications to the statistics until the statistics have been unlocked. Locking procedures are useful in a static environment in which you want to guarantee that the statistics never change.

The DBMS_STATS package provides two procedures for locking (LOCK_SCHEMA_STATS and LOCK_TABLE_STATS) and two procedures for unlocking statistics (UNLOCK_SCHEMA_STATS and UNLOCK_TABLE_STATS).

Setting Statistics

You can set table, column, index, and system statistics using the SET_*_STATISTICS procedures. Setting statistics in the manner is not recommended, because inaccurate or inconsistent statistics can lead to poor performance.

Handling Missing Statistics

When Oracle Database encounters a table with missing statistics, the database dynamically gathers the necessary statistics needed by the optimizer. However, for certain types of tables, Oracle Database does not perform dynamic sampling. These include remote tables and external tables. In those cases and also when dynamic sampling has been disabled, the optimizer uses default values for its statistics, shown in Table 13.8 and Table 13.9.

Table 13.8. Default Table Values When Statistics are Missing

Table Statistic	Default Value Used by Optimizer
Cardinality	num_of_blocks * (block_size - cache_layer)/ avg_row_len
Average row length	100 bytes
Number of blocks	100 or actual value based on the extent map
Remote cardinality	2000 rows
Remote average row length	100 bytes

Table 13.9. Default Index Values When Statistics are Missing

Index Statistic	Default Value Used by Optimizer
Levels	1
Leaf blocks	25
Leaf blocks/key	1
Data blocks/key	1
Distinct keys	100
Clustering factor	800

ESTIMATING STATISTICS WITH DYNAMIC SAMPLING

With **dynamic sampling**, the database augments statistics by issuing recursive SQL to scan a small random sample of table blocks.

This section contains the following topics:

- Purpose of Dynamic Sampling
- Dynamic Sampling Concepts
- Setting Dynamic Sampling Levels.

Purpose of Dynamic Sampling

Dynamic sampling augments missing or insufficient optimizer statistics. Using dynamic sampling the optimizer can improve plans by making better estimates for predicate selectivity. Dynamic sampling can supplement statistics such as table block counts, applicable index block counts, table cardinalities (estimated number of rows), and relevant join column statistics.

Dynamic Sampling Concepts

Dynamic sampling is enabled in the database by default. You can disable the feature by setting the initialization parameter `OPTIMIZER_DYNAMIC_SAMPLING=0`.

Dynamic Sampling Levels

The **dynamic sampling level** controls both when dynamic sampling is triggered, and the size of the sample that the optimizer uses to gather the statistics. You can set the dynamic sampling level using either the `OPTIMIZER_DYNAMIC_SAMPLING` initialization parameter or a SQL statement hint.

Table 13.10 describes the levels. The default level is 2.

Table 13.10 Dynamic Sampling Levels

Level	When the Optimizer Uses Dynamic Sampling	Sample Size (Blocks)
0	Do not use dynamic sampling	n/a
1	Use dynamic sampling for all tables that have not been analyzed, but only if the following criteria are met: • There is at least 1 unanalyzed, nonpartitioned table in the query. • This unanalyzed table has no indexes. • This unanalyzed table has more blocks than the number of blocks that would be used for dynamic sampling of this table.	32
2	Use dynamic sampling if least one table in the statement has no statistics.	64
3	Use dynamic sampling if any of the following conditions is true: • The statement meets level 2 criteria. • The statement has one or more expressions used in the where clause predicates, for example, `WHERE SUBSTR(CUSTLASTNAME,1,3)`.	64
4	Use dynamic sampling if any of the following conditions is true: • The statement meets level 3 criteria. • The statement uses complex predicates (an `OR` or `AND` operator between multiple predicates on the same table).	64
5	Use dynamic sampling if the statement meets level 4 criteria.	128
6	Use dynamic sampling if the statement meets level 4 criteria.	256
7	Use dynamic sampling if the statement meets level 4 criteria.	512
8	Use dynamic sampling if the statement meets level 4 criteria.	1024
9	Use dynamic sampling if the statement meets level 4 criteria.	4086
10	Use dynamic sampling for all statements.	All blocks

When the Optimizer Uses Dynamic Sampling

During compilation, the optimizer decides whether to use dynamic sampling based on a number of factors, including whether the statements use parallel processing or serial processing.

For parallel statements, the optimizer automatically decides whether to use dynamic sampling and which level to use. The decision depends on the size of the tables and the complexity of the predicates. The optimizer expects parallel statements to be resource-intensive, so the additional overhead at compile time is worth it to ensure the best plan. The database ignores the `OPTIMIZER_DYNAMIC_SAMPLING` setting unless set to a nondefault value, in which case the value is honored.

For serially processed SQL statements, the dynamic sampling level depends on the value of the `OPTIMIZER_DYNAMIC_SAMPLING` parameter and is not triggered automatically by the optimizer. Serial statements are typically short-running, so that any overhead at compile time could have a huge impact on their performance.

In both the serial and parallel cases, the database performs dynamic sampling when existing statistics are not sufficient:

- Missing statistics.
  When one or more of the tables in the query do not have statistics, the optimizer gathers basic statistics on these tables before optimization. In this case, the statistics are not as high-quality or as complete as the statistics gathered using the DBMS_STATS package. This tradeoff is made to limit the impact on the compile time of the statement.
- Collected statistics cannot be used or are likely to lead to poor estimates.
  For example, a statement may contain a complex predicate expression, but extended statistics are not available. Extended statistics help the optimizer get good quality cardinality estimates for complex predicate expressions. Dynamic sampling can compensate for the lack of extended statistics.

The database does not use dynamic sampling for queries that contain the AS OF clause.

If no rows have been inserted, deleted, or updated in the table being sampled, then dynamic sampling is repeatable. This means that the optimizer generates the same statistics each time you run dynamic sampling against the table.

Setting Dynamic Sampling Levels

In general, the best practice is not to incur the cost of dynamic sampling for queries whose compile times must be as fast as possible, for example, unrepeated OLTP queries. Dynamic sampling can be beneficial under any of the following conditions:

- You know you are getting a bad execution plan because of complex predicates.
- The sampling time is a small fraction of total execution time for the query.
- The query is executed many times.

When setting the dynamic sampling level, the best practice is to use an ALTER SESSION statement to set the value for OPTIMIZER_DYNAMIC_SAMPLING parameter. Determining a system-wide setting that would be beneficial to all SQL statements can be difficult.

Assumptions

The following tutorial assumes the following:

- You want correct selectivity estimates for the following query, which has WHERE clause predicates on two correlated columns:
  ```
  SELECT * FROM   sh.customers WHERE  cust_city='Los
  Angeles' AND    cust_state_province='CA';
  ```
- The preceding query uses serial processing.
- The sh.customers table contains 932 rows that meet the conditions in the query.
- You have gathered statistics on the sh.customers table.
- You created an index on the cust_city and cust_state_province columns.
- The OPTIMIZER_DYNAMIC_SAMPLING initialization parameter is set to the default level of 2.

To set the dynamic sampling level:

1. You explain the plan for the query as follows:

```
EXPLAIN PLAN FOR
  SELECT *  FROM   sh.customers
  WHERE  cust_city='Los Angeles'
  AND   cust_state_province='CA';
```

The table contains 932 rows that meet the conditions, but the optimizer estimates 53, as shown in the explained plan:

```
------------------------------------------------------------------------
| Id  | Operation          | Name                | Rows  |
Bytes | Cost (%CPU)| Time|
------------------------------------------------------------------------
| 0| SELECT STATEMENT                    |                   |
53| 9593|53(0)|00:00:01|
| 1|  TABLE ACCESS BY INDEX ROWID|CUSTOMERS          |
53| 9593|53(0)|00:00:01|
|*2|   INDEX RANGE SCAN           |CUST_CITY_STATE_IND|
53| 9593| 3(0)|00:00:01|
------------------------------------------------------------------------

Predicate Information (identified by operation id):
------------------------------------------------------------------------

  2 - access("CUST_CITY"='Los Angeles' AND
"CUST_STATE_PROVINCE"='CA')
```

If dynamic sampling had been used, the plan output would have indicated this fact in a note. The optimizer did not use sampling because standard statistics exist and the dynamic sampling level is 2.

2. You set dynamic sampling to level 4 in the session using the following statement:
   `ALTER SESSION SET OPTIMIZER_DYNAMIC_SAMPLING=4;`
3. You explain the plan again:

```
EXPLAIN PLAN FOR
  SELECT *  FROM  sh.customers
  WHERE  cust_city='Los Angeles'
  AND   cust_state_province='CA';
```

The new plan shows a better estimate of the number of rows:

```
PLAN_TABLE_OUTPUT
------------------------------------------------------------------
Plan hash value: 2008213504

------------------------------------------------------------------
| Id  | Operation         | Name      | Rows  | Bytes
| Cost (%CPU)| Time     |
------------------------------------------------------------------
|   0 | SELECT STATEMENT  |           |   932 |
271K|   406   (1)| 00:00:05 |
|*  1 |  TABLE ACCESS FULL| CUSTOMERS |   932 |
271K|   406   (1)| 00:00:05 |
------------------------------------------------------------------
Predicate Information (identified by operation id):
------------------------------------------------------------------
    1 - filter("CUST_CITY"='Los Angeles' AND
"CUST_STATE_PROVINCE"='CA')
```

Dynamic sampling used for this statement (level=4).

The note at the bottom of the plan indicates that the sampling level is 4. The use of the additional statistics leads the optimizer to produce a better estimate for the number of rows: 932 rather than 53.

VIEWING STATISTICS

This section discusses:

- Statistics on Tables, Indexes and Columns
- Viewing Histograms.

Statistics on Tables, Indexes and Columns

The database stores statistics on tables, indexes, and columns in the data dictionary. To view statistics in the data dictionary, query the appropriate data dictionary view (USER, ALL, or DBA). These views include the following:

- DBA_TABLES and DBA_OBJECT_TABLES
- DBA_TAB_STATISTICS and DBA_TAB_COL_STATISTICS
- DBA_TAB_HISTOGRAMS
- DBA_TAB_COLS
- DBA_COL_GROUP_COLUMNS
- DBA_INDEXES and DBA_IND_STATISTICS
- DBA_CLUSTERS
- DBA_TAB_PARTITIONS and DBA_TAB_SUBPARTITIONS
- DBA_IND_PARTITIONS and DBA_IND_SUBPARTITIONS
- DBA_PART_COL_STATISTICS
- DBA_PART_HISTOGRAMS
- DBA_SUBPART_COL_STATISTICS
- DBA_SUBPART_HISTOGRAMS

Viewing Histograms

You can store column statistics as **histograms.** These histograms provide accurate estimates of the distribution of column data. Histograms provide improved selectivity estimates in the presence of data skew, resulting in optimal execution plans with nonuniform data distributions.

Oracle Database uses the following types of histograms for column statistics:

- Height-Balanced Histograms
- Frequency Histograms.

The database stores this type of histogram in the HISTOGRAM column of the *TAB_COL_STATISTICS views (USER and DBA). This column can have values of HEIGHT BALANCED, FREQUENCY, or NONE.

Height-Balanced Histograms

In a **height-balanced histogram**, the column values are divided into buckets so that each bucket contains approximately the same number of rows. The histogram shows where the endpoints fall in the range of values.

Consider a column my_col with values between 1 and 100 and a histogram with 10 buckets. If the data in my_col is uniformly distributed, then the histogram looks similar to Figure 13.1, where the numbers are the endpoint values. For example, the 7th bucket has rows with values between 60 and 70.

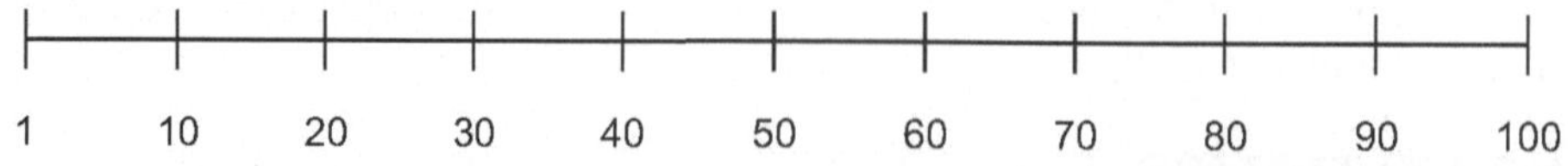

Figure 13.1. Height-Balanced Histogram with Uniform Distribution

The number of rows in each bucket is 10% the total number of rows. In this example of uniform distribution, 40% of the rows have values between 60 and 100.

If the data is not uniformly distributed, then the histogram may look like Figure 13.2. In this case, most of the rows have the value 5 for the column. Only 10% of the rows have values between 60 and 100.

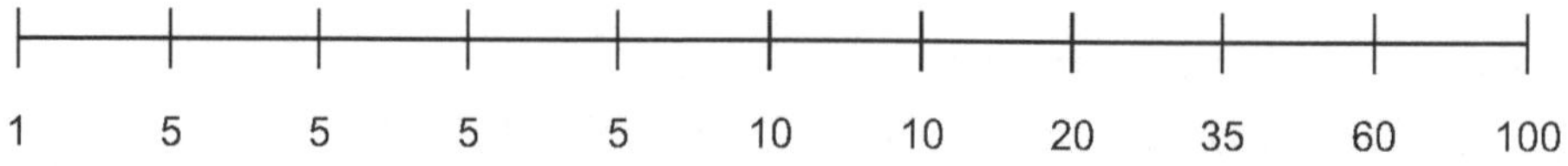

Figure 13.2. Height-Balanced Histogram with Non-Uniform Distribution

You can view height-balanced histograms using the USER_TAB_HISTOGRAMS table, as shown in.

Example 13.1: Viewing Height-Balanced Histogram Statistics

```
BEGIN
  DBMS_STATS.GATHER_table_STATS (
    OWNNAME     => 'OE',
    TABNAME     => 'INVENTORIES',
   METHOD_OPT => 'FOR COLUMNS SIZE 10 quantity_on_hand' );
END;
/

SELECT COLUMN_NAME, NUM_DISTINCT, NUM_BUCKETS, HISTOGRAM
FROM  USER_TAB_COL_STATISTICS
WHERE  TABLE_NAME = 'INVENTORIES' AND COLUMN_NAME =
'QUANTITY_ON_HAND';

COLUMN_NAME   NUM_DISTINCT NUM_BUCKETS      HISTOGRAM
-------------------------------------------------------------------
QUANTITY_ON_HAND                          237          10
HEIGHT BALANCED

SELECT ENDPOINT_NUMBER, ENDPOINT_VALUE
FROM  USER_TAB_HISTOGRAMS
WHERE  TABLE_NAME = 'INVENTORIES' AND COLUMN_NAME =
'QUANTITY_ON_HAND' ORDER BY ENDPOINT_NUMBER;
```

```
ENDPOINT_NUMBER     ENDPOINT_VALUE
---------------     --------------
              0                  0
              1                 27
              2                 42
              3                 57
              4                 74
              5                 98
              6                123
              7                149
              8                175
              9                202
             10                353
```

In the query output, one row (1.10) corresponds to each bucket in the histogram. Oracle Database added a special 0th bucket to this histogram because the value in the 1st bucket (27) is not the minimum value for the `quantity_on_hand` column. The 0th bucket holds the minimum value of 0 for `quantity_on_hand`.

Frequency Histograms

In a **frequency histogram**, each value of the column corresponds to a single bucket of the histogram. Each bucket contains the number of occurrences of this single value. For example, suppose that 36 rows contain the value 1 for column `warehouse_id`. The endpoint value 1 has an endpoint number 36.

The database automatically creates frequency histograms instead of height-balanced histograms under the following conditions:

- The number of distinct values is less than or equal to the number of histogram buckets specified (up to 254).
- It is *not* true that each column value repeats only once.

You can view frequency histograms using the `USER_TAB_HISTOGRAMS` view, as shown in .

Example 13.2: Viewing Frequency Histogram Statistics

```
BEGIN
  DBMS_STATS.GATHER_TABLE_STATS (
    OWNNAME    => 'OE',
    TABNAME    => 'INVENTORIES',
   METHOD_OPT => 'FOR COLUMNS SIZE 20 warehouse_id' );
END;
/

SELECT COLUMN_NAME, NUM_DISTINCT, NUM_BUCKETS, HISTOGRAM
FROM  USER_TAB_COL_STATISTICS WHERE  TABLE_NAME = 'INVENTORIES' AND
COLUMN_NAME = 'WAREHOUSE_ID';

COLUMN_NAME      NUM_DISTINCT NUM_BUCKETS HISTOGRAM
----------------------------------------- ----------  --
WAREHOUSE_ID                           9          9
FREQUENCY
```

```
SELECT   ENDPOINT_NUMBER, ENDPOINT_VALUE
FROM     USER_TAB_HISTOGRAMS
WHERE    TABLE_NAME = 'INVENTORIES' AND COLUMN_NAME =
'WAREHOUSE_ID' ORDER BY ENDPOINT_NUMBER;

ENDPOINT_NUMBER ENDPOINT_VALUE
--------------- --------------
             36              1
            213              2
            261              3
            370              4
            484              5
            692              6
            798              7
            984              8
           1112              9
```

In, the first bucket is for the `warehouse_id` of 1. The value appears 36 times in the table, as confirmed by the following query:

```
oe@PRODs> SELECT COUNT(*) FROM inventories WHERE
warehouse_id = 1;

  COUNT(*)
----------
        36
```

14 Using Indexes and Clusters

Learning Objectives

This chapter provides an overview of data access methods using indexes and clusters that can enhance or degrade performance.

This chapter contains the following sections:

- Understanding Index Performance
- Using Function-Based Indexes for Performance
- Using Partitioned Indexes for Performance
- Using Index-Organized Tables for Performance
- Using Bitmap Indexes for Performance
- Using Bitmap Join Indexes for Performance
- Using Domain Indexes for Performance
- Using Table Clusters for Performance
- Using Hash Clusters for Performance

Indexes are optional structures associated with tables and clusters that allow SQL queries to execute more quickly against a table. Just as the index in this manual helps you locate information faster than if there were no index, an Oracle Database index provides a faster access path to table data. You can use indexes without rewriting any queries. Your results are the same, but you see them more quickly.

Oracle Database provides several indexing schemes that provide complementary performance functionality. These are:

- B-tree indexes: the default and the most common
- B-tree cluster indexes: defined specifically for cluster
- Hash cluster indexes: defined specifically for a hash cluster
- Global and local indexes: relate to partitioned tables and indexes
- Reverse key indexes: most useful for Oracle Real Application Clusters applications
- Bitmap indexes: compact; work best for columns with a small set of values
- Function-based indexes: contain the precomputed value of a function/expression
- Domain indexes: specific to an application or cartridge.

Indexes are logically and physically independent of the data in the associated table. Being independent structures, they require storage space. You can create or drop an index without affecting the base tables, database applications, or other indexes. The database automatically maintains indexes when you insert, update, and delete rows of the associated table. If you drop an index, all applications continue to work. However, access to previously indexed data might be slower.

Create Indexes After Inserting Table Data

Data is often inserted or loaded into a table using either the SQL*Loader or an import utility. It is more efficient to create an index for a table after inserting or loading the data. If you create one or more indexes before loading data, the database then must update every index as each row is inserted.

Creating an index on a table that already has data requires sort space. Some sort space comes from memory allocated for the index creator. The amount for each user is determined by the initialization parameter `SORT_AREA_SIZE`. The database also swaps sort information to and from temporary segments that are only allocated during the index creation in the user's temporary tablespace.

Under certain conditions, data can be loaded into a table with SQL*Loader direct-path load and an index can be created as data is loaded.

Index the Correct Tables and Columns

Use the following guidelines for determining when to create an index:

- Create an index if you frequently want to retrieve less than 15% of the rows in a large table. The percentage varies greatly according to the relative speed of a table scan and how the distribution of the row data in relation to the index key. The faster the table scan, the lower the percentage; the more clustered the row data, the higher the percentage.
- To improve performance on joins of multiple tables, index columns used for joins.

Primary and unique keys automatically have indexes, but you might want to create an index on a foreign key.

- Small tables do not require indexes. If a query is taking too long, then the table might have grown from small to large.

Columns that are Suitable for Indexing

Some columns are strong candidates for indexing. Columns with one or more of the following characteristics are candidates for indexing:

- Values are relatively unique in the column.
- There is a wide range of values (good for regular indexes).
- There is a small range of values (good for bitmap indexes).
- The column contains many nulls, but queries often select all rows having a value. In this case, use the following phrase:
- `WHERE COL_X > -9.99 * power(10,125)`

  Using the preceding phrase is preferable to:

  `WHERE COL_X IS NOT NULL`

  This is because the first uses an index on `COL_X` (assuming that `COL_X is a numeric` column).

Columns that are Not Suitable for Indexing

Columns with the following characteristics are less suitable for indexing:

- There are many nulls in the column and you do not search on the not null values.

`LONG` and `LONG RAW` columns cannot be indexed.

Virtual Columns

You can create unique or non-unique indexes on virtual columns.

Order Index Columns for Performance

The order of columns in the `CREATE INDEX` statement can affect query performance. In general, specify the most frequently used columns first.

If you create a single index across columns to speed up queries that access, for example, `col1`, `col2`, and `col3`; then queries that access just `col1`, or that access just `col1` and `col2`, are also speeded up. But a query that accessed just `col2`, just `col3`, or just `col2` and `col3` does not use the index.

Limit the Number of Indexes for Each Table

A table can have any number of indexes. However, the more indexes there are, the more overhead is incurred as the table is modified. Specifically, when rows are inserted or deleted, all indexes on the table must be updated as well. Also, when a column is updated, all indexes that contain the column must be updated.

Thus, there is a trade-off between the speed of retrieving data from a table and the speed of updating the table. For example, if a table is primarily read-only, having more indexes can be useful; but if a table is heavily updated, having fewer indexes could be preferable.

Drop Indexes that are no Longer Required

Consider dropping an index if:

- It does not speed up queries. The table could be very small, or there could be many rows in the table but very few index entries.
- The queries in your applications do not use the index.
- The index must be dropped before being rebuilt.

Indexes and Deferred Segment Creation

Index segment creation is deferred when the associated table defers segment creation. This is because index segment creation reflects the behavior of the table it is associated with.

Estimate Index Size and Set Storage Parameters

Estimating the size of an index before creating one can facilitate better disk space planning and management. You can use the combined estimated size of indexes, along with estimates for tables, the undo tablespace, and redo log files, to determine the amount of disk space that is required to hold an intended database. From these estimates, you can make correct hardware purchases and other decisions.

Use the estimated size of an individual index to better manage the disk space that the index uses. When an index is created, you can set appropriate storage parameters and improve I/O performance of applications that use the index. For example, assume that you estimate the maximum size of an index before creating it. If you then set the storage parameters when you create the index, fewer extents are allocated for the table data segment, and all of the index data is stored in a relatively contiguous section of disk space. This decreases the time necessary for disk I/O operations involving this index.

The maximum size of a single index entry is approximately one-half the data block size.

Storage parameters of an index segment created for the index used to enforce a primary key or unique key constraint can be set in either of the following ways:

- In the `ENABLE ... USING INDEX` clause of the `CREATE TABLE` or `ALTER TABLE` statement
- In the `STORAGE` clause of the `ALTER INDEX` statement.

Specify the Tablespace for Each Index

Indexes can be created in any tablespace. An index can be created in the same or different tablespace as the table it indexes. If you use the same tablespace for a table and its index, it can be more convenient to perform database maintenance (such as tablespace or file backup) or to ensure application availability. All the related data is always online together.

Using different tablespaces (on different disks) for a table and its index produces better performance than storing the table and index in the same tablespace. Disk contention is reduced. But, if you use different tablespaces for a table and its index and one tablespace is offline (containing either data or index), then the statements referencing that table are not guaranteed to work.

Consider Parallelizing Index Creation

You can parallelize index creation, much the same as you can parallelize table creation. Because multiple processes work together to create the index, the database can create the index more quickly than if a single server process created the index sequentially.

When creating an index in parallel, storage parameters are used separately by each query server process. Therefore, an index created with an INITIAL value of 5M and a parallel degree of 12 consumes at least 60M of storage during index creation.

Consider Creating Indexes with NOLOGGING

You can create an index and generate minimal redo log records by specifying `NOLOGGING` in the `CREATE INDEX` statement.

Because indexes created using `NOLOGGING` are not archived, perform a backup after you create the index.

Creating an index with `NOLOGGING` has the following benefits:

- Space is saved in the redo log files.
- The time it takes to create the index is decreased.
- Performance improves for parallel creation of large indexes.

In general, the relative performance improvement is greater for larger indexes created without `LOGGING` than for smaller ones. Creating small indexes without LOGGING has little effect on the time it takes to create an index. However, for larger indexes the performance improvement can be significant, especially when you are also parallelizing the index creation.

Understand When to Use Unusable or Invisible Indexes

Use unusable or invisible indexes when you want to improve the performance of bulk loads, test the effects of removing an index before dropping it, or otherwise suspend the use of an index by the optimizer.

Unusable Indexes

An **unusable index** is ignored by the optimizer and is not maintained by DML. One reason to make an index unusable is to improve bulk load performance. (Bulk loads go more quickly if the database does not need to maintain indexes when inserting rows.) Instead of dropping the index and later re-creating it, which requires you to recall the exact parameters of the `CREATE INDEX` statement, you can make the index unusable, and then rebuild it.

You can create an index in the unusable state, or you can mark an existing index or index partition unusable. In some cases the database may mark an index unusable, such as when a failure occurs while building the index. When one partition of a partitioned index is marked unusable, the other partitions of the index remain valid.

An unusable index or index partition must be rebuilt, or dropped and re-created, before it can be used. Truncating a table makes an unusable index valid.

Beginning with Oracle Database 11g Release 2, when you make an existing index unusable, its index segment is dropped.

The functionality of unusable indexes depends on the setting of the `SKIP_UNUSABLE_INDEXES` initialization parameter. When `SKIP_UNUSABLE_INDEXES` is `TRUE` (the default), then:

- DML statements against the table proceed, but unusable indexes are not maintained.
- DML statements terminate with an error if there are any unusable indexes that are used to enforce the `UNIQUE` constraint.
- For nonpartitioned indexes, the optimizer does not consider any unusable indexes when creating an access plan for `SELECT` statements. The only exception is when an index is explicitly specified with the `INDEX()` hint.
- For a partitioned index where one or more of the partitions are unusable, the optimizer does not consider the index if it cannot determine at query compilation time if any of the index partitions can be pruned. This is true for both partitioned and nonpartitioned tables. The only exception is when an index is explicitly specified with the `INDEX()` hint.

When `SKIP_UNUSABLE_INDEXES` is `FALSE`, then:

- If any unusable indexes or index partitions are present, any DML statements that would cause those indexes or index partitions to be updated are terminated with an error.
- For `SELECT` statements, if an unusable index or unusable index partition is present but the optimizer does not choose to use it for the access plan, the statement proceeds. However, if the optimizer does choose to use the unusable index or unusable index partition, the statement terminates with an error.

Invisible Indexes

Beginning with Oracle Database 11g Release 1, you can create invisible indexes or make an existing index invisible. An **invisible index** is ignored by the optimizer unless you explicitly set the `OPTIMIZER_USE_INVISIBLE_INDEXES` initialization parameter to `TRUE` at the session or system level. Unlike unusable indexes, an invisible index is maintained during DML statements. Although you can make a partitioned index invisible, you cannot make an individual index partition invisible while leaving the other partitions visible.Using invisible indexes, you can do the following:

- Test the removal of an index before dropping it.
- Use temporary index structures for certain operations or modules of an application without affecting the overall application.

Consider Costs and Benefits of Coalescing or Rebuilding Indexes

Improper sizing or increased growth can produce index fragmentation. To eliminate or reduce fragmentation, you can rebuild or coalesce the index. But before you perform either task weigh the costs and benefits of each option and choose the one that works best for your situation. Table 14.1 is a comparison of the costs and benefits associated with rebuilding and coalescing indexes.

Table 14.1. Costs and Benefits of Coalescing or Rebuilding Indexes

Rebuild Index	Coalesce Index
Quickly moves index to another tablespace	Cannot move index to another table space
Higher costs: requires more disk space	Lower costs: does not require more disk space
Creates new tree, shrinks height if applicable	Coalesces leaf blocks within same branch of tree
Enables you to quickly change storage and tablespace parameters without having to drop the original index.	Quickly frees up index leaf blocks for use.

In situations where you have B-tree index leaf blocks that can be freed up for reuse, you can merge those leaf blocks using the following statement:

```
ALTER INDEX vmoore COALESCE;
```

Figure 14.1 illustrates the effect of an `ALTER INDEX COALESCE` on the index `vmoore`. Before performing the operation, the first two leaf blocks are 50% full. Therefore, you have an opportunity to reduce fragmentation and completely fill the first block, while freeing up the second.

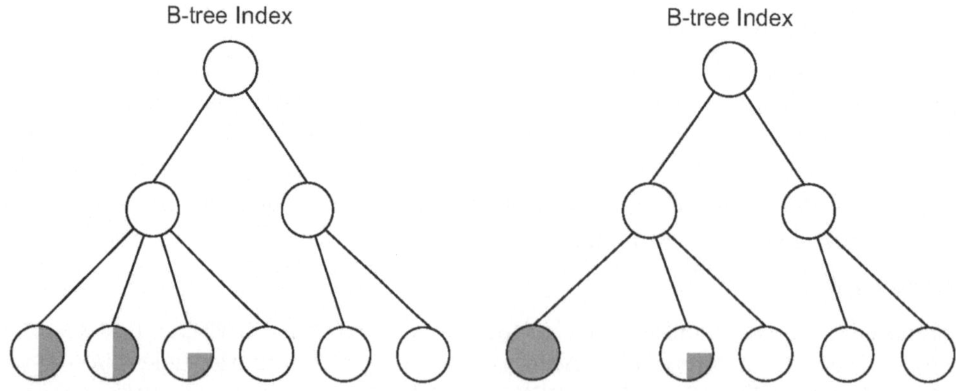

Figure 14.1. Coalescing Indexes

Consider Cost Before Disabling or Dropping Constraints

Because unique and primary keys have associated indexes, you should factor in the cost of dropping and creating indexes when considering whether to disable or drop a `UNIQUE` or `PRIMARY KEY` constraint. If the associated index for a `UNIQUE` key or `PRIMARY KEY` constraint is extremely large, you can save time by leaving the constraint enabled rather than dropping and recreating the large index. You also have the option of explicitly specifying that you want to keep or drop the index when dropping or disabling a `UNIQUE` or `PRIMARY KEY` constraint.

UNDERSTANDING INDEX PERFORMANCE

This section describes the following:

- Tuning the Logical Structure
- Index Tuning using the SQLAccess Advisor
- Choosing Columns and Expressions to Index
- Choosing Composite Indexes
- Writing Statements That Use Indexes
- Writing Statements That Avoid Using Indexes
- Recreating Indexes
- Using Nonunique Indexes to Enforce Uniqueness
- Using Enabled Novalidated Constraints.

Tuning the Logical Structure

Although query optimization helps avoid the use of nonselective indexes within query execution, the SQL engine must continue to maintain all indexes defined against a table, regardless of whether queries make use of them. Index maintenance can present a significant CPU and I/O resource demand in any write-intensive application. In other words, do not build indexes unless necessary.

To maintain optimal performance, drop indexes that an application is not using. You can find indexes that are not being used by using the `ALTER INDEX MONITORING USAGE` functionality over a period that is representative of your workload. This monitoring feature records whether an index has been used. If you find that an index has not been used, then drop it. Make sure you are monitoring a representative workload to avoid dropping an index which is used, but not by the workload you sampled.

Also, indexes within an application sometimes have uses that are not immediately apparent from a survey of statement execution plans. An example of this is a foreign key index on a parent table, which prevents share locks from being taken out on a child table.

If you are deciding whether to create new indexes to tune statements, then you can also use the `EXPLAIN PLAN` statement to determine whether the optimizer chooses to use these indexes when the application is run. If you create new indexes to tune a statement that is currently parsed, then Oracle Database invalidates the statement.

When the statement is next parsed, the optimizer automatically chooses a new execution plan that could potentially use the new index. If you create new indexes on a remote database to tune a distributed statement, then the optimizer considers these indexes when the statement is next parsed.

Note that creating an index to tune one statement can affect the optimizer's choice of execution plans for other statements. For example, if you create an index to be used by one statement, then the optimizer can choose to use that index for other statements in the application as well. For this reason, reexamine the application's performance and execution plans, and rerun the SQL trace facility after you have tuned those statements that you initially identified for tuning.

Index Tuning Using the SQLAccess Advisor

SQL Access Advisor is an alternative to manually determining which indexes are required. This advisor recommends a set of indexes when invoked from Oracle Enterprise Manager or run through the `DBMS_ADVISOR` package APIs. SQL Access Advisor either recommends using a workload or it generates a hypothetical workload for a specified schema.

Various workload sources are available, such as the current contents of the SQL cache, a user-defined set of SQL statements, or a SQL tuning set. Given a workload, SQL Access Advisor generates a set of recommendations from which you can select the indexes to be implemented. An implementation script is provided that can be executed manually or automatically through Oracle Enterprise Manager.

Choosing Columns and Expressions to Index

A key is a column or expression on which you can build an index. Follow these guidelines for choosing keys to index:

- Consider indexing keys that appear frequently in `WHERE` clauses.
- Consider indexing keys that frequently join tables in SQL statements.
- Choose index keys that have high selectivity. The selectivity of an index is the percentage of rows in a table having the same value for the indexed key. An index's selectivity is optimal if few rows have the same value.

Oracle Database automatically creates indexes, or uses existing indexes, on the keys and expressions of unique and primary keys that you define with integrity constraints.

Indexing low selectivity columns can be helpful when the data distribution is skewed so that one or two values occur much less often than other values.

- Do not use standard B-tree indexes on keys or expressions with few distinct values. Such keys or expressions usually have poor selectivity and therefore do not optimize performance unless the frequently selected key values appear less frequently than the other key values. You can use bitmap indexes effectively in such cases, unless the index is modified frequently, as in a high concurrency OLTP application.
- Do not index frequently modified columns. `UPDATE` statements that modify indexed columns and `INSERT` and `DELETE` statements that modify indexed tables take longer than if there were no index. Such SQL statements must modify data in indexes and data in tables. They also create additional undo and redo.
- Do not index keys that appear only in `WHERE` clauses with functions or operators. A `WHERE` clause that uses a function, other than `MIN` or `MAX`, or an operator with an indexed key does not make available the access path that uses the index except with function-based indexes.
- Consider indexing foreign keys of referential integrity constraints in cases in which a large number of concurrent `INSERT, UPDATE,` and `DELETE` statements access the parent and child tables. Such an index allows `UPDATEs` and `DELETEs` on the parent table without share locking the child table.
- When choosing to index a key, consider whether the performance gain for queries is worth the performance loss for `INSERTs, UPDATEs,` and `DELETEs` and the use of the space required to store the index. You might want to experiment by comparing the processing times of the SQL statements with and without indexes. You can measure processing time with the SQL trace facility.

Choosing Composite Indexes

A composite index contains multiple key columns. Composite indexes can provide additional advantages over single-column indexes:

- Improved selectivity.
  Sometimes you can combine two or more columns or expressions, each with poor selectivity, to form a composite index with higher selectivity.
- Reduced I/O.
  If all columns selected by a query are in a composite index, then Oracle Database can return these values from the index without accessing the table.

A SQL statement can use an access path involving a composite index when the statement contains constructs that use a leading portion of the index.

This is no longer the case with index skip scans.

A leading portion of an index is a set of one or more columns that were specified first and consecutively in the list of columns in the `CREATE INDEX` statement that created the index. Consider this `CREATE INDEX` statement:

```
CREATE INDEX comp_ind
ON table1(x, y, z);
```

- `x, xy,` and `xyz` combinations of columns are leading portions of the index
- `yz, y,` and `z` combinations of columns are *not* leading portions of the index.

Choosing Keys for Composite Indexes

Follow these guidelines for choosing keys for composite indexes:

- Consider creating a composite index on keys that appear together frequently in `WHERE` clause conditions combined with `AND` operators, especially if their combined selectivity is better than the selectivity of either key individually.
- If several queries select the same set of keys based on one or more key values, then consider creating a composite index containing all of these keys.

Of course, consider the guidelines associated with the general performance advantages and trade-offs of indexes described in the previous sections.

Ordering Keys for Composite Indexes

Follow these guidelines for ordering keys in composite indexes:

- Create the index so the keys used in `WHERE` clauses make up a leading portion.
- If some keys appear in `WHERE` clauses more frequently, then create the index so that the more frequently selected keys make up a leading portion to allow the statements that use only these keys to use the index.
- If all keys appear in `WHERE` clauses equally often but the data is physically ordered on one of the keys, then place this key first in the composite index.

Writing Statements that Use Indexes

Even after you create an index, the optimizer cannot use an access path that uses the index simply because the index exists. The optimizer can choose such an access path for a SQL statement only if it contains a construct that makes the access path available. To allow the query optimizer the option of using an index access path, ensure that the statement contains a construct that makes such an access path available.

Writing Statements that Avoid Using Indexes

In some cases, you might want to prevent a SQL statement from using an access path that uses an existing index. You may want to take this approach if you know that the index is not very selective and a full table scan would be more efficient. If the statement contains a construct that makes such an index access path available, then you can force the optimizer to use a full table scan through one of the following methods:

- Use the `NO_INDEX` hint to give the query optimizer maximum flexibility while disallowing the use of a certain index.
- Use the `FULL` hint to instruct the optimizer to choose a full table scan instead of an index scan.
- Use the `INDEX` or `INDEX_COMBINE` hints to instruct the optimizer to use one index or a set of listed indexes instead of another.

Parallel execution uses indexes effectively. It does not perform parallel index range scans, but it does perform parallel index lookups for parallel nested loop join execution. If an index is very selective (there are few rows for each index entry), then it might be better to use sequential index lookup rather than parallel table scan.

Recreating Indexes

You might want to recreate an index to compact it and minimize fragmented space, or to change the index's storage characteristics. When creating a new index that is a subset of an existing index or when rebuilding an existing index with new storage characteristics, Oracle Database might use the existing index instead of the base table to improve the performance of the index build.

However, in some cases using the base table instead of the existing index is beneficial. Consider an index on a table on which a lot of DML has been performed. Because of the DML, the size of the index can increase to the point where each block is only 50% full, or even less. If the index refers to most of the columns in the table, then the index could actually be larger than the table. In this case, it is faster to use the base table rather than the index to re-create the index.

Use the `ALTER INDEX ... REBUILD` statement to reorganize or compact an existing index or to change its storage characteristics. The `REBUILD` statement uses the existing index as the basis for the new one. All index storage statements are supported, such as `STORAGE` (for extent allocation), `TABLESPACE` (to move the index to a new tablespace), and `INITRANS` (to change the initial number of entries).

Usually, `ALTER INDEX ... REBUILD` is faster than dropping and re-creating an index, because this statement uses the fast full scan feature. It reads all the index blocks using multiblock I/O, then discards the branch blocks. A further advantage of this approach is that the old index is still available for queries while the rebuild is in progress.

Compacting Indexes

You can coalesce leaf blocks of an index by using the `ALTER INDEX` statement with the `COALESCE` option. This option lets you combine leaf levels of an index to free blocks for reuse. You can also rebuild the index online.

Using Nonunique Indexes to Enforce Uniqueness

You can use an existing nonunique index on a table to enforce uniqueness, either for `UNIQUE` constraints or the unique aspect of a `PRIMARY KEY` constraint. The advantage of this approach is that the index remains available and valid when the constraint is disabled. Therefore, enabling a disabled UNIQUE or PRIMARY KEY constraint does not require rebuilding the unique index associated with the constraint. This can yield significant time savings on enable operations for large tables.

Using a nonunique index to enforce uniqueness also lets you eliminate redundant indexes. You do not need a unique index on a primary key column if that column is included as the prefix of a composite index. You can use the existing index to enable and enforce the constraint. You also save significant space by not duplicating the index. However, if the existing index is partitioned, then the partitioning key of the index must also be a subset of the UNIQUE key; otherwise, Oracle Database creates an additional unique index to enforce the constraint.

Using Enabled Novalidated Constraints

An enabled novalidated constraint behaves similarly to an enabled validated constraint for new data. Placing a constraint in the enabled novalidated state signifies that any new data entered into the table must conform to the constraint. Existing data is not checked. By placing a constraint in the enabled novalidated state, you enable the constraint without locking the table.

If you change a constraint from disabled to enabled, then the table must be locked. No new DML, queries, or DDL can occur, because no mechanism can ensure that operations on the table conform to the constraint during the enable operation. The enabled novalidated state prevents users from performing operations on the table that violate the constraint.

The database can validate an enabled novalidated constraint with a parallel, consistent-read query of the table to determine whether any data violates the constraint. The database performs no locking, so the enable operation does not block readers or writers. In addition, the database can validate enabled novalidated constraints in parallel. The database can validate multiple constraints at the same time and check the validity of each constraint using parallel query.

Use the following approach to create tables with constraints and indexes:

1. Create the tables with the constraints. NOT NULL constraints can be unnamed and should be created enabled and validated. You should name all other constraints (CHECK, UNIQUE, PRIMARY KEY, and FOREIGN KEY) and create them disabled.

By default, constraints are created in the ENABLED state.

2. Load old data into the tables.
3. Create all indexes, including indexes needed for constraints.
4. Enable novalidate all constraints. Do this to primary keys before foreign keys.
5. Allow users to query and modify data.
6. With a separate ALTER TABLE statement for each constraint, validate all constraints. Do this to primary keys before foreign keys. For example,

```
CREATE TABLE t (a NUMBER CONSTRAINT apk PRIMARY KEY DISABLE,
b NUMBER NOT NULL);
CREATE TABLE x (c NUMBER CONSTRAINT afk REFERENCES t DISABLE);
```

Now load data into table t.

```
CREATE UNIQUE INDEX tai ON t (a);
CREATE INDEX tci ON x (c);
```

```
ALTER TABLE t MODIFY CONSTRAINT apk ENABLE NOVALIDATE;
ALTER TABLE x MODIFY CONSTRAINT afk ENABLE NOVALIDATE;
```

At this point, users can start performing INSERT, UPDATE, DELETE, and SELECT operations on table t.

```
ALTER TABLE t ENABLE CONSTRAINT apk;
ALTER TABLE x ENABLE CONSTRAINT afk;
```

Now the constraints are enabled and validated.

USING FUNCTION-BASED INDEXES FOR PERFORMANCE

A function-based index includes columns that are either transformed by a function, such as the UPPER function, or included in an expression, such as col1 + col2. With a function-based index, you can store computation-intensive expressions in the index.

Defining a function-based index on the transformed column or expression allows that data to be returned using the index when that function or expression is used in a WHERE clause or an ORDER BY clause. This allows Oracle Database to bypass computing the value of the expression when processing SELECT and DELETE statements. Therefore, a function-based index can be beneficial when frequently-executed SQL statements include transformed columns, or columns in expressions, in a WHERE or ORDER BY clause.

Oracle Database treats descending indexes as function-based indexes. The columns marked DESC are sorted in descending order.

For example, function-based indexes defined with the UPPER(*column_name*) or LOWER(*column_name*) keywords allow case-insensitive searches. The index created in the following statement:

```
CREATE INDEX uppercase_idx ON employees (UPPER(last_name));
```

facilitates processing queries such as:

```
SELECT * FROM employees WHERE UPPER(last_name) = 'MARKSON';
```

USING PARTITIONED INDEXES FOR PERFORMANCE

Similar to partitioned tables, partitioned indexes improve manageability, availability, performance, and scalability. They can either be partitioned independently (global indexes) or automatically linked to a table's partitioning method (local indexes).

Oracle Database supports both range and hash partitioned global indexes. In a range partitioned global index, each index partition contains values defined by a partition bound. In a hash partitioned global index, each partition contains values determined by the Oracle Database hash function.

The hash method can improve performance of indexes where a small number leaf blocks in the index have high contention in multiuser OLTP environment. In some OLTP applications, index insertions happen only at the right edge of the index. This situation could occur when the index is defined on monotonically increasing columns. In such situations, the right edge of the index becomes a hotspot because of contention for index pages, buffers, latches for update, and additional index maintenance activity, which results in performance degradation.

With hash partitioned global indexes index entries are hashed to different partitions based on partitioning key and the number of partitions. This spreads out contention over number of defined partitions, resulting in increased throughput. Hash-partitioned global indexes would benefit TPC-H refresh functions that are executed as massive PDMLs into huge fact tables because contention for buffer latches would be spread out over multiple partitions.

With hash partitioning, an index entry is mapped to a particular index partition based on the hash value generated by Oracle Database. The syntax to create hash-partitioned global index is very similar to hash-partitioned table. Queries involving equality and IN predicates on index partitioning key can efficiently use global hash partitioned index to answer queries quickly.

USING INDEX-ORGANIZED TABLES FOR PERFORMANCE

An index-organized table differs from an ordinary table in that the data for the table is held in its associated index. Changes to the table data, such as adding new rows, updating rows, or deleting rows, result only in updating the index. Because data rows are stored in the index, index-organized tables provide faster key-based access to table data for queries that involve exact match or range search or both.

A parent/child relationship is an example of a situation that may warrant an index-organized table. For example, a members table has a child table containing phone numbers. Phone numbers for a member are changed and added over time. In a heap-organized table, rows are inserted in data blocks where they fit. However, when you query the members table, you always retrieve the phone numbers from the child table. To make the retrieval more efficient, you can store the phone numbers in an index-organized table so that phone records for a given member are inserted near each other in the data blocks.

In some circumstances, an index-organized table may provide a performance advantage over a heap-organized table. For example, if a query requires fewer blocks in the cache, then the database uses the buffer cache more efficiently. If fewer distinct blocks are needed for a query, then a single physical I/O may retrieve all necessary data, requiring a smaller amount of I/O for each query.

Global hash-partitioned indexes are supported for index-organized tables and can provide performance benefits in a multiuser OLTP environment. Index-organized tables are useful when you must store related pieces of data together or physically store data in a specific order.

USING BITMAP INDEXES FOR PERFORMANCE

Bitmap indexes can substantially improve performance of queries that have all of the following characteristics:

- The `WHERE` clause contains multiple predicates on low- or medium-cardinality columns.
- The individual predicates on these low- or medium-cardinality columns select a large number of rows.
- The bitmap indexes used in the queries have been created on some or all of these low- or medium-cardinality columns.
- The tables in the queries contain many rows.

You can use multiple bitmap indexes to evaluate the conditions on a single table. Bitmap indexes are thus highly advantageous for complex *ad hoc* queries that contain lengthy `WHERE` clauses. Bitmap indexes can also provide optimal performance for aggregate queries and for optimizing joins in star schemas.

USING BITMAP JOIN INDEXES FOR PERFORMANCE

In addition to a bitmap index on a single table, you can create a bitmap join index, which is a bitmap index for the join of two or more tables. A bitmap join index is a space-saving way to reduce the volume of data that must be joined by performing restrictions in advance. For each value in a column of a table, a bitmap join index stores the rowids of corresponding rows in another table. In a data warehousing environment, the join condition is an equi-inner join between the primary key column(s) of the dimension tables and the foreign key column(s) in the fact table.

Bitmap join indexes are much more efficient in storage than materialized join views, an alternative for materializing joins in advance. Materialized join views do not compress the rowids of the fact tables.

USING DOMAIN INDEXES FOR PERFORMANCE

Domain indexes are built using the indexing logic supplied by a user-defined indextype. An indextype provides an efficient mechanism to access data that satisfy certain operator predicates. Typically, the user-defined indextype is part of an Oracle Database option, like the Spatial option. For example, the `SpatialIndextype` allows efficient search and retrieval of spatial data that overlap a given bounding box.

You can also create index types with the `CREATE INDEXTYPE` statement.

USING TABLE CLUSTERS FOR PERFORMANCE

A **table cluster** is a group of one or more tables that are physically stored together because they share common columns and usually appear together in SQL statements. Because the database physically stores related rows together, disk access time improves. To create a cluster, use the `CREATE CLUSTER` statement.

Follow these guidelines when deciding whether to cluster tables:

- Cluster tables that are accessed frequently by the application in join statements.
- Do not cluster tables if the application joins them only occasionally or modifies their common column values frequently. Modifying a row's cluster key value takes longer than modifying the value in an unclustered table, because Oracle Database might need to migrate the modified row to another block to maintain the cluster.
- Do not cluster tables if the application often performs full table scans of only one of the tables. A full table scan of a clustered table can take longer than a full table scan of an unclustered table. Oracle Database is likely to read more blocks because the tables are stored together.
- Cluster master-detail tables if you often select a master record and then the corresponding detail records. Detail records are stored in the same data block(s) as the master record, so they are likely still to be in memory when you select them, requiring Oracle Database to perform less I/O.
- Store a detail table alone in a cluster if you often select many detail records of the same master. This measure improves the performance of queries that select detail records of the same master, but does not decrease the performance of a full table scan on the master table. An alternative is to use an index organized table.
- Do not cluster tables if the data from all tables with the same cluster key value exceeds more than one or two data blocks. To access a row in a clustered table, Oracle Database reads all blocks containing rows with that value. If these rows take up multiple blocks, then accessing a single row could require more reads than accessing the same row in an unclustered table.

- Do not cluster tables when the number of rows for each cluster key value varies significantly. This causes waste of space for the low cardinality key value; it causes collisions for the high cardinality key values. Collisions degrade performance.

Consider the benefits and drawbacks of clusters for the application. For example, you might decide that the performance gain for join statements outweighs the performance loss for statements that modify cluster key values. You might want to experiment and compare processing times with the tables both clustered and stored separately.

USING HASH CLUSTERS FOR PERFORMANCE

Hash clusters group table data by applying a hash function to each row's cluster key value. All rows with the same cluster key value are stored together on disk. Consider the benefits and drawbacks of hash clusters for the application. You might want to experiment and compare processing times with a particular table in a hash cluster and alone with an index.

Follow these guidelines for choosing when to use hash clusters:

- Use hash clusters to store tables accessed frequently by SQL statements with WHERE clauses, if the `WHERE` clauses contain equality conditions that use the same column or combination of columns. Designate this column or combination of columns as the cluster key.
- Store a table in a hash cluster if you can determine how much space is required to hold all rows with a given cluster key value, including rows to be inserted immediately and rows to be inserted in the future.
- Use sorted hash clusters, where rows corresponding to each value of the hash function are sorted on a specific columns in ascending order, when the database can improve response time on operations with this sorted clustered data.
- Do not store a table in a hash cluster if the application often performs full table scans and if you must allocate a great deal of space to the hash cluster in anticipation of the table growing. Such full table scans must read all blocks allocated to the hash cluster, even though some blocks might contain few rows. Storing the table alone reduces the number of blocks read by full table scans.
- Do not store a table in a hash cluster if the application frequently modifies the cluster key values. Modifying a row's cluster key value can take longer than modifying the value in an unclustered table, because Oracle Database might need to migrate the modified row to another block to maintain the cluster.

Storing a single table in a hash cluster can be useful, regardless of whether the table is joined frequently with other tables, as long as hashing is appropriate for the table based on the considerations in this list.

15 Using SQL Plan Management

Learning Objectives

This chapter describes how to manage SQL execution plans using SQL plan management. SQL plan management prevents performance regressions resulting from sudden changes to the execution plan of a SQL statement by providing components for capturing, selecting, and evolving SQL plan information.

This chapter contains the following topics:

- Overview of SQL Plan Baselines
- Managing SQL Plan Baselines
- Using SQL Plan Baselines with SQL Tuning Advisor
- Using Fixed SQL Plan Baselines
- Displaying SQL Plan Baselines
- SQL Management Base
- Importing and Exporting SQL Plan Baselines
- Migrating Stored Outlines to SQL Plan Baselines

OVERVIEW OF SQL PLAN BASELINES

SQL plan management is a preventative mechanism that records and evaluates the execution plans of SQL statements over time. This mechanism can build a **SQL plan baseline**, which is a set of accepted plans for a SQL statement. The accepted plans have been proven to perform well.

Purpose of SQL Plan Baselines

The goal of SQL plan baselines is to preserve the performance of corresponding SQL statements, regardless of changes in the database. Examples of changes include:

- New optimizer version
- Changes to optimizer statistics and optimizer parameters
- Changes to schema and metadata definitions
- Changes to system settings
- SQL profile creation.

SQL plan baselines cannot help in cases where an event has caused irreversible execution plan changes, such as dropping an index.

The SQL tuning features of Oracle Database generate SQL profiles that help the optimizer to produce well-tuned plans. However, this mechanism is reactive and cannot guarantee stable performance when drastic database changes occur. SQL tuning can only resolve performance issues after they have occurred and are identified. For example, a SQL statement may become high-load because of a plan change, but SQL tuning cannot solve this problem until after the plan change occurs.

Common scenarios where SQL plan management can improve or preserve SQL performance include:

- A database upgrade that installs a new optimizer version usually results in plan changes for a small percentage of SQL statements. Most of these plan changes result in either no performance change or improvement. However, some plan changes may cause performance regressions. SQL plan baselines significantly minimize potential regressions resulting from an upgrade.
- Ongoing system and data changes can impact plans for some SQL statements, potentially causing performance regressions. SQL plan baselines help minimize performance regressions and stabilize SQL performance.
- Deployment of new application modules means introducing new SQL statements into the database. The application software may use appropriate SQL execution plans developed in a standard test configuration for the new statements. If the system configuration is significantly different from the test configuration, then the database can evolve SQL plan baselines over time to produce better performance.

Architecture of SQL Plan Baselines

A SQL plan baseline contains one or more accepted plans, each of which contains the following information:

- Set of hints
- Plan hash value
- Plan-related information.

The **plan history** is the set of plans, both accepted and not accepted, that the optimizer generates for a SQL statement over time. Because only accepted plans are in the SQL plan baseline, the plans in the baseline form a susbset of the plan history. For example, after the optimizer generates the first acceptable plan for a SQL plan baseline, subsequent plans are part of the plan history but not part of the plan baseline.

The process of adding plans to a SQL plan baseline is **plan evolution**. To be eligible to be evolved, a plan must be enabled for use by the optimizer.

Figure 15.1 shows a single `SELECT` statement that has two accepted plans in its SQL plan baseline. The SQL plan history includes two other plans for the statement that have not been proven to perform well.

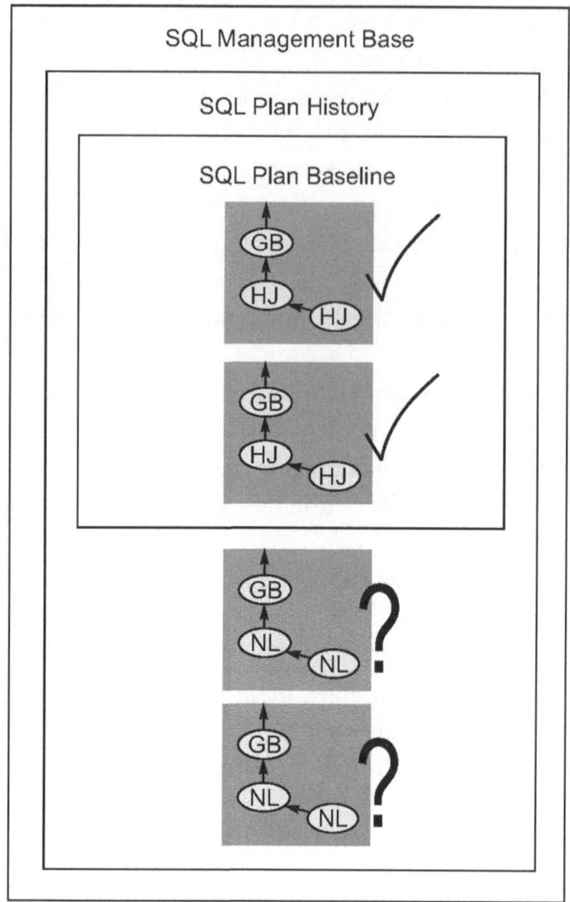

Figure 15.1. SQL Plan Baseline and SQL Plan History

The **SQL management base (SMB)**, which is part of the data dictionary, stores the SQL plan baselines and plan history in the **SYSAUX** tablespace. The SMB also contains SQL profiles. The SMB uses automatic space management.

MANAGING SQL PLAN BASELINES

Managing SQL plan baselines involves the following phases:

- Capturing SQL Plan Baselines
- Selecting SQL Plan Baselines
- Evolving SQL Plan Baselines.

Capturing SQL Plan Baselines

During the SQL plan baseline capture phase, the database detects plan changes and records the new plan so that it can be evolved (verified) by the database administrator. To this end, the database maintains a plan history for individual SQL statements. Because ad hoc SQL statements do not repeat and thus do not suffer performance degradation, the database maintains plan history only for repeatable SQL statements.

To recognize repeatable SQL statements, the database maintains a statement log that contains the SQL ID of various SQL statements that the optimizer has evaluated. The database recognizes a SQL statement as repeatable when it is parsed or executed again after it has been logged.

For each repeatable SQL statement, the database maintains a plan history that contains all plans generated by the optimizer. The set of all accepted plans in the plan history is the SQL plan baseline.

You can configure the SQL Plan Baseline Capture phase for automatic capture of plan history and SQL plan baselines for repeatable SQL statements. Alternatively, you can manually load plans as SQL plan baselines.

This section contains the following topics:

- Capturing Plans Automatically
- Creating Baselines from Existing Plans.

Capturing Plans Automatically

When automatic plan capture is enabled, the database automatically creates and maintains the plan history for SQL statements using information provided by the optimizer. The plan history includes relevant information used by the optimizer to reproduce an execution plan, such as the SQL text, outline, bind variables, and compilation environment.

The optimizer marks the initial plan generated for a SQL statement as accepted for use, and represents both the plan history and SQL plan baseline. The plan history includes all subsequent plans. During the SQL plan baseline evolution phase, the database adds plans to the baseline that have been verified not to cause performance regressions.

To enable automatic plan capture, set the `OPTIMIZER_CAPTURE_SQL_PLAN_BASELINES` initialization parameter to `TRUE`. By default, this parameter is `FALSE`.

Creating Baselines from Existing Plans

You can create SQL plan baselines by manually loading existing plans for a set of SQL statements as plan baselines. The database does not verify manually loaded plans for performance, but adds them as accepted plans to existing or new SQL plan baselines. You can use manual plan loading with or as an alternative to automatic plan capture.

You can perform manual plan loading by:

- Loading Plans from SQL Tuning Sets and AWR Snapshots
- Loading Plans from the Shared SQL Area.

Loading Plans from SQL Tuning Sets and AWR Snapshots: To load plans from a SQL tuning set, use the `LOAD_PLANS_FROM_SQLSET` function of the `DBMS_SPM` package. The following example loads the plans stored in the SQL tuning set named `tset1`:

```
DECLARE
    my_plans PLS_INTEGER;
BEGIN
    my_plans  :=  DBMS_SPM.LOAD_PLANS_FROM_SQLSET(  sqlset_name  =>
'tset1');
END;
/
```

To load plans from Automatic Workload Repository (AWR), load the plans stored in AWR snapshots into a SQL tuning set before using the `LOAD_PLANS_FROM_SQLSET` function as described in this section.

Loading Plans from the Shared SQL Area: To load plans from the shared SQL area, use the LOAD_PLANS_FROM_CURSOR_CACHE function of the DBMS_SPM package. In the following example, Oracle Database loads the plans located in the shared SQL area for the SQL statement identified by its sql_id:

```
DECLARE
    my_plans PLS_INTEGER;
BEGIN
    my_plans := DBMS_SPM.LOAD_PLANS_FROM_CURSOR_CACHE( sql_id =>
'99twu5t2dn5xd');
END;
/
```

You can identify plans in the shared SQL area by:

- SQL identifier (SQL_ID)
- SQL text (SQL_TEXT)
- One of the following attributes:
    - PARSING_SCHEMA_NAME
    - MODULE
    - ACTION.

Selecting SQL Plan Baselines

During the SQL plan baseline selection phase, Oracle Database detects plan changes based on the stored plan history, and selects plans to avoid potential performance regressions for a set of SQL statements.

Each time the database compiles a SQL statement, the optimizer does the following:

1. Uses a cost-based search method to build a best-cost plan
2. Tries to find a matching plan in the SQL plan baseline
3. Does either of the following depending on whether a match is found:
    - If found, then the optimizer proceeds using the matched plan
    - If not found, then the optimizer evaluates the cost of each accepted plan in the SQL plan baseline and selects the plan with the lowest cost.

The best-cost plan found by the optimizer that does not match any plans in the plan history for the SQL statement represents a new plan. The database adds this plan as a nonaccepted plan to the plan history. The database does not use the new plan until it is verified to not cause a performance regression. However, if a change in the system (such as a dropped index) causes all accepted plans to become non-reproducible, then the optimizer selects the best-cost plan. Thus, the presence of a SQL plan baseline causes the optimizer to use conservative plan selection strategy for the SQL statement.

To enable the use of SQL plan baselines, set the OPTIMIZER_USE_SQL_PLAN_BASELINES initialization parameter to TRUE (default).

Evolving SQL Plan Baselines

During the SQL plan baseline evolution phase, the database evaluates the performance of new plans and integrates plans with better performance into SQL plan baselines.

When the optimizer finds a new plan for a SQL statement, the database adds the plan to the plan history as a nonaccepted plan. The database can verify the plan for performance relative to the SQL plan baseline performance. A successful verification of a nonaccepted plan consists of comparing its performance to that of a plan selected from the SQL plan baseline and ensuring that it delivers better performance. When the database verifies that a nonaccepted plan will not cause a performance regression, the database changes it to an accepted plan and integrates it into the baseline.

This section describes how to evolve SQL plan baselines and contains the following topics:

- Evolving Plans with Manual Plan Loading
- Evolving Plans with DBMS_SPM.EVOLVE_SQL_PLAN_BASELINE.

Evolving Plans with Manual Plan Loading

You can evolve an existing SQL plan baseline by manually loading plans from the shared SQL area or from a SQL tuning set. When you manually load plans into a SQL plan baseline, the database adds these loaded plans as accepted plans.

Evolving Plans with DBMS_SPM.EVOLVE_SQL_PLAN_BASELINE

The PL/SQL function `DBMS_SPM.EVOLVE_SQL_PLAN_BASELINE` tries to evolve new plans that have been added by the optimizer to the plan history of existing plan baselines. If the function can verify that the new plan performs better than a plan chosen from the corresponding SQL plan baseline, then the database adds the new plan as an accepted plan.

The following example of the `DBMS_SPM.EVOLVE_SQL_PLAN_BASELINE` function evolves a new plan for a SQL statement identified by its SQL handle, which is its unique SQL identifier in string form. You can find the SQL handle by querying

```
DBA_SQL_PLAN_BASELINES.SQL_HANDLE.
SET SERVEROUTPUT ON
SET LONG 10000
DECLARE
    report clob;
BEGIN
    report := DBMS_SPM.EVOLVE_SQL_PLAN_BASELINE(
                  sql_handle => 'SYS_SQL_593bc74fca8e6738');
    DBMS_OUTPUT.PUT_LINE(report);
END;
/
```

The following output shows that Oracle Database successfully evolved a plan:

```
REPORT
---------------------------------------------------------------
Evolve SQL Plan Baseline Report
---------------------------------------------------------------
Inputs:
--------
    SQL_HANDLE  =     SYS_SQL_593bc74fca8e6738
    PLAN_NAME   =
    TIME_LIMIT  =     DBMS_SPM.AUTO_LIMIT
    VERIFY      =     YES
    COMMIT      =     YES
  Plan: SYS_SQL_PLAN_ca8e6738a57b5fc2
  -----------------------------------
    Plan was verified: Time used .07 seconds.
```

```
    Passed performance criterion: Compound improvement ratio >= 7.32.
    Plan was changed to an accepted plan.
    Baseline Plan     Test Plan   Improv. Ratio
    -------------     ----------  -------------
    Execution Status: COMPLETE    COMPLETE
    Rows Processed:          40         40
    Elapsed Time(ms):        23          8
2.88
    CPU Time(ms):            23          8
2.88
    Buffer Gets:            450         61
7.38
    Disk Reads:               0          0
    Direct Writes:            0          0
    Fetches:                  0          0
    Executions:               1          1

-------------------------------------------------------------------
    Report Summary
-------------------------------------------------------------------
Number of SQL plan baselines verified: 1.
Number of SQL plan baselines evolved: 1.
```

Alternatively, you can use the `DBMS_SPM.EVOLVE_SQL_PLAN_BASELINE` function to specify:

- The name of a particular plan to evolve
- A list of plans to evolve
- No value.
  By specifying no value, you enable Oracle Database to evolve all nonaccepted plans currently in the SMB.

USING SQL PLAN BASELINES WITH SQL TUNING ADVISOR

When tuning SQL statements with SQL Tuning Advisor, if the advisor finds a tuned plan and verifies its performance to be better than a plan chosen from the corresponding SQL plan baseline, then it makes a recommendation to accept a SQL profile. When the SQL profile is accepted, the database adds the tuned plan to the corresponding SQL plan baseline. However, SQL Tuning Advisor does not verify existing unaccepted plans in the plan history.

In Oracle Database 11*g*, an automatically configured task runs SQL Tuning Advisor during a maintenance window. This task targets high-load SQL statements as identified by the execution performance data collected in the Automatic Workload Repository (AWR) snapshots. The automatic SQL tuning task implements the SQL profile recommendations made by SQL Tuning Advisor. Thus, the database automatically adds tuned plans to the SQL plan baselines of the identified high-load SQL statements.

USING FIXED SQL PLAN BASELINES

A SQL plan baseline is fixed when it contains at least one enabled plan whose `FIXED` attribute is set to `YES`. You can use fixed SQL plan baselines to fix the set of possible plans (usually one plan) for a SQL statement, or migrate an existing stored outline by loading the "outlined" plan as a fixed plan.

If a fixed SQL plan baseline also contains non-fixed plans, then the optimizer gives preference to fixed plans over non-fixed ones. Thus, the optimizer picks the fixed plan with the least cost even though a non-fixed plan may have an even lower cost. If none of the fixed plans is reproducible, then the optimizer picks the best non-fixed plan.

The optimizer does not add new plans to a fixed SQL plan baseline. Because the optimizer does not automatically add new plans, the database does not evolve a fixed SQL plan baseline when you execute DBMS_SPM.EVOLVE_SQL_PLAN_BASELINE. However, you can evolve a fixed SQL plan baseline by manually loading new plans into it from the shared SQL area or a SQL tuning set.

When you tune a SQL statement with a fixed SQL plan baseline using SQL Tuning Advisor, a SQL profile recommendation has special meaning. When the SQL profile is accepted, the database adds the tuned plan to the fixed SQL plan baseline as a non-fixed plan. However, as described above, the optimizer does not use the tuned plan when a reproducible fixed plan is present. Therefore, the benefit of SQL tuning may not be realized. To enable the use of the tuned plan, manually alter the tuned plan to a fixed plan by setting its FIXED attribute to YES.

DISPLAYING SQL PLAN BASELINES

To view the plans stored in the SQL plan baseline for a given statement, use the DISPLAY_SQL_PLAN_BASELINE function of the DBMS_XPLAN package. The following example displays one or more execution plans for the specified SQL statement, specified by the handle (sql_handle):

```
SELECT * FROM TABLE(
    DBMS_XPLAN.DISPLAY_SQL_PLAN_BASELINE(
    sql_handle=>'SYS_SQL_209d10fabbedc741',
    format=>'basic'));
```

Alternatively, you can display a single plan by supplying a plan name (plan_name).

This function uses plan information stored in the SQL management base to explain and display the plans. In this example, the DISPLAY_SQL_PLAN_BASELINE function displays the execution plans for the SQL statement specified by the handle

```
SYS_SQL_209d10fabbedc741:
SQL handle: SYS_SQL_209d10fabbedc741
SQL text: select cust_last_name, amount_sold from customers c,sales s
where c.cust_id=s.cust_id and cust_year_of_birth=:yob
--------------------------------------------------------------------
Plan name: SYS_SQL_PLAN_bbedc741a57b5fc2
Enabled: YES   Fixed: NO   Accepted: NO     Origin: AUTO-CAPTURE
--------------------------------------------------------------------
Plan hash value: 2776326082
--------------------------------------------------------------------
| Id |  Operation                              | Name    |
|
--------------------------------------------------------------------
|  0 |  SELECT  STATEMENT                      |
|
|  1 |  HASH  JOIN                             |
```

```
|
| 2 |   TABLE  ACCESS  BY  INDEX  ROWID          |  CUSTOMERS
|
| 3 |   BITMAP  CONVERSION  TO  ROWIDS           |
|
| 4 | BITMAP  INDEX  SINGLE  VALUE    | CUSTOMERS_YOB_BIX
|
| 5 |     PARTITION  RANGE  ALL                  |
|
| 6 |     TABLE  ACCESS  FULL                    | SALES
|
-------------------------------------------------------------------
-------------------------------------------------------------------
Plan name: SYS_SQL_PLAN_bbedc741f554c408
Enabled: YES   Fixed: NO  Accepted: YES    Origin: MANUAL-LOAD
-------------------------------------------------------------------
Plan hash value: 4115973128
-------------------------------------------------------------------
| Id | Operation                               | Name
|
-------------------------------------------------------------------
| 0 | SELECT STATEMENT                          |
|
| 1 |  NESTED LOOPS                             |
|
| 2 |     NESTED LOOPS                          |
|
| 3 |       TABLE ACCESS BY INDEX ROWID         |        CUSTOMERS
|
| 4 |         BITMAP CONVERSION TO ROWIDS       |
|
| 5 | BITMAP INDEX SINGLE VALUE       | CUSTOMERS_YOB_BIX
|
| 6 |       PARTITION RANGE                     |
|
| 7 |       BITMAP CONVERSION TO ROWIDS         |
|
| 8 | BITMAP INDEX SINGLE VALUE                 | SALES_CUST_BIX
|
| 9 | TABLE ACCESS BY LOCAL INDEX ROWID         | SALES
|
-------------------------------------------------------------------
```

You can also display SQL plan baseline information using a SELECT statement directly on the DBA_SQL_PLAN_BASELINES view, as shown in the following example:

```
SELECT SQL_HANDLE, PLAN_NAME, ENABLED, ACCEPTED, FIXED
FROM      DBA_SQL_PLAN_BASELINES;
```

```
SQL_HANDLE                PLAN_NAME                       ENA  ACC  FIX
-------------------------------------------------------------------------
SYS_SQL_209d10fabbedc741  SYS_SQL_PLAN_bbedc741a57b5fc2  YES  NO   NO
SYS_SQL_209d10fabbedc741  SYS_SQL_PLAN_bbedc741f554c408  YES  YES  NO
```

SQL MANAGEMENT BASE

The **SQL management base (SMB)** is a part of the data dictionary that resides in the SYSAUX tablespace. It stores statement logs, plan histories, SQL plan baselines, and SQL profiles. To allow weekly purging of unused plans and logs, the SMB uses automatic space management.

You can also add plans manually to the SMB for a set of SQL statements. This feature is especially useful when upgrading the database from a version before Oracle Database 11*g* because it helps to minimize plan regressions resulting from the use of a new optimizer version.

Because the SMB is located entirely within SYSAUX, the database does not use SQL plan management and SQL tuning features when this tablespace is unavailable.

Disk Space Usage

Disk space used by the SMB is regularly checked against a limit based on the size of the SYSAUX tablespace. By default, the limit for the SMB is no more than 10% of the size of SYSAUX. The allowable range for this limit is between 1% and 50%.

A weekly background process measures the total space occupied by the SMB. When the defined limit is exceeded, the process writes a warning to the alert log. The database generates alerts weekly until one of the following conditions is met:

- The SMB space limit is increased
- The size of the SYSAUX tablespace is increased
- The disk space used by the SMB is decreased by purging SQL management objects (SQL plan baselines or SQL profiles).

To change the percentage limit, use the CONFIGURE procedure of the DBMS_SPM package. The following example changes the space limit to 30%:

```
BEGIN
    DBMS_SPM.CONFIGURE('space_budget_percent',30);
END;
/
```

Purging Policy

A weekly scheduled purging task manages the disk space used by SQL plan management. The task runs as an automated task in the maintenance window.

The database purges plans not used for more than 53 weeks, as identified by the LAST_EXECUTED timestamp stored in the SMB for that plan. The 53-week period ensures plan information is available during any yearly SQL processing. The unused plan retention period can range between 5 and 523 weeks (a little more than 10 years).

To configure the retention period, use the CONFIGURE procedure of the DBMS_SPM PL/SQL package. The following example changes the retention period to 105 weeks:

```
BEGIN
    DBMS_SPM.CONFIGURE( 'plan_retention_weeks',105);
END;
/
```

SQL Management Base Configuration Parameters

You can access the current configuration settings for the SQL management base using the DBA_SQL_MANAGEMENT_CONFIG view. The following query shows this information:

```
SELECT PARAMETER_NAME, PARAMETER_VALUE
FROM      DBA_SQL_MANAGEMENT_CONFIG;
PARAMETER_NAME                        PARAMETER_VALUE
------------------------------ ---------------
SPACE_BUDGET_PERCENT                            30
PLAN_RETENTION_WEEKS                           105
```

IMPORTING AND EXPORTING SQL PLAN BASELINES

Oracle Database supports the export and import of SQL plan baselines using the Oracle Data Pump Import and Export utilities. Use the DBMS_SPM package to define a staging table, which you can use to pack and unpack SQL plan baselines.

To import a set of SQL plan baselines from one system to another:

1. On the original database, create a staging table using the CREATE_STGTAB_BASELINE procedure.

   The following example creates a staging table named stage1:

```
BEGIN
 DBMS_SPM.CREATE_STGTAB_BASELINE(
 table_name  => 'stage1');
END;
/
```

2. Pack the SQL plan baselines you want to export from the SQL management base into the staging table using the PACK_STGTAB_BASELINE function.

   The following example packs enabled plan baselines created by user dba1 into staging table stage1. You can select SQL plan baselines using the plan name (plan_name), SQL handle (sql_handle), or any other plan criteria. The table_name parameter is mandatory.

```
DECLARE
 my_plans number;
BEGIN
 my_plans := DBMS_SPM.PACK_STGTAB_BASELINE(
   table_name => 'stage1',
   enabled => 'yes',
   creator => 'dba1');
END;
/
```

3. Export the staging table stage1 into a flat file using the Oracle Data Pump Export utility.
4. Transfer the flat file to the target system.
5. Import the staging table stage1 from the flat file using the Oracle Data Pump Import utility.
6. Unpack the SQL plan baselines from the staging table into the SQL management base on the target system using the UNPACK_STGTAB_BASELINE function.

   The following example unpacks all fixed plan baselines stored in the staging table stage1:

```
DECLARE
 my_plans number;
BEGIN
 my_plans := DBMS_SPM.UNPACK_STGTAB_BASELINE(
 table_name => 'stage1',
 fixed => 'yes');
END;
/
```

MIGRATING STORED OUTLINES TO SQL PLAN BASELINES

This section explains the concepts and tasks relating to stored outline migration. This section contains the following topics:

- Overview of Stored Outline Migration
- Preparing for Stored Outline Migration
- Migrating Outlines to Utilize SQL Plan Management Features
- Migrating Outlines to Preserve Stored Outline Behaviour
- Performing Follow-Up Tasks After Stored Outline Migration

Overview of Stored Outline Migration

A **stored outline** is a set of hints for a SQL statement. The hints direct the optimizer to choose a specific plan for the statement. A stored outline is a legacy technique for providing plan stability.

Stored outline migration is the user-initiated process of converting stored outlines to SQL plan baselines. A SQL plan baseline is a set of plans proven to provide good performance.

This section contains the following topics:

- Purpose of Stored Outline Migration
- How Stored Outline Migration Works
- User Interface for Stored Outline Migration
- Basic Steps in Stored Outline Migration.

Purpose of Stored Outline Migration

This section assumes that you rely on stored outlines to maintain plan stability and prevent performance regressions. The goal of this section is to provide a convenient method to safely migrate from stored outlines to SQL plan baselines. After the migration, you can maintain the same plan stability that you had using stored outlines while being able to utilize the more advanced features provided by the SQL Plan Management framework.

Specifically, the section explains how to address the following problems:

- Stored outlines cannot automatically evolve over time. Consequently, a stored outline may be good when you create it, but become a bad plan after a database change, leading to performance degradation.
- Hints in a stored outline can become invalid, for example, an index hint on a dropped index. In such cases, the database still uses the outlines but excludes the invalid hints, producing a plan that is often worse than the original plan or the current best-cost plan generated by the optimizer.

- For a SQL statement, the optimizer can only choose the plan defined in the stored outline in the currently specified category. The optimizer cannot choose from other stored outlines in different categories or the current cost-based plan even if they improve performance.
- Stored outlines are a reactive tuning technique, which means that you only use a stored outline to address a performance problem after it has occurred. For example, you may implement a stored outline to correct the plan of a SQL statement that became high-load. In this case, you used stored outlines instead of proactively tuning the statement before it became high-load.

The stored outline migration PL/SQL API helps solve the preceding problems in the following ways:

- SQL plan baselines enable the optimizer to use the same good plan and allow this plan to evolve over time.
  For a specified SQL statement, you can add new plans as SQL plan baselines after they are verified not to cause performance regressions.
- SQL plan baselines prevent plans from going bad because of invalid hints.
  If hints stored in a plan baseline become invalid, then the plan may not be reproducible by the optimizer. In this case, the optimizer selects an alternative reproducible plan baseline or the current best-cost plan generated by optimizer.
- For a specific SQL statement, the database can maintain multiple plan baselines.
  The optimizer can choose from a set of good plans for a specific SQL statement instead of being restricted to a single plan per category, as required by stored outlines.

How Stored Outline Migration Works

This section explains how the database migrates stored outlines to SQL plan baselines. This information is important for performing the task of migrating stored outlines.

Stages of Stored Outline Migration: The following graphic shows the main stages in stored outline migration:

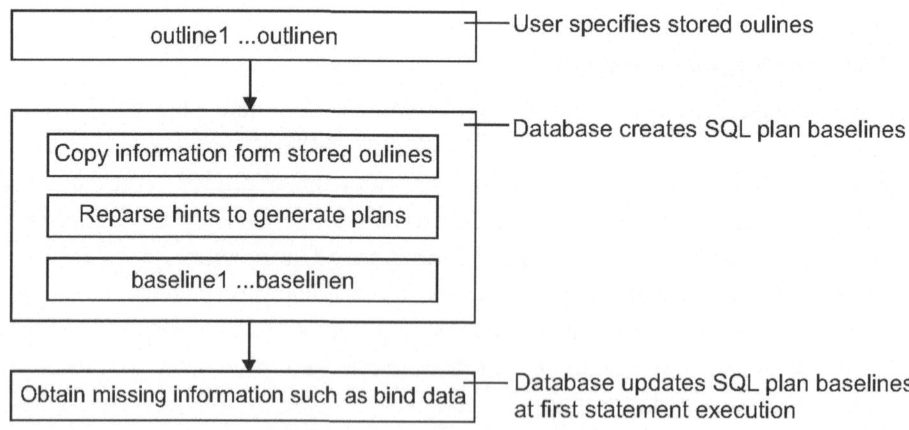

The migration process has the following stages:

1. The user invokes a function that specifies which outlines should be migrated.
2. The database processes the outlines as follows:

(a) The database copies information in the outline needed by the plan baseline.
The database copies it directly or calculates it based on information in the outline. For example, the text of the SQL statement exists in both schemas, so the database can copy the text from outline to baseline.

(b) The database reparses the hints to obtain information not in the outline.
The plan hash value and plan cost cannot be derived from the existing information in the outline, which necessitates reparsing the hints.

(c) The database creates the baselines.

3. The database obtains missing information when it chooses the SQL plan baseline for the first time to execute the same SQL statement.
The compilation environment and execution statistics are only available during execution when the plan baseline is parsed and compiled.

The migration is complete only after the preceding phases complete.

Outline Categories and Baseline Modules: An outline is a set of hints, whereas a SQL plan baseline is a set of plans. Because they are different technologies, some functionality of outlines does not map exactly to functionality of baselines. For example, a single SQL statement can have multiple outlines, each of which is in a different outline **category**, but the only category that currently exists for baselines is `DEFAULT`.

The equivalent of a category for an outline is a module for a SQL plan baseline. Table 15.1 explains how outline categories map to modules.

Table 15.1. Outline Categories

Concept	Description	Default value
Outline Category	Specifies a user-defined grouping for a set of stored outlines. You can use categories to maintain different stored outlines for a SQL statement. For example, a single statement can have an outline in the `OLTP` category and the `DW` category. Each SQL statement can have one or more stored outlines. Each stored outline outline is in one and only one outline category. A statement can have multiple stored outlines in different categories, but only one stored outline exists per category per statement. During migration, the database maps each outline category to a SQL plan baseline module.	`DEFAULT`
Baseline Module	Specifies a high-level function being performed. A SQL plan baseline can belong to one and only one module.	After an outline is migrated to a SQL plan baseline, module name defaults to outline category name
Baseline Category	Only one SQL plan baseline category exists. This category is named `DEFAULT`. During stored outline migration, the module name of the SQL plan baseline is set to the category name of the stored outline. A statement can have multiple SQL plan baselines in the `DEFAULT` category.	`DEFAULT`

When migrating stored outlines to SQL plan baselines, Oracle Database maps every outline category to a SQL plan baseline module with the same name. As shown in the following diagram, the outline category OLTP is mapped to the baseline module OLTP. After migration, DEFAULT is a super-category that contains all SQL plan baselines.

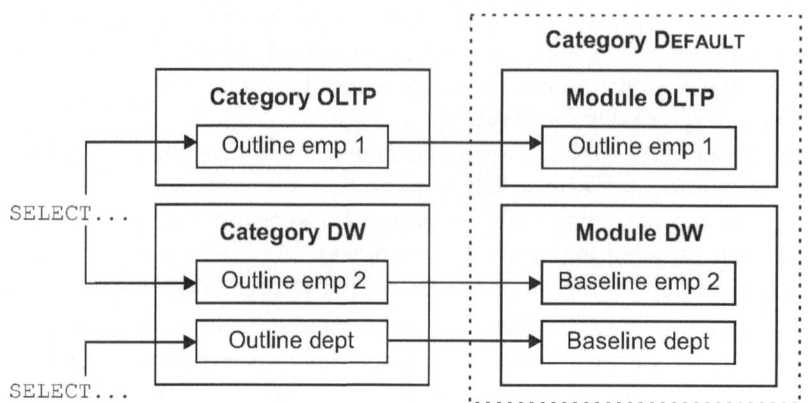

User Interface for Stored Outline Migration

You can use the DBMS_SPM package to perform the stored outline migration. Table 15.2 describes the relevant functions in this package.

Table 15.2. DBMS_SPM Functions Relating to Stored Outline Migration

DBMS_SPM Function	Description
MIGRATE_STORED_OUTLINE	Migrates existing stored outlines to plan baselines. Use either of the following formats: • Specify outline name, SQL text, outline category, or all stored outlines. • Specify a list of outline names.
ALTER_SQL_PLAN_BASELINE	Changes an attribute of a single plan or all plans associated with a SQL statement.
DROP_MIGRATED_STORED_OUTLINE	Drops stored outlines that have been migrated to SQL plan baselines. The function finds stored outlines marked as MIGRATED in the DBA_OUTLINES view, and then drops these outlines from the database.

You can control stored outline and plan baseline behavior with initialization and session parameters. Table 15.3 describes the relevant parameters. See Table 15.5 and Table 15.6 for an explanation of how these parameter settings interact.

Table 15.3 Parameters Relating to Stored Outline Migration

Initialization or Session Parameter	Description
CREATE_STORED_OUTLINES	Determines whether Oracle Database automatically creates and stores an outline for each query submitted during the session.

OPTIMIZER_CAPTURE_SQL_PLAN_BASELINES	Enables or disables the automatic recognition of repeatable SQL statement and the generation of SQL plan baselines for these statements.
USE_STORED_OUTLINES	Determines whether the optimizer uses stored outlines to generate execution plans. **Note:** This is a *session* parameter, not an initialization parameter.
OPTIMIZER_USE_SQL_PLAN_BASELINES	Enables or disables the use of SQL plan baselines stored in SQL Management Base.

You can use database views to access information relating to stored outline migration. Table 15.4 describes the following main views.

Table 15.4. Views Relating to Stored Outline Migration

View	Description
DBA_OUTLINES	Describes all stored outlines in the database. The MIGRATED column is important for outline migration and shows one of the following values: NOT-MIGRATED and MIGRATED. When MIGRATED, the stored outline has been migrated to a plan baseline and is not usable.
DBA_SQL_PLAN_BASELINES	Displays information about the SQL plan baselines currently created for specific SQL statements. The ORIGIN column indicates how the plan baseline was created. The value STORED-OUTLINE indicates the baseline was created by migrating an outline.

Basic Steps in Stored Outline Migration

This section explains the basic steps in using the PL/SQL API to perform stored outline migration. The basic steps are as follows:

1. Prepare for stored outline migration.

   Review the migration prerequisites and determine how you want the migrated plan baselines to behave.

2. Do one of the following:
   - Migrate to baselines to utilize SQL Plan Management features.
   - Migrate to baselines while exactly preserving the behavior of the stored outlines.

3. Perform post-migration confirmation and cleanup.

Preparing for Stored Outline Migration: This section explains how to prepare for stored outline migration.

To prepare for stored outline migration:

1. Start SQL*Plus and log on as a user with SYSDBA privileges or the EXECUTE privilege on the DBMS_SPM package.

For example, do the following to use operating system authentication to log on to a database as SYS:

```
% sqlplus /nolog
SQL> CONNECT / AS SYSDBA
```

2. Query the stored outlines in the database.

   The following example queries all stored outlines that have not been migrated to SQL plan baselines:

```
SELECT NAME, CATEGORY, SQL_TEXT
FROM   DBA_OUTLINES
WHERE  MIGRATED = 'NOT-MIGRATED';
```

3. Determine which stored outlines meet the following prerequisites for migration eligibility:
   - The statement must *not* be a run-time `INSERT AS SELECT` statement.
   - The statement must *not* reference a remote object.
   - This statement must *not* be a private stored outline.
4. Decide whether to migrate all outlines, specified stored outlines, or outlines belonging to a specified outline category.

   If you do not decide to migrate all outlines, then list the outlines or categories that you intend to migrate.
5. Decide whether the stored outlines migrated to SQL plan baselines should use **fixed plans** or **nonfixed plans:**
   - Fixed plans

     A fixed plan is frozen. If a fixed plan is reproducible using the hints stored in plan baseline, then the optimizer always chooses the lowest-cost fixed plan baseline over plan baselines that are not fixed. Essentially, a fixed plan baseline acts as a stored outline with valid hints.

     A fixed plan is **reproducible** when the database can parse the statement based on the hints stored in the plan baseline and create a plan with the same plan hash value as the one in the plan baseline. If one of more of the hints become invalid, then the database may not be able to create a plan with the same plan hash value. In this case, the plan is **nonreproducible**.

     If a fixed plan cannot be reproduced when parsed using its hints, then the optimizer chooses a different plan, which can be either of the following:

     o Another plan for the SQL plan baseline

     o The current cost-based plan created by the optimizer

     In some cases, a performance regression occurs because of the different plan, requiring SQL tuning.
   - Nonfixed plans

     If a plan baseline does not contain fixed plans, then SQL Plan Management considers the plans equally when picking a plan for a SQL statement.
6. Before beginning the actual migration, ensure that the Oracle database meets the following prerequisites:
   - The database must be Enterprise Edition.
   - The database must be open and must *not* be in a suspended state.
   - The database must *not* be in restricted access (DBA), read-only, or migrate mode.
   - OCI must be available.

Migrating Outlines to Utilize SQL Plan Management Features

The goals of this task are as follows:

- To allow SQL Plan Management to select from all plans in a plan baseline for a SQL statement instead of applying the same fixed plan after migration.
- To allow the SQL plan baseline to evolve in the face of database changes by adding new plans to the baseline.

The scenario in this section assumes the following:

- You migrate all outlines.
- You want the module names of the baselines to be identical to the category names of the migrated outlines.
- You do *not* want the SQL plans to be fixed.

  By default, generated plans are not fixed and SQL Plan Management considers all plans equally when picking a plan for a SQL statement. This situation permits the advanced feature of plan evolution to capture new plans for a SQL statement, verify their performance, and accept these new plans into the plan baseline.

To migrate stored outlines to SQL plan baselines:

1. In SQL*Plus, call PL/SQL function `MIGRATE_STORED_OUTLINE`.

   The following sample PL/SQL block migrates all stored outlines to fixed baselines:

```
DECLARE
 my_report CLOB;
BEGIN
 my_report := DBMS_SPM.MIGRATE_STORED_OUTLINE(
attribute_name => 'all' );
END;
/
```

Migrating Outlines to Preserve Stored Outline Behaviour

The goal of this task is to migrate stored outlines to SQL plan baselines and preserve the original behavior of the stored outlines by creating fixed plan baselines. A fixed plan has higher priority over other plans for the same SQL statement. If a plan is fixed, then the plan baseline cannot be evolved. The database does not add new plans to a plan baseline that contains a fixed plan.

This section assumes the following:

- You want to migrate only the stored outlines in the category named `firstrow`.
- You want the module names of the baselines to be identical to the category names of the migrated outlines.

To migrate stored outlines to plan baselines:

1. In SQL*Plus, call PL/SQL function `MIGRATE_STORED_OUTLINE`.

   The following sample PL/SQL block migrates stored outlines in the category `firstrow` to fixed baselines:

```
DECLARE
 my_report CLOB;
BEGIN
 my_outlines := DBMS_SPM.MIGRATE_STORED_OUTLINE(
   attribute_name => 'category',
```

```
    attribute_value => 'firstrow',
    fixed => 'YES' );
END;
/
```

After migration, the SQL plan baselines is in module `firstrow` and category `DEFAULT`.

Performing Follow-Up Tasks After Stored Outline Migration

The goals of this task are as follows:

- To configure the database to use plan baselines instead of stored outlines for stored outlines that have been migrated to SQL plan baselines
- To create SQL plan baselines instead of stored outlines for future SQL statements
- To drop the stored outlines that have been migrated to SQL plan baselines

This section assumes the following:

- You have completed the basic steps in the stored outline migration.
- Some stored outlines may have been created before Oracle Database 10*g*.

Hints in releases before Oracle Database 10*g* use a local hint format. After migration, hints stored in a plan baseline use the global hints format introduced in Oracle Database 10*g*.

This section explains how to set initialization parameters relating to stored outlines and plan baselines. The `OPTIMIZER_CAPTURE_SQL_PLAN_BASELINES` and `CREATE_STORED_OUTLINES` initialization parameters determine how and when the database creates stored outlines and SQL plan baselines. Table 15.5 explains the interaction between these parameters.

Table 15.5 Creation of Outlines and Baselines

CREATE_STORED_OUTLINES Initialization Parameter	**OPTIMIZER_CAPTURE_SQL_PLAN_BASELINES Initialization Parameter**	**Database Behaviour**
FALSE	FALSE	When executing a SQL statement, the database does not create stored outlines or SQL plan baselines.
FALSE	TRUE	The automatic recognition of repeatable SQL statements and the generation of SQL plan baselines for these statements is enabled. When executing a SQL statement, the database creates only new SQL plan baselines (if they do not exist) with the category name `DEFAULT` for the statement.
TRUE	FALSE	Oracle Database automatically creates and stores an outline for each query submitted during the session. When executing a SQL statement, the database creates only new stored outlines (if they do not exist) with the category name `DEFAULT` for the statement.

category	FALSE	When executing a SQL statement, the database creates only new stored outlines (if they do not exist) with the specified category name for the statement.
TRUE	TRUE	Oracle Database automatically creates and stores an outline for each query submitted during the session. The automatic recognition of repeatable SQL statements and the generation of SQL plan baselines for these statements is also enabled. When executing a SQL statement, the database creates both stored outlines and SQL plan baselines with the category name DEFAULT.
category	TRUE	Oracle Database automatically creates and stores an outline for each query submitted during the session. The automatic recognition of repeatable SQL statements and the generation of SQL plan baselines for these statements is also enabled. When executing a SQL statement, the database creates stored outlines with the specified category name and SQL plan baselines with the category name DEFAULT.

The USE_STORED_OUTLINES session parameter (it is *not* an initialization parameter) and OPTIMIZER_USE_SQL_PLAN_BASELINES initialization parameter determine how the database uses stored outlines and plan baselines. Table 15.6 explains how these parameters interact.

Table 15.6. Use of Stored Outlines and SQL Plan Baselines

CREATE_STORED_ OUTLINES Session Parameter	OPTIMIZER_CAPTURE_ SQL_PLAN_BASELINES Initialization Parameter	Database Behaviour
FALSE	FALSE	When choosing a plan for a SQL statement, the database does not use stored outlines or plan baselines.

FALSE	TRUE	When choosing a plan for a SQL statement, the database uses only SQL plan baselines.
TRUE	FALSE	When choosing a plan for a SQL statement, the database uses stored outlines with the category name DEFAULT.
category	FALSE	When choosing a plan for a SQL statement, the database uses stored outlines with the specified category name. If a stored outline with the specified category name does not exist, then the database uses a stored outline in the DEFAULT category if it exists.
TRUE	TRUE	When choosing a plan for a SQL statement, stored outlines take priority over plan baselines. If a stored outline with the category name DEFAULT exists for the statement and is applicable, then the database applies the stored outline. Otherwise, the database uses SQL plan baselines.
category	TRUE	When choosing a plan for a SQL statement, stored outlines take priority over plan baselines. If a stored outline with the specified category name or the DEFAULT category exists for the statement and is applicable, then the database applies the stored outline. Otherwise, the database uses SQL plan baselines. However, if the stored outline has the property MIGRATED, then the database does not use the outline and uses the corresponding SQL plan baseline instead (if it exists).

To place the database in the proper state after the migration:

1. Check that SQL plan baselines have been created as the result of migration.
   Ensure that the plans are enabled and accepted. For example, enter the following query (partial sample output included):

```
SELECT SQL_HANDLE, PLAN_NAME, ORIGIN, ENABLED, ACCEPTED, FIXED,
MODULE
FROM   DBA_SQL_PLAN_BASELINES;
SQL_HANDLE PLAN_NAME     ORIGIN       ENA ACC FIX MODULE
------------------------------        -----------------------------
SYS_SQL_f44779f7089c8fab STMT01       STORED-OUTLINE
YES YES NO   DEFAULT
```

2. Optionally, change the attributes of the SQL plan baselines.
   For example, the following statement changes the status of the baseline for the specified SQL statement to `fixed`:

```
DECLARE
 v_cnt PLS_INTEGER;
BEGIN
 v_cnt := DBMS_SPM.ALTER_SQL_PLAN_BASELINE(
 sql_handle=>'SYS_SQL_f44779f7089c8fab',
                              attribute_name=>'FIXED',
                              attribute_value=>'NO');
DBMS_OUTPUT.PUT_LINE('Plans altered:' || v_cnt);
END;
/
```

3. Check the status of the original stored outlines.
   For example, enter the following query (partial sample output included):

```
SELECT NAME, OWNER, CATEGORY, USED, MIGRATED
FROM   DBA_OUTLINES
ORDER BY NAME;
NAME          OWNER        CATEGORY     USED  MIGRATED
-----------   -------      --------     ----  --------
STMT01        SYS          DEFAULT      USED  MIGRATED
STMT02        SYS          DEFAULT      USED  MIGRATED
```

4. Drop all stored outlines that have been migrated to SQL plan baselines.
   For example, the following statements drops all stored outlines with status `MIGRATED` in `DBA_OUTLINES`:

```
DECLARE
 v_cnt PLS_INTEGER;
BEGIN
 v_cnt := DBMS_SPM.DROP_MIGRATED_STORED_OUTLINE();
DBMS_OUTPUT.PUT_LINE('Migrated stored outlines dropped:'
|| v_cnt);
END;
/
```

5. Set initialization parameters so that:
   - When executing a SQL statement, the database creates plan baselines but does not create stored outlines.
   - The database only uses stored outlines when the equivalent SQL plan baselines do not exist.

For example, the following SQL statements instruct the database to create SQL plan baselines instead of stored outlines when a SQL statement is executed. The example also instructs the database to apply a stored outline in category `allrows` or `DEFAULT` only if it exists and has not been migrated to a SQL plan baseline. In other cases, the database applies SQL plan baselines instead.

```
ALTER  SYSTEM
   SET CREATE_STORED_OUTLINE = false;
ALTER  SYSTEM
   SET OPTIMIZER_CAPTURE_SQL_PLAN_BASELINES = true;
ALTER SYSTEM
   SET OPTIMIZER_USE_SQL_PLAN_BASELINES = true;
ALTER  SESSION
   SET USE_STORED_OUTLINES = allrows.
```

16 SQL Tuning Overview

Learning Objectives

This chapter discusses goals for tuning, how to identify high-resource SQL statements, explains what should be collected, provides tuning suggestions, and discusses how to create SQL test cases to troubleshoot problems in SQL.

This chapter contains the following sections:

- Introduction to SQL Tuning
- Goals for Tuning
- Identifying High-Load SQL
- Automatic SQL Tuning Features
- Developing Efficient SQL Statements
- Building SQL Test Cases

INTRODUCTION TO SQL TUNING

SQL tuning involves the following basic steps:

- Identifying high load or top SQL statements that are responsible for a large share of the application workload and system resources, by reviewing past SQL execution history available in the system.
- Verifying that the execution plans produced by the query optimizer for these statements perform reasonably.
- Implementing corrective actions to generate better execution plans for poorly performing SQL statements.

The previous steps are repeated until the system performance reaches a satisfactory level or no more statements can be tuned.

GOALS FOR TUNING

The objective of tuning a system is either to reduce the response time for end users of the system, or to reduce the resources used to process the same work. You can accomplish both of these objectives in several ways:

- Reduce the Workload
- Balance the Workload
- Parallelize the Workload.

Reduce the Workload

SQL tuning commonly involves finding more efficient ways to process the same workload. It is possible to change the execution plan of the statement without altering the functionality to reduce the resource consumption.

Two examples of how you can resource usage are as follows:

1. If a commonly executed query must access a small percentage of data in the table, then the database can execute it more efficiently by using an index. By creating such an index, you reduce the amount of resources used.
2. If a user is looking at the first twenty rows of the 10,000 rows returned in a specific sort order, and if the query (and sort order) can be satisfied by an index, then the user does not need to access and sort the 10,000 rows to see the first 20 rows.

Balance the Workload

Systems often tend to have peak usage in the daytime when real users are connected to the system, and low usage in the nighttime. If you can schedule noncritical reports and batch jobs to run in the nighttime and reduce their concurrency during day time, then the database frees up resources for the more critical programs in the day.

Parallelize the Workload

Queries that access large amounts of data (typical data warehouse queries) can often run in parallel. Parallelism is extremely useful for reducing response time in a low concurrency data warehouse. However, for OLTP environments, which tend to be high concurrency, parallelism can adversely impact other users by increasing the overall resource usage of the program.

IDENTIFYING HIGH-LOAD SQL

This section describes the steps involved in identifying and gathering data on high-load SQL statements. High-load SQL are poorly-performing, resource-intensive SQL statements that impact the performance of an Oracle database. The following tools can identify high-load SQL statements:

- Automatic Database Diagnostic Monitor
- Automatic SQL tuning
- Automatic Workload Repository
- `V$SQL` view
- Custom Workload
- SQL Trace.

Identifying Resource-Intensive SQL

The first step in identifying resource-intensive SQL is to categorize the problem you are attempting to fix:

- Is the problem specific to a single program (or small number of programs)?
- Is the problem generic over the application?

Tuning a Specific Program

If you are tuning a specific program (GUI or 3GL), then identifying the SQL to examine is a simple matter of looking at the SQL executed within the program. Oracle Enterprise Manager (Enterprise Manager) provides tools for identifying resource intensive SQL statements, generating explain plans, and evaluating SQL performance.

If it is not possible to identify the SQL (for example, the SQL is generated dynamically), then use SQL_TRACE to generate a trace file that contains the SQL executed, then use TKPROF to generate an output file.

The SQL statements in the TKPROF output file can be ordered by various parameters, such as the execution elapsed time (exeela), which usually assists in the identification by ordering the SQL statements by elapsed time (with highest elapsed time SQL statements at the top of the file). This makes the job of identifying the poorly performing SQL easier if there are many SQL statements in the file.

Tuning an Application/Reducing Load

If the whole application is performing poorly, or if you are attempting to reduce the overall CPU or I/O load on the database server, then identifying resource-intensive SQL involves the following steps:

1. Determine which period in the day you would like to examine; typically this is the application's peak processing time.
2. Gather operating system and Oracle Database statistics at the beginning and end of that period. The minimum of Oracle Database statistics gathered should be file I/O (V$FILESTAT), system statistics (V$SYSSTAT), and SQL statistics (V$SQLAREA, V$SQL, or V$SQLSTATS, V$SQLTEXT, V$SQL_PLAN, and V$SQL_PLAN_STATISTICS).
3. Using the data collected in step two, identify the SQL statements using the most resources. A good way to identify candidate SQL statements is to query V$SQLSTATS. V$SQLSTATS contains resource usage information for all SQL statements in the shared pool. The data in V$SQLSTATS should be ordered by resource usage. The most common resources are:
   - Buffer gets (V$SQLSTATS.BUFFER_GETS, for high CPU using statements)
   - Disk reads (V$SQLSTATS.DISK_READS, for high I/O statements)
   - Sorts (V$SQLSTATS.SORTS, for many sorts).

One method to identify which SQL statements are creating the highest load is to compare the resources used by a SQL statement to the total amount of that resource used in the period. For BUFFER_GETS, divide each SQL statement's BUFFER_GETS by the total number of buffer gets during the period. The total number of buffer gets in the system is available in the V$SYSSTAT table, for the statistic session logical reads.

Similarly, it is possible to apportion the percentage of disk reads a statement performs out of the total disk reads performed by the system by dividing V$SQL_STATS.DISK_READS by the value for the V$SYSSTAT statistic physical reads. The SQL sections of the Automatic Workload Repository report include this data, so you do not need to perform the percentage calculations manually.

After you have identified the candidate SQL statements, the next stage is to gather information that is necessary to examine the statements and tune them.

Gathering Data on the SQL Identified

If you are most concerned with CPU, then examine the top SQL statements that performed the most BUFFER_GETS during that interval. Otherwise, start with the SQL statement that performed the most DISK_READS.

Information to Gather During Tuning

The tuning process begins by determining the structure of the underlying tables and indexes. The information gathered includes the following:

1. Complete SQL text from `V$SQLTEXT`.
2. Structure of the tables referenced in the SQL statement, usually by describing the table in SQL*Plus.
3. Definitions of any indexes (columns, column orders), and whether the indexes are unique or non-unique.
4. Optimizer statistics for the segments (including the number of rows each table, selectivity of the index columns), including the date when the segments were last analyzed.
5. Definitions of any views referred to in the SQL statement.
6. Repeat steps two, three, and four for any tables referenced in the view definitions found in step five.
7. Optimizer plan for the SQL statement (either from `EXPLAIN PLAN`, `V$SQL_PLAN`, or the `TKPROF` output).
8. Any previous optimizer plans for that SQL statement.

It is important to generate and review execution plans for all of the key SQL statements in your application. Doing so lets you compare the optimizer execution plans of a SQL statement when the statement performed well to the plan when that the statement is not performing well. Having the comparison, along with information such as changes in data volumes, can assist in identifying the cause of performance degradation.

AUTOMATIC SQL TUNING FEATURES

Because the manual SQL tuning process poses many challenges to the application developer, the SQL tuning process has been automated by the automatic SQL tuning features of Oracle Database. These features are designed to work equally well for OLTP and Data Warehouse type applications:

- ADDM
- SQL Tuning Advisor
- SQL Tuning Sets
- SQL Access Advisor.

ADDM

The Automatic Database Diagnostic Monitor (ADDM) analyzes the information collected by the AWR for possible performance problems with Oracle Database, including high-load SQL statements.

SQL Tuning Advisor

SQL Tuning Advisor optimizes SQL statements that have been identified as high-load SQL statements. By default, Oracle Database automatically identifies problematic SQL statements and implements tuning recommendations using SQL Tuning Advisor during system maintenance windows as an automated maintenance task, searching for ways to improve the execution plans of the high-load SQL statements. You can also choose to run SQL Tuning Advisor at any time on any given SQL workload to improve performance.

SQL Tuning Sets

When multiple SQL statements serve as input to ADDM, SQL Tuning Advisor, or SQL Access Advisor, the database constructs and stores a SQL tuning set (STS). The STS includes the set of SQL statements along with their associated execution context and basic execution statistics.

SQL Access Advisor

In addition to SQL Tuning Advisor, SQL Access Advisor provides advice on materialized views, indexes, and materialized view logs. SQL Access Advisor helps you achieve performance goals by recommending the proper set of materialized views, materialized view logs, and indexes for a given workload. In general, as the number of materialized views and indexes and the space allocated to them is increased, query performance improves. SQL Access Advisor considers the trade-offs between space usage and query performance, and recommends the most cost-effective configuration of new and existing materialized views and indexes.

DEVELOPING EFFICIENT SQL STATEMENTS

This section describes ways you can improve SQL statement efficiency:

- Verifying Optimizer Statistics
- Reviewing the Execution Plan
- Restructuring the SQL Statements
- Restructuring the Indexes
- Modifying or Disabling Triggers and Constraints
- Restructuring the Data
- Maintaining Execution Plans Overtime
- Visiting Data as Few Times as Possible.

The guidelines described in this section are oriented to production of frequently executed SQL. Most techniques that are discouraged here can legitimately be employed in ad hoc statements or in applications run infrequently where performance is not critical.

Verifying Optimizer Statistics

The query optimizer uses statistics gathered on tables and indexes when determining the optimal execution plan. If these statistics have not been gathered, or if the statistics are no longer representative of the data stored within the database, then the optimizer does not have sufficient information to generate the best plan.

Things to check:

- If you gather statistics for some tables in your database, then it is probably best to gather statistics for all tables. This is especially true if your application includes SQL statements that perform joins.
- If the optimizer statistics in the data dictionary are no longer representative of the data in the tables and indexes, then gather new statistics. One way to check whether the dictionary statistics are stale is to compare the real cardinality (row count) of a table to the value of `DBA_TABLES.NUM_ROWS`. Additionally, if there is significant data skew on predicate columns, then consider using histograms.

Reviewing the Execution Plan

When tuning (or writing) a SQL statement in an OLTP environment, the goal is to drive from the table that has the most selective filter. This means that there are fewer rows passed to the next step. If the next step is a join, then this means that fewer rows are joined. Check to see whether the access paths are optimal.

When examining the optimizer execution plan, look for the following:

- The driving table has the best filter.
- The join order in each step returns the fewest number of rows to the next step (that is, the join order should reflect, where possible, going to the best not-yet-used filters).
- The join method is appropriate for the number of rows being returned. For example, nested loop joins through indexes may not be optimal when the statement returns many rows.
- The database uses views efficiently. Look at the `SELECT` list to see whether access to the view is necessary.
- There are any unintentional Cartesian products (even with small tables).
- Each table is being accessed efficiently:

Consider the predicates in the SQL statement and the number of rows in the table. Look for suspicious activity, such as a full table scans on tables with large number of rows, which have predicates in the where clause. Determine why an index is not used for such a selective predicate.

A full table scan does not mean inefficiency. It might be more efficient to perform a full table scan on a small table, or to perform a full table scan to leverage a better join method (for example, hash_join) for the number of rows returned.

If any of these conditions are not optimal, then consider restructuring the SQL statement or the indexes available on the tables.

Restructuring the SQL Statements

Often, rewriting an inefficient SQL statement is easier than modifying it. If you understand the purpose of a given statement, then you might be able to quickly and easily write a new statement that meets the requirement.

Compose Predicates Using AND and =

To improve SQL efficiency, use equijoins whenever possible. Statements that perform equijoins on untransformed column values are the easiest to tune.

Avoid Transformed Columns in the WHERE Clause

Use untransformed column values. For example, use:

```
WHERE a.order_no = b.order_no
```

rather than:

```
WHERE TO_NUMBER (SUBSTR(a.order_no, INSTR(b.order_no, '.') - 1))=
TO_NUMBER (SUBSTR(a.order_no, INSTR(b.order_no, '.') - 1))
```

Do not use SQL functions in predicate clauses or `WHERE` clauses. Any expression using a column, such as a function having the column as its argument, causes the optimizer to ignore the possibility of using an index on that column, even a unique index, unless there is a function-based index defined that the database can use.

Avoid mixed-mode expressions, and beware of implicit type conversions. When you want to use an index on the `VARCHAR2` column `charcol`, but the `WHERE` clause looks like this:

```
AND charcol = numexpr
```

where `numexpr` is an expression of number type (for example, 1, `USERENV('SESSIONID')`, `numcol`, `numcol+0`,...), Oracle Database translates that expression into:

```
AND TO_NUMBER(charcol) = numexpr
```

Avoid the following kinds of complex expressions:

- `col1 = NVL (:b1,col1)`
- `NVL (col1,-999) = ....`
- `TO_DATE()`, `TO_NUMBER()`, and so on

These expressions prevent the optimizer from assigning valid cardinality or selectivity estimates and can in turn affect the overall plan and the join method.

Add the predicate versus using `NVL()` technique.

For example:

```
SELECT employee_num, full_name Name, employee_id
FROM mtl_employees_current_view
WHERE (employee_num = NVL (:b1,employee_num)) AND
(organization_id=:1)
ORDER BY employee_num;
```

Also:

```
SELECT employee_num, full_name Name, employee_id
  FROM mtl_employees_current_view
  WHERE (employee_num = :b1) AND (organization_id=:1)
  ORDER BY employee_num;
```

When you need to use SQL functions on filters or join predicates, do not use them on the columns on which you want to have an index, as in the following statement:

```
varcol = TO_CHAR(numcol)
```

Instead, use them on the opposite side of the predicate, as in the following statement:

```
TO_CHAR(numcol) = varcol
```

Write Separate SQL Statements for Specific Tasks

SQL is not a procedural language. Using one piece of SQL to do many different things usually results in a less-than-optimal result for each task. If you want SQL to accomplish different things, then write various statements, rather than writing one statement to do different things depending on the parameters you give it.

> Oracle Forms and Reports are powerful development tools that allow application logic to be coded using PL/SQL (triggers or program units). This helps reduce the complexity of SQL by allowing complex logic to be handled in the Forms or Reports. You can also invoke a server side PL/SQL package that performs the few SQL statements in place of a single large complex SQL statement. Because the package is a server-side unit, there are no issues surrounding client to database round-trips and network traffic.

It is always better to write separate SQL statements for different tasks, but if you must use one SQL statement, then you can make a very complex statement slightly less complex by using the `UNION ALL` operator.

Optimization (determining the execution plan) takes place before the database knows the values substituted in the query. An execution plan cannot, therefore, depend on what those values are. For example:

```
SELECT info
FROM tables
WHERE ...
AND somecolumn BETWEEN DECODE(:loval, 'ALL', somecolumn, :loval)
AND DECODE(:hival, 'ALL', somecolumn, :hival);
```

Written as shown, the database cannot use an index on the `somecolumn` column, because the expression involving that column uses the same column on both sides of the **BETWEEN**.

This is not a problem if there is some other highly selective, indexable condition you can use to access the driving table. Often, however, this is not the case. Frequently, you might want to use an index on a condition like that shown but need to know the values of `:loval`, and so on, in advance. With this information, you can rule out the **ALL** case, which should not use the index.

To use the index whenever real values are given for :`loval` and :`hival` (if you expect narrow ranges, even ranges where :`loval` often equals :`hival`), you can rewrite the example in the following logically equivalent form:

```
SELECT /* change this half of UNION ALL if other half changes */ info
FROM   tables
WHERE  ...
AND    somecolumn BETWEEN :loval AND :hival
AND   (:hival != 'ALL' AND :loval != 'ALL')
UNION ALL
SELECT /* Change this half of UNION ALL if other half changes. */ info
FROM   tables
WHERE  ...
AND (:hival = 'ALL' OR :loval = 'ALL');
```

If you run **EXPLAIN PLAN** on the new query, then you seem to get both a desirable and an undesirable execution plan. However, the first condition the database evaluates for either half of the **UNION ALL** is the combined condition on whether `:hival` and `:loval` are **ALL**. The database evaluates this condition before actually getting any rows from the execution plan for that part of the query.

When the condition comes back false for one part of the **UNION ALL** query, that part is not evaluated further. Only the part of the execution plan that is optimum for the values provided is actually carried out. Because the final conditions on `:hival` and `:loval` are guaranteed to be mutually exclusive, only one half of the **UNION ALL** actually returns rows. (The **ALL** in **UNION ALL** is logically valid because of this exclusivity. It allows the plan to be carried out without an expensive sort to rule out duplicate rows for the two halves of the query.)

Controlling the Access Path and Join Order with Hints

You can influence the optimizer's choices by setting the optimizer approach and goal, and by gathering representative statistics for the query optimizer. Sometimes, the application designer, who has more information about a particular application's data than is available to the optimizer, can choose a more effective way to execute a SQL statement. You can use hints in SQL statements to instruct the optimizer about how the statement should be executed.

Hints, such as /*+FULL */ control access paths. For example:

```
SELECT /*+ FULL(e) */ e.last_name  FROM employees e
 WHERE e.job_id = 'CLERK';
```

Join order can have a significant effect on performance. The main objective of SQL tuning is to avoid performing unnecessary work to access rows that do not affect the result. This leads to three general rules:

- Avoid a full-table scan if it is more efficient to get the required rows through an index.
- Avoid using an index that fetches 10,000 rows from the driving table if you could instead use another index that fetches 100 rows.
- Choose the join order so as to join fewer rows to tables later in the join order.

The following example shows how to tune join order effectively:

```
SELECT info
FROM taba a, tabb b, tabc c
WHERE a.acol BETWEEN 100 AND 200
AND b.bcol BETWEEN 10000 AND 20000
AND c.ccol BETWEEN 10000 AND 20000
AND a.key1 = b.key1
AND a.key2 = c.key2;
```

1. Choose the driving table and the driving index (if any).
   The first three conditions in the previous example are filter conditions applying to only a single table each. The last two conditions are join conditions.
   Filter conditions dominate the choice of driving table and index. In general, the driving table is the one containing the filter condition that eliminates the highest percentage of the table. Thus, because the range of 100 to 200 is narrow compared with the range of acol, but the ranges of 10000 and 20000 are relatively large, taba is the driving table, all else being equal.
   With nested loop joins, the joins all happen through the join indexes, the indexes on the primary or foreign keys used to connect that table to an earlier table in the join tree. Rarely do you use the indexes on the non-join conditions, except for the driving table. Thus, after taba is chosen as the driving table, use the indexes on b.key1 and c.key2 to drive into tabb and tabc, respectively.
2. Choose the best join order, driving to the best unused filters earliest.
   You can reduce the work of the following join by first joining to the table with the best still-unused filter. Thus, if "bcol BETWEEN ..." is more restrictive (rejects a higher percentage of the rows seen) than "ccol BETWEEN ...", then the last join becomes easier (with fewer rows) if tabb is joined before tabc.
3. You can use the ORDERED or STAR hint to force the join order.

Use Caution When Managing Views

Be careful when joining views, when performing outer joins to views, and when reusing an existing view for a new purpose.

Use Caution When Joining Complex Views

Joins to complex views are not recommended, particularly joins from one complex view to another. Often this results in the entire view being instantiated, and then the query is run against the view data.

For example, the following statement creates a view that lists employees and departments:

```
CREATE OR REPLACE VIEW emp_dept
AS SELECT d.department_id, d.department_name, d.location_id,
e.employee_id, e.last_name, e.first_name, e.salary, e.job_id
FROM  departments d,employees e
WHERE e.department_id (+) = d.department_id;
```

The following query finds employees in a specified state:

```
SELECT v.last_name, v.first_name, l.state_province
  FROM locations l, emp_dept v WHERE l.state_province = 'California'
AND   v.location_id = l.location_id (+);
```

In the following plan table output, note that the emp_dept view is instantiated:

```
----------------------------------------------------------------------
| Operation                       | Name         | Rows    | Bytes    | Cost
| Pstart| Pstop |
----------------------------------------------------------------------
| SELECT STATEMENT                |              |         |          |
|       |       |
|  FILTER                         |              |         |          |
|       |       |
|   NESTED LOOPS OUTER            |              |         |          |
|       |       |
|    VIEW                         |EMP_DEPT      |         |          |
|       |       |
|     NESTED LOOPS OUTER          |              |         |          |
|       |       |
|     TABLE ACCESS FULL           |DEPARTMEN     |         |          |
|       |       |
|     TABLE ACCESS BY INDEX       |EMPLOYEES     |         |          |
|       |       |
|      INDEX RANGE SCAN           |EMP_DEPAR     |         |          |
|       |       |
|   TABLE ACCESS BY INDEX R       |LOCATIONS     |         |          |
|       |       |
|    INDEX UNIQUE SCAN            |LOC_ID_PK     |         |          |
|       |       |
----------------------------------------------------------------------
```

Do Not Recycle Views

Beware of writing a view for one purpose and then using it for other purposes to which it might be ill-suited. Querying from a view requires all tables from the view to be accessed for the data to be returned. Before reusing a view, determine whether all tables in the view need to be accessed to return the data. If not, then do not use the view. Instead, use the base table(s), or if necessary, define a new view. The goal is to refer to the minimum number of tables and views necessary to return the required data.

Consider the following example:

```
SELECT department_name FROM emp_dept
WHERE department_id = 10;
```

The entire view is first instantiated by performing a join of the `employees` and `departments` tables and then aggregating the data. However, you can obtain `department_name` and `department_id` directly from the `departments` table. It is inefficient to obtain this information by querying the `emp_dept` view.

Use Caution When Unnesting Subqueries

Subquery unnesting merges the body of the subquery into the body of the statement that contains it, allowing the optimizer to consider them together when evaluating access paths and joins.

Use Caution When Performing Outer Joins to Views

In the case of an outer join to a multi-table view, the query optimizer (in Release 8.1.6 and later) can drive from an outer join column, if an equality predicate is defined on it.

An outer join *within* a view is problematic because the performance implications of the outer join are not visible.

Store Intermediate Results

Intermediate, or staging, tables are quite common in relational database systems, because they temporarily store some intermediate results. In many applications they are useful, but Oracle Database requires additional resources to create them. Always consider whether the benefit they could bring is more than the cost to create them. Avoid staging tables when the information is not reused multiple times.

Some additional considerations:

- Storing intermediate results in staging tables could improve application performance. In general, whenever an intermediate result is usable by multiple following queries, it is worthwhile to store it in a staging table. The benefit of not retrieving data multiple times with a complex statement at the second usage of the intermediate result is better than the cost to materialize it.
- Long and complex queries are hard to understand and optimize. Staging tables can break a complicated SQL statement into several smaller statements, and then store the result of each step.
- Consider using materialized views. These are precomputed tables comprising aggregated or joined data from fact and possibly dimension tables.

Restructuring the Indexes

Often, there is a beneficial impact on performance by restructuring indexes. This can involve the following:

- Remove nonselective indexes to speed the DML.
- Index performance-critical access paths.
- Consider reordering columns in existing concatenated indexes.
- Add columns to the index to improve selectivity.

Do not use indexes as a panacea. Application developers sometimes think that performance improves when they create more indexes. If a single programmer creates an appropriate index, then this index may improve the application's performance. However, if 50 developers each create an index, then application performance will probably be hampered.

Modifying or Disabling Triggers and Constraints

Using triggers consumes system resources. If you use too many triggers, then performance may be adversely affected. In this case, you might need to modify or disable the triggers.

Restructuring the Data

After restructuring the indexes and the statement, consider restructuring the data:

- Introduce derived values. Avoid `GROUP BY` in response-critical code.
- Review your data design. Change the design of your system if it can improve performance.
- Consider partitioning, if appropriate.

Maintaining Execution Plans Overtime

You can maintain the existing execution plan of SQL statements over time either using stored statistics or SQL plan baselines. Storing optimizer statistics for tables will apply to all SQL statements that refer to those tables. Storing an execution plan as a SQL plan baseline maintains the plan for set of SQL statements. If both statistics and a SQL plan baseline are available for a SQL statement, then the optimizer first uses a cost-based search method to build a best-cost plan, and then tries to find a matching plan in the SQL plan baseline. If a match is found, then the optimizer proceeds using this plan. Otherwise, it evaluates the cost of each of the accepted plans in the SQL plan baseline and selects the plan with the lowest cost.

Visiting Data as Few Times as Possible

Applications should try to access each row only once. This reduces network traffic and reduces database load. Consider doing the following:

- Combine Multiples Scans Using CASE Expressions
- Use DML with RETURNING Clause
- Modify All the Data Needed in One Statement.

Combine Multiples Scans Using CASE Expressions

Often, it is necessary to calculate different aggregates on various sets of tables. Usually, you achieve this goal with multiple scans on the table, but it is easy to calculate all the aggregates with a single scan. Eliminating *n*-1 scans can greatly improve performance.

You can combine multiple scans into one scan by moving the `WHERE` condition of each scan into a `CASE` expression, which filters the data for the aggregation. For each aggregation, there could be another column that retrieves the data.

The following example asks for the count of all employees who earn less then 2000, between 2000 and 4000, and more than 4000 each month. You can obtain this result by executing three separate queries:

```
SELECT COUNT (*)
  FROM employees  WHERE salary < 2000;
SELECT COUNT (*)
  FROM employees  WHERE salary BETWEEN 2000 AND 4000;
SELECT COUNT (*)
  FROM employees  WHERE salary>4000;
```

However, it is more efficient to run the entire query in a single statement. Each number is calculated as one column. The count uses a filter with the `CASE` expression to count only the rows where the condition is valid. For example:

```
SELECT COUNT (CASE WHEN salary < 2000
                   THEN 1 ELSE null END) count1,
       COUNT (CASE WHEN salary BETWEEN 2001 AND 4000
                   THEN 1 ELSE null END) count2,
       COUNT (CASE WHEN salary > 4000
                   THEN 1 ELSE null END) count3
  FROM employees;
```

This is a very simple example. The ranges could be overlapping, the functions for the aggregates could be different, and so on.

Use DML with RETURNING Clause

When appropriate, use INSERT, UPDATE, or DELETE... RETURNING to select and modify data with a single call. This technique improves performance by reducing the number of calls to the database.

Modify All the Data Needed in One Statement

When possible, use array processing. This means that an array of bind variable values is passed to Oracle Database for repeated execution. This is appropriate for iterative processes in which multiple rows of a set are subject to the same operation.

For example:

```
BEGIN
 FOR pos_rec IN (SELECT * FROM order_positions
   WHERE order_id = :id) LOOP DELETE FROM order_positions
      WHERE order_id = pos_rec.order_id AND
        order_position = pos_rec.order_position;
 END LOOP;
 DELETE FROM orders
 WHERE order_id = :id;
END;
```

Alternatively, you could define a cascading constraint on orders. In the previous example, one SELECT and *n* DELETEs are executed. When a user issues the DELETE on orders DELETE FROM orders WHERE order_id = :id, the database automatically deletes the positions with a single DELETE statement.

BUILDING SQL TEST CASES

For many SQL-related problems, obtaining a reproducible test case makes it easier to resolve the problem. Starting with the 11*g* Release 2 (11.2), Oracle Database contains the SQL Test Case Builder, which automates the somewhat difficult and time-consuming process of gathering and reproducing as much information as possible about a problem and the environment in which it occurred.

SQL Test Case Builder captures information pertaining to a SQL-related problem, along with the exact environment under which the problem occurred, so that you can reproduce and test the problem on a separate database. After the test case is ready, you can upload the problem to Oracle Support to enable support personnel to reproduce and troubleshoot the problem.

The information gathered by SQL Test Case Builder includes the query being executed, table and index definitions (but not the actual data), PL/SQL functions, procedures, and packages, optimizer statistics, and initialization parameter settings.

Creating a Test Case

You can access the SQL Test Case Builder from Enterprise Manager or manually using the DBMS_SQLDIAG package.

Accessing SQL Test Case Builder from Enterprise Manager

From Enterprise Manager, the SQL Test Case Builder is accessible only when a SQL incident occurs. A SQL-related problem is referred to as a SQL incident, and each SQL incident is identified by an incident number. You can access the SQL Test Case Builder from the Support Workbench page in Enterprise Manager.

You can access the Support Workbench page in either of the following ways:

- In the Database Home page of Enterprise Manager, under Diagnostic Summary, click the link to Active Incidents (indicating the number of active incidents). This opens the Support Workbench page, with the incidents listed in a table.
- Click **Advisor Central** under Related Links to open the Advisor Central page. Next, click **SQL Advisors** and then **Click here to go to Support Workbench** to open the Support Workbench page.

From the Support Workbench page, to access the SQL Test Case Builder:

- Click an incident ID to open the problem details for the particular incident.
- Next, click **Oracle Support** in the Investigate and Resolve section.
- Click **Generate Additional Dumps and Test Cases**.
- For a particular incident, click the icon in the Go To Task column to run the SQL Test Case Builder.

The output of the SQL Test Case Builder is a SQL script that contains the commands required to re-create all the necessary objects and the environment. SQL Test Case Builder stores the file in the following location, where *inc_num* refers to the incident number and *run_num* refers to the run number:

```
$ADR_HOME/incident/incdir_inc_num/SQLTCB_run num
```

For example, a valid output file name could be as follows:

```
$ORACLE_HOME/log/diag/rdbms/dbsa/dbsa/incident/incdir_2657/SQLTCB_1
```

Accessing SQL Test Case Builder Using DBMS_SQLDIAG

You can also invoke the SQL Test Case Builder manually, using the DBMS_SQLDIAG package. This package consists of various subprograms for the SQL Test Case Builder, some of which are listed in Table 16.1.

Table 16.1. SQL Test Case Builder Procedures in DBMS_SQLDIAG

Procedure Name	Function
EXPORT_SQL_TESTCASE	Generates a SQL test case
EXPORT_SQL_TESTCASE_DIR_BY_INC	Generates a SQL test case corresponding to the incident ID passed as an argument
EXPORT_SQL_TESTCASE_DIR_BY_TXT	Generates a SQL test case corresponding to the SQL text passed as an argument

17 Automatic SQL Tuning

Learning Objectives

This chapter discusses the automatic SQL tuning features of Oracle Database. Automatic SQL tuning automates the manual process, which is complex, repetitive, and time-consuming.

This chapter contains the following sections:

- Overview of the Automatic Tuning Optimizer
- Managing the Automatic SQL Tuning Advisor
- Tuning Reactively with SQL Tuning Advisor
- Managing SQL Tuning Sets
- Managing SQL Profiles
- SQL Tuning Views

OVERVIEW OF THE AUTOMATIC TUNING OPTIMIZER

Oracle Database uses the optimizer to generate the execution plans for submitted SQL statements. The optimizer operates in the following modes:

- Normal mode.
  The optimizer compiles the SQL and generates an execution plan. The normal mode generates a reasonable plan for the vast majority of SQL statements. Under normal mode, the optimizer operates with very strict time constraints, usually a fraction of a second.
- Tuning mode.
  The optimizer performs additional analysis to check whether it can further improve the plan produced in normal mode. The optimizer output is not an execution plan, but a series of actions, along with their rationale and expected benefit for producing a significantly better plan. When running in tuning mode, the optimizer is known as the **Automatic Tuning Optimizer.**

Under tuning mode, the optimizer can take several minutes to tune a single statement. It is both time and resource intensive to invoke Automatic Tuning Optimizer every time a query must be hard-parsed. Automatic Tuning Optimizer is meant for complex and high-load SQL statements that have nontrivial impact on the database.

Automatic Database Diagnostic Monitor (ADDM) proactively identifies high-load SQL statements that are good candidates for SQL tuning. The automatic SQL tuning feature also automatically identifies problematic SQL statements and implements tuning recommendations during system maintenance windows as an automated maintenance task.

The Automatic Tuning Optimizer performs the following types of tuning analysis:

- Statistics Analysis
- SQL Profiling
- Access Path Analysis
- SQL Structure Analysis
- Alternative Plan Analysis.

Statistics Analysis

The optimizer relies on object statistics to generate execution plans. If these statistics are stale or missing, then the optimizer does not have the necessary information it needs and can generate poor execution plans. The Automatic Tuning Optimizer checks each query object for missing or stale statistics, and produces two types of output:

- Recommendations to gather relevant statistics for objects with stale or no statistics
  Because optimizer statistics are automatically collected and refreshed, this problem occurs only when automatic optimizer statistics collection is disabled.
- Auxiliary statistics for objects with no statistics, and statistic adjustment factor for objects with stale statistics.

The database stores this auxiliary information in an object called a SQL profile.

SQL Profiling

A SQL profile is a set of auxiliary information specific to a SQL statement. Conceptually, a SQL profile is to a SQL statement what statistics are to a table or index. The database can use the auxiliary information to improve execution plans.

Access Path Analysis

An access path is the means by which data is retrieved from a database. For example, a query using an index and a query using a full table scan use different access paths.

Indexes can tremendously enhance performance of a SQL statement by reducing the need for full scans of large tables. Effective indexing is a common tuning technique. Automatic Tuning Optimizer explores whether a new index can significantly enhance query performance. If so, then the advisor recommends index creation.

Because the Automatic Tuning Optimizer does not analyze how its index recommendation can affect the entire SQL workload, it also recommends running SQL Access Advisor on the SQL statement along with a representative SQL workload. SQL Access Advisor looks at the impact of creating an index on the entire SQL workload before making recommendations.

SQL Structure Analysis

Automatic Tuning Optimizer identifies common problems with the structure of SQL statements that can lead to poor performance. These could be syntactic, semantic, or design problems. In each case, Automatic Tuning Optimizer makes relevant suggestions to restructure the statements. The suggested alternative is similar, but not equivalent, to the original statement.

For example, the optimizer may suggest replacing the `UNION` operator with `UNION ALL` or `NOT IN` with `NOT EXISTS`. You can then determine if the advice is applicable to your situation. For example, if the schema design is such that duplicates are not possible, then the

UNION ALL operator is much more efficient than the UNION operator. These changes require a good understanding of the data properties and should be implemented only after careful consideration.

Alternative Plan Analysis

While tuning a SQL statement, SQL Tuning Advisor searches real-time and historical performance data for **alternative execution plans** for the statement. If plans other than the original plan exist, then SQL Tuning Advisor reports an alternative plan finding.

SQL Tuning Advisor validates the alternative execution plans and notes any plans that are not reproducible. When reproducible alternative plans are found, you can create a SQL plan baseline to instruct the optimizer to choose these plans in the future.

Shows an alternative plan finding for a SELECT statement.

Example 17.1: Alternative Plan Finding

```
2- Alternative Plan Finding
-------------------------------
 Some alternative execution plans for this statement were found by
searching  the system's real-time and historical performance data.
The following table lists these plans ranked by their average elapsed
time.
See section "ALTERNATIVE PLANS SECTION" for detailed information on
each plan.
id plan hash  last seen   elapsed (s)  origin     note
-------------------------------------------------------------------------
   1 1378942017  2009-02-05/23:12:08  0.000 Cursor Cache
     original plan
   2 2842999589  2009-02-05/23:12:08        0.002 STS
  Information
  -----------
The Original Plan appears to have the best performance, based on the
elapsed time per execution. However, if you know that one alternative plan
is better than the Original Plan, you can create a SQL plan baseline or
it. This will instruct the Oracle optimizer to pick it over any other
choices in the future.
execute dbms_sqltune.create_sql_plan_baseline(task_name => 'TASK_
XXXXX',object_id => 2, task_owner => 'SYS', plan_hash => xxxxxxxx );
```

Shows that SQL Tuning Advisor found two plans, one in the shared SQL area and one in a SQL tuning set. The plan in the shared SQL area is the same as the original plan.

SQL Tuning Advisor only recommends an alternative plan if the elapsed time of the original plan is worse than alternative plans. In this case, SQL Tuning Advisor recommends that users create a SQL plan baseline on the plan with the best performance. In, the alternative plan did not perform as well as the original plan, so SQL Tuning Advisor did not recommend using the alternative plan.

In, the alternative plans section of the SQL Tuning Advisor output includes both the original and alternative plans and summarizes their performance. The most important statistic is elapsed time. The original plan used an index, whereas the alternative plan used a full table scan, increasing elapsed time by .002 seconds.

Example 17.2: Alternative Plans Section

```
Plan 1
-------
  Plan Origin                  :Cursor Cache
  Plan Hash Value              :1378942017
  Executions                   :50
  Elapsed Time                 :0.000 sec
  CPU Time                     :0.000 sec
  Buffer Gets                  :0
  Disk Reads                   :0
  Disk Writes                  :0
```

1. Statistics shown are averaged over multiple executions.
2. The plan matches the original plan.

```
--------------------------------------------
| Id  | Operation             | Name        |
--------------------------------------------
|   0 | SELECT STATEMENT      |             |
|   1 |  SORT AGGREGATE       |             |
|   2 |   MERGE JOIN          |             |
|   3 |    INDEX FULL SCAN    | TEST1_INDEX |
|   4 |    SORT JOIN          |             |
|   5 |     TABLE ACCESS FULL| TEST        |
--------------------------------------------

Plan 2
------
  Plan Origin                  :STS
  Plan Hash Value              :2842999589
  Executions                   :10
  Elapsed Time                 :0.002 sec
  CPU Time                     :0.002 sec
  Buffer Gets                  :3
  Disk Reads                   :0
  Disk Writes                  :0
```

1. Statistics shown are averaged over multiple executions.

```
-------------------------------------
| Id  | Operation             | Name  |
-------------------------------------
|   0 | SELECT STATEMENT      |       |
|   1 |  SORT AGGREGATE       |       |
|   2 |   HASH JOIN           |       |
|   3 |    TABLE ACCESS FULL| TEST  |
|   4 |    TABLE ACCESS FULL| TEST1 |
-------------------------------------
```

To adopt an alternative plan regardless of whether SQL Tuning Advisor recommends it, call `DBMS_SQLTUNE.CREATE_SQL_PLAN_BASELINE`. You can use this procedure to create a SQL plan baseline on any existing reproducible plan.

MANAGING THE AUTOMATIC SQL TUNING ADVISOR

SQL Tuning Advisor takes one or more SQL statements as an input and invokes the Automatic Tuning Optimizer to perform SQL tuning on the statements. The output takes the form of advice or recommendations, along with a rationale for each recommendation and its expected benefit. The recommendation relates to a collection of statistics on objects, creation of new indexes, restructuring of the SQL statement, or creation of a SQL profile. You can choose to accept the recommendation to complete the tuning of the SQL statements.

The database can automatically tune SQL statements by identifying problematic statements and implementing recommendations using SQL Tuning Advisor during system maintenance windows. When run automatically, SQL Tuning Advisor is known as the **Automatic SQL Tuning Advisor.**

This section explains how to manage the Automatic SQL Tuning Advisor:

- How Automatic SQL Tuning Works
- Enabling and Disabling Automatic SQL Tuning
- Configuring Automatic SQL Tuning
- Viewing Automatic SQL Tuning Reports.

How Automatic SQL Tuning Works

Oracle Database automatically runs SQL Tuning Advisor on selected high-load SQL statements from the Automatic Workload Repository (AWR) that qualify as tuning candidates. This task, called **Automatic SQL Tuning**, runs in the default maintenance windows on a nightly basis. By default, automatic SQL tuning runs for at most one hour. You can customize attributes of the maintenance windows, including start and end time, frequency, and days of the week.

After automatic SQL tuning begins, the database performs the following steps:

1. Identifies SQL candidates in the AWR for tuning.

   Oracle Database analyzes statistics in AWR and generates a list of potential SQL statements that are eligible for tuning. These statements include repeating high-load statements that have a significant impact on the database.

   The database tunes only SQL statements that have an execution plan with a high potential for improvement. The database ignores recursive SQL and statements that have been tuned recently (in the last month), parallel queries, DML, DDL, and SQL statements with performance problems caused by concurrency issues.

   The database orders the SQL statements that are selected as candidates based on their performance impact. The database calculates the impact by summing the CPU time and the I/O times in AWR for the selected statement in the past week.
2. Tunes each SQL statement individually by calling SQL Tuning Advisor.

   During the tuning process, the database considers and reports all recommendation types, but it can implement only SQL profiles automatically.
3. Tests SQL profiles by executing the SQL statement.

   If a SQL profile is recommended, the database tests the new profile by executing the SQL statement both with and without the profile. If the performance improvement improves at least threefold, then the database accepts the SQL profile, but only if the

ACCEPT_SQL_PROFILES task parameter is set to TRUE. Otherwise, the automatic SQL tuning reports merely report the recommendation to create a SQL profile.

4. Optionally, implements the SQL profiles provided they meet the criteria of threefold performance improvement.
   The database considers other factors when deciding whether to implement the SQL profile. For example, the database does not implement a profile when the objects referenced in the statement have stale optimizer statistics. SQL profiles that have been implemented automatically show type is AUTO in the DBA_SQL_PROFILES view.
   If the database uses SQL plan management, and if a SQL plan baseline exists for the SQL statement, then the database adds a new plan baseline when creating the SQL profile. As a result, the optimizer uses the new plan immediately after profile creation.

At any time during or after the automatic SQL tuning process, you can view the results using the automatic SQL tuning report. This report describes in detail all the SQL statements that were analyzed, the recommendations generated, and the SQL profiles that were automatically implemented.

Figure 17.1 shows the steps performed by the database during automatic SQL tuning.

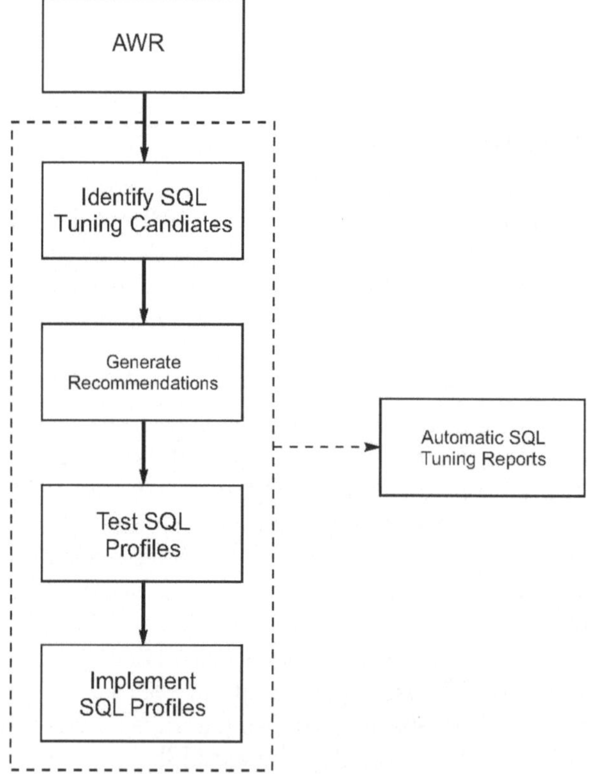

Figure 17.1. Automatic SQL Tuning

Enabling and Disabling Automatic SQL Tuning

Automatic SQL tuning runs as part of the automated maintenance tasks infrastructure.

To enable automatic SQL tuning, use the ENABLE procedure in the DBMS_AUTO_TASK_ADMIN package:

```
BEGIN
  DBMS_AUTO_TASK_ADMIN.ENABLE(
    client_name => 'sql tuning advisor',
    operation => NULL,
    window_name => NULL);
END;
/
```

To disable automatic SQL tuning, use the `DISABLE` procedure in the `DBMS_AUTO_TASK_ADMIN` package:

```
BEGIN
  DBMS_AUTO_TASK_ADMIN.DISABLE(
    client_name => 'sql tuning advisor',
    operation => NULL,
    window_name => NULL);
END;
/
```

You can pass a specific window name using the `window_name` parameter to enable or disable the task in certain maintenance windows only.

Setting the `STATISTICS_LEVEL` parameter to `BASIC` disables automatic statistics gathering by the AWR and, as a result, also disables automatic SQL tuning.

Configuring Automatic SQL Tuning

Starting with Oracle Database 11*g* Release 2 (11.2.0.2), you can use the `DBMS_AUTO_SQLTUNE` package to configure the behavior of the automatic SQL tuning task. For previous releases, use `DBMS_SQLTUNE` instead.

Table 17.2 lists the configurable parameters specific to automatic SQL tuning.

Table 17.1. SET_AUTO_TUNING_TASK_PARAMETER Automatic SQL Tuning Parameters

Parameter	Description
ACCEPT_SQL_PROFILE	Specifies whether to accept SQL profiles automatically.
EXECUTION_DAYS_TO_EXPIRE	Specifies the number of days for which to save the task history in the advisor framework schema. By default, the task history is saved for 30 days before it expires.
MAX_SQL_PROFILES_PER_EXEC	Specifies the limit of SQL profiles that are accepted for each automatic SQL tuning task. Consider setting the limit of SQL profiles that are accepted for each automatic SQL tuning task based on the acceptable level of changes that can be made to the system on a daily basis.
MAX_AUTO_SQL_PROFILES	Specifies the limit of SQL profiles that are accepted in total.

To use the DBMS_AUTO_SQLTUNE package, you must have the DBA role, or have EXECUTE privileges granted by an administrator. The only exception is the EXECUTE_AUTO_TUNING_TASK procedure, which can only be run by SYS.

To Configure Automatic SQL Tuning:

1. Start SQL*Plus, and connect to the database with DBA privileges (or connect as SYS if you plan to run EXECUTE_AUTO_TUNING_TASK).
2. Run the DBMS_AUTO_SQLTUNE.SET_AUTO_TUNING_TASK_PARAMETER procedure. The following example configures the automatic SQL tuning task to automatically accept SQL profiles recommended by SQL Tuning Advisor:

```
BEGIN
DBMS_AUTO_SQLTUNE.SET_AUTO_TUNING_TASK_PARAMETER(
parameter => 'ACCEPT_SQL_PROFILES', value => 'TRUE');
END;
/
```

Viewing Automatic SQL Tuning Reports

Starting with Oracle Database 11g Release 2 (11.2.0.2), you can use the DBMS_AUTO_SQLTUNE.REPORT_AUTO_TUNING_TASK function to generate the automatic SQL tuning report. For previous releases, use the DBMS_SQLTUNE package instead.

The report contains information about multiple executions of the Automatic SQL Tuning task. Depending on the sections that were included in the report, you can view information about the automatic SQL tuning task in the following sections:

- General information.
  The general information section has a high-level description of the automatic SQL tuning task, including information about the inputs given for the report, the number of SQL statements tuned during the maintenance, and the number of SQL profiles created.
- Summary.
  The summary section lists the SQL statements (by their SQL identifiers) that were tuned during the maintenance window and the estimated benefit of each SQL profile, or their actual execution statistics after test executing the SQL statement with the SQL profile.
- Tuning findings.
  This section contains the following information about each SQL statement analyzed by SQL Tuning Advisor:
  - All findings associated with each SQL statement
  - Whether the profile was accepted on the database, and why
  - Whether the SQL profile is currently enabled on the database
  - Detailed execution statistics captured when testing the SQL profile.
- Explain plans.
  This section shows the old and new explain plans used by each SQL statement analyzed by SQL Tuning Advisor.
- Errors.
  This section lists all errors encountered by the automatic SQL tuning task.

To view the automatic SQL tuning report using DBMS_AUTO_SQLTUNE:

1. Start SQL*Plus, and connect to the database with the appropriate privileges.
2. Run the DBMS_AUTO_SQLTUNE.REPORT_AUTO_TUNING_TASK function.

In the following example, the advisor generates a text report to show all SQL statements that were analyzed in the most recent execution, including recommendations that were not implemented.

```
VARIABLE my_rept CLOB;
BEGIN
  :my_rept :=DBMS_AUTO_SQLTUNE.REPORT_AUTO_TUNING_TASK(
    begin_exec   => NULL,
    end_exec     => NULL,
    type         => 'TEXT',
    level        => 'TYPICAL',
    section      => 'ALL',
    object_id    => NULL,
    result_limit => NULL);
END;
/

PRINT :my_rept
```

TUNING REACTIVELY WITH SQL TUNING ADVISOR

You can invoke SQL Tuning Advisor manually for on-demand tuning of one or more SQL statements. To tune multiple statements, you must create a SQL tuning set (STS). A SQL tuning set is a database object that stores SQL statements along with their execution context. You can create a SQL tuning set using command line APIs or Enterprise Manager.

Input Sources

Input for SQL Tuning Advisor can come from several sources, including the following:

- ADDM (Automatic Database Diagnostic Monitor).
  The primary input source is ADDM. By default, ADDM runs proactively once every hour and analyzes key statistics gathered by the Automatic Workload Repository (AWR) over the last hour to identify any performance problems including high-load SQL statements. If a high-load SQL is identified, ADDM recommends running SQL Tuning Advisor on the SQL.
- AWR.
  The second most important input source is the Automatic Workload Repository (AWR). AWR takes regular snapshots of system activity, including high-load SQL statements ranked by relevant statistics, such as CPU consumption and wait time.
  You can view the AWR and manually identify high-load SQL statements. You can run SQL Tuning Advisor on these statements, although Oracle Database automatically performs this work as part of automatic SQL tuning. By default, AWR retains data for the last eight days. You can locate and tune any high-load SQL that ran within the retention period of AWR using this method.
- Shared SQL area.
  The third likely source of input is the shared SQL area. The database uses this source to tune recent SQL statements that have yet to be captured in the AWR. The shared SQL area and AWR provide the capability to identify and tune high-load SQL statements from the current time going as far back as the AWR retention allows, which by default is at least 8 days.

- SQL tuning set.
  Another possible input source for SQL Tuning Advisor is the SQL tuning set. A SQL tuning set (STS) is a database object that stores SQL statements along with their execution context. An STS can include SQL statements that are yet to be deployed, with the goal of measuring their individual performance, or identifying the ones whose performance falls short of expectation. When a set of SQL statements serve as input, the database must first construct and use an STS.

Tuning Options

SQL Tuning Advisor provides options to manage the scope and duration of a tuning task. You can set the scope of a tuning task either of the following:

- Limited.
  In this case, SQL Tuning Advisor produces recommendations based on statistical checks, access path analysis, and SQL structure analysis. SQL profile recommendations are not generated.
- Comprehensive.
  In this case, SQL Tuning Advisor carries out all the analysis it performs under limited scope plus SQL Profiling. With the comprehensive option you can also specify a time limit for the tuning task, which by default is 30 minutes.

Advisor Output

After analyzing the SQL statements, SQL Tuning Advisor provides advice on optimizing the execution plan, the rationale for the proposed optimization, the estimated performance benefit, and the command to implement the advice. You choose whether to accept the recommendations to optimize the SQL statements.

Running SQL Tuning Advisor

The recommended interface for running SQL Tuning Advisor is Enterprise Manager. Whenever possible, run SQL Tuning Advisor using Enterprise Manager. If Enterprise Manager is unavailable, then you can run SQL Tuning Advisor using procedures in the `DBMS_SQLTUNE` package. To use the APIs, the user must be granted specific privileges.

Running SQL Tuning Advisor using `DBMS_SQLTUNE` package is a multi-step process:

1. Create a SQL tuning set (if tuning multiple SQL statements)
2. Create a SQL tuning task
3. Execute a SQL tuning task
4. Display the results of a SQL tuning task
5. Implement recommendations as appropriate.

You can create a SQL tuning task for a single SQL statement. For tuning multiple statements, a SQL tuning set (STS) has to be first created. An STS is a database object that stores SQL statements along with their execution context. You can create an STS manually using command line APIs or automatically using Enterprise Manager.

Figure 17.2 shows the steps involved when running SQL Tuning Advisor using the `DBMS_SQLTUNE` package.

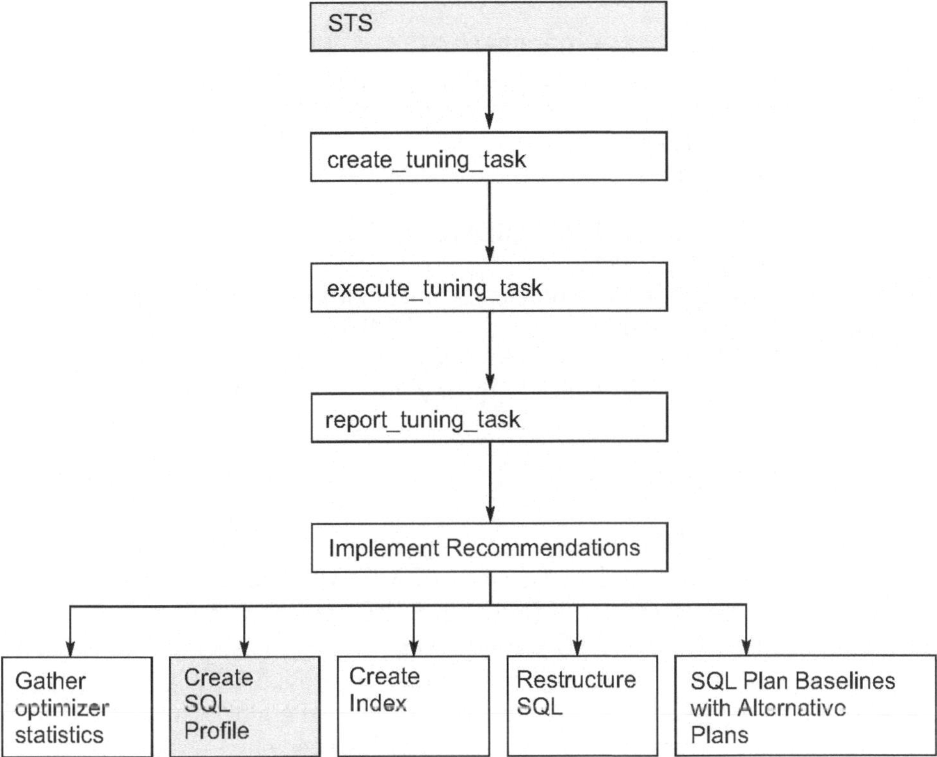

Figure 17.2. SQL Tuning Advisor APIs

This section covers the following topics:

- Creating a SQL Tuning Task
- Configuring a SQL Tuning Task
- Executing a SQL Tuning Task
- Checking the Status of a SQL Tuning Task
- Checking the Progress of SQL Tuning Advisor
- Displaying the Results of a SQL Tuning Task
- Additional Operations on a SQL Tuning Task.

Creating a SQL Tuning Task

You can create tuning tasks from the text of a single SQL statement, a SQL tuning set containing multiple statements, a SQL statement selected by SQL identifier from the shared SQL area, or a SQL statement selected by SQL identifier from AWR.

For example, to use SQL Tuning Advisor to optimize a specified SQL statement text, create a tuning task with the SQL statement passed as a CLOB argument. For the following PL/SQL code, the user `hr` has been granted the `ADVISOR` privilege, and the function is run as user `hr` on the `hr.employees` table.

```
DECLARE
 my_task_name VARCHAR2(30);
 my_sqltext   CLOB;
```

```
BEGIN
 my_sqltext := 'SELECT /*+ ORDERED */ * ' ||
 'FROM employees e, locations l, departments d ' ||
 'WHERE e.department_id = d.department_id AND '  ||
  'l.location_id = d.location_id AND '      ||
  'e.employee_id < :bnd';

 my_task_name := DBMS_SQLTUNE.CREATE_TUNING_TASK
(sql_text    => my_sqltext,
 bind_list   => sql_binds(anydata.ConvertNumber(100)),
 user_name   => 'HR',scope        => 'COMPREHENSIVE',
 time_limit  => 60,task_name    => 'my_sql_tuning_task',
 description => 'Task to tune a query on a specified
 employee');
END;
/
```

In the preceding example, `100` is the value for bind variable `:bnd` passed as function argument of type `SQL_BINDS`, `HR` is the user under which the `CREATE_TUNING_TASK` function analyzes the SQL statement, the scope is set to `COMPREHENSIVE` which means that the advisor also performs SQL Profiling analysis, and 60 is the maximum time in seconds that the function can run. In addition, values for task name and description are provided.

The `CREATE_TUNING_TASK` function returns the task name that you provided or generates a unique name. You can use the task name to specify this task when using other APIs. To view task names associated with an owner, run the following query:

```
SELECT TASK_NAME
FROM   DBA_ADVISOR_LOG
WHERE  OWNER = 'HR';
```

Configuring a SQL Tuning Task

You can fine tune a SQL tuning task after it has been created by configuring its parameters using the `SET_TUNING_TASK_PARAMETER` procedure in the `DBMS_SQLTUNE` package:

```
BEGIN
  DBMS_SQLTUNE.SET_TUNING_TASK_PARAMETER(
    task_name => 'my_sql_tuning_task',
    parameter => 'TIME_LIMIT', value => 300);
END;
/
```

In the preceding example, the maximum time that the SQL tuning task can run is changed to 300 seconds.

Table 17.2 lists parameters that you can configure using the `SET_TUNING_TASK_PARAMETER` procedure.

Table 17.2. SET_TUNING_TASK_PARAMETER Procedure Parameters

Parameter	Description
MODE	Specifies the scope of the tuning task: • LIMITED takes approximately 1 second to tune each SQL statement but does not recommend a SQL profile • COMPREHENSIVE performs a complete analysis and recommends a SQL profile, when appropriate, but may take much longer.
USERNAME	Username under which the SQL statement is parsed
DAYS_TO_EXPIRE	Number of days before the task is deleted
DEFAULT_EXECUTION_TYPE	Default execution type if not specified by the EXECUTE_TUNING_TASK function when the task is executed
TIME_LIMIT	Time limit (in number of seconds) before the task times out
LOCAL_TIME_LIMIT	Time limit (in number of seconds) for each SQL statement
TEST_EXECUTE	Determines if the SQL Tuning Advisor test executes the SQL statements to verify the recommendation benefit: • FULL-Test executes SQL statements for as much of the local time limit as necessary • AUTO-Test executes SQL statements using an automatic time limit • OFF-Does not test execute SQL statements
BASIC_FILTER	Basic filter used for SQL tuning set
OBJECT_FILTER	Object filter used for SQL tuning set
PLAN_FILTER	Plan filter used for SQL tuning set
RANK_MEASURE1	First ranking measure used for SQL tuning set
RANK_MEASURE2	Second ranking measure used for SQL tuning set
RANK_MEASURE3	Third ranking measure used for SQL tuning set
RESUME_FILTER	Extra filter used for SQL tuning set (besides BASIC_FILTER)
SQL_LIMIT	Maximum number of SQL statements to tune
SQL_PERCENTAGE	Percentage filter of statements from SQL tuning set

Executing a SQL Tuning Task

After you have created a tuning task, execute the task and start the tuning process. For example, run the following PL/SQL code:

```
BEGIN
  DBMS_SQLTUNE.EXECUTE_TUNING_TASK( task_name =>
'my_sql_tuning_task' );
END;
/
```

Like any other SQL Tuning Advisor task, you can also execute the automatic tuning task `SYS_AUTO_SQL_TUNING_TASK` using the `EXECUTE_TUNING_TASK API. SQL` Tuning Advisor performs the same analysis and actions as it would when run automatically. You can also pass an execution name to the API to name the new execution.

Checking the Status of a SQL Tuning Task

You can check the status of the task by reviewing the information in the `USER_ADVISOR_TASKS` view or check execution progress of the task in the `V$SESSION_LONGOPS` view. For example, run the following query:

```
SELECT status
FROM   USER_ADVISOR_TASKS
WHERE  task_name = 'my_sql_tuning_task';
```

Checking the Progress of SQL Tuning Advisor

You can check the execution progress of SQL Tuning Advisor in the `V$ADVISOR_PROGRESS` view. For example, run the following query:

```
SELECT SOFAR, TOTALWORK
FROM   V$ADVISOR_PROGRESS
WHERE  USER_NAME = 'HR' AND TASK_NAME =
'my_sql_tuning_task';
```

Displaying the Results of a SQL Tuning Task

After a task has been executed, you display a report of the results with the `REPORT_TUNING_TASK` function. For example:

```
SET LONG 1000
SET LONGCHUNKSIZE 1000
SET LINESIZE 100
SELECT DBMS_SQLTUNE.REPORT_TUNING_TASK( 'my_sql_tuning_task')
FROM   DUAL;
```

The report contains all the findings and recommendations of SQL Tuning Advisor. For each proposed recommendation, the rationale and benefit is provided along with the SQL statements needed to implement the recommendation.

Additional Operations on a SQL Tuning Task

You can use the following APIs for managing SQL tuning tasks:

- `INTERRUPT_TUNING_TASK` to interrupt a task while executing, causing a normal exit with intermediate results

- `RESUME_TUNING_TASK` to resume a previously interrupted task
- `CANCEL_TUNING_TASK` to cancel a task while executing, removing all results from the task
- `RESET_TUNING_TASK` to reset a task while executing, removing all results from the task and returning the task to its initial state
- `DROP_TUNING_TASK` to drop a task, removing all results associated with the task.

MANAGING SQL TUNING SETS

A SQL tuning set (STS) is a database object that includes one or more SQL statements along with their execution statistics and execution context, and could include a user priority ranking. You can load SQL statements into a SQL tuning set from different SQL sources, such as AWR, the shared SQL area, or customized SQL provided by the user. An STS includes:

- A set of SQL statements.
- Associated execution context, such as user schema, application module name and action, list of bind values, and the cursor compilation environment.
- Associated basic execution statistics, such as elapsed time, CPU time, buffer gets, disk reads, rows processed, cursor fetches, the number of executions, the number of complete executions, optimizer cost, and the command type.
- Associated execution plans and row source statistics for each SQL statement (optional).

You can filter SQL statements using the application module name and action, or any of the execution statistics. In addition, you can rank statements based on any combination of execution statistics.

You can use an STS as input to SQL Tuning Advisor, which performs automatic tuning of the SQL statements based on other user-specified input parameters. You can export SQL tuning sets from one database to another, enabling transfer of SQL workloads between databases for remote performance diagnostics and tuning. When poorly performing SQL statements occur on a production database, developers may not want investigate and tune directly on the production database. The DBA can transport the problematic SQL statements to a test database where the developers can safely analyze and tune them. To transport SQL tuning sets, use the `DBMS_SQLTUNE` package.

Whenever possible, you should manage SQL tuning sets using Enterprise Manager. If Enterprise Manager is unavailable, then you can manage SQL tuning sets using the `DBMS_SQLTUNE` package procedures.

Typically, you use STS operations in the following sequence:

1. Create a new STS
2. Load the STS
3. Select the STS to review the contents
4. Update the STS if necessary
5. Create a tuning task with the STS as input
6. Transport the STS to another system, if necessary
7. Drop the STS when finished.

To use the APIs, you need the `ADMINISTER SQL TUNING SET` system privilege to manage SQL tuning sets that you own, or the `ADMINISTER ANY SQL TUNING SET` system privilege to manage any SQL tuning sets.

Figure 173 shows the steps involved when using SQL tuning sets APIs.

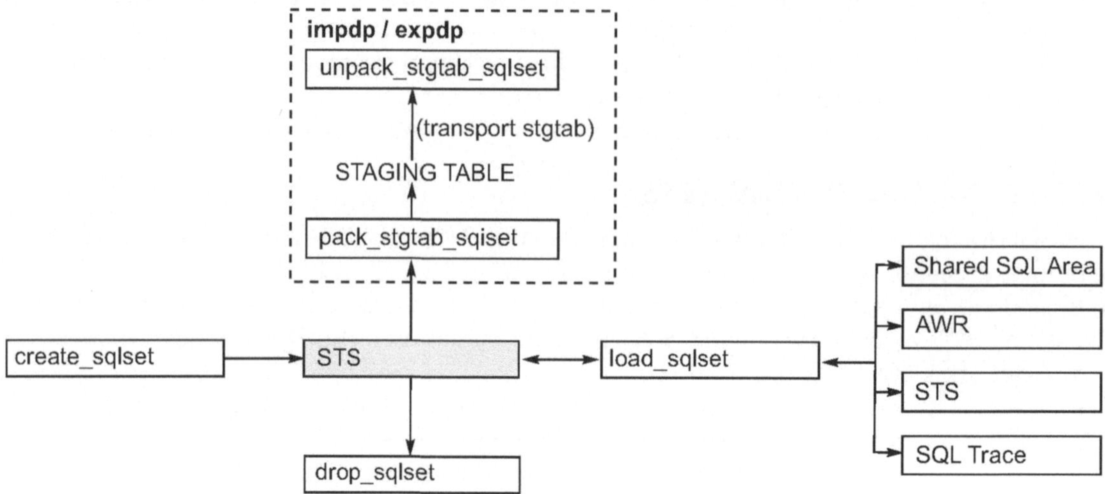

Figure 17.3. SQL Tuning Sets APIs

This section covers the following topics:

- Creating a SQL Tuning Set
- Loading a SQL Tuning Set
- Displaying the Contents of a SQL Tuning Set
- Modifying a SQL Tuning Set
- Transporting a SQL Tuning Set
- Dropping a SQL Tuning Set
- Additional Operations on SQL Tuning Sets.

Creating a SQL Tuning Set

The `CREATE_SQLSET` procedure creates an empty STS object in the database. For example, the following procedure creates an STS object that you could use to tune I/O-intensive SQL statements during a specific period:

```
BEGIN
  DBMS_SQLTUNE.CREATE_SQLSET(
    sqlset_name => 'my_sql_tuning_set',
    description => 'I/O intensive workload');
END;
/
```

In the preceding example, `my_sql_tuning_set` is the name of the STS in the database. `'I/O intensive workload'` is the description assigned to the STS.

Loading a SQL Tuning Set

The `LOAD_SQLSET` procedure populates the STS with selected SQL statements. The standard sources for populating an STS are the workload repository, another STS, or the shared SQL area. For both the workload repository and STS, predefined table functions can select columns from the source to populate a new STS.

In the following example, procedure calls load `my_sql_tuning_set` from an AWR baseline called `peak baseline.` The data has been filtered to select only the top 30 SQL statements ordered by elapsed time. First a ref cursor is opened to select from the specified baseline. Next the statements and their statistics are loaded from the baseline into the STS.

```
DECLARE
 baseline_cursor DBMS_SQLTUNE.SQLSET_CURSOR;
BEGIN
 OPEN baseline_cursor FOR
SELECT VALUE(p) FROM TABLE
(DBMS_SQLTUNE.SELECT_WORKLOAD_REPOSITORY(
  'peak baseline',NULL, NULL,'elapsed_time',
   NULL, NULL, NULL,30)) p;
    DBMS_SQLTUNE.LOAD_SQLSET(
      sqlset_name      => 'my_sql_tuning_set',
      populate_cursor => baseline_cursor);
END;
/
```

Displaying the Contents of a SQL Tuning Set

The `SELECT_SQLSET` table function reads the contents of the STS. After an STS has been created and populated, you can browse the SQL in the STS using different filtering criteria. The `SELECT_SQLSET` procedure is provided for this purpose.

In the following example, the SQL statements in the STS are displayed for statements with a disk-reads to buffer-gets ratio greater than or equal to 75%.

```
SELECT * FROM TABLE(DBMS_SQLTUNE.SELECT_SQLSET(
   'my_sql_tuning_set',
   '(disk_reads/buffer_gets) >= 0.75'));
```

Additional details of the SQL tuning sets that have been created and loaded can also be displayed with DBA views, such as `DBA_SQLSET`, `DBA_SQLSET_STATEMENTS`, and `DBA_SQLSET_BINDS`.

Modifying a SQL Tuning Set

You can update and delete SQL statements from an STS based on a search condition. In the following example, the `DELETE_SQLSET` procedure deletes SQL statements from `my_sql_tuning_set` that have been executed less than fifty times.

```
BEGIN
  DBMS_SQLTUNE.DELETE_SQLSET(
      sqlset_name  => 'my_sql_tuning_set',
      basic_filter => 'executions < 50');
END;
/
```

Transporting a SQL Tuning Set

You can transport SQL tuning sets. This operation involves exporting the STS from one database to a staging table, and then importing the STS from the staging table into another database.

You can transport a SQL tuning set to any database created in Oracle Database 10*g* (Release 2) or later. This technique is useful when using SQL Performance Analyzer to tune regressions on a test database. For example, you can transport an STS in the following scenario:

- An STS with regressed SQL resides in a production database created in Oracle Database 11*g* Release 2 (11.2).
- You are running SQL Performance Analyzer trials on a remote test database created in Oracle Database 11*g* Release 1 (11.1) or Oracle Database 10*g*.
- You want to copy the STS from the production database to the test database and tune the regressions from the SQL Performance Analyzer trials.

To transport a SQL tuning set:

1. Use the `CREATE_STGTAB_SQLSET` procedure to create a staging table where the SQL tuning sets will be exported.

   The following example creates `my_10g_staging_table` in the `dba1` schema and specifies the format of the staging table as 10.2:

```
BEGIN
  DBMS_SQLTUNE.create_stgtab_sqlset(
    table_name  => 'my_10g_staging_table',
    schema_name => 'dba1',
    db_version  => DBMS_SQLTUNE.STS_STGTAB_10_2_VERSION );
END;
/
```

2. Use the `PACK_STGTAB_SQLSET` procedure to export SQL tuning sets into the staging table.

   The following example populates `dba1.my_10g_staging_table` with the STS `my_sts` owned by hr:

```
BEGIN
  DBMS_SQLTUNE.pack_stgtab_sqlset(
    sqlset_name          => 'my_sts',
    sqlset_owner         => 'hr',
    staging_table_name   => 'my_10g_staging_table',
    staging_schema_owner => 'dba1',
    db_version           => DBMS_SQLTUNE.STS_STGTAB_10_2_VERSION );
END;
/
```

3. Move the staging table to the database where the SQL tuning sets will be imported using the mechanism of choice (such as Oracle Data Pump or database link).
4. On the database where the SQL tuning sets will be imported, use the `UNPACK_STGTAB_SQLSET` procedure to import SQL tuning sets from the staging table.

   The following example shows how to import SQL tuning sets contained in the staging table:

```
BEGIN
  DBMS_SQLTUNE.UNPACK_STGTAB_SQLSET(
      sqlset_name  => '%',
      replace  => TRUE,
      staging_table_name => 'my_10g_staging_table');
END;
/
```

Dropping a SQL Tuning Set

The DROP_SQLSET procedure drops an STS that is no longer needed. For example:

```
BEGIN
  DBMS_SQLTUNE.DROP_SQLSET( sqlset_name => 'my_sql_tuning_set' );
END;
/
```

Additional Operations on SQL Tuning Sets

You can use the following APIs to manage an STS:

- Updating the attributes of SQL statements in an STS.
  The UPDATE_SQLSET procedure updates the attributes of SQL statements (such as PRIORITY or OTHER) in an existing STS identified by STS name and SQL ID.
- Capturing the full system workload.
  The CAPTURE_CURSOR_CACHE_SQLSET function enables the capture of the full system workload by repeatedly polling the shared SQL area over a specified interval. This function more efficient than repeatedly using the SELECT_CURSOR_CACHE and LOAD_SQLSET procedures to capture the shared SQL area over an extended period. This function effectively captures the entire workload, as opposed to the AWR—which only captures the workload of high-load SQL statements—or the LOAD_SQLSET procedure, which accesses the data source only once.
- Adding and removing a reference to an STS.
  The ADD_SQLSET_REFERENCE function adds a new reference to an existing STS to indicate its use by a client. The function returns the identifier of the added reference. The REMOVE_SQLSET REFERENCE procedure deactivates an STS to indicate it is no longer used by the client.

MANAGING SQL PROFILES

A **SQL profile** is a set of auxiliary information specific to a SQL statement.

This section contains the following topics:

- Overview of SQL Profiles
- Accepting a SQL Profile
- Altering a SQL Profile
- Dropping a SQL Profile
- Transporting a SQL Profile.

Overview of SQL Profiles

A SQL profile contains corrections for poor optimizer estimates discovered during Automatic SQL Tuning. This information can improve optimizer cardinality and selectivity estimates, which in turn leads the optimizer to select better plans.

The SQL profile does not contain information about individual execution plans. Rather, the optimizer has the following sources of information when choosing plans:

- The environment, which contains the database configuration, bind variable values, optimizer statistics, data set, and so on.

- The supplemental statistics in the SQL profile.

If the environment or SQL profile change, then the optimizer can create a new plan.

You can use SQL profiles with or without SQL plan management. If you use SQL plan management, then the plan chosen by the optimizer must be an enabled plan baseline. If the statement has multiple plans in the baseline, then the profile remains useful because it enables the optimizer to chose the lowest-cost plan in the baseline.

Figure 17.4 illustrates the relationship between a SQL statement and the SQL profile for this statement. The optimizer uses the profile and the environment to generate a query plan. In this example, the plan is in the SQL plan baseline for the statement.

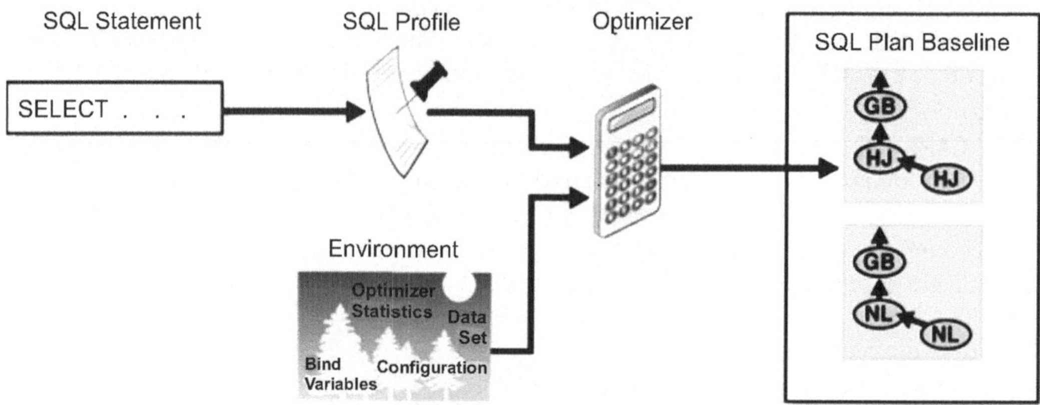

Figure 17.4. SQL Profile

SQL profiles provide the following benefits:

- Unlike hints and stored outlines, profiles do not tie the optimizer to a specific plan or subplan. Profiles fix incorrect estimates while giving the optimizer the flexibility to pick the best plan in different situations.
- Unlike hints, no changes to application source code are necessary when using profiles.

The use of SQL profiles by the database is transparent to the user.

SQL Profile Recommendations

During SQL tuning, you select a statement for automatic tuning and run SQL Tuning Advisor. The database can profile the following types of statement:

- DML statements (`SELECT, INSERT` with a `SELECT` clause, `UPDATE,` and `DELETE`)
- `CREATE TABLE` statements (only with the `AS SELECT` clause)
- `MERGE` statements (the update or insert operations).

SQL Tuning Advisor invokes Automatic Tuning Optimizer to generate recommendations. Recommendations to accept SQL profiles occur in a finding.

Shows that the database found a better plan for a `SELECT` statement that uses several expensive joins. The recommendation is to run `DBMS_SQLTUNE.ACCEPT_SQL_PROFILE` to accept the profile, which should enable the statement to run 98.53% faster.

Example 17.3: Sample SQL Profile Finding

```
-------------------------------------------------------------------------------
FINDINGS SECTION (2 findings)
-------------------------------------------------------------------------------

1- SQL Profile Finding (see explain plans section below)
-------------------------------------------------------------------------------
A potentially better execution plan was found for this statement.
Choose one of the following SQL profiles to implement.

Recommendation (estimated benefit: 99.45%)
-------------------------------------------------------------------------------
Consider accepting the recommended SQL profile.

execute dbms_sqltune.accept_sql_profile(task_name =>
'my_task',object_id => 3, task_owner => 'SH', replace => TRUE);

Validation results
------------------
The SQL profile was tested by executing both its plan and the original
plan and measuring their respective execution statistics. A plan may have
been only partially executed if the other could be run to completion in
less time.

Original Plan  With SQL Profile  % Improved
-------------- ------------------ ---------
Completion Status:              PARTIAL            COMPLETE
Elapsed Time(us):               15467783            226902
98.53 %

CPU Time(us):          5336668            226965        98.52 %
User I/O Time(us):                 0                 0
Buffer Gets:         3375243            18227        99.45 %
Disk Reads:                        0                 0
Direct Writes:                     0                 0
Rows Processed:                    0               109
Fetches:                           0               109
Executions:                        0                 1
```

- The SQL profile plan was first executed to warm the buffer cache.
- Statistics for the SQL profile plan were averaged over next 3 executions.

Sometimes SQL Tuning Advisor may recommend accepting a profile that uses the **Automatic Degree of Parallelism (Auto DOP)** feature. A parallel query profile is only recommended when the original plan is serial and when parallel execution can significantly reduce the response time for a long-running query. When it recommends a profile that uses Auto DOP, SQL Tuning Advisor gives details about the performance overhead of using parallel execution for the SQL statement in the report.

For parallel execution recommendations, SQL Tuning Advisor may provide two SQL profile recommendations, one using serial execution and one using parallel. In this case, the parallel profile is identical to the standard profile except for the directive to run in parallel.

Shows a parallel query recommendation. In this example, a degree of parallelism of 7 improves response time significantly at the cost of increasing resource consumption by almost 25%. You must decide whether the reduction in database throughput is worth the increase in response time.

Example 17.4: Parallel Query Recommendation

```
Recommendation (estimated benefit: 99.99%)
------------------------------------------
Consider accepting the recommended SQL profile to use parallel
execution for this statement.
execute dbms_sqltune.accept_sql_profile(task_name =>
'gfk_task',object_id => 3, task_owner => 'SH', replace =>
TRUE,profile_type => DBMS_SQLTUNE.PX_PROFILE);
Executing this query parallel with DOP 7 will improve its response
time82.22% over the SQL profile plan. However, there is some cost in
enabling parallel execution. It will increase the statement's resource
consumption by an estimated 24.43% which may result in a reduction of
system throughput.
Also, because these resources are consumed over a much smaller duration,
the response time of concurrent statements might be negatively impacted
ifsufficient hardware capacity is not available.
The following data shows some sampled statistics for this SQL from the
past week and projected weekly values when parallel execution is enabled.
 Past week sampled statistics for this SQL
 ----------------------------------------
 Number of executions            0
  Percent of total activity     .29
  Percent of samples with #Active Sessions > 2*CPU  0
  Weekly DB time (in sec)       76.51
 Projected statistics with Parallel Execution
 --------------------------------------------
  Weekly DB time (in sec)      95.21
```

SQL Profile Creation

When you **accept** a profile, the database creates the profile and stores it persistently in the data dictionary. If a user issues a statement for which a profile has been built, then the query optimizer (in normal mode) uses both the environment and the SQL profile to build a well-tuned plan.

If the database uses SQL plan management, and if a SQL plan baseline exists for the SQL statement, then the database adds a new plan to the baseline when a SQL profile is created. Otherwise, the database does not add a new plan baseline.

No strict relationship exists between the SQL profile and the plan baseline. When hard parsing, the optimizer uses the SQL profile to select the best plan baseline from the available plans. In some conditions, the SQL profile may cause the optimizer to select different plan baselines.

SQL Profile APIs

While SQL profiles are usually handled by Enterprise Manager as part of Automatic SQL tuning, you can manage SQL profiles with the `DBMS_SQLTUNE` package. To use the APIs, you must have the `ADMINISTER SQL MANAGEMENT OBJECT` privilege.

Table 17-3 shows the main procedures and functions for managing SQL profiles.

Table 17.3. DBMS_SQLTUNE APIs for SQL Profiles

Procedure or Function	Description
`ACCEPT_SQL_PROFILE`	Creates a SQL Profile for the specified tuning task
`ALTER_SQL_PROFILE`	Alters specific attributes of an existing SQL Profile object
`DROP_SQL_PROFILE`	Drops the named SQL Profile from the database
`CREATE_STGTAB_SQLPROF`	Creates the staging table used for copying SQL profiles from one system to another
`PACK_STGTAB_SQLPROF`	Moves profile data out of the SYS schema into the staging table
`UNPACK_STGTAB_SQLPROF`	Uses the profile data stored in the staging table to create profiles on this system

Figure 17.5 shows the possible actions when using SQL profile APIs.

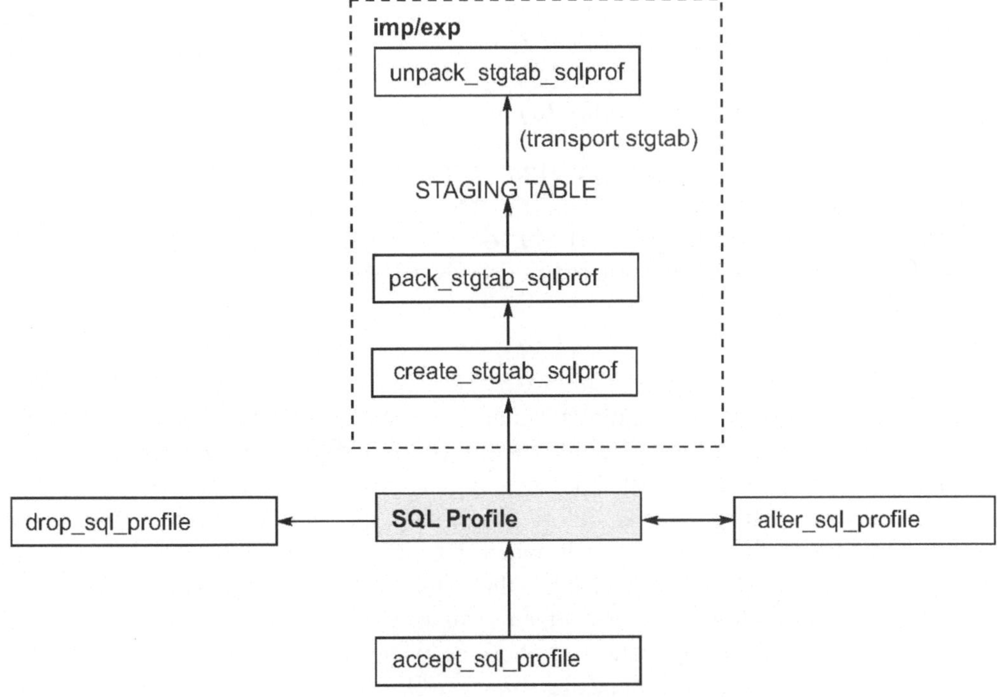

Figure 17.5. SQL Profile APIs

As tables grow or indexes are created or dropped, the plan for a profile can change. The profile continues to be relevant even if the data distribution or access path of the corresponding statement changes. In general, you do not need to refresh SQL profiles.

Over a long period, profile content can become outdated. In this case, the performance of the corresponding SQL statement may degrade. The poorly performing statement may appear as high-load or top SQL. In this situation, the Automatic SQL Tuning task again captures the statement as high-load SQL. You can create a new profile for the statement.

Accepting a SQL Profile

You can use the `DBMS_SQLTUNE.ACCEPT_SQL_PROFILE` procedure or function to accept a SQL profile recommended by SQL Tuning Advisor. This procedure creates and stores a SQL profile in the database.

As a rule of thumb, accept a SQL profile recommended by SQL Tuning Advisor. If both an index and a SQL profile are recommended, then either use both or use the SQL profile only. If you create an index, then the optimizer may need the profile to pick the new index.

In some situations, SQL Tuning Advisor may find an improved serial plan in addition to an even better parallel plan. In this case, the advisor recommends both a standard and a parallel SQL profile, enabling you to choose between the best serial and best parallel plan for the statement. Accept a parallel plan only if the increase in response time is worth the decrease in throughput (see).

To accept a SQL profile:

- Call the `DBMS_SQLTUNE.ALTER_SQL_PROFILE` procedure.
  In following example, `my_sql_tuning_task` is the name of the SQL tuning task and `my_sql_profile` is the name of the SQL profile. The PL/SQL block accepts a profile that uses parallel execution (`profile_type`):

```
DECLARE
  my_sqlprofile_name VARCHAR2(30);
BEGIN
my_sqlprofile_name := DBMS_SQLTUNE.ACCEPT_SQL_PROFILE(
    task_name    => 'my_sql_tuning_task',
    name         => 'my_sql_profile',
    profile_type => DBMS_SQLTUNE.PX_PROFILE,
    force_match  => TRUE );
END;
/
```

  The `force_match` setting controls statement matching. Typically, an accepted SQL profile is associated with the SQL statement through a **SQL signature** that is generated using a hash function. This hash function changes the SQL statement to upper case and removes all extra whites spaces before generating the signature. Thus, the same SQL profile works for all SQL statements in which the only difference is case and white spaces. By setting `force_match` to `TRUE,` the SQL profile additionally targets all SQL statements that have the same text after normalizing literal values to bind variables. This setting may be useful for applications that use only literal values because it allows SQL with text differing only in its literal values to share a SQL profile. If both literal values and bind variables are in the SQL text, or if `force_match` is set to `FALSE` (default), then literal values are not normalized.

  You can view information about a SQL profile in the `DBA_SQL_PROFILES` view.

Altering a SQL Profile

You can alter attributes of an existing SQL profile with the ALTER_SQL_PROFILE procedure. Modifiable attributes are STATUS, NAME, DESCRIPTION, and CATEGORY.

The CATEGORY attribute determines which sessions can apply a profile. You can view the CATEGORY attribute by querying DBA_SQL_PROFILES.CATEGORY. By default, all profiles are in the DEFAULT category, which means that all sessions in which the SQLTUNE_CATEGORY initialization parameter is set to DEFAULT can use the profile.

By altering the category of a SQL profile, you can determine which sessions are affected by profile creation. For example, by setting the category to DEV, only sessions in which the SQLTUNE_CATEGORY initialization parameter is set to DEV can use the profile. Other sessions do not have access to the SQL profile and execution plans for SQL statements are not impacted by the SQL profile. This technique enables you to test a profile in a restricted environment before making it available to other sessions.

To alter a SQL profile:

- Call the DBMS_SQLTUNE.ALTER_SQL_PROFILE procedure.
  In the following example, the STATUS attribute of my_sql_profile is changed to DISABLED, which means the SQL profile is not used during SQL compilation:

```
BEGIN
  DBMS_SQLTUNE.ALTER_SQL_PROFILE(
    name            => 'my_sql_profile',
    attribute_name  => 'STATUS',
    value           => 'DISABLED');
END;
/
```

Dropping a SQL Profile

You can drop a SQL profile with the DROP_SQL_PROFILE procedure. You can specify whether to ignore errors raised if the name does not exist. For this example, the default value of FALSE is accepted

To drop a SQL profile:

- Call the DBMS_SQLTUNE.DROP_SQL_PROFILE procedure.
  The following example drops the profile named my_sql_profile:

```
BEGIN
  DBMS_SQLTUNE.DROP_SQL_PROFILE( name => 'my_sql_profile' );
END;
/
```

Transporting a SQL Profile

You can **transport** SQL profiles. This operation involves exporting the SQL profile from the SYS schema in one database to a staging table, and then importing the SQL profile from the staging table into another database. You can transport a SQL profile to any Oracle database created in the same release or later.

To transport a SQL profile:

1. Use the CREATE_STGTAB_SQLPROF procedure to create a staging table where the SQL profiles will be exported.
   The following example creates my_staging_table in the DBA1 schema:

```
BEGIN
  DBMS_SQLTUNE.create_stgtab_sqlprof(
    table_name  => 'my_staging_table',
    schema_name => 'DBA1' );
END;
/
```

2. Use the PACK_STGTAB_SQLPROF procedure to export SQL profiles into the staging table.
   The following example populates dba1.my_staging_table with the SQL profile my_profile:

```
BEGIN
  DBMS_SQLTUNE.pack_stgtab_sqlprof(
    profile_name         => 'my_profile',
    staging_table_name   => 'my_staging_table',
    staging_schema_owner => 'dba1' );
END;
/
```

3. Move the staging table to the database where the SQL profiles will be imported using the mechanism of choice (such as Oracle Data Pump or database link).
4. On the database where the SQL profiles will be imported, use the UNPACK_STGTAB_SQLPROF procedure to import SQL profiles from the staging table.
   The following example shows how to import SQL profiles contained in the staging table:

```
BEGIN
  DBMS_SQLTUNE.UNPACK_STGTAB_SQLPROF(
      replace  => TRUE,
      staging_table_name => 'my_staging_table');
END;
/
```

SQL TUNING VIEWS

This section summarizes views that shows information gathered for tuning the SQL statements. You need DBA privileges to access these views.

- Advisor information views, such as DBA_ADVISOR_TASKS, DBA_ADVISOR_EXECUTIONS, DBA_ADVISOR_FINDINGS, DBA_ADVISOR_RECOMMENDATIONS, and DBA_ADVISOR_RATIONALE views.
- SQL tuning information views, such as DBA_SQLTUNE_STATISTICS, DBA_SQLTUNE_BINDS, and DBA_SQLTUNE_PLANS views.
- SQL tuning set views, such as DBA_SQLSET, DBA_SQLSET_BINDS, DBA_SQLSET_STATEMENTS, and DBA_SQLSET_REFERENCES views.
- Information on captured execution plans for statements in SQL tuning sets are displayed in the DBA_SQLSET_PLANS and USER_SQLSET_PLANS views.

- SQL profile information is displayed in the DBA_SQL_PROFILES view.
  If TYPE = MANUAL, then the SQL profile was created manually by SQL Tuning Advisor.
  If TYPE = MANUAL, then the profile was created by automatic SQL tuning.
- Advisor execution progress information is displayed in the V$ADVISOR_PROGRESS view.
- Dynamic views containing information relevant to the SQL tuning, such as VSQL, VSQLAREA, V$SQLSTATS, and V$SQL_BINDS views.

18 SQL Access Advisor

Learning Objectives

This chapter illustrates how to use SQL Access Advisor, which is a tuning tool that provides advice on improving the performance of a database through partitioning, materialized views, indexes, and materialized view logs.

This chapter contains the following sections:

- Overview of SQL Access Advisor
- Using SQL Access Advisor
- Tuning Materialized Views for Fast Refresh and Query Rewrite

OVERVIEW OF SQL ACCESS ADVISOR

Materialized views, partitions, and indexes are essential when tuning a database to achieve optimum performance for complex, data-intensive queries. SQL Access Advisor helps you achieve your performance goals by recommending the proper set of materialized views, materialized view logs, partitions, and indexes for a given workload. Understanding and using these structures is essential when optimizing SQL as they can result in significant performance improvements in data retrieval. The advantages, however, do not come without a cost. Creation and maintenance of these objects can be time consuming, and space requirements can be significant. In particular, partitioning of an unpartitioned base table is a complex operation that must be planned carefully.

SQL Access Advisor index recommendations include bitmap, function-based, and B-tree indexes. A bitmap index offers a reduced response time for many types of ad hoc queries and reduced storage requirements compared to other indexing techniques. B-tree indexes are most commonly used in a data warehouse to index unique or near-unique keys. SQL Access Advisor materialized view recommendations include fast refreshable and full refreshable MVs, for either general rewrite or exact text match rewrite.

SQL Access Advisor, using the `TUNE_MVIEW` procedure, also recommends how to optimize materialized views so that they can be fast refreshable and take advantage of general query rewrite.

In addition, SQL Access Advisor can recommend partitioning on an existing unpartitioned base table to improve performance. Furthermore, it may recommend new indexes and materialized views that are themselves partitioned. While creating new partitioned indexes and materialized view is no different from the unpartitioned case, partitioning existing base tables should be executed with care. This is especially true when indexes, views, constraints, or triggers are defined on the table.

You can run SQL Access Advisor from Oracle Enterprise Manager (accessible from the Advisor Central page) using SQL Access Advisor Wizard or by invoking the `DBMS_ADVISOR` package. The `DBMS_ADVISOR` package consists of a collection of analysis and advisory functions and procedures callable from any PL/SQL program.

Figure 18.1 illustrates how SQL Access Advisor recommends access structures for a given workload obtained from a user-defined table or the SQL cache. If a workload is not provided, then it can generate and use a hypothetical workload also, provided the user schema contains dimensions defined by the `CREATE DIMENSION` keyword.

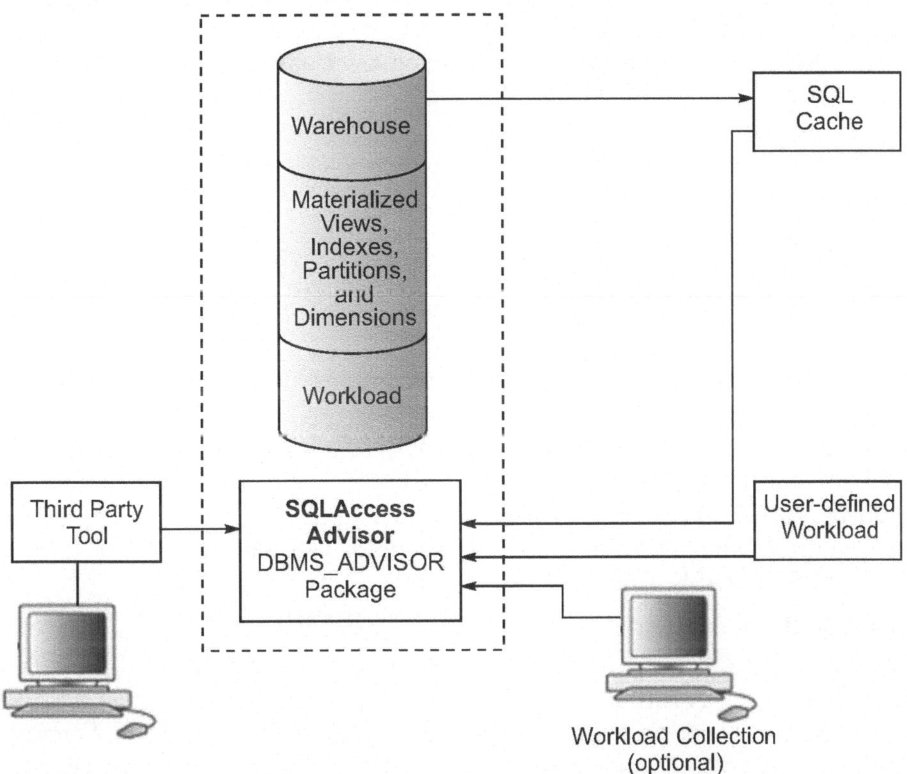

Figure 18.1. Materialized Views and SQL Access Advisor

Using SQL Access Advisor in Enterprise Manager or API, you can do the following:

- Recommend materialized views and indexes based on collected, user-supplied, or hypothetical workload information.
- Recommend partitioning of tables, indexes, and materialized views.
- Mark, update, and remove recommendations.

In addition, you can use SQL Access Advisor API to do the following:

- Perform a quick tune using a single SQL statement.
- Show how to make a materialized view fast refreshable.
- Show how to change a materialized view so that general query rewrite is possible.

To make recommendations, SQL Access Advisor relies on structural statistics about table and index cardinalities of dimension level columns, `JOIN KEY` columns, and fact table key columns. You can gather either exact or estimated statistics with the `DBMS_STATS` package. Because gathering statistics is time-consuming and full statistical accuracy is not required, it is generally preferable to estimate statistics. Without gathering statistics on a given table, queries referencing this table are marked as invalid in the workload, resulting in no recommendations being made for those queries. It is also recommended that all existing indexes and materialized views have been analyzed.

Overview of Using SQL Access Advisor

An easy way to use SQL Access Advisor is to invoke its wizard, which is available in Enterprise Manager from the Advisor Central page. If you prefer to use SQL Access Advisor through the `DBMS_ADVISOR` package, then this section describes the basic components and the sequence in which you must call the procedures.

This section describes the four steps in generating a set of recommendations:

- Create a task
- Define the workload
- Generate the recommendations
- View and implement the recommendations.

Step 1: Create a task

An **advisor task** is a container in the data dictionary that stores the inputs to and the results of an intelligent advisor analysis run. All information relating to the recommendation operation, including the results, resides in the task.

Before SQL Access Advisor can make recommendations, you must create a task using either of the following:

- The wizard in Oracle Enterprise Manager or the `DBMS_ADVISOR.QUICK_TUNE` procedure, which creates the task automatically
- The `DBMS_ADVISOR.CREATE_TASK` procedure

You can control what a task does by defining parameters for the task using the `DBMS_ADVISOR.SET_TASK_PARAMETER` procedure.

Step 2: Define the workload

A **workload** consists of one or more SQL statements, plus statistics and attributes that fully describe each statement. A **full workload** contains all SQL statements from a target business application. A **partial workload** contains a subset of SQL statements. The difference is that for full workloads SQL Access Advisor may recommend dropping unused materialized views and indexes.

You cannot use SQL Access Advisor without a workload. A workload may contain a variety of statements. SQL Access Advisor ranks the entries according to a specific statistic, business importance, or combination of the two, which enables the advisor to process the most important SQL statements first.

SQL Access Advisor may require particular attributes to be present in a valid workload. Although the advisor can perform analysis when items are missing, the quality of the recommendations may be lower. For example, SQL Access Advisor requires a workload to contain a SQL query and the user who ran the query, with other attributes as optional. However, if the workload also contains I/O and CPU data, then SQL Access Advisor can better evaluate statement efficiency.

The database stores a workload as a SQL tuning set. You can access the workload with the DBMS_SQLTUNE package and share it among many Advisor tasks. Because the workload is independent, you must link it to a task using the DBMS_ADVISOR.ADD_STS_REF procedure. After this link has been established, you cannot delete or modify the workload until all advisor tasks have removed their dependency on the workload. A workload reference is removed when a user deletes a parent advisor task or manually removes the workload reference from the task by using the DBMS_ADVISOR.DELETE_STS_REF procedure.

You can create a hypothetical workload from a schema by analyzing dimensions and constraints. For best results, provide a workload as a SQL tuning set. The DBMS_SQLTUNE package provides several helper functions that can create SQL tuning sets from common workload sources, such as the SQL cache, a user-defined workload stored in a table, and a hypothetical workload.

At the time the recommendations are generated, you can apply a filter to the workload to restrict what is analyzed. This restriction provides the ability to generate different sets of recommendations based on different workload scenarios. SQL Access Advisor parameters control the recommendation process and customization of the workload. These parameters control various aspects of the process, such as the type of recommendation required and the naming conventions for what it recommends.

To set these parameters, use the SET_TASK_PARAMETER procedure. Parameters are persistent in that they remain set for the life span of the task. When a parameter value is set using SET_TASK_PARAMETER, it does not change until you make another call to this procedure.

Step 3: Generate the recommendations

After a task exists and a workload is linked to the task and the appropriate parameters are set, you can generate recommendations using the DBMS_ADVISOR.EXECUTE_TASK procedure. These recommendations are stored in SQL Access Advisor Repository.

The recommendation process generates several recommendations. Each recommendation specifies one or more actions. For example, a recommendation could be to create several materialized view logs, create a materialized view, and then analyze it to gather statistics.

A task recommendation can range from a simple suggestion to a complex solution that requires partitioning a set of existing base tables and implementing a set of database objects such as indexes, materialized views, and materialized view logs. When an advisor task is executed, SQL Access Advisor carefully analyzes collected data and user-adjusted task parameters. It then forms a structured recommendation that the user can view and implement.

Step 4: View and implement the recommendations

You can view the recommendations from SQL Access Advisor in either of the following ways:

- Using the catalog views
- Generating a script using the DBMS_ADVISOR.GET_TASK_SCRIPT procedure.

In Enterprise Manager, you may display the recommendations after SQL Access Advisor process has completed.

You need not accept all recommendations. You can mark the ones to be included in the recommendation script. However, when base table partitioning is recommended, some recommendations depend on others. For example, you cannot implement a local index if you do not also implement the partitioning recommendation on the index base table.

The final step is then implementing the recommendations and verifying that query performance has improved.

SQL Access Advisor Repository

All the information needed and generated by SQL Access Advisor resides in the Advisor repository, which is a part of the database dictionary. The benefits of using the repository are that it:

- Collects a complete workload for SQL Access Advisor.
- Supports historical data.
- Is managed by the server.

USING SQL ACCESS ADVISOR

This section discusses general information about, and the steps needed to use, SQL Access Advisor, and includes:

- Steps for Using SQL Access Advisor
- Privileges Needed to Use SQL Access Advisor
- Setting Up Tasks and Templates
- SQL Access Advisor Workloads
- Working with Recommendations
- Performing a Quick Tune
- Managing Tasks
- Using SQL Access Advisor Constants.

Steps for Using SQL Access Advisor

Figure 18.2 illustrates the steps in using SQL Access Advisor and an overview of all parameters in SQL Access Advisor and when it is appropriate to use them.

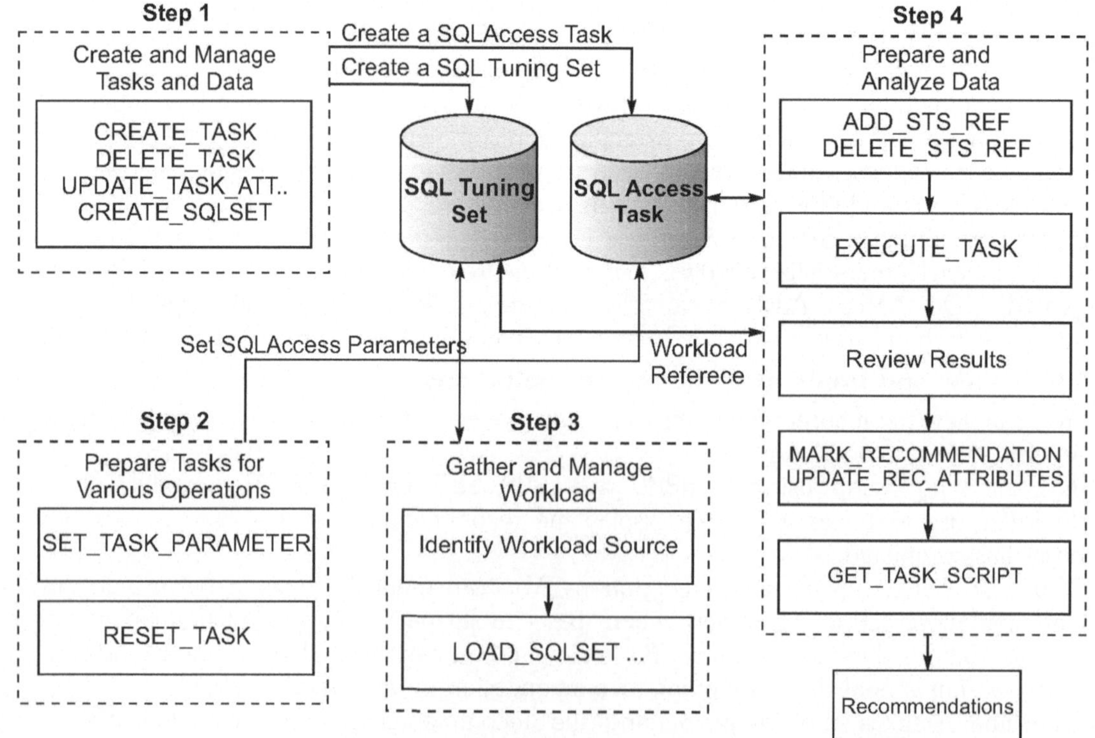

Figure 18.2. SQL Access Advisor Flowchart

Privileges Needed to Use SQL Access Advisor

You must have the ADVISOR privilege to manage or use SQL Access Advisor. When processing a workload, SQL Access Advisor attempts to validate each statement to identify table and column references. The database achieves validation by processing each statement as if it were being executed by the statement's original user.

If the user does not have SELECT privileges to a particular table, then SQL Access Advisor bypasses the statement referencing the table. This behavior can cause many statements to be excluded from analysis. If SQL Access Advisor excludes all statements in a workload, then the workload is invalid. SQL Access Advisor returns the following message:

```
QSM-00774, there are no SQL statements to process for task
TASK_NAME
```

To avoid missing critical workload queries, the current database user must have SELECT privileges on the tables targeted for materialized view analysis. For these tables, these SELECT privileges cannot be obtained through a role.

Additionally, you must have the ADMINISTER SQL TUNING SET privilege to create and manage workloads in SQL tuning set objects. To run the Advisor on SQL tuning sets owned by other users, you must have the ADMINISTER ANY SQL TUNING SET privilege.

Setting Up Tasks and Templates

This section discusses the following aspects of setting up tasks and templates:

- Creating Tasks
- Using Templates
- Creating Templates.

Creating Tasks

In the task, you define what the advisor must analyze and the location of the analysis results. A user can create any number of tasks, each with its own specialization. All are based on the same Advisor task model and share the same repository.

You create a task using the CREATE_TASK procedure. The syntax is as follows:

```
DBMS_ADVISOR.CREATE_TASK (
    advisor_name            IN VARCHAR2,
    task_id                 OUT NUMBER,
    task_name               IN OUT VARCHAR2,
    task_desc               IN VARCHAR2 := NULL,
    template                IN VARCHAR2 := NULL,
    is_template             IN VARCHAR2 := 'FALSE',
    how_created             IN VARCHAR2 := NULL);
```

The following illustrates an example of using this procedure:

```
VARIABLE task_id NUMBER;
VARIABLE task_name VARCHAR2(255);
EXECUTE :task_name := 'MYTASK';
EXECUTE DBMS_ADVISOR.CREATE_TASK ('SQL Access Advisor',
:task_id, :task_name);
```

Using Templates

When an ideal configuration for a task or workload has been identified, you can save this configuration as a template on which to base future tasks and workloads.

A template enables you to set up any number of tasks or workloads that can serve as intelligent starting points or templates for future task creation. By setting up a template, you can save time when performing tuning analysis. This approach also enables you to custom fit a tuning analysis to the business operation.

To create a task from a template, you specify the template to be used when a new task is created. At that time, SQL Access Advisor copies the data and parameter settings from the template into the newly created task. You can also set an existing task to be a template by setting the template attribute when creating the task or later using the `UPDATE_TASK_ATTRIBUTE` procedure.

To use a task as a template, you tell SQL Access Advisor to use a task when a new task is created. At that time, SQL Access Advisor copies the task template's data and parameter settings into the newly created task. You can also set an existing task to be a template by setting the template attribute at the command line or in Enterprise Manager.

Creating Templates

You can create a template as in the following example:

1. Create a template called `MY_TEMPLATE`.

```
VARIABLE template_id NUMBER;
VARIABLE template_name VARCHAR2(255);
EXECUTE :template_name := ‘MY_TEMPLATE’;
EXECUTE DBMS_ADVISOR.CREATE_TASK(‘SQL Access
Advisor’,:template_id, -
:template_name, is_template => ‘TRUE’);
```

2. Set template parameters. For example, the following sets the naming conventions for recommended indexes and materialized views and the default tablespaces:

```
-- set naming conventions for recommended indexes/mvs
EXECUTE DBMS_ADVISOR.SET_TASK_PARAMETER (
   :template_name, ‘INDEX_NAME_TEMPLATE’, ‘SH_IDX$$_<SEQ>’);

EXECUTE DBMS_ADVISOR.SET_TASK_PARAMETER (
   :template_name, ‘MVIEW_NAME_TEMPLATE’, ‘SH_MV$$_<SEQ>’);

-- set default tablespace for recommended indexes/mvs
EXECUTE DBMS_ADVISOR.SET_TASK_PARAMETER (
   :template_name, ‘DEF_INDEX_TABLESPACE’,
 ‘SH_INDEXES’);

EXECUTE DBMS_ADVISOR.SET_TASK_PARAMETER (
    :template_name, ‘DEF_MVIEW_TABLESPACE’, ‘SH_MVIEWS’);
```

3. This template can now be used as a starting point to create a task as follows:

```
VARIABLE task_id NUMBER;
VARIABLE task_name VARCHAR2(255);
EXECUTE :task_name := ‘MYTASK’;
```

```
EXECUTE DBMS_ADVISOR.CREATE_TASK('SQL Access Advisor',
 :task_id, :task_name, template=>'MY_TEMPLATE');
```

The following example uses a pre-defined template SQLACCESS_WAREHOUSE. See Table 18.3 for more information.

```
EXECUTE DBMS_ADVISOR.CREATE_TASK('SQL Access Advisor', -
 :task_id, :task_name,  template=>'SQLACCESS_WAREHOUSE');
```

SQL Access Advisor Workloads

SQL Access Advisor supports different types of workloads, and this section discusses the following aspects of managing workloads:

- SQL Tuning Set Workloads
- Using SQL Tuning Sets
- Linking Tasks and Workloads.

SQL Tuning Set Workloads

The input workload source for SQL Access Advisor is the SQL tuning set. An important benefit of using a SQL tuning set is that because it is stored as a separate entity, it can easily be shared among many Advisor tasks. After a SQL tuning set object has been referenced by an Advisor task, it cannot be deleted or modified until all Advisor tasks have removed their dependency on the data. A workload reference is removed when a parent Advisor task is deleted or when the workload reference is manually removed from the Advisor task by the user.

SQL Access Advisor performs best when a workload based on actual usage is available. You can store multiple workloads in the form of SQL tuning sets, so that you can view the different uses of a real-world data warehousing or transaction-processing environment over a long period and across the life cycle of database instance startup and shutdown.

Using SQL Tuning Sets

The SQL tuning set workload is implemented using the DBMS_SQLTUNE package.

To transition existing SQL Workload objects to a SQL tuning set, the DBMS_ADVISOR package provides a procedure to copy SQL Workload data to a user-designated SQL tuning set. Note that, to use this procedure, the user must have the required SQL tuning set privileges and the required ADVISOR privilege.

The syntax is as follows:

```
DBMS_ADVISOR.COPY_SQLWKLD_TO_STS (
   workload_name           IN VARCHAR2,
   sts_name                IN VARCHAR2,
   import_mode             IN VARCHAR2 := 'NEW');
```

The following example illustrates its usage:

```
EXECUTE
DBMS_ADVISOR.COPY_SQLWKLD_TO_STS('MYWORKLOAD','MYSTS','NEW');
```

Linking Tasks and Workloads

Before the recommendation process can begin, you must link the task to a SQL tuning set. You achieve this goal by using the ADD_STS_REF procedure and using their respective names to link the task and a Tuning Set. This procedure establishes a link between the Advisor task and a Tuning Set. And, after a connection has been defined, the SQL tuning set is protected from removal or update. The syntax is as follows:

```
DBMS_ADVISOR.ADD_STS_REF (task_name IN VARCHAR2,
sts_owner IN VARCHAR2,
sts_name  IN VARCHAR2);
```

The `sts_owner` parameter may be null, in which case the STS is assumed to be owned by the current user.

The following example links the MYTASK task created to the current user's MYWORKLOAD SQL tuning set:

```
EXECUTE DBMS_ADVISOR.ADD_STS_REF('MYTASK', null,
'MYWORKLOAD');
```

Removing a Link between a SQL Tuning Set Workload and a Task

Before you can delete a task or a SQL tuning set workload, if it is linked to a workload or task respectively, then the link between the task and the workload must be removed using the DELETE_STS_REF procedure. The following example deletes the link between task MYTASK and the current user's SQL tuning set MYWORKLOAD:

```
EXECUTE DBMS_ADVISOR.DELETE_STS_REF('MYTASK', null,
'MYWORKLOAD');
```

Working with Recommendations

This section discusses the following aspects of working with recommendations:

- Recommendations and Actions
- Recommendation Options
- Evaluation Mode
- View Intermediate Results During Recommendation Analysis
- Generating Recommendations
- Viewing Recommendations
- Stopping the Recommendation Process
- Marking Recommendations
- Modifying Recommendations
- Generating SQL Scripts
- Special Considerations when Script Includes Partitioning Recommendations
- When Recommendations are no Longer Required.

Recommendations and Actions

SQL Access Advisor makes several recommendations, each of which contains one or more individual actions. In general, each recommendation provides a benefit for one query or a set of queries. All individual actions in a recommendation must be implemented together to achieve the full benefit. Recommendations can share actions.

For example, a `CREATE INDEX` statement could provide a benefit for several queries, but some of those queries might benefit from an additional `CREATE MATERIALIZED VIEW` statement. In that case, the advisor would generate two recommendations: one for the set of queries that require only the index, and another one for the set of queries that require both the index and the materialized view to run optimally.

The partition recommendation is a special type of recommendation. When SQL Access Advisor determines that partitioning a specified base table would improve workload performance, the advisor adds a partition action to every recommendation containing a query referencing the base table. This technique ensures that index and materialized view recommendations are implemented on the correctly partitioned tables.

Recommendation Options

Before the advisor can generate recommendations, you must first define the parameters for the task using the SET_TASK_PARAMETER procedure. If parameters are not defined, then the database uses the defaults.

You can set task parameters by using the SET_TASK_PARAMETER procedure. The syntax is as follows.

```
DBMS_ADVISOR.SET_TASK_PARAMETER (
    task_name            IN VARCHAR2,
    parameter            IN VARCHAR2,
    value                IN [VARCHAR2 | NUMBER]);
```

There are many task parameters and, to help identify the relevant ones, they have been grouped into categories in Table 18.1. Note that all task parameters for workload filtering have been deprecated.

Table 18.1. Types of Advisor Task Parameters and their Uses

Workload Filtering	Task Configuration	Schema Attributes	Recommendation Options
END_TIME	DAYS_TO_EXPIRE	DEF_INDEX_OWNER	ANALYSIS_SCOPE
INVALID_ACTION_LIST	JOURNALING	DEF_INDEX_TABLESPACE	COMPATIBILITY
INVALID_MODULE_LIST	REPORT_DATE_FORMAT	DEF_MVIEW_OWNER	CREATION_COST
INVALID_SQLSTRING_LIMIT		DEF_MVIEW_TABLESPACE	DML_VOLATILITY
INVALID_TABLE_LIST		DFF_MVLOG_TABLESPACE	LIMIT_PARTITION_SCHEMES
INVALID_USERNAME_LIST		DFF_PARTITION_TABLESPACE	MODE
RANKING_MEASURE		INDEX_NAME_TEMPLATE	PARTITIONING_TYPES
SQL_LIMIT		MVIEW_NAME_TEMPLATE	REFRESH_MODE
START_TIME			STORAGE_CHANGE
TIME_LIMIT			USE_SEPARATE_TABLESPACES
VALID_ACTION_LIST			WORKLOAD_SCOPE
VALID_MODULE_LIST			

VALID_SQLSTRING_LIST			
VALID_TABLE_LIST			
VALID_USERNAME_LIST			

In the following example, set the storage change of task MYTASK to 100 MB. This indicates 100 MB of additional space for recommendations. A zero value indicates that no additional space can be allocated. A negative value indicates that the advisor must attempt to trim the current space utilization by the specified amount.

```
EXECUTE DBMS_ADVISOR.SET_TASK_PARAMETER('MYTASK','STORAGE_CHANGE',
100000000);
```

In the following example, set the VALID_TABLE_LIST parameter to filter out all queries that do no consist of tables SH.SALES and SH.CUSTOMERS.

```
EXECUTE DBMS_ADVISOR.SET_TASK_PARAMETER ('MYTASK',
'VALID_TABLE_LIST', 'SH.SALES, SH.CUSTOMERS');
```

Evaluation Mode

SQL Access Advisor operates in two modes: problem-solving and evaluation. By default, SQL Access Advisor attempts to solve access method problems by looking for enhancements to index structures, partitions, materialized views, and materialized view logs. For example, a problem-solving run may recommend creating a new index, adding a new column to a materialized view log, and so on.

When performing evaluation only, SQL Access Advisor comments only on which access structures the supplied workload will use. An evaluation-only run may only produce recommendations such as retaining an index, retaining a materialized view, and so on. The evaluation mode can be useful to see exactly which indexes and materialized views a workload is using. SQL Access Advisor does not evaluate the performance impact of existing base table partitioning.

View Intermediate Results During Recommendation Analysis

SQL Access Advisor now can see intermediate results during the analysis operation. Previously, results of an analysis operation were unavailable until the processing had completed or was interrupted by the user. Now, the user may access results in the corresponding recommendation and action tables even while SQL Access Advisor task is still executing. The benefit is that long running tasks can provide evidence that may allow the user to accept the current results by interrupting the task rather than waiting for a lengthy execution to complete.

To accept the current set of recommendations, the user must interrupt the task. This interruption signals SQL Access Advisor to stop processing and marks the task as INTERRUPTED. At that point, the user may update recommendation attributes and generate scripts. Alternatively, the user can allow SQL Access Advisor to complete the recommendation process.

Note that intermediate results represent recommendations for the workload contents up to that point in time. If it is critical that the recommendations be sensitive to the entire workload, then Oracle recommends that you allow the task execution to complete normally. Additionally, recommendations made by the advisor early in the recommendation process do not contain any base table partitioning recommendations. The partitioning analysis requires a substantial part of the workload to be processed before it can determine whether partitioning would be beneficial. Therefore, if SQL Access Advisor detects a benefit, then only later intermediate results contain base table partitioning recommendations.

Generating Recommendations

You can generate recommendations by using the `EXECUTE_TASK` procedure with your task name. After the procedure finishes, you can check the `DBA_ADVISOR_LOG` table for the actual execution status and the number of recommendations and actions that have been produced. You can query recommendations by task name in `{DBA, USER}_ADVISOR_RECOMMENDATIONS`. You can view the actions for these recommendations by task in `{DBA, USER}_ADVISOR_ACTIONS.`

EXECUTE_TASK Procedure: This procedure performs SQL Access Advisor analysis or evaluation for the specified task. Task execution is a synchronous operation, so control is not returned to the user until the operation has completed, or a user-interrupt was detected. Upon return or execution of the task, you can check the `DBA_ADVISOR_LOG` table for the actual execution status.

Running `EXECUTE_TASK` generates recommendations, where a recommendation comprises one or more actions, such as creating a materialized view log and a materialized view. The syntax is as follows:

```
DBMS_ADVISOR.EXECUTE_TASK (task_name   IN VARCHAR2);
```

The following illustrates an example of using this procedure:

```
EXECUTE DBMS_ADVISOR.EXECUTE_TASK('MYTASK');
```

Viewing Recommendations

You can view each recommendation generated by SQL Access Advisor using several catalog views, such as `(DBA, USER)_ADVISOR_RECOMMENDATIONS`. However, it is easier to use the `GET_TASK_SCRIPT` procedure or use SQL Access Advisor in Enterprise Manager, which graphically displays the recommendations and provides hyperlinks to quickly see which SQL statements benefit from a recommendation. Each recommendation produced by SQL Access Advisor is linked to the SQL statement it benefits.

The following shows the recommendation (`rec_id`) produced by an Advisor run, with their rank and total benefit. The rank is a measure of the importance of the queries that the recommendation helps. The benefit is the total improvement in execution cost (in terms of optimizer cost) of all the queries using the recommendation.

```
VARIABLE workload_name VARCHAR2(255);
VARIABLE task_name VARCHAR2(255);
EXECUTE :task_name := 'MYTASK';
EXECUTE :workload_name := 'MYWORKLOAD';

SELECT REC_ID, RANK, BENEFIT
FROM USER_ADVISOR_RECOMMENDATIONS WHERE TASK_NAME = :task_name;
```

```
    REC_ID       RANK    BENEFIT
---------- ---------- ----------
         1          2       2754
         2          3       1222
         3          1       5499
         4          4        594
```

To identify which query benefits from which recommendation, you can use the views DBA_* and USER_ADVISOR_SQLA_WK_STMTS. The precost and postcost numbers are in terms of the estimated optimizer cost (shown in EXPLAIN PLAN) without and with the recommended access structure changes, respectively. To see recommendations for each query, issue the following statement:

```
SELECT sql_id, rec_id, precost, postcost,
(precost-postcost)*100/precost AS percent_benefit
FROM USER_ADVISOR_SQLA_WK_STMTS
WHERE TASK_NAME = :task_name AND workload_name = :workload_name;
```

```
    SQL_ID     REC_ID    PRECOST   POSTCOST      PERCENT_BENEFIT
---------- ---------- ---------- ----------      ---------------
       121          1       3003        249           91.7082917
       122          2       1404        182            87.037037
       123          3       5503          4           99.9273124
       124          4        730        136            81.369863
```

Each recommendation consists of one or more actions, which must be implemented together to realize the benefit provided by the recommendation. SQL Access Advisor produces the following types of actions:

- PARTITION BASE TABLE
- CREATE|DROP|RETAIN MATERIALIZED VIEW
- CREATE|ALTER|RETAIN MATERIALIZED VIEW LOG
- CREATE|DROP|RETAIN INDEX
- GATHER STATS

The PARTITION BASE TABLE action partitions an existing unpartitioned base table. The CREATE actions corresponds to new access structures. RETAIN recommendations indicate that existing access structures must be kept. DROP recommendations are only produced if the WORKLOAD_SCOPE parameter is set to FULL. The GATHER STATS action generates a call to DBMS_STATS procedure to gather statistics on a newly generated access structure. Note that multiple recommendations may refer to the same action. However, when generating a script for the recommendation, you only see each action once.

In the following example, you can see how many distinct actions there are for this set of recommendations.

```
SELECT 'Action Count', COUNT(DISTINCT action_id) cnt
FROM USER_ADVISOR_ACTIONS WHERE task_name = :task_name;

ACTIONCOUNT        CNT
------------ ---------
Action Count        20
```

```
-- see the actions for each recommendations
SELECT rec_id, action_id, SUBSTR(command,1,30) AS command
FROM user_advisor_actions WHERE task_name = :task_name
ORDER BY rec_id, action_id;

    REC_ID  ACTION_ID COMMAND
----------  ---------  --------------------------
         1          5 CREATE MATERIALIZED VIEW LOG
         1          6 ALTER MATERIALIZED VIEW LOG
         1          7 CREATE MATERIALIZED VIEW LOG
         1          8 ALTER MATERIALIZED VIEW LOG
         1          9 CREATE MATERIALIZED VIEW LOG
         1         10 ALTER MATERIALIZED VIEW LOG
         1         11 CREATE MATERIALIZED VIEW
         1         12 GATHER TABLE STATISTICS
         1         19 CREATE INDEX
         1         20 GATHER INDEX STATISTICS
         2          5 CREATE MATERIALIZED VIEW LOG
         2          6 ALTER MATERIALIZED VIEW LOG
         2          9 CREATE MATERIALIZED VIEW LOG
         ...
```

Each action has several attributes that pertain to the properties of the access structure. The name and tablespace for each access structure when applicable are placed in `attr1` and `attr2` respectively. The space occupied by each new access structure is in `num_attr1`. All other attributes are different for each action.

Table 18.2 maps SQL Access Advisor action information to the corresponding column in `DBA_ADVISOR_ACTIONS`. In the table, "MV" refers to a materialized view.

Table 18.2. SQL Access Advisor Action Attributes

	ATTR1	ATTR2	ATTR3	ATTR4	ATTR5	ATTR6	NUM_ATTR1
CREATE INDEX	Index name	Index tablespace	Target table	BITMAP or BTREE	Index column list / expression	Unused	Storage size in bytes for the index
CREATE MATERIALIZED VIEW	MV name	MV tablespace	REFRESH COMPLETE REFRESH FAST, REFRESH FORCE, NEVER REFRESH	ENABLE QUERY REWRITE, DISABLE QUERY REWRITE	SQL SELECT statement	Unused	Storage size in bytes for the MV
CREATE MATERIALIZED VIEW	Target table name	MV log tablespace	ROWID PRIMARY KEY, SEQUENCE	INCLUD-ING NEW VALUES,	Table column list	Partitioning subclauses	Unused

LOG			OBJECT ID	EXCLUDING NEW VALUES			
CREATE REWRITE EQUIVALENCE	Name of equivalence	Checksum value	Unused	Unused	Source SQL statement	Equivalent SQL statement	Unused
DROP INDEX	Index name	Unused	Unused	Unused	Index columns	Unused	Storage size in bytes for the index
DROP MATERI-ALIZED VIEW	MV name	Unused	Unused	Unused	Unused	Unused	Storage size in bytes for the MV
DROP MATERI-ALIZED VIEW LOG	Target table name	Unused	Unused	Unused	Unused	Unused	Unused
PARTIT-ION TABLE	Table name	RANGE, INTERVAL, LIST, HASH, RANGE-HASH, RANGE-LIST	Partition key for partitioning (column name or list of column names	Partition key for subpartitioning (column name or list of column names)	SQL PARTITION clause	SQL SUBPARTTITION clause	Unused
PARTI-TION INDEX	Index name	LOCAL, RANGE, HASH	Partition key for partitioning (list of column names)	Unused	SQL PARTITION clause	Unused	Unused
PARTI-TION ON MATERI-ALIZED VIEW	MV name	RANGE, INTERVAL, LIST, HASH, RANGE-HASH, RANGE-LIST	Partition key for partitioning (column name or list of column names)	Partition key for subpartitioning (column name or list of column names)	SQL SUBPART-ITION clause	SQL SUBPART-ITION clause	Unused
RETAIN INDEX	Index name	Unused	Target table	BITMAP or BTREE	Index columns	Unused	Storage size in bytes for the index

RETAIN MATERIALIZED VIEW	MV name	Unused	REFRESH COMPLETE or REFRESH FAST	Unused	SQL SELECT statement	Unused	Storage size in bytes for the MV
RETAIN MATERIALIZED VIEW LOG	Target table name	Unused	Unused	Unused	Unused	Unused	Unused

The following PL/SQL procedure can print some of the attributes of the recommendations.

```
CONNECT SH/SH;

CREATE OR REPLACE PROCEDURE show_recm (in_task_name IN
VARCHAR2) IS CURSOR curs IS
SELECT DISTINCT action_id, command, attr1, attr2, attr3, attr4
  FROM user_advisor_actions
  WHERE task_name = in_task_name
  ORDER BY action_id;
  v_action        number;
  v_command      VARCHAR2(32);
  v_attr1        VARCHAR2(4000);
  v_attr2        VARCHAR2(4000);
  v_attr3        VARCHAR2(4000);
  v_attr4        VARCHAR2(4000);
  v_attr5        VARCHAR2(4000);
BEGIN
  OPEN curs;
  DBMS_OUTPUT.PUT_LINE(‘=========================================’);

 DBMS_OUTPUT.PUT_LINE(‘Task_name = ‘ || in_task_name);
  LOOP
   FETCH curs INTO
     v_action, v_command, v_attr1, v_attr2, v_attr3, v_attr4 ;
   EXIT when curs%NOTFOUND;
   DBMS_OUTPUT.PUT_LINE(‘Action ID: ‘ || v_action);
   DBMS_OUTPUT.PUT_LINE(‘Command : ‘ || v_command);
   DBMS_OUTPUT.PUT_LINE(‘Attr1 (name)       : ‘ ||
   SUBSTR(v_attr1,1,30));
   DBMS_OUTPUT.PUT_LINE(‘Attr2 (tablespace): ‘ ||
   SUBSTR(v_attr2,1,30));
   DBMS_OUTPUT.PUT_LINE(‘Attr3              : ‘ ||
```

```
    SUBSTR(v_attr3,1,30));
    DBMS_OUTPUT.PUT_LINE('Attr4                    : ' || v_attr4);
    DBMS_OUTPUT.PUT_LINE('Attr5                    : ' || v_attr5);
    DBMS_OUTPUT.PUT_LINE('----------------------------------------');
    END LOOP;
    CLOSE curs;
    DBMS_OUTPUT.PUT_LINE('==========END RECOMMENDATIONS============');
END show_recm;
/
-- see what the actions are using sample procedure
set serveroutput on size 99999
EXECUTE show_recm(:task_name);
A fragment of a sample output from this procedure is as
follows:
Task_name = MYTASK
Action ID: 1
Command : CREATE MATERIALIZED VIEW LOG
Attr1 (name)       :  "SH"."CUSTOMERS"
Attr2 (tablespace) :
Attr3              :  ROWID, SEQUENCE
Attr4              :  INCLUDING NEW VALUES
Attr5              :
----------------------------------------
..
----------------------------------------
Action ID: 15
Command : CREATE MATERIALIZED VIEW
Attr1 (name)      : "SH"."SH_MV$$_0004"
Attr2 (tablespace): "SH_MVIEWS"
Attr3             : REFRESH FAST WITH ROWID
Attr4             : ENABLE QUERY REWRITE
Attr5             :
----------------------------------------
..
----------------------------------------
Action ID: 19
Command : CREATE INDEX
Attr1 (name)      : "SH"."SH_IDX$$_0013"
Attr2 (tablespace): "SH_INDEXES"
Attr3             : "SH"."SH_MV$$_0002"
Attr4             : BITMAP
Attr5             :
```

Stopping the Recommendation Process

If SQL Access Advisor takes too long to make its recommendations using the procedure EXECUTE_TASK, then you can stop it by calling the CANCEL_TASK procedure and passing in the task_name for this recommendation process. If you use CANCEL_TASK, then SQL Access Advisor makes no recommendations. Therefore, if recommendations are required, consider using the INTERRUPT_TASK procedure.

Interrupting Tasks: The INTERRUPT_TASK procedure causes an Advisor operation to terminate as if it has reached its normal end. As a result, the user can see any recommendations that have been formed up to the point of the interrupt.

An interrupted task cannot be restarted. The syntax is as follows:

```
DBMS_ADVISOR.INTERRUPT_TASK (task_name IN VARCHAR2);
```

The following illustrates an example of using this procedure:

```
EXECUTE DBMS_ADVISOR.INTERRUPT_TASK ('MY_TASK');
```

Canceling Tasks: The CANCEL_TASK procedure causes a currently executing operation to terminate. An Advisor operation may take a few seconds to respond to this request. Because all Advisor task procedures are synchronous, to cancel an operation, you must use a separate database session.

A cancel command effective restores the task to its condition before the start of the canceled operation. Therefore, a canceled task or data object cannot be restarted (but you can reset the task using DBMS_ADVISOR.RESET_TASK and then executing it again). Its syntax is as follows:

```
DBMS_ADVISOR.CANCEL_TASK (task_name   IN   VARCHAR2);
```

The following illustrates an example of using this procedure:

```
EXECUTE DBMS_ADVISOR.CANCEL_TASK('MYTASK');
```

Marking Recommendations

By default, all SQL Access Advisor recommendations are ready to be implemented, however, the user can choose to skip or exclude selected recommendations by using the MARK_RECOMMENDATION procedure. MARK_RECOMMENDATION allows the user to annotate a recommendation with a REJECT or IGNORE setting, which causes the GET_TASK_SCRIPT to skip it when producing the implementation procedure. The syntax is as follows:

```
DBMS_ADVISOR.MARK_RECOMMENDATION (
    task_name            IN VARCHAR2
    id                   IN NUMBER,
    action               IN VARCHAR2);
```

The following example marks a recommendation with ID 2 as REJECT. This recommendation and any dependent recommendations do not appear in the script.

```
EXECUTE DBMS_ADVISOR.MARK_RECOMMENDATION('MYTASK', 2, 'REJECT');
```

If the Advisor makes a recommendation to partition one or multiple previously unpartitioned base tables, then consider carefully before skipping this recommendation. Changing a table's partitioning scheme affects the cost of all queries, indexes, and materialized views defined on that table. Therefore, if you skip the partitioning recommendation, then the Advisor's remaining recommendations on this table are no longer optimal. To see recommendations on your workload that do not contain partitioning, reset the advisor task and rerun it with the ANALYSIS_SCOPE parameter changed to exclude partitioning recommendations.

Modifying Recommendations

Using the UPDATE_REC_ATTRIBUTES procedure, SQL Access Advisor names and assigns ownership to new objects such as indexes and materialized views during the analysis operation. However, it does not necessarily choose appropriate names, so you may manually set the owner, name, and tablespace values for new objects. For recommendations referencing existing database objects, owner and name values cannot be changed. The syntax is as follows:

```
DBMS_ADVISOR.UPDATE_REC_ATTRIBUTES (
   task_name            IN VARCHAR2
   rec_id               IN NUMBER,
   action_id            IN NUMBER,
   attribute_name       IN VARCHAR2,
   value                IN VARCHAR2);
```

The `attribute_name` parameter can take the following values:

- `OWNER`
  Specifies the owner name of the recommended object.
- `NAME`
  Specifies the name of the recommended object.
- `TABLESPACE`

Specifies the tablespace of the recommended object.

The following example modifies the attribute TABLESPACE for recommendation ID 1, action ID 1 to SH_MVIEWS.

```
EXECUTE DBMS_ADVISOR.UPDATE_REC_ATTRIBUTES('MYTASK', 1, 1,
'TABLESPACE','SH_MVIEWS');
```

Generating SQL Scripts

An alternative to querying the metadata to see the recommendations is to create a script of the SQL statements for the recommendations, using the procedure GET_TASK_SCRIPT. The resulting script is an executable SQL file that can contain DROP, CREATE, and ALTER statements. For new objects, the names of the materialized views, materialized view logs, and indexes are auto-generated by using the user-specified name template. You should review the generated SQL script before attempting to execute it.

There are several task parameters that control the naming conventions (MVIEW_NAME_TEMPLATE and INDEX_NAME_TEMPLATE), the owner for these new objects (DEF_INDEX_OWNER and DEF_MVIEW_OWNER), and the tablespaces (DEF_MVIEW_TABLESPACE and DEF_INDEX_TABLESPACE).

The following example shows how to generate a CLOB containing the script for the recommendations:

```
EXECUTE
DBMS_ADVISOR.CREATE_FILE(DBMS_ADVISOR.GET_TASK_SCRIPT('MYTASK'
),'ADVISOR_RESULTS', 'advscript.sql');
```

To save the script to a file, a directory path must be supplied so that the procedure CREATE_FILE knows where to store the script. In addition, read and write privileges must be granted on this directory. The following example shows how to save an advisor script CLOB to a file:

```
--create a directory and grant permissions to read/write to it
CONNECT SH/SH;
CREATE DIRECTORY ADVISOR_RESULTS AS '/mydir';
GRANT READ ON DIRECTORY ADVISOR_RESULTS TO PUBLIC;
GRANT WRITE ON DIRECTORY ADVISOR_RESULTS TO PUBLIC;
```

The following is a fragment of a script generated by this procedure. The script also includes PL/SQL calls to gather statistics on the recommended access structures and marks the recommendations as IMPLEMENTED at the end:

```
Rem  Access Advisor V11.1.0.0.0 - Production
Rem
Rem  Username:        SH
Rem  Task:            MYTASK
Rem  Execution date:  15/08/2006 11:35
Rem
set feedback 1
set linesize 80
set trimspool on
set tab off
set pagesize 60
whenever sqlerror CONTINUE

CREATE MATERIALIZED VIEW LOG ON "SH"."PRODUCTS"
    WITH ROWID, SEQUENCE("PROD_ID","PROD_SUBCATEGORY")
   INCLUDING NEW VALUES;

ALTER MATERIALIZED VIEW LOG FORCE ON "SH"."PRODUCTS"
    ADD ROWID, SEQUENCE("PROD_ID","PROD_SUBCATEGORY")
    INCLUDING NEW VALUES;
..
CREATE MATERIALIZED VIEW "SH"."MV$$_00510002"
    REFRESH FAST WITH ROWID
    ENABLE QUERY REWRITE
    AS SELECT SH.CUSTOMERS.CUST_STATE_PROVINCE C1, COUNT(*) M1
FROM
SH.CUSTOMERS WHERE (SH.CUSTOMERS.CUST_STATE_PROVINCE = 'CA') GROUP BY
SH.CUSTOMERS.CUST_STATE_PROVINCE;
BEGIN
  DBMS_STATS.GATHER_TABLE_STATS('"SH"', '"MV$$_00510002"', NULL,
     DBMS_STATS.AUTO_SAMPLE_SIZE);
END;
/
..
CREATE BITMAP INDEX "SH"."MV$$_00510004_IDX$$_00510013"
    ON "SH"."MV$$_00510004" ("C4");
whenever sqlerror EXIT SQL.SQLCODE
BEGIN
  DBMS_ADVISOR.MARK_RECOMMENDATION('"MYTASK"',1,'IMPLEMENTED');
  DBMS_ADVISOR.MARK_RECOMMENDATION('"MYTASK"',2,'IMPLEMENTED');
  DBMS_ADVISOR.MARK_RECOMMENDATION('"MYTASK"',3,'IMPLEMENTED');
  DBMS_ADVISOR.MARK_RECOMMENDATION('"MYTASK"',4,'IMPLEMENTED');
END;
/
```

Special Considerations when Script Includes Partitioning Recommendations

The Advisor may recommend partitioning an existing unpartitioned base table to improve query performance. When the Advisor implementation script contains partition recommendations, you must take note of the following issues:

- Partitioning an existing table is a complex and extensive operation, which may take considerably longer than implementing a new index or materialized view. Sufficient time should be reserved for implementing this recommendation.
- While index and materialized view recommendations are easy to reverse by deleting the index or view, a table, after being partitioned, cannot easily be restored to its original state. Therefore, ensure that you back up the database before executing a script containing partition recommendations.
- While repartitioning a base table, SQL Access Advisor scripts make a temporary copy of the original table, which occupies the same amount of space as the original table. Therefore, the repartitioning process requires sufficient free disk space for another copy of the largest table to be repartitioned. You must ensure that such space is available before running the implementation script.
  The partition implementation script attempts to migrate dependent objects such as indexes, materialized views, and constraints. However, some object cannot be automatically migrated. For example, PL/SQL stored procedures defined against a repartitioned base table typically become invalid and must be recompiled.
- If you decide not to implement a partition recommendation that the advisor has made, then note that all other recommendations on the same table in the same script (such as `CREATE INDEX` and `CREATE MATERIALIZED VIEW` recommendations) are dependent on the partitioning recommendation. To obtain accurate recommendations, you should not simply remove the partition recommendation from the script. Rather, rerun the advisor with partitioning disabled (for example, by setting parameter `ANALYSIS_SCOPE` to a value that does not include the keyword `TABLE`).

When Recommendations are no Longer Required

The `RESET_TASK` procedure resets a task to its initial starting point. This has the effect of removing all recommendations, and intermediate data from the task. The actual task status is set to `INITIAL`. The syntax is as follows:

```
DBMS_ADVISOR.RESET_TASK (task_name      IN VARCHAR2);
```

The following illustrates an example of using this procedure:

```
EXECUTE DBMS_ADVISOR.RESET_TASK('MYTASK');
```

Performing a Quick Tune

To tune a single SQL statement, the `QUICK_TUNE` procedure accepts as its input a `task_name` and a SQL statement. The procedure creates a task and workload and executes this task. There is no difference in the results from using `QUICK_TUNE`. They are exactly the same as those from using `EXECUTE_TASK`, but this approach is easier to use when there is only a single SQL statement to be tuned. The syntax is as follows:

```
DBMS_ADVISOR.QUICK_TUNE (
   advisor_name           IN VARCHAR2,
   task_name              IN VARCHAR2,
   attr1                  IN CLOB,
   attr2                  IN VARCHAR2 := NULL,
   attr3                  IN NUMBER := NULL,
   task_or_template       IN VARCHAR2 := NULL);
```

The following example shows how to quick tune a single SQL statement:

```
VARIABLE task_name VARCHAR2(255);
VARIABLE sql_stmt VARCHAR2(4000);
EXECUTE :sql_stmt := 'SELECT COUNT(*) FROM customers
               WHERE cust_state_province =''CA''';
EXECUTE :task_name  := 'MY_QUICKTUNE_TASK';

EXECUTE
DBMS_ADVISOR.QUICK_TUNE(DBMS_ADVISOR.SQLACCESS_ADVISOR,
              :task_name, :sql_stmt);
```

Managing Tasks

Every time recommendations are generated, tasks are created. Unless you perform maintenance on these tasks, they grow over time and occupy storage space. You may want to keep some tasks and prevent their accidental deletion. Therefore, you can perform several management operations on tasks:

- Updating Task Attributes
- Deleting Tasks
- Setting the DAYS_TO_EXPIRE Parameter.

Updating Task Attributes

Using the UPDATE_TASK_ATTRIBUTES procedure, you can:

- Change the name of a task.
- Give a task a description.
- Set the task to be read-only so it cannot be changed.
- Make the task a template upon which you can define other tasks.
- Changes various attributes of a task or a task template.

The syntax is as follows:

```
DBMS_ADVISOR.UPDATE_TASK_ATTRIBUTES (
   task_name           IN VARCHAR2
   new_name            IN VARCHAR2 := NULL,
   description         IN VARCHAR2 := NULL,
   read_only           IN VARCHAR2 := NULL,
   is_template         IN VARCHAR2 := NULL,
   how_created         IN VARCHAR2 := NULL);
```

The following example updates the name of an task MYTASK to TUNING1:

```
EXECUTE DBMS_ADVISOR.UPDATE_TASK_ATTRIBUTES('MYTASK', 'TUNING1');
```

The following example marks the task TUNING1 to read-only

```
EXECUTE DBMS_ADVISOR.UPDATE_TASK_ATTRIBUTES('TUNING1',
read_only => 'TRUE');
```

The following example marks the task MYTASK as a template.

```
EXECUTE DBMS_ADVISOR.UPDATE_TASK_ATTRIBUTES('TUNING1',
is_template=>'TRUE');
```

Deleting Tasks

The DELETE_TASK procedure deletes existing Advisor tasks from the repository. The syntax is as follows:

```
DBMS_ADVISOR.DELETE_TASK (task_name  IN VARCHAR2);
```

The following illustrates an example of using this procedure:

```
EXECUTE DBMS_ADVISOR.DELETE_TASK('MYTASK');
```

Setting the DAYS_TO_EXPIRE Parameter

When a task or workload object is created, the parameter DAYS_TO_EXPIRE is set to 30. The value indicates the number of days until the task or object is automatically deleted by the system. To save a task or workload indefinitely, set the DAYS_TO_EXPIRE parameter to ADVISOR_UNLIMITED.

Using SQL Access Advisor Constants

You can use the constants shown in Table 18.3 with SQL Access Advisor.

Table 18.3. SQL Access Advisor Constants

Constant	Description
ADVISOR_ALL	A value that indicates all possible values. For string parameters, this value is equivalent to the wildcard % character.
ADVISOR_CURRENT	Indicates the current time or active set of elements. Typically, this is used in time parameters.
ADVISOR_DEFAULT	Indicates the default value. Typically used when setting task or workload parameters.
ADVISOR_UNLIMITED	A value that represents an unlimited numeric value.
ADVISOR_UNUSED	A value that represents an unused entity. When a parameter is set to ADVISOR_UNUSED, it has no effect on the current operation. A typical use for this constant is to set a parameter as unused for its dependent operations.
SQLACCESS_GENERAL	Specifies the name of a default SQL Access general-purpose task template. This template sets the DML_VOLATILITY task parameter to TRUE and ANALYSIS_SCOPE to INDEX, MVIEW.
SQLACCESS_OLTP	Specifies the name of a default SQL Access OLTP task template. This template sets the DML_VOLATILITY task parameter to TRUE and ANALYSIS_SCOPE to INDEX.
SQLACCESS_WAREHOUSE	Specifies the name of a default SQL Access warehouse task template. This template sets the DML_VOLATILITY task parameter to FALSE and EXECUTION_TYPE to INDEX, MVIEW.
SQLACCESS_ADVISOR	Contains the formal name of SQL Access Advisor. You can specify this name when procedures require the Advisor name as an argument.

Examples of Using SQL Access Advisor

This section illustrates some typical scenarios for using SQL Access Advisor. Oracle Database provides a script that contains this chapter's examples, `aadvdemo.sql`.

Recommendations From a User-Defined Workload

The following example imports workload from a user-defined table, `SH.USER_WORKLOAD`. It then creates a task called `MYTASK`, sets the storage budget to 100 MB, and runs the task. A PL/SQL procedure prints the recommendations. Finally, the example generates a script that you can use to implement the recommendations.

Step 1: Prepare the USER_WORKLOAD table

Load the `USER_WORKLOAD` table with SQL statements as follows:

```
CONNECT SH/SH;
-- aggregation with selection
INSERT INTO user_workload (username, module, action,
priority, sql_text)
VALUES ('SH', 'Example1', 'Action', 2,'SELECT
t.week_ending_dayp.prod_subcategory,
SUM(s.amount_sold) AS dollars, s.channel_id, s.promo_id
FROM sales s, times t, products p WHERE s.time_id =
t.time_id AND s.prod_id = p.prod_id AND s.prod_id > 10
AND s.prod_id < 50  GROUP BY t.week_ending_day,
p.prod_subcategory, s.channel_id, s.promo_id')
/

-- aggregation with selection
INSERT INTO user_workload (username, module, action,
priority, sql_text) VALUES ('SH', 'Example1', 'Action',
2, 'SELECT  t.calendar_month_desc, SUM(s.amount_sold)
AS dollars   FROM     sales s , times t
WHERE    s.time_id = t.time_id
AND    s.time_id between TO_DATE(''01-JAN-2000'', ''DD-
MON-YYYY'') AND TO_DATE(''01-JUL-2000'', ''DD-MON-YYYY'')
GROUP BY t.calendar_month_desc')
/

--Load all SQL queries.
INSERT INTO user_workload (username, module, action,
priority, sql_text)
VALUES ('SH', 'Example1', 'Action', 2,
'SELECT ch.channel_class, c.cust_city,
t.calendar_quarter_desc,SUM(s.amount_sold) sales_amount
FROM sales s, times t, customers c, channels ch
WHERE s.time_id = t.time_id AND s.cust_id = c.cust_id
AND s.channel_id = ch.channel_id AND
c.cust_state_province = ''CA''
AND  ch.channel_desc IN (''Internet'',''Catalog'') AND
t.calendar_quarter_desc IN (''1999-Q1'',''1999-Q2'')
GROUP BY ch.channel_class, c.cust_city,
t.calendar_quarter_desc')
/
```

```
-- order by

INSERT INTO user_workload (username, module, action,
priority, sql_text)
VALUES ('SH', 'Example1', 'Action', 2, 'SELECT
c.country_id, c.cust_city, c.cust_last_name
FROM customers c WHERE c.country_id IN (52790, 52789)
ORDER BY c.country_id, c.cust_city, c.cust_last_name')
/
COMMIT;

CONNECT SH/SH;
set serveroutput on;

VARIABLE task_id NUMBER;
VARIABLE task_name VARCHAR2(255);
VARIABLE workload_name VARCHAR2(255);
```

Step 2: Create a SQL tuning set named MYWORKLOAD

```
EXECUTE :workload_name := 'MYWORKLOAD';
EXECUTE DBMS_SQLTUNE.CREATE_SQLSET(:workload_name, 'test
purposeV);
```

Step 3: Load the SQL tuning set from the user-defined table SH.USER_WORKLOAD

```
DECLARE
  sqlset_cur DBMS_SQLTUNE.SQLSET_CURSOR;    /*a sqlset
cursor variable*/
BEGIN
OPEN  sqlset_cur FOR
SELECT SQLSET_ROW(null, sql_text, null, null, username,
null, null, 0,0,0,0,0,0,0,0,0,null, 0,0,0,0)
   AS ROW FROM USER_WORKLOAD;
DBMS_SQLTUNE.LOAD_SQLSET(:workload_name, sqlset_cur);
END;
```

Step 4: Create a task named MYTASK

```
EXECUTE :task_name := 'MYTASK';
EXECUTE DBMS_ADVISOR.CREATE_TASK('SQL Access Advisor',
:task_id, :task_name);
```

Step 5: Set task parameters

```
EXECUTE DBMS_ADVISOR.SET_TASK_PARAMETER (:task_name,
'STORAGE_CHANGE', 100);
EXECUTE DBMS_ADVISOR.SET_TASK_PARAMETER(:task_name,
'ANALYSIS_SCOPE, INDEX');
```

Step 6: Create a link between the SQL tuning set and the task

```
EXECUTE DBMS_ADVISOR.ADD_STS_REF(:task_name,
:workload_name);
```

Step 7: Execute the task

```
EXECUTE DBMS_ADVISOR.EXECUTE_TASK(:task_name);
```

Step 8: View the recommendations

```
-- See the number of recommendations and the status of
the task.
SELECT rec_id, rank, benefit
FROM user_advisor_recommendations WHERE task_name =
:task_name;

-- See recommendation for each query.
SELECT sql_id, rec_id, precost, postcost,
(precost-postcost)*100/precost AS percent_benefit
FROM user_advisor_sqla_wk_stmts
WHERE task_name = :task_name AND workload_name = :workload_name;

-- See the actions for each recommendations.
SELECT rec_id, action_id, SUBSTR(command,1,30) AS command
FROM user_advisor_actions
WHERE task_name = :task_name
ORDER BY rec_id, action_id;

-- See what the actions are using sample procedure.
SET SERVEROUTPUT ON SIZE 99999
EXECUTE show_recm(:task_name);
```

Step 9: Generate a script to Implement the recommendations

```
EXECUTE
DBMS_ADVISOR.CREATE_FILE(DBMS_ADVISOR.GET_TASK_SCRIPT(:ta
sk_name),'ADVISOR_RESULTS', 'Example1_script.sql');
```

Generate Recommendations Using a Task Template

The following example creates a template and then uses it to create a task. It then uses this task to generate recommendations from a user-defined table.

```
CONNECT SH/SH;
VARIABLE template_id NUMBER;
VARIABLE template_name VARCHAR2(255);
```

Step 1: Create a template called MY_TEMPLATE

```
EXECUTE :template_name := 'MY_TEMPLATE';
EXECUTE DBMS_ADVISOR.CREATE_TASK ( -
   'SQL Access Advisor',:template_id, :template_name,
is_template=>'TRUE');
```

Step 2: Set template parameters

Set naming conventions for recommended indexes and materialized views.

```
EXECUTE DBMS_ADVISOR.SET_TASK_PARAMETER (
:template_name,  'INDEX_NAME_TEMPLATE',
'SH_IDX$$_<SEQ>');
EXECUTE DBMS_ADVISOR.SET_TASK_PARAMETER (
:template_name, 'MVIEW_NAME_TEMPLATE', 'SH_MV$$_<SEQ>');

-- Set default owners for recommended indexes/materialized views.
EXECUTE DBMS_ADVISOR.SET_TASK_PARAMETER (:template_name,
'DEF_INDEX_OWNER', 'SH');

EXECUTE DBMS_ADVISOR.SET_TASK_PARAMETER ( :template_name,
'DEF_MVIEW_OWNER', 'SH');

-- Set default tablespace for recommended indexes/
  materialized views.

EXECUTE DBMS_ADVISOR.SET_TASK_PARAMETER (:template_name,
'DEF_INDEX_TABLESPACE', 'SH_INDEXES');

EXECUTE DBMS_ADVISOR.SET_TASK_PARAMETER(:template_name,
'DEF_MVIEW_TABLESPACE', 'SH_MVIEWS');
```

Step 3: Create a task using the template

```
VARIABLE task_id NUMBER;
VARIABLE task_name VARCHAR2(255);
EXECUTE :task_name := 'MYTASK';

EXECUTE DBMS_ADVISOR.CREATE_TASK ('SQL Access Advisor',
:task_id, :task_name, template => 'MY_TEMPLATE');

--See the parameter settings for task

SELECT parameter_name, parameter_value
FROM user_advisor_parameters WHERE task_name = :task_name
AND (parameter_name LIKE '%MVIEW%' OR parameter_name LIKE
'%INDEX%');
```

Step 4: Create a SQL tuning set named MYWORKLOAD

```
EXECUTE :workload_name := 'MYWORKLOAD';
EXECUTE DBMS_SQLTUNE.CREATE_SQLSET(:workload_name,
'test_purpose');
```

Step 5: Load the SQL tuning set from the user-defined table SH.USER_WORKLOAD

```
DECLARE
sqlset_cur DBMS_SQLTUNE.SQLSET_CURSOR;  /*a sqlset cursor
variable*/
```

```
BEGIN
OPEN sqlset_cur FOR
 SELECT
   SQLSET_ROW(null,sql_text,null,null,username, null,
null, 0,0,0,0,0,0,0,0,0, null,0,0,00) AS row
   FROM user_workload;
DBMS_SQLTUNE.LOAD_SQLSET(:workload_name, sqlsetcur);
END;
```

Step 6: Create a link between the workload and the task

```
EXECUTE DBMS_ADVISOR.ADD_STS_REF(:task_name,
:workload_name);
```

Step 7: Execute the task

```
EXECUTE DBMS_ADVISOR.EXECUTE_TASK(:task_name);
```

Step 8: Generate a script

```
EXECUTE
DBMS_ADVISOR.CREATE_FILE(DBMS_ADVISOR.GET_TASK_SCRIPT(:ta
sk_name),'ADVISOR_RESULTS', 'Example2_script.sql');
```

Evaluate Current Usage of Indexes and Materialized Views

This example illustrates how you can use SQL Access Advisor to evaluate the utilization of existing indexes and materialized views. We assume the workload is loaded into USER_WORKLOAD table. The indexes and materialized views that the given workload are using appear as RETAIN actions in SQL Access Advisor recommendations.

```
VARIABLE task_id NUMBER;
VARIABLE task_name VARCHAR2(255);
VARIABLE workload_name VARCHAR2(255);
```

Step 1: Create a SQL tuning set named WORKLOAD

```
EXECUTE :workload_name := 'MYWORKLOAD';
EXECUTE DBMS_SQLTUNE.CREATE_SQLSET(:workload_name,
'test_purpose');
```

Step 2: Load the SQL tuning set from the user-defined table SH.USER_WORKLOAD

```
DECLARE
  sqlset_cur DBMS_SQLTUNE.SQLSET_CURSOR;  /*a sqlset cursor variable*/
BEGIN
OPEN sqlset_cur FOR
SELECT
  SQLSET_ROW(null,sql_text,null,null,username, null,
  null, 0,0,0,0,0,0,0,0,0,null, 0,0,0,0)
   AS ROW
  FROM user_workload;
DBMS_SQLTUNE.LOAD_SQLSET(:workload_name, :sqlsetcur);
END;
```

Step 3: Create a task named MY_EVAL_TASK

```
EXECUTE :task_name := 'MY_EVAL_TASK';

EXECUTE DBMS_ADVISOR.CREATE_TASK ('SQL Access Advisor',
:task_id, :task_name);
```

Step 4: Create a link between workload and task

```
EXECUTE DBMS_ADVISOR.ADD_STS_REF(:task_name,
:workload_name);
```

Step 5: Set task parameters to indicate EVALUATION ONLY task

```
EXECUTE DBMS_ADVISOR.SET_TASK_PARAMETER (:task_name,
'EVALUATION_ONLY', 'TRUE');
```

Step 6: Execute the task

```
EXECUTE DBMS_ADVISOR.EXECUTE_TASK(:task_name);
```

Step 7: View evaluation results

```
--See the number of recommendations and the status of the
task.
SELECT rec_id, rank, benefit
FROM user_advisor_recommendations WHERE task_name =
:task_name;

--See the actions for each recommendation.
SELECT rec_id, action_id, SUBSTR(command,1,30) AS
command, attr1 AS name
FROM user_advisor_actions WHERE task_name = :task_name
ORDER BY rec_id, action_id;
```

TUNING MATERIALIZED VIEWS FOR FAST REFRESH AND QUERY REWRITE

Several `DBMS_MVIEW` procedures can help you create materialized views that are optimized for fast refresh and query rewrite. The `EXPLAIN_MVIEW` procedure can tell you whether a materialized view is fast refreshable or eligible for general query rewrite. `EXPLAIN_REWRITE` tells you whether query rewrite will occur. However, neither procedure tells you how to achieve fast refresh or query rewrite.

To further facilitate the use of materialized views, the `TUNE_MVIEW` procedure shows you how to optimize your `CREATE MATERIALIZED VIEW` statement and to meet other requirements such as materialized view log and rewrite equivalence relationship for fast refresh and general query rewrite. `TUNE_MVIEW` analyzes and processes the `CREATE MATERIALIZED VIEW` statement and generates two sets of output results: one for the materialized view implementation and the other for undoing the `CREATE MATERIALIZED VIEW` operations. You can access the two sets of output results through views or the external script files created by SQL Access Advisor. These external script files are ready to execute to implement the materialized view.

With the TUNE_MVIEW procedure, you no longer require a detailed understanding of materialized views to create a materialized view in an application because the materialized view and its required components (such as a materialized view log) are created correctly through the procedure.

DBMS_ADVISOR.TUNE_MVIEW Procedure

This section discusses the following information:

- TUNE_MVIEW Syntax and Operations
- Accessing TUNE_MVIEW Output Results

TUNE_MVIEW Syntax and Operations

The syntax for TUNE_MVIEW is as follows:

```
DBMS_ADVISOR.TUNE_MVIEW (task_name IN OUT VARCHAR2,
mv_create_stmt IN [CLOB | VARCHAR2])
```

The TUNE_MVIEW procedure takes two input parameters: task_name and mv_create_stmt. task_name is a user-provided task identifier used to access the output results. mv_create_stmt is a complete CREATE MATERIALIZED VIEW statement that is to be tuned. If the input CREATE MATERIALIZED VIEW statement does not have the clauses of REFRESH FAST or ENABLE QUERY REWRITE, or both, then TUNE_MVIEW uses the default clauses REFRESH FORCE and DISABLE QUERY REWRITE to tune the statement to be fast refreshable if possible or only complete refreshable otherwise.

The TUNE_MVIEW procedure handles a broad range of CREATE MATERIALIZED VIEW statements that can have arbitrary defining queries in them. The defining query could be a simple SELECT statement or a complex query with set operators or inline views. When the defining query of the materialized view contains the clause REFRESH FAST, TUNE_MVIEW analyzes the query and checks to see if it is fast refreshable. If it is fast refreshable, the procedure returns a message saying "the materialized view is optimal and cannot be further tuned." Otherwise, the TUNE_MVIEW procedure starts the tuning work on the given statement.

The TUNE_MVIEW procedure can generate the output statements that correct the defining query by adding extra columns such as required aggregate columns or fix the materialized view logs so that FAST REFRESH is possible. In the case of a complex defining query, the TUNE_MVIEW procedure may decompose the query and generates two or more fast refreshable materialized views or restate the materialized view in a way to fulfill fast refresh requirements as much as possible. The TUNE_MVIEW procedure supports defining queries with the following complex query constructs:

- Set operators (UNION, UNION ALL, MINUS, and INTERSECT)
- COUNT DISTINCT
- SELECT DISTINCT
- Inline views.

When the ENABLE QUERY REWRITE clause is specified, TUNE_MVIEW also fixes the statement using a process similar to REFRESH FAST. The procedure redefines the materialized view so that as many of the advanced forms of query rewrite are possible.

The TUNE_MVIEW procedure generates two sets of output results as executable statements. One set of the output (IMPLEMENTATION) is for implementing materialized views and required components such as materialized view logs or rewrite equivalences to achieve fast refreshability and query rewritablity as much as possible. The other set of the output (UNDO) is for dropping the materialized views and the rewrite equivalences in case you decide they are not required.

The output statements for the IMPLEMENTATION process include:

- CREATE MATERIALIZED VIEW LOG statements: creates any missing materialized view logs required for fast refresh.
- ALTER MATERIALIZED VIEW LOG FORCE statements: fixes any materialized view log related requirements such as missing filter columns, sequence, and so on, required for fast refresh.
- One or more CREATE MATERIALIZED VIEW statements: In the case of one output statement, the original defining query is directly restated and transformed. Simple query transformation could be just adding required columns. For example, add rowid column for materialized join view and add aggregate column for materialized aggregate view. In the case of decomposition, multiple CREATE MATERIALIZED VIEW statements are generated and form a nested materialized view hierarchy in which one or more submaterialized views are referenced by a new top-level materialized view modified from the original statement. This is to achieve fast refresh and query rewrite as much as possible. Submaterialized views are often fast refreshable.
- BUILD_SAFE_REWRITE_EQUIVALENCE statement: enables the rewrite of top-level materialized views using submaterialized views. It is required to enable query rewrite when a composition occurs.

Note that the decomposition result implies no sharing of submaterialized views. That is, in the case of decomposition, the TUNE_MVIEW output always contains new submaterialized view. It does not reference existing materialized views.

The output statements for the UNDO process include:

- DROP MATERIALIZED VIEW statements to reverse the materialized view creations (including submaterialized views) in the IMPLEMENTATION process.
- DROP_REWRITE_EQUIVALENCE statement to remove the rewrite equivalence relationship built in the IMPLEMENTATION process if needed.

Note that the UNDO process does not include the statement to drop materialized view logs. Many different materialized views can share materialized view logs. Some of these logs may reside on remote Oracle database instances.

Accessing TUNE_MVIEW Output Results

There are two ways to access TUNE_MVIEW output results:

- Script generation using DBMS_ADVISOR.GET_TASK_SCRIPT function and DBMS_ADVISOR.CREATE_FILE procedure.
- Use USER_TUNE_MVIEW or DBA_TUNE_MVIEW views.

USER_TUNE_MVIEW and DBA_TUNE_MVIEW Views

After executing TUNE_MVIEW, the results are output into SQL Access Advisor repository tables and are accessible through the data dictionary views USER_TUNE_MVIEW and DBA_TUNE_MVIEW.

Script Generation DBMS_ADVISOR Function and Procedure

The most straightforward method for generating the execution scripts for a recommendation is to use the procedure DBMS_ADVISOR.GET_TASK_SCRIPT. The following is a simple example. First, you must define a directory in which to store the results:

```
CREATE DIRECTORY TUNE_RESULTS AS  '/tmp/script_dir';
GRANT READ, WRITE ON DIRECTORY TUNE_RESULTS TO PUBLIC;
```

Now generate both the implementation and undo scripts and place them in /tmp/script_dir/mv_create.sql and /tmp/script_dir/mv_undo.sql, respectively.

```
EXECUTE
DBMS_ADVISOR.CREATE_FILE(DBMS_ADVISOR.GET_TASK_SCRIPT(:task_name),
'TUNE_RESULTS', 'mv_create.sql');
EXECUTE
DBMS_ADVISOR.CREATE_FILE(DBMS_ADVISOR.GET_TASK_SCRIPT(:task_name,
'UNDO'), 'TUNE_RESULTS', 'mv_undo.sql');
```

Now let us review some examples using the TUNE_MVIEW procedure.

Example 18.1: Optimizing the Defining Query for Fast Refresh

This example shows how TUNE_MVIEW changes the defining query to be fast refreshable. A CREATE MATERIALIZED VIEW statement is defined in variable create_mv_ddl, which includes a FAST REFRESH clause. Its defining query contains a single query block in which an aggregate column, SUM(s.amount_sold), does not have the required aggregate columns to support fast refresh. If you execute the TUNE_MVIEW statement with this MATERIALIZED VIEW CREATE statement, then the resulting materialized view recommendation is fast refreshable:

```
VARIABLE task_cust_mv VARCHAR2(30);
VARIABLE create_mv_ddl VARCHAR2(4000);
EXECUTE :task_cust_mv := 'cust_mv';

EXECUTE :create_mv_ddl := '
CREATE MATERIALIZED VIEW cust_mv
REFRESH FAST
DISABLE QUERY REWRITE AS
SELECT s.prod_id, s.cust_id, SUM(s.amount_sold) sum_amount
FROM sales s, customers cs
WHERE s.cust_id = cs.cust_id
GROUP BY s.prod_id, s.cust_id';

EXECUTE DBMS_ADVISOR.TUNE_MVIEW(:task_cust_mv,
:create_mv_ddl);
```

The original defining query of cust_mv has been modified by adding aggregate columns to be fast refreshable.

The output from TUNE_MVIEW includes an optimized materialized view defining query as follows:

```
CREATE MATERIALIZED VIEW SH.CUST_MV
REFRESH FAST WITH ROWID
DISABLE QUERY REWRITE AS
SELECT SH.SALES.PROD_ID C1, SH.CUSTOMERS.CUST_ID C2,
          SUM("SH"."SALES"."AMOUNT_SOLD") M1,
          COUNT("SH"."SALES"."AMOUNT_SOLD") M2,
         COUNT(*) M3
     FROM SH.SALES, SH.CUSTOMERS
     WHERE SH.CUSTOMERS.CUST_ID = SH.SALES.CUST_ID
     GROUP BY SH.SALES.PROD_ID, SH.CUSTOMERS.CUST_ID;
```

The UNDO output is as follows:

```
DROP MATERIALIZED VIEW SH.CUST_MV;
```

Example 18.2: Access IMPLEMENTATION Output Through USER_TUNE_MVIEW View

```
SELECT STATEMENT FROM USER_TUNE_MVIEW
WHERE TASK_NAME= :task_cust_mv AND
SCRIPT_TYPE='IMPLEMENTATION';
```

Example 18.3: Save IMPLEMENTATION Output in a Script File

```
CREATE DIRECTORY TUNE_RESULTS AS '/myscript'
GRANT READ, WRITE ON DIRECTORY TUNE_RESULTS TO PUBLIC;

EXECUTE
DBMS_ADVISOR.CREATE_FILE (DBMS_ADVISOR. GET_TASK_SCRIPT (:task_cust_ mv),
'TUNE_RESULTS', 'mv_create.sql');
```

Example 18.4: Enable Query Rewrite by Creating Multiple Materialized Views

This example decomposes a materialized view's defining query with set operators UNION, which is not supported by query rewrite, into several submaterialized views, making query rewrite possible. The input detail tables are sales, customers, and countries. These tables do not have materialized view logs. First, you must execute the TUNE_MVIEW statement with the CREATE MATERIALIZED VIEW statement defined in the variable create_mv_ddl.

```
EXECUTE :task_cust_mv := 'cust_mv2';

EXECUTE :create_mv_ddl := '
CREATE MATERIALIZED VIEW cust_mv
ENABLE QUERY REWRITE AS
SELECT s.prod_id, s.cust_id, COUNT(*) cnt, SUM(s.amount_sold)
sum_amount FROM sales s, customers cs, countries cn
WHERE s.cust_id = cs.cust_id AND cs.country_id = cn.country_id
AND cn.country_name IN (''USA'',''Canada'')
GROUP BY s.prod_id, s.cust_id
UNION
SELECT  s.prod_id,  s.cust_id,  COUNT(*)  cnt,  SUM(s.amount_sold)
sum_amount FROM sales s, customers cs
WHERE s.cust_id = cs.cust_id AND s.cust_id IN (1005,1010,1012)
GROUP BY s.prod_id, s.cust_id';
```

The materialized view defining query contains a UNION set operator that does not support general query rewrite. If it is decomposed into multiple materialized views, however, then query rewrite is possible. To support general query rewrite, the database decomposes the MATERIALIZED VIEW defining query.

```
EXECUTE DBMS_ADVISOR.TUNE_MVIEW(:task_cust_mv,:create_mv_ddl);
```

The following recommendation from TUNE_MVIEW contains the materialized view logs and multiple materialized view:

```
CREATE MATERIALIZED VIEW LOG ON "SH"."CUSTOMERS"
WITH ROWID, SEQUENCE("CUST_ID")INCLUDING NEW VALUES;

ALTER MATERIALIZED VIEW LOG FORCE ON "SH"."CUSTOMERS"
    ADD ROWID, SEQUENCE("CUST_ID") INCLUDING NEW VALUES;

CREATE MATERIALIZED VIEW LOG ON
        "SH"."SALES"  WITH ROWID,
SEQUENCE("PROD_ID","CUST_ID","AMOUNT_SOLD")
    INCLUDING NEW VALUES;
ALTER MATERIALIZED VIEW LOG FORCE ON
    "SH"."SALES"
    ADD ROWID, SEQUENCE("PROD_ID","CUST_ID","AMOUNT_SOLD")
   INCLUDING NEW VALUES;

CREATE MATERIALIZED VIEW LOG ON
   "SH"."COUNTRIES"
    WITH ROWID, SEQUENCE("COUNTRY_ID","COUNTRY_NAME")
   INCLUDING NEW VALUES;

ALTER MATERIALIZED VIEW LOG FORCE ON
    "SH"."COUNTRIES"
    ADD ROWID, SEQUENCE("COUNTRY_ID","COUNTRY_NAME")
    INCLUDING NEW VALUES;

ALTER MATERIALIZED VIEW LOG FORCE ON
    "SH"."CUSTOMERS"
    ADD ROWID, SEQUENCE("CUST_ID","COUNTRY_ID")
   INCLUDING NEW VALUES;

ALTER MATERIALIZED VIEW LOG FORCE ON
    "SH"."SALES"
    ADD ROWID, SEQUENCE("PROD_ID","CUST_ID","AMOUNT_SOLD")
    INCLUDING NEW VALUES;

CREATE MATERIALIZED VIEW SH.CUST_MV$SUB1
    REFRESH FAST WITH ROWID ON COMMIT
    ENABLE QUERY REWRITE
    AS SELECT SH.SALES.PROD_ID C1, SH.CUSTOMERS.CUST_ID C2,
        SUM("SH"."SALES"."AMOUNT_SOLD") M1,
COUNT("SH"."SALES"."AMOUNT_SOLD") M2, COUNT(*) M3 FROM
SH.SALES,
SH.CUSTOMERS WHERE SH.CUSTOMERS.CUST_ID = SH.SALES.CUST_ID AND
        (SH.SALES.CUST_ID IN (1012, 1010, 1005))
        GROUP BY SH.SALES.PROD_ID, SH.CUSTOMERS.CUST_ID;

CREATE MATERIALIZED VIEW SH.CUST_MV$SUB2
    REFRESH FAST WITH ROWID ON COMMIT
    ENABLE QUERY REWRITE
    AS SELECT SH.SALES.PROD_ID C1, SH.CUSTOMERS.CUST_ID C2,
      SH.COUNTRIES.COUNTRY_NAME  C3,
```

```
SUM("SH"."SALES"."AMOUNT_SOLD") M1, COUNT("SH"."SALES".
        "AMOUNT_SOLD")
        M2, COUNT(*) M3 FROM SH.SALES, SH.CUSTOMERS,
SH.COUNTRIES WHERE
  SH.CUSTOMERS.CUST_ID        = SH.SALES.CUST_ID AND
SH.COUNTRIES.COUNTRY_ID = SH.CUSTOMERS.COUNTRY_ID
        AND (SH.COUNTRIES.COUNTRY_NAME IN ('USA',
'Canada')) GROUP BY
         SH.SALES.PROD_ID,
        SH.CUSTOMERS.CUST_ID, SH.COUNTRIES.COUNTRY_NAME;

CREATE MATERIALIZED VIEW SH.CUST_MV
    REFRESH FORCE WITH ROWID
    ENABLE QUERY REWRITE
        AS  (SELECT "CUST_MV$SUB2"."C1"
"PROD_ID","CUST_MV$SUB2"."C2"
  "CUST_ID",SUM("CUST_MV$SUB2"."M3")
        "CNT",SUM("CUST_MV$SUB2"."M1") "SUM_AMOUNT" FROM
"SH"."CUST_MV$SUB2"
        "CUST_MV$SUB2" GROUP BY
"CUST_MV$SUB2"."C1","CUST_MV$SUB2"."C2")UNION
        (SELECT "CUST_MV$SUB1"."C1"
"PROD_ID","CUST_MV$SUB1"."C2"
        "CUST_ID",SUM("CUST_MV$SUB1"."M3")
        "CNT",SUM("CUST_MV$SUB1"."M1") "SUM_AMOUNT" FROM
"SH"."CUST_MV$SUB1"
        "CUST_MV$SUB1" GROUP BY
"CUST_MV$SUB1"."C1","CUST_MV$SUB1"."C2");

BEGIN
DBMS_ADVANCED_REWRITE.BUILD_SAFE_REWRITE_EQUIVALENCE
('SH.CUST_MV$RWEQ',
  'SELECT s.prod_id, s.cust_id, COUNT(*) cnt,
         SUM(s.amount_sold) sum_amount
   FROM sales s, customers cs, countries cn
        WHERE s.cust_id = cs.cust_id AND cs.country_id =
  cn.country_id
         AND cn.country_name IN (''USA'',''Canada'')
   GROUP BY s.prod_id, s.cust_id
UNION
   SELECT s.prod_id, s.cust_id, COUNT(*) cnt,
         SUM(s.amount_sold) sum_amount
   FROM sales s, customers cs
   WHERE s.cust_id = cs.cust_id AND s.cust_id IN
 (1005,1010,1012)
   GROUP BY s.prod_id, s.cust_id',
  '(SELECT "CUST_MV$SUB2"."C3"
 "PROD_ID","CUST_MV$SUB2"."C2" "CUST_ID",
          SUM("CUST_MV$SUB2"."M3") "CNT",
```

```
          SUM("CUST_MV$SUB2"."M1") "SUM_AMOUNT"
     FROM "SH"."CUST_MV$SUB2" "CUST_MV$SUB2"
     GROUP BY "CUST_MV$SUB2"."C3","CUST_MV$SUB2"."C2")
    UNION
    (SELECT "CUST_MV$SUB1"."C2"
  "PROD_ID","CUST_MV$SUB1"."C1" "CUST_ID",
          "CUST_MV$SUB1"."M3" "CNT","CUST_MV$SUB1"."M1"
  "SUM_AMOUNT"
     FROM "SH"."CUST_MV$SUB1" "CUST_MV$SUB1")',-1553577441)
END;
/;
```

The DROP output is as follows:

```
DROP MATERIALIZED VIEW SH.CUST_MV$SUB1
DROP MATERIALIZED VIEW SH.CUST_MV$SUB2
DROP MATERIALIZED VIEW SH.CUST_MV
DBMS_ADVANCED_REWRITE.DROP_REWRITE_EQUIVALENCE('SH.CUST_MV$RWEQ')
```

The original defining query of `cust_mv` has been decomposed into two submaterialized views seen as `cust_mv$SUB1` and `cust_mv$SUB2`. One additional column `COUNT(amount_sold)` has been added in `cust_mv$SUB1` to make that materialized view fast refreshable.

The original defining query of `cust_mv` has been modified to query the two submaterialized views instead where both submaterialized views are fast refreshable and support general query rewrite.

The required materialized view logs are added to enable fast refresh of the submaterialized views. Note that, for each detail table, two materialized view log statements are generated: one is the `CREATE MATERIALIZED VIEW` statement and the other is an `ALTER MATERIALIZED VIEW FORCE` statement. The statements ensure that you can run the `CREATE` script multiple times.

The `BUILD_SAFE_REWRITE_EQUIVALENCE` statement is to connect the old defining query to the defining query of the new top-level materialized view. It ensures that query rewrite uses the new top-level materialized view to answer the query.

Example 18.5: Access IMPLEMENTATION Output Through USER_TUNE_MVIEW View

```
SELECT * FROM USER_TUNE_MVIEW
WHERE TASK_NAME='cust_mv2'
AND SCRIPT_TYPE='IMPLEMENTATION';
```

Example 18.6: Save IMPLEMENTATION Output in a Script File

The following statements save the `IMPLEMENTATION` output in a script file located at `/myscript/mv_create2.sql`:

```
CREATE DIRECTORY TUNE_RESULTS AS '/myscript'
GRANT READ, WRITE ON DIRECTRY TUNE_RESULTS TO PUBLIC;

EXECUTE
DBMS_ADVISOR.CREATE FILE(DBMS_ADVISOR.GET_TASK_SCRIPT('cust_mv2'),
'TUNE_RESULTS', 'mv_create2.sql');
```

Fast Refreshable with Optimized Sub-Materialized View

The example illustrates how TUNE_MVIEW can optimize the materialized view so that fast refresh is possible. In the example, the materialized view's defining query with set operators is transformed into one sub-materialized view and one top-level materialized view. The subselect queries in the original defining query are of similar shape and their predicate expressions are combined.

The materialized view defining query contains a UNION set-operator so that the materialized view itself is not fast-refreshable. However, you can combine two subselect queries in the materialized view defining query into one single query.

Example 18.7: Optimized Sub-Materialized View for Fast Refresh

```
EXECUTE :task_cust_mv := 'cust_mv3';
EXECUTE :create_mv_ddl := '

CREATE MATERIALIZED VIEW cust_mv
        REFRESH FAST ON DEMAND  ENABLE QUERY REWRITE AS
        SELECT s.prod_id, s.cust_id, COUNT(*) cnt, SUM(s.amount_sold)
        sum_amount FROM sales s, customers cs
        WHERE s.cust_id = cs.cust_id AND s.cust_id IN
        (2005,1020) GROUP BY s.prod_id, s.cust_id UNION
        SELECT s.prod_id, s.cust_id, COUNT(*) cnt,
        SUM(s.amount_sold) sum_amount       FROM sales s,
        customers cs
        WHERE s.cust_id = cs.cust_id AND s.cust_id IN
        (1005,1010,1012) GROUP BY s.prod_id, s.cust_id';

EXECUTE DBMS_ADVISOR.TUNE_MVIEW(:task_cust_mv,
:create_mv_ddl);
```

The following recommendation will be made by TUNE_MVIEW with an optimized submaterialized view combining the two subselect queries. The submaterialized view is referenced by a new top-level materialized view as follows:

```
CREATE MATERIALIZED VIEW LOG ON "SH"."SALES"
  WITH ROWID, SEQUENCE ("PROD_ID","CUST_ID","AMOUNT_SOLD")
  INCLUDING NEW VALUES

ALTER MATERIALIZED VIEW LOG FORCE ON "SH"."SALES"
  ADD ROWID, SEQUENCE ("PROD_ID","CUST_ID","AMOUNT_SOLD")
  INCLUDING NEW VALUES

CREATE MATERIALIZED VIEW LOG ON "SH"."CUSTOMERS"
  WITH ROWID, SEQUENCE ("CUST_ID")  INCLUDING NEW VALUES

ALTER MATERIALIZED VIEW LOG FORCE ON "SH"."CUSTOMERS"
  ADD ROWID, SEQUENCE ("CUST_ID")  INCLUDING NEW VALUES

CREATE MATERIALIZED VIEW SH.CUST_MV$SUB1
  REFRESH FAST WITH ROWID
  ENABLE QUERY REWRITE AS
  SELECT SH.SALES.CUST_ID C1, SH.SALES.PROD_ID C2,
```

```
    SUM("SH"."SALES"."AMOUNT_SOLD") M1,
    COUNT("SH"."SALES"."AMOUNT_SOLD")M2, COUNT(*) M3
    FROM SH.CUSTOMERS, SH.SALES
    WHERE SH.SALES.CUST_ID = SH.CUSTOMERS.CUST_ID AND
    (SH.SALES.CUST_ID IN (2005, 1020, 1012, 1010, 1005))
    GROUP BY SH.SALES.CUST_ID, SH.SALES.PROD_ID

CREATE MATERIALIZED VIEW SH.CUST_MV
 REFRESH FORCE WITH ROWID ENABLE QUERY REWRITE AS(SELECT
"CUST_MV$SUB1"."C2" "PROD_ID","CUST_MV$SUB1"."C1" "CUST_ID",
   "CUST_MV$SUB1"."M3" "CNT","CUST_MV$SUB1"."M1" "SUM_AMOUNT"
   FROM "SH"."CUST_MV$SUB1" "CUST_MV$SUB1"
   WHERE "CUST_MV$SUB1"."C1"=2005 OR "CUST_MV$SUB1"."C1"=1020)
UNION (SELECT "CUST_MV$SUB1"."C2
"PROD_ID","CUST_MV$SUB1"."C1" "CUST_ID",
"CUST_MV$SUB1"."M3" "CNT","CUST_MV$SUB1". "M1" "SUM_AMOUNT"
      FROM "SH"."CUST_MV$SUB1" "CUST_MV$SUB1"
 WHERE "CUST_MV$SUB1"."C1"=1012 OR
 "CUST_MV$SUB1"."C1"=1010 OR
           "CUST_MV$SUB1"."C1"=1005)

DBMS_ADVANCED_REWRITE.BUILD_SAFE_REWRITE_EQUIVALENCE
('SH.CUST_MV$RWEQ','SELECT s.prod_id, s.cust_id, COUNT(*) cnt,
 SUM(s.amount_sold) sum_amount
 FROM sales s, customers cs
 WHERE s.cust_id = cs.cust_id AND s.cust_id IN (2005,1020)
 GROUP BY s.prod_id, s.cust_id UNION SELECT s.prod_id,
s.cust_id, COUNT(*) cnt,SUM(s.amount_sold) sum_amount
FROM sales s, customers cs WHERE s.cust_id = cs.cust_id
AND s.cust_id IN (1005,1010,1012) GROUP BY s.prod_id,
s.cust_id', '(SELECT "CUST_MV$SUB1"."C2"
"PROD_ID","CUST_MV$SUB1"."C1"
"CUST_ID","CUST_MV$SUB1"."M3" "CNT","CUST_MV$SUB1"."M1"
"SUM_AMOUNT"  FROM "SH"."CUST_MV$SUB1" "CUST_MV$SUB1"
WHERE "CUST_MV$SUB1"."C1"=2005OR "CUST_MV$SUB1"."C1"=1020)
   UNION
   (SELECT "CUST_MV$SUB1"."C2" "PROD_ID",
   "CUST_MV$SUB1"."C1" "CUST_ID",
   "CUST_MV$SUB1"."M3" "CNT","CUST_MV$SUB1"."M1" "SUM_AMOUNT"
    FROM "SH"."CUST_MV$SUB1" "CUST_MV$SUB1"
 WHERE "CUST_MV$SUB1"."C1"=1012 OR "CUST_MV$SUB1"."C1"=1010 OR
   "CUST_MV$SUB1"."C1"=1005)',1811223110);
```

The original defining query of cust_mv has been optimized by combining the predicate of the two subselect queries in the sub-materialized view CUST_MV$SUB1. The required materialized view logs are also added to enable fast refresh of the submaterialized views.

The DROP output is as follows:

```
DROP MATERIALIZED VIEW SH.CUST_MV$SUB1
DROP MATERIALIZED VIEW SH.CUST_MV
DBMS_ADVANCED_REWRITE.DROP_REWRITE_EQUIVALENCE('SH.CUST_MV$RWEQ');
```

The following statements save the **IMPLEMENTATION** output in a script file located at /myscript/mv_create3.sql:

```
CREATE DIRECTORY TUNE_RESULTS AS '/myscript'
GRANT READ, WRITE ON DIRECTORY TUNE_RESULTS TO PUBLIC;

EXECUTE
DBMS_ADVISOR.CREATE_FILE(DBMS_ADVISOR.GET_TASK_SCRIPT('cust_mv3'),'TUNE_RESULTS',
'mv_create3.sql');
```

19 Using Optimizer Hints

Learning Objectives

*You can optimizer **hints** with SQL statements to alter execution plans. This chapter explains how to use hints to instruct the optimizer to use specific approaches.*

This chapter contains the following sections:

- Overview of Optimizer Hints
- Specifying Hints
- Using Hints with Views

OVERVIEW OF OPTIMIZER HINTS

A **hint** is an instruction to the optimizer. When writing SQL code, you may know information about the data unknown to the optimizer. Hints enable you to make decisions normally made by the optimizer, sometimes causing the optimizer to select a plan that it sees as higher cost.

In a test or development environments, hints are useful for testing the performance of a specific access path. For example, you may know that a certain index is more selective for certain queries. In this case, you may use hints to instruct the optimizer to use a better execution plan.

The disadvantage of hints is the extra code that must be managed, checked, and controlled. Changes in the database and host environment can make hints obsolete or even have negative consequences. For this reason, test by means of hints, but use other techniques to manage the SQL execution plans, such as SQL Tuning advisor and SQL Plan Baselines.

Oracle Database supports more than 60 hints, each of which may have zero or more parameters. A statement block can have only one comment containing hints, and that comment must follow the `SELECT`, `UPDATE`, `INSERT`, `MERGE`, or `DELETE` keyword. For example, the following hint directs the optimizer to pick the query plan that produces the first 10 rows from the `employees` table at the lowest cost:

```
SELECT /*+ FIRST_ROWS(10) */ * FROM employees;
```

Types of Hints

Hints can be of the following general types:

- Single-table.
  Single-table hints are specified on one table or view. `INDEX` and `USE_NL` are examples of single-table hints.
- Multi-table.
  Multi-table hints are like single-table hints, except that the hint can specify one or more tables or views. `LEADING` is an example of a multi-table hint. Note that `USE_NL(table1 table2)` is not considered a multi-table hint because it is a shortcut for `USE_NL(table1)` and `USE_NL(table2)`.
- Query block.
  Query block hints operate on single query blocks. `STAR_TRANSFORMATION` and `UNNEST` are examples of query block hints.
- Statement.
  Statement hints apply to the entire SQL statement. `ALL_ROWS` is an example of a statement hint.

Hints by Category

Optimizer hints are grouped into the following categories:

- Hints for Optimization Approaches and Goals
- Hints for Enabling Optimizer Features
- Hints for Access Paths
- Hints for Join Orders
- Hints for Join Operations
- Hints for Online Application Upgrade
- Hints for Parallel Execution
- Hints for Query Transformations
- Additional Hints.

These categories, and the hints contained within each category, are listed in the sections that follow.

Hints for Optimization Approaches and Goals

The `ALL_ROWS` and `FIRST_ROWS(n)` hints let you choose between optimization approaches and goals. If a SQL statement has a hint specifying an optimization approach and goal, then the optimizer uses the specified approach regardless of the presence or absence of statistics, the value of the `OPTIMIZER_MODE` initialization parameter, and the `OPTIMIZER_MODE` parameter of the `ALTER SESSION` statement.

The optimizer goal applies only to queries submitted directly. Use hints to specify the access path for any SQL statements submitted from within PL/SQL. The `ALTER SESSION ... SET OPTIMIZER_MODE` statement does not affect SQL run within PL/SQL.

If you specify either the `ALL_ROWS` or the `FIRST_ROWS(n)` hint in a SQL statement, and if the data dictionary does not have statistics about tables accessed by the statement, then the optimizer uses default statistical values, such as allocated storage for such tables, to estimate the missing statistics and choose an execution plan. These estimates might not be as accurate as those gathered by the DBMS_STATS package, so use DBMS_STATS to gather statistics.

If you specify hints for access paths or join operations along with either the ALL_ROWS or FIRST_ROWS(*n*) hint, then the optimizer gives precedence to the access paths and join operations specified by the hints.

Hints for Enabling Optimizer Features

The OPTIMIZER_FEATURES_ENABLE hint acts as an umbrella parameter for enabling a series of optimizer features based on an Oracle Database release number. This hint is a useful way to check for plan regressions after database upgrades.

Specify the release number as an argument to the hint. The following example runs a query with the optimizer features from Oracle Database 11g Release 1 (11.1.0.6):

```
SELECT /*+ optimizer_features_enable('11.1.0.6') */ employee_id,
last_name FROM employees ORDER BY employee_id;
```

Hints for Access Paths

The following hints instructs the optimizer to use a specific access path for a table:

- FULL
- CLUSTER
- HASH
- INDEX and NO_INDEX
- INDEX_ASC and INDEX_DESC
- INDEX_COMBINE and INDEX_JOIN
- INDEX_JOIN
- INDEX_FFS and NO_INDEX_FFS
- INDEX_SS and NO_INDEX_SS
- INDEX_SS_ASC and INDEX_SS_DESC.

Specifying one of the preceding hints causes the optimizer to choose the specified access path only if the access path is available based on the existence of an index or cluster and on the syntactic constructs of the SQL statement. If a hint specifies an unavailable access path, then the optimizer ignores it.

You must specify the table to be accessed exactly as it appears in the statement. If the statement uses an alias for the table, then use the alias rather than the table name in the hint. The table name within the hint should not include the schema name if the schema name is present in the statement.

For access path hints, Oracle Database ignores the hint if you specify the SAMPLE option in the FROM clause of a SELECT statement.

Hints for Join Orders

The following hints suggest join orders:

- LEADING
- ORDERED

Hints for Join Operations

The following hints instructs the optimizer to use a specific join operation for a table:

- USE_NL and NO_USE_NL
- USE_NL_WITH_INDEX
- USE_MERGE and NO_USE_MERGE
- USE_HASH and NO_USE_HASH
- NO_USE_HASH

Use of the USE_NL and USE_MERGE hints is recommended with any join order hint. Oracle Database uses these hints when the referenced table is forced to be the inner table of a join; the hints are ignored if the referenced table is the outer table.

Hints for Online Application Upgrade

The **online application upgrade hints** suggest how to handle conflicting INSERT and UPDATE operations when performing an online application upgrade using edition-based redefinition:

- CHANGE_DUPKEY_ERROR_INDEX
- IGNORE_ROW_ON_DUPKEY_INDEX
- RETRY_ON_ROW_CHANGE

You can use the CHANGE_DUPKEY_ERROR_INDEX and IGNORE_ROW_ON_DUPKEY_INDEX hints to handle conflicting INSERT operations during an online application upgrade. You can use the CHANGE_DUPKEY_ERROR_INDEX hint to identify unique key violations for a specified set of columns or index. When a unique key violation is encountered during an INSERT or UPDATE operation, an ORA-38911 error is reported instead of an ORA-001. You can use the IGNORE_ROW_ON_DUPKEY_INDEX hint to ignore unique key violations for a specified set of columns or index. When a unique key violation is encountered during a single-table INSERT operation, a row-level rollback occurs and execution resumes with the next input row. Therefore, a unique key violation does not cause the INSERT to terminate or an error to be reported.

You can use the RETRY_ON_ROW_CHANGE hint to handle conflicting UPDATE operations during an online application upgrade. You can use this hint to retry an UPDATE or DELETE operation if one or more rows changed from the time when the set of rows to be modified was determined to the time when the set of rows was actually modified.

Hints for Parallel Execution

The **parallel execution hints** instruct the optimizer about whether and how to parallelize operations. You can use the following parallel hints:

- PARALLEL and NO_PARALLEL
- PARALLEL_INDEX and NO_PARALLEL_INDEX
- PQ_DISTRIBUTE

The following sections group the hints into functional categories.

Hints Controlling the Degree of Parallelism: Hints beginning with the keyword PARALLEL indicate the degree of parallelism for the query. Hints beginning with NO_PARALLEL disable parallelism.

> You can perform conventional inserts in parallel mode using the `/*+ NOAPPEND PARALLEL */` hint.

You can specify parallelism at the statement or object level. If you do not explicitly specify an object in the hint, then parallelism occurs at the statement level. In contrast to most hints, parallel statement-level hints take precedence over object-level hints.

To illustrate the difference between object-level and statement-level parallelism settings, suppose that you perform the following steps:

1. You set the parallelism setting on the `employees` table to `2` and disable parallelism on the `departments` table as follows:

```
ALTER TABLE employees PARALLEL 2;
ALTER TABLE departments NOPARALLEL;
```

2. You execute the following `SELECT` statement:

```
SELECT /*+ PARALLEL(employees 3) */ e.last_name, d.department_name
FROM employees e, departments d
WHERE e.department_id=d.department_id;
```

The `PARALLEL` hint for `employees` overrides the degree of parallelism of `2` for this table specified in Step 1.

In the explain plan in, the `IN-OUT` column shows `PCWP` for parallel access of `employees` and `S` for serial access of `departments`. Access to `departments` is serialized because a `NOPARALLEL` setting was applied to this table in Step 1.

Example 19.1: Explain Plan for uer with PA ALLEL emplo ees Hint

```
---------------------------------------------------------------------
| Id   | Operation       | Name    | Rows    | Bytes                  |
| Cost   (%CPU) | Time |  TQ     | IN-OUT  | PQ Distrib             |
---------------------------------------------------------------------
|  0   |     SELECT STATEMENT  |         |    14         |       588 |
|          5   (20)| 00:00:01    |     |     |        |              |
|  1   |   PX COORDINATOR      |   |   |                             |
|      |   |   |   |   |                                             |
|  2   |   PX SEND QC (RANDOM)   |  :TQ10001    |  14 |  588          |
|          5 (20)|   00:00:01   |  Q1,01   |  P->S    |  QC (RAND) |  |
|* 3   |   HASH JOIN  |    |  14   |  588                            |
|          5   (20)|  00:00:01   |  Q1,01   |  PCWP    |  |          |
|  4   |   BUFFER SORT    |   |   |                                 |
|      |   |  Q1,01   |  PCWC   |    |                              |
|  5   |   PX RECEIVE |    |  4   |  88                              |
|          2  (0)   |  00:00:01   |  Q1,01   |  PCWP    |  |         |
|  6   |   PX SEND BROADCAST |  :TQ10000    |  4  |  88              |
|      2   (0) |   00:00:01    |    |  S->P    |  BROADCAST|         |
|  7   |   TABLE ACCESS FULL|  DEPARTMENTS  |  4  |  88              |
|      2   (0)|  00:00:01  |    |    |   |                          |
|  8   |   PX BLOCK ITERATOR |   |  14  |  280                       |
|          2  (0)| 00:00:01  |  Q1,01  |  PCWC   |   |              |
|  9   |   TABLE ACCESS FULL|  EMPLOYEES  |  14  |  280             |
|      2   (0)|  00:00:01  |  Q1,01  |  PCWP  |  |                  |
---------------------------------------------------------------------
```

You execute the following **SELECT** statement:

```
SELECT /*+ PARALLEL(4) */ hr_emp.last_name, d.department_name
FROM    employees hr_emp, departments d
WHERE   hr_emp.department_id=d.department_id;
```

Because no schema object is specified in the **PARALLEL** hint, the scope of the hint is the statement, not an object. This statement forces the query of the `employees` and `departments` tables to execute with a degree of parallelism of 4, overriding the parallelism setting defined on the tables.

Hints Controlling the Distribution Method for Joins: The **PQ_DISTRIBUTE** hint controls the distribution method for a specified join operation. The basic syntax is as follows, where ***distribution*** is the distribution method to use between the producer and the consumer slaves for the left and the right side of the join:

```
/*+ PQ_DISTRIBUTE(tablespec, distribution) */
```

For example, in a **HASH,HASH** distribution the rows of each table are mapped to consumer query servers, using a hash function on the join keys. When mapping is complete, each query server performs the join between a pair of resulting partitions. This distribution is recommended when the tables are comparable in size and the join operation is implemented by hash join or sort merge join. The following query contains a hint to use hash distribution:

```
SELECT /*+ORDERED PQ_DISTRIBUTE(departments HASH, HASH) USE_HASH
(departments)*/
   e.employee_id, d.department_name
FROM    employees e, departments d
WHERE   e.department_id=d.department_id;
```

Hints Controlling the Distribution Method for Loads: The **PQ_DISTRIBUTE** hint applies to parallel **INSERT ... SELECT** and parallel **CREATE TABLE AS SELECT** statements to specify how rows should be distributed between the producer (query) and the consumer (load) slaves.

For example, a **PARTITION** distribution use the partitioning information of the table being loaded to distribute rows from the query slaves to the load slaves. Use this method when the following conditions are met:

- It is not possible or desirable to combine the query and load operations into each slave.
- The number of partitions being loaded is greater than or equal to the number of load slaves.
- The input data is evenly distributed across the partitions being loaded.

The following sample statement creates a table and specifies the **PARTITION** distribution method:

```
CREATE /*+ PQ_DISTRIBUTE(lineitem, PARTITION) */ TABLE lineitem
   NOLOGGING PARALLEL 16
   PARTITION BY HASH (l_orderkey) PARTITIONS 512
   AS SELECT * FROM lineitemxt;
```

In contrast, a **NONE** distribution combines the query and load operation into each slave. Thus, all slaves load all partitions. Use this distribution to avoid the overhead of distribution of rows when there is no skew. The following sample SQL statement specifies a distribution of **NONE** for an insert into the `lineitem` table:

```
INSERT /*+ APPEND PARALLEL(LINEITEM, 16) PQ_DISTRIBUTE(LINEITEM, NONE)
*/
   INTO lineitem
   (SELECT * FROM lineitemxt);
```

Hints for Query Transformations

Each of the following hints instructs the optimizer to use a specific SQL query transformation:

- NO_QUERY_TRANSFORMATION
- USE_CONCAT
- NO_EXPAND
- REWRITE and NO_REWRITE
- MERGE and NO_MERGE
- STAR_TRANSFORMATION and NO_STAR_TRANSFORMATION
- FACT and NO_FACT
- UNNEST and NO_UNNEST

Additional Hints

The following are several additional hints:

- APPEND, APPEND_VALUES, and NOAPPEND
- CACHE and NOCACHE
- PUSH_PRED and NO_PUSH_PRED
- PUSH_SUBQ and NO_PUSH_SUBQ
- QB_NAME
- CURSOR_SHARING_EXACT
- DRIVING_SITE
- DYNAMIC_SAMPLING
- MODEL_MIN_ANALYSIS

SPECIFYING HINTS

Hints apply only to the optimization of the block of a statement in which they appear. A statement block is any one of the following statements or parts of statements:

- A simple SELECT, UPDATE, or DELETE statement
- A parent statement or subquery of a complex statement
- A part of a compound query.

For example, a compound query consisting of two component queries combined by the UNION operator has two blocks, one for each component query. For this reason, hints in the first component query apply only to its optimization, not to the optimization of the second component query.

The following sections discuss the use of hints in more detail.

Specifying a Full Set of Hints

When using hints, in some cases, you might need to specify a full set of hints to ensure the optimal execution plan. For example, if you have a very complex query, which consists of many table joins, and if you specify only the INDEX hint for a given table, then the optimizer must determine the remaining access paths to be used, and the corresponding join methods. Therefore, even though you gave the INDEX hint, the optimizer might not necessarily use that hint, because the optimizer might have determined that the requested index cannot be used due to the join methods and access paths selected by the optimizer.

In, the LEADING hint specifies the exact join order. The join methods are also specified.

Example 19.2: Specifying a Full Set of Hints

```
SELECT /*+ LEADING(e2 e1) USE_NL(e1) INDEX(e1 emp_emp_id_pk)
USE_MERGE(j)   FULL(j)   */  e1.first_name,   e1.last_name,   j.job_id,
sum(e2.salary) total_sal FROM employees e1, employees e2, job_history j
WHERE e1.employee_id = e2.manager_id
   AND e1.employee_id = j.employee_id
   AND e1.hire_date = j.start_date
   GROUP BY e1.first_name, e1.last_name, j.job_id
   ORDER BY total_sal;
```

Specifying a Query Block in a Hint

To identify a query block in a query, you can use an optional query block name in a hint to specify the block to which the hint applies. The syntax of the query block argument is of the form `@queryblock`, where `queryblock` is an identifier that specifies a block in the query. The `queryblock` identifier can either be system-generated or user-specified.

Note the following guidelines:

- You can obtain the system-generated identifier by using `EXPLAIN PLAN` for the query. You can determine pre-transformation query block names by running `EXPLAIN PLAN` for the query using the `NO_QUERY_TRANSFORMATION` hint.
- You can set the user-specified name with the `QB_NAME` hint.

Assumptions

This tutorial assumes the following:

- You intend to create a join view of `employees` and `job_history` that contains a nested query block.
- You want to query all rows in the view, but apply the `NO_UNNEST` hint to the query block only.

To apply the NO_UNNEST hint to the query block:

1. Start SQL*Plus and log in as user `hr`.
2. Create the view.

For example, run the following statement:

```
CREATE OR REPLACE VIEW v_emp_job_history AS
   SELECT e1.first_name, e1.last_name, j.job_id,
sum(e2.salary) total_sal
   FROM employees e1, (SELECT * FROM employees e3) e2, job_history j
        WHERE        e1.employee_id = e2.manager_id
        AND          e1.employee_id = j.employee_id
        AND          e1.hire_date = j.start_date
        AND          e1.salary = (SELECT max(e2.salary)
                                  FROM employees e2
   WHERE e2.department_id = e1.department_id)
   GROUP BY e1.first_name, e1.last_name, j.job_id
   ORDER BY total_sal;
```

3. Explain the plan for a query of `v_emp_job_history`.

   For example, run the following SQL statement:

```
   EXPLAIN PLAN FOR SELECT * FROM v_emp_job_history;
```

4. Query the plan table.
   For example, run the following SQL statement:
   ```
   SELECT PLAN_TABLE_OUTPUT
   FROM TABLE(DBMS_XPLAN.DISPLAY(NULL, NULL, 'ALL'));
   ```
   The database displays the plan.
5. In the query plan output, obtain the operation ID associated with the query block, and then use the ID to find the query block name.
   For example, the following plan shows that the full scan of the `employees` table occurs in operation `11`, which corresponds to query block `@SEL$4`:

```
----------------------------------------------------------------------
|Id| Operation              |Name
|Rows|Bytes|Cost |Time
----------------------------------------------------------------------
|0 | SELECT STATEMENT       |      |1     |46
|9(34)|00:00:01|
.
.
.
|11|     TABLE ACCESS FULL | EMPLOYEES |107
|749 |3(0) |00:00:01|
.
.
.
----------------------------------------------------------------------
Query Block Name / Object Alias (identified by operation id):
----------------------------------------------------------------------
   1     - SEL$2980E977 / V_EMP_JOB_HISTORY@SEL$1
   2     - SEL$2980E977
   8     - SEL$8F9407EC / VW_SQ_1@SEL$32F848CB
   9     - SEL$8F9407EC
   11    - SEL$8F9407EC / E2@SEL$4
```

6. Query the view using the `NO_UNNEST` hint.
   For example, run the following SQL statement to apply the `NO_UNNEST` hint to query block `@SEL$4` (sample output included):

```
SQL> SELECT /*+ NO_UNNEST( @SEL$4 ) */ * FROM
v_emp_job_history;
FIRST_NAME                 LAST_NAME          JOB_ID
TOTAL_SAL
----------------    --------------------    --------------    -
Michael                    Hartstein          MK_REP
6000
```

Specifying Global Table Hints

Hints that specify a table generally refer to tables in the `DELETE`, `SELECT`, or `UPDATE` query block in which the hint occurs, not to tables inside any views referenced by the statement. When you want to specify hints for tables that appear inside views, Oracle recommends using global hints instead of embedding the hint in the view. You can transform the table hints described in this chapter into a global hint by using an extended `tablespec` syntax that includes view names with the table name.

In addition, an optional query block name can precede the `tablespec` syntax. Hints that specify a table use the following syntax, where `view` specifies a view name and `table` specifies the name or alias of the table:

tablespec::=

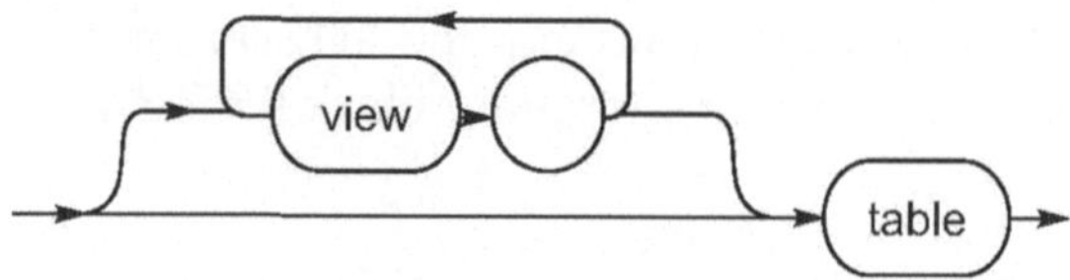

If the view path is specified, then the database resolves the hint from left to right, where the first view must be present in the `FROM` clause, and each subsequent view must be specified in the `FROM` clause of the preceding view.

Creates a view `v` to return the first and last name of the employee, his or her first job, and the total salary of all direct reports of that employee for each employee with the highest salary in his or her department. When querying the data, you want to force the use of the index `emp_job_ix` for the table `e3` in view `e2`.

Example 19.3: Using Global Hints Example

```
CREATE OR REPLACE VIEW v AS
SELECT e1.first_name, e1.last_name, j.job_id, sum(e2.salary) total_sal
FROM employees e1, ( SELECT * FROM employees e3) e2, job_history j WHERE
e1.employee_id = e2.manager_id
    AND e1.employee_id = j.employee_id
    AND e1.hire_date = j.start_date AND e1.salary = ( SELECT
    max(e2.salary) FROM employees e2 WHERE e2.department_id =
    e1.department_id ) GROUP BY e1.first_name, e1.last_name,
    j.job_id ORDER BY total_sal;
```

By using the global hint structure, you can avoid the modification of view v with the specification of the index hint in the body of view `e2`. To force the use of the index emp_job_ix for the table e3, you can use one of the following statements:

```
SELECT /*+ INDEX(v.e2.e3 emp_job_ix) */ * FROM v;
SELECT /*+ INDEX(@SEL$2 e2.e3 emp_job_ix) */ * FROM v;
SELECT /*+ INDEX(@SEL$3 e3 emp_job_ix) */ * FROM v;
```

Oracle Database ignores global hints that refer to multiple query blocks. For example, the `LEADING` hint is ignored in the following query because it uses the dot notation to the main query block containing table `a` and view query block `v`:

```
SELECT /*+ LEADING(v.b a v.c) */ *
FROM a, v
WHERE a.id = v.id;
```

To avoid this issue, Oracle recommends that you specify a query block in the hint using the `@SEL` notation:

```
SELECT /*+ LEADING(A@SEL$1 B@SEL$2 C@SEL$2)*/
FROM a a, v v
WHERE a.id = v.id;
```

Example 19.4: Using Global Hints with NO_MERGE

The global hint syntax also applies to unmergeable views as in.

```
CREATE OR REPLACE VIEW v1 AS
   SELECT *
   FROM employees
   WHERE employee_id < 150;
CREATE OR REPLACE VIEW v2 AS
   SELECT   v1.employee_id   employee_id,   departments.department_id
department_id
   FROM v1, departments
   WHERE v1.department_id = departments.department_id;
SELECT /*+ NO_MERGE(v2) INDEX(v2.v1.employees emp_emp_id_pk)
   FULL(v2.departments) */ * FROM v2
   WHERE department_id = 30;
```

The hints cause `v2` not to be merged and specify access path hints for the employee and department tables. These hints are pushed down into the (nonmerged) view `v2`.

Specifying Complex Index Hints

Hints that specify an index can use either a simple index name or a parenthesized list of columns as follows:

indexspec::=

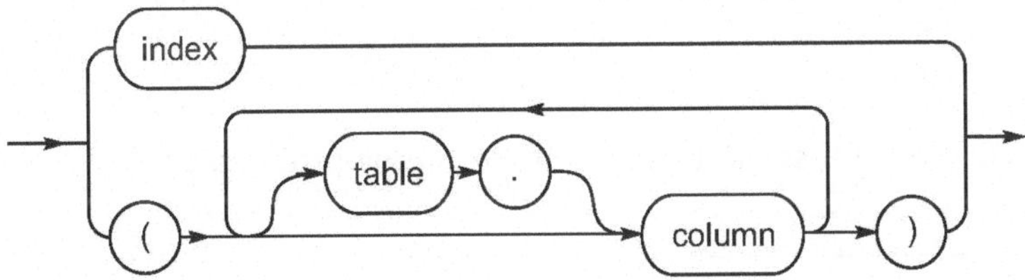

The semantics are as follows:

- `table` specifies the name.
- `column` specifies the name of a column in the specified table.
  - o The columns can optionally be prefixed with table qualifiers allowing the hint to specify bitmap join indexes where the index columns are on a different table than the indexed table. If tables qualifiers are present, then they must be base tables, not aliases in the query.
  - o Each column in an index specification must be a base column in the specified table, not an expression. Function-based indexes cannot be hinted using a column specification unless the columns specified in the index specification form the prefix of a function-based index.

- `index` specifies an index name.
  When `tablespec` is followed by `indexspec` in the specification of a hint, a comma separating the table name and index name is permitted but not required. Commas are also permitted, but not required, to separate multiple occurrences of `indexspec`.

The hint is resolved as follows:

- If an index name is specified, then the database only considered the specified index.
- If a column list is specified, and if an index exists whose columns match the specified columns in number and order, then the database only consider this index. If no such index exists, then any index on the table with the specified columns as the prefix in the order specified is considered. In either case, the behavior is exactly as if the user had specified the same hint individually on all the matching indexes.

For example, in the `job_history` table has a single-column index on the `employee_id` column and a concatenated index on `employee_id` and `start_date` columns. To specifically instruct the optimizer on index use, you can hint the query as follows:

```
SELECT /*+ INDEX(v.j jhist_employee_ix (employee_id start_date)) */ *
FROM v;
```

USING HINTS WITH VIEWS

Oracle does not encourage hints inside or on views (or subqueries) because you can define views in one context and use them in another. Also, such hints can result in unexpected execution plans. In particular, hints inside views or on views are handled differently, depending on whether the view is mergeable into the top-level query.

To specify a hint for a table in a view or subquery, the global hint syntax is preferable.

If you decide to use hints with views, then the following sections describe the behavior.

Hints and Complex Views

By default, hints do not propagate inside a complex view. For example, if you specify a hint in a query that selects against a complex view, then this hint is not honored, because it is not pushed inside the view.

If the view is on a single table, then the hint is propagated.

Unless the hints are inside the base view, they might not be honored from a query against the view.

Hints and Mergeable Views

A **mergeable view** is a view that Oracle Database can replace with the query that defines the view. For example, suppose you create a view as follows:

```
CREATE OR REPLACE VIEW emp_view AS
   SELECT last_name, department_name FROM employees e, departments d
   WHERE e.department_id=d.department_id;
```

This view is mergeable because the database can optimize the following query to use the `SELECT` statement that defines the view, avoiding use of the view itself.

```
SELECT * FROM emp_view;
```

Optimization Approaches and Goal Hints in Views

Optimization approach and goal hints can occur in a top-level query or inside views.

- If such a hint exists in the top-level query, then the database uses this hint regardless of any such hints inside the views.
- If there is no top-level optimizer mode hint, then the database uses mode hints in referenced views as long as all mode hints in the views are consistent.
- If two or more mode hints in the referenced views conflict, then the database discards all mode hints in the views and uses the session mode, whether default or user- specified.

Access Path and Join Hints on Views

Access path and join hints on referenced views are ignored unless the view contains a single table or references an Additional Hints view with a single table. For such single-table views, an access path hint or a join hint on the view applies to the table inside the view.

Access Path and Join Hints Inside Views

Access path and join hints can appear in a view definition.

- If the view is an inline view (that is, if it appears in the `FROM` clause of a `SELECT` statement), then all access path and join hints inside the view are preserved when the view is merged with the top-level query.
- For views that are non-inline views, access path and join hints in the view are preserved only if the referencing query references no other tables or views (that is, if the `FROM` clause of the `SELECT` statement contains only the view).

Hints and Nonmergeable Views

With nonmergeable views, optimization approach and goal hints inside the view are ignored; the top-level query decides the optimization mode.

Because nonmergeable views are optimized separately from the top-level query, access path and join hints inside the view are preserved. For the same reason, access path hints on the view in the top-level query are ignored.

However, join hints on the view in the top-level query are preserved because, in this case, a nonmergeable view is similar to a table.

20 Using Plan Stability

Learning Objectives

This chapter describes how to use plan stability to preserve performance characteristics. Plan stability also facilitates migration from the rule-based optimizer to the query optimizer when you upgrade to a new Oracle Database release.

This chapter contains the following topics:

- Using Plan Stability to Preserve Execution Plans
- Using Plan Stability with Query Optimizer Upgrades

Stored outlines will be desupported in a future release in favor of SQL plan management. In Oracle Database 11*g* Release 1 (11.1), stored outlines continue to function as in past releases. However, Oracle strongly recommends that you use SQL plan management for new applications. SQL plan management creates SQL plan baselines, which offer superior SQL performance and stability compared with stored outlines.

USING PLAN STABILITY TO PRESERVE EXECUTION PLANS

Plan stability prevents certain database environment changes from affecting the performance characteristics of applications. Such changes include changes in optimizer statistics, changes to the optimizer mode settings, and changes to parameters affecting the sizes of memory structures, such as `SORT_AREA_SIZE` and `BITMAP_MERGE_AREA_SIZE`. Plan stability is most useful when you cannot risk any performance changes in an application.

Plan stability preserves execution plans in stored outlines. An outline is implemented as a set of optimizer hints that are associated with the SQL statement. If the use of the outline is enabled for the statement, then Oracle Database automatically considers the stored hints and tries to generate an execution plan in accordance with those hints.

Oracle Database can create a public or private stored outline for one or all SQL statements. The optimizer then generates equivalent execution plans from the outlines when you enable the use of stored outlines. You can group outlines into categories and control which category of outlines Oracle Database uses to simplify outline administration and deployment.

The plans that Oracle Database maintains in stored outlines remain consistent despite changes to a system's configuration or statistics. Using stored outlines also stabilizes the generated execution plan if the optimizer changes in subsequent Oracle Database releases.

If you develop applications for mass distribution, then you can use stored outlines to ensure that all customers access the same execution plans.

Using Hints with Plan Stability

The degree to which plan stability controls execution plans is dictated by how much the Oracle Database hint mechanism controls execution plans, because Oracle Database uses hints to record stored plans.

There is a one-to-one correspondence between SQL text and its stored outline. If you specify a different literal in a predicate, then a different outline applies. To avoid this situation, replace literals in applications with bind variables.

Oracle Database can allow similar statements to share SQL by replacing literals with system-generated bind variables. This works with plan stability if the outline was generated using the `CREATE_STORED_OUTLINES` parameter, not the `CREATE OUTLINE` statement. Also, the outline must have been created with the `CURSOR_SHARING` parameter set to `FORCE` or `SIMILAR`, and the parameter must also set to `FORCE` or `SIMILAR` when attempting to use the outline.

Plan stability relies on preserving execution plans at a point in time when performance is satisfactory. In many environments, however, attributes for data types such as `dates` or `order numbers` can change rapidly. In these cases, permanent use of an execution plan can result in performance degradation over time as the data characteristics change.

This implies that techniques that rely on preserving plans in dynamic environments are somewhat contrary to the purpose of using query optimization. Query optimization attempts to produce execution plans based on statistics that accurately reflect the state of the data. Thus, you must balance the need to control plan stability with the benefit obtained from the optimizer's ability to adjust to changes in data characteristics.

How Outlines Use Hints

An outline consists primarily of a set of hints that is equivalent to the optimizer's results for the execution plan generation of a particular SQL statement. When Oracle Database creates an outline, plan stability examines the optimization results using the same data used to generate the execution plan. That is, Oracle Database uses the input to the execution plan to generate an outline, and not the execution plan itself.

Oracle Database creates the `USER_OUTLINES` and `USER_OUTLINE_HINTS` views in the `SYS` tablespace based on data in the `OL$` and `OL$HINTS` tables, respectively. Direct manipulation of the `OL$`, `OL$HINTS`, and `OL$NODES` tables is prohibited.

You can embed hints in SQL statements, but this has no effect on how Oracle Database uses outlines. Oracle Database considers a SQL statement that you revised with hints to be different from the original SQL statement stored in the outline.

Storing Outlines

Oracle Database stores outline data in the OL$, OL$HINTS, and OL$NODES tables. Unless you remove them, Oracle Database retains outlines indefinitely.

The only effect outlines have on caching execution plans is that the database uses the outline category name in addition to the SQL text to determine whether the plan is in cache. This ensures that Oracle Database does not use an execution plan compiled under one category to execute a SQL statement that the database should compile under a different category.

Enabling Plan Stability

Settings for several parameters, especially those ending with the suffix _ENABLED, must be consistent across execution environments for outlines to function properly. These parameters are:

- QUERY_REWRITE_ENABLED
- STAR_TRANSFORMATION_ENABLED
- OPTIMIZER_FEATURES_ENABLE

Using Supplied Packages to Manage Stored Outlines

The DBMS_OUTLN and DBMS_OUTLN_EDIT package provides procedures used for managing stored outlines and their outline categories.

Users need the EXECUTE_CATALOG_ROLE role to execute DBMS_OUTLN, but public has execute privileges on DBMS_OUTLN_EDIT. The DBMS_OUTLN_EDIT package is an invoker's rights package.

Some of the useful DBMS_OUTLN and DBMS_OUTLN_EDIT procedures are:

- CLEAR_USED—Clears specified outline
- DROP_BY_CAT—Drops outlines that belong to a specified category
- UPDATE_BY_CAT—Changes the category of outlines in one specified category to a new specified category
- EXACT_TEXT_SIGNATURES—Computes an outline signature according to an exact text matching scheme
- GENERATE_SIGNATURE—Generates a signature for the specified SQL text.

Creating Outlines

Oracle Database can automatically create outlines for all SQL statements, or you can create them for specific SQL statements. In either case, the outlines derive their input from the optimizer.

Oracle Database creates stored outlines automatically when you set the initialization parameter CREATE_STORED_OUTLINES to true. When activated, Oracle Database creates outlines for all compiled SQL statements. You can create stored outlines for specific statements using the CREATE OUTLINE statement.

When creating or editing a private outline, the outline data is written to global temporary tables in the SYSTEM schema. These tables are accessible with the OL$, OL$HINTS, and OL$NODES synonyms.

You must ensure that schemas in which outlines are to be created have the CREATE ANY OUTLINE privilege. Otherwise, despite having turned on the CREATE_STORED_OUTLINE initialization parameter, no outlines appear in the database after you run the application.

Also, the default system tablespace can become exhausted if the CREATE_STORED_OUTLINES initialization parameter is enabled and the running application has many literal SQL statements. If this happens, then use the DBMS_OUTLN.DROP_UNUSED procedure to remove those literal SQL outlines.

Using Category Names for Stored Outlines

You can categorize outlines to simplify the management task. The CREATE OUTLINE statement allows for specification of a category. The DEFAULT category is chosen if unspecified. Likewise, the CREATE_STORED_OUTLINES initialization parameter lets you specify a category name, where specifying true produces outlines in the DEFAULT category.

If you specify a category name using the CREATE_STORED_OUTLINES initialization parameter, then Oracle Database assigns all subsequently created outlines to that category until you reset the category name. Set the parameter to false to suspend outline generation.

If you set CREATE_STORED_OUTLINES to true, or if you use the CREATE OUTLINE statement without a category name, then Oracle Database assigns outlines to the category name of DEFAULT.

Using Stored Outlines

When you activate the use of stored outlines, Oracle Database always uses the query optimizer. Outlines rely on hints. To be effective, most hints require the optimizer.

To use stored outlines when Oracle Database compiles a SQL statement, set the system parameter USE_STORED_OUTLINES to true or to a category name. If you set USE_STORED_OUTLINES to true, then Oracle Database uses outlines in the default category. If you specify a category with the USE_STORED_OUTLINES parameter, then Oracle Database uses outlines in that category until you reset the parameter to another category name or until you suspend outline use by setting USE_STORED_OUTLINES to false. If you specify a category name, and if Oracle Database does not find an outline in that category that matches the SQL statement, then the database searches for an outline in the default category.

To use a specific outline rather than all the outlines in a category, execute the ALTER OUTLINE statement to enable the specific outline. To use the outlines in a category except for a specific outline, use the ALTER OUTLINE statement to disable the specific outline in the category that is being used. The ALTER OUTLINE statement can also rename a stored outline, reassign it to a different category, or regenerate it.

The designated outlines only control the compilation of SQL statements that have outlines. If you set USE_STORED_OUTLINES to false, then Oracle Database does not use outlines. When you set USE_STORED_OUTLINES to false and you set CREATE_STORED_OUTLINES to true, Oracle Database creates outlines but does not use them.

The USE_PRIVATE_OUTLINES parameter lets you control the use of private outlines. A private outline is an outline seen only in the current session and whose data resides in the current parsing schema. Any changes made to such an outline are not seen by any other session on the system, and applying a private outline to the compilation of a statement can only be done in the current session with the USE_PRIVATE_OUTLINES parameter. Only when you explicitly choose to save your edits back to the public area are they seen by the rest of the users.

While the optimizer usually chooses optimal plans for queries, there are times when users know things about the execution environment that are inconsistent with the heuristics that the optimizer follows. By editing outlines directly, you can tune the SQL query without having to alter the application.

When the USE_PRIVATE_OUTLINES parameter is enabled and an outlined SQL statement is issued, the optimizer retrieves the outline from the session private area rather than the public area used when USE_STORED_OUTLINES is enabled. If no outline exists in the session private area, then the optimizer does not use an outline to compile the statement.

Any CREATE OUTLINE statement requires the CREATE ANY OUTLINE privilege. Specification of the FROM clause also requires the SELECT privilege. This privilege should be granted only to those users who would have the authority to view SQL text and hint text associated with the outlined statements. This role is required for the CREATE OUTLINE FROM command unless the issuer of the command is also the owner of the outline.

The USE_STORED_OUTLINES and USE_PRIVATE_OUTLINES parameters are system or session specific. They are not initialization parameters.

You can test whether the database is using an outline with the V$SQL view. Query the OUTLINE_CATEGORY column in conjunction with the SQL statement. If the database applied an outline, then this column contains the category to which the outline belongs. Otherwise, it is NULL. The OUTLINE_SID column tells you whether this particular cursor is using a public outline (value is 0) or a private outline (session's SID of the corresponding session using it).

For example:

```
SELECT OUTLINE_CATEGORY, OUTLINE_SID
   FROM V$SQL
   WHERE SQL_TEXT LIKE 'SELECT COUNT(*) FROM emp%';
```

Viewing Outline Data

You can access information about outlines and related hint data that Oracle Database stores in the data dictionary from the following views:

- USER_OUTLINES
- USER_OUTLINE_HINTS
- ALL_OUTLINES
- ALL_OUTLINE_HINTS
- DBA_OUTLINES
- DBA_OUTLINE_HINTS

Use the following syntax to obtain outline information from the USER_OUTLINES view, where the outline category is mycat:

```
SELECT NAME, SQL_TEXT
   FROM USER_OUTLINES
   WHERE CATEGORY='mycat';
```

Oracle Database responds by displaying the names and text of all outlines in category mycat.

To see all generated hints for the outline name1, use the following syntax:

```
SELECT HINT
   FROM USER_OUTLINE_HINTS
   WHERE NAME='name1';
```

You can check the flags in _OUTLINES views for information about compatibility, format, and whether an outline is enabled. For example, check the ENABLED field in the USER_OUTLINES view to determine whether an outline is enabled or not.

```
SELECT NAME, CATEGORY, ENABLED FROM USER_OUTLINES;
```

Moving Outline Tables

Oracle Database creates the USER_OUTLINES and USER_OUTLINE_HINTS views based on data in the OL$ and OL$HINTS tables, respectively. These tables and the OL$NODES table reside in the outln schema.

The outln schema stores data in the SYSTEM tablespace. If outlines use too much space in the SYSTEM tablespace, then you can move them. To achieve this goal, create a separate tablespace and move the outline tables into this tablespace.

The default system tablespace could become exhausted if the CREATE_STORED_OUTLINES parameter is on and if the running application has many literal SQL statements. In this case, use the DBMS_OUTLN.DROP_UNUSED procedure to remove the literal SQL outlines.

To move outline tables into a new tablespace:

1. Use the Oracle Data Pump Export utility to export the OL$, OL$HINTS, and OL$NODES tables.
   The following example exports these tables to the exp.dmp file located in the directory that maps to the outln_dir object:

```
% expdp outln DIRECTORY=outln_dir DUMPFILE=exp.dmp
TABLES=OL$,OL$HINTS,OL$NODES
Password: password
```

2. Start SQL*Plus and connect to the database as the outln user, as shown in the following example:

```
SQL> CONNECT outln
Enter password: password
```

3. Remove the previous OL$, OL$HINTS, and OL$NODES tables, as shown in the following example:

```
SQL> DROP TABLE OL$;
SQL> DROP TABLE OL$HINTS;
SQL> DROP TABLE OL$NODES;
```

4. Create a new tablespace for the tables.
   The following example connects as SYSTEM and creates a tablespace named outln_ts:

```
SQL> CONNECT SYSTEM
Enter password: password
SQL> CREATE TABLESPACE outln_ts DATAFILE 'tspace.dat' SIZE 2M
DEFAULT STORAGE ( INITIAL 10K NEXT 20K MINEXTENTS 1 MAXEXTENTS 999
PCTINCREASE 10 ) ONLINE;
```

5. Change the default tablespace for the outln schema.
   The following statement changes the default tablespace to outln_ts:

```
SQL> ALTER USER OUTLN DEFAULT TABLESPACE outln_ts;
```

6. To force the import into the outln_ts tablespace, perform the following tasks:
   (a) Set the quota for the SYSTEM tablespace to 0K for the outln user.

(b) Revoke the UNLIMITED TABLESPACE privilege and all roles, such as the RESOURCE role, that have unlimited tablespace privileges or quotas.

(c) Set a quota for the outln tablespace.

7. Use the Data Pump Import utility to import the OL$, OL$HINTS, and OL$NODES tables, as in the following example:

```
% impdp outln DIRECTORY=outln_dir DUMPFILE=exp.dmp
TABLES=OL$,OL$HINTS,OL$NODES
Password: password
```

When the import completes, the OL$, OL$HINTS, and OL$NODES tables are re-created in the schema named outln and reside in the outln_ts tablespace.

8. Optionally, adjust the tablespace quotas for the outln user appropriately by adding any privileges and roles that were removed in a previous step.

USING PLAN STABILITY WITH QUERY OPTIMIZER UPGRADES

This section describes procedures you can use to significantly improve performance by taking advantage of query optimizer functionality. Plan stability provides a way to preserve a system's targeted execution plans with satisfactory performance while also taking advantage of new query optimizer features for the rest of the SQL statements.

While there are classes of SQL statements and features where an exact reproduction of the original execution plan is not guaranteed, plan stability can still be a highly useful part of the migration. Before the migration, outline capturing of execution plan should be turned on until all or most of the applications SQL-statement have been covered.

If performance problems for some specific SQL-statement occur after migration, then you can turn on the stored outline for the specified statement as a way of restoring the old behavior. Stored outlines are not always the best way of resolving a migration related performance problem because they prevent plans from adapting to changing data properties. However, stored outlines add to the arsenal of techniques that you can use to address such problems.

Topics covered in this section are:

- Moving from RBO to the Query Optimizer
- Moving to a New Oracle Release under the Query Optimizer.

Moving from RBO to the Query Optimizer

If an application was developed using the rule-based optimizer, then a considerable amount of effort might have gone into manually tuning the SQL statements to optimize performance. You can use plan stability to leverage the effort that has gone into performance tuning by preserving the behavior of the application when upgrading from rule-based to query optimization.

By creating outlines for an application before switching to query optimization, the plans generated by the rule-based optimizer can be used, while statements generated by newly written applications developed after the switch use query plans. To create and use outlines for an application, use the following process.

Carefully read this procedure and consider its implications before executing it!

1. Ensure that schemas in which outlines are to be created have the **CREATE ANY OUTLINE** privilege. For example, from **SYS**:

```
GRANT CREATE ANY OUTLINE TO user-name
```

2. Execute syntax similar to the following to designate; for example, the **RBOCAT** outline category.

```
ALTER SESSION SET CREATE_STORED_OUTLINES = rbocat;
```

3. Run the application long enough to capture stored outlines for all important SQL statements.
4. Suspend outline generation:

```
ALTER SESSION SET CREATE_STORED_OUTLINES = FALSE;
```

5. Gather statistics with the **DBMS_STATS** package.
6. Alter the parameter **OPTIMIZER_MODE** to **CHOOSE**.
7. Enter the following syntax to make Oracle database use the outlines in category **RBOCAT**:

```
ALTER SESSION SET USE_STORED_OUTLINES = rbocat;
```

8. Run the application.
   Subject to the limitations of plan stability, access paths for this application's SQL statements should be unchanged.

If a query was not executed in step 2, then you can capture the old behavior the query even after switching to query optimization. To achieve this goal, change the optimizer mode to **RULE**, create an outline for the query, and then change the optimizer mode back to **CHOOSE**.

Moving to a New Oracle Release Under the Query Optimizer

When upgrading to a new Oracle Database release under query optimization, some SQL statements may have their execution plans changed because of changes in the optimizer. While such changes benefit performance, you might have applications that perform so well that you would consider any changes in their behavior to be an unnecessary risk. For such applications, you can create outlines before the upgrade using the following procedure.

Carefully read this procedure and consider its implications before running it!

1. Enter the following syntax to enable outline creation:

```
ALTER SESSION SET CREATE_STORED_OUTLINES =
ALL_QUERIES;
```

2. Run the application long enough to capture stored outlines for all critical SQL statements.
3. Enter this syntax to suspend outline generation:

```
ALTER SESSION SET CREATE_STORED_OUTLINES = FALSE;
```

4. Upgrade the production system to the new version of the RDBMS.
5. Run the application.

After the upgrade, you can enable the use of stored outlines, or alternatively, you can use the outlines that were stored as a backup if you find that some statements exhibit performance degradation after the upgrade.

With the latter approach, you can selectively use the stored outlines for such problematic statements as follows:

1. For each problematic SQL statement, change the `CATEGORY` of the associated stored outline to a category name similar to this:

```
ALTER OUTLINE outline_name CHANGE CATEGORY TO problemcat;
```

2. Enter this syntax to make Oracle database use outlines from the category `problemcat`.

```
ALTER SESSION SET USE_STORED_OUTLINES = problemcat;
```

Upgrading with a Test System

A test database, separate from the production database, is useful for conducting experiments with optimizer behavior after an upgrade. You can migrate statistics from the production system to the test system using import/export. This technique alleviates the need to fill the tables in the test database with data.

You can move outlines between the systems by category. For example, after you create outlines in the `problemcat` category, export them by category using the query-based export option. This is a convenient and efficient way to export only selected outlines from one database to another without exporting all outlines in the source database. Use the Data Pump Export utility with the `QUERY` parameter as in the following example (note the use of the line continuation character):

```
expdp outln DIRECTORY=outln_dir DUMPFILE=exp_file.dmp
TABLES=OL$,OL$HINTS,OL$NODES QUERY='WHERE
CATEGORY="problemcat"'
Password: password.
```

21 Using Application Tracing Tools

Learning Objectives

Oracle Database provides several tracing tools that can help you monitor and analyze applications running against an Oracle database.

End to End Application Tracing can identify the source of an excessive workload, such as a high load SQL statement, by client identifier, service, module, action, session, instance, or an entire database. This isolates the problem to a specific user, service, session, or application component.

Oracle Database provides the trcsess command-line utility that consolidates tracing information based on specific criteria.

The SQL Trace facility and TKPROF are two basic performance diagnostic tools that can help you monitor applications running against the Oracle database.

This chapter contains the following sections:

- End-to-End Application Tracing
- Using the Trcsess Utility
- Understanding SQL Trace and TKPROF
- Using the SQL Trace Facility and TKPROF
- Avoiding Pitfalls in TKPROF Interpretation
- Sample TKPROF Output

END-TO-END APPLICATION TRACING

End to End Application Tracing simplifies the process of diagnosing performance problems in multitier environments. In these environments, a request from an end client is routed to different database sessions by the middle tier, making it difficult to track a client across database sessions. End to End Application Tracing uses a client ID to uniquely trace a specific end-client through all tiers to the database.

This feature could identify the source of an excessive workload, such as a high load SQL statement, and allow you to contact the specific user responsible. Also, a user having problems can contact you. You can then identify what this user's session is doing at the database level.

End-to-End Application Tracing also simplifies management of application workloads by tracking specific modules and actions in a service.

End-to-End Application Tracing can identify workload problems for:

- Client identifier-specifies an end user based on the logon ID, such as `HR.HR`.
- Service-specifies a group of applications with common attributes, service level thresholds, and priorities; or a single application, such as `ACCTG` for an accounting application.
- Module-specifies a functional block, such as Accounts Receivable or General Ledger, of an application.
- Action-specifies an action, such as an INSERT or UPDATE operation, in a module.
- Session-specifies a session based on a given database session identifier (SID), on the local instance.
- Instance-specifies a given instance based on the instance name.

After tracing information is written to files, you can consolidate this information with the `trcsess` utility and diagnose it with an analysis utility such as `TKPROF`.

To to create services on single instance Oracle databases, you can use the `CREATE_SERVICE` procedure in the `DBMS_SERVICE` package or set the `SERVICE_NAMES` initialization parameter.

The module and action names are set by the application developer. For example, you would use the `SET_MODULE` and `SET_ACTION` procedures in the `DBMS_APPICATION_INFO` package to set these values in a PL/SQL program.

The recommended interface for End-to-End Application Tracing is Oracle Enterprise Manager. Using Enterprise Manager, you can view the top consumers for each consumer type, and enable or disable statistics gathering and SQL tracing for specific consumers. Whenever possible, you should use Enterprise Manager to manage End to End Application Tracing. If Oracle Enterprise Manager is unavailable, then you can manage this feature using the `DBMS_MONITOR` APIs, as described in the following sections:

- Enabling and Disabling Statistic Gathering for End-to-End Tracing
- Viewing Gathered Statistics for End-to-End Application Tracing
- Enabling and Disabling for End-to-End Tracing
- Viewing Enabled Traces for End-to-End Tracing.

Enabling and Disabling Statistic Gathering for End-to-End Tracing

To gather the appropriate statistics using PL/SQL, you need to enable statistics gathering for client identifier, service, module, or action using procedures in the `DBMS_MONITOR` package.

You can gather statistics by the following criteria:

- Statistic Gathering for Client Identifier
- Statistic Gathering for Service, Module, and Action

The default level is the session-level statistics gathering. Statistics gathering is global for the database and continues after an instance is restarted.

Statistic Gathering for Client Identifier

The procedure `CLIENT_ID_STAT_ENABLE` enables statistic gathering for a given client identifier. For example, to enable statistics gathering for a specific client identifier:

```
EXECUTE DBMS_MONITOR.CLIENT_ID_STAT_ENABLE(client_id => 'OE.OE');
```

In the example, `OE.OE` is the client identifier for which you want to collect statistics. You can view client identifiers in the `CLIENT_IDENTIFIER` column in `V$SESSION`.

The procedure CLIENT_ID_STAT_DISABLE disables statistic gathering for a given client identifier. For example:

```
EXECUTE DBMS_MONITOR.CLIENT_ID_STAT_DISABLE(client_id => 'OE.OE');
```

Statistic Gathering for Service, Module, and Action

The procedure SERV_MOD_ACT_STAT_ENABLE enables statistic gathering for a combination of service, module, and action. For example:

```
EXECUTE DBMS_MONITOR.SERV_MOD_ACT_STAT_ENABLE(service_name =>
'ACCTG', module_name => 'PAYROLL');
EXECUTE DBMS_MONITOR.SERV_MOD_ACT_STAT_ENABLE(service_name =>
'ACCTG', module_name => 'GLEDGER', action_name => 'INSERT ITEM');
```

If both of the previous commands are executed, then statistics are gathered as follows:

- For the ACCTG service, because accumulation for each service name is the default
- For all actions in the PAYROLL module
- For the INSERT ITEM action within the GLEDGER module.

The procedure SERV_MOD_ACT_STAT_DISABLE disables statistic gathering for a combination of service, module, and action. For example:

```
EXECUTE DBMS_MONITOR.SERV_MOD_ACT_STAT_DISABLE(service_name
=> 'ACCTG', module_name => 'GLEDGER', action_name => 'INSERT ITEM');
```

Regarding statistics gathering, when you change the module or action using these procedures, the change takes effect when the next user call is executed in the session. For example, if a module is set to module1 in a session, and if the module is reset to module2 in a user call in the session, then the module remains module1 during this user call. The module is changed to module2 in the next user call in the session.

Viewing Gathered Statistics for End-to-End Application Tracing

You can display the statistics that have been gathered with several dynamic views.

- The accumulated global statistics for the currently enabled statistics can be displayed with the DBA_ENABLED_AGGREGATIONS view.
- The accumulated statistics for a specified client identifier can be displayed in the V$CLIENT_STATS view.
- The accumulated statistics for a specified service can be displayed in V$SERVICE_STATS view.
- The accumulated statistics for a combination of specified service, module, and action can be displayed in the V$SERV_MOD_ACT_STATS view.
- The accumulated statistics for elapsed time of database calls and for CPU use can be displayed in the V$SERVICEMETRIC view.

Enabling and Disabling for End-to-End Tracing

To enable tracing for client identifier, service, module, action, session, instance or database, execute the appropriate procedures in the DBMS_MONITOR package. You can enable tracing for specific diagnosis and workload management by the following criteria:

- Tracing for Client Identifier
- Tracing for Service, Module, and Action

- Tracing for Session
- Tracing for Entire Instance or Database.

With the criteria that you provide, specific trace information is captured in a set of trace files and combined into a single output trace file.

Tracing for Client Identifier

The CLIENT_ID_TRACE_ENABLE procedure enables tracing globally for the database for a given client identifier. For example:

```
EXECUTE DBMS_MONITOR.CLIENT_ID_TRACE_ENABLE(client_id =>
'OE.OE', waits => TRUE, binds => FALSE);
```

In this example, OE.OE is the client identifier for which SQL tracing is to be enabled. The TRUE argument specifies that wait information will be present in the trace. The FALSE argument specifies that bind information will not be present in the trace.

The CLIENT_ID_TRACE_DISABLE procedure disables tracing globally for the database for a given client identifier. To disable tracing, for the previous example:

```
EXECUTE DBMS_MONITOR.CLIENT_ID_TRACE_DISABLE(client_id => 'OE.OE');
```

Tracing for Service, Module, and Action

The SERV_MOD_ACT_TRACE_ENABLE procedure enables SQL tracing for a given combination of service name, module, and action globally for a database, unless an instance name is specified in the procedure.

```
EXECUTE DBMS_MONITOR.SERV_MOD_ACT_TRACE_ENABLE(service_name => 'ACCTG' ,waits
=> TRUE, binds => FALSE, instance_name => 'inst1');
```

In this example, the service ACCTG is specified. The module or action name is not specified. The TRUE argument specifies that wait information will be present in the trace. The FALSE argument specifies that bind information will not be present in the trace. The inst1 instance is specified to enable tracing only for that instance.

To enable tracing for all actions for a given combination of service and module:

```
EXECUTE DBMS_MONITOR.SERV_MOD_ACT_TRACE_ENABLE(service_name =>
'ACCTG',module_name => 'PAYROLL', waits => TRUE, binds =>
FALSE,instance_name => 'inst1');
```

The SERV_MOD_ACT_TRACE_DISABLE procedure disables the trace at all enabled instances for a given combination of service name, module, and action name globally. For example, the following disables tracing for the first example in this section:

```
EXECUTE DBMS_MONITOR.SERV_MOD_ACT_TRACE_DISABLE(service_name =>
'ACCTG',instance_name => 'inst1');
```

This example disables tracing for the second example in this section:

```
EXECUTE DBMS_MONITOR.SERV_MOD_ACT_TRACE_DISABLE(service_name =>
'ACCTG', module_name => 'PAYROLL', instance_name => 'inst1');
```

Tracing for Session

The SESSION_TRACE_ENABLE procedure enables the trace for a given database session identifier (SID), on the local instance.

To enable tracing for a specific session ID and serial number, determine the values for the session to trace:

```
SELECT  SID,          SERIAL#,      USERNAME FROM V$SESSION;
        SID           SERIAL#       USERNAME
----------            ----------    ------------------------------
        27            60            OE
```

Use the appropriate values to enable tracing for a specific session:

```
EXECUTE DBMS_MONITOR.SESSION_TRACE_ENABLE(session_id => 27, serial_num
=> 60,waits => TRUE, binds => FALSE);
```

The TRUE argument specifies that wait information will be present in the trace. The FALSE argument specifies that bind information will not be present in the trace.

The SESSION_TRACE_DISABLE procedure disables the trace for a given database session identifier (SID) and serial number. For example:

```
EXECUTE DBMS_MONITOR.SESSION_TRACE_DISABLE(session_id => 27,
serial_num => 60);
```

While the DBMS_MONITOR package can only be invoked by a user with the DBA role, any user can also enable SQL tracing for their own session by using the DBMS_SESSION package. A user can invoke the SESSION_TRACE_ENABLE procedure to enable session-level SQL trace for the user's session. For example:

```
EXECUTE DBMS_SESSION.SESSION_TRACE_ENABLE(waits => TRUE, binds =>
FALSE);
```

The TRUE argument specifies that wait information will be present in the trace. The FALSE argument specifies that bind information will not be present in the trace.

The SESSION_TRACE_DISABLE procedure disables the trace for the invoking session. For example:

```
EXECUTE DBMS_SESSION.SESSION_TRACE_DISABLE();
```

Tracing for Entire Instance or Database

The DATABASE_TRACE_ENABLE procedure enables SQL tracing for a given instance or an entire database. Tracing is enabled for all current and future sessions. For example:

```
EXECUTE DBMS_MONITOR.DATABASE_TRACE_ENABLE(waits => TRUE, binds =>
FALSE, instance_name => 'inst1');
```

In this example, the inst1 instance is specified to enable tracing for that instance. The TRUE argument specifies that wait information will be present in the trace. The FALSE argument specifies that bind information will not be present in the trace. This example results in SQL tracing of all SQL in the inst1 instance.

The DATABASE_TRACE_ENABLE procedure overrides all other session-level traces, but will be complementary to the client identifier, service, module, and action traces. All new sessions will inherit the wait and bind information specified by this procedure until the DATABASE_TRACE_DISABLE procedure is called. When this procedure is invoked with the instance_name parameter specified, it will reset the session-level SQL trace for the named instance. If this procedure is invoked without the instance_name parameter specified, then it will reset the session-level SQL trace for the entire database.

The DATABASE_TRACE_DISABLE procedure disables the tracing for an entire instance or database. For example:

```
EXECUTE DBMS_MONITOR.DATABASE_TRACE_DISABLE(instance_name => 'inst1');
```

In this example, all session-level SQL tracing will be disabled for the inst1 instance. To disable the session-level SQL tracing for an entire database, invoke the DATABASE_TRACE_DISABLE procedure without specifying the instance_name parameter:

```
EXECUTE DBMS_MONITOR.DATABASE_TRACE_DISABLE();
```

Viewing Enabled Traces for End-to-End Tracing

An Oracle Enterprise Manager report or the DBA_ENABLED_TRACES view can display outstanding traces. In the DBA_ENABLED_TRACES view, you can determine detailed information about how a trace was enabled, including the trace type. The trace type specifies whether the trace is enabled for client identifier, session, service, database, or a combination of service, module, and action.

USING THE TRCSESS UTILITY

The trcsess utility consolidates trace output from selected trace files based on several criteria:

- Session ID
- Client ID
- Service name
- Action name
- Module name.

After trcsess merges the trace information into a single output file, the output file could be processed by TKPROF.

trcsess is useful for consolidating the tracing of a particular session for performance or debugging purposes. Tracing a specific session is usually not a problem in the dedicated server model as a single dedicated process serves a session during its lifetime. You can see the trace information for the session from the trace file belonging to the dedicated server serving it. However, in a shared server configuration a user session is serviced by different processes from time to time. The trace pertaining to the user session is scattered across different trace files belonging to different processes. This makes it difficult to get a complete picture of the life cycle of a session.

Syntax for Trcsess

The syntax for the trcsess utility is:

```
trcsess [output= output_file_name]
        [session=session_id]
        [clientid=client_id]
        [service=service_name]
```

```
        [action=action_name]
        [module=module_name]
        [trace_files]
```

where,

- `output` specifies the file where the output is generated. If this option is not specified, then the utility writes to standard output.
- `session` consolidates the trace information for the session specified. The session identifier is a combination of session index and session serial number, such as `21.2371`. You can locate these values in the `V$SESSION` view.
- `clientid` consolidates the trace information given client ID.
- `service` consolidates the trace information for the given service name.
- `action` consolidates the trace information for the given action name.
- `module` consolidates the trace information for the given module name.
- *`trace_files`* is a list of all the trace file names, separated by spaces, in which `trcsess` should look for trace information. You can use the wildcard character (*) to specify the trace file names. If you do not specify trace files, then `trcsess` takes all the files in the current directory as input.

You must specify one of the `session`, `clientid`, `service`, `action`, or `module` options. If more then one of the `session`, `clientid`, `service`, `action`, or `module` options is specified, then the trace files which satisfies all the criteria specified are consolidated into the output file.

Sample Output of Trcsess

This sample output of `trcsess` shows the consolidation of traces for a particular session. In this example the session index and serial number equals `21.2371`.

You can invoke `trcsess` with various options. In the following case, all files in current directory are taken as input:

```
trcsess session=21.2371
```

In this case, several trace files are specified:

```
trcsess session=21.2371 main_12359.trc main_12995.trc
```

The sample output is similar to the following:

```
[PROCESS ID = 12359]
*** 2002-04-02 09:48:28.376
PARSING IN CURSOR #1 len=17 dep=0 uid=27 oct=3 lid=27 tim=868373970961
hv=887450622 ad='22683fb4'
select * from cat
END OF STMT
PARSE
#1:c=0,e=339,p=0,cr=0,cu=0,mis=0,r=0,dep=0,og=4,tim=868373970944
EXEC #1:c=0,e=221,p=0,cr=0,cu=0,mis=0,r=0,dep=0,og=4,tim=868373971411
FTCH
#1:c=0,e=791,p=0,cr=7,cu=0,mis=0,r=1,dep=0,og=4,tim=868373972435
FETCH
#1:c=0,e=1486,p=0,cr=20,cu=0,mis=0,r=6,dep=0,og=4,tim=868373986238
*** 2002-04-02 10:03:58.058
```

```
XCTEND rlbk=0, rd_only=1
STAT #1 id=1 cnt=7 pid=0 pos=1 obj=0 op='FILTER'
STAT #1 id=2 cnt=7 pid=1 pos=1 obj=18 op='TABLE ACCESS BY INDEX ROWID
OBJ$'
STAT #1 id=3 cnt=7 pid=2 pos=1 obj=37 op='INDEX RANGE SCAN I_OBJ2'
STAT #1 id=4 cnt=0 pid=1 pos=2 obj=4 op='TABLE ACCESS CLUSTER TAB$J2'
STAT #1 id=5 cnt=6 pid=4 pos=1 obj=3 op='INDEX UNIQUE SCAN I_OBJ#'
[PROCESS ID=12995]
*** 2002-04-02 10:04:32.738
Archiving is disabled
Archiving is disabled
```

UNDERSTANDING SQL TRACE AND TKPROF

The SQL Trace facility and TKPROF let you accurately assess the efficiency of the SQL statements an application runs. For best results, use these tools with EXPLAIN PLAN rather than using EXPLAIN PLAN alone.

Understanding the SQL Trace Facility

The SQL Trace facility provides performance information on individual SQL statements. It generates the following statistics for each statement:

- Parse, execute, and fetch counts
- CPU and elapsed times
- Physical reads and logical reads
- Number of rows processed
- Misses on the library cache
- Username under which each parse occurred
- Each commit and rollback
- Wait event data for each SQL statement, and a summary for each trace file.

If the cursor for the SQL statement is closed, then SQL Trace also provides row source information that includes:

- Row operations showing the actual execution plan of each SQL statement
- Number of rows, number of consistent reads, number of physical reads, number of physical writes, and time elapsed for each operation on a row.

Although it is possible to enable the SQL Trace facility for a session or for an instance, it is recommended that you use the DBMS_SESSION or DBMS_MONITOR packages instead. When the SQL Trace facility is enabled for a session or for an instance, performance statistics for all SQL statements executed in a user session or in the instance are placed into trace files. Using the SQL Trace facility can have a severe performance impact and may result in increased system overhead, excessive CPU usage, and inadequate disk space.

Oracle Database provides the trcsess command-line utility that consolidates tracing information from several trace files based on specific criteria, such as session or client ID.

Understanding TKPROF

You can run the TKPROF program to format the contents of the trace file and place the output into a readable output file. TKPROF can also:

- Create a SQL script that stores the statistics in the database
- Determine the execution plans of SQL statements.

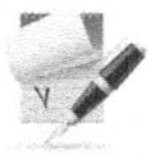

If the cursor for a SQL statement is not closed, then TKPROF output does not automatically include the actual execution plan of the SQL statement. In this situation, you can use the EXPLAIN option with TKPROF to generate an execution plan.

TKPROF reports each statement executed with the resources it has consumed, the number of times it was called, and the number of rows which it processed. This information lets you easily locate those statements that are using the greatest resource. With experience or with baselines available, you can assess whether the resources used are reasonable given the work done.

USING THE SQL TRACE FACILITY AND TKPROF

Follow these steps to use the SQL Trace facility and TKPROF:

1. Set initialization parameters for trace file management.
2. Enable the SQL Trace facility for the desired session, and run the application. This step produces a trace file containing statistics for the SQL statements issued by the application.
3. Run TKPROF to translate the trace file created in Step 2 into a readable output file. This step can optionally create a SQL script that you can use to store the statistics in a database.
4. Interpret the output file created in Step 3.
5. Optionally, run the SQL script produced in Step 3 to store the statistics in the database.

The following sections discuss each step in depth.

Step 1: Setting Initialization Parameters for Trace File Management

When the SQL Trace facility is enabled for a session, Oracle Database generates a trace file containing statistics for traced SQL statements for that session. When the SQL Trace facility is enabled for an instance, Oracle Database creates a separate trace file for each process. Before enabling the SQL Trace facility:

1. Check the settings of the TIMED_STATISTICS, MAX_DUMP_FILE_SIZE, and USER_DUMP_DEST initialization parameters. See Table 21.1.

Table 21.1. Initialization Parameters to Check Before Enabling SQL Trace

Parameter	Description
TIMED_STATISTICS	This enables and disables the collection of timed statistics, such as CPU and elapsed times, by the SQL Trace facility, as well as the collection of various statistics in the dynamic performance tables. The default value of false disables timing. A value of true enables timing. Enabling timing causes extra timing calls for low-level operations. This is a dynamic parameter. It is also a session parameter.
MAX_DUMP_FILE_SIZE	When the SQL Trace facility is enabled at the instance level, every call to the server produces a text line in a file in the operating system's file format. The maximum size of these files (in operating system blocks) is limited by this initialization parameter. The default is 500. If you find that the trace output is truncated, then increase the value of this parameter before generating another trace file. This is a dynamic parameter. It is also a session parameter.

USER_DUMP_DEST	This must fully specify the destination for the trace file according to the conventions of the operating system. The default value is the default destination for system dumps on the operating system.You can modify this value with ALTER SYSTEM SET USER_DUMP_DEST= *newdir*. This is a dynamic parameter. It is also a session parameter.

2. Devise a way of recognizing the resulting trace file.
   Be sure you know how to distinguish the trace files by name. Oracle Database writes them to the user dump destination specified by USER_DUMP_DEST. However, this directory can soon contain many hundreds of files, usually with generated names. It might be difficult to match trace files back to the session or process that created them. You can tag trace files by including in your programs a statement like SELECT '*program_name*' FROM DUAL. You can then trace each file back to the process that created it.
   You can also set the TRACEFILE_IDENTIFIER initialization parameter to specify a custom identifier that becomes part of the trace file name. For example, you can add *my_trace_id* to subsequent trace file names for easy identification with the following:

   ```
   ALTER SESSION SET TRACEFILE_IDENTIFIER = 'my_trace_id';
   ```

3. If the operating system retains multiple versions of files, then ensure that the version limit is high enough to accommodate the number of trace files you expect the SQL Trace facility to generate.
4. The generated trace files can be owned by an operating system user other than yourself. This user must make the trace files available to you before you can use TKPROF to format them.

Step 2: Enabling the SQL Trace Facility

Enable the SQL Trace facility for the session by using one of the following:

- DBMS_MONITOR.DATABASE_TRACE_ENABLE procedure (recommended)
- DBMS_SESSION.SET_SQL_TRACE procedure
- ALTER SESSION SET SQL_TRACE = TRUE;

Caution

Because running the SQL Trace facility increases system overhead, enable it only when tuning SQL statements, and disable it when you are finished. Oracle recommends that you use the DBMS_SESSION or DBMS_MONITOR packages to enable SQL tracing for a session or an instance.

You may need to modify an application to contain the ALTER SESSION statement. For example, to issue the ALTER SESSION statement in Oracle Forms, invoke Oracle Forms using the -s option, or invoke Oracle Forms (Design) using the statistics option. For more information on Oracle Forms, see the *Oracle Forms Reference*.

To disable the SQL Trace facility for the session, enter:

```
ALTER SESSION SET SQL_TRACE = FALSE;
```

The SQL Trace facility is automatically disabled for the session when the application disconnects from Oracle.

You can enable the SQL Trace facility for an instance by setting the value of the SQL_TRACE initialization parameter to TRUE in the initialization file.

```
SQL_TRACE = TRUE
```

After the instance has been restarted with the updated initialization parameter file, SQL Trace is enabled for the instance and statistics are collected for all sessions. If the SQL Trace facility has been enabled for the instance, then you can disable it for the instance by setting the value of the SQL_TRACE parameter to FALSE.

Setting SQL_TRACE to TRUE can have a severe performance impact.

Step 3: Formatting Trace Files with TKPROF

TKPROF accepts as input a trace file produced by the SQL Trace facility, and it produces a formatted output file. TKPROF can also be used to generate execution plans.

After the SQL Trace facility has generated trace files, you can:

- Run TKPROF on each individual trace file, producing several formatted output files, one for each session.
- Concatenate the trace files, and then run TKPROF on the result to produce a formatted output file for the entire instance.
- Run the trcsess command-line utility to consolidate tracing information from several trace files, then run TKPROF on the result.TKPROF does not report COMMITs and ROLLBACKs that are recorded in the trace file.

Sample TKPROF Output

Sample output from TKPROF is as follows:

```
SELECT * FROM emp, dept
WHERE emp.deptno = dept.deptno;
call     count        cpu     elapsed         disk         query    current
rows
----  -------    -------   ---------     --------    ----------    --------
Parse        1       0.16        0.29            3            13           0
0
Execute      1       0.00        0.00            0             0           0
0
Fetch        1       0.03        0.26            2             2           4
14

Misses in library cache during parse: 1
Parsing user id: (8) SCOTT
Rows     Execution Plan
-------  -----------------------------------------------------------
14       MERGE JOIN
4        SORT JOIN
4        TABLE ACCESS (FULL) OF 'DEPT'
14       SORT JOIN
14       TABLE ACCESS (FULL) OF 'EMP'
```

For this statement, TKPROF output includes the following information:

- The text of the SQL statement
- The SQL Trace statistics in tabular form
- The number of library cache misses for the parsing and execution of the statement.
- The user initially parsing the statement.
- The execution plan generated by EXPLAIN PLAN.

TKPROF also provides a summary of user level statements and recursive SQL calls for the trace file.

Syntax of TKPROF

TKPROF is run from the operating system prompt. The syntax is:

```
tkprof filename1 filename2 [waits=yes|no] [sort=option] [print=n]
   [aggregate=yes|no] [insert=filename3] [sys=yes|no]
[table=schema.table]
   [explain=user/password] [record=filename4] [width=n]
```

The input and output files are the only required arguments. If you invoke TKPROF without arguments, then the tool displays online help. Use the arguments in Table 21.2 with TKPROF.

Table 21.2. TKPROF Arguments

Argument	Description
filename1	Specifies the input file, a trace file containing statistics produced by the SQL Trace facility. This file can be either a trace file produced for a single session, or a file produced by concatenating individual trace files from multiple sessions.
filename2	Specifies the file to which TKPROF writes its formatted output.
WAITS	Specifies whether to record summary for any wait events found in the trace file. Values are YES or NO. The default is YES.
SORTS	Sorts traced SQL statements in descending order of specified sort option before listing them into the output file. If multiple options are specified, then the output is sorted in descending order by the sum of the values specified in the sort options. If you omit this parameter, then TKPROF lists statements into the output file in order of first use. Sort options are listed as follows:
PRSCNT	Number of times parsed.
PRSCPU	CPU time spent parsing.
PRSELA	Elapsed time spent parsing.
PRSDSK	Number of physical reads from disk during parse.
PRSQRY	Number of consistent mode block reads during parse.
PRSCU	Number of current mode block reads during parse.
PRSMIS	Number of library cache misses during parse.
EXECNT	Number of executes.

EXECPU	CPU time spent executing.
EXEELA	Elapsed time spent executing.
EXEDSK	Number of physical reads from disk during execute.
EXEQRY	Number of consistent mode block reads during execute.
EXECU	Number of current mode block reads during execute.
EXEROW	Number of rows processed during execute.
EXEMIS	Number of library cache misses during execute.
FCHCNT	Number of fetches.
FCHCPU	CPU time spent fetching.
FCHELA	Elapsed time spent fetching.
FCHDSK	Number of physical reads from disk during fetch.
FCHQRY	Number of consistent mode block reads during fetch.
FCHCU	Number of current mode block reads during fetch.
FCHROW	Number of rows fetched.
USERID	Userid of user that parsed the cursor.
PRINT	Lists only the first integer sorted SQL statements from the output file. If you omit this parameter, then TKPROF lists all traced SQL statements. This parameter does not affect the optional SQL script. The SQL script always generates insert data for all traced SQL statements.
AGGREGATE	If you specify AGGREGATE = NO, then TKPROF does not aggregate multiple users of the same SQL text.
INSERT	Creates a SQL script that stores the trace file statistics in the database. TKPROF creates this script with the name *filename3*. This script creates a table and inserts a row of statistics for each traced SQL statement into the table.
SYS	Enables and disables the listing of SQL statements issued by the user SYS, or recursive SQL statements, into the output file. The default value of YES causes TKPROF to list these statements. The value of NO causes TKPROF to omit them. This parameter does not affect the optional SQL script. The SQL script always inserts statistics for all traced SQL statements, including recursive SQL statements.
TABLE	Specifies the schema and name of the table into which TKPROF temporarily places execution plans before writing them to the output file. If the specified table exists, then TKPROF deletes all rows in the table, uses it for the EXPLAIN PLAN statement (which writes more rows into the table), and then deletes those rows. If this table does not exist, then TKPROF creates it, uses it, and then drops it. The specified *user* must be able to issue INSERT, SELECT, and DELETE statements against the table. If the table does not exist, then the user must also be

	able to issue CREATE TABLE and DROP TABLE statements. This option allows multiple individuals to run TKPROF concurrently with the same user in the EXPLAIN value. These individuals can specify different TABLE values and avoid destructively interfering with each other's processing on the temporary plan table. If you use the EXPLAIN parameter without the TABLE parameter, then TKPROF uses the table PROF$PLAN_TABLE in the schema of the user specified by the EXPLAIN parameter. If you use the TABLE parameter without the EXPLAIN parameter, then TKPROF ignores the TABLE parameter. If no plan table exists, TKPROF creates the table PROF$PLAN_TABLE and then drops it at the end.
EXPLAIN	Determines the execution plan for each SQL statement in the trace file and writes these execution plans to the output file. TKPROF determines execution plans by issuing the EXPLAIN PLAN statement after connecting to Oracle Database with the user and password specified in this parameter. The specified user must have CREATE SESSION system privileges. TKPROF takes longer to process a large trace file if the EXPLAIN option is used.
RECORD	Creates a SQL script with the specified *filename4* with all of the nonrecursive SQL in the trace file. You can use this script to replay the user events from the trace file.
WIDTH	An integer that controls the output line width of some TKPROF output, such as the explain plan. This parameter is useful for post-processing of TKPROF output.

Examples of TKPROF Statement

This section provides two brief examples of TKPROF usage.

TKPROF Example 1: If you are processing a large trace file using a combination of SORT parameters and the PRINT parameter, then you can produce a TKPROF output file containing only the highest resource-intensive statements. For example, the following statement prints the 10 statements in the trace file that have generated the most physical I/O:

```
TKPROF ora53269.trc ora53269.prf SORT = (PRSDSK, EXEDSK, FCHDSK) PRINT
= 10
```

TKPROF Example 2: This example runs TKPROF, accepts a trace file named examp12_jane_fg_sqlplus_007.trc, and writes a formatted output file named outputa.prf:

```
TKPROF examp12_jane_fg_sqlplus_007.trc OUTPUTA.PRF
EXPLAIN=scott/tiger  TABLE=scott.temp_plan_table_a  INSERT=STOREA.SQL
SYS=NO
SORT=(EXECPU,FCHCPU)
```

This example is likely to be longer than a single line on the screen, and you might need to use continuation characters, depending on the operating system.

Note the other parameters in this example:

- The EXPLAIN value causes TKPROF to connect as the user scott and use the EXPLAIN PLAN statement to generate the execution plan for each traced SQL statement. You can use this to get access paths and row source counts.

> If the cursor for a SQL statement is not closed, then TKPROF output does not automatically include the actual execution plan of the SQL statement. In this situation, you can use the EXPLAIN option with TKPROF to generate an execution plan.

- The TABLE value causes TKPROF to use the table temp_plan_table_a in the schema scott as a temporary plan table.
- The INSERT value causes TKPROF to generate a SQL script named STOREA.SQL that stores statistics for all traced SQL statements in the database.
- The SYS parameter with the value of NO causes TKPROF to omit recursive SQL statements from the output file. In this way, you can ignore internal Oracle Database statements such as temporary table operations.
- The SORT value causes TKPROF to sort the SQL statements in order of the sum of the CPU time spent executing and the CPU time spent fetching rows before writing them to the output file. For greatest efficiency, always use SORT parameters.

Step 4: Interpreting TKPROF Output

This section provides pointers for interpreting TKPROF output.

- Tabular Statistics in TKPROF
- Row Source Operations
- Wait Event Information
- Interpreting the Resolution of Statistics
- Understanding Recursive Calls
- Library Cache Misses in TKPROF
- Statement Truncation in SQL Trace
- Identification of User Issuing the SQL Statement in TKPROF
- Execution Plan in TKPROF
- Deciding Which Statements to Tune.

While TKPROF provides a very useful analysis, the most accurate measure of efficiency is the actual performance of the application in question. At the end of the TKPROF output is a summary of the work done in the database engine by the process during the period that the trace was running.

Tabular Statistics in TKPROF

TKPROF lists the statistics for a SQL statement returned by the SQL Trace facility in rows and columns. Each row corresponds to one of three steps of SQL statement processing. Statistics are identified by the value of the CALL column. See Table 21.3.

Table 21.3. CALL Column Values

CALL Value	Meaning
PARSE	Translates the SQL statement into an execution plan, including checks for proper security authorization and checks for the existence of tables, columns, and other referenced objects.
EXECUTE	Actual execution of the statement by Oracle. For INSERT, UPDATE, and DELETE statements, this modifies the data. For SELECT statements, this identifies the selected rows.
FETCH	Retrieves rows returned by a query. Fetches are only performed for SELECT statements.

The other columns of the SQL Trace facility output are combined statistics for all parses, all executes, and all fetches of a statement. The sum of query and current is the total number of buffers accessed, also called Logical I/Os (LIOs). See Table 21.4.

Table 21.4. SQL Trace Statistics for Parses, Executes, and Fetches

SQL Trace Statistic	Meaning
COUNT	Number of times a statement was parsed, executed, or fetched.
CPU	Total CPU time in seconds for all parse, execute, or fetch calls for the statement. This value is zero (0) if TIMED_STATISTICS is not turned on.
ELAPSED	Total elapsed time in seconds for all parse, execute, or fetch calls for the statement. This value is zero (0) if TIMED_STATISTICS is not turned on.
DISK	Total number of data blocks physically read from the data files on disk for all parse, execute, or fetch calls.
QUERY	Total number of buffers retrieved in consistent mode for all parse, execute, or fetch calls. Usually, buffers are retrieved in consistent mode for queries.
CURRENT	Total number of buffers retrieved in current mode. Buffers are retrieved in current mode for statements such as INSERT, UPDATE, and DELETE.

Statistics about the processed rows appear in the ROWS column. See Table 21.5.

Table 21.5. SQL Trace Statistics for the ROWS Column

SQL Trace Statistic	Meaning
ROWS	Total number of rows processed by the SQL statement. This total does not include rows processed by subqueries of the SQL statement.

For SELECT statements, the number of rows returned appears for the fetch step. For UPDATE, DELETE, and INSERT statements, the number of rows processed appears for the execute step.

The row source counts are displayed when a cursor is closed. In SQL*Plus, there is only one user cursor, so each statement executed causes the previous cursor to be closed; therefore, the row source counts are displayed. PL/SQL has its own cursor handling and does not close child cursors when the parent cursor is closed. Exiting (or reconnecting) causes the counts to be displayed.

Row Source Operations

Row source operations provide the number of rows processed for each operation executed on the rows and additional row source information, such as physical reads and writes. The following is a sample:

```
Rows    Row Source Operation
------- ---------------------------------------------------------
0 DELETE (cr=43141 r=266947 w=25854 time=60235565 us)
28144 HASH JOIN ANTI (cr=43057 r=262332 w=25854
   time=48830056 us)
51427 TABLE ACCESS FULL STATS$SQLTEXT (cr=3465 r=3463 w=0
   time=865083 us)
647529 INDEX FAST FULL SCAN STATS$SQL_SUMMARY_PK
   (cr=39592 r=39325 w=0 time=10522877 us) (object id 7409)
```

In this sample TKPROF output, note the following under the Row Source Operation column.

- `cr` specifies consistent reads performed by the row source
- `r` specifies physical reads performed by the row source
- `w` specifies physical writes performed by the row source
- `time` specifies time in microseconds.

Wait Event Information

If wait event information exists, then the TKPROF output includes a section similar to the following:

```
Elapsed times include waiting on following events:
Event waited on Times Max. Wait                  Total Waited
--------------------------------------           Waited ----------
        db file sequential read                    8084
0.12                           5.34
        direct path write                           834
0.00                           0.00
        direct path write temp                      834
0.00                           0.05
        db file parallel read                         8
1.53                           5.51
        db file scattered read                     4180
0.07                           1.45
        direct path read                           7082
0.00                           0.05
        direct path read temp                      7082
0.00                           0.44
```

```
        rdbms ipc reply                         20
0.00                        0.01
        SQL*Net message to client                1
0.00                        0.00
        SQL*Net message from client              1
0.00                        0.00
```

In addition, wait events are summed for the entire trace file at the end of the file.

To ensure that wait events information is written to the trace file for the session, run the following SQL statement:

```
ALTER SESSION SET EVENTS '10046 trace name context forever, level 8';
```

Interpreting the Resolution of Statistics

Timing statistics have a resolution of one hundredth of a second; therefore, any operation on a cursor that takes a hundredth of a second or less might not be timed accurately. Keep this in mind when interpreting statistics. In particular, be careful when interpreting the results from simple queries that execute very quickly.

Understanding Recursive Calls

Sometimes, to execute a SQL statement issued by a user, Oracle Database must issue additional statements. Such statements are called recursive calls or recursive SQL statements. For example, if you insert a row into a table that does not have enough space to hold that row, then Oracle Database makes recursive calls to allocate the space dynamically. Recursive calls are also generated when data dictionary information is not available in the data dictionary cache and must be retrieved from disk.

If recursive calls occur while the SQL Trace facility is enabled, then TKPROF produces statistics for the recursive SQL statements and marks them clearly as recursive SQL statements in the output file. You can suppress the listing of Oracle Database internal recursive calls (for example, space management) in the output file by setting the SYS command-line parameter to NO. The statistics for a recursive SQL statement are included in the listing for that statement, not in the listing for the SQL statement that caused the recursive call. So, when you are calculating the total resources required to process a SQL statement, consider the statistics for that statement and those for recursive calls caused by that statement.

Recursive SQL statistics are not included for SQL-level operations.

Library Cache Misses in TKPROF

TKPROF also lists the number of library cache misses resulting from parse and execute steps for each SQL statement. These statistics appear on separate lines following the tabular statistics. If the statement resulted in no library cache misses, then TKPROF does not list the statistic.

Statement Truncation in SQL Trace

The following SQL statements are truncated to 25 characters in the SQL Trace file:

```
SET ROLE
GRANT
```

```
ALTER USER
ALTER ROLE
CREATE USER
CREATE ROLE
```

Identification of User Issuing the SQL Statement in TKPROF

TKPROF also lists the user ID of the user issuing each SQL statement. If the SQL Trace input file contained statistics from multiple users, and if the statement was issued by multiple users, then TKPROF lists the ID of the last user to parse the statement. The user ID of all database users appears in the data dictionary in the column ALL_USERS.USER_ID.

Execution Plan in TKPROF

If you specify the EXPLAIN parameter on the TKPROF statement line, then TKPROF uses the EXPLAIN PLAN statement to generate the execution plan of each SQL statement traced. TKPROF also displays the number of rows processed by each step of the execution plan.

Trace files generated immediately after instance startup contain data that reflects the activity of the startup process. In particular, they reflect a disproportionate amount of I/O activity as caches in the system global area (SGA) are filled. For the purposes of tuning, ignore such trace files.

Deciding Which Statements to Tune

You need to find which SQL statements use the most CPU or disk resource. If the TIMED_STATISTICS parameter is on, then you can find high CPU activity in the CPU column. If TIMED_STATISTICS is not on, then check the QUERY and CURRENT columns.

With the exception of locking problems and inefficient PL/SQL loops, neither the CPU time nor the elapsed time is necessary to find problem statements. The key is the number of block visits, both query (that is, subject to read consistency) and current (that is, not subject to read consistency). Segment headers and blocks that are going to be updated are acquired in current mode, but all query and subquery processing requests the data in query mode. These are precisely the same measures as the instance statistics CONSISTENT GETS and DB BLOCK GETS. You can find high disk activity in the disk column.

The following listing shows TKPROF output for one SQL statement as it appears in the output file:

```
SELECT * FROM emp, dept
WHERE emp.deptno = dept.deptno;

call      count       cpu     elapsed        disk      query      current
rows
----   -------    -------   ---------    --------   -------      -------
Parse        11      0.08        0.18           0          0            0
0
Execute      11      0.23        0.66           0          3            6
0
Fetch        35      6.70        6.83         100      12326            2
824
```

```
---------------------------------------------------------------------
total        57      7.01         7.67         100     12329          8
826

Misses in library cache during parse: 0
```

If it is acceptable to have 7.01 CPU seconds and to retrieve 824 rows, then you need not look any further at this trace output. In fact, a major use of TKPROF reports in a tuning exercise is to eliminate processes from the detailed tuning phase.

You can also see that 10 unnecessary parse call were made (because there were 11 parse calls for this one statement) and that array fetch operations were performed. You know this because more rows were fetched than there were fetches performed. A large gap between CPU and elapsed timings indicates Physical I/Os (PIOs).

Step 5: Storing SQL Trace Facility Statistics

You might want to keep a history of the statistics generated by the SQL Trace facility for an application, and compare them over time. TKPROF can generate a SQL script that creates a table and inserts rows of statistics into it. This script contains:

- A CREATE TABLE statement that creates an output table named TKPROF_TABLE.
- INSERT statements that add rows of statistics, one for each traced SQL statement, to the TKPROF_TABLE.

After running TKPROF, you can run this script to store the statistics in the database.

Generating the TKPROF Output SQL Script

When you run TKPROF, use the INSERT parameter to specify the name of the generated SQL script. If you omit this parameter, then TKPROF does not generate a script.

Editing the TKPROF Output SQL Script

After TKPROF has created the SQL script, you might want to edit the script before running it. If you have created an output table for previously collected statistics, and if you want to add new statistics to this table, then remove the CREATE TABLE statement from the script. The script then inserts the new rows into the existing table.

If you have created multiple output tables, perhaps to store statistics from different databases in different tables, then edit the CREATE TABLE and INSERT statements to change the name of the output table.

Querying the Output Table

The following CREATE TABLE statement creates the TKPROF_TABLE:

```
CREATE TABLE TKPROF_TABLE (
DATE_OF_INSERT        DATE,
CURSOR_NUM            NUMBER,
DEPTH                 NUMBER,
USER_ID               NUMBER,
PARSE_CNT             NUMBER,
PARSE_CPU             NUMBER,
PARSE_ELAP            NUMBER,
PARSE_DISK            NUMBER,
PARSE_QUERY           NUMBER,
```

```
PARSE_CURRENT        NUMBER,
PARSE_MISS           NUMBER,
EXE_COUNT            NUMBER,
EXE_CPU              NUMBER,
EXE_ELAP             NUMBER,
EXE_DISK             NUMBER,
EXE_QUERY            NUMBER,
EXE_CURRENT          NUMBER,
EXE_MISS             NUMBER,
EXE_ROWS             NUMBER,
FETCH_COUNT          NUMBER,
FETCH_CPU            NUMBER,
FETCH_ELAP           NUMBER,
FETCH_DISK           NUMBER,
FETCH_QUERY          NUMBER,
FETCH_CURRENT        NUMBER,
FETCH_ROWS           NUMBER,
CLOCK_TICKS          NUMBER,
SQL_STATEMENT        LONG);
```

Most output table columns correspond directly to the statistics that appear in the formatted output file. For example, the `PARSE_CNT` column value corresponds to the count statistic for the parse step in the output file.

The columns in Table 21.6 help you identify a row of statistics.

Table 21.6. TKPROF_TABLE Columns for Identifying a Row of Statistics

Column	Description
SQL_STATEMENT	This is the SQL statement for which the SQL Trace facility collected the row of statistics. Because this column has data type LONG, you cannot use it in expressions or WHERE clause conditions.
DATE_OF_INSERT	This is the date and time when the row was inserted into the table. This value is not exactly the same as the time the statistics were collected by the SQL Trace facility.
DEPTH	This indicates the level of recursion at which the SQL statement was issued. For example, a value of 0 indicates that a user issued the statement. A value of 1 indicates that Oracle Database generated the statement as a recursive call to process a statement with a value of 0 (a statement issued by a user). A value of *n* indicates that Oracle Database generated the statement as a recursive call to process a statement with a value of *n*-1.
USER_ID	This identifies the user issuing the statement. This value also appears in the formatted output file.
CURSOR_NUM	Oracle database uses this column value to keep track of the cursor to which each SQL statement was assigned.

The output table does not store the statement's execution plan. The following query returns the statistics from the output table.

```
SELECT * FROM TKPROF_TABLE;
```

Oracle Database responds with something similar to:

```
DATE_OF_INSERT CURSOR_NUM    DEPTH    USER_ID    PARSE_CNT    PARSE_CPU
PARSE_ELAP
------------   ---------     -----    -------     -------     --------
21-DEC-1998         1          0         8           1           16
22

PARSE_DISK PARSE_QUERY PARSE_CURRENT PARSE_MISS EXE_COUNT EXE_CPU
--------- --------- --------- ---------- --------- -------- ---
                    3          11         0          1           1
0
EXE_ELAP EXE_DISK EXE_QUERY EXE_CURRENT EXE_MISS EXE_ROWS FETCH_COUNT
--------        --------   -------- --------    --------    --------
0                   0          0         0          0           0
1

FETCH_CPU       FETCH_ELAP  FETCH_DISKFETCH_QUERY          FETCH_CURRENT
FETCH_ROWS
--------        --------   -------- --------    --------    --------
2                   20         2         2                      4
10

SQL_STATEMENT
---------------------------------------------------------------------
SELECT * FROM EMP, DEPT WHERE EMP.DEPTNO = DEPT.DEPTNO
```

AVOIDING PITFALLS IN TKPROF INTERPRETATION

This section describes some fine points of TKPROF interpretation:

- Avoiding the Argument Trap
- Avoiding the Read Consistency Trap
- Avoiding the Schema Trap
- Avoiding the Time Trap.

Avoiding the Argument Trap

If you are not aware of the values being bound at run time, then it is possible to fall into the argument trap. EXPLAIN PLAN cannot determine the type of a bind variable from the text of SQL statements, and it always assumes that the type is varchar. If the bind variable is actually a number or a date, then TKPROF can cause implicit data conversions, which can cause inefficient plans to be executed. To avoid this situation, experiment with different data types in the query.

To avoid this problem, perform the conversion yourself.

Avoiding the Read Consistency Trap

The next example illustrates the read consistency trap. Without knowing that an uncommitted transaction had made a series of updates to the NAME column, it is very difficult to see why so many block visits would be incurred.

Cases like this are not normally repeatable: if the process were run again, it is unlikely that another transaction would interact with it in the same way.

```
SELECT name_id FROM cq_names
WHERE name = 'FLOOR';
call       count    cpu elapsed      disk      query    current    rows
-----      -----      -----          -----      -----     -----     -----
Parse        1          0.10          0.18        0         0         0
0
Execute      1          0.00          0.00        0         0         0
0
Fetch        1          0.11          0.21        2        101        0
1
Misses in library cache during parse: 1
Parsing user id: 01 (USER1)

Rows    Execution Plan
----    ---------   ----
   0    SELECT STATEMENT
   1    TABLE ACCESS (BY ROWID) OF 'CQ_NAMES'
   2    INDEX (RANGE SCAN) OF 'CQ_NAMES_NAME' (NON_UNIQUE)
```

Avoiding the Schema Trap

This example shows an extreme (and thus easily detected) example of the schema trap. At first, it is difficult to see why such an apparently straightforward indexed query needs to look at so many database blocks, or why it should access any blocks at all in current mode.

```
SELECT name_id
FROM cq_names
WHERE name = 'FLOOR';

call  count   cpu     elapsed    disk    query   current        rows
----  -----   ---     -------    ----     -------------     -------
Parse            1       0.06    0.10                   0          0
0     0
Execute          1       0.02    0.02                   0          0
0     0
Fetch            1       0.23    0.30                  31         31
3     1
Misses in library cache during parse: 0
Parsing user id: 02 (USER2)
Rows    Execution Plan
------- -------------------------------------------------------
   0 SELECT STATEMENT 2340      TABLE ACCESS (BY ROWID) OF
   'CQ_NAMES'
   0 INDEX (RANGE SCAN) OF 'CQ_NAMES_NAME' (NON-UNIQUE)
```

Two statistics suggest that the query might have been executed with a full table scan. These statistics are the current mode block visits, plus the number of rows originating from the Table

Access row source in the execution plan. The explanation is that the required index was built after the trace file had been produced, but before TKPROF had been run.

Generating a new trace file gives the following data:

```
SELECT name_id
FROM cq_names
WHERE name = 'FLOOR';

call     count      cpu     elapsed       disk      query    current    rows
----    ------    -----    --------     ------     ------    -------    ----
Parse        1     0.01        0.02          0          0          0       0
Execute      1     0.00        0.00          0          0          0       0
Fetch        1     0.00        0.00          0          2          0       1

Misses in library cache during parse: 0
Parsing user id: 02 (USER2)
Rows    Execution Plan
------- ---------------------------------------------------
   0    SELECT STATEMENT
   1    TABLE ACCESS (BY ROWID) OF 'CQ_NAMES'
   2    INDEX (RANGE SCAN) OF 'CQ_NAMES_NAME' (NON-UNIQUE)
```

One of the marked features of this correct version is that the parse call took 10 milliseconds of CPU time and 20 milliseconds of elapsed time, but the query apparently took no time at all to execute and perform the fetch. These anomalies arise because the clock tick of 10 milliseconds is too long relative to the time taken to execute and fetch the data. In such cases, it is important to get lots of executions of the statements, so that you have statistically valid numbers.

Avoiding the Time Trap

Sometimes, as in the following example, you might wonder why a particular query has taken so long.

```
UPDATE cq_names SET ATTRIBUTES = lower(ATTRIBUTES)
WHERE ATTRIBUTES = :att

call     count      cpu    elapsed       disk  query current     rows
----    ------    -----   --------     ------          ------    ----
Parse                 1       0.06       0.24               0       0
0            0
Execute               1       0.62      19.62              22     526
12           7
Fetch                 0       0.00       0.00               0       0
0            0
Misses in library cache during parse: 1
Parsing user id: 02 (USER2)
Rows    Execution Plan
------- ---------------------------------------------------
   0    UPDATE STATEMENT
   2519 TABLE ACCESS (FULL) OF 'CQ_NAMES'
```

Again, the answer is interference from another transaction. In this case, another transaction held a shared lock on the table cq_names for several seconds before and after the update was issued. It takes a fair amount of experience to diagnose that interference effects are occurring. On the one hand, comparative data is essential when the interference is contributing only a short delay (or a small increase in block visits in the previous example). However, if the interference contributes only modest overhead, and if the statement is essentially efficient, then its statistics may not require analysis.

SAMPLE TKPROF OUTPUT

This section provides an example of TKPROF output. Portions have been edited out for the sake of brevity.

Sample TKPROF Header

```
TKPROF: Release 10.1.0.0.0 - Mon Feb 10 14:43:00 2003
(c) Copyright 2001 Oracle Corporation. All rights reserved.
Trace file: main_ora_27621.trc
Sort options: default
*************************************************************
count    =     number of times OCI procedure was executed
cpu      =     cpu time in seconds executing
elapsed =      elapsed time in seconds executing
disk     =     number of physical reads of buffers from disk
query    =     number of buffers gotten for consistent read
current =      number of buffers gotten in current mode (usually for
update)
rows     =     number of rows processed by the fetch or execute call
*************************************************************
```

Sample TKPROF Body

```
call   count  cpu  elapsed       disk   query       current       rows
------- ------   --------   ----------  ----------   ---------- ---
Parse        1        0.01          0.00            0            0
0          0
Execute      1        0.00          0.00            0            0
0          0
Fetch        0        0.00          0.00            0            0
0          0
------- ------   --------   ----------  ----------   ---------- ---
total        2        0.01          0.00            0            0
0          0
Misses in library cache during parse: 1
Optimizer mode: FIRST_ROWS
Parsing user id: 44
Elapsed times include waiting on following events:
 Event waited on Times Max. Wait Total Waited
 ---------------------------------------------- Waited      ------
 SQL*Net message to client 1 0.00 0.00
 SQL*Net message from client 1 28.59 28.59
*************************************************************
```

```
select condition
from cdef$ where rowid=:1

call    count  cpu  elapsed      disk      query       current    rows
------- ------    --------    ----------  ----------    ----------  ---
Parse       1        0.00          0.00           0             0
0         0
Execute     1        0.00          0.00           0             0
0         0
Fetch       1        0.00           0.0           0             2
0         1
------- ------    --------    ----------  ----------    ----------  ---
total       3        0.00          0.00           0             2
0         1
Misses in library cache during parse: 1
Optimizer mode: CHOOSE
Parsing user id: SYS (recursive depth: 1)
Rows    Row Source Operation
----   ------   -----   --------   ------   ------   -------   ----
   1    TABLE ACCESS BY USER ROWID OBJ#(31) (cr=1 r=0 w=0 time=151 us)
*************************************************************

SELECT last_name, job_id, salary
   FROM employees
WHERE salary =
   (SELECT max(salary) FROM employees)

call    count  cpu  elapsed      disk      query       current    rows
------- ------    --------    ----------  ----------    ----------  ---
Parse       1        0.02          0.01           0             0
0         0
Execute     1        0.00          0.00           0             0
0         0
Fetch       2        0.00          0.00           0            15
0         1
------- ------    --------    ----------  ----------    ----------  ---
total       4        0.02          0.01           0            15
0         1
Misses in library cache during parse: 1
Optimizer mode: FIRST_ROWS
Parsing user id: 44

Rows    Row Source Operation
------- ---------------------------------------------------------
   1    TABLE ACCESS FULL EMPLOYEES (cr=15 r=0 w=0 time=1743 us)
   1    SORT AGGREGATE (cr=7 r=0 w=0 time=777 us)
   107  TABLE ACCESS FULL EMPLOYEES (cr=7 r=0 w=0 time=655 us)
Elapsed times include waiting on following events:
Event waited on Times Max. Wait Total Waited
------------------------------------------------ Waited ------
```

```
SQL*Net message to client 2     0.00
0.00
   SQL*Net message from client  2
9.62    9.62
********************************************************************
********************************************************************

delete
   from stats$sqltext st
   where (hash_value, text_subset) not in
   (select —+ hash_aj
   hash_value, text_subset
   from stats$sql_summary ss
   where ( ( snap_id < :lo_snap
   or snap_id > :hi_snap
   )
   and dbid = :dbid
   and instance_number = :inst_num
   )
   or ( dbid != :dbid
   or instance_number != :inst_num)
   )
call     count  cpu  elapsed     disk       query    current    rows
------- ------   --------   ----------  ----------   ---------- ---
Parse        1       0.00          0.00           0           0
0          0
Execute      1      29.60         60.68      266984       43776
131172     28144
Fetch        0       0.00          0.00           0           0
0          0
------- ------   --------   ----------  ----------   ---------- ---
total        2      29.60         60.68      266984       43776
131172     28144
Misses in library cache during parse: 1
Misses in library cache during execute: 1
Optimizer mode: CHOOSE
Parsing user id: 22
Rows    Row Source Operation
------- -----------------------------------------------------------
0  DELETE (cr=43141 r=266947 w=25854 time=60235565 us)
28144   HASH JOIN ANTI (cr=43057 r=262332 w=25854 time=48830056 us)
   51427      TABLE  ACCESS  FULL  STATS$SQLTEXT  (cr=3465  r=3463  w=0
time=865083 us)
   647529     INDEX FAST FULL SCAN STATS$SQL_SUMMARY_PK
   (cr=39592 r=39325 w=0 time=10522877 us) (object id 7409)
Elapsed times include waiting on following events:
 Event waited on Times Max. Wait Total Waited
```

```
----------------------------------------------  Waited -------
         db file sequential read                     8084
0.12                              5.34
         direct path write                            834
0.00                              0.00
         direct path write temp                       834
0.00                              0.05
         db file parallel read                          8
1.53                              5.51
         db file scattered read                      4180
0.07                              1.45
         direct path read                            7082
0.00                              0.05
         direct path read temp                       7082
0.00                              0.44
         rdbms ipc reply                               20
0.00                              0.01
         SQL*Net message to client                      1
0.00                              0.00
         SQL*Net message from client                    1
0.00                              0.00
**********************************************************************
```

Sample TKPROF Summary

```
OVERALL TOTALS FOR ALL NON-RECURSIVE STATEMENTS
call   count      cpu    elapsed     disk    query  current   rows
------- ------  --------  ----------  ----------  ---------- ---
Parse       4      0.04         0.01           0            0
0          0
Execute     5      0.00         0.04           0            0
0          0
Fetch       2      0.00         0.00           0           15
0          1
------- ------  --------  ----------  ----------  ---------- ---
total      11      0.04         0.06           0           15

0          1
Misses in library cache during parse: 4
Misses in library cache during execute: 1
Elapsed times include waiting on following events:
Event waited on Times Max. Wait Total Waited
---------------------------------------------- Waited -------
SQL*Net message to client     6                    0.00
0.00
SQL*Net message from client   5                   77.77
128.88
OVERALL TOTALS FOR ALL RECURSIVE STATEMENTS
```

```
call  count   cpu   elapsed     disk  query   current      rows
------- ------   --------   ----------  ----------   ----------  ---
Parse       1       0.00          0.00           0           0
0           0
Execute     1       0.00          0.00           0           0
0           0
Fetch       1       0.00          0.00           0           2
0           1
------- ------   --------   ----------  ----------   ----------  ---
total       3       0.00          0.00           0           2
0           1
Misses in library cache during parse: 1
   5    user SQL statements in session.
   1    internal SQL statements in session.
   6    SQL statements in session.
.....................................................................
Trace file: main_ora_27621.trc
Trace file compatibility: 9.00.01

Sort options: default
     1     session in tracefile.
     5     user SQL statements in trace file.
     1     internal SQL statements in trace file.
     6     SQL statements in trace file.
     6     unique SQL statements in trace file.
    76     lines in trace file.
   128     elapsed seconds in trace file.
```

Index

A

B

C

D

E

F

G

H

I

J

K

L

M

N

O

P

Q

R

S

T